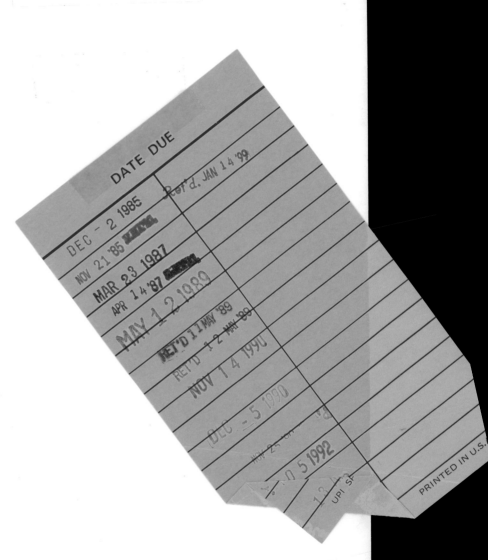

# LUTHER

*Also by Richard Friedenthal*
GOETHE

# LUTHER

## HIS LIFE AND TIMES

# *Richard Friedenthal*

*Translated from the German by John Nowell*

*A Helen and Kurt Wolff Book*
*Harcourt Brace Jovanovich, Inc.*
*New York*

Copyright © 1967 by Richard Friedenthal

English translation copyright © 1970 by John Nowell

First American edition

Originally published in Germany under the title *Luther, sein Leben
und seine Zeit* by R. Piper & Co. Verlag

ISBN 0-15-154785-8

Library of Congress Catalog Card Number: 72-124834

Printed in the United States of America

A B C D E

# Contents

*Part Three*

## THE WITTENBERG REFORMER

# Illustrations

vii

*Part One*

# Evolution of a Rebel

# I

# The miner's son of peasant stock

LUTHER was born in 1483. According to the history books this was still the Middle Ages, and there has been much argument as to whether Luther himself belongs to the Middle Ages or to the opening years of modern times. This division of history into large blocks which, when we glance back over several centuries, all too easily acquire a monolithic appearance, has become increasingly suspect. The Middle Ages have been subjected to the most varied appraisals, people's notions of them ranging from the long-accepted view that they were an era of darkness and unenlightenment to the Romantic view of the entire life of those days as bathed in the golden light of medieval painting. Eventually, after ingredients of every kind had been poured into the retorts – scraps of colour from paintings of the saints, moss from the great cathedrals and a good deal of mysticism – a mythical 'man of the Middle Ages' was created. Large, if vague, traces of this idealized creation still remain: the notion of an immensely pious and devout west, for example, living in enviable unity under pope and emperor and capable of great things, of a time in which everyone felt safe and secure in his divinely ordained place within the existing order of society, until the presumptuous unrest of certain individuals drove him to uncertainty. Luther, the most prominent among these individualists, has been regarded as the great subverter and divider of this unity of the Middle Ages, a unity which existed less in reality than in the great cathedrals of thought erected by theologians and philosophers. It would be truer to say that the late Roman emperors had left a heritage of schism and division, and the following centuries a Church split into the Eastern, or Greek, Church and the Western Church, or Church of Rome. The fact that during the greater part of the complex known as the Middle Ages the Eastern Church was as important as the Church of Rome, and at times considerably more important, has been progressively ignored and obscured by a historic tradition moulded exclusively by western European thought, a tradition given force by the decay of the great Byzantine Empire, the only empire that can justly be said to have lasted a 'thousand years', beginning with the conquest and terrible sack of Constantinople by the 'devout' Crusaders in 1204 and ending with the destruction of this great bastion of the Christian world by the Turks in 1453. By the time Luther was born, however, a change had already taken place. The grand duchy of Moscow had wrenched itself free from Tartar domination, Ivan III marrying the Byzantine princess Zoë and taking the Greek title of autocrat. The 'Orthodox' Church once again experienced a great resurgence; claiming to be the 'third Rome' it assumed the mission of bringing salvation to the world – a missionary idea that under another guise has survived until today. When, on his first public appearance in Leipzig, Luther questioned the pope's claim to be the supreme head of Christendom, he specifically cited the Greek Church and protested against its adherents being called 'heretics', or even 'unbelievers', to fight whom one was justified in undertaking crusades and collecting indulgences.

But even within western Europe the unity of the Church had been subjected to very severe shocks. The great schism, which split Europe into two and finally into three camps, with two and even three popes indulging in mutual condemnation, had been healed only with difficulty at the Council of Constance in 1414–18; the burning of the Czech reformer Hus had led to almost twenty years of Hussite wars and left the legacy of an unconquered Bohemia as a heretic church, which the Curia was forced reluctantly to endure. At Constance the idea of the Council as the supreme authority, standing above the pope, had triumphed, and since then had never been lost sight of. As the great hope of a 'root and branch' reform, it determined thought and politics; it was also of decisive importance in paving the way for Luther. In 1483, when Luther was born, the Holy See was occupied by Pope Sixtus IV, the first of the Rovere dynasty and the earliest representative of the Renaissance papacy, which by then had become predominantly an Italian territorial principality, having forfeited its position as arbitrator among nations. At the head of these nations, which now went their own ways, was France; it had already created its own 'Gallican' national Church, the temporal ruler being vested with a power to dispose of Church property and appoint ecclesiastical dignitaries unknown in any other country. The German emperors had failed in their attempts to do likewise, and in the end had been crushed by the great popes of the High Middle Ages. The French kings remained victorious, thus acquiring control over a tightly-knit political body of immense power. 1483 was also the year of accession to the French throne of Charles VIII, who took opposition to the Curia in Rome a fateful step further by invading Italy with military might and causing the collapse of the whole Italian political system, which the popes had hoped to direct. This initiated a struggle in which all the European powers took part and which continued throughout Luther's life, exercising a decisive influence on the fate both of himself and the Reformation. In so far as it is possible to speak of a split in the unity of the west – the existence of any such unity being very questionable – it was prepared and brought about in the field of French politics, before anyone had heard of the Wittenberg monk or imagined that Germany might play a part in it.

When Luther was born the German throne was occupied by the Emperor Frederick III, the most supine of all rulers, the Habsburg who achieved unmerited historic significance solely by the obstinacy and cunning with which he pursued his dynastic and material policies. He was scarcely ever seen in public within the empire, and was frequently threatened with the loss of his throne: even in his Austrian patrimonial lands his position was very insecure. Almost destitute, he borrowed from the citizens of his own towns, even from the city gatekeeper in Vienna; politically he was almost equally bankrupt. It was for his house alone that, in the form of contracts of inheritance and dynastic alliances, he placed huge time-bombs everywhere which, exploding in unexpected ways, were to change fundamentally the whole European landscape. To ascribe exceptional wisdom to him on this account smacks a little of hindsight. He could hardly have anticipated that no fewer than six prior claimants would die and thus permit his great-grandson Charles to ascend the throne of Spain; still less could he have foreseen that the great Jagellon Empire, which in his day dominated the whole of eastern Europe and extended from the Baltic to the Black Sea, would collapse as quickly as it did, and that one day Hungary and Bohemia would fall to his other great-grandson, Ferdinand, and form the basis of a great Habsburg possession.

In Germany, which had been completely neglected by its titular emperors, the real rulers had long been the temporal and spiritual princes: the electors, archbishops, dukes, princes, counts, and other still less important princelings. It was in the territory of one of these miniature potentates, in Eisleben in the county of Mansfeld on the southern edge of the Harz mountains, that Martin Luther was born on 10 November 1483. The whole lamentable German political situation, which far from being a recent creation was centuries old and was to continue for centuries to come, can be seen in miniature in this dwarf territory; moreover it was of the greatest importance for Luther, and for the fate of the movement he unleashed, that he was born into such irremediably entangled and fragmented conditions. This county – was it a state, a country? It was barely a shire, and could not even be said to have a ruler. Two 'lines' of the ruling family were still struggling for possession; both lived in the ancestral castle at Mansfeld, apart and in bitter enmity. They were known as the 'anterior' and 'posterior' lines, from the parts of the castle in which they lived; later a third, 'interior', line was added, and the whole structure disintegrated so completely as a result of inheritances and family feuds that, a few decades after Luther's death the county, deeply in debt, was sequestered by the feudal overlords in Magdeburg, Halberstadt and the electorate of Saxony. The last journey undertaken by the old reformer, who died in Eisleben where he was born, was made in an attempt to bring about agreement between the quarrelling counts. In the last letter he wrote, to his wife Käthe, he spoke hopefully of the cheerful sound of bells that came from the sleigh-ride with which the younger members of the family were celebrating the reconciliation of the anterior and posterior lines. It was a short-lived reconciliation.

A coloured map of the Holy Roman Empire looks like the patch-work of a jester's costume, and even then there is no way of representing the family divisions within the little patches, the criss-cross patterns of feudal rights or those superimposed by the ecclesiastical authorities. And this held good not only in Thuringia, where these scattered possessions continued to exist into our own day, but almost everywhere. The end of the fifteenth century, as though in prelude to the apocalyptic times that were to follow, of which dark prophecies were already in circulation, was the heyday of the fool, in plays, in pageants, in dress, and in a literature which in Sebastian Brant's *Narrenschiff* ('Ship of Fools') provided a German poet with a European reputation for the first time and in the popular tale of Till Eulenspiegel created an immortal character. In every tiniest court the fool sat at the feet of his lord, often cleverer than his master, often a pitiful semi-idiot like his prince. Sometimes the 'comic counsellor' rose to a position of great eminence, like the Emperor Maximilian's court fool, Kunz von der Rosen, who behind the throne became privy chancellor to the throne and amassed a large fortune with his jester's bladder. The jokes were coarse and merciless, but people laughed at them. The story was told with relish of a special show put on by Kunz at one of the diets: having tethered a fat pig to a stake in the market place, he assembled the blind people of the town, handed each of them a club and promised the pig to the one who killed it; to the accompaniment of roars of laughter from princes and people the blind, mad with greed, clubbed and belaboured each other in a bloody fight. This macabre scene may serve as an allegory of the times.

But in spite of the hundred and more feast days and holidays that crowded the motley calendar of saints, people worked hard in Mansfeld. The county was rich in mineral resources. The Mansfeld copper-

Sixteenth-century German mine

mining industry, which had been started in the twelfth century, flourished until the end of the nineteenth century, and maintained the oldest and largest mining concern in Germany. The extensive seam, however, was very thin, being scarcely twenty inches thick, of which only the lowest stratum of some four inches was worth mining; the copper content varied from two to three per cent and was mixed with a certain amount of silver. The metal, of cardinal importance in those days, could be extracted only at the cost of enormous effort and with the aid of very advanced dressing and smelting techniques. Because of divisions of inheritance and family quarrels among the counts, the lucrative business had already greatly deteriorated by the middle of the fifteenth century. This in its turn gave small groups of workers the opportunity to combine and take over shafts or prospect on their own account, financial backing being provided by the copper merchants in Mansfeld and Eisleben. One of these mineworkers was Luther's father, Hans Luder. He worked his way up from pickman until finally he became a business partner in a whole series of small shafts in Mansfeld; he also had a leaseholder's interest in three smelting works, in all probability only tiny undertakings, but they assured him a good income. He never became rich, but nevertheless was able to acquire a house and give his son Martin an education. When he died in 1534 he left the modest sum of 1,250 guilders.

In those days the German mining industry was the most important in Europe, and to it we owe the first great classic technical works on the subject. In view of this it seems strange that Luther, son of a miner and brought up in industrial surroundings, referred so seldom to his father's trade. In his table-talk he would say: 'I come of peasants. My father, my grandfather, my forebears were true peasants.' His ancestors, who cannot be traced very far back, were indeed peasants, a widespread clan whose home was Möhra in the Thuringian Forest. The name, a derivative of the Christian name Lothar, was written Luder or Lüder, although it also occurs as Loder or Lotter; it was only when he began to publish his writings that Luther chose the form by which he is known. The Luders were very far from being oppressed and serf-like peasants; they were relatively well placed and free proprietors, paying only a modest quit-rent to their overlord, the elector of Saxony. In the village communities to which they belonged they were blessed with an autonomy that was only rarely interfered with from above. They enacted their own local laws, decreed their own punishments and fines, and administered their own local finances. Among the local laws was one governing inheritance, and it was strictly enforced: the youngest, not the eldest, son inherited the homestead. The elder sons had to seek their fortune elsewhere. Luther's father was the eldest of four sons. Leaving home soon after his marriage, he took his young wife, Margarethe, into the county of Mansfeld, settling first in Eisleben, where their son Martin was born, and a year later moving to Mansfeld, where he remained until he died.

Contemporaries described the Luders, or Luthers, as 'small and swarthy'. It was desirable for men working in the mines to be small; they had to work in a very narrow shaft, and at the face often in a crouching position. The work was hard. Safety measures scarcely existed, and the ventilation was very inadequate; there was constant danger from gas and flooding. Hans Luder was a hard worker and a hard man. The portraits of him and his wife which Lucas Cranach painted in their old age reveal coarse features and the deeply ingrained marks that come from lives of unremitting toil; the wife bears some resemblance to Albrecht Dürer's mother, exhausted by her many confinements. Nine children came at regular intervals; there may have been more, because we do not know for certain how many died. It seems to have been only in later years, after his son Martin had already left home, that Hans Luder's circumstances improved to any extent; in the Mansfeld records he also appears as councillor. During Luther's early childhood the family, while not actually in want, must have had to observe the strictest economy; ruthless discipline was also observed. In spite of Luther's respect for his parents, he complained bitterly of being thrashed unmercifully for the slightest offence; he had only to sneak a nut and his mother would beat him black and blue. On one such occasion his father punished him so severely that he ran away. Luther brought up his own children very differently; in his home, which was run by his wife Käthe, discipline was easy-going and at times downright negligent. Jacob Burckhardt once said that a world history of the rod could be extremely revealing; peoples are its victims as well as children. That the father's disciplinary methods, with their strict adherence to the old adage 'spare the rod and spoil the child', left an indelible mark on the boy seems certain. Luther's characteristic defiance, which so often led him into trouble, was awakened at an early age, especially when he was punished unjustly. The idea that he was at the mercy of a relentless judge, with no possibility of appeal to either good conduct or merit – and this was the general view taken of the Heavenly Father too – became confirmed in him; in weak natures such a conviction leads to servility and numb obedience, in strong to the development of all the inherent powers of resistance. It took a long time for these to mature in Luther, but when they did they burst forth with redoubled power.

We shall do better to regard Hans Luder as a model husband and father, in accordance with the notions current in his day, than as exceptionally tyrannical. His son has told us that, like all miners, he enjoyed a good drink and sometimes returned home the worse for it; on these occasions, however, he walked in erect and pleasantly tipsy, and 'not like a savage as you do, you scoundrel' – as the reformer once angrily remarked in later years to one of his nephews who had been brought up in the Luther household. The hard-working Hans Luder can never have been a drunkard. He must also have had a gift for getting on with his fellow miners, a vital requirement for successful work in the desperately cramped working conditions of the small enterprises; early in his career they made him their speaker and representative in dealing with the town council. One thing he unquestionably passed on to his son: his capacity for dogged, tireless, hard work.

Of family life in the Luder household we know nothing. In view of the large number of children it cannot have been exclusively patriarchal and strict; one feels more inclined to imagine the boys and girls being left to play on their own with their friends, while the father worked in the heavy, black, slaty marl of the pit, and the mother got on with the housework, or brought in the kindling wood on her back, as Luther tells us she did. When engaged on these tasks she would hum her favourite song – not a very cheerful one, it must be admitted: '*Mir und dir ist keiner hold, das ist unser beider Schuld*' ('We two must take the blame alone that you and I are loved by none'). There was much talk of misfortune and evil spirits. A miner's life was beset by thoughts of spiteful and malicious spirits, demons and devils, who were behind all the numerous accidents; returning home from work, Luther's father told of one of his companions who had died in agony after Satan's minions had torn the skin off his back. His mother was convinced that the death of one of her children had been caused by a neighbour who was a witch. Every hailstorm and thunderstorm brought denunciations of witches from the pulpit. The defence of turning his back on devils and demons, to which Luther clung all his life, had been instilled into him as a child at home. An ancient legacy of heathen magic, consisting of herbs and benedictions, mixed with the Christian customs of sprinkling holy water on household utensils, or spreading palm leaves crosswise above the fireplace, was in vogue. In emergencies St Anne, the patron saint of miners, was invoked. Whether prayers were said apart from this Luther has not told us. The house contained no Bible, nor even one of the popular devotional books of the day; in all probability it contained no books of any kind. Like most men of his class, Hans Luder set little store by priests and monks, and it was one of the bitterest disappointments of his life that his talented eldest son wanted to enter this calling of chanters and bigots instead of becoming a skilled lawyer, and thus raising the Luder family to the highest status open to it, that of advisers to princes and city councils.

Convinced of his son's intelligence, he seems to have conceived this ambition when Martin was still a child. When the boy was only five he sent him to the grammar school in Mansfeld, an older relative having to carry him to school pick-a-back because the journey was too much for his infant legs. A new era of beating now began. Luther had not a single good word to say of the eight years he spent at Mansfeld grammar school; he referred to it only as an 'asses' stable and devils' school,' run by 'tyrants and jailers', a 'hell and purgatory'. In a single morning, so he tells us, the master birched him fifteen times. A birch the size of a garden broom, as the sceptre of every schoolmaster, is proudly displayed on the title page of all the pedagogic tracts of the day. In most cases the teacher was some poor wretch, ill-paid and ill-equipped, who had to cope with a horde of children of all ages, from those just learning to read to more advanced pupils; his task was simply to teach them to read and write, and above all to teach them Latin, with the aid of time-honoured school books such as those by the fourth-century grammarian Donatus and those by Alexander de Villa Dei of the twelfth century. Latin, the Late Latin of the Middle Ages, was the language of the Church, of officialdom and of business and was thus the key to all subsequent careers, whether within the Church or outside it; it was ruthlessly crammed down the pupils' throats. The wielder of the birch, sitting at his high desk, was aided by a well-developed system of espionage and denunciation: anyone uttering a word of German, instead of Latin, was denounced with the cry 'wolf', a special 'wolf card' being used to record the culprits' names. In addition to the birch there were wooden asses' halters, hung round the pupils' necks as a disgrace. Nevertheless Luther learned to write at the school – throughout his life he cultivated an admirably fine and clear hand – and to master Latin, in which he expressed himself with confidence and force. But it is curious that from his fifth to his thirtieth year the greatest master of the German language of his century remained pinioned within the strait-jacket of a foreign idiom; when, finally, he was able to throw it off, his mother tongue yielded to him in the most wonderful way.

The school provided no instruction in German, or indeed in any other subjects at all; religion entered the picture only to the extent of the calendar of saints, which was used as a means of teaching Latin, and the Paternoster and Ave Maria. More significant for Luther's subsequent career than what he learned was what he did not learn. He learned not a word of the history either of his own country or of the rest of the world. In later life Luther greatly regretted this and in the fine petition he addressed to members of the councils of the great cities he forcefully stressed the advantages of a knowledge of history, and the benefits of the modern system of education. He, and above all Philipp Melanchthon, were responsible for the change, the scope and consequences of which it is impossible to over-estimate. He learned not a word about politics or civic affairs, and this was to have disastrous consequences when Luther was drawn into the political life of his time. What did the children learn of the Holy Roman Empire in which they lived? There was not even a reliable scholarly work on the subject, let alone a school book; moreover it would have been difficult to encompass within a single volume this monstrous complex of dynastic, ecclesiastical, secular-ecclesiastical and extraterritorial patterns. No geography was taught and no natural science. The earth was flat, a disc, with its centre at Rome or Jerusalem. News of the great voyages of discovery had at the most penetrated into the studies of certain scholars. As a boy Luther certainly never set eyes on a map, and did so subsequently only very rarely. He did not even learn arithmetic; the famous arithmetic books of Adam Riese did not appear until many years later. He was never any good at figures, and even gave the year of his birth wrongly; nor did calculation ever enter his mind where time or work was concerned. The catalogue can be extended at will. Certain grammar schools gave a somewhat wider education. At Mansfeld Latin alone was crammed into the pupils, to the beat of the birch.

His father, intent on advancing the education of his eldest son, and saving every penny to do so, sent him to the great city of Magdeburg, where the 'Brothers of the Common Life' ran a better school that had a wide reputation. But the boy spent only a year there, and it is doubtful whether he received more than fleeting impressions of the piety of this community, which was so utterly different from anything he had known at home. All he retained was the picture of a devout penitent who attracted attention in the streets because he was a prince of Anhalt; this man went about dressed as a simple Franciscan, carrying his beggar's scrip and reduced to a skeleton by incessant fasting. The fourteen-year-old Martin also had to beg and earn part of his keep as a door-to-door chorister; this was not considered in any sense a disgrace, being the normal practice even for boys in better circumstances. Begging was still a hallowed institution: it was practised by monks, even by those of the wealthy mendicant orders, as a means of raising funds to help the poor, as a church custom at every church door, and by large, highly organized beggar guilds under their picturesque beggar kings, who were often heavily armed leaders of gangs; the Curia's system of raising money by indulgences and the granting of pardons was also really a form of begging on a grand scale. In any case Luther learned to sing in this way, and music was to be the only art with which he had any real affinity.

The boy, now a strapping young lad, was next sent to Eisenach, where the Luders had relatives; here, in the house of the Schalbe family, he seems for the first time to have found a more congenial home life. These Eisenach people were devout and maintained close relations with the Franciscan monastery at the foot of the Wartburg. Here Luther had another experience which remained in his memory: the brothers had immured one of their number for life for making dangerous prophecies, which he had taken from the prophet Daniel. In later life Luther's thoughts often reverted to this man, Johannes Hilten, who, along with his gloomy predictions of cataclysms and the end of the world, is said to have given 1516 as the date of a great turning-point in the history of the world, and in so doing erred by only a few months.

The parish school of St George was a good one, and young Martin's hard-earned mastery of Latin now stood him in good stead: he felt at home in it, wrote it quickly and well, and was also able to compose the compulsory verses. He soon outstripped the other pupils in the top class. Among the friends of the Schalbe family he made stimulating contacts and found patrons with whom he continued to remain in touch in after years. Later he spoke of 'his dear Eisenach', an expression he used for no other place in which he lived. The days of the birch were over. People at that time did not worry their heads over the problems of puberty, and to replace the gaps in our knowledge with present-day theories is to indulge in pure speculation. Like everything else he said in retrospect, Luther's few statements about his boyhood and his parents' house, which are the only sources we have for his life prior to his late 'teens, should be treated with caution. At the age of seventeen he must have been a 'lively, cheerful fellow', to quote his fellow students: short, stockily built, headstrong, with keen, deep-set brown eyes and brown hair. He went the rounds with his singing companions, cheerfully playing the role of *Partekenhengst*, as it was called, whose job was to collect the tiny gifts of alms; at feasts held to celebrate the slaughter of pigs or cattle they did better. As an older pupil he cheerfully looked after little Heinrich Schalbe, both on his way to school and at his studies. The word cheerful (*fröhlich*) is inseparable from Luther's character. It occurs constantly in his writings, and not by accident. He used it even in his important polemic works, and in the preface to his translation of the Bible. In immediate juxtaposition to this cheerfulness, however, was his heritage of severe melancholy, his tendency to brood, to torment himself, which he referred to as the 'knots' in his soul; they long resisted all efforts to untie them. In Eisenach he was hardly aware of them. The world was a friendly place. Things were also going better

13

for his hard father, Hans Luder, who decided to use the first money he was able to save, after paying his debts to the copper merchants, for Martin's further education. The university he chose was the famous one at Erfurt. The young man made his way there on foot, being entered at the end of April 1501 as *Martinus Ludher ex Mansfeldt*.

# 2

# At Erfurt University

LUTHER spent four years at Erfurt University, studying first the 'liberal arts', in the faculty of arts, and then law, not theology. These four years comprised a by no means insignificant part of his life and education, and yet, in the eyes of later observers and in his own eyes too, his subsequent conversion and life as a monk completely overshadowed these university days. These years between the ages of eighteen and twenty-two are usually considered decisive in the development of a gifted young man. Luther tells us almost nothing about them, although he was only too ready to speak of his struggles in the monastery – but everything Luther said in retrospect was highly coloured. When people accused him of having inadequate book knowledge, he would defend himself: not at all, he had learnt all that thoroughly; his teachers had been excellent, only they had been unable to instil into him anything that 'really mattered'. He claimed that in Erfurt he held a Bible in his hands for the first time – a claim we can readily believe – but said he took only a cursory glance at it. Mathesius, his pupil and first biographer, portrays him as in every respect a model young man: 'He may have been a gay and lively young lad, but he began his studies each morning with heart-felt prayer and attendance at church, thus living up to his motto: prayer is more than half-way to learning. He never went to sleep over his lessons or neglected them, liked to ask his tutors questions and discuss things with them deferentially, often went over his work with his fellow students, and when there were no lectures spent all his time in the University library.' In other words no time for frivolities, no departure from the straight and narrow path laid down for the great reformer. He took his examination in the shortest permissible time: his bachelor's degree after only a year, coming thirtieth out of fifty-seven candidates, and two years later his master's degree, in which he came second out of seventeen. His father was overjoyed and from this moment addressed the son who had achieved such distinction with the respectful *Ihr* instead of the familiar *du*. He also presented him with a sumptuous gift in the form of a complete edition of the *Corpus juris*, for he hoped to see

Early sixteenth-century schoolroom

his son Martin become a great lawyer, a legal adviser to princes and city councils, like his university teacher Professor Henning Goede.

Almost everything else that has been recorded about this period relates exclusively to Luther's metamorphosis into the rebel and reformer; and in the search for pre-Reformation trends and personalities almost everyone who ever uttered a word against the pope or against indulgences has been dragged within the meshes of a widespread net, a method lacking somewhat in historical perspective. Criticism, and criticism of the most biting kind, had always been exercised against the conditions prevailing in the Church, even when the papacy was at its zenith; moreover this criticism was often expressed in stronger terms than those used by Luther. During the previous century such criticism had, if anything, become rather more moderate, at least in expression; it was rare for anyone to be so bold as to call the pope – least of all a pope as forceful as Gregory VII, who established the Curia as a world power – his 'Satanic Holiness', a 'wolf' and a 'tiger'. St Petrus Damiani, however, had done precisely this; he had also cast his bishopric of Ostia, the highest honour that could be bestowed on a cardinal, at his primate's feet – a gesture no one was ever to make again – and withdrawn into his hermit's cloister to write the four volumes of his *Sodom and Gomorrah of the Priesthood*. As life in all its aspects became more bourgeois – itself a result of increasing bureaucracy in the management of the Church – talk centred more and more exclusively on money matters, taxes and other material burdens, and the unlawful uses to which these moneys were put in Rome. In 1490, for example, the

Erfurt chronicler, a Benedictine monk and loyal churchman named Nikolaus, complained that the people would willingly be good sheep if only they had a good shepherd! But the shepherd wanted more than simply to shear them and protect them from the wolves: 'He also wants to tear the flesh from their bodies and devour it; but in the way of comfort and piety he has little, if anything, to offer. What kind of shepherd is this?' This metaphor recurs constantly; the biblical tradition of 'feeding the sheep' was the great authority on which the Church took its stand. But the attitude of the sheep had changed; they were no longer so willing to submit patiently to shearing. The people of Erfurt were particularly sensitive, and for good reasons. Their shepherd was the archbishop of Mainz, their temporal as well as their spiritual master – if indeed the two offices can be distinguished. Erfurt provides a typical example of the extraordinary confusion that prevailed in the Holy Roman Empire at this time and our justification for taking a glance at it is that Luther spent the decisive years of his life there.

In the Middle Ages the world was conceived in terms of one's town, not one's country. Even Augustine, the patron saint of Luther's religious order and his constant model, had taken as his starting point the divine city of his imagination; Thomas Aquinas had also based his idea of the world entirely on the city, which he thought of as at best surrounded by 'provinces'. Erfurt was a city in this sense, and it was the centre of a very considerable province, comprising seventy-six villages and small market towns and divided into nine administrative districts; in size it was second only to Nuremberg, whose sphere of influence made it almost comparable to a principality. Thus it was a valuable possession, and its importance was further increased by the fact that, situated as it was in the middle of Germany and at the intersection of great trade routes, it had grown rich as a commercial centre. In addition it was also the centre of what in those days was a highly lucrative industry, Thuringia having virtually a monopoly in the production of dyer's blue, which was made of woad obtained from the now almost forgotten *crucifer isatis*; the leaves were crushed, mixed with water to form a pulp, and then, by a process of fermentation and oxidization through contact with the oxygen in the air, turned into the greatly prized dye for which, in the colour-loving Middle Ages, there was an enormous demand. Erfurt also boasted a very competent armed force, which it employed over a wide area to subdue the Thuringian robber knights; when one of their strongholds had been overrun and destroyed the proud citizens, as a token of victory, scattered woad seeds over the ploughed-up territory of the defeated knight – certainly a more profitable custom than the usual one of scattering salt. Proud, belligerent and rich, they strained incessantly against the yoke imposed on them by the overlordship of the archbishop in distant Mainz. Unlike other great cities, Erfurt, although it was one of the three or four largest cities in Germany – the population statistics are all inaccurate – was never able wholly to shake off this yoke and win the status of a 'free' city of the empire; in size it was scarcely inferior to Rome, whose population at that time was about 60,000, though this figure, too, is only approximate. It would be quite wrong to picture Luther during these years as a student in a small, out-of-the-way town, such as Wittenberg was when he went there ten years later. It would be more accurate to think of him studying in a great metropolis and at a leading university whose reputation extended far beyond the borders of the empire. Erfurt was the most modern German university of its day. The philosophic school of thought prevailing in it was the *via moderna* of nominalism, though humanism at first also found powerful support there, and in its brief heyday – which was brought to an end by the events of the Reformation – Erfurt University even took the unprecedented step of giving the faculty of philosophy pride of place over the faculty of theology, which reigned undisputed everywhere else. This revolution in academic life caused almost as much horror among adherents of the old order as the rebellion of the Wittenberg monk. Even before Luther burned the Bull of Excommunication a young Erfurt University teacher named Hermann von dem Busche had solemnly committed to the flames the hallowed textbooks of tradition. The student body, gathered from many different countries, was one of the most turbulent for many miles around. Nowhere else were there so many disturbances and skirmishes, some of them violent in the extreme, and when the struggle began no other university was so ardent in its support of Luther.

There was nothing revolutionary or modern about the students' reception and dress. Unlike most other universities Erfurt had not followed the example of Paris and divided its students by grouping compatriots together; on his arrival every student had to enrol in a *Burse*, or students' hostel, where he lived as a boarder under strict supervision. Jealously as the students paraded their status before the townspeople, they had to toe the line like schoolboys in their hostels, where life was almost monastic, their meals, their prayers, their coming and going being prescribed and supervised. The syllabus of work was controlled; any student wishing to attend a lecture that was not compulsory had to get permission from the rector. The students wore uniform, to make them easily identifiable in the town; university bulldogs, as well as proctors, kept a lookout. The choice of books was not left to the students, and we may safely assume that Luther hardly ever held a book in his hand which deviated, however slightly, from what his professors regarded as the true path. Hence we may conceive of the young Luther as an obedient and model pupil, who rose with the bell at four o'clock each morning and went to bed, in obedience to the rules, at eight o'clock at night.

Of course this was not all. On entering the university the new student was subjected to 'deposition', an old custom, carried out pretty roughly, that consisted of 'deposing' the 'brutish' non-student, symbolized by a cap surmounted with horns and asses' ears which was torn off him, and 'christening' him as a new-born undergraduate by ducking him in the water-butt. Luther afterwards cited this custom in a sermon as an instructive example of the need for humility and patience: in life one was always 'humbled' in this way, officials were 'deposed and tormented by townspeople and peasants, married couples by women' – it was symbolic of human existence in general. The uniform resembled that of a priest, and this in any case was what most of the students were going to be; at the side of his gown, however, each student carried a short sword, and it was not worn merely for decoration. Despite the strict daily schedule, brawls were frequent; Luther's closest friend, whose name we do not know, was killed in one such affray, and his death is said to have influenced Luther's decision to enter a monastery. The official drink at meals, which were very copious, was beer, but we may be certain that not everyone contented himself with this. Luther's hostel was popularly known as the *Biertasche*, or beer pot, but there were many better places for a drink in the town. Among the professors were some very gay spirits, though not, of course, among those of the older and more devout school. Luther's teacher, Usingen, was one of the latter; in his fifties he followed his pupil's example and entered the Augustinian monastery as a monk. The humanist professors, who called themselves proudly 'the poets' and turned out their Latin verses, had found precedents among the ancients to justify a somewhat freer life. Their leader was the handsome Eobanus Hessus, a gifted man of unquenchable optimism, famous for his ability to write verses in the style of Ovid, his capacity for liquor, his brilliant rhetoric and the lively delivery of his lectures. During his mild reign as 'King Eoban' the university enjoyed a short period of glory, he and his associates looking to Erasmus as their patron – but this was after Luther had gone to Wittenberg. Under his headship there emerged a prototype of the later students' fraternity or association, with strict regulations as to drinking, its own officers, and ceremonial dinners at the George Inn. A member of his student audience, recalling in later years Eoban's commanding presence at his lectures, attributed it to the dignity and gravity of his bearing, with the modification, however: 'When Eoban was sober rather than when he was drunk.' Audiences of over a thousand were

19

claimed at his lectures, but this is hard to reconcile with the entrance figures for the university.

Not all the Erfurt humanists were like Eoban. There was Crotus Rubianus, a man of great talent known to have been a fellow student and friend of Luther, who later, under conditions of great secrecy, became author-in-chief of the *Epistolae obscurorum virorum*, a work of which we shall have more to say. Then there was Euricius Cordus, a sour, discontented individual who wrote satiric epigrams; he has left us the most intimate accounts of the Erfurt of his day. One of his enemies – people quarrelled interminably – declared that Cordus was more at home in the Cavaten than in the lecture rooms; the Cavaten were large vaults, beneath the high, sloping sides of the cathedral, where the brothels were housed – in the Middle Ages these were generally located in the shadow of a church. Cordus undoubtedly knew his way about them, as he did the *Sperlingsgasse*, which was later re-named after Doctor Faust, who at about this time gave one of his performances in Erfurt. Canon Mutian of Gotha, the mentor and Maecenas of the Erfurt humanists, who heard Faust 'playing the braggart' in an inn, dismissed him summarily as a chiromant, boaster and fool. Luther mentions Faust in his table-talk, and Melanchthon, annoyed because the man's name was also linked with Wittenberg where he even wanted to take the degree of master or doctor, called him a 'cesspool of many devils'. The aura of mystery, which later surrounded this master magician and turned him into a mythical figure, was then only in the process of formation; he was seen rather as one of numerous vagabond story-tellers. All the same it is significant that this figure also spirited his way into Luther's life.

Cordus mentions a much more harmless academic entertainer, who brought great wisdom from Italy and gave free lectures in the courtyard of the inn *Zum goldenen Kreuz* (The Golden Cross). Earning not only resounding applause but financial reward, he spoke extempore 'in the Italian manner' from a rostrum he set up by the fountain in the courtyard, while his listeners sat tightly packed on piles of books or old casks. He announced himself as the messenger of Apollo, who for his benefit had transformed these evil-smelling surroundings into a 'fragrant poet's study', chatted about Horace and Juvenal, and generally gave himself out as a 'new prophet'. In the lecture rooms a young assistant professor, a Swabian named Emser, who later became Luther's inveterate enemy, read a paper on the newly published comedy *Sergius*, by the great humanist teacher Reuchlin, which ridiculed a charlatan monk; another university master once gave a lecture on one of the first dialogues of Ulrich von Hutten.

In addition to his set books Luther also read some of the ancient classics; of these the one he liked best was Virgil, whom the Church had raised to the status of a great Christian poet on the strength of his alleged prophecy of the birth of Christ in the fourth Eclogue. But he never felt any real affinity with the poetry of antiquity, and when he quoted a Greek poet it was only because a phrase struck him didactically as an 'aphorism'; in all probability he got such passages out of the usual anthologies. His model was Aesop, whose fables he found 'full of good, fine precepts, morals, educative virtues and experience'; Terence he considered useful for teaching the language. The whole humanist inspiration was alien to him, even as a student; later it became far more so. He turned out no Latin epigrams, no verses to some Chloe; nor did he engage in the customary mutual panegyrics in which a fellow student was inevitably hailed as a new Horace, Pindar or Martial. He was not unsociable, but he never attached himself to a 'group'.

A very distinct group, and one that acquired temporary importance, was the circle which clustered round Canon Mutian in nearby Gotha, a man whose influence and reputation are not easy to explain. Mutian, whose real name was Konrad Muth, was one of those men who like to operate by stealth, to attach wires and then manipulate them; he had an almost morbid fear of publicity and never published a line. His great delight was to exercise authority over young people, to guide them, and sometimes also to incite them; if they 'went too far' he withdrew in alarm into his study. Nevertheless with these rather meagre talents he managed to spin a veritable spider's web over a very wide area. To be praised or recommended by Mutian was considered almost as important as to be able to produce a few words of recommendation from Erasmus; even the Elector Frederick of Saxony, normally so painfully cautious, listened to him and tried to win him for his new university at Wittenberg. Mutian was not to be enticed by any offer; the silent power he wielded from his pleasant canonry was enough for him, and for a few years this power was great. But he was fated to live in an age that refused to tolerate such silence. When the cold winds blew they tore his web to shreds, and in the closing years of his life Mutian was a pitiful figure, without means, dependent on the charity of his patrons, mistrusted everywhere. It is not surprising that Luther was never able to feel any sympathy for him, either in Erfurt or later.

But this group round Mutian was of peripheral importance in Erfurt; the unremitting correspondence and self-adulation of its members brought it disproportionate fame. The centre of this town of many spires was dominated by the cathedral and the church of St Severus, a fortress-like complex whose silhouette is the most picturesque and fanciful that has survived from the Middle Ages; it did not consist merely of churches and chapels, but was a town within a town, housing the highly privileged chapters and their canons, an aristocracy within the hierarchy of the Church. The townspeople looked upon them as 'outsiders', and the canons were in fact recruited largely from the 'foreign aristocracy'. Their ample prebends enabled them to live in comfort, their residences being as beautifully appointed as their magnificently carved choir stalls in the cathedral, which stressed very clearly the fact that these lords of the Church considered themselves to be something quite apart from and better than the common people, who sat on benches in the nave. They sat at finely inlaid tables and drank well, the full extent of their vast wine cellars being revealed only when the storm broke and the impious mob made free with the precious Malmsey and Franconian wines. They had their concubines too, this being the general practice in those days of cathedral canons in every country; in the words of a popular song: '*Er hat ein Hur von Würzburg bracht/Er ist vierzehn Jahr ein Domherr gewesen/Und hat noch nie kein Mess gelesen*' ('He brought a whore from Würzburg town, full fourteen years a canon here, he's never yet said Mass I fear'.) The 'immorality' of what went on caused less dismay than the fact that, instead of staying quietly at home or in bed, which might have been condoned as human frailty, these ladies paraded arrogantly about the town, 'showing no consideration for either the townswomen or the nobility', heavily made up, laden with jewellery and claiming almost the same precedence as their protectors. Even these sometimes had to suffer from the dominating ways of their ladies, and when a sharply worded though, as always, ineffective order came from higher authority to the effect that in future the canons were only to keep 'servants', Cordus wittily remarked that no priest kept a servant, she was always his *domina*, his mistress. Instead of saying Mass, the canons eagerly studied the registers of revenues and rents – the burning of which later became one of the main objectives of the revolts – and ruthlessly exacted their dues. They were exempt from all taxes and contributions, and for this reason were also extremely unpopular with the city council. Since they had received their privileges from the archbishop of Mainz, they naturally formed the core of his sovereignty over Erfurt, a sovereignty that was fought tooth and nail and always in vain.

Surrounding this stronghold there were numerous smaller bastions scattered throughout the town, all similarly privileged and exempt from taxes, all intent on supervising their revenues. At this time there were over ninety churches and chapels in Erfurt, as well as thirty-six monasteries and convents. The Augustinian monastery which Luther entered was one of the smaller ones. Almost every religious order was represented, giving rise to a corresponding variety of dress, ways of life and behaviour. Some, the 'reformed' foundations, were strict, but these were a minority; from time to time a great figure would appear preaching repentance, denouncing abuses in thunderous sermons and occasionally crusading against the sellers of indulgences, who invaded the town to present their own privileges and means of grace, which they claimed were better and more effective than those of the local custodians of sacred relics. But these were only isolated exceptions. The rule to which the 'regulars', the monks, in fact adhered was that of the free and easy life. For the most part they kept neither to their monasteries nor to their regulations, and swarmed all over the town. They were to be seen at every festivity and amusement, feasting jovially with the people whenever there was anything to feast on; some could hardly be blamed for this – alongside the heavily endowed foundations there existed a large clerical proletariat who prowled about begging in shabby, tattered habits. The class structure of the priesthood, which in theory was supposed to feature only one class, corresponded fairly closely to that of ordinary life; there was an aristocracy, a bourgeoisie and a plebs. The great difference was that the high privilege of the *character indelebilis*, the indestructible dignity of ordination, was claimed unconditionally on every occasion, even when a member of the priesthood stole, committed adultery or actually committed murder. The dispute engendered by this judicial privilege stood at the head of the long list of complaints against the Church.

In reading the complaints and exhortations to repentance, however, let us not be misled into seeing only the picture of gloom painted in these records. Erfurt celebrated its great festivals and held its great processions. Work went on on the construction of churches and chapels, on the over-elaborate carving and costly tombstones, some of which, like that for Luther's teacher Henning, were supplied by Peter Vischer's celebrated foundry in Nuremberg. The goldsmith's art was responsible for huge quantities of monstrances and chalices, not many of which survived the great revolt against the priesthood. St Severus lay in a magnificent solid silver coffin; later the city council had this melted down and turned into coins, which circulated for many years under the name *Sargpfennige*, or coffin pennies. The monasteries were not filled only with fairground-haunting monks; among them were also men who spent their time in quiet meditation and prayer, as Martin Luther was to do. Nevertheless, this does not change the overall picture. It does not explain why all the colour and splendour, the remains of which today afford us so much aesthetic pleasure, collapsed as they did under the axes of the enemies of the Church and the pamphlets of the Wittenberg monk. The whole social structure had become rotten, if indeed it had ever been sound; the spiritual foundations were shaken still more profoundly and turned out to be still less stable.

We have no means of knowing how much Luther in his Erfurt days understood of what was going on around him, but it seems certain that a young man with his acuteness of perception and comprehension must have assimilated a great deal more than the mere book knowledge imparted by his professors. He appears to have taken almost no part in the wilder aspects of student life; had he done so his later enemies would certainly have proclaimed the fact with relish, especially as they themselves – Emser and Eck for example – were well informed on the subject. But Luther was a 'gay and lively fellow', surely not content only with enquiring deferentially of his tutors which chapter of the dialectic he should study next. He accomplished his allotted task with great energy – throughout his life he was a tremendous worker – perfecting himself in the prescribed method, which laid particular stress on the ability to engage in disputations. The scholastic technique consisted of disposing of objections deftly and aptly, in 'fencing with arguments'; it was much less important for an argument to be 'true' or 'profound' than for it to be shrewd and telling. Luther retained his enjoyment of the cut and thrust of disputations throughout his life; the story of the Reformation is composed of one long series of great disputations. He became a master in this art at an early age. His fellow students called him the 'philosopher', which implied, not that he had a taste for philosophic speculation – this never interested him in the slightest – but that he was adept in the manipulation of ideas, logic and the presentation of arguments. The faculty of arts, in which he was enrolled, had the task of schooling students in this; it was intended as an introduction to the higher, true faculty of theology. Luther's impatience to get to grips with this subject, for him the most important of all, led him in retrospect to complain that all he had done before this was to thresh empty straw. Later, when he used the cudgel, the frequent bluntness of his language easily blinds us to the accuracy of his aim and the debt he owed to his training in the dialectical method.

He was a good keen pupil; he sharpened his mind, prayed assiduously and passed his examinations in quick succession. But to his fellow students he was known not only as the philosopher but also as 'the musician'. All his life music was the art closest to him. But although it was included in the university syllabus, it was treated there as a mathematical exercise, a study in musical theory, and was taught as scholastically as any other set of rules, being yoked irrevocably to the authorities, the Late Latin philosopher Boëthius and his successors. The words 'music', 'mathematics', 'astronomy', found in the prescribed course of study, bore almost no relation to the terms as we use them today. The whole canon of university study, which had remained unaltered for centuries, was based on the mystical number seven.

Grammar was the first and noblest of the 'Seven Free Arts', whereas painting and sculpture were excluded as manual, mechanical, inferior exercises, while music was accepted only because it was 'mathematical'. The 'arts' taught in the faculty of arts were 'sciences'. Grammar, rhetoric and dialectic formed the leading triad, the *trivium*, after which came the four mathematical arts, or *quadrivium*, consisting of arithmetic, geometry, music and astronomy. They were called 'free', or liberal, because they were worthy of a free man; yoked to the doctrines of the the Church, it was the Church they had to serve, not the self-sufficient forces of free thought, 'art for art's sake', or scientific research. Their task was to explain the God-ordained harmony of the universe; the express mission of dialectics was to establish 'the truth', while astronomy pointed to the stars in the heavens as the unalterably fixed signs of the zodiac. Music, too, had to express this harmony down to the smallest detail. The music introduced to Luther in the lecture room was based on the theoretical work of Johannes de Muris, written some two hundred years before and itself based on the still earlier music of the twelfth and thirteenth centuries; at the same time, however, it provided a very thorough training in the theory of intervals, the church modes and musical proportion.

Luther mastered this too. But he also made music of a different, more practical, kind. As a boy he had sung in the *Kurrende*, the boys' choir which went round singing from door to door; he had a good voice. Now he played the lute, a costly and difficult instrument. With the exception of the top, or melody, string, the strings were double-strung; the tuning alone took a quarter of an hour and required a good ear, which Luther had. To Luther's contemporaries, whose hearing had not been blunted and sated by constant subjection to music, the tone that came out of the lute's bulbous, arched body sounded quite powerful. In importance the lute ranked immediately after the organ, being used as an orchestral instrument for another hundred years, until the violin family took over. The finger positions were not easy, and the music was written in a special tablature, which made use of letters; the first printed manuals did not appear until some years later. We know neither from whom Luther learned the art nor what he played or sang. It was the heyday of the so-called 'folk song', which drew on an ancient treasury of religious and secular airs. People rang the changes on these indiscriminately, and the first song collections printed religious and secular songs side by side; it was quite usual for a love ditty to be sung to a religious air, and vice versa. Verses making fun of handicrafts, like that of the tailor, were old favourites and were also sung. Politics played a great part, as did a wide variety of propaganda; the song became a weapon, a news sheet that often gave more information about events of the day than the dispatches of diplomats. Songs were sometimes danced as rounds; here too a satiric note crept in when, for example, the 'proud nuns', facing the monks on the village green, curtsied to their lovers with a solemn '*Herr Domine*', and they in turn wished their 'bride a good year'. In the late Middle Ages people danced to more pious strains than this, and in some places, though not in Erfurt, even in church.

While it seems unlikely that Martin Luther, as a young undergraduate, took part in this kind of singing and dancing, it is impossible to picture him at this stage as the stern reformer prepared only to accept the hymnal. When that time came he wanted to ban loud laughter and joking: 'Music should rejoice the soul; the tongue finds no pleasure in it. When we sing diligently, the soul takes its place in the body, plays for us, and finds a special delight in so doing.' Above all, however, he saw in music a source of comfort in sadness and temptation: Satan was the spirit of gloom, he could not tolerate joy; thus to no one was music so alien as it was to Satan. Even in Luther's younger days his friends would bring him his lute when he was in the grip of one of his frequent severe attacks of melancholy. Once they found him stretched out almost lifeless on the floor; when they handed him his instrument he ran his fingers over the strings and, on hearing the music, stood up.

Gaiety and gloom were inseparable companions in Luther's life. In one of the folk song parodies the ditty '*Es hat ein Meidlin sein Schuh verlorn*' ('There is a lass has lost her shoe') is at once transformed into the devout '*Gottes Huld hab ich verlorn*' ('The grace of God is lost to me'). The first version he may have sung to lute accompaniment in the presence of gay companions; the second now became his personal melody. He had passed his master's examination brilliantly and had been acclaimed for it. As an old man his thoughts wandered sadly back to the colourful celebrations of those days: 'What a majestic and splendid occasion it was when the masters received their degrees; people went in front of them carrying torches and they were honoured'; and when doctor's degrees were conferred they celebrated by riding all over the town – 'It is all past and gone. But if I had had my way it would have been preserved.' He was now to begin the study of law, this being his father's wish. The *Codex juris* of Justinian lay in front of him, a huge volume, over half the pages of which were filled with innumerable notes and commentaries; this was supplemented by still further volumes written by commentators, which Luther had also acquired. No expense was too great for the father when it came to realizing his life's dream to see his son take his place among the newly rising class of lawyers. He even had a wealthy bride in view. His teachers thought highly of him. An assured career lay ahead.

According to Justas Jonas, a fellow student at the university who was also studying law, Luther had bought his books in Gotha. He was returning to Erfurt on foot 'when a terrifying vision appeared from heaven, which he interpreted there and then to mean that he was to become a monk. As soon as he reached Erfurt he secretly sold all his law books and had a magnificent collation, a dinner, prepared ... invited a number of scholars, modest and virtuous girls and women, and became excessively gay in their company. When the time came to leave they thanked him courteously and left in a cheerful mood, not knowing what he had in mind. But he, Martin Luther, at once went by night into the Augustinian monastery in Erfurt, for this is what he had decided to do; and he became a monk.'

Elsewhere we are told that at this farewell dinner Luther, 'as was his habit, gave a musical performance, for he was a good musician.' Many people attended this farewell; no one but Luther saw the fearful storm and lightning flash which threw him to the ground and made him vow to become a monk. Like everything else he recounted after the change in him that took place in the monastery, his own words on the subject are not quite reliable, being a 'justification' of his subsequent conduct. Immediately after taking the fateful step he had to justify himself to his father, to whom he had said nothing beforehand, well knowing how little sympathy he would receive from that quarter. This seems to be one of the most important aspects of the whole business: for the first time in his life Luther refused obedience, ranging himself, as a man with a will of his own, against his father, the highest authority he then knew, and committing himself to a higher authority, the Church. The break was not easy for him. The family was the nucleus of his outlook on life, his father the supreme judge who, in addition to punishing and thrashing him, had also helped him and furthered his studies most generously. Luther would hardly have made this decision had there not been other thunderstorms prior to the one that broke near Stotternheim in the summer of 1505.

There has been much speculation on this point. External events have been adduced, such as the death of a close friend and the deaths of others; the plague was threatening again and was soon to carry off two of his brothers. Reference has been made to an earlier journey on which, just outside Erfurt, he ran his sword into his body and severed an artery; he is said to have only just escaped bleeding to death, the bandage breaking open again even after he had been taken back to his hostel in the university. He thought he was going to die and turned to the Blessed Virgin for help. The incident is puzzling in the extreme. People do not go around playing with drawn swords; they leave them in their scabbards and draw them only in case of danger, of which there is no mention in this instance. Like all men of strong character and creative genius, Luther was subject to frequent attacks of severe depression, but he admitted this much more frankly and emphatically than other people; his friend Melanchthon has told of attacks of this nature in later years too. 'Depression' was a sign of the times; a 'low' had spread across Europe, a cloud that found powerful expression in the painting and art of the day. The dance of death had become the favourite symbol of the transitoriness of all earthly things, and, until Holbein gave it a somewhat pleasanter humanistic note, was depicted with all the horror of fleshless bones. In justifying his action to his father, Luther himself spoke of fear of death and agony surrounding him like a wall. Later, when he had to explain the further, still more decisive step of breaking his monk's vows, he quoted the well-known saying: 'Despair is the making of a monk.'

But what was the reason for this despair? To enter a monastery was not a desperate step to take; many people took it in order to be well looked after. Luther mentioned this to his father too, saying that he had not become a monk for his 'stomach's sake'. Disgust and boredom with the world, of which up till that time he had not seen very much, can hardly have been the incentive, while the reason he gave later, that his parents' upbringing had been too severe – 'it was the serious strict life they forced me to lead which made me subsequently go into a monastery' – strikes us as strongly coloured by hindsight, especially in view of the fact that latterly his life had been comparatively free.

Possibly Luther was seeking an authority to which his intractable will could submit. He always retained his belief in authority, often indeed to a fatal extent. His father's authority was no longer adequate. That of scholastic learning had already worn thin, especially since he began to study the law commentaries; he constantly criticized their practice of offsetting 'it can be seen like this' with 'it can also be considered otherwise.' At this stage it was the Church whose foundations seemed to him secure. Only when, during the course of his life as a monk, he began to lose faith in this too, did he turn directly to God as the supreme authority, to God as proclaimed by the Bible, about whom no scruples could be entertained. To the end of his life the Bible remained his sole authority; nothing else had any validity.

Phenomena such as religious conversions obey no hard and fast rules; every attempt to explain them briefly ignores the fact that a young genius is an extremely complex creature. But there is no harm in considering the plain facts: when the lightning struck at his side Luther made a vow which, because of his uncompromising nature, he intended to keep, no matter how much his friends tried to dissuade him and argue that there was no need to take it so dreadfully seriously. It is also possible that, despite the lute playing and gay company, the notion of sin had already been awakened in him even at this early date; the very fact that he was unaware of any particular sins in himself, but regarded his whole existence as sinful, may have brought this about. Today such sentiments are hard to appreciate. Awareness of sin has largely disappeared; it is absent in the most hideous of crimes. But in Luther's time it was a great force. It was instilled into people from childhood; in Luther's case it was literally hammered in and never afterwards lost sight of. Life itself was felt to be 'filthy', the body, the 'flesh', to be an encumbrance, and the 'desires of the flesh', not merely sexual desires but even eating and drinking, a burden of impurity. 'The more we wash, the less clean we become,' Luther once said to a friend as they were washing their hands. If this sounds old fashioned, it is worth recalling that almost the same words were used by Franz Kafka; fundamentally he, too, was a man whose life was determined by religion and whose longing for cleanliness and disgust at the 'filth of the world' corresponded exactly to the temper of the late Middle Ages. 'I am sinful to the last corner of my being,' we read in one of his diaries; even to talk to other people was 'polluting'. He expressed a passionate desire for 'unreflecting solitude', and Luther's main problem during his time as a monk finds a parallel in his own words: 'In my ear I hear the constant supplication: if only thou wouldst come, thou invisible judgment!'

Solitude is the only escape from the filth of the world. A monastery was the accepted sanctuary. 'When I was young,' Luther was to relate, 'they commended the adage "keep yourself apart and you keep a pure heart", to which they added St Bernard's saying that every time he had mixed with people he had defiled himself. And in the lives of the Church Fathers there is the story of a hermit who desired no one to visit him and to speak to no one, because, as he said, "the angels cannot visit us if we consort with men".' Luther chose the monastery of the Augustinian anchorites, where he lived as a recluse, although the rules did not stipulate this. There he came face to face with the invisible judgment, with the wrathful judge, which is how he had been taught to fear God. When subsequently he explained his development, his conversion became a challenge that was applicable to others as well as himself: 'God strikes us in order that we shall turn to Him and be converted; but instead of turning to Him we flee from Him. Under the papacy they entered monasteries, whereas what we need to do is turn to Him who strikes us; it is to Him that we must be converted.'

# 3

# The monk

LUTHER spent the decisive years of his early manhood, the years of his real struggle, in the monastery. Very little evidence concerning these years has survived. It is curious how extraordinarily little information about him was provided by his fellow monks after he had become famous, although they were besieged with questions from all sides. As is only natural, his own statements about this period are mostly polemic in character, laying passionate stress on the torments inflicted on the people by the papacy and the agonies he underwent himself.

'We had enough to eat and drink in the monastery, but our hearts and consciences were heavy with suffering and torment, and the suffering of the soul is the greatest suffering of all. I often took fright at the name Jesus, and when I looked at Him on the cross it was like seeing a flash of lightning,' he said later. 'In the monastery I did not think about women, money or possessions, but my heart trembled and pounded at the thought of God's mercy to me.'

'Nor was it only our worldly possessions we gave up, we also sacrificed our bodies with fasting, mortification and other heavy and intolerable burdens, so that some often went mad as a result, all their strength failing them until finally they lost even their souls. I also was one of these and have been tormented by the recipes of that pharmacy more than many others. It took me a long time before I could bring myself to disregard the pope's order. It went hard with me to eat meat on Fridays and to think that the pope's law and decrees went for nothing. Heavens! what I went through before I summoned up courage to defy the laws of the Church.'

He spoke also of the severest temptation, of the temptation peculiar to saints, 'which is commonly called *desertio gratiae*, because in his heart man feels exactly as if God had forsaken him with His grace and wanted nothing more to do with him.'

Obedience, poverty, chastity – these were the vows of a monk. He was required to withdraw from the world and devote himself exclusively to prayer. In a monastery a man was in any case shut off from the world;

it was a small isolated island. Obedience was demanded to those senior in the order, in the community of monks of that particular observance, each such community being distinguished from the others by dress, rules and customs. A long history of development lay behind the monasticism into which Luther now entered. His appearance marked its end as one of the great forces exercising a decisive influence on the west. Monasticism continued to exist, and the old orders still continued, even later, to produce great and distinguished figures, but they never again played their former dynamic role in the world.

Towards the end of the fifteenth century, after a history extending over more than a thousand years, a final stage had unmistakably been reached. These thousand and more years are important; to people living at the time they were, to all intents and purposes, equivalent to eternity. 'As long as man can remember,' it would be said, and man's memory did not go very far back. Even in its very earliest forms monasticism's underlying principle had in fact been the suspension of time, as one of the essential factors controlling human life. One might almost ascribe to these early forms of monasticism the invention of infinity, of eternity; at all events they introduced the concept into the awareness of the west. To take the vow of chastity, to deny sexuality, means more than merely to accept the challenge of an exceptionally difficult problem, the solution of which frees one from everything 'temporal' and opens the way to exclusive contemplation of the eternal. In taking it the ascetic also divorces himself from the passing of the generations, which in children and children's children presents an image of the evolutionary process in one's flesh and blood far more arresting than any obtained by computing time. It was of the greatest consequence for Luther's life that he spent his crucial formative years in such an atmosphere of timelessness, and that then he was suddenly cast into the world, in which, not only year after year but month after month and day after day, he was confronted by decisions requiring him to take action. He often longed to be back in the quiet of the monastery, especially at first; it was only reluctantly that he allowed himself to be wrenched away from it. He himself said this plainly enough, and there is every reason to believe him. The daylight and the glare of daily events blinded him; as he himself put it, in his inimitably dramatic way, he charged off in the opposite direction like a 'blinded horse'.

In the very early days a hermit had been a fugitive. The original meaning of *anachoret*, the Greek word for anchorite, was the very worldly one of a *fellah*, or Egyptian peasant, who ran away from the intolerable burden of taxation – which under the extremely efficient bureaucracy of the late Egyptian Empire was levied with unusual brutality – and hid in the desert, where no one felt any inclination to follow him. The first hermits were *fellaheen,* simple people, uneducated and opposed to education. No theological work of any significance is attributable to them; there are only legends, but these were a basic element of all medieval life and thought. The timelessness of their existence, which they devoted exclusively to prayer and the weaving of rush mats, is caught most beautifully in the tale of the dying Paul of Thebes, the progenitor of all the desert monks. It was not even known how old he was, 113 being the age finally given when St Anthony, himself a man of ninety, sought him out in the disused coiner's workshop that was his cave – a meeting which Matthias Grünewald has depicted on the altarpiece of Isenheim. Paul, on the verge of death, asked Anthony: 'Tell me, I beg you, how things are now with the human race? Do new houses in the old towns have roofs? Whom does the kingdom of the world belong to now? ... if indeed any people at all survive, ensnared in the fallacies of the demons ...'

Demons, the devil in many guises, were the sole companions of these solitaries. They paid frequent visits, because however rigorously and uncompromisingly ascetism was practised it offered no protection against temptation. Luther too, as we know, was subjected to frequent visitations of this kind, even when he no longer lived ascetically. But in those earliest days people wanted to be put to the test; they sought harshness, and even martyrdom, once the real and fearful martyrdoms at the hands of the Roman state and executioner were over. The legend of Paul of Thebes states this explicitly: one prayed to be allowed to die by the sword but the devil, the insidious enemy, thought up tortures that brought a slower death; it was the soul, not the body, he wished to kill.

Temptation meant first and foremost woman, the lust of the flesh. It was through the Egyptian monks that the rabid contempt for woman as the source of all evil found its way into the Church; once inside it took root. As late as Luther's day the temptation of St Anthony remained the favourite subject of painters; it was often treated with secret relish. The old Church Fathers, who neither knew nor tolerated art in any form, took it far more seriously. A hermit, carrying his aged mother across a river, was careful to wrap his cloak round his hands; when she asked him why he did it, he replied: 'A woman's body is fire. And even as I touched you the thought of other women entered my soul.' Anti-feminism underwent many transformations in the Church; later it became somewhat modified because of the gradually increasing veneration for the Virgin Mary. But it continued to exist, at least in the rules and instructions of the religious orders. According to the rules of the Augustinian Order merely to set eyes on a woman was fraught with danger; if the gaze 'lingered' it was a sin, and it was the duty of the culprit's fellow monks, who were under a general obligation to keep a watch on each other, to report it. If a sin of the flesh was actually committed the punishment was prison, with the feet manacled and a diet of bread and water. Luther has recorded that in his monastery days he was seldom aware of sexual desire. He never looked at a woman, even when, as a priest, he had to hear her confession: 'I did not wish to see her face while I heard her. In Erfurt I never heard a woman's confession, and in Wittenberg three times in all.' In view of the nature of his voluntary confessions, which were always characterized by an extreme honesty, amounting at times to brutality, we need have no hesitation in believing this. In this same connection he also spoke quite frankly of pollutions, forced on him 'by the needs of the body'. This was a problem which caused the authorities concern, and Gerson, the great scholastic, wrote a tract on the subject. The difficulty was to distinguish precisely where the border lay between sinful intention and the innocent action of the body; and in the pleasure they took in analysing distinctions the scholastics exceeded even the psycho-analysts of our own day. Luther's statements, however, are so bold, and at times so blunt, that little opportunity seems to be left for complicated interpretation; we willingly leave them to the professionals in this field, along with the question of how much sense of guilt he may have had in regard to masturbation. When he speaks of the 'needs of the body' he means it in a very forthright sense; indeed he referred to all the needs of the body so frankly by name that the more delicate susceptibilities of later times were shocked. It is worth stressing that, in complete contrast to ourselves, people in his day lived together so closely and so entirely without inhibitions – sleeping with several others in the same room and attending to their needs in full view of everyone, or in the closest proximity to other people – that the taboos which today play so large a role could scarcely have arisen.

Because of the undue prominence given to sex in our lives today, it is the sexual problems of monastic life that receive special attention. Undoubtedly they existed, but generally, as we shall see, they were solved much more simply in those days. In Luther's case there is another important fact: quite clearly he had very little aptitude for visions and ecstatic transports. This is most evident in his attitude towards mysticism, which lived on visions and in its acceptance of them went extremely far; it accepted, for example, the imaginings of the mystic nuns who claimed, as 'brides of Christ', to feel the tangible, bodily embrace of the Saviour, were 'sprinkled' with his blood, and celebrated mystic weddings. All this Luther rejected quickly and decisively; what attracted him to the teachings of the German mystics, and then only for a relatively short time, was their attempt to find direct access to God. This struck an answering chord in him.

To put it briefly, we may assume that while in the monastery he lived faithfully in accordance with the order's rules on this point. And none of his opponents, zealous though they were in their enquiries and investigations, was able to bring to light anything whatever indicative of a 'lapse into sin'.

Decisive for his spiritual development, on the other hand, was the fact that, anticipating modern psychology, he was genuinely convinced that libido, or sexual desire, penetrated the whole man and the whole of life. For this he had ready to hand the scholastic notion of *concupiscentia*, which meant simply desire and referred not only to sex. But it led him to his concept of sin, of sinful man, that cardinal thesis of the Church which had brought about the historic break with the ideas of antiquity. According to this the 'flesh' was not simply a part of the body, the phallus, which the ancients had revered as divine, and which had its own god of fertility. The flesh was the physical man with all his characteristics, in glaring contrast to the soul, which was gravitating towards God. And so in enumerating the temptations through which he had passed, Luther listed merely 'anger, impatience, desire', and he did not say that sexual desire had been the greatest of these.

These were the old monastic vices, enumerated first by the desert fathers and then catalogued as the 'seven deadly sins': pride, covetousness, lust, anger, gluttony, envy, sloth. In his prayers Luther did not rattle off the complete list, and some of them, indeed, can have had no special significance for a monk. If he took seriously the commands to forgo all possessions and live a life of constant fasting, how could 'covetousness', 'greed', or 'gluttony' affect him? Or 'envy', if he regarded the solution of his problems as dependent on himself? He would have been more likely to recall, and with far better reason, that the old monks were familiar with the deadly sin they called *accidia* or 'slothfulness of heart'. The earliest commentators on the catalogue of sins had declared that sorrow, *hypochondria*, was their constant companion and was capable of leading to thoughts of suicide. In Luther's day, as a result of the theory of the four humours, melancholy had become a fashionable idea; doctors, translating the term literally, attributed it to the 'black choler'. Luther suffered again and again from severe melancholic and hypochondriac depressions which he attributed to overexertion in the monastery, but in all probability he had a predisposition to them when he entered it. The need to fight against such slothfulness and apathy of heart became a leading point in his opposition to the usual, easy-going routine of religious faith. His anger was never fiercer than when he spoke of the 'lukewarm' people, who thought they had done enough when they had done a bare minimum. His whole fight was over the fact that the Church – the Church as he saw it, that is – regarded this minimum as sufficient.

Anger was also one of the deadly sins; it was a stumbling block to Luther and he often succumbed to it. The rules of his order laid down that disputes between the brothers – and because of the close quarters at which they lived this was a constant problem – were to be settled at once. As if drawn up with Luther in mind, the rules also stated that a brother who, though tempted by anger, was quick to make amends was better than one who, though slow to anger, was more difficult to move to forgiveness. Luther's sudden savage anger and his subsequent, and often excessive, attempts at pacification were two of his characteristic qualities. They often led him into dangerous situations, while at the same time revealing pronounced conciliatory traits; during all the excitement of the Leipzig disputation, for example, when his life was at stake, he wrote a kind letter to Tetzel, his first and bitterest enemy, as he lay dying.

Pride, haughtiness, *superbia*, was another deadly sin; indeed it was placed first, as being the vice from which all other vices sprang. The hermit's isolation, by means of which he hoped to secure for himself a privileged position relative to the 'ordinary', lesser brethren and sisters, was in reality a form of pride. The thesis that there can exist only a small band of 'perfect' or near-perfect individuals, while the main bulk must consist of 'weaker brethren', can be traced still further back, to the earliest days of the Church's formation.

Because of their asceticism pride had already become a danger to the desert fathers, whom there is reason to mention at greater length, because the hothouse atmosphere of the desert gave birth to all the basic forms of monasticism, often in extravagant variations. The term 'asceticism' originally referred to the severe training of professional athletes in ancient times. The first hermits called themselves 'God's athletes', and they began at once to compete, like sportsmen, for record performances. The very first were gentle and mild. They had no code of rules, and even when they began to form groups and monasteries punishments were virtually unknown. They wanted only to be 'different' from the heathen. They wore dark or black smocks, in order to dissociate themselves from the white philosopher's coat of the Greeks, they had a contempt for personal hygiene, which in late antiquity had been taken to such a pitch that people became physically enervated and sat interminably in hot baths, and they ate only what was absolutely necessary. But very soon the heroes among them won a reputation for performing wonders and for setting an example by achieving records in asceticism. At first these records were records in solitude. With astonishing speed, however, visitors and admirers appeared from the towns; these wanted miracles and more miracles, and superhuman or inhuman feats of mortification. Out of this emerged the type of 'God's athlete' who weighed down his body with ever-increasing loads of chains and iron collars, lived buried in the earth in an earthen barrel or suspended high in the air in an openwork cage; one of these fakirs had a cage made for himself that rotated on drums, as though he were a tame squirrel. The pinnacle was attained by the celebrated Simon Stylites, a peasant's son of unimaginable fitness and toughness; first he had himself buried for two years, after which he climbed out on to a boulder of rock, on which he had further boulders piled until finally he stood on a pedestal sixty feet high, where he proceeded to spend the last thirty years of his life – the first of the 'pillar monks'. Moreover, he did not just stand there, but cast himself on his knees in prayer in an endless series of rhythmic movements. The formula adopted by these penitents was to get as close to heaven as possible, in a physical sense, and to perfect themselves by the simple process of numerical repetition; less heroic variations of the formula continued until Luther's day. One of Simon's admirers tried to count the master's exercises, but abandoned the attempt after reaching the figure 1,244. After the death of the saint a place of pilgrimage was constructed round the 'pillar' or platform; a magnificent piece of architecture, it was one of the greatest monastic buildings of late antiquity. Far from being a curiosity, Simon was a great glory and pride of the Church. The custom of reckoning penances purely numerically continued, and was one of the points selected by Luther for attack.

But it was also in the desert that the other primitive form of monasticism came into existence: the monastery, with a fixed code of rules, under an *abba* (father), or abbot, and with well-developed commercial activities. Idleness was recognized as a danger even for the hermits, who spent their whole time weaving rush mats. The monasteries, however, went further in this respect. Anthony with his picturesque temptations became world famous; the other Egyptian, Pachom, the founder of this form of organized monastery, which was to exert world-wide influence, was soon forgotten. There was nothing about him to excite the imagination and create legends. He was a great organizer, a man of order; thanks to these qualities he became one of the outstanding founders of the west, which talked ceaselessly of order while living in indescribable disorder. The monastery, as devised by him, not only turned out mats and baskets on a commercial scale, it had its own agents, who disposed of the goods in the towns, as well as its own ships on the Nile; it acquired lands and had its own builders, tailors and shoemakers. The monastery became an industrial centre for the district, and it was not long before it was also held in high regard by the government authorities. Perhaps its most significant contribution was to put an end to the hermit's deliberate rejection of all education; every monk had to be able to read and write and the Bible was learnt by heart. Fixed rules were laid down for the brothers and sisters, convents having been established for the latter. Strict discipline – not at the discretion of individuals but under the eye of superiors – was a basic element of these new creations. And this was the form of monastery into which Luther entered.

It had been in existence for over a thousand years since the time of Pachom, who died in the middle of the fourth century, and, although undergoing many changes, had remained far less altered in its main features than any other institution of the Church. The fact that Luther grew up in this earliest form of Church life would seem also to be of importance. Time and time again he appealed to, and invoked, the early days of Christianity, and other movements at the time of the Reformation stressed this even more than he did; admittedly he was thinking of the very earliest Christian period, before monasteries and hermits had come into existence. Nevertheless he was dominated by the idea that a steady 'decline' had set in, by the notion of the 'last days', which inevitably would lead to a complete reversal. This was something that had been constantly prophesied; hardly a century has passed in which there have not been passionate protests calling attention to the imminent 'end of everything'. At the time of the Hohenstaufens Abbot Joachim de Fiore, in Calabria, the protégé of the powerful Pope Gregory IX, had systematized it into a historical theory. It was in this age of strife between emperor and pope that Luther's Augustinian Order, as well as the other mendicant orders of Franciscans and Dominicans, came into existence.

A new foundation, it once more followed the 'decline' and downfall of the other great monastic orders; the whole history of monasticism is that of ceaseless rise and fall. The idea of 'reformation' had been present throughout the history of the Church, as a constantly recurring necessity. When Luther entered the Augustinian Order it was split, like almost all other orders, into two factions, one supporting reform and the other opposing it. The orders not only fought each other, they engaged in the most bitter internal feuds. In the Franciscan Order the 'observants', the advocates of strict obedience to the code of rules laid down by the order's founder, Francis of Assisi, shook the Church to its foundations for almost two centuries before they submitted, or, as one can also put it, until the 'radicals' were bloodily exterminated and suppressed.

Obedience was one of the vows taken by a monk. It was treated seriously so far as his relations with the superiors of his own order were concerned; but interminable quarrels and disobedience occurred over

the other institutions of the Church, not least over the papacy, and in
this the Franciscans were not alone. It is noteworthy that, of all the
orders, Luther's Augustinians were regarded as the Curia's most loyal
sons and defenders; indeed they prided themselves on the fact that, in
contrast to almost all the other orders, they had never produced a heretic
– until Luther came on the scene. The other vow was poverty. It had
already been eroded in the monastic foundations of Egypt. The individual monk possessed nothing, but the monastery grew rich; a
great abbot not only kept discipline among the brothers, he was also a
great administrator and, where possible, an 'empire builder'. In addition the great monasteries of the early Middle Ages built up, or at
least preserved, the treasures of the mind, and what they achieved in
this field remains a precious heritage. They also raised the standard of
living in their neighbourhoods by turning desert into arable land,
planting new crops, providing accommodation for travellers and
caring for the sick; all this, moreover, was constantly pleaded as justification for their existence. There was no more talk of poverty. They
were great patrons of the arts. They became great landed proprietors;
certain abbots justifiably bore the title prince-abbot, and lived like
princes. They became rich, and the most powerful of the orders of
knights, the Templars, perished on this account, being exterminated in
the most atrocious case of judicial murder of the Middle Ages; the grand
master and many of the brothers of the order were burned and their
fortune, which had been amassed by means of extensive banking
operations, confiscated in what was the first secularization of the Middle
Ages. The memory of it was still alive in Luther's day, although it
was referred to only in uneasy whispers. The radical Franciscans'
'struggle for poverty', which claimed many more victims, had never
been quite forgotten either; it had arisen because the 'left wing' of the
order, intent on obeying to the letter the injunctions regarding poverty
laid down by the founder, Francis of Assisi, rejected possessions of any
kind, whereas the 'right wing', the 'conventuals', wanted to make
immediate use of the many possessions and legacies that had accrued to
the order. In Luther's day the Franciscans had long since reverted to
obedience. Their theses survived to undergo a revival.

In Luther's Augustinian monastery there was no question of poverty.
He himself said: 'We had enough to eat and drink'; fasts were observed
with moderation. The Augustinians were not one of the wealthy orders,
like the Benedictines, but they owned extensive property, individual
monasteries owning varying amounts. Some of them owned large
numbers of farms, stretching far into the surrounding countryside, with
their own managers, bailiffs and rent collectors. These possessions had
been acquired in the course of centuries; they had never diminished.

Once the Church acquired property it remained hers 'in perpetuity', whereas secular possessions underwent inevitable change of ownership. In the late phase, during the sixteenth century, the accumulation of possessions, rights, dues and privileges had reached such proportions that a modification of this state of affairs was inevitable. The 'greed' of the secular powers for ecclesiastical property, which was the Church's way of putting it, had been a constant source of dispute down the centuries; and the Church's greed for more and more property was resented by the laity. Even in Spain, most Catholic of all countries, Emperor Charles v was implored by his subjects to put a stop to the constant transfer of land to the 'Dead Hand'; if he failed to do so, they pointed out, there was a danger that nothing would be left to the laity, on whom fell the whole burden of national taxation. Since, in principle at any rate, Church property could not be called upon to contribute to the perennially hard-pressed finances of the country, this was a strong argument. How much Church property existed in individual countries has never been established precisely; in England it was calculated to be a third of the whole, and in Germany it must have been at least as much. It was often the best and most fertile land, as well as the best cultivated, that was in the hands of the Church and the monasteries.

The Augustinian friars possessed their share of this third of the Holy Roman Empire; in Germany they had one hundred and two monasteries, most of them dating from the thirteenth century, although there were some very recent ones among them. Luther's monastery in Erfurt dated from 1256, the year in which the order had been consolidated by papal decree. Luther wore the order's black habit with its black leather belt; over it he wore a white scapular and under it a white woollen shirt. Even at night he had to wear a scapular with a white cowl, although normally people slept naked in those days. He retained the habit long after he had broken with the Church; he lived in the Wittenberg monastery until he died.

Luther's chief concern during this time as a monk was to meditate on his sinfulness, on his 'suffering and torment of heart and conscience,' and on his heart, which 'trembled and pounded at the thought of God's mercy to me.' He was indeed the monk, as we imagine the type in the sense of the old monastic fathers, exposed both to the temptations of demons and to those of the monastic vices listed in the catalogue of sins, to pride, anger, melancholy, indecision of heart, and it drove him to despair. He kept all his monk's vows with the exception of one, obedience. He had no desire to be one of 'God's athletes' or to set up any records in asceticism. Nor did he wish to become a saint, an idea that could occur very easily to a monk and one which his order would have greatly liked to see realized; it distressed the Augustinians that they

could point to no saint of their own, whereas the Franciscans and Dominicans had the names of their founders in the catalogue of saints.
What Luther really wanted was something quite simple: to find a
merciful God. His disobedience consisted of attempting to do this in his
own way. In their solitude many monks and hermits had had thoughts
of their own; the Church could not and would not concern itself with
them. The fact that Luther proclaimed a way of his own and in so doing
influenced others, or 'led them astray', was the form of disobedience
named heresy, and the punishment for it was death.

# 4

# Life in the monastery

THE monastery at Erfurt, true to the course of development taken by monasticism, was an organization with a strictly hierarchic structure and a system of precisely differentiated ranks. At its head stood the prior, a sort of petty monarch or pope in miniature; he was surrounded by 'principals', the sub-prior, sacristan, procurator and novice master, the last three responsible respectively for matters connected with the services, administration and finance, and the training of new arrivals. The monks were divided into *patres*, the aristocracy, who had been ordained as priests and were learned, or at least well read, and *fratres*, or common friars, who, although they had taken the vows, were un-educated and were, in fact, supervised to ensure that they did not learn to read and write; they served as doorkeepers and singers, looked after the sick and the clothes store, and did other menial tasks. Luther's monastery at Erfurt was not poor, but it was not outstandingly wealthy like some of the others, which often had staffs of hundreds or even thousands of 'commoner friars', servants and administrators, and formed small towns, or even small principalities, of their own. In some countries monasteries still kept slaves, a practice which, in the hier-archic structure of the Church and the great systems of thought devised by the Doctors of the Church, was considered entirely in keeping with the divine order of things. The order was international and extra-territorial, with its general in Rome as commander-in-chief and its own ambassador to the pope, who was its supreme head. Thus it was subject directly to the Curia; it also enjoyed judicial autonomy – a little church within the Church. The German region was divided into four provinces; the fact that these had nothing whatever to do with the normal frontier demarcations emphasized the order's superiority to all worldly régimes. Luther, hitherto a Mansfelder, became an Augustin-ian. Generally speaking it was still usual for a man entering a monastery to drop his own name and take a new one; at first Luther was known as Augustinus, but he soon reverted to Martin – a step in which we can fancy, if we wish, some symbolic element. The order had its own constitution, which was drawn up with very much greater precision than that of the indeterminate Holy Roman Empire; together with the rules it was read out once a week at mealtime. The order also had its own tradition and appointed role in the overall plan of the Church. Its primary duty was to preach. The Augustinians counted no great scholars and thinkers among their number; in these the Dominicans and Franciscans, the other two mendicant orders, had won a virtual monopoly, claiming almost all the leading names in scholasticism. They were, however, in demand as teachers at universities, and it was in this capacity that Luther began the career which was to take him out of the order.

At first he was simply a novice; moreover he was regarded with some distrust by the other brothers because of his academic standing, behind which, they suspected, lurked pride. Acceptance into the order was not hurried; the novice was given time to reach his final decision. Initially Luther was put into the monastery's guest-house for observation. As an obedient son he had told his parents of his decision. His father was beside himself at the disobedience of this promising young man whom, following the award of his master's degree, he had just started to address with the respectful '*Ihr*', and who had given every sign of justifying the highest hopes; he now wrote to him as '*Du*', and 'denied me entirely his favour and paternal goodwill'. His mother declared she wanted to have nothing more to do with him. It was only after the loss of two other sons, in one of the constantly recurring plague epidemics, that the old miner, now supervisor of a smelting works, was persuaded to give his consent. Reluctantly he declared: 'So be it; God grant it may turn out well'. The story of the sudden conversion amid thunder and lightning was not at all to the taste of the hard-headed realist; later, when Luther officiated at his first Mass, he still referred to it sceptically in front of everyone, saying: 'Would to God there was no chance of it being a vision of the devil!' This first break with a God-ordained authority – and the family was the nucleus of the whole order of things – caused Luther deep concern.

Luther stepped straight from the variety and colour of university life into a world of black and white, from brightness into half-light, from the gay company of good friends, with their impulsive movements and loud laughter, into strict discipline. Laughter was forbidden on principle, and so was every unseemly gesture. As a monk he had to learn to be silent. One of the doctors of his order had decreed: 'It is the business of the monks to weep, to be silent, and to wait in wholesome quietude.' The gaze had to be directed downwards, the hands held in the sleeves of the habit. When he drank, the monk had to hold the goblet with both hands, not frivolously with one. There was no talking at meals, which were communal; passages were read from the legends of the order, or from a devout text by some accepted authority. Every detail of the day, which began in the middle of the night, was regulated, prayers being said, and responses from the Psalms sung, in the choir seven times in the twenty-four hours; this began at two o'clock in the morning and ended with evening prayer. The first meal was midday lunch. The cell was small and unheated, no other brother was allowed to enter it; when the cold was very severe, a heated common-room was available. The cell door could not be locked and was provided with an aperture for observation; no ornaments were allowed, not even the image of a saint. The bed consisted of a straw mattress with a woollen blanket.

Thus silence reigned and quietness. The monks were forbidden to talk to themselves even in their cells; with each other they might communicate only by signs. Prayers were said, and faults discussed, in the choir, under strict supervision and control. At least once a week, on Fridays, the *Schuldkapitel*, or recital of faults, was heard. The prior began: 'Let us consider our faults.' The brothers threw themselves to the ground. The prior asked: 'What are you reciting?' The answer came: 'Our faults.' They were permitted to rise and confess their faults individually. These had to consist exclusively of contraventions of the rules and statutes; all other sins were reserved for the confessional. Examples of offences were being late and going to sleep in the choir, or, more serious, telling lies, breaking the rule of silence and looking at a woman; still more serious offences were blasphemy, disobedience to the prior and drunkenness. The most serious transgressions of all were forging letters or documents, violation of the secrets of the confessional, and sins of the flesh. The prescribed punishments ranged from school punishments, such as eating one's meals sitting on the floor or reciting psalms, to beating and, finally, imprisonment. The essence of this recital of faults was that it was an exercise in community existence: it was the duty of every brother to indict his fellows, observe and check up on them, and present his observations, though not in the form of a personal accusation. The guilty brother might be referred to only in the third person: a brother had done this or done that. The brother concerned was then expected to own up and confess. This 'group therapy' is familiar to us from present-day forms of systematic training and education, and we know how extraordinarily effective it can be.

The confession was a different thing again; it had to be made personally to the prior, or to one of the father confessors appointed by him, and, as a sacrament of penance, was an essential part of Catholic teaching. By its means the Church, through its priests, made its most direct approach to the individual believer, undertaking to reconcile the sinner to God. In his personal practice Luther retained the confession to the end of his life, but in a changed form that accorded with his ideas: for him there was no necessary intermediate authority in the form of a priest, a human being; he turned direct to Christ. It was Christ who absolved: 'Christ sits there, Christ hears, Christ answers, not a human being.' Even during the stormy days of the Diet of Worms Luther made his confession, in the old, prescribed form, to the archbishop of Trier; attempts were made to induce the latter to violate the strict secrecy of the confessional, but this he refused to do. Later on Luther selected friends from among those round him to act as 'partners' in his form of confession.

As with everything he undertook, Luther made an impetuous start to his days as a monk; not a murmur of rebellion, or of the slightest disobedience, has ever been reported. Being a probationer, or postulant, he stood to one side among the brethren of lower rank during the chanting of the horary prayers. He asked to be sent with his beggar's scrip into the villages to beg, an activity that, for the wealthier mendicant orders, was no longer any more than a traditional gesture; like much else, this rule of the order had become a fiction. It seems that his fellows intentionally gave Martin, the university graduate, a hard time, stressing the fact that now he was merely one among others; this lasted only about two months and then, after a year, the novice was accepted and took the solemn vow as a brother. He took the oath of obedience, renunciation of possessions, and chastity 'unto death, according to the precepts of the blessed Augustine.'

The quiet and discipline did the intractable young man good. Despite his many later complaints he felt well and at ease during his first years in the monastery. But he very soon began to brood. Unlike most of the others he could not treat merely as routine the perpetual references to guilt even in the most trivial and superficial matters. He felt a constant need to confess, to discover sins in himself; his superiors knew his type and how to deal with it. Even in later life Luther still felt grateful to the novice master, that 'fine old man', who every now and then gave him a good scolding for his continual references to the wrath of God: 'You are a fool; God is not angry with you – it is you who are angry with Him!' Altogether he was shown great consideration and great understanding; he was a 'difficult brother', but one who, if he were guided rightly, might develop into a great luminary of the order. This, of course, was the great mistake; Luther did not want to be directed. He wanted to 'break through' on his own to God, to his God; in the eighteenth century pietism formulated a whole doctrine and technique of penitential struggle and breakthrough. He could find no comprehension of his point of view; it was opposed to the teaching of the Church. But he was touchingly appreciative of the slightest encouragement, and in Staupitz, the head of the congregation of his order, he found for the first time in his life a 'father' who was truly fatherly.

What sins, lapses and trespasses Luther claimed to have discovered in himself, and recited in the confessional, we do not know. We know only that once, when he wailed to Staupitz 'Oh my sins, my sins, my sins!' the latter told him emphatically that, in the true sense of the word, he had committed no sins at all. Really to sin meant to murder one's parents, to blaspheme in public, to scorn God, to commit adultery and so on. 'If Christ is to help you, you must keep a list of real, honest-to-goodness sins and not go hobbling around nursing toy ones, imagining you commit a sin every time you fart!' The wording is Luther's; the aristocratic Staupitz would have expressed himself differently. But the understanding approach, the comfort, the consideration for the young brother's pangs of conscience – these all reveal Staupitz's influence. This experienced man of the world, of old and noble lineage, influential at court, a favourite in cultured circles because of his brilliant sermons, must often have been taken aback by the scruples of this young peasant, with his prominent cheekbones and deep-set eyes. Such intensity was certainly foreign to him and a little uncanny; probably it seemed superfluous as well. But clearly he recognized the spark of genius in Luther before anyone else. Attempts have been made to identify 'early forms' of Luther's teaching in Staupitz's sermons and writings, but this would seem to be going too far; Luther himself has led the way here by placing the name of Staupitz at the beginning of his transformation into a reformer. At any rate it is impossible to exaggerate the importance to Luther of having this 'father' and solicitous friend by his side, and in authority over him, during these years of bewilderment and confusion.

It was this bewilderment and confusion that tormented him. Later he put the blame for them on 'the papacy' and the Church, basing an important part of his teaching on this. He never tired of telling his followers, who knew of monastic life only from hearsay, how he and his fellow monks had been persecuted in the monastery. Every slightest lapse – if they stammered over a prayer, for example, or inadvertently touched one of the sacred vessels – had been turned into a sin; the great Doctors of the Church, they were told, had declared that anyone who omitted so much as a syllable in the choir would have to answer for it on the Day of Judgment. The others were not unduly disturbed; they took it in their stride, as they did their punishments when they were caught. To Luther the Day of Judgment meant something very different from a day of reckoning for slipped syllables. He saw constantly before him the wrathful God, the wrathful Christ, the judges who could pronounce sentence of damnation.

It is usual to call such anxieties morbid and hysterical, or at any rate absurdly exaggerated. There is no doubt that Luther suffered from severe attacks of a psychopathic nature, and not only in the monastery. It would not be easy to name anyone of genius, let alone anyone of genius in the religious sphere, who did not exhibit such symptoms. His enemies went so far as to call Luther an epileptic, and there is no reason whatever to doubt that he used to fall down, or rather throw himself, on the ground. There is a record of one such episode. It was at Conventual Mass, and when the passage from St Mark's Gospel (I. 23) was read in which the man with the unclean spirit cries out 'Let us alone; what have we to do with thee, thou Jesus of Nazareth? Art thou come to destroy us? I know thee who thou art, the Holy One of God,' Luther fell down, moaning, 'It isn't me, it isn't me.' It is Cochläus, his later enemy, who tells the story, adding the pious observation that even in those days his fellow monks considered him to be possessed by a demon. In a higher sense he was.

Luther himself tells us how he trembled with fear and alarm when he said his first Mass, because the words troubled him and he could not rid himself of the thought: 'Who is this you are speaking to?' He wanted to run away from the altar and, if it had not been for his preceptor, would have done so.

'Who is this you are speaking to?' It could not be put more simply and more nobly. But in asking himself this Luther also posed the further question: 'Who am I that speaks thus to God?' This was a far cry from the hierarchic view of the Church, which reserved to the priest a position well above that of the 'mere believer'. In taking this attitude he had already, though as yet quite unconsciously, stepped out of the framework of traditional ideas.

No one sensed this. The ecstatic, the 'psychopath', was a well-known and indeed welcome phenomenon; as the penitent tormented by demons he had become familiar, and been legitimized, in numerous stories of the saints. Luther's superiors, excellent men and strict members of their order, had not the slightest hesitation in promoting this brother as quickly as possible and entrusting him with a succession of new and increasingly responsible posts. Staupitz was not his only patron. Even Professor Nathin, one of his more surly theological superiors, was so impressed by the young brother and by his zeal that he presented him to the nuns at the convent in Mühlhausen as a 'second Paul'.

Only Luther's father adhered stubbornly to his reservations concerning his son's conversion. Immediately after being accepted as a brother, Luther had been told to prepare himself for the next step on the road to the priesthood; he was later ordained sub-deacon, deacon and finally priest by the suffragan bishop of Erfurt. These were all important stages in the life of a monk and in the organization of the Church. The first

Mass of an ordained priest was a solemn occasion and its celebration was not confined to the Church. In the ordinary way a monk was permitted scarcely any contact with his family and former friends; Luther had already been forgotten by his fellow students at the university. Now he was allowed to issue invitations. He sent well composed letters and compliments to his father, his friends, his old teachers, and Hans Luder did not decline this opportunity to present himself as the well-to-do works manager he had now become. He donated to the monastery kitchens the sum of twenty guilders – almost enough to buy a small house. He arrived on horseback with twenty attendants, an entrance that caused one of the monks to remark: 'You must have a good friend to mean so much to him.' A copious banquet was served. Luther went up to his father's table: he felt the need to justify once more his decision to enter the Church. The father remained obdurate, although in addressing his son he now reverted to the more respectful '*Ihr*'. 'Did you give no thought to the Fourth Commandment: honour thy father and thy mother?' And mention of the lightning flash drew from him the comment that it was an apparition of the devil. Luther, deeply hurt, defended himself by saying that he could serve his parents and friends better by prayer and devotion than in some worldly position; 'Would to God that were true,' retorted Hans Luder. 'On hearing these words of my father's,' said Luther, according to his first biographer, 'I was so shocked that I felt as if a sword had pierced my heart – to think that I needed him to draw my attention to the Ten Commandments. After that I could never get what he had said out of my mind.' The old father became reconciled only when Luther married and presented him with a grandson to carry on the Luder-Luther line. 'Then my father restored me to his favour and I became once more his dear son.'

Life in the monastery did not consist entirely of discipline, singing the hours, and confessing one's faults; the incessant complaints made subsequently by Luther about the 'torment' suffered were coloured by his polemics. What he said about the 'gluttony of the monks', when members of his monastery paid a visit at the time of the annual fair to their brothers in Zerbst, was also biased. The day started with a procession, when the streets were strewn with flowers; afterwards the city council gave a banquet in the open market square: 'We made our way there, ate and drank and put God behind closed doors for a while ... so that he should not look askance; when we were full and had drunk ourselves tipsy we took him out again.' Luther was never one to scorn a good drink. The only curious thing is that his enemies later checked up so mercilessly on every glass he drank, although feasting of a very different order was a daily occurrence in monasteries and abbeys.

47

It would be wrong, however, to imagine this relatively strict congregation of the Augustinians as typical. They represented only a small
minority within their own order and a vastly smaller one in the total
monastic community. There were stricter orders, in particular the
Carthusians (from whom, during the Counter-Reformation, the most
determined opposition groups were formed), but these were tiny fragments and, despite the most zealous endeavours, champions of the old
order have been unable to identify more than a handful of the 'right-
eous'. Monasteries and abbeys in which life was very worldly and
agreeable, however, were scattered liberally throughout every country.
The kitchens of the monasteries were famous, as their beers and liqueurs
still are today, these last being the only things many people associate
with the names Benedictine and Chartreuse. The pictures of rotund
monks, glowing with the pleasures of the table as they sample the wine,
their rosaries hanging casually from their belts, were not an invention
of nineteenth-century *genre* painters. The brewing, milling and other
commercial activities, which were carried on on a large scale and very
successfully, also had their social side: a great part of the quarrel to
come was over these things and not over questions of belief or dogma.
The monks were exempt from all taxes and levies, although originally
it was not intended that they should use this exemption to engage in
commerce and injure the tax-ridden citizens by competing with them.
They sold wine retail, and thus incensed the innkeepers. They operated
mills, and the millers protested. They were supposed to read Masses for
the dead, and for this purpose had been given lands and money, but in
many monasteries this had been completely forgotten. They were
supposed to live in poverty, but had grown rich. They had taken the
vow of chastity, but only a few even paid lip-service to it. The lascivious
monk was the constant butt of popular sayings and satire, as well as of
serious exhortations to repentance; the mendicant friar, who wandered
about free of all supervision, was regarded more or less everywhere as a
lecher and seducer.

The monasteries were supposed to be subject to inspection and when
things got too bad – which happened repeatedly – to reform. The fact
that they were autonomous, and not under the jurisdiction of the
bishops and archbishops of their dioceses, was one of the permanent,
as well as one of the most explosive, points at issue within the Church;
it was never resolved. It is also doubtful whether the high prelates, whose
own lives were even more dissolute, would have had the moral authority
to step in and improve matters. Generally, therefore, things were allowed
to slide. It was only when, as the result of some particularly flagrant case,
the secular courts, the ruling princes or the civic authorities intervened
that something was occasionally done; more often than not, however,

their intervention was rejected because it encroached on the sacred liberty of the Church. The chronicles tell how the monks and nuns lived together quite unmolested; travellers knew exactly which convents to visit on their journeys, if they wished to be sure of a good reception. The excuses were sometimes disarming: the convent had become so poor that the nuns had no other way out if they did not want to starve.

Among the inspection reports one, referring to a convent in Württemberg, caused a sensation that extended far beyond the country's borders, eventually reaching the Curia and unleashing a whole series of feuds. Among the documents of this report are preserved the oldest private letters in Germany – love letters from monks to the nuns. Offending articles discovered in the nuns' cells are also recorded: escutcheons bearing the legend 'To thee alone', women's pointed shoes, bodices and worldly ditties. Details of the nuns' numerous progeny were common knowledge for miles around. The letters are touching, ranging from ingenuous endearments to recipes for the right way of preserving salmon and warnings against the wicked 'envious ones'. The 'envious ones', in this case, had a hard time of it. The abbess firmly refused inspection and reform – this was some decades before the Reformation – and help had to be sought from the secular powers, the Church authorities having tried in vain for fifty years – so the statement runs – to effect an improvement. The matter was taken up by the Dominicans, who were jealous of the Franciscans as the guilty party. Half the nuns, being pregnant, were driven out but immediately found sanctuary across the border with the Duke of Bavaria, who was anxious to pick a quarrel with his Württemberg neighbour. Some went to Ulm and quite clearly lived as harlots. Others were brought back through the intervention of aristocratic relatives – princes joined in the affair too – and the former abbess returned in triumph to her kingdom.

There had been a similar occurrence in the Klingenthal convent near Basle; it is referred to in the letters preserved with the report just described. In this case the nuns were expelled for their excessively scandalous activities, but were returned under force of arms by their powerful relatives, the people of Basle being compelled under severe threats to pay them a large cash indemnity for the wrongs they had suffered. This affair, too, was reported to Rome by the Dominicans; in a letter to his sweetheart one writer says in triumph that the preaching monks were poorer by many thousands of guilders, which they had paid out in Rome, but to no avail.

These two cases show how involved the 'successive stages of appeal' were, and how powerful was the influence of the secular powers, whether their intention was 'to reform' or simply to protect their aristocratic relatives in the convents, no matter how they behaved there. The fact that many convents were no more than institutions for maintaining the superfluous daughters of the prolific aristocratic families was to cause Luther and the other reformers a great deal of trouble. The command to be chaste was looked upon tacitly, and even overtly, as a superhuman requirement, to be fulfilled only by saints and the elect, who were regarded with special veneration. And when the 'weaknesses of the body' could not be denied, the saints intervened, or the Blessed Virgin, and put the whole thing right. The most widely used devotional book, the *Legenda aurea*, contained the story of the abbess who was tireless in maintaining discipline and order in her convent, ruling it with a rod of iron. 'Then God ordained that she should become pregnant.' The sisters, delighted to be able to say something shameful about her, denounced her to the bishop. But before he could intervene, the abbess implored the Blessed Virgin's help in her extremity. 'And Our Lady spoke to the angels and told them to deliver her of the child, which they did.' The child was taken by the angels to a hermit, who reared it. The bishop went to inspect the convent, found the abbess free from reproach and punished the nuns for slandering her. The story ends on a more edifying note: the abbess fell to her knees in the confessional and confessed her sins as well as the help of the Blessed Virgin. The bishop, greatly pleased by the miracle, sent to the hermit, demanded the child from him and took it into his own home; when he died 'it was elected bishop in his stead.'

No one took exception to this sort of pious legend; on the contrary it lent a new and touching glow to the veneration of the Virgin. In an age when the popes themselves presented their illegitimate offspring quite openly and with great pomp, not only appointing them to bishoprics but marrying them into the great ruling houses, there could scarcely be criticism.

It was not only celibacy that had become a fiction; the rapid collapse of many monasteries at the time of the Reformation had other causes as well. Some abbots, like their monks, regarded the property as their own, something with which they could do as they pleased, and when threatened with inspection, resisted it fiercely. In the monastery of Helmershausen the unwanted visitors were tied up and thrown out, one of them dying from his maltreatment. The monks defied all the rules, pawned the Church treasures and led a gay life in the taverns; the abbot, more circumspect, sold the lands and went off with the money. At the monastery gate he said: 'Farewell, Helmershausen, may we never meet again!'

Such was the background. The foreground, for us, is occupied by Luther in his monastery, where he lived as brother of a congregation of observants who took their rules seriously. There is no inconsistency in the fact that the great Protestant movement emanated from such a place and found such a passionate response in Germany, the most obedient and most credulous territory within the far-flung authority of the papacy.

Luther took the rules a great deal more seriously than his fellow monks. It was for this that he was commended by his superiors as a 'second Paul'. They had no suspicion of the hidden meaning that lay in this comparison, because for Luther Paul became the leader, the great authority. The story of the apostle's conversion already had a secret bearing on his own conversion. Now he began to read and adopt the theology of Paul, the Church's first theologian. The Bible became for him pre-eminently the Pauline preaching, as handed down in the letters of the great missionary.

As he was destined to become one of the learned monks, the *patres*, Luther had been given the use of a red, leather-bound copy of the complete Bible, in the prescribed Latin translation of St Jerome. This was a privilege. The lesser brothers, as we have seen, never had a Bible in their hands and heard it only in carefully chosen extracts. In fact Staupitz had been the first to distribute copies of the Bible, for purposes of study, to the *patres* in the monasteries of his congregation. It is not true, as Luther afterwards asserted, that within the Catholic Church the Scriptures were 'unknown', or forbidden; but their use was strictly controlled and rationed, and limited to the canonic Latin version or extracts in the vernacular. The struggle over the translation of the Bible reflects fairly accurately the various heretical movements, from those of the Waldenses in northern Italy and the Albigenses in Provence by way of Wyclif and Hus to Luther. A principal point in the charges against, and persecution of, the heretics, had been the fact that they possessed, or attempted to produce, a Bible in their own language, together, of course, with the fact that from it they evolved teachings which were in conflict with the official doctrines of the Church. Luther's own translation of the Bible into German was to be his greatest work, by far the greatest achievement of his whole career; it lay at the very heart of the Reformation movement and is the most enduring testimony to his activities.

He now read the traditional Latin text for the first time. He read it, re-read it and memorized it, until he knew the book virtually by heart; he was always able to quote from it with the greatest ease. In reading it he translated the text at once into ideas, not into German ideas but into Lutheran ideas. His thinking was still influenced by the Latin that was the obligatory language in the monastery; but even when he rendered what he read into Latin, it was Lutheran Latin. It would be premature to see a system, the beginnings of a doctrine, in his work at

51

this time. Luther, indeed, was never very systematic – a fact that has been remarked often enough. What 'appealed' to him, he read with feeling, with passion. It would have been impossible for the complete text, compiled from a literature extending over a millennium, to speak to him in its every line, every book. He was no philologist, and 'textual criticism' was not his field, although he was soon to apply himself to it. What he sought at this time was the 'clear' transparent text, the 'naked truth'. Luther's constantly repeated reference to the 'shining word of God', which became a watchword, is perhaps still more characteristic. It was in direct contrast to the 'darkness' of tradition, which emphasized ceaselessly that the difficult original text could be understood and expounded only by scholars, by teachers recognized by the Church, and was to be made available to the general public only with discretion.

Luther's Bible reading soon attracted attention. He said later that they had taken the red leather-bound book away from him, but this is certainly an exaggeration. One feels more inclined to believe the comment made by Professor Usingen, the preceptor, when he found him at his studies: 'Ah, Brother Martin, what is the Bible? One should read the old teachers; they extracted the sap of truth from the Bible. The Bible gives rise to every kind of tumult and revolt.' This was the confirmed standpoint and practice of the Church, which could quote sufficient cases in which irresponsible reading of the Bible had indeed caused tumult and revolt. Revolt on a still more serious scale was to come. To this day the Christian world remains divided into two great denominations, one of which takes as its basis the individual reading of the Bible, the other traditional interpretation and selection.

Luther himself has become the founder of a tradition. Here in the monastery he was a beginner, a seeker, and in the opinion of his superiors ill-equipped for the reading he was doing. Long established and recognized commentaries were available. It was his duty to know them; this was a more binding obligation than knowledge of the Scriptures, to establish the true meaning of which had been the purpose of the Fathers of the Church and of the greatest minds since their day.

He read the Bible and had to study the commentaries, which were prescribed reading for an Augustinian friar. They are volumes whose names mean little to us today and which cost even specialists a considerable effort to read – a physical effort too, since one tome weighs several pounds. In most cases the labours of these specialists are devoted to establishing a thesis, again by means of 'selected passages' – the process seems unending – in accordance with teachings current today; for example the thesis that the nominalism taught in the Erfurt monastery was dangerous heterodoxy, or the opposite thesis that it was with

Ockham that the liberating thought of modern times began. We must follow, in its outlines, this battle of Luther's too. It was scarcely less important for him than the penitential battle and the struggle to find a 'merciful God', because between God and the obedient monk stood the picture of God painted by the Doctors of the Church.

# 5

# Battle with the Commentaries

THE picture to which Luther now gave his attention had darkened greatly in the course of the centuries. It had been varnished, cleaned and overpainted afresh. The Fathers of the Church, whose line had come to an end at roughly the same time as the Roman Empire, were recognized as the earliest and most eminent authorities, and to take one's stand on them was to be on firm ground. They had already expounded, commented on and interpreted the Scriptures, and in so doing had by no means always been of one mind. Origen, the earliest and most prolific of them – two thousand of his writings, taken down from dictation by seven stenographers, were recorded – was suspected of heresy soon after his death. The dispute between Arius and Athanasius had split the western world for several centuries; during Luther's first year his novice master put into his hands a tract by Athanasius, which the 'fine old man' had copied out himself from an old codex – books were a rarity in the monastery. Since the belligerent bishop had succeeded in getting his doctrine, that the Son was of the same Nature as the Father, accepted at the Council of Nicaea, Athanasius had been sound orthodox reading. It was only later, when Luther went rather more thoroughly into the history of the Church, that he learnt of the grave dissensions to which this teaching had given rise. Augustine, the last and greatest of the Fathers of the Church, was also the patron of Luther's order and on this ground alone his supreme authority; he turned to him again and again. Luther had the advantage of being able to read Augustine in the original, in the magnificent and very idiosyncratic Latin of the last important writer of the universal language of antiquity, whereas he knew the Greek Fathers only in translation, and for the most part only from quotations and anthologies.

After Augustine's death there had been an almost unimaginably long fallow period, half a millennium of genuinely dark ages that produced only copies, compilations and paraphrases; not until the inrush of Arabic and Jewish philosophers, with their own translations of classic authors and their own original thought, was the west able

54

once again, in self-defence and after fierce struggles, to create new schools of theology and philosophy. The masters of the schools – those cathedral schools, and the universities which grew out of them, to which the name 'scholasticism' was given – became the next great group whose authority was recognized. When the struggle began Luther himself usually referred to them contemptuously as 'the sophists'; the humanists saw them in much the same light and vied with one another in their scornful rejection of these once all-powerful figures of the intellectual world. Their very names, that of the great Duns Scotus for example, became bywords for pedantry and narrow-mindedness. People forgot that 'scholasticism', far from being a unity, had been extremely heterogeneous, that, far from being limited in outlook, its existence had been endangered by its almost limitless attempts to extend and explore the realm of thought in every direction. Forgotten, too, were the fierce battles that had been fought, above all in Paris, 'the university' of the High Middle Ages, battles literally for life and limb, mainly of Dominicans or Franciscans. The stake was a more immediate threat to these men than it was to Luther and his con-temporaries, and some of them met their deaths either in this way or rotting in prison. For the most part the conflict had been forgotten even by the Church itself. Recently the twelfth century has been called the open or 'receptive' century, because it opened its doors so readily to the powerful currents that flowed in from the east, and because its people engaged in such vehement and frank discussions; and yet it left many questions, among them the crucial ones, unanswered. Then the frontiers of the mind were closed again. It was a repetition of the period that succeeded the Fathers of the Church: the mills continued to grind, only commentaries and excerpts were produced. Luther and his con-temporaries knew the masters of the schools only in extracts or in the elucidations of 'late scholasticism'.

So completely was the great battle forgotten that the men who had once been the bitterest enemies of the papacy, having now been rendered completely harmless, had become 'teaching material', a fate similar to that habitually suffered by erstwhile revolutionaries. The teachings of the English Franciscan, William of Ockham, were now considered authoritative, and yet Ockham, under the ban and anathema of the Church, had had to seek shelter from the stake in Munich, at the court of his patron King Louis of Bavaria, who himself had been excommunicated. For a century the Ockhamists, representing the *via moderna*, the modernist teaching, had dominated the leading universities; foremost among these was Paris, which still ranked as the greatest academic authority, but their number also included many German universities, among them Erfurt. Luther's teachers had grown

up in this school. It was not the only school, however. The authorities
had long since adapted themselves to the battlefield. There were
professorships in the teachings of the great Thomas Aquinas, prescribed
reading for the Dominicans, and in the Scotist school, which revered as
its leader Duns Scotus, the former opponent of Thomas; in some universities the professorships were on an equal footing. Ockham, once
branded as a heretic, was now *doctor invincibilis*, the invincible, Duns
Scotus was *doctor subtilis*, the man of subtle distinctions, while Thomas
Aquinas was *doctor angelicus*. Thomas's teacher, Albert, was known as
Albertus Magnus, because of his universal intellect which had mastered
the entire range of knowledge of his day. As the great Doctors they
formed a class of their own, ranking just below the Fathers of the
Church.

Hardly any names of comparable standing had been added to these,
although Luther was an enthusiastic reader of the Paris Ockhamist
Gerson, who had played a significant role at the Council of Constance;
but despite his great reputation he was extremely unpopular with the
Curia, owing to his energetic support of the Council principle. In
any case the men in Rome had followed the philosophic trends only
from a distance; they were often uneasy about them, occasionally they
intervened, but they never took part in the discussion. None of the
popes exercised any personal influence on scholasticism as an individual
thinker. Their very background made the great majority of them either
lawyers or great administrators. The monument which took shape
under their guidance, and with the collaboration of the University of
Bologna, was the canon law, the Church's register of its structure and
organization as this had evolved since the twelfth century. The main body
of it consisted of papal decrees; in Luther's day it was referred to as the
'decretals'. At the famous scene outside the gates of Wittenberg,
Luther was to burn the decretals because they were the root-stock on
which the Church of Rome was founded; the Bull of Excommunication
was thrown on the flames only as an inessential extra.

Luther did not read this register of the Church in the monastery.
His first task there was to master the commentaries, which, in fact,
were commentaries on the commentaries of the Fathers of the Church.
For over three hundred years Petrus Lombardus, with his great book of
Sentences, had occupied first place among the 'Masters of the Sentences'. Teaching technique in the Middle Ages did not work with
systems, it employed theorems, almost as mathematics does. The
fundamentals of every truth had been established once and for all; the
teacher's task – as well as that of the philosopher and theologian,
because the three were indivisible – was to demonstrate these truths.
Abelard, the originator of the scholastic method and himself a victim of

persecution – he ended his days imprisoned in a monastery – had brilliantly introduced dialectics in thesis, antithesis and synthesis. The method used was to place side by side, in *pro* and *contra*, the often contradictory, or 'apparently' contradictory, theses of the Fathers of the Church, and then to extract the 'true meaning'. The technique thus developed, that of thinking in terms of Sentences or theses, was also retained by Luther in his early days; his ninety-five theses conformed strictly to this tradition. His first academic task, as *sententiarius*, was to deliver and expound Sentences; his notes on Lombardus are the earliest surviving evidence of his work. For Bible interpretation he had another authority at his disposal: the five-volume collection of 'everlasting sermons' on the Old and New Testaments by the Franciscan Nikolaus de Lyra.

How did one read in those days? Very differently from today, even physically. The book, invariably a heavy folio volume bound in heavy wooden boards and written or printed on heavy paper, was placed on a reading desk; there were no light, small books in the monastery. The monk took hold of it with both hands, just as he had to take his drinking goblet in both hands. A book was seldom read in its entirety, and since it was composed of Sentences this was hardly necessary. People generally made use of anthologies, selections, collections of quotations, or those forerunners of the encyclopaedia which contained 'everything worth knowing' in a single volume. Editions of the great scholastics were often inscribed *Quodlibet* (as you please) and were opened at random. It is almost impossible to imagine a more erratic and arbitrary approach to reading; but it is equally impossible for the modern reader fully to appreciate the intensity with which everything that 'made an appeal', that lit a spark, was absorbed. No one thought twice about picking up his pen and noting in the wide margins of the book his answers, questions and doubts; some of Luther's books, covered with his wild scrawls, still exist. It was all or nothing with every question, no matter how haphazardly it turned up in the round of Sentences.

Not everyone read in this way. On opening these old editions of Petrus Lombardus or Nikolaus de Lyra a refreshing sense of pleasure emanates from the variegated ornaments, sportive beasts and grotesques drawn in the margins; these witnesses to the humour of the monks, which was often extremely gay and exuberant, had a sequel in the initials and woodcuts that adorned the grimmest tracts and pamphlets of the Reformation era. One likes to think that Luther too, whose humour was one of his most endearing qualities, occasionally let his eyes wander from the Sentences and definitions.

What is important, however, is the selection Luther made in his reading. Here again prevailing notions are exaggerated and unhistoric.

His reading was not done in the well-stocked library of a theological seminary containing 'complete critical editions', together with all the important supplementary literature. It may be worth noting that even today complete critical editions do not exist of all the great classics of scholasticism. In considering the charges later levelled against him, that he had left so much unread and that his ignorance of the best and doctrinally crucial authors had such disastrous consequences, it is well to remember that no more than a handful of books was available to him. As contemporary pictures show, the bookcase even of a great scholar in those days consisted of no more than two or three shelves in a niche in the wall; even these were rarely filled. The monastery library would have contained rather more books and manuscripts than this, but it would certainly have been far from imposing.

Thus Luther's reading, consisting of an intensive study of Sentences undertaken within the confines of a small community, covered a very narrow field devoted exclusively to theological literature. His life in the monastery was timeless and quite devoid of any sense of history. This, too, was of decisive importance for his subsequent career. He knew nothing whatever about his own country, about its geography, form of government or history; he often regretted this later and urged that history be taught to the young. When he was thrown into the world, and himself made history, his ignorance of it had fearful consequences. He cannot, however, be held responsible for this.

But even in the field of theology the modest guidance and instruction he received left much to be desired. In his day theology itself left much to be desired; his teachers were well-meaning, worthy men of a worthy average, but this average was low, in the world-famous University of Paris and the great University of Oxford as well as in Erfurt. In the fifteenth century there had still been a few great and lonely figures such as Nicholas Cusanus of Kues on the Mosel, a man of peasant extraction like Luther, in whom present-day scholarship is inclined to see the beginning of modern thought and research. It is very doubtful whether any of his works had made their way into the Black Monastery at Erfurt, unless by those devious underground channels that discoverers of influences so love to nose out. A great deal may have reached Luther by such underground channels; he said once that even the name of Hus, the great heretic, had come to his ears and that one of his teachers had expressed a guarded opinion that he had been condemned unjustly. What faced him on the cumbrous reading desk was the darkened, overpainted picture of that late period known in the history of art as Late Gothic.

Late Gothic woodcuts adorned the worthy tracts of his teachers at Erfurt. When we open them we find ourselves suddenly face to face with the world in which Luther lived as a monk, a world separated not merely by hundreds of miles but by centuries from the airy, classical halls of Italy and from the Rome of the Renaissance masters, of the popes and the elegant, sceptical authors whom they patronized and employed as secretaries. Gnarled and tangled roots, their origins in the forests, still creep and climb everywhere; the faces are coarse and often grotesque, the allegories down to earth. In a work called the *Himm-lische Fundgrube*, or Celestial Storehouse – a storehouse of arguments supporting indulgences, which were widely preached by its author Father Johann Paltz, a teacher in Luther's Augustinian monastery – there is a woodcut so startling that we can scarcely believe our eyes. There in front of us stands the *'feste Burg'*, the safe stronghold, high-walled and well fortified, surrounded by a world full of devils, who are storming it by force and with great cunning. Was it this picture that first gave Luther the idea for his battle song? In Luther's song every-thing is infinitely simpler, lapidary, reduced to a few trenchant phrases; simplicity was the secret of his effectiveness. Father Paltz's book, its text as well as its illustrations, is still riddled with creepers and tendrils, with pedantic one-two-three arguments; banderols flutter everywhere. The devils, their four armies armed with pikes and spiked clubs, advance against the stronghold of the Church, whose task, the tract tells us, is to defend indulgences. The fortress is defended by angels occupying four turrets; they are using up-to-date and effective weapons – bombards, mortars, culverins – representing the authority of the Church, as well as small-arms intended to represent somewhat more modestly the rational arguments. (See Plate 4.)

The murmuring over indulgences had never quite died down; there had also been plenty of public protests. The picture of the stronghold with its bombarding angels was intended for the simpler people, who could not read the Latin text; Father Paltz, however, was also address-ing scholars and his arguments were hardly less naïve. Luther, who still sat at Paltz's feet torturing himself with the very questions which the latter found so easy to answer, fell foul of him over these. In Paltz's view all arguments over the origin of indulgences – though he was forced to admit that such things did take place – were quite superfluous: 'The Church approves indulgences and dispenses them, therefore they exist – *ergo sunt*.' This was the basic thesis; it underwent many and frequent modifications. The pope, by virtue of his supreme position, could not be questioned. The order of precedence within the Church was determined according to the Bible's words about 'feeding the sheep'. They were interpreted by Paltz quite ingenuously, the word 'feed', or graze, applying also to the wool of the sheep, the sheepfold and the sheepdogs. These were the religious orders, each of which was allotted a corner of the fold, again in a quadruple arrangement: the black and white Dominicans, the grey Franciscans, the white Carmelites, and, as the fourth, the black Augustinians, his own order. The dog was not a figment of Paltz's imagination. The Dominicans proudly called themselves *domini canes*, the hounds of God. The hound was included in their coat-of-arms because of a dream which, according to legend, the saint's mother had had; she was to bear a son in the likeness of a dog and out of his mouth would issue a flame that would set fire to the whole world. The great painting of the Church militant and triumphant by Andrea da Firenze, in Santa Maria Novella in Florence, shows at the bottom the speckled hounds, the Dominicans, chasing the heretic; at the very edge, huddled in the corner, is the frightened heretic. In his extremity he tries to tear the offending pages out of his book before his fate overtakes him. (See Plate 5.)

Luther did not know this painting, but he read Paltz and other works of a similar nature. Not that at this time he was yet protesting or even aware of any feeling of revulsion. But this trite theological literature gives a clear picture of the world from which he came and against which he later rebelled. The good Father Paltz was soundly orthodox, though at times too zealous in his arguments; later, when the situation had become hopeless, he was identified as the author of highly 'questionable' theses which were far from reflecting the 'correct view' of the Church. These misgivings were afterthoughts; the 'correct views' of the Church were hidden away, remote from Luther's age, in the works of the great classics of three and four hundred years earlier and in his day were read by no one, either in the Erfurt monastery or in Rome. The practice of the Church – and this is what mattered – wore a different look.

Another teacher and another woodcut: Gabriel Biel, the Tübingen theologian, one of the shining lights of late Scholasticism, as we say today, one of the most modern and learned authorities, as was said then; his books were widely published, even reaching Spain. On the title page of his sermon on the Passion his professor's desk, inscribed 'Gabriel Biel', is superimposed quite unblushingly on an illustration of the Crucifixion; at his side the soldiers cast lots for Christ's garment, at his head stands the Blessed Virgin. He has opened his book – he, too, holds it with both hands – and is lecturing. His principal work was *The Mass in its Mystic and Literal Interpretations*, a folio volume of four hundred pages, each printed in two columns; Luther read it and even in his old age could still quote large sections of it by heart. With enormous application he mastered the huge volume in a few months; not only did he not find it forbidding, he found it extremely interesting, the last word in theology, the *via moderna* of Ockhamism.

Luther had no sense of philosophy at all; very soon he engaged in his first battle against it and the practice of philosophizing over questions of religious belief. Today scholasticism is usually treated as a chapter in the history of philosophy, but this has many disadvantages. Philosophy in our modern sense did not exist in the Middle Ages. It was accepted only as the 'handmaid of theology', a humble servant allowed to fetch water and carry wood. Kant made the nice comment that one can never be sure whether the handmaid 'is bearing the torch before her mistress or carrying her train behind her'; this was the presumptuous voice of the Age of Enlightenment and the voice of a layman. In the Middle Ages no layman could make any contribution to philosophic questions; they were the exclusive province of the clergy and above all of the religious orders. The Dominicans and Franciscans virtually held the sole rights in philosophic matters. Luther was hardly aware of the battles that had taken place between them; in his day their noise had died away. Only one great battle, though perhaps the most important of all, was still unresolved. In retrospect the so-called 'dispute over universals' has been seen as a mere battle of words, a 'squabble between monks'. It was of far greater significance. It settled the question as to which was to have priority: the hierarchic structure, with its monarchic summit, or individual man.

There were two main opposing factions – the realists and the nominalists. The 'universals' over which they quarrelled were the universal concepts. According to the realists these constituted an entity, known as reality, to which individual things were subordinate; the nominalists saw in them only names, *nomina*. To begin with it had been simply a quarrel over names and nomenclature; but in the Middle Ages nothing could be discussed in the context of independent thought. Every problem inevitably became a theological question of conscience. The first nominalist turned his attempts at thinking – they were hardly more than that – to the very thorny problem of the Trinity and was led, in this way, to resolve it into three separate divinities. Having done this he disappeared, and we know his view only from quotations made by his opponents. Thinking in those days really was 'universal': everything was related to the universality of the Church, of the Church's system of belief, and to serve this was also philosophy's task. As we see it today, these were problems in the theory of knowledge; but all attempts to explain medieval thought by means of later terminology are fraught with danger. Every word, every idea, in those days had as its background a completely different world; the language itself was different, being Latin, a Late Latin that mocks every attempt to translate it. Moreover behind every word looms the authority of the Church; many of the boldest thinkers are known to us only from condemnations and theses selected for censure, and these can be misleading. The concept of a higher 'reality', or entity, of which earthly things are only a reflection, would today be termed 'hyper-idealism'; the meaning we give to 'realism' is not that given to it in the Middle Ages. In order to guard against any feeling of superiority on our part it is well to remind ourselves that scarcely any other word can be applied so variously as realism; even today an expression like 'social realism' can mean, or be made to mean, something that presents man not as he is but as he ought to be according to a particular ideology. Scholasticism proceeded in exactly the same way. Man had to be allotted his place in the universal structure of the hierarchic Church, and in this structure universal ideas were a reality.

The disputes extended over a long period with fluctuating fortunes, and the difficulties of incorporating the fixed and eternal truths of religious belief into the framework of philosophical interpretation led to all sorts of compromises; of these the most important was the 'mitigated realism' of Thomas Aquinas. His teachings in general were moderate, well-proportioned and balanced to a superhuman, and indeed to an almost inhuman, degree. There was no place in them for any personal element reflecting either the author or contemporary history, the latter being ignored completely, in a way not to be found in any other medieval thinker; no sound of the violent struggles between emperor and pope was allowed to penetrate the quiet of these halls, designed by the son of one of the eminent men in the entourage of the heretic Hohenstaufen Emperor Frederick II. The great word he introduced into the discussion was reason. He envisaged a unity composed of reason and faith – a unity that conformed to his own nature – as the pattern for the whole world order of things; he saw as rational and God-ordained the strictly hierarchic social order typified by the Church.

It was only after Luther's death, however, with the Council of Trent, and subsequently in numerous variations of neo-Thomism, that Thomas Aquinas became compulsory teaching for the Church of Rome. That Luther did not read him or, when he did so, rejected him categorically was not a fortuitous circumstance occasioned, say, by the fact that the great master of the Dominicans was regarded by his own order as undesirable. Nor did he reject him simply because he was put off by the impersonal note in Thomas Aquinas, though this may have been a contributory factor. There are affinities of temperament, and on this ground alone Luther was closer to Augustine, and also to Bernard of Clairvaux, whom he esteemed as a great preacher and man of the people. In such cases individual theses or dogmatic propositions play a less important part than the popular practice of comparing definitions would lead us to believe. First and foremost Luther was an opponent of the practice of philosophizing over questions of religious belief. Luther's chief objection to Thomas Aquinas was that he had been instrumental in introducing, and procuring the acceptance of, Aristotle – whom at first the Church had categorically rejected – as 'the philosopher', 'the authority': 'He is responsible for the fact that Aristotle, that wrecker of every form of piety, is now enthroned.' He detested the speculations, the 'hundred questions', taken from the pagan philosopher – 'not a word calculated to give a man confidence in Christ.' He talks perpetually, 'because metaphysics seduces him,' was Luther's final verdict on Aquinas.

To Luther metaphysics meant simply drawing philosophic conclusions, the deductions and definitions learnt from classical philosophy. Disdainfully he called the Greek philosopher 'that rank Aristotle', meaning that the master had passed through so many hands – he had been translated from Greek into Arabic and from Arabic into Latin, and so on – that he was no longer fresh. The great natural philosopher, who had sought to master the knowledge of his day in its entirety, had become a sort of Father of the Church *honoris causa*, to whom one could turn in safety and confidence. The conclusion he had reached by thinking along physical lines – that the fact of motion postulated a first and supreme principle, the immovable mover, and that this supreme principle should be called God – had been incorporated by the scholastics in their logical proof of the existence of God, as had the whole series of ascending proofs deriving from this. All this was alien to Luther. He had no use for this kind of architectonic structure. Also alien to him was the whole doctrine of ascending steps, according to which the road to perfection was divided into clearcut stages; of these the last was unattainable in this earthly existence, the second, though attainable in theory, was seldom reached, but the first, or bottom, step was accessible to all who put their trust in God 'habitually' – this is how the scholastics had defined it. Gabriel Biel began at once at this bottom step, with the 'ordinary man', whom the Church, in its wise regard for the weakness of its children, had in mind. These were mere patterns of thought and bore no relation to practical life; the last and final stage, in any case, was reserved to saints. Luther rebelled against this highly aristocratic order of precedence. He wanted to stand face to face with God, as person to person, without the use of steps and handrails. For this he needed no mathematically and logically worked-out proofs of God's existence; so far as he was concerned this was not a subject for question and counter-question. Moreover he desired no mediation on the part of other human beings; for him the Church was a man-made institution. This became his great battlecry. It was to be heard far and wide.

But great changes had also taken place in the realm of thought and Luther did not remain untouched by them, fiercely though he fought against the influence of the 'sophists'. Thomas Aquinas's impressive doctrine of unity had been followed by the rather evasive and questionable stopgap of separating scholarly investigation and religious belief and proclaiming the so-called 'dual truth': because a thing was true in the sphere of philosophy, it did not necessarily follow that it was true in the sphere of religious belief – a formula that by no means died out with scholasticism.

Only with the victory of the nominalists was a clearcut decision reached: on the one hand religious belief, on the other scholarly investigation. God, as the inscrutable being, was reserved for religious belief; knowledge of, and enquiry into, the things of this world were left to individual man, whose business they were. Universals were not 'realities' but only indications or signs, conceived by man and relating to those things of this world that were accessible to experience. From this evolved the whole development of the sciences, with its focus on experience and research. It was the most radical inroad suffered by medieval thought. According to Ockham God was not concerned with worldly institutions; He was free, wholly independent and not subject to the laws that govern our comprehension. In order to drive his thesis home Ockham resorted to paradox: God could have created a world quite different from the existing one; had He chosen to do so He could have identified Himself with the characteristics of a stone or a piece of wood, indeed He could have come into the world in the form of an ass. Paradox, the provocatively pointed assertion, which was to play a great role in Luther's life and work, was immensely popular; no one was shocked by it. Ockham, however, as was only to be expected, fell out with the papacy, for which no satisfactory place was provided in this system of things.

Ockham marks the point of development at which the masters of the schools emerged from the academic business of teaching. They were no longer concerned solely with abstract problems and definitions but quite specifically with questions of power and the affairs of their world and times. By assigning God a place so immeasurably far above human experience, the pope, as His representative and the keeper of the keys of heaven, was brought considerably nearer; he became a possible subject for discussion. And discussed he was, in a most thoroughgoing way. A whole literature of highly critical and highly dangerous polemic writings sprang into existence. The position of the papacy, as being far above everything worldly, was disputed and the theses of Marsilius of Padua, who demanded that its functions be limited strictly to tasks of a purely ecclesiastical nature, were never again allowed to pass into oblivion; they experienced a revival at the time of the Reformation.

Luther was familiar with Ockhamism mainly in its late, attenuated form, and although he referred to Ockham as his 'master', it is not very clear how much of his work he had read and understood. Only some of the master's writings had been published; much of his work did not come to light again until the nineteenth century. Luther read Gabriel Biel. Later, in discussing Ockhamism with his followers, he said that he himself had also been a 'terminist', a nominalist, and that to nominalists the terminology did not denote the higher 'reality' but simply conventional references agreed on by men. The name terminists, he said, was given to 'a sect in the Schools, to which I also belonged. They opposed the Thomists, Scotists and Albertists and were also called Occamists, after Occam their founder; it was the very newest sect and in Paris, too, it was the most powerful.' More characteristically he also said that as a terminist one had to call things by their correct and appropriate *termini*, or technical names, 'and not put strange and reckless constructions on words ... in talking to a carpenter I must use the right technical terms ... axe and not chopper. In the same way one should also leave Christ's words alone ...'

Interpretation and allegory – these were the two coats with which the picture had been overpainted and obscured. The Bible had been the subject of allegorical interpretation in the very early days; for this the ancient philologists, who had already interpreted Homer – the most unsuitable of all subjects – in this way, were taken as models. When Christianity came into conflict with the culture of Greece and Rome and, in the days of the Fathers of the Church, was forced to assert and defend itself and prove its superiority, the Scriptural texts, as they stood, were not enough. They had to be given a 'deeper' meaning and a distinction was made between the 'merely' literal, the spiritual and the mystic meanings. 'Objectionable' passages were given a new interpretation, while others were endowed with a philosophical meaning, intended to put them beyond the reach of the frequently malicious criticism of the heathen. Throughout the Middle Ages the Song of Solomon was accepted allegorically as the 'Church's betrothal' to Christ; from this arose the description of the Church as the 'bride'. Eventually a fourfold interpretation of every Scriptural text became canonical: 'historical', meaning the literal interpretation; 'allegorical'; 'tropological' or figurative; and 'anagogical', leading to its deeper meaning. Luther had toiled over these in the monastery and angrily rejected them: 'In their day the Fathers took a special delight in allegories, trotting them around everywhere and messing up all their books with them. So far as allegories are concerned Origen is a prince, a king; he filled the whole Bible with secret interpretations of this kind, which aren't worth a damn. The reason was that they all followed their own conceits, thoughts and opinions, as they thought fit, instead of St Paul, who lets the Holy Ghost speak for itself.'

It was not only in Bible interpretation that the allegory, as the younger and frailer daughter of symbolism, had become all-powerful. The whole of life was expressed in allegories; they had found their way into art, literature, popular performances and even politics. The allegory had the advantage of being generally intelligible in an age when the spoken word was rare, the printed word rarer still and read by few; pictorial representation was accessible to all. This state of affairs lasted until into the Reformation era. Everybody could understand death as a skeleton, the dance of death, the favourite allegory of the fifteenth century. Everybody knew what was meant when he saw a picture of the pope with two huge keys, capable of unlocking or locking the Kingdom of Heaven. The entire animal and plant worlds were seen allegorically. They made a triumphant entry into heraldry, which was regarded as one of the leading arts or sciences and had enormous political significance. The beasts of prey all became virtues; a flower could mean impending claims and war. The whole iconography of the Church had become allegorical and heraldic, until finally even popes and cardinals discarded the ancient symbols of their office in favour of their family coats-of-arms. All this had undeniably led to flatness and insipidity. Individualism was astir. Art began to rebel. Luther rebelled against the fourfold allegorical interpretation of the Bible, against the fourfold overpainting of the Scriptures. He wanted the simple text, the 'clear, shining word', not paraphrases. This meant fighting a thousand years of tradition and three hundred years of commentaries, which had been further confirmed and expounded in the commentaries of the great Doctors. It meant fighting the philosophers, the 'sophists', too. It meant fighting authority in its entirety. Looking back he said: 'I have been a strange man towards my brothers,' or, more graphically, 'I have been Our Lord's quicksilver which he cast into the pond, in other words among the monks.' He himself was very modest in those days, frequently indeed apprehensive. A single word of encouragement could hearten him almost absurdly; the slightest hint of doubt cast him into the depths. As his eyes wandered round the books in the library at Erfurt he said to himself, as he admitted later: 'Look at the authority of the Pope and the Church, how great it is. Are you the only wise one? You could be wrong...'

# 6

# Arrival in Wittenberg

LUTHER advanced rapidly. He had been ordained priest, completed a number of teaching courses, worked his way through the great commentaries and taken a glance at scholasticism. Only a year later he was ordered by his superiors to go to Wittenberg, as assistant professor and lecturer in moral philosophy. He was reluctant to go. He was still far from having resolved his doubts and the questions troubling his conscience, and this, so far as he was concerned, was his 'main business', his real task; it was far more important to him than studying the Sentences and their interpretation. The quiet of the monastery had done him good; it had also left him time for contemplation. If, in the course of this, he had tormented himself, it was because he wanted to do so; the first monks had also sought martyrdom, trials and temptations. His superiors recognized the symptoms; the wise Staupitz saw that the time had come to give him something to do. Luther was twenty-five.

From the wealthy and famous city of Erfurt, with its old-established university, he went to Wittenberg, which was poor and small, a village rather than a town. The country round it was said to be almost a wilderness, the people unfriendly. As a university teacher he still remained within his order and subject to its control. For reasons of economy the university, which had been founded only a few years previously, was staffed partly by Augustinians. Luther lived in the Wittenberg monastery; he remained there for the rest of his life. We must not be misled by the name 'university' into visualizing something too big and important. There were twenty-two professors, of whom very few would conform to our present-day notions of a professor, and less than two hundred students, some of whom were scarcely more than children; in those days the entrance age for a university was between twelve and fifteen, and not much was expected of the applicant. The elector had established Wittenberg University mainly out of rivalry: his cousin and enemy possessed a university at Leipzig, for the duchy of Saxony, and he was determined to have a similar institution of his own for the electorate of Saxony. This antagonism continued well into the period of

Luther's own struggles; initially very academic affairs, the first battles were fought out between Leipzig and Wittenberg. Leipzig, as one of the oldest German universities, considered itself by far the more distinguished of the two; it had been founded in 1409, when German teachers and students left Prague as the result of a dispute with the Bohemians. Hus had been the cause of this, and even at that time heresy was at the bottom of it, the Germans, who were 'orthodox', accusing the Czechs of adopting the false doctrines of Wyclif, of whom Hus was a follower. The name of Hus, the great heretic who had been burned at the stake in Constance, and still more the memory of the disastrous Hussite wars that followed, remained more vividly in people's minds in Leipzig than elsewhere; the Leipzigers were thus especially keen to prove their loyalty to the Church. Duke George, the ruler of this half of Saxony, was also uncompromisingly conservative; opposed to innovation of every kind, he later became a lifelong and implacable enemy of Luther. Apart from this he was an excellent administrator of his widespread possessions, an 'old German warrior', as they said in those days, with an enormous beard that fell in grey-white strands to his waist. He also tried, though in vain, to bring some kind of order and discipline into his monasteries, abbeys and convents, and he was one of those who, at meetings of the Diet, always voiced the old complaints against Rome and the mismanagement of the Church.

His cousin, the Elector Frederick – called the 'Wise' in the history books of later times – was a very different type of man. 'Wise' is hardly the right word to describe him – cautious would be better, or sly; no 'warrior', he was resolutely averse to all warlike adventures, a trait in which one can in fact discern a wisdom lacked by each and every one of his peers. He never wanted to wage a war, or even to conduct a campaign, and never played the role of 'empire builder'. He was peaceable to the point of being thought half asleep – a very unjust assessment, because he was capable of looking after his interests with extreme prudence and discretion. His features are misleading, if we trace them in the many portraits of him done by his court painter Lucas Cranach; at times they seem weak and flabby, and at Worms Aleander, the papal nuncio, described him in his malicious, biting way as a 'fat dormouse'. At other times his face reveals the almost peasant features that were more coarsely marked in his brother and co-regent John, known as the 'Constant'. Eventually Dürer caught him in the full splendour of his majesty and girth; in this portrait the eyes sparkle with an energy that enables us to understand how this otherwise excessively cautious ruler came to be regarded as the most significant figure among his indecisive peers, the majority of whom could compete with him only in physical bulk. He embodied all these characteristics; much else, that never came out, may well have lain dormant in him. He was reserved to the point of shunning human society and kept people, even his advisers, waiting till they were almost in despair. He never married, but whether from preference – he had three illegitimate children – or because of his indecision and obesity is not clear. He was a devout churchman and in his younger days had made an expensive pilgrimage to the Holy Land, bringing home costly relics, to which he added by constant purchases. This collection was his greatest treasure; his cousin George, in contrast, amassed hard cash. The precious objects were displayed in the Schloss-kirche, the church of the ducal castle, in Wittenberg, to whose door Luther was later to nail his theses condemning indulgences. The blessings of this endowment became widely known through a guide written, and illustrated with woodcuts, by the court painter Lucas Cranach. The collection comprised 5,005 relics, the precise number being recorded as well as the precise efficacy of the corresponding indulgences; devout contemplation of the collection could procure a person 1,443 years' remission of purgatory. Included were tiny 'particles', such as a piece of straw from the Manger, one of the Blessed Virgin's hairs and a drop of her milk; side by side with these was a complete corpse of one of the children murdered by Herod in Bethlehem. Closely linked to this endowment was the university. Frederick remained true to his faith all his life; he never received Luther personally. But he was proud of his University of Wittenberg and never so proud of it as when it acquired worldwide fame through the monk. This was probably not his only reason for protecting Luther. Nor does he seem to have been deeply affected by the new teaching – by the time he came face to face with it he was already old and inflexible. More probably he felt quite simply that injustice was being done, that one of his protégés was being treated badly, and he was not prepared to countenance it. Is this an oversimplification? Possibly, but at the same time it is well to remind ourselves how excessively rare it is to be able to record such simple virtues. They can even, as in this case, affect the history of the world.

Frederick's purchases were not confined to relics. Concealed within this huge ungainly man, whose chief recreation was hunting, was also an astonishingly sensitive connoisseur of art. The small eyes, behind their rolls of fat and muscle, were keen, and picked out the best masters in Germany before they became famous. He employed Albrecht Dürer, when he was still almost unknown, and engaged and retained Lucas Cranach; the latter's studio, before long almost a small factory employing large numbers of assistants, was to become scarcely less important for the 'pictorial propaganda' of the Reformation than printing. He also brought in painters from the Netherlands and even from

Italy, the slightly mysterious Jacopo de'Barbari of Venice introducing a touch of the spirit of Italy into the tortuous scrollwork of the German masters. When Luther went to Wittenberg the Stiftskirche there contained nineteen altarpieces by Dürer, Cranach and Dutch, Italian and French painters; nothing of their work survived the iconoclasm.

Vivid and graphic though his language was, Luther had no feeling whatever for the fine arts. Unless painting served a didactic purpose it meant nothing to him; architecture meant nothing to him either, whether in stone or in the ethereal edifices of the great scholastics. For music alone of all the arts did he have any affinity, a fact that was to be of importance in the development of Protestantism. To music, however, must be added the art of language, of which he became a supreme master. An early opportunity to practise this, and to enrich his vocabulary, presented itself on his way to Wittenberg. He went on foot, the prescribed form of travel for a monk. It was his first journey of any length. During his life Luther travelled a great deal, for a long time on foot but later also on horseback or by carriage, thus becoming familiar with a large part of Germany, as well as with Switzerland and parts of Italy; it has been calculated that during the course of his life he covered some twelve or thirteen thousand miles in this way. The roads in those days were very different from the roads of today. From the quiet of the monastery he stepped into an immensely colourful world; it was wild and dangerous too. Highway robbery was as common then as bank robbery is now. Latterly, during an exceptionally lawless period, the robber knights had taken to hacking off merchants' hands in order to strike more terror into people's hearts. One valiant noblewoman, Agathe Odheimer, gave her horsemen the specific instruction: 'When a merchant does not keep his word, cut off his hands and feet and leave him.' There were discharged *Landsknechte* (German mercenary soldiers) on the roads – which were nothing more than deeply rutted field paths; they, too, plundered and stole wherever they could. There were vagabonds, beggars, tricksters attempting to awaken pity by displaying their appallingly mutilated bodies, poor scholars, monks, lay brothers and lay sisters of the Beghards and Beguines, regarded with extreme suspicion by the Church authorities because of the freedom of their views and lives. All of these differed in their clothing, their distinguishing marks and the language they spoke. The rules required a monk to walk with downcast eyes, his hands tucked into the sleeves of his habit; his eyes were not to wander and above all were never to rest on a woman. Luther must have proceeded in this way. But his ear was very sharp. He had already begun to 'look the ordinary man in the mouth', as he put it later in his letter on translating. The richness of his language had its origins in the street and in the market place; his vocabulary included the many technical terms used by craftsmen, the quiet prayers of the pious, the savage oaths and coarse invective of the drivers. The roads reflected the whole anarchy of the time in all its colour and variety. People sang and begged, were born and died on them, and in the cornfields alongside couples made love – a favourite subject for painters; on the outskirts of the towns and of civilization stood witnesses to the pitiless justice of the day, in emulation of the wrathful judge in heaven who so disturbed Luther: gallows with rotting corpses, or with hands, feet and other parts of the body nailed to them.

On this first journey Luther received an object lesson in the variety and dismemberment of the German territories; he had heard no word of this in the monastery. From Erfurt the road took him to Weimar, then already containing a castle and a seat of the dukes of Saxony. He passed through Naumburg, an important ecclesiastical see with an imposing church and magnificent carvings, which he did not notice. Halle was his next stop, another great ecclesiastical see, a residence of the archbishop of Mainz, whose territories meandered across half Germany. He entered the duchy of Saxony, which belonged to his later enemy Duke George, and then the electorate of Saxony, where his future ruler and protector reigned. His way led him north to the farthest corner of the land, where Wittenberg was situated; 'on the edge of barbarism' was the humanists' description of it. Beyond lay the march of Brandenburg with its sand, swamps, forests, poor soil and a population that was half Slav. Even on his way to Wittenberg Luther passed through villages where only Wendish was spoken, villages that were circular in the Slav style instead of stretched out along the village street, where the customs and clothes were strange, where white was worn for mourning instead of black; and it was as black from white that the peasants stood out from the rest of the population, despised as an 'inferior race' and therefore not inclined to be friendly to the traveller. This Saxony was an outpost, a colonial land.

Germany has never had a centre, it has had neither a capital city nor a dominant cultural focal point. Its movements, spiritual, intellectual and political, have originated in the border provinces – a phenomenon found also in other parts of the world. Christianity originated in a border province of the Roman Empire; Augustine came from the colonial territory of north Africa and may even have been an African. It was into this border town of Wittenberg, a grubby little place on the Elbe, which was spanned by what we should consider a very rickety-looking wooden bridge, that Luther now made his way; it had two thousand inhabitants, fortifications, a castle and the Schlosskirche containing the elector's collection of relics.

Luther's first letters from his new home have been published. The expressions 'borders of civilization' and 'close to barbarism' are his. The rector of the university, a cultured humanist named Pollich who had previously been the elector's personal physician, put it still more strongly when he said that living in Wittenberg was like living 'in a knacker's yard'. The university prospectus made vain and not entirely honest claims; in the first years of the university's existence the attendance had already dropped to half. Living in Wittenberg was cheap, the prospectus announced, and this may well have been true – a student needed only eight guilders a year; the air was excellent, it continued, and no one had any need to fear the plague – a somewhat premature claim because the town suffered continually from epidemics, probably due in part to sanitary arrangements that to us seem hair-raising. The university, the propaganda went on, had more and better scholars even than Padua, the goal of all the more ambitious German students, or Bologna. This was simply not true. Admittedly Pollich, the university's founder, was a man of note and doctor in three faculties, although the distinction between these was less clear-cut then than it is today; he lectured on philosophy, theology and medicine, and in this last field, at least, left behind him a manual which influenced medical thought for two hundred years. To open his anatomy, which was based on the Italian text of an old thirteenth-century master, at the title page is to be confronted with the old world and modern times side by side: the teacher sits, book in hand, in a heavy Gothic armchair, the book quite certainly being a classic work by Galen, whose authority in medicine was as unquestioned as that of the Fathers of the Church in theology. But laid out on the dissecting table in front of him is a body which his assistant, a little nervously and uncertainly, has opened up. In those days this was still a very bold thing to do, and many people considered it an outrage; even in Italy, where everything was so much freer, Leonardo could get the body he needed for his studies only by secretly removing that of a hanged man from the gallows. Pollich was a 'modern' in philosophical matters as well, and considered the classical poets and thinkers more profitable than the scholastics. This involved him in a dispute with Konrad Koch, one of the other professors who had been brought to Wittenberg and who assumed the name Wimpina, from the town of Wimpfen where he had spent his youth. There was talk of 'heresy', always a favourite word; but Pollich had the ear of the elector and Wimpina moved on to Brandenburg, to the newly formed university at Frankfurt on the Oder. The story is worth telling only because Wimpina intervened again, from Frankfurt now, immediately the quarrel with Luther began, again employing the accusation of heresy – an effective argument in disputes between university teachers – as ammunition against him.

More important than this man was Jodokus Trutfetter, the 'Eisenach doctor', a truly great figure; in this small Saxon world he was the 'Prince of Aristotelians', though scarcely known beyond its borders. He had written a book on logic and was considered a great dialectician in the scholastic manner; he was also author of a *Summa* covering the whole field of physics, a term under which he included whatever of natural science was accessible to him. The scope of the book is much the same as the scope of Luther's own knowledge. It treats in very summary fashion of the heavens, the stars and the earth, touching on stones, metals, plants, animals and also man, of whom it contains a diagram revealing his inner organs, though it stops short modestly at the bladder. There is also some discussion of psychology, physiognomy, palmistry and geography, this last being illustrated by a map of the world which includes a very vague representation of America. It is striking how little attention the great majority of people at that time paid to the New World; Luther was not alone in this. The wind, represented by plump-cheeked angels – as it was by Dürer too – blows from every quarter on to the sparse little map, whose outlines can be made out only with difficulty. But even the Emperor Charles V himself, as sovereign over the new continent, gave no more than a passing thought to this vast new possession.

The Eisenach doctor and other eminences of Wittenberg University gave the young monk from Erfurt a very cool reception. Luther wrote of the 'cold, haughty north wind of the Wittenberg world of learning.' At the same time, however, it is not easy to see what he had to offer as assistant professor. Moreover part of his task was to lecture on Aristotle, whom he detested, and, still worse, on physics, of all subjects the most alien to him and of which he knew nothing whatsoever; he had also to lecture on ethics, and was supposed somehow to find time to continue his own studies.

Nevertheless he was promoted, given his bachelor's degree and entrusted with every imaginable teaching task, a sign that at least his capacity for hard work had been recognized. He climbed the academic ladder to become *sententiarius*, or sententiary, complaining in the meantime to a friend in Eisenach that all this was getting him no nearer to theology, 'the kernel of the nut, the marrow of the bone'. Before he could extract the marrow from the bone he was suddenly transferred back to Erfurt. Here his reception was still more unfriendly than in Wittenberg. The authorities would not recognize the examinations of the brand new and, to Erfurt eyes, very inadequate University of Wittenberg. There was a dispute over dues, which Luther could not pay because he did not want to ask his father, who was still grumbling, for the money. Finally he received permission to expound the Sentences in his old monastery to a few of the brothers whom the prior had detailed for the purpose. He rescued himself from this drudgery by starting to learn Hebrew in order to be able to read the Bible in the original; he had only the scantiest means available, such as Reuchlin's *Rudimenta*, which literally supplied merely the rudiments of the language.

The quiet of the monastery was disturbed by a dispute of a different and quite unacademic nature, in the course of which Luther made his first acquaintance with tumult and revolt. In all probability Father Luther understood very little of what the dispute, which came to be known as the 'year of madness', was about. Although he rejected the scholastics and their teachings, the pattern of social order introduced by them was also his own; built on a strictly hierarchic and class basis, it started with the slaves, in their God-ordained place at the bottom, and worked up by way of serfs, peasants, citizenry and nobility to a monarchic summit. What did he know of the centuries of bitter strife in the towns between plebeians and patricians, the latter considering themselves no less noble in birth than the knights living in the surrounding countryside? What did he know of the peasant revolts? All the chronicles were full of them, but these chronicles had not been included in the reading matter available to the monk; at most he had heard of the conflict between the emperor and the pope, and for the time being was unhesitatingly on the side of the pope. In Erfurt the situation was particularly difficult because the city came within the jurisdiction of the elector of Mainz, although it enjoyed a high degree of independent self-government and never lost sight of the coveted goal of free city of the empire, a status it was never to achieve. The trouble was always caused by the elector, as sovereign prince, wanting to interfere from outside in the city's internal affairs; a large part of the citizenry regarded him as a public enemy, and being a priest he was loathed by all who inveighed against the rule of the great prelates. In this controversy the university and the monasteries, as was to be expected, took the part of the elector. They were privileged, and they paraded the fact with considerable arrogance.

The row began over questions of taxation, always a ticklish business in an age when people had not yet learnt to accept taxes meekly. The city authorities had plunged the town into debt by raising loans and then pocketing the money themselves. The citizenry wanted to know 'when the taxes would cease' and demanded a statement of accounts. A delegation approached the 'high and mighty Gentlemen' and a scribe recorded the proceedings. Reluctantly the council supplied some information, but confined itself to this; meanwhile it had reported the matter to the elector, whose landsknechts were on their way. With all the haughtiness of his patrician blood, Alderman Kellner shouted at the scribe, when a sum of a hundred guilders could not be accounted for: 'If you don't know what I spent it on, put down "brothels"!' At this weapons were drawn. The citizenry banded together and there was fighting in the streets against the archbishop's landsknechts. Students from the university joined in, were set upon and came off considerably the worse. The main building of the university was burnt down, the library destroyed and a new city council appointed in which the plebeians, the smaller craftsmen and journeymen, were in a majority. After a summary trial the hated Kellner was strung up for his insolent remark. The conflict was thus a class struggle, but with additional complications that confuse the 'clear picture' presented by today's summary view of the matter: the citizenry also called in 'foreign' aid and turned to the elector of Saxony, to whom they wanted to hand over the city; other princes and bishops also took a hand in the affair. Like all revolts in those days it ended in compromise and an armistice. The archbishop retained the city, the citizenry winning the right to elect the city council and demand statements of account for expenditure. A few years later there was a new revolt, during which the council's syndic was quartered; this was the usual punishment for high treason, the spectacle being enjoyed by the public with hideous relish. In the Peasants' War Erfurt was again to be the scene of bitter fighting.

The whole of Germany at this time resembled a landscape of volcanic mud in which small eruptions continually broke the surface and subsided again. Luther remembered these events all his life and constantly referred to them. 'It is no simple matter to break up a government,' he declared later, adding that for twenty years there had been no proper government in Erfurt. It is almost ironical that on this occasion he found himself on the side of the selfsame archbishop of Mainz who, a few years later, became his first great enemy and the cause of his forsaking monastic life to enter the world. Sebastian Franck, whom Luther classed among the 'fanatics', stated in his *German Chronicle* that he had scarcely ever read of an uprising 'in which the common people behaved with greater wisdom than in this clearly necessary revolt.' Luther never forgot that the people of Erfurt hanged their alderman. The incident planted in him his first distaste for '*Herr Omnes*', as he called the masses; he always regarded them as blind and liable to commit blind outrages.

Whether he took sides at all in Erfurt at this time may be regarded as uncertain; he saw only the fighting in the streets, the burning university buildings, the mangled books. The humanists had fled and did not return until later. A number of members of the old city council had also made timely escapes to safety, to wait until the archbishop and his fellow bishops had restored some measure of order. It was in this shifting, unstable world, in this dishonourable state of suspense, in which no group or faction rested, or could rest, content, in which each sought momentary advantage for itself and in which *Herr Omnes* lacked both cohesion and leadership – being ready at one moment to strike out and the next to knuckle under again – that Luther spent the years that were decisive both for himself and for German history.

At the moment, however, he was still tied to his lecture notes, which were giving him a great deal of trouble. Shortly afterwards, on instructions from the superiors of his order, he was recalled to Wittenberg.

# 7

# Journey to Rome

BEFORE Luther could resume his lectures in Wittenberg he received another assignment: he was to go to Rome on business connected with his order. According to later legends this was the great break, the cardinal experience: 'He saw with his own eyes the corruption of the Church and made up his mind to fight it'. Most legends contain an element of truth; the journey meant a great deal to the young monk. The city of Rome was the goal of every devout pilgrim. To go there guaranteed a large indulgence. To have seen the holy places was for many the most ardent desire and the greatest experience of their lives. Such must have been the attitude of the young Father Luther.

The reason for his journey was one of the many internal disputes within the order; most of them were over questions of organization and were too petty to merit discussion here. Reformers quarrelled with those who did not want to be reformed, and within the factions were still further opposition groups. They all tried to cover themselves by appealing to Rome and it was to one of these appeals – in a fairly hopeless cause – that Luther owed this journey; he went as travelling companion to a delegate sent by the Erfurt monastery. And so, in 1510, in dull November weather, two monks set out to make the pilgrimage on foot. Physically alone this was an arduous undertaking. The Alps had not yet become the haunt of tourists eager to admire the magnificent mountain scenery; with their gloomy walls of rock they were regarded as both a serious obstacle and a dangerous region, the wildest spots being given names from hell. It never entered anyone's head to climb one of the mountains; 'threatening' was the epithet invariably applied to them. The Septimer pass, which led to Milan, was lined with crosses to mark the spots where travellers had met their deaths. All Luther remembered of Switzerland was the robust physique of its people; 'robustissimi' was the word he used to contrast them with the much less sturdy Thuringians. There was only pasturage, he remarked, no agriculture, and the rest of the population had to 'look elsewhere' for its livelihood; this meant enlisting as mercenaries in the service of France or the pope. On another occasion, when comparing the various races, he praised the Swiss as the 'leading Germanic race, lively and upright'. But in general his verdict on Switzerland was: 'It is really nothing but mountains and valleys'. Like all who came from Germany, he was lost in wonder as he descended into the Lombard plain. Below him he saw riches, an elaborately cultivated landscape criss-crossed with canals and conduits, a prospect totally unlike the miles of desolate heathland that surrounded Wittenberg: 'Very good country, fertile and cheerful.' The people were polite, never forgetting to use the proper forms of address or say thank you, they sang and hummed as they went along, and the wine was good, having more body than the German wine to which he was accustomed. Accommodation was no problem for the two monks, who walked one behind the other in the required manner; they simply made their way from one Augustinian monastery to another, their order being especially well represented in Lombardy where, in addition, it was sympathetic to Staupitz's views on observance. In Milan Luther wanted to say Mass, in gratitude for having survived the perils of the journey, but to his astonishment learned that it was celebrated quite differently there and was conducted according to the jealously preserved Ambrosian rites handed down from St Ambrose. 'You cannot celebrate Mass here,' he was told. Once again he discovered how very different the world was from the world he had heard about in the monastery, and how much more varied.

The two monks crossed the Apennines in rainy weather and encountered their first snowstorms. Luther complained of the treacherous Italian air and the 'deadly water', from the effects of which, on one occasion, he and his companion were saved only by eating pomegranates. In Florence he was taken ill, probably with the bowel complaint that attacked all the early travellers to Italy. Although he had no eyes for the splendour of this city of the Medicis, he was full of praise for its hospitals: 'Regal buildings, with the finest food and drink, attentive service, very learned physicians and clean beds' – all of which was new to him. When the patient entered the hospital a legally attested inventory was made of his clothes, then he was dressed in a white shift and put into a 'beautifully painted bed.' Drinks were brought in clean glasses carried on a plate: 'they do not touch them with a single finger.' Gentlewomen in veils were in charge of the patients; relieved each day by others, they cared even for the poor stranger. He also admired the foundling hospitals, where the children were admirably brought up and looked after; 'they dress them all alike in the same colour and take care of them in a fatherly way.'

Sometime towards the end of the year they arrived in Rome. At his first glimpse of the city Luther threw himself on the ground, exclaiming

'Hail, holy city of Rome!' Entering through the Porta del Popolo, they found Santa Maria, the Augustinian monastery where they were to stay, immediately on their left; it had been staffed by the order with specially chosen monks, so that the Augustinian friars should be represented as fittingly as possible in the papal city. Barely twenty years after Luther's visit the monastery fell a victim to the ravages of the Emperor Charles's soldiery in the sack of Rome in 1527; but the church of Santa Maria del Popolo, where he performed his devotions, still stands. Luther had no eye for the city's art treasures, of which, in any case, many fewer were to be seen than vague ideas of Renaissance Rome would lead us to believe. A poor, insignificant German monk had no chance whatsoever of gaining admission to one of the palaces where the collections were housed.

What Luther saw was the Rome of the Middle Ages. When he first caught sight of the Holy City from the Ponte Molle the panorama was not dominated by the dome of St Peter's as it has been for all later generations. The foundations of the new building had only just been laid, and throughout Christendom money was being raised for it by means of special indulgences; these were also to play a role in Luther's life. Towers of castles belonging to the great Roman families rose everywhere from the ruins like spearheads; they had been built as strongholds. The great houses of the cardinals were strongholds too. The Vatican was a fortress and forming its centre was the mighty and impregnable Castle of St Angelo, in which the popes used to take refuge and in which they were still often forced to do so in Luther's day. Ancient ruins stood out on the hilltops, considerably higher then than they were later, after they had served as quarries for the construction of churches and the vast Palazzo Farnese. Parts of the topmost tiers of the Colosseum still stood, as did the vaults of the great Roman baths with their massive arches, which later became the inspiration for buildings of the baroque period. Of the total area of the ancient city, with its million inhabitants and walls that now extended 'far into the surrounding country', what remained was little more than a pathetic fragment. It was as if it had slithered down to the river to form a few congested centres of habitation honeycombed with narrow 'Gothic' lanes; the whole city contained about 60,000 people, scarcely more than German cities like Nuremberg and Augsburg and not to be compared with great and magnificent cities such as Venice or Paris, to say nothing of Constantinople. The narrow streets, with their many nooks and corners that led nowhere, meandered completely at random. The first to give his attention to them was the reigning pontiff, Pope Julius II, who used a mailed fist to get things done; he had an imposing marble tablet erected to commemorate his achievement in opening up the

St Peter's Square and the Vatican in 1520

streets. It proclaimed, in fine old Roman lettering: 'To Pope Julius II, who extended the borders of the Papal State, liberated Italy and embellished the city of Rome, which was too congested and lacked proper thoroughfares, with new streets worthy of the Empire's majesty'; at the bottom appeared the names of his municipal officers in the style of ancient Rome.

Luther came upon a building site and a rubble heap. He remarked observantly how far ancient Rome had sunk: 'Where houses now stand there used to be roofs, so deep does the rubble go; one can see this clearly in the Tiber, which is two pike lengths deep in rubble.' Contemporary views of Rome, in so far as they are not merely idealized reminiscences of the splendours of antiquity, show heaps of piled up rubble elsewhere – reaching as high as the first arcades of the Colosseum or standing higher than a man round the triumphal arches – rank grass, vegetation on the ruins, herds of cattle on the Forum, and undulating ground that was neither levelled, paved nor at any point recognizable as a street.

As a mendicant friar he made his pilgrimage to all the prescribed Stations. In the monastery he had been handed the usual printed guide, modelled on the *Mirabilia Romae* which was already well known in the Middle Ages; but it did not contain, nor could it have contained, any mention of the new art treasures and new buildings. The Sistine Chapel was still hidden by tall, wooden scaffolding on top of which Michelangelo lay painting the ceiling. In the private apartments of the Vatican Raphael was busy painting the pope's rooms, his first big commission in Rome; today these rooms, known as the Stanze, are the showpiece of the Vatican museum, but then they could be seen only by a few intimates and were still far from complete. It is fascinating to think that Luther could have met the painter; he was almost his own age, had just become famous and was the spoilt favourite of the miserly Pope Julius, who haggled over every penny he had to pay Michelangelo. The monk could only have gazed in astonishment at the beautifully dressed artist, who never went to work without a whole train of attendants and who used to take one of his mistresses with him to the Vatican to provide distraction; this kind of thing was unknown in Germany, where even the greatest artists were still only master craftsmen. Luther has been rather naïvely criticized because he failed to notice any of the new art treasures in Rome; but the same criticism can be levelled against Erasmus and many others who were a long way from being mendicant friars. There is no doubt, however, that Raphael's Camera della Signatura, which was just finished, would have struck Luther as very strange; it was a completely different world from his own. What could he have seen in the spacious halls of the 'School of

Athens', a painting that contained the figure of his detested Aristotle? And what in that supreme glorification of the Church, painted in this same year, the so-called Disputà, in which no one is disputing anything but in which a well-ordered assembly of the Fathers of the Church reflects the divine order that hovers over them; they are demonstrating to the pope, in the person of Julius's uncle Sixtus IV, the beauty and balanced perfection of the hierarchic edifice.

Succeeding centuries have admired Raphael's paintings as models of composition and design; they were not conceived from this standpoint. It was the pope's wish that they should serve his central idea of the Church dominant and militant, an idea that was similarly expressed in his plan for St Peter's; every last dogmatic detail in them was precisely stipulated by the painter's theological advisers. This tends to be overlooked when the paintings are seen from a purely stylistic and aesthetic viewpoint. Contemporaries marvelled at the powerful Julius, who had re-established the Caesarist claims of the earlier popes and who was pleased when people linked his name of Julius with Caesar. With mailed fist, and literally weapon in hand, he had once again demonstrated that the Church militant was a power to be feared.

Even as a pilgrim Luther found cause to praise the harsh rule of this pontiff. After years of disorder, during which Rome had been a veritable den of thieves, Julius had taken drastic action. As Luther tells us: 'The chief of police, who is both captain and judge, rides round the town every night with three hundred men, maintaining a strict patrol. Anyone caught on the streets has to take the consequences; if he is armed he is either hanged, drowned and thrown into the Tiber, or racked.' The prescribed round of the seven pilgrim churches was still a risky undertaking, some of them being situated far outside the town. Luther's guide stipulated as the first Station San Paolo fuori le Mura, on the way to Ostia. The route taken by the pilgrims passed through rough wasteland to what was then the greatest church in the west; built in the days of Constantine, it still retained in their full splendour its rows of classic columns. The way was considered unsafe because of marauders, who made regular incursions from the river; all the surroundings of Rome had a bad name, which they kept until the nineteenth century. Important personages rode with a personal guard and an armed retinue; lesser pilgrims were careful to go in groups, but even so were often set upon and robbed. The arduous pilgrimage, which had to be completed in a day, started at this church of San Paolo; from here the way led to San Sebastiano on the Appian Way, near the Catacombs containing the graves of the martyrs, thence to the Lateran, to Santa Croce, with its memories of the Holy Cross which Constantine's mother, Helena, had dug up in Jerusalem, to San Lorenzo,

Santa Maria Maggiore and finally St Peter's. It was a good day's march, in sand and clay, over narrow paths and bad roads. 'I believed everything', Luther said later; he even claimed to have been almost sorry that his parents were still alive, because the 'large indulgence' he had earned could have made them happy in the life beyond. The 'large indulgence' was due above all to the Lateran, as the oldest papal residence; according to legend the Emperor Constantine had presented it to the pope as a sign that the whole of the west had now been handed over to him. In Luther's day it was a large, oddly assorted complex of buildings, some parts of it, with their towers and buttresses, ancient and some medieval; here, too, mountains of rubble had piled up. The pilgrim's way also took him to the most sacred place of all, to the steps up which Christ had climbed to Pilate's palace; they had been brought intact to Rome by angels. To climb the twenty-eight steps on one's knees guaranteed a nine years' indulgence for each step; the step on which Christ had stumbled – it was marked by a cross – counted double. Luther would have liked to say Mass in the Lateran but there were too many people: 'I could not get near it, so I ate a pickled herring instead', he said later with heavy sarcasm. He ate nothing; the pilgrim had to arrive at St Peter's, the last Station, fasting so that he could partake of the sacrament there.

Luther said very little about St Peter's; it was a vast building site. Part of the old basilica of Constantine was still standing and was partitioned off for divine worship. From the wide, unpaved square in front of the entrance steps led up to a façade composed of narrow colonnades, with bare patches of wall on either side. The monk said his prayers before several of the many altars. All that he remembered were some curiosities: the rope with which Judas hanged himself, a stone with a furrow as broad as a man's finger caused by Peter's tears after he had denied Christ.

Luther stayed four weeks in Rome. The mission on which they had gone was handled by his companion, who was the delegate; the result was satisfactory. Luther accompanied him on his various calls and obtained some idea of the vast administrative apparatus of the Church. He admired the systematic way in which things were done: 'The business and legal aspects of the matter were heard, assessed, judged and discussed in an admirably orderly way.' But he also remembered the pay counters that stood outside every door in the long corridors, each for the receipt of specific dues, such as those for annulment of vows, dispensation from obstacles to marriage, legitimization of bastard children – in other words for all the countless 'exceptions' which formed the rule governing the Curia's financial policy. He estimated the number of 'scribes', some of whom were distinguished secretaries,

humanists and authors of witty writings, at three thousand; like everything else he said later about Rome, this was a slight exaggeration.
But he was not far wrong in saying that what went on in the papal
chancellery was no different from what went on in the great markets of
Venice and Antwerp.

In spite of his disappointment at the Lateran, he was able to say Mass
in other churches and for a monk visiting Rome this was even more
important than the general confession. Great numbers of priestly
pilgrims converged on Rome from every country. The thing had to be
done in a hurry and not infrequently there were two saying Mass at
the same time; the Italian priests, who called out to him '*passa, passa,*
come on, make way,' 'turned out a Mass in a trice.' People from northern countries were always put off by the way in which divine service was
conducted in Rome; they found it superficial.

Of the ancient monuments the only one to attract Luther's attention was the Pantheon; this, too, was in a deplorable state – half of
the great, columned entrance portico was bricked up and its top
surmounted by a crooked quadrangular tower. Very much the monk,
he saw 'all the heathen's gods' expediently assembled by Providence in
this one place, so that Christ could 'send them all flying' with a single
blow. The Capitol, a barren hill on top of which stood the massive
block of the church of Ara Coeli, was for him a sign that, although the
Romans possessed all the treasures in the world, they would come to
grief, inevitably and in accordance with God's will. This monument
of former imperial greatness had survived because it was 'cast together'
with such huge stones 'that it was indestructible'. As a devout pilgrim
he visited the Catacombs, where the descent was made by torchlight;
this undertaking was also considered especially meritorious. He
accepted credulously the story that they contained the bodies of 46
martyred popes and 176,000 ordinary martyrs.

We must not think of Luther as a tourist, intent on 'doing' all the
places of interest. For him what mattered was the absolution of the
general confession, which was the climax of the pilgrimage to Rome.
He must have spent much of his time in the Augustinian monastery in
prayer. There were no great Church festivals during his stay; he did
not see the pope. Julius was away on one of his incessant military
campaigns, extending the borders of his empire, as the marble tablet
proclaimed. When engaged on his devotions in the chapels of Santa
Maria del Popolo Luther, had he been enlightened by a knowledgeable
brother, could have read on the monuments the whole history of the
House of Rovere, from which Julius came, as well as some of the ex-
ploits of other recent popes.

Unfortunately all he heard was the usual monastery gossip. In the

Rome of those days, before the structure of the Church, which seemed so secure, was seriously threatened, people were outspoken and carefree. There was no official censorship; this was first introduced with the Counter-Reformation, in the middle of the century. The only danger, as in the whole preceding period, lay in questions touching on Church dogma or in questioning fundamentally the institutions of the Church. What mattered was the basic dogmatic thesis, proclaimed over and over again, that the office, whether that of pope, cardinal or ordinary priest, was above any unworthiness in its holder. Great saints had called Rome a brothel, the cesspit of Christianity, and no one had taken offence. Great popes had not hesitated to impute to their predecessors every imaginable vice, if it seemed expedient to them. It was a well-known saying in Rome that Saint Golden Coin and Saint Silver Piece were the two most eminent saints: without their intercession nothing could be achieved. Priests of the mendicant orders exhorting people to repentance knew very well that their best chance of attracting large congregations was to inveigh passionately against the pomp of the prelates, illustrating their sermons with highly dramatic incidents taken from life. Moreover it was the ready wit of the Romans which had created the original form of the lampoon. The Pasquino, a mutilated, ancient statue in front of the Palazzo Braschi, was used as a display board for the poems and contentious verses that were the delight of great and humble alike. The pope's secretaries still had their own room or 'lie centre', the *bugiale*, in the very heart of the Curia, from which they circulated their charming drolleries and malicious libels. People wrote anonymously because it was prudent; with an energetic pope in office they could expect severe punishment. After the death of the pontiff, however, a stream of abuse would flood the squares and market places, soon to dry up again until it was the next one's turn. An anthology of these writings could be compiled that would far exceed anything Luther ever said about Rome and the popes. Moreover, Luther confined himself almost entirely to generalities, whereas the Roman school for scandal found its main pleasure in intimate, personal details, in allusions to the popes' love affairs, their bastards, their boy friends, and their bodily infirmities, which were lampooned mercilessly.

Of all this activity Luther retained merely the general impression that Rome had crawled with 'vermin and vileness' to an extent unknown even in ancient Babylon. From his fellow monks in the monastery he heard the current stories of corruption in the papal chancellery: offerings to Saint Golden Coin had brought a courtier twenty-two incumbencies, seven provostships and a further forty-two benefices. There were tales of unprincipled Roman clerics who poked fun at the mystery of the eucharist and murmured during Mass: 'Bread thou art and bread thou shalt remain.' Such things had pained him, he said later. The brothers pointed out to him the strange mural relief at a street corner in front of St Peter's; archaeologists have explained it as an ancient representation of Mithras. In those days it was thought to be a woman carrying her child and to be a portrait of the well-known woman, pope Johanna, who gave birth to her child during a procession, in full view of everyone. Said to have come from Mainz, and to have been called Jutta, she had been brought by her lover to Rome dressed as a man; there she had studied, become a celebrated Doctor of the Church and, because of her learning, been elected pope. The legend had been accepted throughout the Middle Ages and in Rome it was familiar to every class of the population; it was only the Holy Father who avoided the street where the relief was to be seen, or so the brothers told Luther.

'I believed everything', said Luther. He also believed what he was told in a hushed whisper of the latest scandal in Rome: Pope Alexander Borgia, who had recently died of poison he had intended for a rich cardinal, had had incestuous relations with his bastard daughter Lucrezia. Today we have a better knowledge of this large-scale erotomaniac, both from the accounts of Burkhard, his master of ceremonies, who noted down the misdeeds of his employer coolly and without any spicy additions, and from other sources. It is worth remarking that moral indignation over his activities became really intense only in the moralizing eighteenth century; in Luther's day, and in Luther's own writings, there is very little mention of it. What made people indignant were the pomp and splendour, the payments, the system of benefices and the pope's constant wars. The homosexuality which was carried on quite openly in Rome was also a current topic of conversation; but the more intimate details of the private lives of the popes were reserved for Italians and ambassadors, whose reports contain very factual information on the various 'Ganymedes' or mistresses, their earnings and the high honours bestowed on them.

Because it fell in Luther's lifetime, the reign of Pope Alexander VI has been regarded as the nadir in the history of the papacy and as the explanation of its fearful collapse. This greatly oversimplifies the matter. The Borgia epoch represents merely an intensification in a process of development; to our eyes it stands out particularly clearly, but the development itself had been going on for a long time. It would have been impossible for a single unworthy pope to jeopardize the institution; to this extent the thesis of the independence of the office from its holder was correct.

'Simony' (corruption and sale of ecclesiastical offices) and 'nepotism' (favouritism shown by the popes to their 'nephews') had long been in vogue but had increased greatly in the course of the preceding century.

It was scarcely ever claimed any longer that any pope had been elected without simony; legation reports gave precise details of payments and promises of high honours made during the elections. The sale of ecclesiastical offices, of both high and medium rank, had become a recognized practice; the cardinals themselves pressed the pope to resort to this well-tried means when money was short. A further well-known custom, and one that was bitterly contested, especially abroad, was 'pluralism' – the bestowal of three, four and up to as many as ten or fifteen high offices on a single favoured individual; it was forbidden under canon law but practised widely without compunction. In Luther's day there was hardly a cardinal who did not enjoy the rich rewards of four or five highly lucrative offices, in many cases abroad; usage permitted these to be transferred to members of the family, thus creating a further nepotism within the great nepotism of the popes. But the establishment of their nephews and cousins in high office by the popes, which had been going on for centuries, now developed on a really big scale; the papal families became great Italian landowners. Duchies and even kingdoms were demanded for the clan. These had to be wrested from someone and this necessitated wars and campaigns, which were waged with all the means of 'ecclesiastical power', including excommunication and interdict. Italy became a battle-field, above all when the foreign powers – France, Spain, Germany – were drawn in. The great decisions of a century were fought out on Italian soil. Neither the times in which Luther lived nor the crucial turning points in his own destiny can be understood except in this context.

These general observations may be seen graphically exemplified in the mortuary monuments which adorn Santa Maria del Popolo, the church in which Luther used to pray. Here, Cardinal Ascanio Sforza, sculpted by Sansovino in an unusually lifelike pose, could tell an absorbing story of the pluralist life he led, and of simony during papal elections where figures ran so high that even his hardened countrymen could find no parallel. The Borgia family is represented by Giovanni Borgia, the eldest son of Alexander VI, who was murdered by his younger brother Cesare. Next to him lies his mother, Vanozza, the richest and most celebrated of all the papal mistresses and a woman with a gift for politics, which she exercised. She had invested her fortune wisely in house property and owned the best known inns in the city; these were patronized by eminences and diplomats, who in this way obtained information that was otherwise hard to get. But the church was mainly the family vault of the della Roveres, the first of the great Renaissance dynasties; they were followed by the Borgias and then by the Medicis, who were in power throughout the critical period

87

of the Reformation. Julius II succeeded to the papacy as the nephew of his uncle Sixtus IV, and with Sixtus began the era of the princes who 'lacked all taint of morals', to use Nietzsche's expression, and used the holy see simply as a basis for furthering their reckless plans to extend their own power and family influence.

The della Roveres came from a family of modest craftsmen; starting as a mendicant friar of the Franciscan Order, originally dedicated to poverty, Sixtus, prior to being elected pope by simony, had risen to become general of his order. His nephew Julius was one of the first to be appointed cardinal; four other nephews and one of his illegitimate sons, who made their way into Roman society under the name Riario, were also raised to the purple. The term 'nephew' was charitably vague. The scandalous gossip of Sixtus's day fully bears comparison with that of the Borgia epoch. Worse, however, was the new policy of territorial aggrandizement. Sixtus's small son, Girolamo Riario, was to be made duke, or king, of Naples. Anathemas were tossed around and withdrawn again. The della Rovere pope wanted to secure Florence for his family by committing 'murder in the cathedral'; the eldest Medici was killed in church, on a sign from the cardinal-nephew during the celebration of High Mass. The plot misfired because the younger Medici brother, though badly wounded, escaped. Sixtus pronounced an anathema on the 'rebellious' city; a synod of Tuscan bishops retaliated with a memorandum in which the pope was described as 'pander to his mother the Church, and the devil's vicar' – the phraseology will be worth remembering when that of the Luther era is under discussion. The nephew remained a cardinal; as an old man he served on the council which elected the first Medici pope, Leo X, the son of the Lorenzo who was to have been murdered.

Julius della Rovere had grown up and become powerful in the school of his uncle Sixtus; under the latter's successor, the Genoese Innocent VIII, he was already known as the 'second pope', the power behind a pope who wore his tiara uneasily and was concerned mainly with looking after his family interests. It was from the time of Innocent that Italian chroniclers dated the papal custom of presenting illegitimate children openly instead of under the shamefaced name of 'nephew'. The wedding of his illegitimate son to a Medici was celebrated with pomp in the Vatican, and from then on it became usual even for the great, princely families to feel honoured and politically strengthened if they were connected by marriage to the sons and daughters of popes. After Innocent came the Borgia pope, during whose rule Julius was forced to flee to France; this resulted in a further portentous development when the exiled Julius della Rovere led the first French expedition into Italy. The territorial policy of the popes, which outside Italy could

Pope Julius II

still be ignored to a large extent, led to their entanglement in international politics and, no matter what their dynasty, they were never again able to extricate themselves from this net. They sent for the French and, when these became too successful, tried to drive them out of Italy again; they formed alliances against them with other powers and imported Swiss mercenaries. All the forces of the day were set in motion. This went on, back and forth, for over half a century. During this period the word 'theatre' was first used to describe the scene of fighting. The word 'theatrical' describes equally well the fearful anathemas, the great proclamations announcing a crusade, the eloquent words about the universal peace which the holy father assured his people he was trying to secure, while he pursued one campaign after another, mostly with the object of acquiring tiny fragments of territory. People in Luther's day were far more concerned over this incessant warfare than over the gay life that went on behind the high walls of the Vatican.

At the beginning of 1511, when Luther carried out his duties as a pilgrim, Julius was away on one of these campaigns. He had the habit of forming alliances and speedily dissolving them again; the Holy League was the name given to the alliance of the day. He conceived a project to crush Venice and put the city under an interdict; then, when his French allies proved too overbearing, Venice was tendered absolution and the papal blessing. On his return to Wittenberg, Luther referred to this affair in his lectures. He still unreservedly sided with the pope: the Venetians, it was true, had seized Church property unlawfully; but, he added, someone ought to have advised the pope to show clemency – 'Be forbearing, such is God's will.' Julius, however, had taken the position that he was pursuing his lawful right, and it had all led to terrible bloodshed.

Clemency was not the great Julius's way. After Venice had been humbled he continued to wage further war, this time against France, his recent ally. He wanted to conquer Ferrara, Parma, Piacenza and the County of Mirandola. The widowed countess of Mirandola defended her old family castle for her children. The sixty-eight-year-old pope recklessly embarked on a winter campaign, although his generals had advised him against it. Julius himself rode right up to the front line, where a cannon ball killed two grooms at his side; he had the ball hung from the ceiling of the pilgrim church of San Loretto in memory of his deliverance. When the castle wall was breached the countess surrendered. Before the barricaded doors could be opened Julius had himself hoisted over the breach in a wooden cage, so that he would be the first to enter the captured castle. In one of his sudden switches from violent anger to a mood of conciliation, or astute diplomacy, he treated the brave woman graciously; contenting himself with driving her from her ancestral home, he accompanied her personally through the castle gate.

The campaigns continued. Bologna had been taken and lost again; Michelangelo's huge statue of the pope was shattered and recast into cannon. War in Italy remained the watchword for decades. Those cardinals who were on the side of France met in Pisa, where they held a council to depose the pope; Julius convened an opposition council in Rome, which anathematized the cardinals. The ageing pope fell ill from overstrain and was expected to die. For a moment his whole imperial edifice seemed on the point of collapse. The Romans, under the command of Bishop Pompeo Colonna, stormed the Capitol and proclaimed a republic. But the mighty man recovered and the uproar blew over. The leaders of the opposition left Rome to await a better opportunity to return.

We have presented a brief cross-section of events during this single year of 1511. It would be wrong, however, to confine ourselves to the principal actor, Julius II, whom his countrymen, in awed admiration, called 'Il Terribile'. Papal history has too often focused its attention solely on the occupant of the holy see, but the rest of the cast is no less important and it fills the stage to overflowing. 'Rome', the target of so many bitter complaints, encompassed also the cardinals, the 'nephews', the great aristocratic families of the Colonna and Orsini and their retinues; for all of them the paltry word 'corruption' is quite inadequate. To take but one of the wearers of the red hat: the cardinal of Pavia, whom the papal nephew Francesco Maria of Urbino coolly murdered in the street. With 'hands raised to Heaven', the chronicler tells us, the cardinals gave thanks that the hated upstart had been eliminated, this man whom the pope had elevated from nothing, showered with riches and kicked out of his presence only to reinstate; there is no lack of the usual charges of 'unspeakable vices'. The old man's weakness for this Alidosi – in all probability a wretched specimen of humanity – is more plausibly explained by Julius's obstinacy and limitless contempt for mankind than by assuming Alidosi to have been the papal 'Ganymede'. But he was by no means the only one of his kind; similar favourites crop up constantly, and when the cardinals turned against them it is safe to assume that their aim was not reform but a larger share of the vast spoils; they were willing to resort to violence in order to safe-guard their position. The weakness of the papacy was not simply a theological one; it was due also to the fact that, with every change of dynasty, the new family invariably began by robbing its predecessor's 'nephews' of as much as possible in order to make provision for its own members. Thus the Church's mainstay, its tradition, was replaced by a new usage, each papal election resulting in a sort of revolution. With each new election the existing balance of power and distribution of property was repudiated and revoked, a new balance being created, which in turn lasted only so long as the new pope remained in office.

In the history of the Church the papacy of Julius II can be summed up as the period in which the papal states were re-established. On his marble tablet he had himself honoured as the man who had liberated Italy from foreign domination, a claim which, being little more than a pious hope, was very soon proved untrue. In the history of art he is rightly acclaimed as the great patron of Bramante, Raphael and Michelangelo. Erasmus made him the subject of a small satire *Julius exclusus*, or Julius excluded from heaven – that is to say the work can be ascribed with a fair amount of confidence to Erasmus, although he persistently denied its authorship. On his death Julius appears at the gate of heaven and tries to open it with the keys which have proved so efficacious on earth. But they do not fit, having been made only to open the money chest. On hearing the din set up by the impatient Julius Peter hurries to the spot, but fails to recognize him as his successor, more especially as Julius, in telling of the services he has rendered, stresses his great feats of arms. Finally Julius lays siege to heaven itself, declaring that the souls of warriors who have fallen in his campaigns will hurry to his aid as soon as they enter heaven.

From the safe distance of centuries such 'Renaissance figures' as Pope Julius have been admired; to his contemporaries, he was 'The Terrible'. The tremors set up by him undermined the ground and caused it to collapse under the feet of his successors.

How much of all this Luther sensed when he was in Rome we do not know. Armed with a rich store of indulgences he made his way home on foot, like the good monk he was; the long journey took him past Padua, over the Brenner Pass to Augsburg and then up to the little town of Wittenberg. To his friends and acquaintances he spoke only of the greatness of the Eternal City – a good German mile across, 'as far as from Wittenberg to the Poltersberg'. Not until after his battle had begun did he speak of the corruption of the Church, which 'I saw with my own eyes', and fill out the gaps in his own experience by adding things told him by others. Like many other pilgrims he saw on his journey only 'certain grievances' and small blemishes on the shining escutcheon of the Church. They could, he was convinced, have been removed quite easily by a good pope undertaking the 'root and branch' reform of the Church for which everyone was hoping. Until this happened all an individual could do was try to improve things within his own small sphere of action. It was for this that the homecomer was needed in Wittenberg and in his order.

# 8

# Promotion in the Order

LUTHER always received rapid promotion. Within a few years of his return from Italy he had risen to the highest position in the local congregation of his order. In Erfurt, it is true, he had not been appreciated and was regarded as aggressive and disturbing, but in Wittenberg he was needed. Staupitz needed him; years of disputes over organizational matters had reduced his conciliatory nature to a state of resignation and he looked forward to receiving active help from the young and ardent Father Luther.

Staupitz was not content merely to console Luther and encourage him when he was worried by qualms of conscience. He urged him on and forced him to find his vocation, doing this at first by the purely academic and practical means of appointing him to new posts. Luther himself was faint-hearted and at times despaired altogether. He attributed this to the life he had led in the monastery; it seems more likely, however, that it was the incubatory period of uncertainty and hesitation which, in great men, so often precedes the breakthrough to their appointed task. He fought against this breakthrough. He pretended he was ill and weak, telling his patron he would not live long. Nonsense, replied Staupitz with humour, he was still needed and even were he to go to heaven God could use a smart doctor; he was to take his doctor's degree and begin preaching as well – 'that would keep him busy'. Still adhering closely to the methods of Scholasticism, Luther set out fifteen reasons why he could not do this. Staupitz became more insistent and drew Luther's attention to the discipline of his order: 'My dear fellow, don't try and know better than the whole monastery!' 'Herr Staupitz', wailed Luther, 'you will be the death of me. I shan't endure it for three months'.

Staupitz appointed him preacher in the Wittenberg monastery, got him his doctor's degree and handed over to him his own chair at the university, which, because of his numerous journeys and missions, he had been unable to occupy effectively. With some difficulty he persuaded the thrifty elector to pay the fairly high graduation fee for the penniless monk, assuring him that in doing so he would be acquiring a very valuable addition to his university. The letters he exchanged with the elector reveal in all its pettiness the economy of what was at that time the largest territorial unit in Germany. The question at issue was 'a quantity of bricks', which Staupitz asked the elector to allocate from work on the royal castle to the Augustinian monastery, where there seemed no prospect of the buildings ever being finished. The monastery services were held in a tiny half-timbered chapel that was out of alignment and supported by beams to prevent it collapsing, and whose pulpit was made of rough wooden boards – little better than 'a painter's version of the Bethlehem manger' is how a visitor described it later. There was, however, a small garden, with a pear tree beneath which Luther and Staupitz carried on their conversations; there was also an old brewery. The monks' dormitory and the brewery were connected by another building and it was in the tower-like upper storey of this that the young professor was allotted a tiny room. For the first time in his life Luther, now aged thirty, had a room of his own where he could work undisturbed and without supervision; it remained his workroom for the rest of his life. Luther was proud of this little room. It had belonged to the original monastery, and when he himself had become a part of history he felt sad to think that the new fortifications 'were going to gobble up his poor little room, from which he had stormed the papacy'; it would have been worth preserving for posterity.

The Word was now his world. He was made lecturer in Bible studies in the faculty of theology; this comprised five professors. Karlstadt, the dean of the faculty, invested him with his doctor's hat, which from now on he wore in place of the monk's cowl, and put the silver doctor's ring on his finger – this, too, had been provided by the elector. The formalities, extending over two days, included a disputation, several hours of learned addresses, the pealing of bells and processions through the town. The dean handed Luther first a closed and then an open Bible.

The following day Luther gave his first lecture, at seven o'clock in the morning; the monks rose early. Opening the Bible at Genesis he began to lecture before an audience of scarcely more than a dozen listeners. His title of doctor, which Staupitz had had such difficulty in persuading him to take, always meant a great deal to him; he regarded it as a special calling, never as a mere academic honour. 'Doctor of the Holy Scriptures' was how he signed himself in his first. letter to Archbishop Albrecht of Mainz, the document with which the great battle of his life began. He often said that, when faced by the hostility of both emperor and pope, and by the whispered 'you have not been called' of the devil, he would comfort himself with the thought that he was a doctor and bound by his oath to teach the Scriptures. On taking his doctor's degree, however, he had also had to swear never to expound any 'strange' doctrine of any kind that had been condemned by the Church, and to report to the faculty at once anyone who did so.

His activities as doctor and lecturer made up only a part of his duties. He had to preach, at first to the monks but soon in the parish church as well; as yet there was no sign of the tremendous force he was to become as a preacher. His sermons were worked out in Latin; he did not preach extempore, nor did he ever adopt the style of the popular Capuchin or Augustinian sermon, which was still used with brilliant effect in the seventeenth century by his fellow Augustinian, Abraham a Santa Clara, whose edifying tales, with their rich vocabulary and use of puns, appealed to an enormously wide public. He was strict, as he was in everything he did at this period. When he referred to topics of the day, they were local topics, things that happened in the village of Wittenberg and its immediate neighbourhood. The students drank; this was normal, students drank prodigiously and many were the times that Luther's temper flared up on the subject of the 'drunken Germans'. But during their drinking bouts they danced with the daughters of Wittenberg citizens and then things occurred that horrified him. It came to his ears that the girls had put on the students' caps and the students the girls' chaplets. He denounced this with such vehemence that the parents, grateful for the hint, kept their marriageable daughters at home; as a result the Augustinian father won 'a following, large congregations, honour and praise from the most distinguished citizens.' It was rare in those days for such harmless dancing to provoke such a stern rebuke from the pulpit, although one can well imagine that the word 'chaplet' may have been a euphemism for a girl's virginity.

In carrying out the obligations of his order he maintained an iron discipline, both in regard to himself and as supervisor of the other brothers. He was careful always to pray the required seven times a day, and if, when away on outside missions, he fell in arrears he did his best to make good the Hours he had missed, sometimes exhausting himself in the process; his attitude astonished his fellow monks, who seldom took their duties so strictly. He was elected sub-prior and district vicar, in which capacity he had to visit a dozen other monasteries; his visits must have been feared. In Gotha he made a speech condemning slander, which had repercussions far beyond the walls of the monastery; his target was the monks, for their everlasting denunciations of their fellows, the 'little saints', who arrogantly considered themselves so superior to the other brothers. Soon he was writing to a friend: 'To get through my work I need two secretaries or clerks; I do almost nothing all day but write letters . . . I have to preach in the monastery, preside at meals, am sent for every day to preach in the parish church, I am supervisor of studies, vicar, which is like being prior of eleven monasteries, inspector of our fishpond near Litzkau and intercessor in matters concerning the Herzberg monks in Torgau, I lecture on St Paul, collect material on the Psalms, and this, as I say, all has to be done in addition to letter writing, which is the work that takes up most of my time. With all these temptations of the flesh, the world and the devil I seldom have time to say my Hours or say Mass. So you see how I idle away my time.' In addition to this the plague, a constant threat, had broken out again. He was advised to go away. 'Where to? I hope the world will not come to an end just because Brother Martin does. If the epidemic gets worse I shall send the brothers to all the ends of the earth; I have been placed here and it is my duty to obey.'

On later occasions, too, Luther remained in Wittenberg when the plague threatened, almost always against the advice or urgent pleas of his friends; his legendary 'Here I stand' at the Diet of Worms was very far from being an isolated attitude.

The word 'pestilential', which was in such common use, was not employed figuratively but with the very real and tangible implication of the immediate danger of infection, with a quick death as the almost inevitable result. The threatening presence of epidemics – whether of bubonic plague or typhoid, cholera or typhus – also played a considerable part in the constant recrudescence of chiliastic movements prophesying the imminent end of the world.

As we have seen, the life Luther led in the monastery during these years did not consist exclusively of penitential struggles and tussles with his conscience. This is how he simplified it later, and commentators have accepted his version. For the development of his teaching there is no doubt that it was the decisive aspect and we shall have more to say about it. But for the development of the future great leader of a mighty movement, of the tireless worker, the importance of the time spent during this preparatory period on the everyday tasks of a busy life should not be underestimated. He was never very methodical, nor was he a great organizer like Calvin. But he acquired a knowledge of human nature at this time; he saw, to use Goethe's expression, 'the frenzied confusion of the antheap', and throughout his life retained an extremely realistic attitude to the ants. His language became richer; so did his conception of life in the towns and villages and on the roads, reflecting as it did all the varied social strata which filled the Germany of those days to bursting point with unrest, dissension and hope. Politics were hammered out on the roads; in the towns, where everybody knew everybody else, people were usually more reticent. Conversations on the highroads – between a peasant and a nobleman, a mendicant friar and an abbot on horseback, a brothel keeper and a university scholar – were the sources from which sprang the inflammatory writings and dialogues that reflect the tumult of the times so much more truly than the dull records of meetings of diets and their evasive announcements.

Luther travelled these roads on foot. No sooner had he been appointed to Wittenberg than he had to tramp right across Germany to Cologne, to a convention of his order; the journey there and back took him two months, walking over sandy tracks in the inadequate footwear of a mendicant friar. The visits he carried out as district vicar were also made *per pedes apostolorum*. Luther's anger in Rome at seeing prelates riding their mules, seated high above the ordinary people, or his fury because the pope 'has men to carry him in unprecedented pomp like an idol, although he is strong and healthy', was based on his personal experience as a mendicant friar. But even from the purely physical standpoint these ceaseless journeys on foot, year after year, were a formidable achievement. It seems doubtful whether Luther could ever have accomplished the tasks ahead of him if, as he declared, he had really spent fifteen years doing nothing but writhing in agonies of conscience. It is also doubtful whether his physique, tough as it was, would have survived the coming exertions without this thorough and very beneficial acquaintance with fresh air and mother nature. The freshness and vigour of his writing were not born of study and the stale air of a monk's cell. He loved flowers, a love he shared with the Middle Ages as a whole; at the dispute in Leipzig, when his life was at stake, he faced his enemies wearing a small bunch of flowers attached to his habit. The pear tree, under which Staupitz had reasoned with him, stayed in his memory. But neither he nor his contemporaries referred to nature or scenery. On his wanderings the monk was only too happy to reach the door of the next monastery, either wet through or, in summer, drenched with sweat. The instructions he issued as district vicar expressly required that the practice of washing a wayfarer's feet should on no account be neglected. The washing of feet was still a sacred act.

Some of the many letters he claims to have written at this time have survived. In them the stern superior of his order sometimes shows the more conciliatory side of his nature. A monk had run away; many did so. The 'fugitive monk' was a well-known figure. Sometimes he turned up in gangs, of which people lived in fear; sometimes he attached himself to highwaymen. In this particular case the monk, after a certain amount of wandering, had sought refuge in another monastery, and Luther asked the prior to send the lost sheep to him, 'so that we can put an end to the disgrace'. There was no need for the man to be afraid, he told him, he could come without any misgivings. 'I know, I know, that offences are inevitable. It is no wonder that a man falls; the only wonder is that he rises again. Did not Peter himself fall, so that he might realize he was only a man? ... and even one of the angels in heaven [Lucifer], which surpasses all wonder, and Adam in Paradise? No wonder then that such a faltering reed is shaken by the wind.'

The roads were lined with pilgrims, and a pilgrimage to some newly famous shrine was by no means always an orderly procession led by the Church authorities. The sermons of all those preaching repentance were full of complaints. Fathers of families complained that their young people and womenfolk made devout pretexts to run off, and that on such pilgrimages they were exposed, or willingly exposed themselves, to 'dangers' of every kind. Servants used these sacred occasions to shirk their work, which in any case was no sinecure and lasted, according to patriarchal custom, from cockcrow to dusk. Among his other rights the master or mistress of a household still had the right to inflict corporal punishment. The sellers of marvels and relics, who mixed among the pilgrims without authority and with forged authentications, excited Luther's anger, unlike the objects in the elector's collection, which were guaranteed under seal. Everywhere there was lack of supervision and control. These were supposed to be exercised by the bishops, but they had other worries. He saw only 'snoring priests' and 'darkness worse than in Egypt'.

This was not the rebel and reformer speaking, but the worried Augustinian monk; it was the events which followed that gave his words such an ominous sound. Many similar voices were to be heard at this time. The behaviour of the bishops and high prelates was a universal scandal. 'This is how the bishops live', declared Geiler von Kayserberg, a preacher in Strasbourg Cathedral, 'they ride with many horses, are the recipients of great honour, fill their purses, eat succulent chickens and chase the harlots.' To protect himself he added that there were also devout prelates, citing three German bishops within the Holy Roman Empire. The title of bishop was largely a façade, a cloak to hide a very worldly, and often very powerful, position, intended for sons of princes and the high nobility. The cathedral chapters, who elected their bishops, applied strict tests of nobility as a means of entrenching themselves against inroads by the common people; although from time to time an ordinary citizen was admitted, they preferred the protection of a high-ranking noble from some neighbouring territory to electing someone who, not being an aristocrat, would inevitably see his vineyard overrun by the robber princes of the district. The sight of a bishop in armour riding off to fight some local battle aroused virtually no attention; bitterness was caused by the fact that these clerics did not fight only with clubs but with the additional, and completely

Pilgrims at the Schöne Maria shrine, Regensburg

inadmissible, 'spiritual weapons' of excommunication and interdict, to which their lay enemies had no answer. But the spiritual lords did not rely exclusively on excommunication, the effectiveness of which had already been greatly reduced; they went to battle with their artillery. Sermons exhorting people to repentance are always a somewhat questionable source of information, but the chronicles and histories of the times are full of the subject. The campaigns went by the fairly innocuous-sounding name *Stiftsfehden*, or quarrels between religious bodies, but like other campaigns they were fought primarily over open country. The practice was to ravage the enemy's territory, burn down his villages and pauperize his peasants, who were poor enough already; the well-fortified towns and bishops' palaces, with their bastions and battlements, were usually left unmolested.

Anarchy of this sort came under the general heading of 'certain grievances', and people wanted to know why a timely stop was not put to it. It was for the holy father to intervene but, as we have seen, he, like the bishops, had other worries. The great hope lay in a council; but the experiences at Constance and Basle had shown this to be a very flimsy hope. Could the bishops and prelates, being the sort of men they were, be expected to reform themselves? Or the princes, who had filled the bishoprics with their relatives? Or the lesser nobility, whose daughters filled the convents? It is not only we who ask these questions, they were asked incessantly at the time. No one had an even tolerably satisfactory answer.

Luther had no answer either, except to go on working in his own small sphere of activity. Once he summarily dismissed a prior who could not control his unruly flock; on another occasion he consoled a fellow monk who suffered from melancholia, trying to comfort him with the same words which he used to console himself. All this restlessness and uneasiness was caused only by the so-called 'wisdom' of the senses, by the 'eye' as he termed it, using the Bible expression, which was evil and treacherous. 'Speaking of myself, heavens! what misery it has caused me; it has shaken me to my very core.' The cross of Christ was the only help; by its means curses were turned into blessings.

His own 'restlessness', which accompanied him like a descant, was not satisfied by this active existence, although another man would have found it fully adequate as a way of life. At the end of his half-humorous letter to his friend, in which he listed his duties as preacher, inspector of the fishpond and intercessor in matters concerning one of his monasteries, he also spoke of studying Paul and the Psalms. He now began to pore over these, and this was the starting point of his transformation into the rebel and reformer.

# 9

# The first controversial lectures

IT WAS the wish of his superiors that Luther should carry out his lecturing activities as a member of his order. In placing him at the disposal of the university they had done the elector a good turn; a thrifty man, he did not want to spend much money on his new foundation. Luther, who was still wrestling with himself and was as yet by no means clear about his own 'teaching', began to teach and in so doing to learn. He found his first enthusiastic audience, and before long the fame of Wittenberg University, hitherto completely unknown, had spread far and wide. Students of every nationality flocked to it, and through one of them, Prince Hamlet, its name finally made its way into world literature.

The university was still small when Luther began to lecture. He had a good name both within his order and at court. Staupitz hoped that one day he might become a luminary of the Augustinian Order and of the Holy Church, which was in urgent need of new lights; the old ones seemed to have burned themselves out. But Luther did not burn with the peaceful, consecrated flame of tradition; he entered the lecture room brandishing a torch.

In fact he walked to his desk with measured tread and downcast eyes, as the rules of his order required him to do; all violent movements were forbidden to its members. He opened his carefully prepared notes and began to lecture – like any other lecturer. He was a modern professor, a follower of the *via moderna* of nominalism, and for the New Testament used the original Greek text in the edition just published by Erasmus; this had found very little support among university teachers, many of them considering it superfluous or even open to suspicion. He used the approved commentaries, some three hundred years old, some more recent, and interpreted the Scriptures according to their 'fourfold meaning'. He showed himself very progressive again in having a special text printed for his students, in large type and with the lines widely spaced, in which they could insert their professor's explanations. He lectured on the two books of the Bible that were closest to his heart: the Psalms and Paul's Epistle to the Romans.

Paul was his teacher, the Epistle to the Romans his authority. Outwardly, even here, his lectures were planned in the usual way. But the substance of what he told his twelve or twenty listeners was utterly different. It was rebellion or, from another standpoint, sheer anarchy, in spite of the many traditional trappings in which it was clothed. It was untamed, sombre, extreme, full of unconditional demands. His style was personal and he spoke freely and without respect against all authority, whether written or living, that represented the great powers of the Church. The young professor even spoke with disrespect of the great secular figures. He gave determined advice to Duke George of Saxony on how to handle his quarrel with the Frisian Count Edgar. Saxony had claims on the remote province of Friesland, right on the far side of Germany, which it had been prosecuting over many decades, sometimes by negotiation, sometimes by force of arms. Luther disapproved strongly. He was very much a man of peace, however violent the storms that raged within him. He admonished, though in circumspect terms, the reigning pope, Julius II, for his bloody war against Venice, but then went on to make furious accusations. Was what was happening in Rome not a sin? The appalling corruption of the Curia, the mountains of vice, the pride, the greed, the blasphemy?

However, the political sallies were only peripheral or were incorporated in purely theological trains of thought. Fundamentally what mattered to Luther was not what went on in Rome, or anywhere else in the world, but his own salvation. Was he damned because he was a sinner or could he gain salvation? Was he sure of this or must he remain in continued anxiety to the end of his life? He was a wholehearted advocate of anxiety, of fear and trembling, of constantly recurring temptation, with which one is forced to grapple. He argued ceaselessly against the lukewarm and the self-righteous, the *justitiarii* as he called them, who imagined themselves already justified before God, whereas they had no right whatever to feel so certain. He protested again and again at the practice and teaching of the Church, which gave excessive consideration to the weak and the mediocre, of whom it did not wish to demand too much. He was for the strong, who were not afraid even of the most extreme consequences. Speaking far over the heads of his listeners – who diligently wrote down what he said and made many mistakes in doing so – he asked himself: am I damned or not? A man had to be strong enough to accept damnation if God, in his inscrutable providence, had condemned him to it. But he must still continue to love God.

In spite of this, and in all good faith, he stood firm in his belief in the Church. He stated quite sincerely that, in the last resort, the authority which he constantly challenged must decide what was to be taught. Accordingly the teacher of false doctrines, the heretic, however pious the airs he assumed, spoke only for himself, a fact of which he might well even have been proud: 'Execration, the anathema, is the very powerful weapon with which such people are hurled to the ground,' he proclaimed, or rather stated decorously in Latin.

Would this teacher of false doctrines, this rebel, be seized immediately and burned at the stake – or at least locked up for the rest of his life in one of the monastery prisons in which so many others had already disappeared? There was not so much as a murmur of criticism. The elector, delighted at being told he had such a gifted teacher, even wanted to have the lectures on the Psalms published, but this plan came to nothing. The most controversial lectures of all, those on the Epistle to the Romans, vanished without sound and without trace, as did the transcripts made by the students. So completely did they vanish that they were not referred to either in Luther's trial for heresy, which took place shortly afterwards and for which they would have provided rich material, or during the whole course of the Reformation. Luther's collected works were published during his lifetime; after his death there were repeated editions, as well as whole libraries of writings for and against him. Not until four hundred years later did this crucial document come to light. The most astonishing aspect of the affair, and for the tireless burrowings and commentaries of scholarly research the most humiliating, was that the manuscripts – among them Luther's own clear and beautifully written original – were not lying buried in some remote castle but were reposing, properly registered and recorded, in two of the greatest libraries in the world: the Vatican Library and the Berlin State Library. In the former one of the students' transcripts was found and used extensively by the Dominican scholar Father Denifle, the Vatican librarian, in his great attack on Luther, and the first stages of his influence, published in 1904; this work, which opened a new era of controversy, at the same time afforded Protestant scholars much new insight. Only after the publication of this book was Luther's own manuscript produced intact from the treasures of the Berlin library, where it had lain, conscientiously preserved and quite unread, since the eighteenth century. This curious story demonstrates the longevity of the medieval custom of working from Sentences and commentaries to Sentences, and the eternal truth of the humanists' watchword 'back to the sources'.

As a result of the controversies over the great work of the nineteenth-century Dominican scholar, Father Denifle, a new portrait of Luther emerged and, while individual Sentences still continued to play their part, serious efforts were made to give the portrait a broader basis. The whole theology of the Middle Ages was deliberately introduced into the debate; scholasticism was re-examined and, to all intents and purposes, discovered. Luther appeared as ignorant and very inadequately informed on the works of the great masters; these, in fact, were now being adequately published and explored for the first time, while additional basic writings were discovered lying forgotten in the archives. Exposed to twentieth-century scholarship, with its centuries of background, its well-stocked libraries and worldwide network of specialist journals, and not least to dogmatic viewpoints which in the meantime had been clarified and formulated, this series of lectures delivered by a young university teacher in 1517 cut a very sorry figure. The things he had not read, had disregarded or had misunderstood! And how badly his teachers, who had always considered themselves loyal members of their order, showed up too; how much of what they had taught, whether innocently or in an excess of zeal, was open to attack! How utterly dubious the whole nominalist creed, even though it had been the most widespread movement of the entire century, both before and during Luther's day, and had been championed by the University of Paris, the supreme authority in the world of learning! Finally, theology as a whole in Luther's day was seen to have been weak, to say the least, insufficiently equipped to embark on a fight, complacent and almost 'uncatholic'. Luther's fundamental thesis of justification had been the cause of serious disagreement within the Church of Rome even during his own lifetime and immediately after his death; one cardinal had been forced to defend himself against the not unjustified charge that he was advocating a doctrine almost identical with Luther's on this point. Among the Protestants themselves there had been many changes of attitude and many splits over this central question. The newly discovered document, and other early records which had lately come to light, raised many questions. How far had Luther developed his system, or his basic ideas, when he started to lecture? Was he already certain in his mind about salvation or was he still undecided? To what extent did he still occupy a position within the Church and to what extent had he already left it?

Theology has been described by Karl Barth as a 'continuous pilgrimage', incapable of satisfying the natural desire of human thought for completeness and integration; disjunct in thought and speech, always approaching the same subject from different angles by means of individual ideas and theses. This would seem to apply with extreme accuracy to Luther and this earliest phase of his development. It is easy to demonstrate the flaws in his arguments, his incompleteness, his lack of system. He was engaged on a pilgrimage, and it was a pilgrimage of a very different kind from the colourful affairs of his day, which so often were gay, boisterous and even frivolous. Luther was never frivolous; he took everything seriously, nothing lightly. He did not stride out unconcerned, certain now of his teaching and its promise. He waded upstream, as it were, constantly fighting against a current which threatened to drag him down with it; it was being dragged down, being at the bottom, that he was afraid of. All men are sinners: everyone knew this and was quite reconciled to it; people confessed, repented, atoned and paid their fines – doing their best to keep them within bounds – and were thus freed from anxiety. Luther was more Catholic than Catholic doctrine, more completely the monk than his fellow monks, for whom the regulations, so practically adapted to human imperfections, were intended. All this he found inadequate. He was already arguing furiously against the teachers of scholasticism and their readiness to concede that a man could discover certain 'indications' in himself, proving that he was the recipient of God's grace. This was pestilence of the very worst kind, he thundered. He was never at a loss for powerful and telling language, and in many passages the greatest of all controversialists was already clearly to be seen. Speaking of those who were so complacent and sure of themselves he lapsed involuntarily from the prescribed Latin into German. To one who had nothing to show but 'good intentions', the devil answered: 'Snuggle close, pussy dear, we are going to have guests – in hell.' Or to those who were vain: 'How pretty you look, little owl, have you grown peacock feathers?' Of those who considered themselves so exquisite and spotless, but in the spiritual sense were covered in dirt, he demanded: 'When you were a child in your mother's arms, did you never do anything on her breast that made a bad smell? Do you exude such a sweet aroma that one day a chemist is going to make a precious ointment out of you? If your mother had taken this attitude you would have perished in your own filth!'

This sounds more like a popular sermon than a lecture, and one can imagine that such passages drew a sigh of relief from the students. The rest of what their teacher offered them was heavy going. Luther always expected a great deal of people, in fact he expected so much that at times it verged on the impossible. They had to change and to change radically. This was one of the expressions he had taken from the Greek original, and philology at once became for him a religious teaching, a religious demand. The realization that the Greek word *metanoia*, translated in the Latin text recognized by the Church as *poenitentia*, repentance, in fact meant change of heart, was a revelation and became the key to his whole thought and faith. It unlocked the Kingdom of Heaven to him; he did not need the pope's keys for this, as Church doctrine insisted, nor did he need the accumulated practice which had attached itself to the doctrine of the power of the keys. For penitence was no longer simply repentance, it had become associated with the penitential punishments and the indulgences attached to them. A whole powerful apparatus had grown up around this, culminating in one of the most important offices of the Curia, with the Cardinal Grand Penitentiary at its head. It was there in Rome that the decisions were made concerning atonement, punishment and mitigation of the punishment by means of indulgences. There in Rome, as a result of the bureaucratization and centralization of ecclesiastical administration – which far surpassed anything that any other world power could boast – a central office had been established with quantities of rooms, anterooms, officials, pay tables, balance sheets and imposing conference halls in which international financial transactions of the greatest political significance were negotiated. On his visit to Rome Luther had admired the orderliness and dispatch with which this institution was run. But now it seemed to him intolerable that it should have the last word in matters of conscience and that, moreover, this last word should be connected with money and payments. To him change of heart meant that a man had to improve fundamentally within himself and commit himself unreservedly to God's mercy.

This was the starting-point of his fight, now no longer a struggle against the enemy within his own breast but a fight directed beyond himself against tradition, against the Church. He was still quite unaware of this. He lectured and stated his 'opinions', believing they would receive wide recognition, even in Rome, provided the people there were correctly informed. All that was necessary was to remove the obstacles which had accumulated 'latterly' – by which he meant the previous three or four hundred years, the period during which the Church's whole administrative structure and the corresponding interpretation of ideas had been created and built up. What the monk could not foresee was that to do this would mean a revolution, because it involved not only theological ideas but international politics and finance and social decisions of the most far-reaching kind – in other words questions of power and influence that were inextricably bound up with the things of this world. As we have already seen, he told his students quite openly of the anathema that would crush the heretic who thought for himself, should he rebel against the authority of the Church. And no one took offence. On the contrary, Luther's colleagues, much older and of much higher standing than he was, sat in the lecture room and listened to him. The sensitive humanist, anatomist and philosopher Pollich, the first rector of the university, was one of them. He said – whether in fear or hope we do not know – 'This monk will introduce a new teaching.'

## 10

# Rebel and reformer

NOTHING was further from Luther's thoughts than to become a rebel. He was fundamentally conservative and in many respects always remained so. He accepted the order of things as God, in his view, had created it. He adapted himself to the hierarchy of the Church and was about to take his place in the centuries-old structure. He preached on the saints, he respected his superiors in the order and its supreme patron, the pope. He based his studies on the most celebrated authorities, and in regarding Augustine, the patron saint of his order, as the best authority of all he was acting only in accordance with the vast majority of the Doctors of the Church, for whom 'Augustinianism', in a wide variety of forms, had been the true doctrine.

But he lived in a furious, rebellious age and became its greatest son, a revolutionary such as the world had rarely known. The currents converged on him from every direction, even when he was sitting in his little tower room bent over the Bible, intent only on reading and discerning the 'clear text'. While engaged on this reading he was caught up in one of the most powerful movements of the day: humanism. The meaning of this term has become very vague and has been made even vaguer by misuse; the word humanist, for example, has come to mean someone of a gentle, humanitarian nature with a horror of war and homicide, a person honoured when nothing is at stake but ignored the moment things grow serious. The humanists of Luther's day were cast in a very different mould – with the single exception of the great Erasmus of Rotterdam, who succeeded in giving dignity to the idea of reconciliation and mediation, although he himself became a tragic figure. Apart from him the humanists were of sterner stuff and conciliation never entered their heads. It would be more accurate to describe them as militant and quarrelsome, heroes of the pen and of feuds that were not always confined to paper. Many carried weapons and drew them when occasion arose, and most of them led lives very different from those of scholarly bookworms. Even as students they moved around; they started begging as quite young schoolboys and continued to beg even after they had become famous, asking a gift in return for a dedication, instead of an honorarium which did not exist in those days. Few of them died in the place where they were born; rarely, indeed, did any of them stay long in any place. They were the first bohemians of modern times, successors to the itinerant scholars of the Middle Ages, the medieval and the new being inextricably blended in them, as in all who lived in that period which we lazily call 'transitional'.

For us the new is the more important; we can forget their super-stitions and their Latin, although in their Latin they began to show themselves rebels with their cry 'back to the sources', *ad fontes*. The first humanists rediscovered forgotten manuscripts of the ancients, one of the earliest triumphs of these explorers of sources being the discovery of Plautus in a convent; by 'back to the sources' they meant back to the true Latin, as distinct from the monastic Latin of the scholastics, who had developed a language of their own, a very vivid, individual Latin whose word forms and, above all, meanings differed from those the ancients had known. It was Church Latin, written and conceived by monks; even when they believed themselves to be quoting Aristotle, it was not the classic sage but a master who had been transformed into a Doctor of the Church and from whom they borrowed certain basic forms of thought, dialectic and argument.

On religious questions the pagan could have no voice, and this was the attitude Luther took to the great authority. To the true Latin Greek was now being added. Homer was published in Florence, by one of the scholars who had fled from Constantinople and the Turks. Plato, hither-to little more than a name and exercising covertly a neo-Platonic, or rather Plotinian, influence, now appeared in all his majesty. In the same year in which Luther was making his penitential pilgrimages in Rome, Raphael put Plato next to Aristotle in the centre of his 'School of Athens'; in those days this painting conveyed a programme, it was the solemn documentation of a great process of change that had affected the whole Italian humanist world. Luther paid virtually no attention to Plato and, in any case, what the humanists of his day read into the Greek poet-philosopher had little to do with antiquity. But Greek, the language of the New Testament, now became available. 'Back to the sources' meant that one could read the 'original text' and was no longer dependent on the Latin translation of St Jerome. In addition to this the Hebrew of the Old Testament was beginning to be known, although its study was beset by difficulties; help had to be sought from the Jews, an expedient much disliked by the authorities, but to which there was no alternative. It led to violent conflicts, in one of which Luther, after his return from Rome, found himself involved.

At first these conflicts were purely academic, being concerned with linguistic questions, aims of scholarly research, erudite philological problems. They developed into a battle of youth against age. Considered in terms of years the humanists were the younger generation; some of them, like Melanchthon and Luther's enemy Eck, became famous almost as children because they knew Greek, a rare and valuable attainment. They formed a new class, a secular fraternity. The old order, in which the fields of knowledge, culture and research, within prescribed limits, were the responsibility and prerogative of the monks, was breached. The humanists captured the universities. They were installed, or rather wandered, everywhere, often exiled and threatened and threatening others with their satires, epigrams and polemics. An 'intelligentsia' emerged, that restless intellectual class and constant bane of the authorities, who in every age have considered it 'seditious', 'subversive', 'individualistic'. The great days, in which the humanists promised themselves a famous victory and resounding glory, were soon over. With Erasmus at their head they had hoped to establish a reign of calm, lucid scholarship, a florescence of learning, encouraged by wise and discerning popes, emperors and princes; they exulted incautiously in the joy of living, like Ulrich von Hutten, or more cautiously like Erasmus, who also believed that a golden age, with a better understanding of the classics, had dawned. The ancients had relegated the golden age to a mythical, remote past and followed it with a silver and finally with an iron age. The humanists lived in an iron age without knowing it; they were to discover it all too soon from the iron jaws of cannon and musket.

But they were still full of courage and joyful anticipation, fighting their campaigns with their native weapons of wit and satire. As a lecturer at the university, where he already had a reputation as a teacher, Luther was asked by the court chaplain, Spalatin, to prepare a report on the 'Reuchlin dispute'; the case had caused a stir throughout the humanist world. This world was not as big as the humanists imagined it to be, but its representatives were everywhere, still closely knit, in ceaseless correspondence with one another and keeping the printing presses, which now started to exercise great power, constantly busy. The great controversies of the Middle Ages, though no less bitterly contested, had been fought out on parchment – with a very limited number of copies available – and confined to the universities, which in most cases meant only Paris. Now printing presses had been set up everywhere, often in the most out-of-the-way places, and were disseminating the writings, for and against, of the contestants in slim volumes and pamphlets, illustrated with satirical woodcuts. Everything was printed, immediately pirated and circulated; every eulogy to a friend and fellow thinker, every piece of personal spite or revenge, every begging letter and every defence of everything, however obscure. Of all this chaotic mass of material only one small pamphlet has survived: the *Epistolae Obscurorum Virorum* ('Letters of the Obscurantists'), published in 1515 in the remote Alsatian town of Hagenau. The dismemberment and disunity of the Holy Roman Empire had at least one good result: there was almost complete freedom of the press, not because no censorship existed, but because each town reserved the right of censorship to itself. A work forbidden in one place was immediately published in another; printers and publishers, often influential citizens, added their word too and did well out of the party battles, especially as, in principle, they had no fees to pay.

In the pamphlet *Letters of the Obscurantists* the opposing parties were the 'Obscurantists', in other words the Dominicans in Cologne, and the young humanists as the champions of 'more light'. The two sides were very unequal in strength; the theologians in Cologne had behind them the whole authority and machinery of the Church and, because they were the Church's official inquisitors, this included the power to burn both books and men. Their assailants were young men of letters who either had just run away from monasteries or still had one foot behind the walls; they were called sarcastically the 'poets' by their enemies. They remained anonymous because what they were doing could mean death; the individual authors have never been adequately identified and much of what they wrote was simply high-spirited teamwork or the result of discussions among friends. Some certainly came from Erfurt; Crotus Rubianus was one of these and the young Hutten another. A geography of the main centres of opposition was emerging in outline, and it applied for the whole Luther era; Erfurt had long had the reputation of being tainted with heretical ideas, of being a sort of 'modern Prague', while Cologne and the neighbouring town of Louvain were the strongholds of the old spirit of scholasticism and orthodoxy. In Cologne the theologians were proud of the ancient fame of their university, which numbered Albertus Magnus and Duns Scotus among its founders; Erfurt had followed the *via moderna* of nominalism and had already gone considerably beyond it. In Cologne, in 1489, the inquisitors Institoris and Sprenger had published the celebrated *Malleus Maleficarum* ('The Witches' Hammer'), the first thorough and comprehensive manual on the prosecution of witches and sorcerers; it opened a new epoch in the prosecution of 'demons', hitherto carried out in a somewhat haphazard manner, and received papal approval from Innocent VIII. This was perhaps the greatest achievement of the 'School of Cologne', which otherwise had contented itself with the established commentaries and their old-fashioned Latin. The younger generation in Erfurt spoke and wrote the new Latin, which they claimed to be the true Latin of the ancient classics, and they wrote it with wit, verve and aggression. The 'Reuchlin case' was simply made an excuse for insolent satire. Scholasticism was made ridiculous; monks, their way of life, from which the young authors had just run away, and the whole system of relics were pilloried.

The satire took the form of unconscious self-revelation: the Obscurantists correspond quite spontaneously with one another and in so doing reveal their lack of education and stupidity. They enjoy their food and drink, they like to sleep and make love and for everything they do find authority in the Bible. They quote Ecclesiastes: 'Live joyfully with the wife whom thou lovest all the days of the life of thy vanity', or 'If two lie together, then they have heat: but how can one be warm alone?' This is followed by hackneyed monastery anecdotes: a Dominican, surprised in the act, jumps naked from the window of his mistress's room, or a mistress takes her lover's habit in lieu of payment and at home cuts it up to use, so that the saying, 'They parted my garments among them', shall be fulfilled. Indulgences are ridiculed and the monks are full of the slanderous talk they have to listen to everywhere about the system of prebends and the drift of German money to Rome – all long-standing and common complaints, only here they are given rather more witty expression than usual. But throughout the satire runs the sinister thread of the proceedings against the humanists' hero Reuchlin, whom the Obscurantists are determined to bring to account, and accompanying it is a strong smell of burning because the fire, intended in the first instance for the books and after that for their authors, is close at hand. The high-spirited, insolent tone of the little work can easily make us forget that its authors and their friends were constantly risking life and limb. But the young poets were fighting in a great cause. The innovators and critics of the existing order found their ammunition in the wrath of the Old Testament prophets. In these *Letters of the Obscurantists* they counter the monks' preference for Solomon's easygoing philosophy of life by quoting the judgment and day of wrath announced by Zephaniah: 'I will search Jerusalem with candles, and punish the men that are settled on their lees: that say in their heart, The Lord will not do good, neither will He do evil.' The 'lees' is the old, worn-out theology on which the Obscurantists rest; the 'candles' are the light lit by Erasmus and Reuchlin, the new and true doctrine whose inspiration is to be found in a knowledge of the languages of antiquity.

This was the crux of the matter. Were the Dominicans in Cologne to be allowed to forbid all scholarly investigation, even when its aim was to reveal the true Word of God? Was it to be counted heresy simply to read the original Hebrew text instead of St Jerome's 'hallowed' Latin translation? Was it a crime merely to suggest that, in rendering his considerable services, the great Father of the Church might have mis-understood, or possibly mistranslated, a word here and there? Today such things excite no one; philology long ago won the right to exist, but we forget how hard it had to fight in order to win this victory. The Latin text had become hallowed, and it was the authority of the Church that had hallowed it. To dispute this text was to proclaim oneself a rebel.

Reuchlin, who had unleashed the whole conflict, was no rebel. He was a loyal son of the Church who died professing the old faith, although he had been condemned. Moreover he started, not as a scholar or philologist, but as a lawyer; as such he had travelled widely in France and Italy and led a long and active life in diplomatic missions and high judicial office. It was only later that he turned to the study of languages, 'for rest and recreation after much hard work and the tumult of court life,' as he put it. On his small country estate he bred white peacocks and intended to settle down to a life of quiet study; instead of which he found himself drawn into the most strident argument of his life and in greater danger than he had ever been in politics. A layman, a dilettante, he became the greatest Hebrew authority of his day and the author of the first Hebrew grammar to appear in Germany. This brought him into 'conflict with the professionals', a conflict that had an almost grotesque air about it because the professionals, the Dominican theologians who wanted to destroy him, knew not one word of Hebrew. They regarded the language with the gravest suspicion, as something better left to the accursed Jews; they had the approved and proven Latin of St Jerome and that was all anyone needed. Reuchlin had taken enormous pains to learn Hebrew; not a rabbi passed but he was invited to the house and asked to explain some phrases to him. He had acquired most of his knowledge in Italy, where, in the small town of Soncino, some fifty Hebrew writings had been published under the auspices of a rich Jewish family. The Italian humanists had produced a great authority on the ancient language in the person of Count Pico della Mirandola, a Platonist who envisaged a universal religion composed of Hellenism, Judaism and Christianity. Pico even ventured on a study of the Talmud and, still more danger-ously, of the Cabbala, which was regarded as a book of magic and a key to buried treasure.

In taking these occult sciences back with him from the liberal atmosphere of Italy – even at the papal court people appreciated the value of Hebrew studies – to the much more sultry air of Germany, Reuchlin was hoping to find treasure of a very different kind. He be-lieved they contained a comprehensive explanation of the universe; by following in the footsteps of the Cabbala one would be able to progress from symbol to symbol until one reached the ultimate and purest form of spirit. He was a mystic in the field of language, believing that the original language of mankind, dating from the time when God still walked among men, had been preserved within the language of the ancient Jewish patriarchs, and that through them it had been transmitted to the peoples who came after them. But the mysticism of numbers also played a role in his inquiries. Here, without knowing it, he was on the right track; recent research has also been concerned with the extraordinarily difficult problems of interpreting the words and signs contained in the Cabbala and they seem to be connected with cosmic values and relations. For Reuchlin the book was something else; it was a prophecy of the New Testament and thus of Christ, and very welcome as supplementing the Old Testament prophecies concerning the Messiah. By adding another letter he interpreted the characters for God to mean Jesus; elsewhere he found characters that foretold the Trinity. To him the Word meant first and foremost spirit, the secret of the divine nature. God, who delighted in associating with the soul, wished to transform Himself into it: 'God is spirit, the word is his breath, man breathes, God is the Word.' Innocent enough to our eyes; blasphemous presumption and the heresy of a layman to the theologians in Cologne. Although they understood neither the Cabbala nor the Talmud, they were convinced that the devil was behind them both. Their successors, with equally inadequate knowledge but commanding still greater means of persecution, have continued to exist into our own day.

Such knowledge as the Dominicans possessed of the ancient Hebrew texts they owed to a baptized Jew named Johann Pfefferkorn, who became the pitiable local figure of the whole conflict. Possessed by the fanatical zeal of the convert, and the self-hatred not uncommon among Jews, Pfefferkorn wanted to convert his former co-religionists. To achieve this it was necessary first to destroy their writings, so he submitted extracts, in a highly biased and questionable form, to prove they contained only 'blasphemies'. If after this they still remained obdurate, they were to be banished. In Spain this had already been done to a very large extent by the all-powerful Inquisition, acting in close association with King Ferdinand and Queen Isabella, the necessary basis of 'scholarship' having been supplied by another converted Jew, who had risen to become archbishop of Burgos and whose writings circulated in Germany under his new name Paulus de Sancta Maria. The Dominicans in Cologne thought they could carry out an action on a similar scale. They encouraged their protégé, and Pfefferkorn obtained from the peripatetic Emperor Maximilian, who was encamped outside Padua, a mandate for all Jewish writings to be confiscated and handed over to Pfefferkorn, who would examine and destroy them. The zealot called on Reuchlin and invited him to participate in the worthy task. Reuchlin refused, and thus began the conflict in which for the first time the humanists combined to form a great party. It was to be the prelude to the 'Luther case', which followed a similar course even down to details: charges, summonses, delays on political grounds and finally conviction.

The Jewish question was only secondary; the humanists did not hesitate to use the popular anti-Jewish lines of attack against Pfefferkorn and delightedly dragged his pretty wife into the controversy as well. For them the conflict was a fight for freedom of knowledge; they saw it threatened, as indeed it was. Reuchlin issued a report attacking Pfefferkorn's procedure. In it he was careful to distinguish between the Hebraic writings, energetically defending his beloved Cabbala and finding only two small works, both disclaimed by the Jews themselves, worthy of condemnation. So far as converting the Jews was concerned, this should be done 'gently and amicably' by means of 'reasonable disputations' and to this end professorships in Hebrew should be established.

Reuchlin did not have in mind an edict calling for tolerance. The idea of tolerance was foreign to his century as a whole and it was to be a long time before it gained acceptance even for a short period. But his was a first, if still tentative, voice for reason and conciliation. It immediately met with unconciliatory rebuttal. Pfefferkorn published a pamphlet entitled *Handspiegel* ('Hand Mirror'), containing crude libels: Reuchlin had no knowledge of Hebrew, he had been bribed by the Jews – always a favourite accusation. Reuchlin answered with *Augenspiegel* ('Pair of Spectacles' – they are reproduced symbolically on the title page); he did not pull his punches either. Then the Dominicans stepped in. The chief inquisitor, Jakob van Hochstraten, from the small Brabant town of Hoegstraaten, became the champion of orthodoxy and for a long time to come the *bête noire* of the humanists. Later it was said in his defence that he wrote a Latin by no means as bad as that of which he was accused in the *Letters of the Obscurantists*, and that he was also the author of a very useful discourse on moral philosophy. To us this 'cultivated' informer and burner of heretics is even less sympathetic than the crude zealot. Hochstraten was ceaselessly and tirelessly active, issuing warnings and demands for the most severe measures; very soon he was also directing his efforts against Luther, to whom, in his attack on Reuchlin's Cabbala, he urgently called the pope's attention: 'Arise, Leo, with the lion's courage of your name', and he urged Leo to do battle with the foxes which were 'ravaging God's vineyard' – words which recurred in the bull of excommunication issued against Luther.

The proceedings against Reuchlin came immediately before those against Luther, and overlapped them. Hochstraten, in his capacity as inquisitor, summoned the elderly scholar to Mainz. He had already erected a pyre for the burning of Reuchlin's *Augenspiegel* when an order from the archbishop forbade the sentence to be carried out; the matter had to be submitted to the pope. Leo X assigned the case to the bishop of Speyer, whose advisers snubbed Hochstraten; they even sentenced him to pay 111 guilders compensation and to keep silent in future. Hochstraten had no intention of complying; he made his own appeal to the pope and procured testimonials from the theological faculties of Louvain and Paris. In Rome a committee of eighteen prelates acquitted Reuchlin, the sole dissenting voice being that of Silvester Mazzolini, court theologian to the pope, who a few years later was to be Luther's first accuser. The humanists celebrated prematurely by publishing an illustrated pamphlet *Triumphzug* ('Triumphal Procession') in which their hero Reuchlin enters like a Roman emperor followed by his defeated enemies, Hochstraten and his associates, who can only gasp helplessly 'To the flames! To the flames!' 'Reuchlinist' became the party cry, and in their letters the humanists addressed each other and signed themselves with this name; some fifty pamphlets were exchanged. Ulrich von Hutten persuaded his great friend Sickingen, the condottiere, to intervene; he threatened the theologians in Cologne, forced them to accept the Speyer verdict and pay Reuchlin his expenses, and even compelled them temporarily to suspend Hochstraten as chief inquisitor. It was not until the still greater excitement over Luther that the Reuchlin case was reopened and finally settled by the pope in 1520: Reuchlin's book was to be banned – it favoured the Jews and was condemned; he was to pay the costs of the case which, because he had been summoned to Rome, were considerable. Reuchlin bowed to the decision, as well as to the Church's imposition of silence; he died shortly afterwards. When he heard that his beloved great-nephew Melanchthon – whom he had sent as a very young man with Abraham's blessing to teach at Wittenberg University – had joined Luther, he never wrote him another line.

Reuchlin was no rebel, nor was he a fighter, but he was a dignified figure; even in appearance he was impressive and, with his great height and confident bearing, looked like a senator of ancient Rome. He had an international reputation as a scholar and led an unexceptionable life. Only zealots could have questioned his faith. That the advocates of orthodoxy should have selected this particular man as their victim shows how hopelessly rigid their front had become; it also became evident how greatly they had overestimated their influence. Shortly before Luther's appearance on the scene, however, the whole stage was lit by this conflict: the emperor nervously restless, Pope Leo hesitant and uncertain, the humanist party, already powerful, undergoing its first trial of strength. But the humanists immediately revealed their weakness. On seeing the first signs of the gathering storm, many began to whisper anxiously and advise against carrying the matter further; in this they were led by Erasmus, who at first had smiled his approval but whose smile had soured when the young hotheads became too free with their praises and use of his name. Once it became clear that more was at stake than a dispute between scholars and the study of Hebrew the humanists very soon dispersed.

To Father Luther – his name still untarnished when, with the case against Reuchlin hanging in the balance in Rome, he had to prepare his report for the elector – the matter seemed simple enough. He strongly supported Reuchlin, for whom he had a high regard and whose Hebrew grammar was indispensable for his study of the Bible. In any case, he declared, in saying that the Jewish writings were of value Reuchlin had only expressed an 'opinion', he had not laid down a 'doctrine'. Did that amount to heresy? If this attitude prevailed the theologians in Cologne would soon be 'straining at gnats and swallowing camels', as the Bible put it. He vigorously opposed such carping; the censors in Cologne, he asserted, should turn their attention to more urgent matters, to things that were a hundred times more important, to the 'enemy within', to idolatry. It was here that the inquisitors could exercise their wisdom and zeal, and their 'love' as well, instead of occupying themselves with such far-fetched questions.

So far as the Jews were concerned, his view was that the proselytism of the Cologne theologians was a violation of the express word of the Bible, according to which it must be left to God to change the Jews' hardness of heart. It was for God alone to accomplish this work, from within; it did not become man to attempt it. In those days Luther still believed in a conversion of this kind; in his old age he spoke very differently, wishing to leave the matter not to God but to the elector, whom he enjoined to drive out the Jews in some of the wildest and most pitiless attacks he ever wrote.

Now he was still calm, at least outwardly. What concerned him, as he stressed in this report, was the 'inner man'; basically this meant his own inner man, still greatly disturbed because of the many activities associated with his various offices. It was here that the battle had first to be fought out; the satirical pamphlets of the humanist fraternity struck him as trivial and superficial. When some of them turned to him with their usual flattery, expecting a service in return – because his name was already becoming known – he would have nothing to do with them. He never really 'belonged to them' and was never a humanist, whether as a member of their party, in his studies or in the sense in which we use the word today.

Luther studied what he called the 'clear' text of the Bible. For this he used Reuchlin's Hebrew grammar and the Greek edition of the New Testament, just published by Erasmus. Luther proved himself a true scholar in his search for the truths contained in the Bible, using the latest aids, which promised an understanding hitherto undreamed of; even single words, becoming clear for the first time as he read the original text, sometimes acquired supreme importance and became decisive for his interpretation. But once again all this was only 'external', only a means to an end, a stimulus, like the consoling words spoken to him by Staupitz. His own highly personal doubts and temptations formed the starting point, suggested by the devil as he put it, remarking in his bold and acutely paradoxical way that the devil was the 'father of his theology'; had it not been for these temptations he would never have learnt to know God's grace. And this grace, which for him did not mean a gentle, kindly favour emanating of its own accord, but a redemption from anguish and torment that could be won only with difficulty and for which one had to struggle constantly, became the central idea of his teaching. It could be attained only through faith.

He remarked characteristically that he had been forced to 'choke' over the Bible when all previous interpretations had failed to speak to him. 'It is much better to see with one's own eyes than with someone else's'; there spoke the rebel. The entire doctrinal system of the Church was based on the principle that the individual had to adapt himself to the whole, that he could not be left to see with his own eyes. Right up to the time of the Diet of Worms, and in the official record of its verdict, this rebellion was regarded as Luther's decisive act, his act of temerity. 'It is certain that an individual monk is wrong if he opposes his own point of view to that of the whole of Christendom, with its thousand years of existence – according to this point of view Christendom may always have been in error.' Thus the young emperor, expressing his will independently for the first time, formulated the case when he condemned Luther. This, too, was a personal opinion but it corresponded exactly to the views of the Church; it still remains the standpoint of the Catholic Church today. The Roman Catholic scholar Joseph Lortz has recently given a very open-minded appraisal of Luther's character and importance in his book on the Reformation in Germany. He stresses the fact that Luther's development was a highly individual process: 'He sees and is aware only of himself; everything else he rejects, or else he reads his own ideas into the text.' This, Lortz claims, opens up great opportunities for criticism, which in the past has usually contented itself with trivialities; God's revelation, as presented in the Old and New Testaments, is a comprehensive promulgation and allows for every human situation. 'No single individual, however, can preserve undiluted a comprehensive promulgation of this kind. On his own he will make a one-sided selection. Only an organism that is as much God's work as the revelation of the Word can preserve this comprehensive possession; this organism is the Church. Essentially Luther gave no heed to this representative of God. Nor did he preserve the whole compass of the revelation, but reacted heretically and sporadically.'

In quoting an authority of our own day we need not enumerate all the opposing arguments. Luther did not regard himself as in any sense a heretic, either then or at any other time. He wanted to bring about reform. Certainly he took as his point of departure his own experience – it is hard to see what else he could have done, especially in an age when leadership and direction had become very uncertain, if indeed they existed at all. Time and again it has been a lone monk, to use the Emperor Charles's contemptuous expression, who has had to tackle the key questions and give them new meaning; the history of the Church is composed of such monks, just as the history of human thought comprises many individual minds outside the walls of the cloister, and mankind has found many different ways of expressing its ideas.

The great difficulty of explaining Luther's fight is due to the widely divergent evidence we have concerning its development. The struggle of the theologian to free himself from the traditional categories and interpretations, which seemed inadequate to him, went hand in hand with the practice of the pastor, who saw before him the abuses of the day and felt the need to bring about an improvement. When speaking of faith, he felt all around him the lack of it; in passionately opposing the false belief that man could find salvation through 'works alone', he did not consult the subtle definitions of earlier teachers but what was going on around him. That from time to time the Church and the world were in urgent need of a revival in matters of faith was not just a presumptuous thesis put forward by Father Martin; history consists of the ceaseless alternation of decline and reform.

Luther, the Augustinian Father and university lecturer, did not yet want to reform the Church, let alone rebel. He wanted to be clear in his own mind, and as soon as he thought he had achieved this clarity he wanted to start evangelizing to make his viewpoint known. He regarded it as only an 'opinion', just as he had declared Reuchlin's views on the usefulness of the Jewish writings to be an opinion that could not be held to be a doctrine. His missionary spirit led him quite logically to Paul, the first missionary as well as the first theologian, and to Augustine, the missionary to the heathen world of the Romans and the foremost theologian of the Church of Rome. To Luther 'back to the sources' meant back to this early period, and not back to classical antiquity as it did to the humanists. In this he was in agreement with the 'best authorities'; what came later he saw only as an addition, an expansion, as confusion and unnecessary complication. To this extent he was a true disciple of Ockham, the master whose famous maxim – known as the 'razor' – ran: essentials should not be multiplied unnecessarily. Using his own language Luther said: 'Doctors of the Scriptures are not the sort of people who begin with heaven or start by putting on the roof. Such people become chamois hunters and break their necks.'

The scholastics of the Middle Ages began on principle with the roof; their thought processes started at the top and worked downwards. Heaven was their starting point, an absolute postulate; if anyone raised his voice, however modestly, to point out that God was incomprehensible and beyond the range of man's knowledge, the reply was immediate: the hierarchy of heaven was described minutely. Only then did the scholastics descend to earth, where once more they started at the top, with the saints, and descended step by step to the lowest rank, to ordinary, sinful man.

Luther recognized no classification or 'orderly disposition' – the favourite concept of the medieval thinker, from which their romantic descendants tried, in their enthusiasm, to deduce a corresponding orderliness within the life of ordinary, sinful man in the Middle Ages. In spite of his monastic training, Luther was 'undisciplined'. He wanted to stand in the immediate presence of God, carrying only his Bible, the book which contained everything.

He needed no proof of God's existence, whether of a logically mathematical or of a metaphysical nature. God's existence was as evident to him as the amens he said in church and in his prayers. He spoke to Him as man to man, although he was very well aware of the huge gulf that separated them. He saw himself as an utterly miserable, puny creature, subject like everyone else to original sin, exposed to constant sinning and confronted by a terrible judge who could grant him only mercy. Only mercy, not justice; he could boast of no merits, however blameless his life. The only evidence of God's pity and mercy to man was the fact that in Christ He had sent His own son and let Him suffer on the cross. Man was 'justified' only when he believed this. Luther always thought 'only' in terms of exclusives, hence his 'only through grace', *sola gratia*, 'only through faith', *sola fide*, 'only through Christ' – these later became the three crucial declarations of the Reformation. They were simple and intelligible, a triad far easier to grasp than the mystery of the Trinity, whose interpretation had already led, in the first centuries of Christianity, to the most serious schisms. Simplicity was the secret of Luther's appeal.

But the way by which he arrived at these propositions had not been simple at all. His starting-point had been his own scruples. He had confessed his sins – though what they were we do not know – and found no relief. 'The flesh' in general was a sin, his whole existence, his intractable will. He even went so far as to consider it a sin for a man to attempt to reach salvation through the exercise of his own will, of his own accord; he rejected 'free will' in the strongest terms and proclaimed as a fundamental thesis of his teaching that the will was in bondage. In this Paul was his teacher, as he was in all the main lines of his thought. Here, too, Luther proceeded in a very personal way: of all the books in the Bible one in particular appealed to him, Paul's Epistle to the Romans, and at first it was a single sentence from it. Luther's theology was Pauline theology as stated in this book, and until very recently the whole theology of Protestantism repeatedly took its stand on this Epistle. 'This Epistle is the true centrepiece of the New Testament and the purest gospel,' he wrote at the beginning of the preface to his translation. It was a book to be learned by heart and made one's daily companion, and this was how he himself treated it. It is possible to include all his fundamental viewpoints, as well as his conduct in life and attitude to the state, within the framework of a commentary to this Epistle.

In contrast to the historical view taken today, he did not see Paul separated by a certain distance from the Gospels, as a very early missionary working among a community he could not yet rely upon, and threatened from without and from within, as an apostle who was himself threatened without knowing it by the heritage of the Jewish tradition in which he had grown up and through whose theological school he had passed as a rabbi. Paul for him was the Bible itself. The Gospels at this time remained in the background for the very man who was to become the founder of the evangelical movement; they were made use of only in so far as they were mentioned by Paul or explained him. In this Luther was a theologian and the disciple of a theologian.

But another book of the Bible also occupied a central position for him, the Psalms. It appealed to him because of its great poetry and music. At first the theologian in him followed tradition, laboriously explaining the Psalms according to their fourfold interpretation and associating every line with Jesus, whose voice it was, not David's, he heard in the poetry and song. The whole of his later work, in fact, is rooted in the Psalms, above all the strength and ardour of its language and its wealth of feeling. Rabbinical tradition associated the origin of the Psalms with poetic and musical inspiration: David lay down and slept. Above his head in the darkness hung a harp, which began to sing in the midnight wind until the king awoke and set his words to its strains; when morning came his work was done. Luther's first publication was intended for the 'eight-stringed psaltery', which had a compass of an octave, and it was to the Psalms that he devoted his earliest lectures and with them found his first enthusiastic audience. The Psalms formed the basis of his whole output of hymns, and the Reformation derived more power from song than from its arguments and disputes. Later the Psalms were the only 'ornament' permitted French Protestants in their church services, while also becoming their war songs. For Luther the penitential and militant Psalms were the most important; his favourite was the second which, it seemed to him, might have been written expressly for his cause: 'The kings of the earth set themselves, and the rulers take counsel together, against the Lord and against His anointed, saying, Let us break their bands asunder, and cast away their cords from us.'

The university lecturer was not yet thinking on such rebellious lines as these. He was still very much under the influence of tradition and his training. But his development cannot be explained solely on the basis of 'Scriptural extracts' taken from surviving documents or of his subsequent recollections in which he singled out specific experiences that had struck and illuminated him 'like a flash of lightning'. A spiritual lightning flash of this kind ignites only when it strikes inflammable material. Today we are apt to be preoccupied with the theory of evolution and may often go too far in this. 'Influences' are traced to their remotest sources. In earlier ages sudden crises and changes were the preferred criteria, and they had been hallowed by great examples, such as the conversions of Paul and Augustine. In later life Luther referred to a particular moment of illumination when studying the Epistle to the Romans in his little tower room; it was at this moment, after he had wandered in utter darkness, that the 'gate to Paradise' had opened to him for the first time and he had seen Christ in the clearest light. Only then did he believe he had found the key: faith not as a human act but as the grace of God. Recently attempts have been made to date this 'tower experience' more accurately, but it is a forlorn hope. There have even been grotesquely fervent, but deadly serious, arguments as to whether the scene of the inspiration was Luther's little study or the 'heimliches Gemach', which an abbreviation in the handwriting of a pupil reveals to have been the monks' lavatory. In view of Luther's well-known outspokenness it is very possible that he did say something of the kind, but in any case this, like the attempts to give the occurrence a precise date, seems to the present writer totally unimportant. Luther always used the most impassioned imagery: he felt as if he had been struck 'by an axe', he 'raged', he was hounded this way and that by anxiety, one remark would cast him into hell, another transport him to heaven, and far from complaining about all this he regarded it as necessary for his salvation. The very worst temptation, he said, was not to feel tempted at all.

A further stream of thought, in addition to humanism, impinged on him; this was German mysticism, and it has been made substantially responsible for his development. By chance, during these years, he came across a short mystical text in powerful, old-fashioned German, published in Frankfurt. He re-published it immediately, in 1516, under the title *A German Theology*, calling it 'a noble little book that distinguishes correctly between the old and the new man.' It was his first publication for a wide public. The original author was unknown, but Luther considered the book to be the work of a Dominican preacher named Tauler, some of whose sermons he had read.

The great age of German mysticism had flourished a century and a half earlier and little was known about it in Luther's day; very little was published and of the works of Eckhart, its greatest master, nothing at all. So Luther knew nothing of Eckhart, with whom all inter-pretation of German mysticism today begins. He really knew nothing of 'German mysticism'. Eckhart's dialectic, with its strong emphasis on intellect and reason, would most probably only have repelled him. But he had no need to bother with it; the great man's writings had been either dispersed or completely destroyed. What Luther got hold of were the merest odds and ends, a few pages of a great movement, which lived on under cover, in small conventicles, among initiates who under-stood, or thought they understood, the secret language. Indeed the great importance of German mysticism was that it was a movement of this kind, whose teachings were passed from hand to hand and above all from mouth to mouth. It was a sign that many people were dissatisfied with life within the Church. From the standpoint of the Church these people were individualists, lone wolves; they wanted to find their own way to God, without mediators. This made them rebels, like Luther, and it was entirely logical for the Church to condemn and try to suppress them. It was hard to lay hands on these 'quiet ones of the land'; they lived secluded, and for the most part exemplary, lives and often communicated with each other simply by attitudes, gestures and signs, things it was hardly possible to censor. The writings that have survived represent only a tiny part of this widely ramified movement, and for this reason alone it is extremely difficult to get a clear picture of it and explain its often contradictory viewpoints. But as a network of 'cells of resistance' its importance is hard to overestimate. It was from such spiritually minded groups that the 'Friends of God' were recruited;

they had their adherents in the 'Devotio moderna' movement of Gerrit Groote, and in the *Imitation of Christ* – which appeared under the name of Thomas à Kempis – they produced one of the most widely disseminated devotional books and one which, because its poetry was melancholy and lacked the bold imagery of the other mystics, was regarded as permissible.

To a great extent these groups are intangible to us; like all movements regarded as heretical they come to the surface only when they are persecuted. Moreover they are forced constantly to disguise themselves and one can easily be misled by what they say, and still more easily by what their opponents say about them. Much is intended to have a double meaning; 'lamb-like' words of submission can easily deceive us, and Christ as the lamb was the principal symbol of these devout people. Behind it may lurk a stubborn resistance more determined than any verbal protest. The intentional ambiguity in the writings of the mystics often leads to an imagery that is extremely hard to decipher, balanced on the borderline between the physical and the spiritual. Divine intoxication is extolled in a song of 'eight lads in the church tavern': the dice they use are the 'deep, keen senses, which they throw to the Divinity', 'they lie down with the dregs, they drink wine by whole kegs, nothing suffices, God is the highest good.' This trifling with God and Love is taken to its furthest point in the sayings of the Eleven Virgins, one of whom declares: 'I languish for love of Christ in heart and body, I can hide it no more, it drives me to bed with Him.'

These underground groups of mystics, who often had their representatives in the most reputable convents and best-run schools, while always leading secluded lives themselves, were not alone. In the outside world there were more conspicuous groups. The best known of these were the Beghards and Beguines, who travelled the countryside preaching their unorthodox sermons and living 'free' lives. They subsisted on charity and thus came into competition with the mendicant orders of monks; they spread disturbing prophecies and gloomy predictions. The sayings of the Beghards ranked as 'lies' but were widely circulated; the Beguines were frequently accused of being harlots. To what extent vagabond riff-raff attached itself to them is hard to say; what connection their mystical doctrines bore to 'true mysticism' is virtually impossible to trace. They avoided surveillance of any kind and were driven away and condemned, sometimes by solemn orders of the councils, which were constantly renewed. The convictions pronounced by bishops who, with their concubines, led lives of far less restraint are not quite above suspicion. But the thesis that a life wholly devoted to God made man wholly free, since, no longer having any will of his own, he could no longer sin even if he committed 'sins of the flesh', does seem to have produced a number of dissolute sects, who went about half-naked and were bloodily persecuted. Mysticism had many faces: the face of selfless devotion, the face strained with the exertions of arduous thinking, the grotesquely distorted face. The extreme elements cannot be excluded from the picture without falsifying and prettifying it.

Luther found in *A German Theology* more wisdom than in 'all the books by the teachers of the schools', whose learning, by comparison, was 'iron and earthen'. He was not speaking as a university lecturer but as a popular educator, and warned the reader against forming a hasty judgment because some of the contents might strike him as insubstantial or unusual, 'floating on the surface like foam on water, whereas in fact they have been plucked from the bed of the River Jordan by a true Israelite', whose name unfortunately could not be established. Luther also regarded the sermons of Tauler, the putative author of *A German Theology*, as superior to all the theologians of the schools. The title-page of Tauler's sermons in the edition he had read proclaimed them to be the 'true way to walk in the spirit through the overlaying senses'; but Luther did not adhere to the mystic sense that lay behind the words. He put his own construction on them and wrote it in the margins. He was delighted to find these two old books and make them available to others; what moved him more than anything else was that they both spoke 'from the bottom of the heart' and in his own language. But he had no affinity with the basic ideas of mysticism, and this first brief acquaintance he soon put behind him. He was insensitive to the visions and raptures of the mystics: 'To come trotting along with your own thoughts and try to clamber up to heaven has got precious little to do with seeing God', he declared impatiently. No one was able to see God with his physical eyes, he could be seen 'only through faith'.

Here again he was looking at the text with his own eyes. Other currents caught hold of him. We have mentioned humanism and mysticism. The strongest current, the social and political ferment of the times, Father Luther hardly noticed; it was not mentioned in any of the books he read. But its huge waves rose around him and on his wanderings he caught sight of some of their crests. It was only when he stepped out of his cell and monastic existence that he was seized, carried away and overwhelmed by the power of this ferment.

*Part Two*

# The Conflagration

# 11

# The ninety-five theses

IN 1517 Luther emerged from the timelessness of his cell to enter history. At about midday on 31 October, tradition tells us, he nailed his ninety-five theses on the practice of indulgences to the door of the Schlosskirche at Wittenberg. Very recently the date has been contested; in fact it has been argued that he never nailed his theses to the door at all. It is not certain whether the notice was handwritten or printed; both forms were customary in making an announcement 'on the university notice-board', which is the purpose for which the church door was used; theses had been nailed to it before. Neither Luther's historic notice nor one of the original printed copies, if these were ever issued, has survived. But the affair caused a stir. The text was widely circulated: both small and poster-size copies were made, it was printed, translated into German, read, debated, and read aloud to those unable to read; it was quoted in the form of slogans. Luther said later that 'in a fortnight' it made its way 'almost across the length and breadth of Germany, because everyone was complaining about indulgences.' This much is certain: everyone was indeed complaining and everyone either read or knew about these theses. Even though the story of Luther nailing his protest to the church door with resounding hammer blows may not be literally true, his theses constituted a fearful blow against the existing Church. The Protestant churches celebrate the nailing of the theses to the door in Wittenberg as their foundation day.

Luther had no 'blow against the Church' in mind. What he intended was to invite academic circles to a disputation, to be conducted in scholarly language on specialized theological questions. This was the general practice where controversial or difficult problems were concerned; the whole of university life was enacted in a setting of theses and discussions on theses.

He said in after years: 'I was preacher in the monastery here and a young doctor, fresh from the forge, passionately absorbed in the Holy Scriptures.' He also said he did not really know what indulgences were, 'no one knew what they were'; he had begun to preach about them because he had heard so much about the traffic in indulgences that seemed to him vexing and harmful. He had even preached on the subject at the castle in Wittenberg, in front of his sovereign the elector, and 'got into his bad graces for doing so,' because Duke Frederick was proud of his great collection of relics and the indulgences they guaranteed – the duke was also careful to see that the money they earned stayed in the country. It was only with the arrival of a certain Johannes Tetzel, a 'Cheap Jack' as Luther called him, a charlatan, that he had started to look more seriously into the indulgence problem and debate it.

Before it came to this, the 'passionate' young doctor had engaged in a sort of preliminary skirmish on purely academic soil. His powers had developed; he had learned by his teaching and found acclamation, pupils and a following. It would be wrong to underestimate the self-assurance either of the university lecturer, who felt such wide support for his views, or of the preacher, who perceived the effect of his sermons. Luther was both university lecturer and pastor. The action he fought was rooted in these two offices.

It was as a teacher in the university that he took his first step. The trends of his teaching had begun to exert an influence, especially his fight against scholastic theology and the theologico-philosophical interpretations associated with the name of Aristotle. He wrote exultantly to his friend Lang in Erfurt, where the 'old school' was still firmly in the saddle: 'Our theology and St Augustine continue to make good progress and, thank heavens, dominate our university. Aristotle, forced to relinquish his throne, is on his way to ruin, perhaps for ever. Lectures on the Sentences have become quite astonishingly unpopular.' He arranged a disputation on ninety-seven theses for one of his pupils, had them printed and circulated them, hoping for a lively debate. In spite of their extremely provocative criticism of accepted doctrines, no one responded to these ninety-seven 'proto-theses'. No one noticed that in them Luther had already raised fundamental points. They fell completely flat. The world of learning simply paid no attention.

His next step was taken in his capacity as pastor and preacher, and with it Luther found his public. His confessants had told him of the sermons on indulgences preached by the Dominican Tetzel; certain details upset and angered him. Luther never heard Tetzel personally. The Dominican was unable to preach in Wittenberg because the elector, afraid for the indulgences accruing from his own collection of relics, and also on political grounds, had forbidden him to enter the electorate. But no doors were barred to him in nearby Brandenburg, and the faithful hurried across the border, to Jüterbog, Zerbst and

The Schlosskirche, Wittenberg

other towns, to secure the coveted indulgence certificates. They told amazing stories of the impressive pomp with which Tetzel made his appearance, of the ringing of bells and official receptions; they described the large, red cross erected in the church between two red banners emblazoned with the pope's arms, the carriage, decked with letters of indulgence, in which Tetzel drove past, and his impressive sermons delivered in a powerful voice that revealed a great and strong man. What Tetzel actually said we do not know for certain; no one wrote these sermons down. Very soon they were to be the cause of serious conflict. Luther claimed he had been told of monstrous goings-on: 'I have received such dispensation from the pope,' Tetzel was supposed to have proclaimed, 'that even if you had got the Virgin Mary with child I could grant you forgiveness, provided you put a suitable contribution into the chest'. Tetzel, needless to say, denied this under oath when the great conflict began, and the story sounds improbable. There is no reason to doubt, however, that this warrior of many indulgence campaigns conducted his business with considerable gusto, and the celebrated verse 'Once you hear the money's ring, the soul from purgatory is free to spring' corresponds fairly accurately to the tone of Tetzel's surviving discourses and writings. Luther quoted other wild assertions made by the preacher: that the pope's red indulgence cross, for example, was as effective as the cross of Christ, or that if Peter himself were in Tetzel's place he could not dispense more grace than he.

We may be sure that point and bite were added later to Tetzel's phrases by Luther, especially when he included them in one of his polemics; but we can be equally sure that the whole business smacked of charlatanry. At this time, however, Luther was not particularly concerned with individual words and phrases. He was angered much more by the traffic as a whole than by the details connected with it, which were by no means unusual. For decades sellers of indulgences had been touring the countryside, sometimes with great showmanship and led by a cardinal, sometimes more modestly. The offertory chests, heavily reinforced with iron, were set up everywhere and notices were displayed giving the precise tariff: princes of the blood twenty-five guilders, prelates and barons ten guilders, the better-class citizenry six guilders, the poorer citizenry one guilder, down to the ordinary people who could get a letter of indulgence for a half or quarter of a guilder. Women, it was expressly stated, could acquire indulgences even against the wishes of their husbands; they formed the main body of purchasers and 'ran like mad to Jüterbog'; the men were more sceptical. That there was considerable opposition among all classes to this pious traffic Luther had already gleaned from the writings of

Paltz, his teacher in Erfurt. The princes complained because the money was leaving the country, men of learning raised all manner of objections to dogmatically insidious theses and assertions; there was much murmuring, and even blaspheming, among the ordinary people. Questions were asked about where the vast sums of money really went, and whether they were not put to very different uses from those stated. Some inkling of all this had reached Luther's ears on his wanderings through the countryside.

But it was not these more superficial aspects of the matter that occupied Luther's mind. He had tormented himself over the problem of God's grace, and now he was faced with the question whether this 'means of grace' was the door to salvation, or whether it might not be merely 'good works' that gave man the comforting feeling that he had done all that was required of him. He had long been worried by the thought that the Church attached too much importance to such outward means; he had referred to the matter both in his lectures and in his sermons. He did not yet question indulgences as such, any more than he questioned the authority of the pope; he merely believed that certain abuses had found their way into the practice – thus showing himself to be a faithful and obedient monk. He only had to appeal to the proper authorities, or so he imagined, and they would realize the need to put an end to the offences.

This he proceeded to do, and it was his decisive step. He wrote – in modest and reverential language – to the appropriate ecclesiastical authority. The archbishop of Mainz had announced the indulgences; Luther as yet did not know the dismal story that lay behind this. He also wrote to the bishop of Brandenburg, in whose diocese Wittenberg was situated; he seems to have written to other high prelates as well, but these letters have not survived. He could hardly have acted more circumspectly or correctly. In his letters he referred not only to what his confessants had told him of Tetzel's behaviour, but also to the specific instructions regarding sermons on indulgences issued by the archbishop of Mainz after consultation with his spiritual and temporal advisers. Here he felt himself to be on absolutely safe ground so far as the dogmatic aspect of the problem was concerned. Speaking to the people a preacher might well be carried away from Church doctrine; but any document issued officially by the highest ecclesiastical dignitary in the empire must surely reflect the views of the Church. A great deal has been written on this particular point, and Luther's subsequent battle made it easy for his opponents to overlook this side of the matter. But we are still in October 1517.

He wrote his letter to the archbishop on the 31st of that month, but it had to pass through many hands before reaching the archbishop himself – Luther, rightly considering this letter to be one of the most important documents of his life, was careful to keep a copy of it. In it he begged the archbishop to admonish his preachers on indulgences and withdraw the instructions issued to his commissioners for indulgences. This he did with all the necessary forms of address and protestations of the writer's unworthiness, who 'has to live in awe of his Lord and Pastor in Christ'; he had hesitated for a long time, but now his conscience drove him to act. Enumerating the things that had come to his ears, he made it clear that he himself had never heard Tetzel preach on indulgences; but it disturbed him that people were being led astray by such talk and acquiring wrong ideas. 'Merciful God,' he exclaimed, 'the poor souls in Your keeping are being led into death with teaching of this kind.' Carried away by passion, he dropped the submissive tone of his opening and closing formulae: one day the archbishop would have to account for the harm being done. He enclosed his theses, having emphasized their main points in his letter as well.

He asked naïvely, 'What am I to do?,' and could only beg the Lord Archbishop and Noble Prince 'to do away with' the 'little book', in other words the printed instructions to commissioners for indulgences, and give his paternal attention to this matter. He added modestly that, should he care to do so, the Noble Lord might cast a glance at the enclosed theses; he would see from them how 'uncertain' the opinions on indulgences were, whereas the preachers proclaimed them to be absolutely 'certain'.

It is not known whether the Noble Lord did glance at the theses. At all events he realized that the great indulgence scheme was in jeopardy. He considered the monk's proposals 'insolent' and told his advisers that the matter was of no personal concern to him; he was afraid, however, that the 'people in their foolishness would be provoked and led astray' and therefore was taking the necessary steps. The theses were submitted to the University of Mainz, with the purpose of instituting a *processus inhibitorius*, which would prohibit any further comments on the matter. As was the usual practice, the archbishop referred to the traffic in indulgences as this 'sacred business'. In their report the local theologians singled out only one of the ninety-five theses as contrary to tradition – that advocating a limitation of the pope's power to grant indulgences. They advised against any formal condemnation of Luther. At all events the archbishop referred the awkward matter to the pope in Rome, partly to get it off his hands and partly to forestall any possible censure from the Curia.

At this point it is necessary to say something about the 'sacred business', and the attitude to it at this time, since this was what the ensuing conflict was about. Luther declared that he did not really know what indulgences were – a very barbed statement. Even in his theses he fully acknowledged indulgences as a practice of the Church; his only quarrel was with their misuse and with what he considered to be the excessively loose interpretation of them. These were the points he wished to dispute. The archbishop of Mainz, too, was conversant only with the practice of indulgences; he had never given thought to the problems of theology and dogma involved. Indeed he was not a theologian at all but a young Hohenzollern prince who had reached his high office as a result of extremely dubious political and financial manœuvring. Luther was unaware of this when he wrote his letter. His teachers in the monastery did not know much about indulgences either, and such opinions on the subject as they expressed in their writings were indefinite and questionable in the extreme. How much Pope Leo may have known about indulgences is equally unclear; he, too, was no theologian but by birth and upbringing a Medici prince and a diplomat. The theologians, in so far as they had discussed the issues, had only added to the confusion; there was no binding and authoritative teaching on the subject, there were only 'viewpoints' and references to statements in papal bulls. Both the archbishop and Pope Leo relied on the expert opinion of their professional theologians. Being a professional theologian and professor, Luther considered himself fully competent to submit his views to debate; this was, and long remained, his attitude. But the learned discussion he aimed at never materialized. The matter at once passed into the sphere of politics and gained wide publicity.

Indulgences had first been introduced on a large scale as a measure to promote the first Crusade. For this no developed 'theory' was necessary: as their devout enterprise was beset with toils and dangers, the Crusaders were anxious to obtain both the Church's blessing and absolution for their sins, of which not a few had built up an ample store. It is true that the indulgence was a remission of ecclesiastical penalties, not a forgiveness of sins, but from the outset there was confusion between the notions of the theologians and the more down-to-earth views of the ordinary people. The decisive factor was always the practice and not the theory, which lagged permanently behind. With the Crusades indulgences, which hitherto had been in the hands of local bishops, became the privilege of the popes. In its practice the Curia took into account the constantly increasing demand for this means of grace: instead of taking part in a Crusade a man could redeem his vow by paying an appropriate sum of money. The demand grew and the basis of the system was continually broadened. The great popularity of indulgences was due to the extraordinarily realistic attitude of people in the Middle Ages; they feared punishment for their sins and

were ready to make full compensation, in cash. This was the old
Germanic concept of law, in which the word 'atonement' was used for
monetary compensation, even in cases of murder and manslaughter.
For the Church atonement had another meaning, but this had validity
only in the theoretical propositions of the Doctors of the Church; the
people clung to their simple notion that guilt was expiated by a cash
payment. And thus the matter stood until Luther's day, poised between
popular belief and the higher theoretical view of the dogmaticians.

Theory was unable to keep pace with the constant increase in this
wholesale traffic. The Crusades soon proved inadequate to satisfy the
desire for more and yet more indulgences. War against heretics, as
well as against enemies of the pope, was declared to be a Crusade that
guaranteed indulgences; the history of indulgences is also a history of
war. It is also an economic and financial history of the Middle Ages,
because none of the many taxes and tributes levied by the Church
brought in comparable sums, and none was so directly the privilege and source of income of the Curia, which, since the captivity
of the popes in Avignon, had created and built up its vast administrative apparatus. The Italian banks, then in process of establishing
themselves, were drawn in and the transfer of the indulgence moneys
constituted their first large-scale transactions; in Luther's day the
indulgence business, at any rate for central Germany, eastern Europe
and Scandinavia, was in the hands of the Augsburg banking house of
Fugger. People in the Middle Ages had an extreme aversion towards
paying taxes; even temporal rulers had the greatest difficulty in extracting payments from their subjects and in most cases could do so
only on a short-term basis or for specific purposes. It is understandable
that these rulers made repeated efforts to cash in on the rich flow of
indulgence money, and under favourable international political circumstances they received their share; the tough, acrimonious negotiations on the subject fill many pages of history. By Luther's day the
continually diminishing political power of the papacy had brought
about a situation in which kings and princes took for granted their
participation in the indulgence trade; the pope might be able to count
on a third, or at most a half, of the takings.

Initially an indulgence, as interpreted by the theologians, was simply
a remission of ecclesiastical penalties, such as fasting, pilgrimages and
banishment. Later, it was considerably extended. The pope, it was
argued, was master of all temporal forms of punishment, and one of
these temporal forms was purgatory. Hell remained outside his jurisdiction because it was eternal and subject only to the will of God.
Over purgatory, however, which existed for the purpose of cleansing
and purging sinful man, the pope could exercise jurisdiction, and do so

here on earth; it belonged, in a sense, to his diocese. A seven years' indulgence meant that seven years were deducted from the punishment; the total punishment was never stated, but even a remission of this order was well worth having. In the Middle Ages people as a rule feared purgatory more than they feared hell. Hell, being eternal, was beyond man's comprehension; purgatory, being 'temporal', offered the hope that the purging process might be brought to an end. Scholasticism justified the enormous power over men's souls vested in papal authority by arguing that the pope controlled the secret treasure, the Thesaurus of the Church, a treasure accumulated through the surplus merits of Christ and the saints. The idea that every believer, as a member of the mystic body of the Church, could share in these merits was an old one, but the doctrine that this store was entrusted to the pope, to be used by him – like petty cash as it were – on behalf of every man of good will, was first formulated in the thirteenth and fourteenth centuries. It was no accident when Pope Clement VI, the Avignon pope under whom the new tax policy of the Curia and a huge accumulation of funds on a scale hitherto unknown reached their culmination, expressly established this doctrine in his bull *Unigenitus* in 1343. We shall see later how this bull came to Luther's attention; in the monastery he had never heard of it.

On the other hand he was well aware of the distinctions existing between 'plenary' and 'partial' indulgences; plenary indulgences were the prerogative of the pope. He knew also about the establishment of the Jubilee Year which, dating from 1300, was associated with a plenary indulgence and drew the first considerable pilgrimages to Rome: the indulgence was conditional on the pilgrim visiting the seven pilgrimage churches, a task which Luther also completed. The observance had proved such a success that it was repeated at increasingly shorter intervals; the original hundred years were first decreased to fifty, then to thirty-three, as representing the life-span of Christ, and finally to twenty-five, corresponding roughly to man's expectation of life in those days. Here, too, the use of 'substitutes' was immediately introduced: one could send a substitute pilgrim to Rome or fulfil one's obligation by making a cash payment equal to the cost of the journey. But this was by no means all. In the fifteenth century indulgences were offered on every conceivable pretext: for building churches, for the very practical purpose of constructing dykes in Holland, for the Turkish wars – an effective catchword much in use since the times of the Crusades – and for the pope's wars in Italy against the enemies of the day. The desire to pass on the benefit to dead relatives in purgatory led to a further extension of the practice. The theologians had serious misgivings about this, but were overruled by the Curia's legal experts. The innovation, introduced only fifty years before Luther appeared on the scene, was an enormous success. Even with this, however, the inflation of indulgences was not over. It became possible to buy whole sheaves of letters of indulgence for dead relatives; there were indulgences for the obligation to fast, the so-called 'butter letters', indulgences for vows, as well as for the dubious acquisition of worldly goods, provided the rightful owner could no longer be found. Dismissory letters gave permission to dispense with confession to the local priest, which was frequently embarrassing, and obtain an indulgence from the priest of one's choice, a provision of which the preachers on indulgences also took advantage, to the great annoyance of the secular priesthood.

The indulgence question had been a source of annoyance, and even of revolt, from its inception. In the fourteenth century Wyclif had protested; Hus was burned for his opposition to the traffic in indulgences, although this was not the sole reason why he was sent to the stake. His case is of particular interest because it demonstrates how completely the system of indulgences was tied to the politics of the Curia, and also because, from the moment Luther appeared, he was threatened with the dangerous charge of being a 'Bohemian', a 'second Hus'. Hus preached against an indulgence offered by the antipope John XXII for participation in a 'Crusade' against his enemy King Ladislas of Naples or for subscribing money for this campaign. As soon as he heard that Hus had preached against his indulgence, and was also expounding other dangerous theses concerning the pope's authority, he fulminated a ban against him as a heretic. Shortly afterwards he himself was deposed by the Council of Constance as an unworthy man who had arrogated to himself the papal authority; the detailed charges accused him of heresy, simony, unchastity and the murder of his predecessor, who had died suddenly. These charges were not necessarily all true, but the Church removed his name from its records and recognized in his place the antipope Gregory, one of three popes who, all appointed as the result of questionable elections, split the west into three factions. The sermons which Hus preached against John XXII's 'Crusaders' indulgence' led to wild demonstrations in Prague; the letters of indulgence were burned, students dragged through the streets a cart containing two whores with letters of indulgence hung around their necks, King Wenceslas intervened, there were disputations among the theologians, and finally Hus was summoned before the Council and sentenced to be burned as a heretic. He was a victim of the policy of unification pursued by the great Ecclesiastical Council which, although it postponed the hoped for 'root and branch reform', was anxious nevertheless to preserve, the authority of the Church and the papacy by impressive means. In order to put an end to the schism the

Council elected a new fourth pope, the first of a new line which has remained unbroken to this day. The schism caused by the proceedings against Hus remained; its consequences, shown in the bloody Hussite wars and the creation of a separate church in Bohemia, were felt until Luther's day. The gruesome irony that Hus had opposed the authority of a pope who was condemned as unworthy by the same Council which sentenced Hus was either overlooked or disregarded by the Council's members. The principle that the office was above any unworthiness on the part of its holder emerged victorious.

In Luther's day indulgence practice was governed by bulls of indulgence, covering specific fields and purposes, issued by the pope after long and detailed negotiations. Commissioners, who were sometimes cardinals nominated as legates with this special mission, were appointed; directives, like that of the archbishop of Mainz, issued; and experienced preachers installed who, in turn, engaged large staffs of assistants. Some of the campaigns for the launching of new indulgences needed careful preparation and were waged in military fashion, with strategic and tactical headquarters; there were also diplomatic obstacles to be cleared. This was an expensive procedure, and the costs often swallowed up most of the receipts. The commissioners, assistant commissioners and other functionaries shared in the proceeds on a widely differing percentage basis; as their public appearances were often surrounded by considerable splendour, further inroads were made into the takings. Even before Luther intervened there had been complaints from Rome about the indulgence policy of the archbishop of Mainz; the authorities were disturbed by reports of poor results, and the archbishop had to reprove Tetzel, his commissioner, for excessive expenditure and admonish him about the 'unseemly' behaviour among his staff, both in their sermons and in the inns, where clearly they had not been conducting themselves in a very decorous way. The collecting boxes, heavily reinforced with iron bands, were to be opened only in the presence of a representative from the bank – in Germany this was the House of Fugger – and a legally attested record was to be made of the contents. Embezzlement was frequent and a great deal of false or debased coinage was found, which, in view of the general monetary confusion, was hardly surprising. The House of Fugger's responsibility did not end with this 'retail trade'; it was also responsible for the wholesale trade, the cash transfers to Rome. The bank floated large new indulgence loans, exactly in the manner of the later state loans, and mortgaged them in advance. The whole indulgence business had become an integral part of papal financial policy.

Within this vast framework, which spanned the whole of Europe, the unfortunate Tetzel, whose name so unexpectedly made its way into

history, was no more than a speck. Since his own lifetime he has unjustly been made a scapegoat, the subject of innumerable caricatures
and calumnies. He was said to have been condemned to death by the
Emperor Maximilian for his vices, being pardoned only on the entrea-
ties of the elector of Saxony; to have had several illegitimate children;
and to have acquired a fortune for himself. Luther considered these
accusations unjust and protested against them, although he believed
the stories of Tetzel's past. When Tetzel lay on his death-bed Luther
wrote him a conciliatory letter, consoling him with the words 'the child
had quite a different father', meaning the indulgence dispute, not one
of Tetzel's alleged offspring.

One has to concede, however, that the popular legend about Tetzel
is to some extent justified. Probably he was a hard worker, more
efficient than a multitude of others engaged in the same business –
there were many Tetzels – and in another context he might easily have
been an excellent preacher; but since this was the branch he chose,
he came to stand for all those too numerous to list and remember and
must bear the blame before history for the sins of his many colleagues.
His shoulders were broad enough for this. He was not primarily a
charlatan, although charlatanry came naturally enough to him.

An exceptionally good organizer, he knew how to deal with ruling
princes and public authorities, and how to manage his large staff. He
travelled with a whole retinue of assistant commissioners, servants and
even bank officials, who wanted to be present when the accounting was
done and who frequently also dispensed indulgences, thus making very
bad blood indeed. Tetzel had travelled widely in his indulgence campaigns and had proclaimed the great indulgence of 1504 for the benefit
of the Order of Teutonic Knights in Prussia, which was engaged in
severe fighting with the Russians; adherents of the Eastern Church
were classed out of hand as 'unbelievers'. He had preached in Saxony
and Silesia, where he firmly swept aside every obstacle placed in his
path; one mayor, who pointed out that a different indulgence had been
scheduled for his town, was told bluntly that Tetzel's indulgence was
much better than that of his competitor and thus took precedence.
Moreover, declared the preacher, very sure of himself, 'when I have
been to a place others do not follow very quickly.'

Tetzel was convinced he was working in a good cause and was not
unduly worried by scruples over the means he employed. If his assistants made exaggerated and questionable statements – and these may
have been at the bottom of some of the scandalous comments quoted
about him – it was no concern of his. In taking this attitude he could
plead the example of his superiors, right up to the very summit in Rome.
No instance is known in which abuses of the indulgence system, well

Sale of indulgences

known and deplored though they were, led to any rebuke from the responsible higher authority. Quite the contrary: every bull of indulgence threatened heavy penalties for anyone obstructing the preacher or making his work more difficult. According to one of the chronicles Tetzel, who as a Dominican prior was also an inquisitor, threatened: 'All those who criticize my sermons and indulgences will have their heads ripped off and be kicked bleeding into hell; heretics I will have burned until the smoke billows over the walls.' His sermons surely had the same popular ring; the authentic extant examples, being master copies of what he himself said, are naturally couched in more guarded terms. But even in them it is the experienced agitator who speaks. The poor souls in purgatory implore those left behind to have mercy on them, they are suffering agonies, whereas a few alms will set them free: 'Do not be so cruel as to let us languish in the flames.' A letter of indulgence costs only a quarter of a guilder and 'thanks to this you can bring the divine, immortal soul safe and free into the fatherland of Paradise.' Tetzel, undaunted, addresses the 'murderers, usurers, thieves and profligates: now is the time to listen to the voice of God; He does not want the sinner to die but to be converted.'

There is no doubt that indulgences were extraordinarily popular, and not only with murderers and profligates. They promised security in an age of great insecurity. There was something comforting in the very precision of the tariffs; everyone was assigned his proper place in the class dominated order of society – if not always to his satisfaction, as must have been the case among the poorer classes and peasants. Tetzel had his greatest success in the towns. There he could call on the town councils and local church authorities, though they often resented his use of his status to forbid any other church services to be held while he was there. Indulgences took priority. The preacher on indulgences was the direct representative of the pope; his warrant gave him full authority to dispense the same favours as the holy see, a small number of serious cases excepted. To attack indulgences was thus to make a direct attack on the authority of the pope and this, though Professor Luther was still quite unaware of it, was the cause of the great conflict. In drawing up his theses Luther was concerned with questions of conscience; he had no idea what he was letting himself in for. If 'everyone complained', as he said, the overriding reason was not pangs of conscience but hard cash. The percentages due to the sellers of indulgences were calculated on the basis of their heavy expenses. The princes calculated too and haggled for their share; the Curia did the same. It was a question of money and of nothing else.

Indulgences, as we have already seen, were part of the prevailing economy. Virtually all large-scale and complicated construction works, including bridges and dykes, had to be financed through them. As late as the nineteenth century cathedral lotteries were established to enable soaring towers to be added to unfinished Gothic cathedrals. An indulgence, however, was not a lottery, although it has been compared to one. It more nearly resembled our modern insurance policy; not a life insurance policy but a policy for the far more important insurance of the life beyond. The ability to handle figures and make calculations played a decisive role; this was true not only of indulgences but of Masses for the dead and ecclesiastical practice generally. In those days it could be assumed that almost no one could handle figures, and that numbers, such as the number seven, still held their ancient magic significance. A promise of 'seven years' indulgence' meant more than the bare figures mean today. The higher numbers had a still greater indefinable power; the number a thousand, for instance, encompassed the notion of something monstrous, as well as suggesting the end of the world. Only a few initiates could handle figures of this order, and it was this that gave the banks, whose function was still an occult science, their unrivalled supremacy. The Fuggers were the first to introduce the alchemy of double-entry book-keeping into Germany from Italy, making great use of it in their indulgence business.

Believers, in this world of figures, acquired with their letters of indulgence a priceless sense of reassurance: they had 'done their part' and settled their account, and had done so in a clearly defined and recognized manner. The giving of alms had always been preached as one of the foremost duties of a Christian; but it had been left entirely to the discretion and pious sentiments of the individual. Anyone who subscribed to the indulgences, Masses and other causes prescribed or considered desirable by the highest ecclesiastical authority was able to rest assured of his 'piety'. This piety could be measured; it could be displayed and was acknowledged with respect by the community. All the chronicles contain detailed accounts of these gifts, singling them out for honourable mention. Even a merchant decried as a merciless usurer – all tradesmen were considered usurers, and were so in fact, according to the Church's ban on interest – was able to feel 'justified' if he contributed in this way. It was over this point that Luther's 'doctrine of justification', which was something entirely different, clashed most sharply with reality.

Luther could not calculate, in the broadest sense. He literally could not do sums and manage figures; he had not been taught arithmetic at school and all his life remained unable to understand it. At the same time he had no use for security, a fact that can be clearly deduced from his ninety-five theses: a man was to wage an incessant fight with his sinful heritage. 'Thou shalt repent: the believer's whole life must be repentance, as Christ said', was the first of his theses. He had fought this battle out for himself, and now he proclaimed it for all. There must be no rest, no easy balancing of accounts. No one, no human being, could come to one's help, and for Luther the pope, too, was a human being; everyone stood alone before his judge, as an individual. No one could be sure that his repentance was sufficient, still less that he was completely forgiven and least of all through a letter of indulgence. Forgiveness could be brought about only through a person's own true repentance, through constantly renewed repentance and atonement; man must follow Christ through suffering, death and hell, through temptation, and not through the 'peace' that was preached, he said at the conclusion of his theses. What he wanted to proclaim, literally with hammer blows, was not 'peace, peace, when there is no peace' but 'the Cross, the Cross'.

This was Luther's challenge, and he began and ended his notice with it. He could not calculate the outcome of this challenge. He still believed that such theses or 'opinions' could be debated. But he was also, though without being fully aware of it, a powerful agitator. His theses were political dynamite. He did not contest indulgences on principle, but relegated them to a subordinate place. He did not contest the position of the pope, but he reduced his powers considerably. He did not deny the doctrine of the 'Church's treasure', but preached unequivocally that the Gospel was the true treasure of the Church. And the treasure of the Gospel, he said with extreme political provocation, was 'hated because it declares that the first shall be last', whereas the treasure of indulgences made the last first, and that was 'pleasant to hear'.

Luther was very much a man of the people and appointed himself their advocate: he quoted 'caustic remarks' he had heard about indulgences on his travels, pointing out that they could not be forcibly suppressed because to do so would make a laughing-stock of the Church and the pope. The people, in their naïve way, were asking why the pope did not make a present of indulgences instead of charging for them; he was enormously rich, so why did he not build St Peter's with his own money? And if he had power over the souls in purgatory, why did he not make a clean sweep of purgatory and have done with it, instead of allowing the poor souls to linger there? Or again: the pious had created endowments for the souls of the departed; if these were no longer effective, and had to be replaced by new payments, why did the pope not return the endowments?

His intention, he stressed, was only to report what the people were saying; in his opinion these 'caustic remarks' could easily be silenced if indulgences were preached in the way the pope meant and wished them to be. He was still fully convinced that Pope Leo, about whom he knew no more than he knew about Archbishop Albrecht of Mainz, was a good and benevolent Holy Father who was being deceived by unprincipled subordinates. This long remained his conviction. He also believed that the bishops were in a position to ensure that the preachers on indulgences did not propound 'their own dreams instead of the things the pope had instructed them to say.' He immediately went on to make practical suggestions for preaching without 'dreams': it would, for instance, be better to give the money to the poor and needy than to spend it on an indulgence, which was used for one's own ends in order to escape punishment. No fewer than ten theses proclaimed his practical Christianity.

The theses as a whole do not add up to a doctrine or system; this would scarcely have been possible. They are a detached series of propositions of the type needed to form the basis of a disputation. Some are almost like soliloquies and deal with Luther's innermost personal convictions, others have the ring and zest of political battle-cries, yet others provide a sermon for an as yet invisible congregation. Much can be read into this single sheet of paper, and many interpretations put on it; this was done even at the time. The document is held together only by the iron brace of its beginning and end, in which Luther confesses his faith.

Thus the sheet went out into the world. The impact it made came as the greatest surprise to Luther. The scholars to whom it was addressed did not respond; no one came to the disputation. But the people responded, and they responded throughout the social scale: simple folk, citizens, intellectuals, artists. Albrecht Dürer in Nuremberg sent a parcel of his woodcuts and engravings as a present to the devout monk. The clergy, too, were stirred by it, princes were interested, each extracting something different from it. Each individual thesis appealed to a different social class; the poor pricked up their ears when they heard that the first should be last and the last first. The sheet was not only read, it was nailed up and displayed, and 'translated' to the uneducated. Finally, and by no means least, people were impressed by the fact that here at last was a man who pleaded his cause without fear. There had always been 'mumblings'; even the Diets made their everlasting weak-kneed complaints, and there had been no lack of satirical allusions and Latin epigrams. At times scholars had made guarded criticisms. But here was a simple monk, who said aloud what needed to be said – this at any rate was how the theses were understood. It is of no account that Luther was misunderstood, or that people read a 'programme' into his theses. History has seldom been made by definite, clearcut programmes. It was precisely the general nature and variety of his theses that guaranteed their effectiveness; together, of course, with the feeling, which cannot be ascribed to any individual thesis, that behind this sheet of paper lay enormous strength and determination, courage and conviction – qualities conspicuously absent in German history; for more than two hundred years, no such voice had been heard.

Everyone was complaining, said Luther in later years. 'And because all the bishops and doctors held their peace and there was no one willing to bell the cat – for the simple reason that the Dominican inquisitors had put everyone in fear of the stake – it was said in Luther's praise that here at last was a doctor who did something.'

He added that he had not enjoyed the fame; 'the song was pitched too high for my voice'.

# The Holy Roman Empire

WHAT sort of world was it in which Luther found himself? Let us begin with Luther himself. As a monk and member of a religious order he belonged to an international organization possessing, or claiming, extraterritorial rights, with its head in Rome and using the international language of Latin, which he himself still used for his theses and retained in half of his works and correspondence. Born a native of Mansfeld he had become an Augustinian, and it was as an Augustinian that he taught at the university of the Electorate of Saxony in Wittenberg, which belonged to Duke Frederick the Wise. Since the division of the inheritance in the previous century there had been two Saxonys – this much Luther knew: the electorate belonging to Frederick and the other belonging to Duke George, Frederick's cousin. He was soon to be made acutely aware of this division. There were many other such divisions among the principalities; the entire Holy Roman Empire was a patchwork of temporal and ecclesiastical possessions with an emperor as its titular head. Luther had no idea of the details of this picture. It is necessary constantly to reiterate and stress his ignorance of worldly matters, because he was now brought face to face with them and day after day, month after month, required to make decisions and take action. He had become the 'man of the hour'. The nation listened to him. The quiet monastic life, regulated by horary prayers, was a thing of the past, as was the orderly, predictable activity of the monk and university lecturer. He was now assailed by unpredictable claims, expectations and wild hopes from every class and stratum of society. He had to deal with bishops and archbishops, and soon with cardinals, the pope and the emperor; this involved him in the maze of international politics, which was even more tangled and impossible to grasp than that of the German Empire, then hardly an empire at all. It is understandable that, at first, he was afraid and lay low. The overwhelming echo from his theses alarmed him, 'the song was pitched too high'. Luther had a very sensitive ear; he began to perceive shrill, high-pitched sounds as well as a deafening clamour, the anxious voices of friends and wellwishers, and rising above the rest the strident voices from the chancelleries of higher authority calling him to order. From Mainz came a 'ban on speaking and writing'.

It was a key to which Luther was not accustomed. As his fellow monks affirmed, he had complied loyally with the freely accepted precepts of his order. He had been praised and promoted, and had been spoiled by his success as a preacher and university teacher. He had gained influence at court and was on the best of terms with all the authorities he knew. Now, suddenly, he clashed with another, higher authority that wanted nothing to do with the 'presumptuous monk' in Wittenberg. He had been worried and had turned trustingly to the archbishop of Mainz, but the Noble Lord had not answered; all he had received were threats and an order from his secretariat.

Who was this archbishop whom Luther addressed as 'My dear Father' and referred to as his 'Shepherd'? We shall begin our survey of the patchwork of the Holy Roman Empire with him. In his letter Luther gave him the title 'Archbishop of Mainz and Magdeburg, Primate of All German Archbishops and Margrave of Brandenburg'. The young prince was also incumbent of the great bishopric of Halberstadt and, in his capacity as elector of Mainz, Lord High Chamberlain of the Holy Roman Empire – an unusual accumulation of honours, and acquired in an unusual way. Albrecht of Mainz was the younger brother of Joachim, the reigning margrave of Brandenburg; he was one of numerous Hohenzollern margraves, some of whom had their seats in the family ancestral homeland of Franconia. At this period the Hohenzollerns were by no means the dominant power they were to become later, but they had aspirations and were in the ascendant; this was in sharp contrast to some of the older princely houses, and especially to the House of Saxony, which in Luther's day was considered the foremost dynasty. Dynastic politics were not limited to temporal possessions but were focused equally on ecclesiastical appointments, almost all of which were obtained by the high aristocracy or the younger sons of princes. Thus, in capturing Mainz, the Brandenburgs could chalk up a notable success. In addition to this, another cousin was grand master of the Order of Teutonic Knights in Prussia; the order was in serious difficulties, it is true, and lay beyond the frontiers of the empire, but nonetheless it could be reckoned an important outpost. All this caused a great deal of anxiety to Frederick the Wise who, politically often somnolent and indecisive, had been outplayed. The antagonism remained, and played its part in Luther's destiny; the margrave of Brandenburg became his most persistent opponent in all the diets, seeing in the monk the champion of his Saxon rival.

With Brandenburg and Mainz the Hohenzollerns now disposed of two of the seven votes in the electoral college, which had the privilege of electing the emperor. It was also mainly thanks to this elective assembly that the young Albrecht had been appointed to his high position, for which according to canon law he was not eligible. The House of Fugger had engineered the matter in Rome. The Fuggers played an active part in the indulgence business, in the financial transactions of the Curia when high prelates were appointed, and in elections, including those of kings and emperors; Jacob Fugger, the head of the banking house, was known as the 'King-maker' as well as the 'Wealthy'. He deserved the name. Charles v's election was financed by him, and later his house secured the throne for Charles's brother and successor. It would be as correct to speak of the age of Fugger as of the age of Luther.

Canon law forbade an accumulation of high ecclesiastical offices. Albrecht had been made archbishop of Magdeburg at the early age of twenty-three; this was a bitter blow to the elector of Saxony, whose brother had previously held the see. To this had been added the bishopric of Halberstadt. For the third and highest appointment the pope expected, as balm for his canonic scruples, a large sum in compensation, in addition to the other moneys due to him. Three archbishops of Mainz had died in rapid succession, and the authorities there shrank from incurring this new expense. The House of Fugger stepped into the breach and advanced the required sum. Jacob the Wealthy shrewdly made provision for the speedy amortization of the debt by arranging for the issue of an indulgence which, officially intended for the construction of St Peter's, was in fact made over to Mainz. His officials supervised the execution of the plan and had to keep a check on Tetzel; they settled with Albrecht and with Rome. The cost of the transaction was roughly equal to the entire annual revenue of the imperial German government.

Like Tetzel, the young Prince Albrecht must be seen, not as an exception but as representative of his class. Unlike other high ecclesiastical dignitaries, who rode off in armour to their private wars and campaigns, he was not a belligerent prince; the sword crossed with the bishop's crook, which appears on the medals he had struck, had only heraldic significance. It was meant to show that he was both an archbishop and a ruler of his widespread territories; these, in addition to his domains along the Rhine and the Main, comprised large possessions in central Germany together with Halle, which was his residence there, Erfurt and further lands in Hesse. Brought together over the centuries, these possessions had constantly been added to. The fact that they remained intact was what mainly distinguished the ecclesiastical principalities from their temporal counterparts; these were forever being broken up and splintered until in Luther's day there were some half-dozen Guelf duchies and principalities. In size alone Mainz was the largest and most powerful of the three ecclesiastical electorates; Trier and Cologne were the other two.

In Albrecht himself, however, there was no trace of the mighty ruler, powerful as some of his predecessors had been; one of them, with all the priestly pride of the High Middle Ages, had had himself represented on his tombstone as a towering figure blessing with gracious fingers two diminutive German kings, one on either side of him. Albrecht's ambitions were on a lesser scale; timid and vacillating all his life, he also suffered from uncertain health, due in part to his various love affairs. He was ambitious and made big plans, which, however, he did not carry through; unlike others among his peers, he was incapable of pursuing an intrigue single-mindedly. He was fond of good living; in this he could point to the example of his eminent superior, Pope Leo, who, on assuming office, had made it very clear that he now intended to enjoy life. He also resembled Leo in his love and patronage of the arts: Matthias Grünewald was his court painter, he corresponded with Dürer, employed Lucas Cranach and appointed humanists, including the young Ulrich von Hutten, to his court. He liked to be painted in the guise of St Jerome, book in hand and cardinal's hat hanging on the wall, or as a saint in the wilderness, a less suitable pose because he was sociable and wanted to be popular. Later he developed a basic respect and secret admiration for Luther, in spite of the rough way in which he was treated by him. In the course of his many vacillations he toyed with the idea of marrying and turning his electorate into a secular duchy, as his Brandenburg cousin – another Albrecht – had done in Prussia. As with so much else that he projected, nothing came of it. His large, fleshy face, with the long curving nose and the small, twisted mouth of one of fortune's darlings, is that of a fair connoisseur of the good things of life whose rather sad eyes show that he does not really know how to abandon himself to enjoyment.

There were many such mediocrities in the higher ranks of the German clergy. They all remained nervously in the background when the great storm broke; many, like Albrecht, looked anxiously round for some way to safeguard their possessions in the event that the new faith should prove the stronger. Nothing shows more clearly how empty the name 'Prince of the Church' had become. Not one of them distinguished himself as a champion of the faith to which he owed his position. Not one of them assumed any major role at all. If we compare them with such impressive Princes of the Church as Cardinal Wolsey, who ruled England like a dictator and made possible the course taken by Henry VIII, or Cardinal d'Amboise in France, whose hold on the reins of French politics was hardly less firm, these German prelates appear as provincial, bourgeois pigmies in spite of the pomp and splendour with which they decked themselves out. England, like France, had a king, a central authority, a capital city; it was a nation, a state. In Germany there existed the fiction of the Holy Roman Empire which, in the course of the previous century, had acquired the additional title 'German Nation'; this was no proud boast, but a renunciation of the once-prevailing idea of an Empire that would comprise the whole of the west. This also had scarcely ever been more than an idea; its inspiration had been Charlemagne, the only emperor who can truly be said to have given the title pith and substance. Whatever the German emperors of the Middle Ages may have been, and there were towering personalities among them, they were worsted in their fight with the papacy.

It was the humanists who first gave new life to the memory of a great age, a memory that had long lain dormant or at best lived on in legends of a mighty emperor who would return and revive the empire's splendour. They created the rudiments of an idea of history, or at least of an awareness of history, and with it a feeling of nationhood that until then had been extremely vague and nebulous. Tacitus, whom they had just discovered, and his *Germania* provided them with a national hero in Arminius. His victory over the Roman cohorts in the Teutoburg forest was used to exemplify a new fight against Rome. The virtues ascribed by Tacitus to the ancient Germans were held up, exactly as he had held them up, as the model for a race that had grown weak and flabby. A whole literature of praise and glorification began to appear, and it was badly needed because the self-confidence of the Germans had long been at a low ebb and they had to dig far into their past to recover any sense of pride.

For two centuries there had been no really great figure in the German lands. Modern historians, with their more precise judgment, have been at pains to find some redeeming features among the rulers of the fourteenth and fifteenth centuries; but to Luther's contemporaries Charles IV, who had lived in Prague, was the 'stepfather' of the empire, and Frederick III, whose reign continued endlessly, the 'skinflint' and unprincely semi-bourgeois. Now the next Habsburg was on the throne: Maximilian, the 'last of the knights'. He at least looked the part, with his huge, aquiline nose, flashing eyes, and passion for the chase and war. He was liked by the humanists, writers and artists; no other monarch has ever been touted by such an array of written and pictorial propaganda as was turned out by the printing presses, then enjoying their first flush of prosperity. In an enormous woodcut, big enough to occupy a whole wall, Dürer erected a great triumphal arch to him; it bore the inscription: 'The Gate of Honour and Might'.

The might existed on paper. Maximilian had plans on the largest and most comprehensive scale for reforming the empire, for internal peace and for imperial administration; he waged war incessantly and achieved virtually nothing apart from strengthening the position of his House by marriages – this was the Habsburg family recipe and was to prove its efficacy in undreamt-of political combinations. Like his predecessors, he too treated the empire as a secondary consideration, however grandiosely he expressed his intention to make it great. He too appeared in public only on ceremonial occasions; his primary interests were in Austria and above all in Burgundy, which he had acquired by marriage. He laid great stress on his German chivalry, but had his children and grandchildren brought up to speak French and wrote to them exclusively in the more elegant language. His unreliability, both in figures and politics, was a byword everywhere; within a few years he had no credit left, either diplomatic or financial. His money difficulties became the laughing stock of Europe, especially as they went hand in hand with increasingly far-flung schemes. He wanted to 'draw' Scandinavia, Hungary and even Portugal into the empire, advancing ancient claims of the vaguest authenticity. He seriously considered becoming pope but the idea fell through, mainly because of opposition on the part of his financial backers. How serious his intentions were in any of his projects, however, is a moot point. His most important adviser – at court he became almost omnipotent – was his 'diverting councillor' and court fool Kunz von der Rosen. Kunz was one of the chief figures, and a historic one, in the great fool's prelude that introduced the great tragedy. Maximilian's whole reign was a tournament and fool's turn.

On one occasion Luther said that on his journey to Rome he had heard of Shrovetide plays in which fun was poked at the emperor's poverty. The doge entered with a well-filled money bag, lavishing gold ducats on all and sundry. Following him came Maximilian, dressed in a plain, grey hunting jacket and wearing a little hat; he also carried a purse and wanted to distribute some coins, but when he put his hand inside his fingers came out through the holes in the bottom. Luther interpreted this patriotically as indicating the arrogance of the Italians, who would be severely punished by the will of God. But this clutching at nothing symbolizes Maximilian's nature; what he thought he held eluded him.

These gibes at the emperor's poverty were justified; the 'knightly' contractor of debts owed his insolvency to his indulgence in pomp and splendour. Maximilian borrowed everywhere and on the most petty scale; he was not above accepting gifts of cloth or products of the soil. He mortgaged the mineral resources of his patrimonial lands, and in doing so paved the way for the Fuggers' and other large bankers' domination of Germany. He used the money he obtained to prosecute his wars and establish his supremacy, his object in every case being to promote the interests of the House of Habsburg. This policy of family aggrandizement, which was pursued on a vast scale by his grandson and successor Charles v, determined the entire German politics of the day, and it was not due solely to the princes' jealousy and self-interest that Maximilian was refused compliance and payment whenever possible. The self-interest of the princes and other estates was certainly great; they wanted an emperor who was representative and, if possible, not too powerful, but they had no intention of contributing anything themselves. Meanness and miserliness, of which people liked to accuse others, were rampant in Germany, and in this the princes were at one with the towns; they disagreed only on how the expenses should be distributed, the princes insisting that the towns should bear the main burden. But whatever amounts may have been sanctioned as a result of such pettyfogging bargaining, they were a mere pittance compared with the sums readily lavished by other nations. Imposing though his title sounded, a German emperor was rarely able to pay even for his journeys and inn accommodation. The Emperor Sigismund, acclaimed for a century as the ruler who finally brought the great schism to an end and convened the Council of Constance, had to pawn in Holland the silver presented to him in England in order to get to Constance at all; unable to pay his bill there, he stole secretly out of the town, leaving behind his table linen. It was still there many years later, as the chronicler of the Council complained bitterly: 'no one wanted to buy it' because it was decorated with huge, heraldic eagles.

Maximilian also disappeared quite frequently when his creditors pressed him too hard; he would go off hunting or instruct the towns which he favoured with a visit to settle his accounts. The German emperors had no capital city, the country had no centre; the Holy Roman Empire was held loosely together by nothing but a very wide network of traditional relationships. The king was crowned in Aix-la-Chapelle, elected in Frankfurt and the imperial crown jewels, without which no election was valid, were kept in Nuremberg Castle. Augsburg, however, was the commercial and financial capital and it was there that the great financiers, who controlled the elections, lived. A tenuous link bound the empire to Rome in order to justify the name 'Roman': traditionally the German king received the title emperor only on being crowned in Rome by the pope.

Germany itself had no centre and no frontiers. It would be hopeless to try and describe the utterly improbable tangle of the border territories; all we can do is take a look at some of the salient edges of the patchwork that are of significance for the history of Luther's day. Under the constitution half of Burgundy, in other words of the Netherlands, belonged to the empire; the territories bordering on France were French fiefs. The situation was so confused that even Margaret of Austria, the regent of the Netherlands, was at a loss and asked her nephew, the emperor, to explain it to her. Switzerland, too, belonged to the empire only nominally, and for all practical purposes, since Maximilian's foolish and costly war with the confederation, it no longer belonged to it at all. In the north-east a similar state of affairs existed. Prussia, the land of the Order of Teutonic Knights, was officially an 'ecclesiastical' possession of the knights of what had formerly been a devout order, with vows of chastity and enforced obedience. It had never been incorporated into the empire and, since the terrible defeat at Tannenberg, the order had been forced increasingly under the protection of the king of Poland instead of that of the emperor; eventually it became a fief. In Italy claims to fiefdom, which had originated in feudal times, were pressed or dropped according to the military situation; these claims were contested throughout Luther's lifetime. Savoy and Provence were fiefs of the empire; officially the boundary with France ran west from Verdun and Toul across the Argonne. For decades all these territories had been the subjects of campaigns, wars and quarrels; in addition to these the landscape was dotted with still smaller independent, or semi-independent, particles like the duchy of Bouillon, which the devout crusader Godfrey had been forced to mortgage to the bishop of Liège in order to defray the expenses of his Crusade; the quarrel over this possession, which had started in the eleventh century, was still going on in the sixteenth and was finally settled only by the French Revolution.

It is impossible to draw a map of this labyrinthine agglomeration. Contemporary maps dispensed entirely with boundary lines, which even in reality did not exist; there were no frontier posts, let alone the ditches, fences and walls of today. There were no imperial taxes, although Maximilian had tried to levy an impost which was not paid, and no imperial customs duty, although this too had been considered in theory. There was no army, no police force and no imperial law; there was only an imperial high court of justice, which was intended to secure peace when necessary but which, owing to lack of funds and because no one obeyed its mandates, eked out a shadowy existence. Uncertainty about the law – this again in marked contrast to other countries like England, where common law prevailed – was perhaps the greatest evil, and this was further exacerbated by the fact that the Church's canon law claimed precedence and intruded everywhere, even in secular matters. In addition there were also the old Saxon code of law, formulated in the

*Sachsenspiegel*, Roman law, which was just begining to penetrate into Germany, and the right of feud and vehmic law.

Germany had no centre but it was a central country, in size and population the greatest in Europe, with thriving towns, the foremost mining industry of the time, the most inventive arts and crafts. Printing had been invented in Mainz, and German printers had taken the new art into Italy and Spain. Nuremberg craftsmen made clocks and measuring instruments as well as the first terrestrial globes and celestial charts; the work of Copernicus was published in Nuremberg during Luther's lifetime, introduced, to Luther's annoyance, by a Protestant clergyman. German geographers processed information about the New World, giving it the name America by mistake. Its towns were the empire's glory and strength; their activities extended far beyond its indeterminate frontiers. The Hanseatic League, although its political power had already been greatly reduced, still had its outposts in London, Scandinavia and Russia, well secured enclaves with their own legal competence. The Fuggers had offices in Rome, Cracow, Antwerp and Madrid; they owned the Hungarian copper mines, the Transylvanian salt mines and the mercury mines in Almadén. The Augsburg House of Welser founded a settlement in Venezuela and had representatives in Lisbon and India. The Höchstetters, Paumgartners and, in Nuremberg, the Tuchers were scarcely less important. No German potentate had a larger sphere of influence; they quibbled over their boundaries or, in obedience to the supreme dynastic and political wisdom of the day, tried to acquire some piece of land or other by marriage. These traders, however, were 'regal merchants'. Their objective was acquisition. They had their own envoys, who were listened to with far greater attention than those of the electors. They had their own couriers, who provided a very much quicker postal service than the kings' messengers. Their news service provided the first newspapers; important business information, naturally, was reserved for office use.

On the confused map of Europe we ought to place an overlay showing the footholds, branches and outposts of these business houses, together with their roads and lines of communication; these provided a safe network of access across every obstacle set up – in the form of bonded warehouses, transit duties and toll bridges – by the towns, countries and legal systems. Order and discipline reigned only on this overlay. Accounts were kept and meticulously recorded on regular balance sheets in which debits were set off against credits – an occult science unknown to princes and emperors alike. Only here were to be found people who understood the mysteries of the five hundred different currencies and their silver content, of the two thousand local weights and measures. The superiority of these men over their contemporaries is beyond compare; not even the great financial powers of our own day can rival them.

As the great 'monopolies' the business houses were well known to Luther and his generation – the idea of monopoly was not a nineteenth-century invention. There were just as many complaints about them as about the extortions of Rome. People were utterly helpless in the face of them. Their power was bewailed by the estates in the diets; decrees were enacted and ignored. The emperor immediately intervened. He made some small use of the imperial enactments to persuade the banks to new and higher loans, and then released them from any unpleasant consequences of the decrees by creating one of the normal 'exceptions', which also formed the rule in the practice of the Curia.

The real strength of the empire lay in the cities. They were sovereign – the imperial cities being subject only to the emperor – and not accountable to any other authority. They concluded their own alliances, mounted their own campaigns, possessed their own mercenaries and their own artillery, which was often excellent; not a few of them, like Nuremberg, had control over substantial territory. They were on the worst imaginable terms with the reigning princes, whose aspirations were constantly rising; their relations with the princes of the Church were even worse. The volumes of local chronicles are full of their battles with the bishops and archbishops, and usually the towns won. Not many of the high ecclesiastical potentates who bore the title of a city – Cologne, Augsburg, Mainz or Bremen for example – could reside in it or had any voice in its affairs; they had their seats in Bonn, Aschaffenburg or Halle, in other words 'outside', and controlled their widespread official territories from there. The city councils kept a jealous watch, armed if necessary, to ensure that their city freedoms were preserved. Freedom of the cities, liberty of the princes – these were the watchwords; the freedom of the rest of the population of the Holy Roman Empire was not mentioned. Of this rest the peasants still comprised almost ninety per cent.

But inside the cities too, with their powerful city councils, their well-armed police and their strictly regulated constitutions, there were very severe tensions. The struggle between the patricians and the plebeians, between the privileged aldermanic families and the representatives of the guilds, had raged down the centuries and had generally ended in a victory, or semi-victory, for the guilds. Within these the ferment continued; even the journeymen and labourers wanted power. And still lower down were groups of highly restive elements, the 'lumpenproletariat'; often reinforced by vagabonds or discharged mercenaries, they were ready to band together at the slightest provocation, to storm, to plunder and to vanish again very quickly. They all carried weapons.

Slogans abounded, not exclusively slogans of class warfare; at any rate the clearly defined classes and strata of today may be applied only arbitrarily to the picture of those disordered times. Religious, or pseudo-religious, slogans could be just as effective as economic and material incentives. To storm a synagogue and drive out the Jews, as was done in Regensburg or Nuremberg, was no less popular than the call to evict the priests.

Ferment, unrest, feuds, war, extreme economic prosperity, world-wide connections and projects, stark poverty among the great masses of the people – this list of contrasts might be continued indefinitely. It was into this unrest that Luther's sheet of paper fell. Its effect can be understood only in the light of the historical background, and the historical realities of the day determined subsequent developments. There was rebellion everywhere. The princes and the estates were rebellious and mutinous toward the supreme head whom they had elected; the whole country was in rebellion against the 'tyranny of Rome', as the supremacy of the Church was called. The cities were in rebellion against the ruling princes and the bishops, and within the cities the plebeians were in a state of war with the patricians; the peasants were ready to rise. All the reports of the day, every parliamentary discussion, expressed a fear of the unexpected. In most cases it was a vague anxiety. Gloomy prophecies from long ago were still in circulation among the people, foretelling the approaching end of the world or the dawn of a new and juster age in which the last would be first, as Luther had quoted in his theses. Since the Council of Constance people had talked and written constantly of reform; one anonymous and widely circulated publication, strongly infused with social ideas, had even maintained naïvely that the Emperor Sigismund, one of the most untrustworthy of all the German kings, had had a programme for reform. But that was long ago; in those days 'a hundred years ago' was tantamount to 'from time immemorial'. Sigismund had grown into a splendid figure of an emperor and Dürer painted him side by side with Charlemagne, giving each a magnificent beard to signify his status as man and ruler.

Rebellion and tradition existed side by side, the desire for reform and belief in a mythical, mystical emperor who would bring order and better-ment at a single stroke. How this was to come about no one knew. No large-scale integration seemed attainable, whereas England, France and Spain were taking very definite steps to consolidate themselves into states and nations. The Hanseatic League, the greatest force of the preceding era, had disintegrated because of the egotism of the individual member cities. The Swiss Confederation, the most powerful separate group, had seceded, or been driven, from the empire. The only effective combination of any size and strength was the Swabian League in South Germany, a frequently changing federation of princes and cities with changing aims; its last role, and that a dangerous one, was in the Peasants' War, after which it dissolved. The lesser nobility dreamed of combining to form a Knights' League, but as an estate it was already completely decadent without knowing it. The peasants had inscribed their banners with the slogan 'Bundschuh', this being the peasant's leather shoe, tied at the ankle by a leather strap. No word was in such common use as Bund ('alliance'), while every tie or commitment, except among the closest associates, was rejected. Every agreement broke down before the ink on the contract was dry. Germany was exposed on every side. The unrest began long before Luther appeared on the scene and continued throughout the country.

One can also paint a different picture, and it has been done; the picture of a devout, hard-working people, living according to the amply filled calendar of saints, observing its festivals and decorating its churches magnificently. And this would be true also. It is also true that in the religious sphere, as well as in the practical and social spheres, an enormous, oppressive power was vested in tradition – however open to question this had become – an emphasis that was to make itself decisively felt in the sequel. When the struggle began wide areas, whole regions and countries, remained neutral and almost unaffected, or else temporized. In the main it was specific 'centres' of unrest that emerged as the focal points; they were often quite small places on the map. Here again the cities played the dominant role; without them the Reformation movement would very soon have come to a stop. They had been the mainstays of culture and civilization since the High Middle Ages; the minsters and cathedrals they had built were as much tokens of their civic pride as of their devoutness. One could wax lyrical over these cities, but the song would end on a sad note. None was able to assume the leadership; all were equally strong, all equally jealous of the others, all enclosed within their high walls and carefully shut off from the outside world, all equally blind to the dangers that threatened them. One after another they fell into the hands of the ruling princes. They had grown soft at the core. Their most powerful and prominent families, led by the hard-headed Fuggers and Welsers whose keen eyes had been focused on South America, Africa and the Far East, were soon looking for nothing better than to secure themselves estates, titles and small domains about the flat countryside. With the approaching bankruptcy of Charles v, whom they had financed so extravagantly, their worldwide concerns were liquidated. The various stages of the liquidation of the Holy Roman Empire lasted longer; it was finally completed under the eyes of commissioners of the French Revolution.

Along with the splendour of the imperial cities and some thousand domains directly subject to the emperor, there also vanished the ecclesiastical electorates. Mainz, which up till the end had hoped to survive, was the last to go.

We must now return to the year 1517 and Albrecht of Mainz. He had sent Luther's theses, together with a report on him, to Rome. The pope – and in this he was quite correct – considered that the vicar-general of Luther's order, as supreme head of the Augustinian friars, should deal with the matter. Tetzel, however, was a Dominican monk and an inquisitor. As soon as he saw Luther's notice he declared: 'In three weeks I shall have this heretic thrown to the flames.' He found immediate support among his fellow Dominicans. At first the ensuing conflict was regarded as a 'squabble between monks' of two rival orders, and as such was even welcomed by those unsympathetic to the orders. People laughed, jeered and waited eagerly for the outcome. This too throws an oblique, unholy light on conditions in the great, central land that bore the name Holy Roman Empire of the German Nation.

# 13

# Augustinians and Dominicans

FROM the court of the archbishop of Mainz, where he was then living and where the mendicant orders, whether Dominicans, Franciscans or Augustinians, commanded little respect, Ulrich von Hutten wrote to a friend early in 1518: 'I wonder if you have heard about it? A faction in Wittenberg in Saxony is trying to rebel against the authority of the pope; another faction is defending the papal indulgences. Monks are leading the two camps into battle. These imperturbable generals, hot-headed, vehement and frivolous, howl, bellow, shed tears and wail to heaven; others again sit down and write and run to the libraries. Theses, counter-theses, arguments, deadly articles ... I hope they succeed in killing each other off...'

Three hundred years later Lessing, in one of his youthfully fiery and irreverent early publications, also saw the affair as a squabble between monks and brought to light a report from Luther's time. According to this letter from a humanist in Antwerp to a fellow humanist in Spain – they corresponded from country to country everywhere and, like the Fuggers, had their own network of postal services and stages all over Europe – the business most probably arose out of envy and jealousy. 'The Augustinian is jealous of the Dominican, the Dominican of the Augustinian, and both are jealous of the Franciscans – what can one expect but discord of the most violent kind?' Lessing went on to quote a remark of Pope Leo x which, although unsubstantiated, is perfectly plausible: 'Brother Martin has a good head on him; it is only a squabble between monks.'

This is how the conflict in its early stages appeared to many people at the time. The Dominicans were the only ones to take it completely seriously from the start. They had already prosecuted the 'Reuchlin case' on the assumption that it was their specific responsibility, and it was not yet settled; now Luther's case was added to it and before long the whole prelude was forgotten. Tetzel had already threatened the stake. His brother Dominicans took up the cry. It became an argument between the two orders. The Dominicans, marshalling their forces, held a great conference in the university at Frankfurt on the Oder.

The Augustinians, on the other hand, were utterly despondent. Luther's prior implored him to keep silent; the Dominicans, he said, whose own record was not without its black patches, were 'already jumping for joy' because now it was the Augustinians' turn to come under suspicion of heresy. He was not thinking of Eckhart, who had been forgotten, but possibly of Savonarola, whose memory was still very much alive, and above all of the four Dominican monks who some years earlier had been sent to the stake at Bern because, allegedly, they had simulated a miracle by artificially producing the stigmata of Christ on the body of a novice. The affair had caused a great stir, and a whole series of publications, some in verse form, had carried news of it to the countries of the empire. And now, so the prior had heard, one hundred and six counter-theses attacking Luther had been drawn up by the great Dominican convention at Frankfurt on the Oder. Nor did they stop at this academic gesture. The convention decided to denounce Luther formally in Rome as a heretic; this was a much more dangerous move than that of the archbishop of Mainz. In Frankfurt they announced from the pulpit that within a few weeks Luther would go to the stake, and this again was of considerably greater significance than the private statements made by Tetzel. The affair progressed from week to week and Luther was forced to grapple with the problem.

He was not nervous but, or so he said later, he still felt as if he were 'blinded'. He did not receive much help from those round him. The university professors were careful to keep their distance from him and regretted that their university had been drawn into the conflict. A clergyman in Hamburg was reported to have said: 'You speak the truth, good Brother Martin, but you will accomplish nothing. Go to your cell and say, "God have mercy on me".' He had to wait for the first friendly, or enthusiastic, echo to come from a great distance. Largely because he felt so misunderstood, Luther added explanatory notes to his ninety-five theses. Here again he acted very correctly, sending them to the bishop of Brandenburg, his ecclesiastical superior, with the request that he correct and delete whatever he found objectionable or else annul the whole document. 'Nothing is so difficult,' he declared, 'as to establish what the true teaching of the Church is,' adding that he knew what a grievous sinner he was; in his letter he emphasized once more his loyalty to the pope. But Luther himself now advanced week by week, going beyond the views expressed in his theses; he became more and more doubtful about indulgences and about the sovereign power of the pope. He boldly described as a 'hellish invention', and a late one at that, the medieval doctrine of the 'two swords', the pope's and the emperor's, from which the Curia had developed the claim that the pope had the right of supreme jurisdiction over all countries and kingdoms; this doctrine did not exist in earlier times, he said, and the Greek Church had never submitted to it – a point he was soon to take up and defend. He also referred to the practice of burning heretics: he could find nothing on the subject in his Bible, either in Paul or the Gospels.

All Luther's early writings are volcanic: they have a soft crust overlaid with his protestations of loyalty to the Church, which undoubtedly were sincere; underneath the lava glows, ready at any moment to burst forth. Quite unconsciously he was supplying the Dominicans with wood for their stake which, at the moment, was surrounded only by a little rather wet kindling. Up till now he had stated his views in Latin, in 'opinions' intended as subjects for debate; all at once he wrote in German a sermon 'On Indulgences and Grace'. It was this little volume that made the first really widespread impact. More than twenty different editions have been identified, an unbelievably high number when one considers how few people could read and how laborious book distribution was, the books having to be transported from place to place in wooden kegs either on horseback or in carts; added to this was the constant threat of local censorship, tax laws and staple laws. Luther, incidentally, received no honorarium either for this or for any other of his works. As a monk he also received no academic salary; his order had lent him to the elector. On several occasions he even had to ask humbly for the new habit that had been promised him; the superfluous expense was repeatedly refused by Pfeffinger, one of the electoral councillors, until finally Luther's patrons at court bestirred themselves and had the black gown sent to him. It was in truth a beggarly monk who now joined battle with a world power of unlimited resources.

In this booklet Luther addressed himself not to the scholars but to the people. He spoke concisely and compellingly in twenty articles – 'firstly, secondly' – and, as though overnight, the language obeyed him. So they wanted to label him a heretic? 'Well and good, but I don't pay much attention to such bawling.' They were only 'obscured minds, who have never smelt the Bible, never read the Christian teaching, never understood their own teachers'; they put forward only their own 'torn and tattered opinions.' They were 'new teachers' who had introduced new teachings and these teachings were false. Indulgences came of evil; let those who wanted them make use of them, but they were only for the 'lazy and sleepy Christians'. It was much better to give to those in need, to care for one's fellow beings, for one's own neighbours; and if anything were left over – which was quite possible if such were God's will – it might be contributed to the pope in far-off Rome, to help in the building of the new St Peter's, or 'some other place'. Everyone

159

understood this, including the 'other place', since there was very general doubt whether the money would actually be used for St Peter's. 'If anyone tells you anything different, he is misleading you or looking for your soul in your purse, and should he find a penny in it he will rejoice more than over any soul.' This was the voice people wanted to hear. Luther had become the nation's spokesman, and the language he used had never been heard before. No one noticed, however, that he was concerned with other things than the penny in the purse.

The bishop of Brandenburg, for his part, overlooked phrases in Luther's exegesis of his theses that were genuinely dangerous. Luther's ignorance of all worldly matters has been stressed; but the ignorance of high Church dignitaries of the time in matters concerning their office and theology is truly astonishing. The Hohenzollern prince in Mainz had paid scant attention to the theses of the impudent monk; the bishop of Brandenburg, Schulze by name, simply did not read the material Luther had sent him and asked him to correct. At first he remarked pleasantly and candidly that he had no time to give to the document. Then he sent an abbot from the monastery at Lehnin to Luther with a gracious letter in his own handwriting: there was nothing uncatholic in Luther's work; he, too, found the activities of the preachers on indulgences 'immodest'. The best thing now would be to keep silent. Clearly he thought the storm would soon blow over. Moreover Bishop Schulze, a lawyer and administrator, presumably did not want to add fuel to the tension between Brandenburg and Saxony. A few weeks later he even gave Luther permission to print his two works – the German sermon and the Latin exegisis of his theses. Luther did so, thinking that this would be the end of the matter; he was longing to devote himself in peace to his further studies. He had become increasingly involved in the study of ecclesiastical law and Church history, and in the investigation of the antecedents of the indulgence traffic.

He was allowed no time for this. The 'bawling' he so airily thought he had put an end to continued. The counter-theses of his opponents now also appeared in print and were dispatched in a thick bale to Wittenberg. The students, regarding them as an arrogant attack on the honour of Wittenberg University, burned them in the market place. Luther was far from pleased; he disapproved of the proceedings and preached a sermon on the subject. He wanted to keep silent, true to the promise he had given the bishop.

But the Dominicans had no intention of keeping silent. They received support from a great scholar, the celebrated Dr Eck, professor at Ingolstadt, who became Luther's chief opponent. The matter was now seen as a dispute between Eck and Luther instead of as an argument between two religious orders. There is a pettiness about this which runs counter to our notions of great historical events or of a struggle between great spiritual movements; nevertheless, the attitude prevailed, down to the details of the proceedings against Luther. It was Eck who pursued the case with furious energy when it showed signs of flagging; it was Eck who brought it to trial and prolonged it for years and decades. Like Luther he was a fighter by nature and both men used the same crude weapons; it can hardly be said, however, that Eck was motivated by passionate struggles over questions of conscience. Only at the end of his life, resigned and also disillusioned by the Church he had served so zealously with endless pen-feuds and missions, did he withdraw and work as pastor of his flock in Ingolstadt, coming close to obeying Luther's admonition that a man should do good to those nearest to him.

But this was still far ahead in the future. Eck, like Luther, came of peasant stock; he was tall, powerfully built, thick-set, had a loud voice and was blessed with an excellent memory, which in disputations enabled him to defeat all his opponents with quotations from the most obscure authorities. His knowledge was always textbook knowledge, based on prescribed reading; one can only be astounded by what he claims to have read before he 'finished' at the age of twelve, a prodigy like Melanchthon, and went to the university. In his reminiscences he begins his list with Cato, the censor, going on to say that he has also read Seneca, Isidore's five books on dialectic, together with the canon law, the greatest authority of all, and the commentaries to it; the decretals he had 'learned by heart in alphabetical order' and quoted constantly to the discomfiture of those who did not have them on the tips of their tongues. He even claims to have studied the work of the Augustinian Trionfo on the power of the pope; the most fantastic of all the books of its kind, it asserts that the position of the Holy Father is not merely similar but equal to that of God. All this Eck had assimilated by the time he was ten or eleven; at fifteen he had taken his master's degree, having by then absorbed scholasticism in its entirety. He matured young and never developed further. For a time he joined the humanists, whose star was rising, and then came down firmly on the side of authority. He was now able to satisfy his overweening ambition: he could appear as the confidant of cardinals, he was the great Eck, the useful Eck, his name was on everyone's lips. He became indispensable.

He was the only one who, as a writer, kept pace in some degree with the indefatigable Luther. But his writing was dry and didactic, and he never succeeded in writing a phrase that caught fire; his volumes, most of them thick, remained unread and unsold. Because of his bluntness he was not popular even with his own side; the cardinals, annoyed by his persistent begging for benefices, fobbed him off with a few modest livings. His opponents, using one of the indispensable weapons of the day, slandered him as a whoremonger and drunkard; one of his former humanist friends maliciously published a Latin elegy on the death of the 'best of Doctor Eck's concubines'. A Nuremberg pamphlet, which caused a great deal of amusement, ridiculed him as *Eckius Dedolatus*, the corner (*Eck*) from which the rough edges had been planed off. None of this disturbed him much. He continued to drink happily and the city councils sent him complimentary presents of wine as well. Later he declared that he was now repenting the sins of his youth, and that was that. His recipe for attack was simple: 'Catch the foxes while they are young', eradicate every trace of heresy in the bud, and 'this devil can only be driven out by pain and torture'. He was that most terrible of all zealots, the eternal schoolmaster, and said proudly of himself: 'I intend to remain a schoolmaster all my life.' His great sorrow was that people did not pay sufficient attention to him, either at home or in Rome. His proposals for organizing an effective defence against the growing inroads of heresy were made in vain. He saw, quite rightly, that the arguments were too weak, the theological basis too sketchy. The pope should appoint dynamic nuncios, and give them as assistants energetic men of great knowledge who were well informed about Germany. Such men were rare birds, he admitted with concern; in the whole of his Bavarian homeland he knew perhaps three – among whom, presumably, he counted himself. Even the reformers' most biting criticism cannot vie with the unintentional and annihilating disclosures of his memoranda to the Curia.

In these this unsympathetic man appears as a limited, though honest, warrior dealing out blows indiscriminately. The bishops in particular fascinated him. Luther had accused them of being asleep. Eck went into details. Why did they tolerate their priests having concubines? Why did they even accept payment for this tolerance? Why did they not exercise their functions instead of leaving them to miserable, underpaid deputies who then proceeded to sell the means of grace to the poor people, this also on instructions from their superiors (the price for adultery was four guilders, if between married people six, and fornication with a nun cost ten guilders)? He aimed his blows further afield, too, and thundered against Rome: the abuse of Church livings, the reckless intervention in secular jurisdiction. It sounds like the voice of Luther. But it is the voice of Dr Eck. Works of spiritual penance had been scandalously exchanged for cash payments – a practice that went back to the eighth century as the doctor, well versed in ecclesiastical history, was aware; this was a practice unknown to the Early Church, it was 'the work of man', and so, instead of cures for the soul, all that remained in the papal penitentiary was gold and silver. Church offices were sold to people who knew as much about the Bible and theology as a donkey about singing. The great offenders, the usurers and the sodomites, went free, but poor little devils who could not pay their tribute were excommunicated. And how was Mass said in Rome? The father confessors were interested only in the dues, and disposed of the penitents as quickly as possible, so that large numbers could be dealt with. Luther told the same story of his experiences in Rome. On whom were the great favours bestowed? On foreigners and immature young boys. 'The ground ought to open and swallow up these merchant souls.' There is something eerie about the way in which Eck propounded almost word for word the very theses for which, without a scruple in the world, he wanted to see Luther and his followers burned.

He was orthodox only in expecting all salvation to come from the pope – all, that is, apart from the speedy application of pain and torture, or strict censorship exercised by an enlightened board of professors. Just as the Germans hoped for a good emperor, he hoped for a good, strict and wise pope; he would have to set about him with a rod of iron. Brought up in the school of decretals since he was ten, Eck knew nothing but decrees, bulls and interdicts. His inner aridity and inadequacy are disarmingly revealed in his memoranda to the Holy See where he recommends that the papal breves should contain 'something' of the divine nature, 'something' of the Bible – 'in so far as this is possible.'

Naturally these proposals for reform were shelved in Rome. The old warrior had become superfluous and a nuisance. It is to his credit that he did not withdraw into bitterness, but set to work looking after his small parish. From his hated opponent he had learnt that preaching must not be neglected, so he preached tirelessly, as few others have done, and carefully recorded his sermons in a parish register that still exists. These sermons, it is to be feared, must have been as dry as his writings.

The latter were menacing enough to Luther when the battle began; but later he spoke almost pleasantly of Eck: 'He kept me on my toes.' Heretics were useful, he quoted, and called his Bible to witness. Eck ought really to have been pope; 'apart from him they haven't anybody.'

When Luther joked like this he had grown old and heavy. Eck's first arrows struck a monk who was still brooding and far from sure of himself; among them were some very well-aimed shots. With a sure eye Eck had seen that there were no real prospects in a discussion on the extremely unpopular indulgence question and its still unelucidated dogmatic assumptions. He switched it to the subject of papal authority, which Luther had attacked. Making use of his excellent memory, and a knowledge of papal decretals far superior to Luther's, he cited the Bull *Unigenitus*, of which we have already spoken and which Luther was forced to admit he did not know. Luther put his trust in faith, which was a matter of grace and necessarily took precedence over any sacrament; Eck quoted the papal authority of Clement VI of Avignon. This at once forced Luther into an awkward, defensive position: to dispute a papal bull was very much worse than to criticize the abuses of the indulgence system; it was tantamount to an attempt to undermine the foundations of the Church.

Eck, manœuvring very effectively, now introduced another theme into the debate: he called Luther's views 'Bohemian heresy', thus invoking the universal abhorrence of the heretic Hus and the memory – still very much alive – of the horrors of the Hussite wars, in which Saxony had suffered particularly severely. This stirred up political resentments, because during the twenty years of those wars the Germans had been defeated again and again. They had been put to flight by the Bohemian armies under their great commander Ziska and the no less remarkable Prokop; they had taken to their heels – and this was something no one wanted to be reminded of – at the mere sound of the approaching Bohemians' fearful battle song, with its opening line 'warriors we of God' and the closing shout 'Kill, kill, kill, kill them every man!' The children, and their children after them, told the tale of the blind Ziska who, with closed eyes, led his people from victory to victory and, when he lay dying, ordered his skin to be stretched across a drum so that he should still lead them. The Hussites had penetrated deep into Germany; they had besieged Magdeburg, and one troop had reconnoitred as far north as Bremen. They had threatened to pillage the whole of the Rhineland, and many towns had bought immunity only at the cost of crippling payments; in parts of Saxony there were still deserted villages which they had burned down. What had been forgotten were the causes of these wars, the perfidy of the emperor, who had promised Hus safe conduct, the provocations of the Crusaders, who, flourishing their banners, had marched into Bohemia under the image of the Blessed Virgin, vowed to exterminate the heretics lock, stock and barrel, and, just as ruthless as their opponents, had plundered and killed the anti-heretics as well as their Hussite enemies. That the crown of Bohemia had been considered one of the most glittering jewels of the Holy Roman Empire, and still had a decisive voice in the electoral Council which elected the emperors, had become almost entirely forgotten. 'Bohemian' was synonymous with 'national enemy'; the mere word struck terror into German hearts.

No other accusation was as dangerous as this, which Eck was the first to advance. No other did Luther so much harm or caused him such anxiety; in the end he was driven by Eck to an attitude of defiant revolt, declaring himself a supporter of Hus. In this way he was prodded and pushed until it may be said that step by step he was manœuvred out of the Church, Eck proving himself a more skilful tactician than the Dominican. Eck opened his campaign against the Bohemian Luther with petty skirmishing. He committed his sharply barbed innuendoes to paper under the title *Obelisks*, the name given to marginal marks on manuscript pages indicating questionable passages. After long hesitation Luther answered with *Asterisks*, another symbol for marginal comments. His real wish was to swallow and digest this 'offal' in silence and apply himself to his study of ecclesiastical law, of which, as we have seen, he was still fairly ignorant. But his friends were pressing him: something had to be done to save the honour of Wittenberg and Saxony. The quarrel was still between religious orders, an academic argument.

The Augustinians too held a big convention, in Heidelberg, at which Luther was to be presented. Staupitz expressly assigned him the leading role in the scholarly disputations, without which such an occasion was unthinkable. Once again Luther set off on foot; the journey was not without its dangers, because the cry of heretic had already stirred up large areas. Luther was warned that his enemies might seize him and deliver him to Rome; the elector was doubtful about the undertaking, and gave him ample letters of introduction. The journey was Luther's first triumph before a wider public. It also did him good physically and he came back looking fitter and stronger. In Heidelberg the first supporters from the more distant parts of Germany rallied to Luther; some of them were later to play significant roles. Among them were also members of other orders, including even Dominicans. He was looked upon as the man of the younger generation; the older professors, including his former Erfurt teachers, were less seduced by his arguments, which once more, and for the last time, were directed against philosophic doctrines and the 'rank' Aristotle. There was no mention in the public discussions of the current dispute over indulgences, though there must have been talk in private. Conventions of this kind were also social occasions, and Luther wrote home to his friend Spalatin that 1518 had been a particularly good year for wine. People became aware of his gift for graphic and striking table-talk. His young listeners wrote enthusiastic letters from Heidelberg to all and sundry praising the 'delightful exchange of ideas'. Luther's sharply cut, almost emaciated head made an impression, as did his passion and fire; but people were also struck by his trenchancy and quick repartee, as well as by his assurance in quoting the Bible, still a comparatively rare accomplishment. Perhaps an even greater impression was made by his warm, sincere approach; it was evident that he expected nothing in return, as the humanists did, and was also quite prepared to attack his friends if he thought it necessary. Luther always had the gift of winning enthusiastic friends and supporters; many of them he lost again, and cursed roundly. As yet, alignments were still vague and 'undogmatic', depending entirely on personal impressions. These, however, were strong. The rudiments of a Luther party were formed in Heidelberg. Luther had been notorious; he now became famous.

The battle continued, and this time it was Luther who took a new, bold step forward. There was already talk of his excommunication, although no decision could yet have been made in Rome. Luther returned from Heidelberg so strengthened and in such high spirits that he wrote scoffingly to a friend, as though he had already been condemned: 'The more these people threaten me the more confident I feel. I have already provided for my wife and child and assigned my land, home and possessions; my name and reputation have already been torn to shreds. All I have left is my wretched, frail body. Let them have it, at the most it will shorten my life by an hour or two; they cannot rob me of my soul.' Whoever took it upon himself to proclaim the Word, he said, had to reckon on persecution and death. Then he added: 'A short while ago I preached a sermon to the people on excommunication and its virtues. I rebuked the tyranny and ignorance of the whole filthy pack of officials, commissioners and vicars. Everyone was aghast, they had never heard anything like it; now they are all waiting to see what evil will befall me as a result. I have lit a new fire, but this is what happens with the word of truth.'

A new fire and a burning new problem. Luther did not proceed by reason but by unerring instinct: together with indulgences, the use of excommunication was one of the most universally deplored scandals. Fear of it was much greater than fear of purgatory – with which most people felt they would somehow be able to cope – because it impinged directly on life. This weapon of the Church, once reserved for great and important cases, now threatened everyone from the richest to the poorest, the poor much more than the great. Excommunication was no longer a solemn anathema issued from the summit and flung at emperors, kings and great heretical figures; in the wake of the ever-increasing bureaucracy in the administration of Church finances, it had become an easy and very widely applied means of tax enforcement. Simple people who did not pay their tithes promptly were excommunicated. Abbots, bishops and archbishops who were in arrears with payments for confirmation in office by the Curia were excommunicated – even before the end of the fourteenth century several hundred such cases have been counted. Meanwhile inflation of this means of punishment had developed; abbots and bishops, as well as all the ecclesiastical bodies, excommunicated people on their own account and often for the most worldly reasons. Complaints in Luther's day were always over the same economic issues: religious foundations and monasteries were selling goods, beer and wine free of duty; convents were selling fabrics. If a town council intervened, or attempted to exact dues, it was excommunicated; if it did not desist, the town was placed under an interdict forbidding all church rites and observances.

Excommunication was classified so that it applied in the first instance to the individual, in the second – following continued refusal to pay or non-compliance – to his family, and in the third to his fellow citizens. With the development of canon law and its intrusion into numerous aspects of daily life, the original punishment of exclusion from the community of the faithful by refusal of the sacraments had been extended to include a ban on all business transactions with the excommunicated person, as well as exclusion from marriage and burial. The practice had taken on such proportions that in the autumn, when payments were due, a whole series of excommunication dates came to be established. Crowds of excommunicated persons, who had lost house and home, then went round begging. The total lack of consideration with which payment was extorted often led to people being murdered, as Luther pointed out in his sermon. At the same time he praised the secular authorities, who refused to countenance such a misuse of the Church's anathema in territories under their jurisdiction. The problem was keenly debated. The demands of the two sides grew and clashed constantly. Excommunication, like indulgences, had become a social, economic and political question. For the second time Luther had raised a controversial issue.

Here also, as in everything else, he did not speak only of abuses and economic problems; he approached the problem from the standpoint of his newly won articles of faith. By being refused communion a man could be excluded from the community of the faithful but not from his inner communion with God: 'No man, no bishop, pope, nor even an angel can give or take away this communion'; no excommunication could do that. Only after making this point did Luther turn to the outward, 'physical' excommunication. This was an old practice, he said, but had been so extended that it now also forbade 'burial, purchases, sales, commercial activities and all manner of human intercourse, and finally also, as they say, water and fire'. Even this did not satisfy the excommunicators, so they also harnessed the temporal forces of sword, fire and war against those they excommunicated; all of which was contrary to the tenor of the Holy Scriptures and not proper to the spiritual estate. And to go so far as 'to excommunicate for money, or some other temporal end, is a new invention.' The Apostles and Christ knew nothing of this. Luther's 'discovery', from which his early writings drew their power, was that he constantly referred to the simple phrases of the Bible and ignored entirely the whole complex structure that had been built on it. Everyone understood what he said and everyone naturally inferred from it something different. The secular authorities were delighted when he acknowledged their right to intervene. The poor pricked up their ears when he said that the 'big fellows', the usurers, were left in peace and only the little men were made to suffer, for debts which were often so small 'that the letters and expenses involve a much greater sum than the debt itself.' The Church authorities understood his meaning perfectly when he fulminated that excommunication 'harmed and endangered no one more than those who imposed it.' Might they not be more guilty before God than hundreds of those they had excommunicated?

Before he himself was excommunicated there now began an extremely unsavoury interlude of spying, eavesdropping and all the usual apparatus of denunciation. As he was soon to discover, there had already been 'abominable spies' among the congregation when he delivered his sermon; they had taken it down and sent in reports – of varying accuracy – on these new and dangerous theses. On another occasion, when Luther preached in Dresden, he received an invitation to visit Emser, the court chaplain, in the evening; a monk of Tetzel's order stood behind the door while a Leipzig master of arts tried to involve Luther in a heated discussion about what he was supposed to have said in Wittenberg. Reports were sent to Cajetan, the papal legate, who was attending the diet in Augsburg; he forwarded them to Rome, with an accompanying letter from the emperor requesting that Luther's excommunication be announced with all possible speed. Whether the emperor had ever read any of Luther's authentic writings is very doubtful; he was already in poor health, in a nervous state because of the failure of his latest grand designs, as carelessly planned as his earlier ones, and in the midst of difficult negotiations with his refractory estates. It is likely that the main reason for his taking this step was to underline his new and somewhat unexpected policy of close co-operation with the Curia. His letter, however, made a great impression. The papal auditor now declared the case opened: Luther was denounced as a notorious heretic. Pope Leo x sent a brief to Cardinal Cajetan: Luther was to be taken into custody and carefully guarded until further orders. A second letter was sent to the elector of Saxony demanding Luther's extradition; a third went to the vicar-general of Luther's order who was instructed to send a delegate and have the heretic seized and duly bound hand and foot. The whole clumsy machinery for bringing a heretic to trial was set in motion, great care being taken to ensure that the correct procedure was observed.

So far only one denunciation had been preferred; it had been made the subject of a preliminary enquiry. A report was to be submitted on the degree to which Luther's teachings were questionable. This task was entrusted to the Curia's specialist on doctrinal matters, Sylvester Mazzolini, 'Master of the Holy Palace'; known as Prierias, after his birthplace, he too was a Dominican. He was an old man of nearly seventy, author of a *Summa summarum* on the teachings of scholasticism and a handbook on questions of conscience. At least he had in front of him Luther's ninety-five theses and not merely the spy report that had sufficed for the emperor. Nevertheless, he made short work of his task, completing it in three days, as he announced proudly in his booklet which, having literary ambitions, he published at once. Mazzolini's work was not conceived as a solemn document appearing at a great moment in history; he presented the controversy in a stylized way, as a 'Dialogue on Martin Luther's Presumptuous Assertions Concerning the Papacy'. He emphasized the fact that, being an old man, he was no longer accustomed to 'sword play'; he did not attack with a foil either. He merely called Luther names – the very thing Luther himself is always accused of, except that he was much better at it. There were sneering insinuations: If the holy father had bestowed a bishopric on you, Martin, you would have found that everything was in order, wouldn't you? Luther was called out like a boy in class: Stand up! He was then made to recite his theses one after the other, each being promptly refuted by Mazzolini. The only passage of any real importance was the opening; here the position and authority of the pope, regarded both from above and from below, was explained clearly and concisely: essentially the Universal Church was represented by the Church of Rome, which in turn was represented by the cardinals and most fully by the pope, who could no more err than could the Church. Thus anyone who maintained that, in the matter of indulgences, the Church could not act as in fact it did was a heretic. In Mazzolini's opinion nothing more needed to be said; the classroom interrogation was intended only as a sort of bonus. Rarely was a pope served so cursorily or so badly in a matter that was to prove so important for the Church. This soon became clear to the more discerning members of the Curia; Mazzolini was called a 'dolt', and even Leo x, who at least had taste in matters of style, is said to have remarked: 'He would have done better to work on it for three months instead of three days.'

When Luther received the booklet he merely sighed: 'Is the thing now to come before the Pope?' He composed a reply, in gentle terms, considering his unruly nature: 'I do not propose to exchange abuse with you, My Father.' He only touched in passing on Mazzolini's insinuation about the bishopric: 'In saying this are you not judging me a little by your own views, Reverend Father?' – he was quite well aware of the methods by which people in Rome could acquire a bishopric or other benefice. For the rest Luther thought he was dealing simply with a prattler and a busybody. Clearly the pope had been inadequately informed; he even declared: 'I know that in Leo x we have the best of popes.' He called him a 'Daniel in the lions' den', who was in danger of his life, this being an allusion to the recent action against certain cardinals who had conspired to murder Leo x. Neither excommunication nor the stake had any power to frighten him so long as the execration came from 'you and those like you'; 'look for someone else whom you can frighten'. And Luther, like Mazzolini, also stressed the fact that he did not take the matter too seriously: 'You see, Reverend Father, I have given you my answer in all haste, in two days.'

Luther even considered the booklet useful – it might serve to show the Germans how they were treated in Rome; so he had Mazzolini's Dialogue reprinted in Leipzig. His faith in the pope was still unshaken. He had personally sent Leo his explanatory notes on the theses, accompanied by the most humble letter imaginable: for greater safety he was issuing this work under the pope's name 'so that all readers of good will may see how pure my sentiments are in attempting to probe the nature of the Church's power, and with what reverence I respect the papal authority.' He assumed that the holy father, like the archbishop of Mainz and the bishop of Brandenburg, had not found time to look into the matter thoroughly.

So far he had merely been served with a summons from the Curia to report personally in Rome in order to defend himself. This seemed to him risky. Wittenberg friends who were well versed in the law advised him to lodge an appeal and demand a hearing in Germany, as Reuchlin had done. This was a demand often made during political debates in the diets, a protest against Rome's claim to sovereignty in legal disputes; a German should be brought to trial only on German soil. Both Mazzolini's report and the summons, however, were merely preliminaries. The case was officially opened only after the emperor's intervention. It was Maximilian's action that led to Luther's conviction.

In its early stages Luther's case had been regarded as a dispute between the Dominicans and the Augustinians, an academic affair between rival universities. For Luther himself it was a burning question of conscience. Now the case was brought before the Curia and into the turmoil of international politics.

## 14

# Examination before Cardinal Cajetan in Augsburg

MAXIMILIAN's last public appearance was in 1518 at the Diet of Augsburg; he was old and had difficulty in maintaining his celebrated vigour through all the physical exertions of crossbow shooting, jousting and hunting. He had even taken to drinking water, a most unusual habit in a knight in those days of reckless drunkenness, and one that was remarked on with astonishment; even during meetings of the diet drinking often interrupted the proceedings for days on end. His great plans for reform had all miscarried and vanished into oblivion; if good intentions were a sign of greatness he would have to be counted among the great monarchs. When he died an old nobleman put it very succinctly: 'Great heavens, Sir! As soon as My Lord the Emperor took it into his head to reform the government, and tried to keep too close an eye on things, his plan came to grief.' The only matter to which the emperor still gave attention, with a stubbornness and persistence unusual in him, was the future of his house, of the Habsburg-Burgundian dynasty. He intended his grandson Charles, king of Spain and duke of Burgundy, to continue the line of Habsburg emperors. Only a short time previously Maximilian had offered this throne at a very high price to the Jagellon king of Hungary and to Henry VIII of England, while he himself thought of retiring to Naples as king; but this, like numerous other projects, came to nothing from lack of money, and now this election was going to cost a great deal. The election of the German emperor was an auction; the winner would be the highest bidder. The coffers of the House of Habsburg were empty. The scheme would have to be financed by the House of Fugger. But even this richest of all banking houses could not do this single-handed; a consortium was necessary. The bribes that had to be paid to the princes, their advisers and other influential persons were estimated at a round million gold florins.

The emperor stayed at the Fugger palace, the most sumptuous modern building north of the Alps; he himself had no residence to compare with it. It was here that the discussions took place which were to decide the country's future. It was also here that the 'presumptuous monk' appeared before one of the chief personages of the diet, Cardinal Cajetan, the papal legate. This, however, was only a postlude, a small but tiresome incidental matter to the lords and princes who were playing high politics with their usual wiles and stratagems.

Very high politics indeed were envisaged, involving much manœuvring; the unity of pope and emperor was to be demonstrated once more, as it had existed at the height of the Middle Ages. The almost forgotten doctrine of the two swords, the temporal sword of the emperor and the spiritual sword of the pope, was resuscitated, regardless of the disunity to which this theory had led. Only recently Maximilian, in one of his many vacillations, had inclined towards the opposition council of cardinals in Pisa which, under French influence, wanted to depose Pope Julius; second thoughts had turned him to the new Pope Leo, the Medici prince who, for his part, was considering a plan to prevent any further Habsburg succession and was negotiating with France for this purpose. For the moment these schemes had been shelved. Cardinal Cajetan was to announce the new rapprochement between the emperor and the Curia, and Maximilian proposed to use this glorious omen to announce a large imperial tax, an old plan that hitherto had always been defeated. As an attractive catchword a Crusade against the 'Turkish infidel' was contemplated, another throwback to the Middle Ages, which, it was hoped, would make an impression.

The cardinal made his appearance with great pomp. According to the Roman view a cardinal legate took precedence over 'kings of any kind.' Cajetan insisted on entering the city on a white palfrey caparisoned in purple; he also demanded that the rooms allotted to him be lined with purple satin, and then continued to make so many further demands that the emperor's master of ceremonies, accustomed though he was to protocol, was in despair. In the cathedral Cajetan celebrated a solemn High Mass, attended by the princes, temporal and spiritual. He placed the cardinal's hat on the head of Archbishop Albrecht of Mainz, whose important vote on the electoral council the Curia was anxious to win, and handed the emperor a consecrated sword, symbolic of the doctrine of the two swords. He preached with subtlety and finesse, for he was a great scholar, famous for his commentaries on Thomas Aquinas. He was also looked upon as a great politician, and his work *On the Power of the Pope* had won him the red hat at the last creation of a new college of cardinals as well as his position as vicar-general of the Dominican Order. He did not touch on the delicate problems of the day. Instead, he recalled, in a broad historical review, that the date 1 August was the anniversary of the victory at Actium which had given Augustus mastery of the world. Now, as in ancient Rome, both the temporal empire and the empire of the Church must be advanced to the frontiers of the world; the time had come for the final defeat of the infidel Turk, the enemy of Christendom – Maximilian's task was to recapture Constantinople and Jerusalem.

The emperor listened complacently. The princes and representatives of the estates reverently lowered their heads; they had no intention of allowing themselves to be confused by such grandiose prospects. A new tax to fight the Turks? Would the money really be used for this purpose? The old battle-cry was no longer convincing; it had been used too often, both by the Curia and the House of Habsburg, to further quite different plans. The Habsburg dynasty was known to have designs on Hungary and Bohemia; it had already acquired Spain and Naples, as well as the Netherlands, leaving the empire stuck in the middle. And the Curia? Had it ever contributed anything to the Turkish wars? What it was really interested in was its share of the new contributions, if they were sanctioned, which would then be added to the regular dues that flowed to Rome in the form of appointment fees or annuities; latterly these had been demanded, on threat of excommunication and interdict, not only on the appointment of bishops but from abbeys and provostships as well, and on down to individual ministers. This was the subject to be discussed first, before proceeding to the conquest of Constantinople or Jerusalem, dear as this was to every Christian.

And discussed it was, very thoroughly. The chief speaker was one of the high dignitaries of the Church in Germany, Erhard von der Mark, bishop of Liège; he belonged to the high nobility, as did his whole cathedral chapter, and was lord of a great and ancient possession sandwiched between the two territories of the House of Burgundy – the Netherlands and the Franche-Comté – and for this reason habitually coveted by the dukes of Burgundy. He nursed all manner of complaints both against this house and against Rome, which obstinately withheld from him the cardinal's hat. He now entered the arena armed with a detailed catalogue, in writing, of all the sins of the Curia; seldom had they been set out so clearly. Very different from the rather vague charges of the paltry little monk from Wittenberg, who in any case had little accurate information on the subject, the catalogue had been compiled with the expert, intimate knowledge of an eminent churchman who was fully informed on the constantly increasing charges for confirmation in Church appointments, on the special dues and perquisites of the papal chancellery and on the infringement of patronage rights. He also referred to the incessant violation of the Concordat, whose terms in any case were unfavourable to the empire, whereas by means of the Pragmatic Sanction France, as was well known, had made sure of a position of independence, in relation to the Curia, which Germans could only look upon with envy and concern. The princes and estates took delighted note of this *exposé*. The bishop did not confine himself to dry facts. He spoke of the Roman sons of Nimrod, of the great hunters who were forever chasing benefices, thinking day and night only of how they could set at nought the canon law. German money, comparable in weight to Mount Atlas, was speeding over the Alps.

This put an end to the imperial tribute under the name of the Turkish tax. There followed a string of further lively complaints about injustice, feuds, price increases within the empire, and the imperial high court of justice, which was intended to remedy the confusion but was powerless to do so because the electors claimed exemption from its decisions. Other princes failed to maintain the *Landfrieden* or public peace; the duke of Geldern was at that moment waging war in neighbouring Holland, and a good half-dozen major feuds were in progress with a few hundred villages always in flames. Complaints poured in from all sides and each prince had his own particular complaint against the House of Habsburg. The plan to put another member of this dynasty on the throne was bitterly opposed. The emperor could hardly keep track of the situation, and his advisers had a difficult time. They scurried from one prince to another and between whiles to the bankers; capitulations for the coming election were arranged and sealed, promises were made and securities demanded for them, prospects of marriage – a leading device of dynastic politics – were offered.

Cardinal Cajetan had a difficult time too. Still labouring under the delusion that the Germans were a devout, well-disposed if perhaps somewhat difficult people, he had promised himself a quick triumph. He now felt very uneasy, despite the exceptional hospitality of his hosts. To begin with he did not like the climate. Small and delicate, he was a scholar at heart and even in Augsburg continued to work on his study of Thomas Aquinas; he had just completed the 'second part of the second volume'. He froze and longed for the sun, as Dürer did when he returned from Venice. Hutten, who was attending the diet, at which he wanted to read a paper he had written, jeered at him, saying that Cajetan had threatened to excommunicate the sun if it did not make provision for some warmth in the cold of Germany. Hutten also mocked the cardinal's luxurious style of living, of which he had heard stories from the domestic staff at the Fugger palace: clothed in his purple robe and screened by an opulent curtain he would eat only off silver plates; no German dish was delicate enough for him, the bread was too coarse, the partridges too tough, the wine too acid.

We must not judge the cardinal by such attacks nor yet by Rabelais, whose Pantagruel heard Cajetan's 'bray' among the old, leather-bound volumes of scholastics in the Paris library. But quite apart from the mutual national prejudices, the contrast between the Italians and the Germans was striking and had its effect on the talks with Luther. Cajetan was the first Church dignitary of real stature with whom the monk had come face to face; there can be no doubt that he regarded Luther simply as an insignificant mendicant friar, a *fratellino* as he described him afterwards, a word that carries an implication of shabbiness. The fact that the order to which he himself belonged was officially a mendicant order – even though in practice this had long ago been forgotten – never bothered him. He was now a cardinal, one of the great figures of the Curia, and he was unquestionably annoyed that the mannerless Germans did not sufficiently accord him the precedence he claimed. The birds were not the only things he found tough; these sly, stubborn princes, for ever grumbling about Rome and then cringing again, incapable of reaching any decisions except to obstruct every move, were just as bad. The crude excesses of their shouting, tippling and gorging revolted him; for him they were literally barbarians, Goths.

Cajetan's career had been a story of rapid advance, achieved as a result of elegantly conducted arguments with the Italian humanists. He had engaged in a theological joust with the celebrated Platonist and scholar of Hebrew, Pico della Mirandola, and defeated the pseudo-philosopher, the dangerous Pomponazzi, whose speculations had brought him to the point where he wanted to deny the immortality of the soul; at the Lateran Council he had been responsible for having such teachings condemned as the 'Arabian influence' of Averroës. He had been born in Gaeta, as Tommaso de Vio, in the same year in which his order had made Thomas Aquinas a general teacher of the church. Starting his career in the order as the 'man from Gaeta', or Cajetanus, he invested Thomism, which had long since faded into the background, with new life by his great commentaries. He was a staunch advocate of strict hierarchic thinking and the supreme authority of the pope – proving himself here a true follower of Thomas Aquinas – and it was a work on this subject that recommended him so warmly to the Curia. Fully aware of the shortcomings of the system, and by no means uncritical, he was also fully alive to the possibility that one day there might be a bad pope. Under these circumstances, he declared, the Church, which was bound to slavish obedience, could only pray faithfully that things might improve. Later he issued a warning saying that the Church 'had taken leave of its senses', had sunk into the depths of ignorance, and that its profligacy was an offence even to the Turks. After the great catastrophe of 1527, when Rome was sacked by the troops of Charles v, an event which to many seemed to herald the end of the world or at least of the papacy, he admitted frankly: 'We should have been the salt of the earth, but we had sunk so low that we cared for nothing but outward ceremony and external well-being.' It is useless to speculate on what would have happened if he had spoken so discerningly to Luther or if the talks had been conducted by a more understanding dignitary of the Church. History recognizes only the 'right moment'.

The reason Luther had been summoned to Augsburg to justify himself before Cajetan, however, was not the Church's need for reform. The voice of the elector of Saxony in the forthcoming election of the emperor had suddenly become of prime importance to the Curia. Rome wanted at all costs to prevent the election of Charles, the Habsburg candidate. Saxony was not to be antagonized. For this reason the indictment for heresy, which had been so hurriedly set in motion, was at first allowed to fall into abeyance. Maximilian, as ever constantly changing his position, but also counting on the elector of Saxony's vote to implement his plans, suddenly decided that the monk could be a useful card to play against Rome. So he wrote to his dear cousin of Saxony urging him to shield the man carefully from danger, 'we may need him one day.'

The dangers, which the emperor himself had provoked by his letter to Rome, were not inconsiderable. To lay hold of a heretic, even before the official excommunication had been promulgated, was the right and God-fearing thing to do and a man's bounden duty; Luther had already been summoned to Rome and had not complied. He was very doubtful if he could remain in Wittenberg; the elector, who had also been wavering, remained strictly aloof. Spalatin, the elector's secretary and court chaplain, tried to get the emperor's safe conduct for Luther's journey to Augsburg; Maximilian, unreliable as ever, refused. Only when the cardinal himself declared that as legate he had full authority to assume responsibility on the pope's behalf did Luther's friends feel sufficiently reassured to let Luther set out.

On this occasion Luther's journey – he was accompanied only by another Augustinian monk – was not the cheerful affair his trip to Heidelberg had been. The elector had already left Augsburg and their paths crossed; Frederick the Wise, however, thought it wiser not to meet his professor and merely sent Luther twenty guilders for his journey when he stopped at Weimar. The monks in the Augustinian monasteries where Luther stayed warned him: 'They will burn you. Turn back.' His friend Link, now prior of the Augustinian monastery at Nuremberg, shocked at Luther's down-at-heel appearance, gave him a better habit so that at least he could present a decent appearance before the cardinal, and accompanied him to Augsburg. Luther contracted gastric cramp and some miles outside the city had to be put in a carriage. He continued to brood. No other of his many journeys had been made in such a gloomy mood; never before had he found the going so hard. The symptoms of his illness were simply the result of his state of mind; he sensed that he was now faced with the decision: could he remain in the

Frederick the Wise of Saxony and his brother John

Church or would he have to break away from it? Of the web of high-level political intrigues enveloping him he was completely unaware.

Nor did he know that his position was a great deal more precarious than he had been given to understand in Wittenberg. Since arriving in Augsburg the cardinal had received new instructions from Rome – the Curia's instructions were constantly superseded by new ones: the heretic was to be brought before the cardinal and made to recant; should he refuse, he was to be taken into custody and sent to Rome. All who shielded or protected him were to be threatened with excommunication and interdict; all authorities were to arrest him at once should he fail to appear. Cajetan could only shake his head over the conflicting orders from Rome. It was obvious that the people there were quite inadequately informed of the mood in Germany. To threaten whole towns with interdict was no way to improve it.

Cajetan intended to solve the ticklish problem by diplomacy. Being also a conscientious scholar, however, he made his preparations, noting down some ideas on the indulgence question which, as a distinguished theologian, he admitted was still in need of clarification and which he had already discussed in a tract the previous year. In a number of passages his phrasing was near Luther's but for him the deciding factor was the voice of authority: Clement vi had spoken in the Bull *Unigenitus*; this was no theologian's 'opinion', it was dogma and everyone had to accept it.

Luther put up at the Carmelite monastery where he had many visitors, among them his elector's advisers, who were still in Augsburg; he was not allowed to show himself in the streets. Eventually the advisers secured him a safe conduct; faced by this disagreeable problem Maximilian had done what he had done before on similar occasions – he had made himself scarce and gone hunting. Before starting his examination of Luther, the cardinal sent an Italian diplomat to the monk; his name was de Serralonga, and he was the envoy of one of the numerous Italian princes who also had interests to pursue at meetings of the diet.

From his own point of view de Serralonga's proposals were 'very sound', Luther told Spalatin in a letter written that same evening: simply agree with the legate, obey the Church and recant; the little word *revoco* had only six letters and was easy to say. Luther pointed out that he must justify the statements he had made. De Serralonga: Do you want to engage the cardinal in a jousting match? (He quoted an example from history: a few centuries earlier the abbot Joachim de Fiore had stirred up the Franciscans with his wild prophecies, which were still in circulation; he was certainly a heretic, but he recanted and that settled the matter.) As regards indulgences, it is surely a trifling matter if the preachers sometimes say things that are not true but nevertheless fill the coffers; such a thing might well be allowed to happen in a good cause. Luther: No. De Serralonga: Do you want to dispute the pope's authority? Ho! ho! Do you want to joust with him? Do you imagine that your elector will take up arms on your behalf? Luther: Hardly. De Serralonga: Where will you go then? Luther: Somewhere under heaven ...

The diplomat took his leave. Luther wrote that he had shown the tempter the door; but he added: 'I am now suspended between hope and fear.'

On 12 October Luther, accompanied by his friend Link, his host the Carmelite prior and some other monks, set out for the Fugger palace. He had been given precise instructions on how to behave in the presence of so eminent a man as the cardinal legate. He prostrated himself in the required manner; when the cardinal motioned him to rise Luther rose to his knees, but stood up only on receiving a further sign. He apologized for keeping the cardinal waiting, but the safe conduct had not been issued in time; he was convinced he would hear nothing but the truth from the cardinal.

Cajetan, surrounded by a whole group of his Italian courtiers, was gracious and addressed Luther as his 'dear son'. He was quite determined to settle the matter with due decorum and show himself a fatherly superior. He even complimented Luther on his scholarship and his gratifying activity as teacher and lecturer in Wittenberg. Then he came to the point. He had three demands to make: firstly, Luther must recant his errors; secondly, he must give an assurance not to continue such teaching; thirdly, he must undertake not to disturb the peace of the Church again. These, he said, were the demands contained in the pope's brief. Luther asked to see the letter. Cajetan refused; the letter actually said something quite different, and to have produced it would only have made the talks more difficult. Luther then asked which of his errors he was to recant. Cajetan, who had studied Luther's theses carefully, cited two: the one about the Church's treasure, adequately refuted by the Bull *Unigenitus*, and the far more important one – decisive at least for Luther – that justification was achieved not through the sacraments but by faith. This is a new doctrine, my son, Cajetan declared, and therefore false.

Luther had already made the contrast between 'new' and 'old' doctrine a leading point in his writings, and he now had to defend it before the legate; he had described everything he could not find in the Bible as 'new doctrine', regarding it as the work of man, an addition of later times. This was the core of the subsequent discussion: 'I prefer the passages from the Scriptures which I quote in my theses,' Luther stated. Cajetan, still in fatherly fashion, explained to him that the pope was the authority one had to follow; the pope was above the Scriptures and above the Councils too – as witness Pope Nicholas v's condemnation of the Council of Basle. Cajetan not unjustly sensed in Luther the nominalist and adherent of the dangerous conciliar theory (according to which the General Council was the highest authority of the Church, superior even to the pope), which was still current; the great Paris theologian Jean Gerson had won a victory for this theory at the Council of Constance, and he still enjoyed a high reputation. Cajetan told Luther to his face: 'You are a Gersonist, my son, and all Gerson's followers are condemned along with him.' This was not quite true, because the Church had been careful not to pronounce such a verdict. Cajetan spoke as a Thomist, as the champion of a teaching he had just re-established. Where was the examination leading? The scholar in Cajetan allowed himself to be carried away. Luther, too, now became the academic opponent and ventured to draw the eminent cardinal's attention to the fact that Paris, Gerson's old university, had quite recently made an explicit request for a General Church Council. 'And the Parisians will have to answer for it,' Cajetan replied irritably. It was obvious that he was getting impatient. He had not summoned this insignificant monk to a disputation. Luther observed that the Italians in the cardinal's entourage sniggered derisively every time he quoted the Bible as his witness; they were certainly not well disposed towards this monk who was creating such unexpected difficulties, who drew himself up higher and higher, spoke louder and louder and showed no trace of deference. The diplomat de Serralonga tried to enter the debate, but the cardinal waved him aside. He was intent on settling the matter not only diplomatically but as a great scholar, the superior of this upstart Wittenberg lecturer. Moreover, he was undeniably speaking from deep conviction. Conviction opposed conviction. Luther took his stand on faith, as the only means to grace, not on the sacraments. Cajetan, on the other hand, argued: did a communicant receiving the sacrament know if he had the true and full faith? Was he not necessarily uncertain and doubtful whether he would attain grace or not? Only the Church could save him from these doubts; salvation lay in its objective authority, represented by the sacraments, and not in the soul of the individual, which was always subject to error. On this point agreement was impossible; Luther had put this doubt behind him.

But in his writings he had also expressly stated that he was prepared to submit unconditionally to the pope's authority. The cardinal, certain of his ground here, kept on confronting Luther with papal decretals he could not dispute. Paternally, forcefully, and finally sternly Cajetan stressed the question: 'Do you or do you not believe? Recant, acknowledge your errors; this and nothing else is what the pope desires you to do.' Luther replied that he certainly believed, subject to what the Bible said. Cajetan threw his proviso back at him; it was the pope who interpreted the Bible.

The discussion, often degenerating into excited exchanges and therefore unlikely to have been very accurately reported in the accounts of the participants, ended in stalemate. Luther heard only the command: recant. He asked for time to think it over. This Cajetan generously conceded. He detected uncertainty in the monk's request, and willingness to comply. In the course of the talks the shrewd theologian and experienced canonist had also been struck by an extremely awkward point, which clearly had been overlooked in Rome where things were done hurriedly and erratically: the indulgence had never been established authoritatively as a dogma at the highest level. This would have to be remedied without delay. The monk was actually on quite firm ground in constantly reiterating that there was room for an exchange of 'opinions' on the subject; this ground must now be taken from under his feet. At the moment the important thing to do was to stress the pope's authority. This the monk made no attempt to deny. He would give way, as many others had done before him.

The hearing continued for several more days. Luther had to confer with the elector's councillors and with his friends. To his great relief his 'father' Staupitz turned up in Augsburg; influential people in the city took up his cause. The diet was already as good as over, but the debates had had an effect. When high prelates of the Church like the bishop of Liège spoke so openly against Rome, and when the estates without exception protested against the constant interference of the Church in matters under their jurisdiction and against excommunication and interdict, the 'Luther case' could no longer be treated simply as a squabble between monks. The theologians could argue over dogmatic details to their hearts' content, the point at issue was whether Rome had the right to subpoena, condemn and perhaps burn a man and to do so, moreover, in a matter over which everyone was worked up and indignant. Luther no longer felt alone; he was now aware not merely from letters and reports, but intimately and personally, of the great current that was to bear him forward.

He was in great need of encouragement. His doubts persisted. He did not want to break with the Church. He still believed that the pope was simply ill-informed and that once he was in a better position to judge he would acknowledge Luther to be right and call to order those who trafficked in indulgences. Subsequently he often declared that had this happened he would have retired to his cell, his mind at rest. No one can be certain about this. What we may take as certain, however, is that the final decision was made before Cajetan in Augsburg and not three years later in Worms, when Luther was sure of his ground and the possibility of retreat no longer existed for him.

He was advised at length but with great caution. Even Staupitz, with his conciliatory nature and experience gained in many missions, sought a way out. He loved his son Martin and admired him for his daring, a quality he himself lacked. In any case he released him from his vows of obedience to his superiors in the order. It is possible that he did this in order to be able to intervene more effectively on Luther's behalf 'from outside'; this at any rate is the kindest interpretation. Luther composed a written protest and appeared once more before the cardinal, this time with a larger group of supporters that included both Staupitz and a notary. He read his statement in the presence of his witnesses: he could not recant until he was refuted. He had said nothing against the Holy Scriptures, the Fathers of the Church or the decretals; he was liable to error and would bow to the verdict of the Church. So far so good, and Cajetan could voice his approval with satisfaction. But now came the snag, and it was a serious one: Luther wanted a public disputation, in Augsburg or elsewhere but in any case on German soil. If that was not granted, he wished his views to be submitted in writing to the judgement of the universities; he named Basle, Freiburg, Louvain and finally Paris. In Luther's day public discussion was the only means of being heard beyond a very restricted circle; it was that period's form of publicity. It was also the normal way to proceed in academic circles, and Luther's reference to universities shows the extent to which he still thought as a university lecturer.

The cardinal confined himself to drawing Luther's attention once more to the Bull *Unigenitus*, which seemed to him to be the heart of the matter. Luther remarked somewhat incautiously that he did not want to quarrel over it again. Cajetan corrected him: 'I have not quarrelled with you, my son.' He pointed out that there could be no question of a dispute between them; it was only consideration for the elector that made him willing to hear him and try to reconcile him with the pope. Staupitz now intervened and Cajetan, once again very forbearing, gave permission for Luther to submit a further written answer. On taking his leave the cardinal said benevolently that he was anxious to deal with the matter like a father and not like a judge.

Luther took up his pen again, and it is one of the characteristics of this man, whom we are apt to think of as a formidable speaker, that he had a much more powerful command of words when he put them on paper in the quiet of his little study. In a fascinating way he was both a man of solitude and a public figure with the widest appeal. His 'alone with God' was the innermost citadel of his faith; only there did he feel absolutely sure of himself, even though he had constantly to battle with his temptations. As soon as he stepped out and faced the world in order to proclaim his message – which for him was a categorical imperative – he became uncertain of himself, loud-voiced. He often shouted and then regretted his precipitancy and vehemence, quite frequently going to extremes and unhesitatingly withdrawing his rash statements; it is this that makes his statements so contradictory and lays them open to such varied interpretations. There is unity only in his life and deepest convictions: here he never hesitates and never recants.

But Cajetan wanted nothing less than recantation. Only armed with this could he settle the case. And so when Luther came back with his closely written sheets of paper he changed to a much sharper tone: Recant! Recant! He quoted the Bull *Unigenitus* yet again as the mainstay of papal authority; he lectured, he explained and Luther, now also excited, tried to interrupt him. The discussion grew more and more unseemly, they quarrelled over passages in the texts relating to the treasure of the Church and over the interpretation of terms, they reached for books, which they had at their sides, and Luther exclaimed: 'Surely my Father is not under the impression that the Germans know no grammar!' The cardinal, carried away by his pride of learning, and in order to demonstrate how necessary the Church's authority was in interpreting the Scriptures, allowed himself to be tempted into saying that the Bible itself was not free from error. Only when he had said this did he recall his instructions. Ashamed at having engaged in such an altercation with the monk, he now quoted the pope's letter, the true contents of which he had so far withheld: 'I am authorized to pronounce excommunication on you and on all who take your part and to lay all places that shelter you under the interdict. Recant!'

Luther remained adamant. The long-awaited threat made hardly any impression on him. Cajetan, now abandoning any attempt to be benevolent, cried: 'Go! Do not let me see you again unless it is to recant.' As Luther and his companions turned to go he cried out again: 'Recant!' This moment, though no one present realized it, marked Luther's break with the Church and the Church's break with Luther.

But the cardinal must have noticed the horror and alarm on the faces of Luther's companions; Luther's own gaunt head, with its deep-set eyes, must have struck him as that of a haunted fanatic. The aristocratic Staupitz, a member of the old nobility and experienced at court, seemed to him the most suitable person with whom to discuss the matter further. He sent for him and for Luther's friend Link. With exceptional courtesy he told them that Luther had no better friend than himself; he had only to recant. Staupitz evaded the question. He had always tried, he said, to influence Luther, but he was no match for him either in knowledge or intellect; personally he submitted to the Church in all humility. But, he added with a certain irony, the cardinal, as the Curia's representative, was the only one present called upon to settle the case. Cajetan declined any further talks; he was prepared only to supply a list of the articles to be retracted. In his audience with Link Cajetan went further: Luther need only retract his statements concerning the Church's treasure. Link, clearly very relieved, agreed. Once again the matter seemed on the point of being settled, and this example of a change of heart at the very moment when a violent collision seemed inevitable was later to be repeated at other critical moments in Luther's destiny. What was always lacking, however, was the final saving word, the small gesture of reconciliation, the willingness to yield even an inch, that 'would have altered everything'. It is not our task to correct history: in Luther's case it is made up of rejected opportunities and intransigence – on both sides.

Cajetan was convinced that this time he had really settled the case, and said mockingly to members of his entourage: 'This Brother Martin should have brought fresher goods to market.' As he saw it everything hinged on the question of the Church's treasure; the quarrel over indulgences, which was giving the Church so much trouble, went back to this. If the monk recanted on this point it would be much easier to discredit the whole damaging campaign.

Very different forces now intervened. The machinery which had been set in motion by the Curia's overlapping instructions took effect. Staupitz, who had spoken so cautiously and diplomatically to the cardinal, became alarmed: he had suddenly found out that the vicar-general of the Augustinian Order, his supreme superior, had already given instructions for Luther's arrest and his own as well. He complained of the cardinal's methods, of his fine, empty phrases that were so typical of Rome; all the man was really looking for was a way to destroy Luther's 'innocent blood'. But what mattered most of all was that orders had been given to throw both Luther and himself into prison.

Staupitz considered that Luther's only course was to flee; he would not be safe even in Wittenberg. He suggested Paris, the headquarters of the 'Gersonists', the nominalist school; now that he was a famous university lecturer he would be well received there and also find sympathy for his plan to appeal to the Council, as the supreme authority, should the pope condemn him. Staupitz made vain efforts to persuade the Augsburgers to give his protégé money for the journey; they sympathized with the fearless monk, they were impressed and pleased with the way he had conducted himself, but they shrank from siding so openly with him. Staupitz felt it wiser to leave the city himself and so did Link. Luther stayed on alone. With the aid of the elector's councillors, and in the presence of a notary, he drew up an appeal 'from the inadequately informed pope to the pope who should be better informed.' In it he rejected the previously appointed papal commissioners on the grounds of prejudice. He could not agree to being examined in Rome, where even Pope Leo's own life was not safe, but would agree to some other place. To Cajetan he addressed a detailed letter in which he made a last, extreme offer. He admitted having been too vehement and disrespectful of the pope. He was prepared not to discuss indulgences again provided his opponents kept the peace, and would announce this from the pulpit. He would submit to every condition, even to the extent of refraining in future from all utterances, whether spoken or written, of the kind that had led him 'into this tragedy'. He would willingly recant – 'in so far as my conscience allows me to.' This, of course, was a matter on which no one, however well intentioned, could advise him. Becoming increasingly aggressive, as he always did when he wrote, Luther permitted himself a dig at Cajetan's Thomism: neither the teachings of Saint Thomas nor those of 'the other' masters of scholasticism could satisfy him; to be convinced he would need better reasons. It was the Thomist versus the Ockhamist – and this was how people regarded the encounter. But in reality Luther faced Cajetan in a life-and-death struggle.

Cajetan did not reply. Luther took formal leave; there was nothing left for him to do in Augsburg. 'I am leaving now and shall make my way elsewhere.'

The cardinal said nothing. Luther's friends were worried; they told him he had no alternative but to flee like Staupitz and Link. Everyone assumed that Cajetan would have Luther arrested. But the cardinal was much too experienced and cautious; he had no desire whatever to see the odium of such a step laid at the door of the papal legate. It was for the elector to execute the order, and it was to him that he now wrote, severely and urgently: it was his duty to deliver the unimportant little monk to Rome as an obvious heretic or at least to banish him from his duchy. Cajetan also at once set about producing the draft of an official doctrine on indulgences; this he intended to dispatch to Rome with a request for its immediate publication under the pope's name.

The walls and gates of the imperial city of Augsburg were closely guarded. Luther's patrons, among them a canon of the cathedral, had a small gate in the city wall opened for him and provided him with two horses and a city groom. Dressed in his habit Luther swung himself on to his mount and rode for eight hours without stopping; on drawing rein he fell down exhausted on the straw of the stable, without a bite to eat or a drop to drink. Not until reaching Nuremberg did he feel moderately safe and dare to make a proper stop. He rode on, losing his way between Leipzig and Wittenberg. When at last he was back in his cell in the Black Monastery he wrote to Spalatin, the court chaplain, to say he was safely home; he did not know, however, how long he would remain in Wittenberg. 'I feel cheerful and at peace. It surprises me that the danger I am in seems of importance to so many and such distinguished people.' He sat down at his desk and prepared for publication a detailed report of his examination before the cardinal; he also prepared a new appeal, this time over the head of the pope to an as yet non-existent Council. His intention was simply to complete these tasks and then set out for France. He had been encouraged in this plan by the news that the University of Paris had just taken a step similar to his in angry protest against the repeal of the concordat known as the Pragmatic Sanction, which had been looked upon as an important achievement in conformity with the 'Gallican Liberties'.

Luther was now entirely alone. Never was he more magnificent than in these weeks. We no longer hear a word about his gastric troubles or his melancholy, which usually attacked him when he had leisure to devote himself to his doleful thoughts; when fighting he was eager and fit, indeed cheerful. During these weeks the devil, normally so close to him, is not mentioned once. We see a Luther calm, lucid and filled with a wary energy.

Through his vacillations the Elector Frederick had gradually lost the leading position he had once occupied in the empire. Now he was faced with deciding what was to be done with his Professor Luther. The cardinal's letter to him had contained a veiled threat that even a prince of the Holy Roman Empire might find himself paying the price of excommunication and interdict. Frederick, as was his habit, turned the contents of the letter over and over in his mind; he would have preferred to put it aside in the hope that the affair would solve itself. This, in fact, was his one strong point and the tactic that had won him his greatest successes. He would have been still better pleased if Luther had not returned from Augsburg at all. He sent him the cardinal's letter and asked for his comments on it.

Luther understood what was expected of him: 'I hereby declare that I am leaving your country with the intention of going wherever the merciful God wishes me to be.' But this was only one of the sentences in his very circumstantial letter, which was both a masterly statement and a brilliant piece of pleading; among other things it showed that his father had not been far wrong in wishing to see him become a great lawyer. With a sure touch he put his finger on the weakest point in his opponents' armour: so far no official, binding doctrine on the indulgence question had been announced by the Church; therefore he had been entirely justified in discussing the problem, and to condemn him as a heretic for doing so was a totally arbitrary action. Thus Cajetan's demand for his extradition to Rome was murder pure and simple, more especially since the pope's own life was not safe there, as the recent case, in which the whole of Europe had taken part, against the cardinals for their murderous plot had proved.

But there was much more to Luther's letter than this; he had written it for publication, for a wider, and indeed for the widest, public. It contained an account of his talks with the cardinal. His views on indulgences were explained more clearly and convincingly than ever before, his previous writings on the subject having been of a provisional, tentative nature. His own questions of conscience were by no means ignored, but they became part of an integrated whole. He addressed Cajetan again, at the same time addressing the entire world and the scholarly world of the theologians in particular. He turned effortlessly from the theologians to the laity, making it clear to the simplest intelligence – exemplified by the elector to whom he was writing – what was at stake. Where was it written that Christ's merits had been entrusted to the Church to form a treasury of indulgences? It was not in the Scriptures. And if it was contained in the papal decretals, how old were these? When had they been issued? The word of the Scriptures had held true for twelve hundred years of Christendom; only after that did the decretal make its appearance in the extragavances of the canon law. Let these people instruct him from the Scriptures! They could condemn him, declare him wrong, persecute him, have him banished and move heaven and earth, but he would not recant until they taught him something better. He himself invoked heaven and earth and indulged in the boldest paradoxes, which sound like blasphemies when taken out of their context. He too called on both mankind and the Divinity to condemn him, had he been in error: 'I shall speak from certain knowledge and not from mere opinion.' Luther pulled out every stop in his organ, the caustic and ironic ones as well, and in a single short sentence cast doubt on the whole apostolic succession: he could be wrong, he repeated, even 'Peter erred and indeed after the Holy Ghost had descended on him – is it not possible for even a cardinal to be wrong, however learned he may be?' The letter was an effective defence, a confession, a politically discreet counter-attack, a theologically effective exposition; it was passionate, cool almost to the point of being calculating, and above all courageous. He closed on a half-ironic, half-respectful note: his many words would assuredly have been too much for his Noble Prince. Commending himself to the elector, but still more readily to the mercy of his Lord in Heaven, and omitting his academic titles, he signed himself simply 'Brother Martin Luther, Augustinian'.

The elector made no reply. Luther got ready to leave; he had not many preparations to make. At the end of November a letter arrived from Frederick: he was in whole-hearted agreement with Luther's departure. Luther invited his friends to a farewell dinner in the monastery; he intended to leave during the night for France.

# 15

# The Miltitz interlude

TOWARDS the end of the farewell dinner a new letter arrived from the
elector: Luther was to stay. What had happened? A further special
envoy from Rome had turned up with completely new instructions,
and the elector no longer saw any need to let his professor go off
'somewhere under heaven'. The great tragedy had a harlequinade as
its prologue; from time to time it was also to be interrupted by a
half-comic, half-serious interlude. A Herr von Miltitz was announced,
calling himself a nuncio and bringing important messages from the
pope. The authorities in Rome had been dissatisfied with Cardinal
Cajetan, and since his return he had been received very coolly; on the
other hand the move may simply have been one of the blind throws
in the political game of dice in which the Curia habitually indulged.
Pope Leo was a great gambler who also, in fact, enjoyed the homely
pleasures of the gaming table; the debts he incurred in indulging this
pleasure represented a considerable item in the limitless monetary
needs of the court and in the huge liabilities of his estate – no one
expected any distinction to be made between personal and official
expenditure. Twenty-eight-year-old Miltitz, an entertaining companion with a ready tongue who for some years had held the title of
Gentleman-in-Waiting to His Holiness, had caught the pope's attention. One of Leo's favourite forms of relaxation was to watch the
comedies of Ariosto, and lesser authors, staged with Raphael's settings;
these performances also included dancers, tightrope artists and a monk
whose trousers fell down and who was then beaten on his bare bottom
for his clumsiness – the Medici prince was not fastidious.

Miltitz was not a monk but he held ecclesiastical rank, although this
influenced his behaviour as little as it did that of the higher-ranking
young cardinals who were his companions on his drinking bouts and
escapades in Rome; a member of the lesser nobility and poor, he had
hoped to make his fortune in Rome through the patronage of his uncle,
who was a confidant of the Medici secretary of state. So far he had not
got further than a subordinate position. He lived off small commissions;

he had bought relics for the elector of Saxony's great collection in Wittenberg and carried out other assignments for him. One of these missions had been to negotiate for the award to Frederick of the Golden Rose, the highest distinction the pope could bestow. This decoration, given to high-ranking potentates for special merit and services to the Curia, was greatly coveted by Frederick; he had long urged his claim by drawing attention to his devout way of life. Miltitz was now to present it to him. Miltitz also brought another gift, although it had no immediate connection with devout living; it consisted of two dispensations from the pope annulling the stigma of illegitimate birth. They were intended for Frederick's two sons by Anna Weller; now they could qualify for high ecclesiastical posts, carrying with them abbeys or other benefices. It was well known in the Curia that Frederick took this provision for his children no less seriously than other princes, whose bastard sons had been found bishoprics or other high positions.

In his diplomatic bag Miltitz also carried other letters patent, the sale of which he hoped would cover his travelling expenses and enable him to put a little aside as well; there were appointments to the post of papal notary and other dignities – a sheaf of thirty titles in all. Finally, however, the large leather bag contained harsh bulls and proclamations of excommunication – seventy of them, as Miltitz boasted – to be displayed in every locality should the elector prove obdurate in the Luther affair.

Officially Miltitz was subordinate to Cardinal Cajetan and supposed to report his actions to him; but he was in luck, Cajetan had left Augsburg in order to follow the emperor to Austria. And so, having taken the precaution of depositing the Golden Rose with the Fuggers, the gentleman-in-waiting continued his journey in a cheerful frame of mind, intending to carry out a great mission on his own initiative and if possible clear up the whole unpleasant Luther business once and for all. As a visitor from Rome, who could gossip in the most intimate detail about that fount of all honours and great events, he was well received everywhere. Speaking as a fellow countryman, and not as an Italian, he became expansive; the gossip he retailed spread like wildfire everywhere and later made its way into Protestant history books and chronicles. The pope, said Miltitz, had spoken in an extremely uncomplimentary way of Tetzel, calling him a *porcaccio*, a swine; the pope held no brief for the Dominicans either, with their hue and cry, and as for that fool Mazzolini, he had given him a good dressing down for his superficial report. Furthermore Cardinal Cajetan, with his well-known irascibility, obviously had not tackled the matter properly, which was hardly surprising seeing that he was an Italian. If the case were put to the pope in the right way he would take a lenient view;

Leo was good-natured, generous and open-minded – all of which was more or less true. At the same time Miltitz did not forget to brandish the threats he carried in his leather case.

Without informing Cajetan, the gentleman-in-waiting, proudly calling himself Nuncio and Privy Councillor to His Holiness, proceeded to Saxony and presented himself to the elector. Once again he deemed it wise to announce the two means he had at his disposal, the Golden Rose and the anathema. The least the elector could do, he maintained, was to expel Luther. Where to, asked the sleepy old monarch? Did he suggest Bohemia, where heresy was rampant enough already? Even reconciliation with the pope was possible, Miltitz declared; he had the best connections, he would undertake to bring it about. It might be worth trying, was Frederick's comment. He sent a messenger to Luther with instructions to present himself in Altenburg for a talk with Miltitz.

Miltitz, who was not without some knowledge of the lower levels of diplomacy, now decided to make an example of Tetzel. It was he who had engineered the whole business, or so everyone assured him; if Tetzel were eliminated, all the excitement would die down. The accepted way of doing this was to discredit him morally, the stock charges being dissolute living and embezzlement. Miltitz circulated the story that in his youth Tetzel had only just escaped death by drowning as punishment for his vices—quickly adding that he had been saved only by the goodness of the Elector Frederick; he was reputed also to have two illegitimate children. The embezzlement charge necessitated criminal proceedings. Miltitz subpoenaed Tetzel to defend himself. The old man, now thoroughly frightened, wrote from Leipzig to say he was unable to come; he was discredited everywhere, he complained, even as far away as Bohemia and Poland, was in danger of being done to death by Luther's followers, and dared not leave the house. The gentleman-in-waiting and nuncio went to Leipzig, where he summoned the provincial of the Dominican Order and the Fuggers' agent and confronted Tetzel with the bank's statement of accounts. There it stood: eighty guilders a month into his own pocket—according to other reports it was one hundred and thirty; to this had to be added ten guilders for servants, three horses, provender, free board and lodging and possibly other stolen money as well. Tetzel collapsed completely. He could have defended himself; such percentages were by no means unusual and in some cases may have been still higher, but speech failed the great speaker. He had thought of leaving Leipzig in any case, he declared. So there was danger of flight! The only answer, Miltitz decided, was to confine him in a monastery. The provincial, also thoroughly subdued, agreed. Miltitz said he would make a report to the pope. Tetzel, forsaken even by his order, vanished into his cell, fell into depressions and died shortly afterwards. Even the letter in which Luther admonished him not to take it too much to heart ('the child had quite a different father') was powerless to console him.

Miltitz reached Altenburg in the best of spirits and with high hopes. Luther was already there, and so were the elector's councillors who really hoped for a solution. A sort of standstill agreement was reached: Luther was to keep silent, provided his opponents did the same – this condition was stipulated by Luther. He was prepared to notify the public accordingly, by posting the necessary notice, and to write a personal letter to the pope. It remained a plan; Miltitz realized at once that he could not present himself in Rome with this letter, for although Luther affirmed his humility in the most deferential terms, he said not a word about recanting. Would it improve matters if he did? he asked the Pope. On the contrary, it would only make things worse. His writings had had a wider circulation than he had dared hope for and had made a stir everywhere; 'even our Germany today can boast a veritable flowering of scholarly and discriminating minds,' and they were not going to be stilled. He, Luther, was not the guilty one. 'They are the ones, my Father, those whom I have opposed. It is they who in our country harm and disgrace the Church of Rome', those people whose sermons on indulgences, preached in the pope's name, served only the ends of avarice. Perhaps, all the same, he had been too severe on these prattlers, and he regretted it.

Luther was ready to make still another attempt. He had doubts about the man who was bringing the offer. His suspicions aroused, he attended a dinner with Miltitz given by the elector's councillors at the castle. 'I had thought of you, Martin,' Miltitz began, 'as an old, grey-haired theologian debating with himself by his own fireside. Now I see before me a man in the full vigour of his youth. I would not dare to haul you off to Rome, even with 25,000 armed men at my back!' Luther remained unmoved. Miltitz resorted to flattery: on his journey he had asked people everywhere what they thought of Luther – 'For everyone who supported the pope there were three in favour of you and against the pope,' he joked. Luther had no time for such chatter. For him the crux of the matter had not been the trade in indulgences, nor had it been old Tetzel; it had not even been Archbishop Albrecht of Mainz. It was the pope, the pope himself, who was really the guilty one; it had been he who, by his demands for money, had driven the archbishop into the business.

Miltitz changed his tune. He spoke emotionally of the fearful consequences of a schism in the Church; according to Luther he even wept. He recalled the Hussite wars. Every conflict over religious questions had brought untold misery on the world. Luther would have to bear the responsibility for this. This made an impression on Luther; it confirmed his own misgivings. The advisers reasoned with him. Luther gave way and agreed to accept the condition of silence. He then published the printed announcement, which was couched in the most conciliatory terms; indeed it went so far that later his followers deplored this document as a departure from the straight and narrow way they liked to imagine rising steeply to the summit.

At the end of the talks Miltitz, moved, embraced and kissed him. He had a new proposal to make in conformity with Luther's demand for a hearing on German soil: the archbishop of Trier, a friend of the House of Saxony, could be persuaded to conduct this. He continued to pursue this idea for some time but Cajetan, who was his superior, insisted on attending; Luther indignantly refused this condition, and the plan came to nothing. Miltitz travelled doggedly about, sending his reports to Rome. His memoranda must have made a deep impression, because Pope Leo decided to write personally to Luther, thus contributing what is surely the most astonishing document in the whole dispute.

In this letter, composed in smooth and flowing Latin by the great Latin scholar Sadoleto and addressed to his 'dear son Martin Luther', Professor of Theology, the pope said with what joy he had read in a letter from his envoy Miltitz that Luther was willing to take a conciliatory attitude. Perhaps at the hearing Luther had been needlessly intimidated by his other dear son, Cardinal Cajetan, who, it seemed, had been rather too severe: 'The spirit is willing, but the flesh is weak.' Many things might have been said in the heat of the moment that on maturer reflection would have better remained unsaid. 'The Lord says: I take no pleasure in the death of a sinner, but that he may turn from his wickedness and live'; Luther should come to Rome and answer to the pope in person, who would be a kindly father to him.

Luther never saw this letter. It was sent through the Elector Frederick, who withheld it because he doubted whether Luther would accede to the request. But still stranger proposals came from Rome. The Emperor Maximilian had died, a new election was imminent. For a long time the pope had been vainly trying to get Francis I of France nominated as candidate. When his legates told him there was no chance of this, he put all his hopes on the Elector Frederick: anything but a Habsburg. Offer succeeded offer, each new one outbidding the last: he informed Frederick that he would recognize him even if only a minority of the electors voted for him. Order after order was rushed to Germany, to Frankfurt where the electors had assembled for preliminary discussions; and in Frankfurt Miltitz had another great day: on instructions from Orsini, the papal legate, he visited Frederick and tried to persuade him to agree to the pope's wishes and accept election. Should he comply, he would be granted, among other things, the appointment of a cardinal of his own choice from among his entourage. Care was naturally taken to avoid mentioning Luther by name and the suggestion was later represented as a figment of the imagination. In view of the almost weekly changes in the game played by the Curia, it would not seem at all improbable; a great deal of juggling with red hats and other high honours was part and parcel of the negotiations over the election.

Barely a week later the scene had changed. The latest information from his legates convinced Pope Leo that further opposition to the Habsburg was pointless. He hastened to give instructions that Charles was to be assured of his special goodwill. Miltitz continued his travels for a while; the people in Rome had already forgotten him, as they had the offer of the red hat. Eventually it occurred to them, however, that the Golden Rose could not be left with the Fuggers, and that the Elector Frederick was still an important person. Miltitz was entrusted with its delivery. Frederick, having been kept waiting so long, did not even receive him; acceptance of the precious gift, consecrated with holy oil, perfumed with rare essences and having power to grant special indulgences, was left to his advisers. Miltitz, having expected a large reward and received what he regarded as merely a tip, for a long time afterwards went on vainly petitioning the Saxon court for compensation for his expenses. Then, after trying his luck in minor roles at other courts, he disappears from sight; he is said to have fallen overboard on a boating trip and been drowned.

He was a small-part actor, who had to speak his lines and take his bow. Like Tetzel, he is important only as representing a whole class; there were many Miltitzes in the service of the Curia. The elector was wise enough not to accept candidature, although he discussed the matter at length with friends and advisers. The election of the emperor itself, however, is worth a brief examination because it decided the fate of Germany and the whole of Europe for the rest of Luther's lifetime. No one could have foreseen this. The candidate, Charles of Burgundy and Spain, was a young man of eighteen whose health, according to all reports, was not to be relied upon; he was a completely unknown quantity. Many saw the election simply as an intermezzo, and in the event it was played out as a farce. At first the choice had been entirely open. Who had not applied for the part! There were Henry VIII and the young Jagellon Louis. Francis I, at one time the most promising candidate, had paid out almost half a million ducats to the electors; he also had powerful supporters within the empire, but he made the mistake of vaunting his prowess as a fighting man, his brilliant victories in Italy, his energy and vigour – this was precisely the type of ruler the

German electors did not want. His chances were still further damaged by the fact that the pope patronized him so openly, pressing his nomination to the point of tactlessness; the ill-feeling against Rome was widespread.

The young Charles seemed merely harmless; he was said to be wholly under the thumb of his advisers, and it was hoped to maintain this state of affairs, with a different entourage, for a long time to come. The propaganda on his behalf represented him as 'a young nobleman of ancient German lineage', although his mother was Spanish and his grandmother, Joanna the Mad, Portuguese; nevertheless, as Maximilian's grandson he inherited his reputation.

The deciding factor, however, was quite simply money. The House of Fugger rallied its syndicate, which embraced Italian banks as well as the Welsers, and outbid the French by almost double. Pope Leo's offer of his blessing was of no avail, nor was his offer of the red hat to the electors of Cologne and Trier and the offer to appoint the archbishop of Mainz, who was already a cardinal, to be a permanent legate. A number of those taking part changed front several times, and each change meant new revenue. The Elector Frederick of Saxony also played this game, but with extreme caution as always; he let it be known that he was completely incorruptible and had strictly forbidden his councillors to accept any gifts – even the great Erasmus allowed himself to be inveigled into spreading this information through his large correspondence. But the gifts are recorded in the account books of the House of Fugger: Frederick had been promised the hand of a Spanish Infanta for his nephew, the prince elector, and the settlement of debts outstanding from the time of Maximilian as well. Charles's councillors took another important step: they engaged the noted and able condottiere, Franz von Sickingen, who had recently been in the service of the King of France; Sickingen's troops, who took up their positions in the vicinity of Frankfurt, where the elections were to be held, also exerted an influence.

The final scene of this pathetic piece of mummery took place in the symbolic semi-darkness of the little chapel in the choir of Frankfurt Cathedral. Charles was elected unanimously. He had readily subscribed to all the surrender terms, in which there was much talk of freedom and which stipulated that all official positions were to be held by Germans and that German, which he did not even understand, was to be used exclusively for all negotiations and at all meetings of the diets. It is hardly necessary to add that the electors' interests – called by them the 'princely liberty' – were emphasized in the strongest terms, and extended to include participation in the government and a voice in all decisions regarding war, alliances and taxation. These were all long familiar demands, which had been submitted to Maximilian, agreed by him and then ignored.

Charles was not even present at the ceremony; the only people who put in an appearance in Frankfurt were his councillors and representatives of the House of Fugger. The emperor elect was in Barcelona, where he staged a week of grand celebrations with allegorical processions and masquerades. His reign was to last for nearly forty years, one of the longest and most fateful in German history; of this whole period only eight years were spent in Germany, and even these were split into separate visits, many of them quite short. He had no permanent residence and spent the years of his reign in travel, moving from place to place, and not least in conducting campaigns against half the princes who had elected him. Titian painted him in armour, lance in hand, as the victor of Mühlberg riding through a desolate landscape in which not a soul is to be seen – Luther's Saxony.

# 16

# Seventeen days' disputation

LUTHER kept the pact of silence for two months, and to keep it as long as that must have been difficult for him. He was seething inside; at the urgent request of the elector's advisers he had given in once again, an action he very soon regretted because his enemies had no intention whatever of remaining silent. Luther had by now gone beyond the indulgence question. Cajetan had switched the ground to the pope's authority. Luther began to look into the bulls and decretals in earnest. His knowledge of Church and papal history was still fairly sketchy; he now studied everything he could find on the subject. It was not much, because this extremely delicate field had been greatly neglected. Where was there a man prepared to venture on a description of the deeds and misdeeds of the popes? He would run the constant risk of being indicted as a heretic. Where a man with the courage to expose the highly political background which lay behind the enactment of all the great obligatory bulls? The great compilation of the canon law was still regarded, almost universally, as the authoritative pronouncement of the Church, as the effective weapon in every quarrel; to quote from it was to dispose of every objection. It was the Church's constitution and doctrine in one, as well as the authority on questions of everyday life; moreover it claimed to be superior to all secular law. Luther studied it, and it was this study, rather than any personal experience, which was the starting-point of his fight against the papacy.

He still believed in Pope Leo's essential goodness and willingness to reform, once he realized that improvements were necessary; he imagined him surrounded by cunning, ambitious minions planning to take his life – there had been plenty of talk of this. Of Leo, the great patron of the arts, he knew nothing, nor would he have been interested in this side of him. But for centuries there had been talk of the sinful life in Rome; people were used to hearing sermons and complaints on the subject and to hope that one day an 'angelic pope' would put everything right. Luther now began to have doubts about the whole institution. The angelic pope had never appeared; instead the holy see had been occupied by personalities who seemed to confirm the old sayings and prophecies that for a change to take place Antichrist had first to appear.

Consequently at this period we find Luther using the term Antichrist for the pope; it crops up first in letters to his friends. As a synonym for his Sovereign Lord it sounds incredibly blasphemous on the lips of a monk, but Luther had become convinced that his Sovereign Lord was Christ and not a human being, however powerful he might be, who, what is more, lived in the sink of iniquity that was Rome. The legend of Antichrist was very ancient and very obscure, but it had the force of an inexorable historical concept. In the twelfth century the abbot Joachim de Fiore had proclaimed the doctrine of succeeding 'kingdoms', periods whose sequence had been predetermined by God; only through the coming of Antichrist would the way be made clear for the new and final 'kingdom', the Age of the Spirit, of freedom and love among men. The radical Franciscans had carried on his teaching and been anathematized by the pope for doing so. Repeated reference to the doctrine had been made by every apocalyptic movement, the coming of Antichrist being inseparably bound up with all ideas of the last days; the world's end was expected whenever there was a great catastrophe. Joachim had searched for a 'scientific basis', in the manner of modern interpretations of history, and he had sought it in the only language he knew, the language of theology: the world and its affairs would run their course inevitably and logically in foreordained and easily comprehensible stages.

Joachim had taken his idea of the new age from the Book of Revelation: 'And I saw another angel fly in the midst of heaven, having the everlasting gospel to preach unto them that dwell on the earth, and to every nation, and kindred, and tongue, and people'. The revolutionary element in Joachim's interpretation is overwhelming; it represented a complete reversal of the hitherto accepted picture of history. The viewpoint was switched from backwards to forwards. Mankind had become reconciled to the fact that the world was getting constantly worse, that the 'golden age' lay in the past. Now it became attainable here on earth and not only in heaven, in the hereafter; indeed it was at hand and, what is more, promised as something the date of which could be calculated precisely. The mysticism of numbers played its part, and the exact dates announced by Joachim's followers for the coming of Antichrist and the beginning of a new age caused vast upheavals and fearful disappointments. For Joachim the mysticism of numbers determined the division into three periods, the trinity of kingdoms corresponding to the Holy Trinity; in our own day the Third Reich has made us familiar with the mysticism of numbers. Joachim defines the first age as that of the Old Testament, of the law, the Father; the second as that of the New Testament, the Son; the third as the coming age, that of the Spirit. It sounded harmless enough and was not contested. It was only the interpretation that was revolutionary and endangered the Church: the second age was the age of the existing Church; it had not yet attained the fullness of the Spirit and of freedom. From among the monks a man would arise and open the way to the third kingdom. God's plan of salvation was progressive – this was the crux of the matter. It did not stand still. It continued to progress, beyond the Church and beyond the clergy.

Joachim was never regarded as the 'leader' of the new movement; he was only its John the Baptist. The search for the inspired monk continued. It assumed the most varied forms. St Francis was seen as the hoped-for saviour, his disciples being immediately split into the peaceful followers of Joachim, who renounced the world, and the fiercely mundane, who preached revolution by force; they were all held in the deepest suspicion by the Church and hence suppressed, often bloodily. But the prophecy of the monk who was to come with great tidings endured. In 1515, shortly before Luther entered the scene, Joachim's prophecies were published in Bologna by a Dominican and dedicated in all innocence to Cardinal Medici, the papal secretary of state. Ten years later a disciple of Luther's brought out a German edition in Nuremberg to prove that Luther was the monk foretold in the prophecy. In this Luther is pictured as a monk holding Saturn's sickle in his hand; with it he is severing the unworthy papacy, symbolized at the side by the stump of a leg.

The new kingdom could be brought about only by means of a catastrophe, the last days. Until Joachim's time the Last Judgment had been thought of as the end; he replaced this by the end of the second kingdom. It would be effected by Antichrist, whose historic mission was thus almost free from all taint of devilry; provision had been made for him in God's universal plan. The doctrine of the necessary catastrophe, not unknown in the thought of every age, demanded upheaval on the most colossal scale, 'that the days may be fulfilled' – an idea that had already dominated the earliest Christian presentation of the doctrine, that of the Revelation of St John. In his early years Luther never wearied of speaking of upheaval, of fighting, of war and the sword. He did so even before the Diet of Worms: God wanted conflict, not peace. He meant it in the spiritual sense; it was understood in the worldly sense.

It is difficult to determine how much Luther knew of the legends of Antichrist; myths and fables circulate mostly by word of mouth. As recently as 1516 a small tract had been published in Erfurt on the life and rule of Antichrist, telling 'how he was turning the world upside down with his false doctrine'; only through the two prophets Enoch and Elijah would Christendom turn again to the true faith. Luther may have read this. In any case what was now unmistakable was the emergence in his thought of the idea that Rome was the seat of Antichrist. All the ancient, whispered signs seemed to confirm this. The Antichrist would compare himself presumptuously with God. He would send his messengers to all the ends of the earth. He would turn the heads of the people and create confusion everywhere. Before he could be overthrown the Church would have to suffer a fearful punishment for its worldliness; as a result of this the last would become the first. These sayings had been handed down through the centuries.

In March 1519 Luther wrote to Spalatin: 'Let me whisper something in your ear: I do not know if the pope is Antichrist or an apostle of Antichrist'. But in the same breath he could still affirm that he had never considered renouncing the pope: 'I am quite satisfied that he should be called, and indeed is, Lord of the world'. There was, however, an undertone to this: *Dominus mundi*, lord of this world, was also the name given to Satan; Luther, in his famous battle song, later called him the prince of this world. The pope could rule this world, but 'let him leave the Gospel untouched by his decretals, and then I shall not raise so much as my little finger, even though he takes everything else from me'. In that case, Luther would also observe 'rigidly' the agreed demand for silence.

It did not come to this; a chain of events intervened. In order to put an end to all excuses that there was no binding doctrine on the subject, Cajetan had arranged for the decretal on indulgences, drawn up by him, to be published. This in itself was enough to rouse Luther – a new decretal! News that his excommunication was being prepared also reached his ears. Mazzolini published a new work, his pamphlet *On the Power of the Pope*, which was an out-and-out parody of Joachim's theory of ages: he specified five 'kingdoms' instead of three, and the fifth and greatest of them was already a reality in the form of the existing Church militant. The Gospel, too, had been proclaimed and would continue to convert further peoples over whom the pope was to reign; he was the sole judge over the monarchical and hierarchical kingdom of the Church, his jurisdiction extending even over unbelievers, over the heathen and the Jews. Everyone owed allegiance to the laws he enacted and to his commands, on pain of losing eternal bliss. The pamphlet also contained a controversial statement about the claims of secular rulers who styled themselves 'by the Grace of God': 'He [the pope] alone receives his power and authority from God. No one can depose him, neither a Council nor any other power, and no one can condemn him, even though he cause offence.'

This was a current topic; the possibility of deposing the pope by means of a Council was under constant discussion even among the cardinals, and at the Council of Pisa Julius II had come near enough to meeting this fate. But to Luther these theses were like a red rag to a bull. He saw the old prophecy fulfilled in all seriousness: Antichrist, the final disorder, had come; whether as the second or the fifth monarchy he did not care—he never had much feeling for the mysticism of numbers. And now Eck chose this moment to attack him again; following his preliminary skirmish with the obelisks he had actually made advances to Luther, although his motives can hardly have been honest. Luther felt the time had come to enter the arena once more. Fighting was his element. He had kept his pledge of silence; his enemies had paid no attention to it. Now he wanted to strike.

His whole nature is summed up in a letter he wrote to a friend after Eck's first attack on him: 'The more they rage, the bigger my strides. I give up my first position, they yap at my heels, I move on to the next, and they yap at me there.' The first position had been the dispute over indulgences, the next was the question of the pope's authority. Luther possessed an instinctive power and orderliness of procedure which alone explains his effectiveness: he did in fact stride from one position to the next in an almost logical sequence, reaching by this method a peak not attained before, either by the emperors or by the numerous thinkers and literary opponents of the papacy. Of course, one can also say that the 'days were fulfilled' or, more modestly, that the time was ripe, but the time always needs the man to formulate and announce the liberating word, a man forceful enough to overcome the opposition.

This was still formidable enough and might have daunted anyone but Luther. What was he? A university lecturer who had almost lost his job, a shabby mendicant friar in the eyes of the authorities in Rome, who at this very moment, and with the help of both Mazzolini and Cajetan, were in the act of excommunicating him formally, finally and in circumstantial detail. So far as Luther was concerned the elector was more or less an unknown quantity. His only anchor was the University of Wittenberg, which was proud of the startling increase in numbers it had achieved in the last two years, thanks to Luther. The attendance at lectures had doubled, there were students from all over the world, and Wittenberg, originally quite insignificant, could now compete with the ancient, great universities; its other outstanding luminary was Professor Karlstadt. Quite recently, and on Reuchlin's own recommendation, Reuchlin's great-nephew, Philipp Melanchthon, had joined the faculty as lecturer in Greek; still very boyish-looking, frail, inconspicuous and with a slight lisp, he was looked upon at first as a very modest acquisition. But his lectures, delivered in brilliant humanist Latin, very soon made people change their opinion; a scintillating address, in which he submitted a comprehensive programme for reforming the syllabus of studies at the university, made him famous and gave early hints of future greatness. Before long his lectures were attracting audiences by the hundreds, making the older universities jealous of Wittenberg and its twenty-two-year-old professor with the modest title of 'master of arts'; he remained master of arts all his life, even when he became the world-famous Melanchthon.

The University of Leipzig, jealous in any case of the competition of its rival in the electorate, decided to hold a great disputation with the object of cutting Wittenberg's fame down to size. The chief victim was to be Karlstadt, who had ventured into print with some very audacious theses and publications and had also come out in support of Luther, whose doctorate he had sponsored. Eck intended to oppose him. In doing so he looked forward to delivering an annihilating blow at the whole Wittenberg movement, Karlstadt then being regarded as one of its leading figures and not merely as a follower of Luther. A savage preliminary skirmish had already been fought with theses and counter-theses, and this had made it plain to Luther that the main action was to be directed against him. He wanted to take part, and made efforts to do so, but this was not so easy because, while not yet officially excommunicated, he was under extreme suspicion of being a heretic, and it was known that he had been summoned to Rome. The theological faculty in Leipzig had misgivings, and the reigning prince, Duke George of Saxony, was anything but well disposed towards Luther; soon he was to become one of his bitterest enemies. But he was annoyed at the pusillanimity of his professors, of whom at any rate he had no very high opinion; he called them 'a timid lot', who recoiled at every volley. He was even more annoyed by seeing Wittenberg advancing so rapidly in comparison with Leipzig; he intended to redress the balance. The famous Eck would contribute to this. Finally, he promised himself a notable theological joust; an ardent amateur theologian himself, he later exchanged polemics with Luther, which in sharpness of tone could vie with those of his fellow-ruler Henry VIII of England.

The pleasure and interest taken in theological disputations before large audiences is something we can no longer appreciate, but in those days it was general; the discussions, after all, centred on politics and the burning questions of the day. Full-dress intellectual tournaments had been popular since the High Middle Ages, in the world of Islam as well. They were valued at court as entertainments, and women could attend them; Spain, in particular, had been the scene of many such contests. There were jousts over the immortality of the soul, over new doctrines and dangerous old ones; a Jew might, or might be forced to, defend his faith against a Christian, and with it all lives might be at stake, at any rate on one side, and this only heightened the suspense. Here in Leipzig a life was certainly at stake, and this may well have been a spur to Duke George; unlike his cousin Frederick he was mettlesome, he loved plain speaking and forceful gestures.

A disputation

It began as a very local affair, as a dispute between Wittenberg and Leipzig. Duke George had given it a magnificent setting in the great hall of the Pleissenburg Castle; the room was hung with tapestries, the desk to be used by Eck, the favourite, was adorned with a picture of St George and the Dragon, while that for the Wittenbergers was decorated politely with Luther's patron saint Martin. The proceedings opened with a special service. The choir of the Thomaskirche, still famous today, chanted an elaborate twelve-part Mass specially composed for the occasion by the cantor, Georg Rhau, who later went to Wittenberg, where he earned a well-deserved reputation as a musical pedagogue. The professor of poetics made a two-hour speech on the correct method of conducting a disputation. The civil guard, accompanied by a pipe band, paraded every day in armour, the authorities fearing trouble. The Wittenberg contingent arrived in two carriages, accompanied by two hundred students, all of whom were heavily armed; the Leipzig students carried daggers and swords in their belts. Bloody brawls were still an everyday part of academic life, and the atmosphere on both sides was tense.

There had also been introductory debates on procedure and the 'order of the day'. Eck, who relied on his powerful voice and gift for extemporizing, insisted that the disputation be conducted in the Italian manner; he objected even to the publication of a verbatim report. Karlstadt was more cautious, insisting on a verbatim record to be attested before a notary. The report was important, since it was to be submitted to the Universities of Paris and Erfurt as the supreme arbiters. Eck wanted to add to these the pope, as the supreme arbiter-in-chief, but Luther objected. Even the report of this discussion on reporting was recorded before a notary. The full formality of the bureaucratic machine was maintained throughout the disputation, which lasted seventeen days.

If Eck had had his way it might have gone on for six weeks – he said so himself with pride. He held a large repertoire of Sentences and passages from the decretals in his remarkable memory. In the mornings he refreshed himself by going for a ride, on a horse readily provided by the city council, accompanied by a municipal groom; entering the debating hall, riding whip in hand, he paced casually up and down, the great artist in spontaneous argument, turning his back on his desk and the dragon-slayer. He poked fun at the undersized Karlstadt, clinging anxiously to his desk and notes, for ever referring to his books, which he had piled up round him, and always intent that the notaries should neither omit nor misquote anything he said. His theses were almost as far-reaching as Luther's; they dealt with the vast problem of whether the will was free or subject.

This question had almost split the Church in its very earliest days. It was only thanks to St Augustine – whom Luther always revered as his model – with his impressive mastery of the language of ancient Rome and his no less remarkable power of persuasion, that Pelagius, the arch-heretic and corrupter, had been overcome once and for all; but the name Pelagius has persisted throughout the history of the Church and is still solemnly denounced by the Anglican Church today. To take one's stand on the human exercise of free will was Pelagian heresy; even to accord it a part in the attainment of salvation was 'semi-Pelagianism'. Beginning with St Augustine the question had been disputed for two hundred years. The fight went on and is still by no means settled; it will always be renewed. No work by this man who shook the world has survived; we know only that he came from the British Isles, led a humble, god-fearing life, was condemned by Innocent I, bishop of Rome, and reinstated by his successor Zosimus. Exiled by order of the emperor and outlawed, he vanished into obscurity. His teaching, in so far as it can be established, was clear and simple, perhaps even matter-of-fact, but its implications were terrifying: man was created by God capable of good; sin was not inherited, but freely committed by each individual. Adam's fall was only to serve as an example; it did not taint every human being for ever afterwards. Death was a natural occurrence, and Christ, whose life was sinless, overcame it. The temptations to which mankind was exposed were only obstacles to perfection; they could be overcome by Christ's teaching and example. We know these intimidating theses only from quotations made by opponents, above all by St Augustine. But why the indignation? The emergent Church could not tolerate free will on the part of the individual, even if the intention was godly; the very term seemed an invitation to disobedience and has always been so understood. Any teaching that even approximated to those of Pelagius was suspect, stigmatized as semi-Pelagianism, and suppressed. What survived was the notion of Pelagian heresy.

But in one of its strangest reversals the Church had arrived at doctrines which ceded at least a certain standing to 'semi-Pelagianism', although the name would have been vehemently opposed. Eck, indignant and offended, protested that Karlstadt had accused him of 'Pelagian' ideas. Karlstadt seems undoubtedly to have been on the right track, but he was a poor debater. Later, in a further switch of fronts, it was Luther who saw the fight against the doctrine of 'free will' as one of his main tasks. In his great treatise *On the Bondage of the Will* he defended his standpoint against Erasmus. The idea that man of his own accord could contribute anything whatsoever to his own salvation, and least of all through good works, ran contrary to his doctrine of grace. Like Augustine he saw in Pelagius the 'rational' man, who put his trust not in God but in himself, in his own judgment. Here in Leipzig, however, he was fighting his first great battle against the papacy which, because it claimed to be the supreme and sole authority, was not prepared to concede any place to his, Martin Luther's, judgment. His 'free will' rebelled against this.

We have mentioned Pelagius, not merely because his name was dragged into this disputation, but because his is an outstanding, indeed the most astonishing, case of defamation in the history of the human mind; it is unexampled if only because he has been unable to defend himself against the accusations and misinterpretations to which every century has subjected him – good care was taken that not one of his works survived in its original text. Only his name was carefully preserved, as that of one of the first and most dangerous of all heretics. And it was with the question to what extent Luther himself was a heretic that the Leipzig disputation was concerned. Eck's plan, carried out coolly, skilfully and commandingly, was to establish this charge against him; he was the victor in this disputation, and honoured as such not only by the people of Leipzig, who had sided with him from the beginning.

Tactically alone he displayed great acumen in treating Karlstadt as the leader, although he rightly regarded him as by far the weaker opponent; inevitably the weeks-long dispute with an adversary who, even physically, was so much smaller than himself proved exhausting for the listeners and onlookers. The attention of the audience flagged, and from time to time the Leipzig professors of theology went quietly to sleep; on such occasions the physical impression made by the contestants played a considerable role, and in this respect Eck, 'our Eck', had a distinct advantage. The whole proceeding would have passed off still more effectively had he been able, as he intended, to exclude Luther altogether. It was with difficulty that Luther made his way to the desk that bore St Martin's effigy. Being a notorious heretic, his every step was watched and regarded with suspicion, every detail even of his clothing was remarked. Whenever, during the whole week in which Karlstadt was toiling away, he took a stroll through the town, the Dominicans immediately hid the sacred vessels containing the sacrament in the sacristy, in order to protect them from the pestilential heretical aura. The superstitious claimed to have seen a magic ring on Luther's finger, in which diabolical powers were undoubtedly concealed; others were convinced that his Satanic assistant was hidden in a capsule in the ring. It caused a commotion when the monk, flouting established custom, mounted his desk holding a small bunch of carnations, whose perfume he inhaled from time to time. This little bunch of flowers, which to us is one of the most endearing features of the whole interminable affair, at once became a legend; he was said to have walked brazenly through the town, his head garlanded with flowers, and at the end to have left garbed in this way. The local poets celebrated the unprecedented occurrence:

> *I stood one day in Leipzig market square –*
> *My sweetheart had assigned to meet me there –*
> *When, garlanded with flowers, the monk that way did chance*
> *And I bethought me, now the monk is making off to dance.*

In the deluge of letters and publications that flooded the lands of Germany during the three weeks of the disputation and immediately afterwards, nothing was omitted, not the slightest mis-step, not the smallest hesitation. In addition to the official notaries, no less than thirty of the audience claimed to have taken down the proceedings verbatim; the memoranda and reports fill a small library and most were printed at the time.

Eck wanted to prove that Luther was a heretic, not only over the indulgence question but in his whole basic attitude. The brutality with which he set about it sickened some of those taking part. The young humanist Mosellanus, who as professor of poetics had given the inaugural address, described him as a tall, burly man with a powerful chest and a full, 'authentically German' voice, whose behaviour, however, was more reminiscent of a butcher or landsknecht than a theologian. Luther, on the other hand, was 'of only medium height and gaunt, so worn out with cares and much study that when one is close to him one can count every bone in his body. But he is still in the prime of life. His voice rings bright and clear.'

Luther needed all his confidence because Eck pressed him dangerously. With a sure touch he had already singled out the question of the pope's authority in the first encounter. Now he returned to it, adding the accusation that Luther's views were 'Bohemian heresy'. Luther, already very heated, denied this. Eck retorted slyly: 'Is the Reverend Father really so opposed to the Hussites? If so, why does he not use all his eminent intellectual gifts to attack them in his writings?' Luther, now still more worked up, refused to tolerate such remarks; he was seething inside, which was precisely what Eck, who knew his opponent, intended. After the midday recess Luther fell headlong into Eck's trap. Without stopping to reflect he blurted out: 'Certainly, there are very many truly Christian and evangelical tenets among the articles of Hus and the Hussites.' Then, still more thoughtlessly: 'Among them are tenets the Church cannot condemn.' Wild disorder arose in the debating chamber. With arms akimbo, Duke George jumped up from his seat: 'The man's a maniac!' He was thinking of the arch-heretics who had ravaged his land of Saxony and forced the founders of his University of Leipzig to flee from Prague. Moreover, a guilty conscience made him especially sensitive: his mother was a daughter of the heretic king of Bohemia, George of Podebrad, after whom he was named; as a result, he was suspected of secret sympathy with that heretic country, a fact that had hardened his already gruff nature into extreme harshness and severity. The word Hussite meant revolt and rebellion, revolt against Church and state. Eck did not let go, and continued to manœuvre with care. So the Church 'could not condemn'? But the Council of Constance had expressly condemned both Hus and his articles. Did Father Luther then deny the authority of the Sacred Council? Luther became hesitant; he had said nothing against the Council of Constance. Is that so? said Eck. He would prove that he had; in any case he was a patron, a defender, of the Hussite teachings. Lies! protested Luther, in still greater confusion. He really had no grounds for protest; Eck had used underhand methods, but what he had said was true. The day ended in tumult and excitement. And this was Eck's greatest success; its repercussions were long-lasting. The term 'Bohemian heretic, Hussite' stuck to Luther like a leech, he could not shake it off; it was repeated incessantly as proof of the dangerous nature of his views, and at the Diet of Worms it was to be one of the main arguments leading to his condemnation.

Luther was as ill-informed as Eck about Hus and the Hussites. They both knew only the Council's verdict, the Sentences and articles which it had condemned. To Eck the matter was clear: the Church had spoken, the details were irrelevant. Among the condemned articles Luther had found theses that agreed with his own viewpoints, although these were still far from clearly formulated. It was a dispute conducted on mediaeval lines over Sentences, over single phrases, stops and dashes. And as in the case of Pelagius the vaguest possible accusation, that of heresy, proved the most effective. It was of little or no importance that the Hussites had not been a united party, but had very quickly split into two bitterly opposed schools of thought, the radical Taborites and the more moderate party, who called themselves Utraquists after the doctrine that the Communion should be celebrated in both forms, with bread and wine. Nor did it matter that the Utraquists had inflicted a bloody defeat on the Taborites in a suicidal battle, the most disastrous in the whole history of the country. Neither Luther nor Eck had the slightest knowledge of Czech history or indeed of any history at all. Duke George knew a little more, and it was this very fact that intensified his dislike of the monk, who was raking up things that should have remained buried. George's devout mother had always urged him to pray, and to pray in the orthodox manner; she was both afraid and proud. She was proud because her father had been a powerful king, who had even thought of joining the German crown to the Bohemian, which his Czech nobles had awarded him in gratitude for his victory over the radical Taborite rabble. She was afraid because he had always remained a heretic, taking the Communion cup which the Church forbade, and had acknowledged the old Church only in secret, because this was something he had to keep from his subjects. She had grown up in this dishonesty, in the atmosphere of a dishonest peace between the Church and the race from which she came, for the Church, likewise, had concluded its pact with Bohemia only with secret reservations, granting the country a special position, enjoyed by no other, in which Communion in both its forms was reluctantly permitted. This was the background to George's boyhood. Bohemia had remained a 'source of infection' which at any moment might provoke the most appalling dangers, primeval dangers going back to the Waldenses and Picards; it was the home of heresy in Europe, and with its deviationist teachings was a threat to the social and political order of the world.

George's horror was genuine, and as he was anxious to support law and order he used his position as chairman of the debate to instruct his deputies to prohibit any further discussion of the delicate question. Eck had been able to treat the subject at length and that was sufficient. Moreover he wanted no personal recriminations.

Luther remained agitated but, keeping quite logically to the matter in hand, he now came to the crucial point for which he had been preparing: what was the truth about the primacy of the pope? Was he appointed by divine right or only by human? This was the 'second position' in his advance; the first, the indulgence question, had really been of secondary importance. The pope issued indulgences, but from where did he take his authority to do so? What was the origin of the supreme position he claimed for himself? Was it founded on the Bible, or had it been created in the course of centuries by 'human agency'? If so, in which centuries? Luther now struck with great power at a rock against which hitherto scarcely anyone had so much as lifted a finger. The doctrine of the 'rock' on which the Church was built had remained inviolate, and for the monk to dare to contest it was monstrous. The Bible was invoked, the Church quoting as its authority the passage in which Christ said to his disciple: 'Thou art Peter, and on this rock I will build my Church.' Obviously Peter had been chosen to be the principal apostle; he had gone to Rome, and the popes had descended in an unbroken line from him. The papacy had been established by Christ and was thus the sole authority with a direct and unquestionable claim to exist 'by the Grace of God'. Explanation or interpretation of scriptural passages could be undertaken only with the pope's approval. The only recognized viewpoints were those of the Fathers of the Church, who ranked as saints. Any individual, any 'innovator', who now came and wanted to base his views as he pleased on his own interpretation was a heretic. This was Eck's standpoint too. Cyprian had spoken, he cried, Origen, Augustine, Hilary, Chrysostom and many others had spoken, the Eighth Council and the Council of Chalcedon had spoken – 'I have more faith in the saints than in a young doctor.' Peter was the rock, the pope his vicar. Luther's standpoint was 'that the writings of every teacher, however sacred, however learned they may be, should be put to the test and judged by the Word of the Bible, as Christ, Paul and John have commanded us.'

The battle concerned words too, and here it was fought with imperfect means on both sides. Luther's Greek was still far too inadequate for him to have known what was meant in the Bible by 'rock', that it was a play on words, the name Peter meaning stone or rock; as for Eck, such things simply did not concern him. Following Augustine, Luther explained the rock as Christ; this view being too dangerous for Eck to attack, he contented himself with maintaining that the rock was 'Peter too'. This was only one of many misunderstandings and differences. What left no room for misunderstanding, however, was the fact that two fundamental viewpoints were opposed: that of the individual and that of authority. From this standpoint the wearisome discussion at Leipzig was a paradigm of recurring conflicts.

Luther did not stop at the interpretation of words. He denied that Peter had been the first among the Apostles. Hence the claims of Peter's successors – the claim that the papacy existed by 'divine right', for instance – had no validity for him; the pope was a human being, 'and before God master and servant, great and small, poor and rich are equal,' as Paul expressly said, including in his statement the Apostles as well. In claiming divine right for the pope Eck had referred to the Council of Constance, but that too was a law of man not of God. Against the thesis of divine right Luther cited the case of the Greek Church: it had not recognized the pope for 1,400 years. Were all Greek Christians to be condemned, including such universally revered holy fathers as Basil the Great, Gregory of Nazianzus and so many others? Luther cited the Council of Nicaea, the most sacred of all since it had established for the first time the basic principles of the confession: was it also to be condemned as heretical because it was ignorant of the primacy of the pope in Rome?

Once more, guided only by his instinct, he had broached one of the burning issues of the time, a historical problem that causes fierce argument even today: what was the position regarding the greatest of all the schisms in Christendom? Could it be healed, as had been variously attempted, or would it have to continue for ever? When, in fact, did the break with the Greek Church occur? Disputes still continue over these questions, as they do even more bitterly over the seemingly insoluble question as to the status of the bishop of Rome in the early centuries and the date from which he can be regarded as 'pope' in the later sense of the word. Only very inadequate information on the subject was available to Luther. In fact he had little else to go on than the history of the popes written in the middle of the previous century by the papal librarian Platina, who treated the extensive material he found in the huge Vatican library in a very cursory manner. Platina was an ambitious and skilled humanist, but he was no historian; among his friends he had a reputation as a gourmet, and in addition to his history of the popes, which was reprinted in every country, he wrote an equally celebrated cookery book under the seductive title: *On the Permissible Voluptuous Pleasures of the Body: Eating, Drinking and Diversions of every Kind.*

Luther ventured even further, questioning not only the 'divine right' of the pope's authority but maintaining that the Councils had also been liable to error. They had made mistakes and refuted one another; the decisions of both the last two great ecclesiastical Councils at Constance – which Eck had just cited as evidence against him – and Basle had been contested by the pope on a number of essential points. Purely theological and ecclesiastical as the whole disputation appeared to be, Luther was already calling in question the entire hierarchy of the Church. Eck defended it. Though still a dispute between two doctors and two universities, it contained the seeds of a world conflict.

The affair had dragged on for nearly three weeks. It was not always conducted with decorum. The participants jeered and shouted and Luther himself became abusive; Mosellanus, who otherwise in his eye-witness account praised him for his learning and remarkable knowledge of the Bible, found him too 'caustic', a man 'who goes his own way', and his views too 'risky' for a theologian, who ought to behave with greater modesty. Nevertheless the opponents endeavoured to observe the formalities and address each other by their proper titles.

The performance was brought to an end by the approach of a royal visit from Brandenburg, which meant more to Duke George than the jousting of the doctors. The Wittenberg contingent returned home, with Luther by no means satisfied at the result. The students had set out on the return journey earlier, after numerous clashes with their Leipzig counterparts; three weeks in a strange and substantially more expensive town had proved too much for most of the penniless scholars. Eck remained in Leipzig as the victor and accepted the plaudits; Duke George sent him a fine stag and the city council the traditional gift of wine. The verbatim reports were sent to the Universities of Paris and Erfurt for their verdict. Erfurt refused to pronounce judgment on such distinguished scholars. The Sorbonne asked a fee of thirty gold crowns for each of the twenty-four members of their committee, and this put an end to the matter; Duke George had no intention of paying as much as that.

Memoranda passed back and forth; Karlstadt and Luther defended themselves to their elector, Eck tried to goad Frederick by sending him a biting report on his Doctor Luther: it was his duty to take action 'before the vermin got the upper hand'. Back in Ingolstadt he was acclaimed again, this time by his own university, which also presented him with gifts. He did not rest on his laurels. In Leipzig he had already spoken to the elector of Brandenburg; it had been easy for him to influence the Hohenzollern against Wittenberg and Frederick of Wettin. Eck wrote to the chief inquisitor, van Hochstraten, in Cologne; he issued pamphlets, he was indefatigable.

As if to corroborate his suspicion two priests now wrote to Luther from Prague. The letters had been opened and must have confirmed Duke George in his opinion that there was a very real fear of infection from Bohemia; they were immediately put to use by the court chaplain, Georg Emser, a new enemy of Luther's, but continued on their way and reached Luther. The two Czechs assured Luther that he was widely read in Prague and that he was not without friends in the attacks he suffered at the hands of his many enemies; they also sent him, as a precious gift, the essay *On the Church* by Hus, 'the apostle of the Bohemians, so that you may see what kind of a man he was' from his own words, and not from what was commonly said about him. Luther was suspicious, thinking it was probably a new trap on Eck's part, and put the work aside for several weeks. But when eventually he read it he was overwhelmed and wrote to his friend Spalatin that for a long time he had clearly been following the same road as the Bohemian. 'We are all Hussites without knowing it, Paul and Augustine as well. I am too astonished to know what to think when I consider God's terrible judgment on the man: in him the crystal clear and true Gospel was publicly burned a hundred years ago; it is still condemned today, and no one may confess his belief in it.'

The verbal contests had not been to his liking, and he had not come out of them very well; the whole academic system of disputations seemed to him out of date. He derived little pleasure from the flood of brochures and pamphlets that followed in the wake of Leipzig, even though people from far and wide sang his praises or attacked him abusively, venomously and with subtle taunts. He wanted now to appear before an entirely different public. During the discussions on reporting the debate he had already expressed a wish, though in vain, to have the verdict delivered not by the faculties of theology but by the 'whole universities'. He had made a submission to Duke George on the subject: 'By God's grace and through the great increase in good books the young people are more skilled than the old,' and 'everything that gleams and glitters is regarded with suspicion by all classes.' It was to the young people, and not to the old theologians, that he now intended to turn, and to 'all classes', and so began the greatest and most momentous period of his life. He wrote, and his writings appeared in print.

# 17

# The three primary treatises

LUTHER always wrote fast, in a fine, delicate hand, with not a trace of brute force in it, even when he fired his heaviest broadsides. His capacity for work was admired even by his enemies; in the early days of his battle he was already tossing off twenty to thirty publications a year – mostly small pamphlets – and these would be revised while actually going to press. Sometimes he had three printers on tenterhooks at once. Apprentices brought the proofs, waited outside his door, raced off again and returned the next day. Luther did all this work alone, in his little room over the passage between the monastery and the brewery, without a secretary or any other help. A whole printing industry, judged by the standards of the day, came into existence, and the printer-publishers grew rich. Luther himself received no fee. Most of what was published was reprinted outside Wittenberg, often in ten or more editions, a wide network of printing centres and literary bases being established, especially in south Germany. The publishing strongholds were the powerful free imperial cities, but even tiny out-of-the-way places had their printing presses and could step in when the censorship of the municipal councils in the big cities grew too bothersome. Basle became the main stronghold, the home of the great printing magnates and publishers, who employed famous humanists as proof-readers and editors; here were published the first epoch-making editions of the Bible and the original text of the New Testament, the Fathers of the Church in huge volumes, the ancient classics and the works of Erasmus. The books were illustrated and decorated by the best artists, by Holbein among others, and were exported everywhere. As early as 1519 a complete edition of the hitherto published writings of Luther appeared in Basle, with an introduction by a young humanist named Capito who – writing from Albrecht's court in Mainz where he, like Hutten, was still able to go on living for a time – exclaimed: 'The conscience of the laity is now awakened, let it resist the tutelage of the professional theologians.' Froben, the publisher, wrote to Luther on more practical lines: six hundred copies had gone to Italy and yet others to the Netherlands and England, 'I have only ten copies left in stock. I have never done so well with a book before.'

Everything Luther wrote was printed, down to the most trivial leaflet. His works in turn produced a flurry of polemics, pamphlets, theses, counter-theses, weighty refutations and defences. The complaint that the flood of print is reaching absurd dimensions has been voiced in every century; the age of the Reformation started with an inundation. Vulgarities and calumnies abounded. One of the chief delights was to make play with opponents' names; the favourite accusations of drunkenness and debauchery were used *ad nauseam*, and a writer able to convict his opponent of a grammatical blunder smacked his lips in triumph. Luther participated to the full in these activities, and when it came to rudeness no one could touch him. He never greatly bothered his head over philological niceties. He too was fighting over words and interpretations, but it was always the 'Word' that mattered to him, that was decisive. His fighting spirit often asserted itself, and he took pleasure in it: 'A good strong burst of anger refreshes the system,' he said, and he sometimes rushed his most furious pamphlets into print without even reading them over.

Luther had incomparable powers of language. It is hard to understand where this gift came from; he had spent fifteen years as a monk, using an exclusively Latin vocabulary. When addressing the world of learning or writing for abroad he continued to use Latin; he was as adept at the humanist letter, with its flattery and courtship of alliance, as he was at the rough dispatch of an unworthy opponent. But it was in the German which he may have picked up on the road during his journeyings that his full powers were revealed. People spoke forcibly in those days; he had at his command a variety of locutions that gave him a dozen names for every object and a richly articulate professional jargon for every craft. Theological discussions were conducted in Sentences, the laity spoke in proverbs; Luther was well supplied with both. 'Here is the beast in its stable, said the devil as he shoved a fly up his mother's backside', was one of his more respectable phrases. But it was not only the richness of his vocabulary that made his language so trenchant; above all it was its cadence and rhythm, and in this his gift for music helped him. Much of this cadence is lost on the modern reader, because nothing is so subject to change as the ear for quantity. To us the music of Luther's day, even that of the love songs and jaunty riding songs, with its ponderous minims and semibreves, sounds 'solemn' and chant-like. The same is true of the written word; we no longer have much patience for the verbiage, with its endless repetitions and accumulations of words, or for the sermonizing of which Luther makes frequent use. In those days the effect was quite different; it was powerful, rousing, striking. If we want to recapture this effect we have to change the tempo – to use the language of music – into allegro, presto or 'furioso'.

But Luther was also a master of the short, telling phrase, an art in which he far excelled all his contemporaries: 'Buckle to! Though you don't want to, you must!' He had at his finger tips phrases rich in imagery, verbs charged with action; he enjoyed onomatopoeia, and playing with words in general. He would 'prelude'; he calls his decisive polemic *On the Babylonian Captivity of the Church of God*, the work which marked his final break with Rome, a 'praeludium'; he writes that he is shortly going to break into another 'little song' in a still higher key, as if he were engaged in a light-hearted singing contest. He joked with grim humour, often very calmly and collectedly, sometimes with irony directed at himself. Then he would launch into unrestrained, furious outbursts, which the sensitive Erasmus was not alone in finding insufferable. In this mood he recognized no limits, and his fury, known even then as the *furor teutonicus*, drove him to forms of expression so dangerous that misunderstanding was inevitable; in fact it is hard to say whether this language was not actually intended to incite to kill. 'If we punish thieves on the gallows, robbers with the sword and heretics at the stake, why do we not also take up arms against those who teach falsely, against the cardinals, popes and the whole Roman Sodom which persistently despoils God's Church, and wash our hands in their blood?' It was in vain for him to protest that this was not meant as an incitement to murder, and equally in vain to call the Bible to witness, where David, in the 58th Psalm, castigates the godless, the hypocritical liars, in almost the same terms. Not everyone was as familiar with the Psalms as he was; moreover people were not agreed as to how far the words of the psalmist were to be understood only in a 'metaphorical sense'. The effect of sentences like this was appalling; they pursued Luther like murderous spectres.

Armed with the power of his language Luther now set out to overthrow the papacy. It was a remarkable operation because it was entirely single-handed. Before him lay only the confused tangle of Germany, from which came sporadic acclamation, often from people he mistrusted. He could not count even on the elector, and it was by no means certain that he would be able to remain in Wittenberg. His excommunication was on its way and it might well involve the elector and the whole country, which in any case represented only half of Saxony; the other half, under Duke George, was already hostile to Luther and was becoming more so every week. He had neither a group of followers nor any firmly established doctrine, no positive programme of any kind for bringing about this downfall of a centuries-old world order. Least of all did he have any clear idea what was to replace the order he was attacking. All he had was his Bible and the conviction that it would tell him what was to be done. God had called him and He would take care of things if they were in accordance with His will; should He ordain otherwise, He would abandon him.

Most astonishing of all is the mood and attitude with which the 'paltry little friar', the 'presumptuous monk', went to work. He cheerfully set about demolishing institutions which had stood like rocks against the mightiest rulers. His polemical writings, now seen as historical documents that have changed the world, were dashed off for the moment, even with preliminary joking, as if he were merely tuning the strings of his lute. *On Improving the Christian Estate, An Address to the Nobility of the German Nation,* was the name he gave to the first of the three treatises.

By 'nobility' he meant not so much the knights, who had offered him help and protection through Hutten and others, as the princes and the emperor, the 'noble young man'. It was the laity he now intended to approach, it was they who would have to take the matter in hand, since he had turned in vain to the theologians and ecclesiastical authorities. He made the most modest reservations, well aware that it appeared presumptuous in a monk, who was poor and despised and had actually renounced the world, to address men of such lofty standing 'as if there were no one else in the world but Doctor Luther to espouse the cause of the Christian Estate.' Those who wished to censure him could do so: 'Perhaps I owe it to my God and to the world to do something foolish; this is what I have resolved to do.' And still more composedly, as if he already knew what to expect, he said that his excuses should be offered to those of 'moderate intellect', because he did not know how to win the grace and favour of those of exceptional intellect: 'I have so often tried very hard to do this, but henceforth I neither want, nor intend, to heed them. God help us to seek, not our glory, but His alone. Amen.' And in the middle of his treatise, before starting to develop his proposals for reform, he repeats yet again: 'And so, come what may at the hands of secular power or General Council, I intend to sing and proclaim my piece of folly to the best of my understanding.' We may well ask whether any revolutionary before or since has set about his task in such a mood.

To some extent this was the usual phraseology used by monks to convey humility; Luther had used it before in his writings. Now, however, it was replaced by the new and unmistakable Luther note, and it was precisely those of 'moderate intellect' who understood it; those of 'exceptional intellect' remained aloof. Luther switched abruptly from his gentle key. 'May God now help us and give us the trumpets' that blew the walls of Jericho to the ground: the papacy had surrounded itself with three walls; these were made only of straw and paper, he would blow them down.

The first wall was the 'invented' division between the spiritual and temporal estates, leaving the pope, priests and monastics on one side and the princes, lords, craftsmen and peasants on the other. No one should let himself be 'intimidated' by such a division, because 'all Christians really belong to the spiritual estate and there is no distinction between them.' This was what Paul had said: they were 'all one body', but each member had his own work to do in order that he might serve the others. The clergy also had their work, their 'office'. Through baptism they were all spiritual, called and ordained as priests. 'For any creature that has crawled from its baptism can boast that he is already ordained to be priest, bishop or pope, although not everyone is fitted to exercise such office.' The priest was an 'official' so long as he held his office; on being removed from office he became a peasant or citizen like the rest. The indestructible character, the *character indelebilis*, of the priest was a fabrication. 'A cobbler, a blacksmith, a peasant, each man, whatever his craft, has his office and work,' in the exercise of which he should help the others. The community was composed of these as the body was of its members. And so the first of the paper walls fell.

The second wall was the thesis that the pope alone could not err in faith, 'be he evil or devout', that he alone might interpret the Scriptures. The Bible did not say this. On the contrary it said: 'We have all one Spirit of faith'. Thus we should 'be courageous and free, and not allow the spirit of freedom (as Paul calls it) to be intimidated by words invented by the popes, but go straight ahead, judging everything they do and permit according to our faithful understanding of the Scriptures and compelling them to obey the better, not their own, understanding.'

Luther went straight ahead, too, through the third wall erected by the papacy: the pope alone was authorized to convene a Council. There was nothing in the Bible to support this either. Would it not be unnatural if a fire broke out 'and everyone were to stand around and let whatever was burning go on burning for ever simply because no one had the mayor's authority or because the fire had started in the mayor's house?' Was it not the duty of each citizen 'to stir and summon the others?' How much truer this was of the spiritual city when a fire of offence broke out. The Church had power only to improve; if a pope used this power to prohibit a Council whose aim was to improve the Church, it should be ignored and his excommunications and thunderings should not frighten people.

Ten pages of this treatise were enough to demolish the walls. As we can see if we translate Luther's phrases into our own language and terminology, he told the people they had come of age and made them responsible. This had consequences far beyond the sphere of religion, though this was all that mattered to him. For the individuals whom he called to arms it meant the most bitter conflicts, pangs of conscience and mental anguish. It caused endless unrest and fearful antagonisms that continued through the centuries to come. The struggle continues into our own day. In large areas of the world the individual has been subjected to binding authoritarian doctrines, with new-old forms of excommunication, punishment and trials of heretics. New walls have been erected, sometimes quite literally. Even in the so-called 'free world' the individual is increasingly subjected to the constraint of mass movements, and it is only in the 'privacy of his own room' that he can unburden himself to his God.

His treatise went further. He outlined the decisions to be made by a Council if it were convened – which was the great hope in every country. Here, too, his suggestions, though rapidly sketched, had momentous consequences. The pope could remain in office; he had no desire to remove him. But he should relinquish the claim that the triple crown gave him right of dominion over all other crowns. He should devote himself to prayer, to spiritual welfare. His household, with all its finery and pomp, and above all its huge 'crawling mass' of functionaries, officials, money-collectors and lawyers, should be reduced to modest proportions. The College of Cardinals was to be reformed. The never-ending payments to Rome were to be discontinued at once; 'this brings us to the heart of the matter.' In popular language he urged what had been recommended repeatedly at every imperial diet, always without the slightest effect. He called what were habitually referred to as the 'gravamina' of the German nation simply 'thievery and robbery' or 'machinations', and cited examples, such as that of his first antagonist, Archbishop Albrecht of Mainz. It had all 'become stale and customary in Rome', the only changes being the new machinations thought up. Rome was a city of 'buying, selling, changing, exchanging, tippling, lying, deceiving, robbing, stealing, boasting, whoring, knaving' – the fairs at Antwerp and Venice were nothing in comparison. He did not forget to mention the mighty Fuggers, who took such a prominent part in these activities. And where were the bishops, priests and doctors who were supposed to be pledged by their oath and paid in their office to raise their voices against such scandals? 'Turn the page and you have the answer.'

He made further proposals, each touching long-tender spots: reform of the system of confirming bishops in their appointments, which must not be left to Rome; reform of the monasteries, the judicial system, begging, the last to be replaced by poor relief. He attacked celibacy, again with savage reference to existing conditions: priests lived with women in any case, the pope allowed it, forbidding only marriage; dispensation was granted for cash, but not permission to marry. So the poor pastors were forced 'to languish in disgrace and a heavy conscience'. The women were known as priests' whores, the children as priests' children. He made the very practical comment: 'It is not every pastor who can do without a woman, not so much out of frailty as for the sake of his household. In this case he should keep a wife' – God's commandment was that no one should part man and wife.

Here Luther was touching on a particularly acute problem, and even strictly orthodox powers had long been giving thought to the question of celibacy and the possibility of lifting the ban on marriage; in Spain, the most strictly orthodox of all his lands, Charles v himself could not forgo the revenue arising from dispensations for 'priests' children'. Until after Luther's death he still continued to table discussions – during the various attempts to bring about a reunion of the churches – on permission for priests to marry; it was one of the points on which it was hoped to reach agreement.

Luther made many more suggestions for reform: excommunication and interdict should be abolished; there should be a reduction in the excessive number of Church festivals, which degenerated into wild abandon, in pilgrimages and in the raising of 'new saints', which only meant 'people flocking together and money flowing in', more taverns and more whoring. The question of money being drained out of the country cropped up incessantly; it was the strongest argument, and Luther was not the only one to use it, nor was he using it here for the first time. But Luther went further and raised questions of international politics, declaring that the Church's quarrel with the Bohemians should be terminated: 'It is high time for us also to tackle this matter of the Bohemians seriously and truthfully, to unite them to us and us to them.' Here again the secular powers were to intervene: 'on no account should a cardinal or inquisitor' be sent, but peace must be established rationally; the Bohemians should be allowed to retain their Communion cup, which was neither un-Christian nor heretical. The universities were in great need of reform. Luther stormed against the luxurious clothing and intemperance of the Germans, against the 'silk and satin merchants' who encouraged unnecessary luxury. Of usury and interest rates he said: 'The Fuggers and similar concerns must be bridled. How is it possible for one man's life to be piled high with worldly goods on such a kingly scale? I do not know the answer.'

The treatise omitted almost nothing that occupied and disturbed people's minds at that time. Luther, however, raised one further question of overriding importance: what was the source of the papacy's right to intrude into every sphere of human activity in Germany and demand obedience even in secular matters? The Middle Ages had accepted the legend that the pope had conferred the empire on the emperor in the first place. In order to substantiate this legend it had invented the myth of the so-called 'Donation of Constantine': on making Christianity the state religion he was alleged to have given Pope Sylvester Italy and the whole of the west, while he withdrew to the east and his new capital, Constantinople. There had been a deed, signed by the Emperor Constantine and dated. The whole of the Middle Ages had believed in this legal basis of the papacy; it was the foundation of the Pope's claim to primacy over the emperor, the outward sign of this being that the emperor had to 'hold the stirrup' for the pope, to indicate that the ruler was only the Holy Father's 'man' or vassal. The deed was an eighth-century forgery with which Pope Stephen II had confronted the Frankish King Pippin, who could neither read nor write. It had never been questioned, though it had been attacked by many of the emperors, who did not want to submit to the constantly increasing claims of the popes. In the passage in the *Inferno* in which he sends all the popes of his day to hell for their simony, Dante exclaims: 'Ah, Constantine! what ills were gendered there – no, not from thy conversion, but the dower the first rich pope received from thee as heir!'; he traces the whole decline of the Church to this association with wealth and money. But it was only in the fifteenth century that the ability to read and write, hitherto the privilege of the clergy, became sufficiently widespread for serious doubts to be raised about this deed, which had become a part of canon law. Cardinal Nicholas Cusanus had already questioned the document's authenticity; one of the humanists in the entourage of Pope Nicholas V, Lorenzo Valla, papal secretary and elegant Latin scholar, produced a rhetorical study which demonstrated conclusively that this document, so vital to the pope's position, was a forgery. Pope Nicholas allowed the work to pass as a successful essay in humanism; other popes were more on their guard and tried to suppress it. In Germany it was a long time before anything was known about this study, only a few people passing copies furtively from hand to hand. Hutten got hold of one of these manuscripts and published it with an impudent dedication to the reigning pope, Leo X, pointing out that, as the friend of truth and knowledge, he could not but welcome the appearance of this frank document. Luther had got hold of a copy of this edition before he started work on his pamphlet; it strengthened his conviction that Antichrist ruled in Rome. Lies, confusion, conflict were the distinguishing characteristics of Antichrist: had any lie ever done so much mischief as this lie about Constantine's 'donation' of the west to the pope?

He went on to enlarge on this in a historical review of the 'fictitious little discovery'. His knowledge of history was small but, as so often, his instinct had nosed out a genuine scent in the chaos of mediaeval history: endless wars and conflicts had broken out, 'untold shedding of blood', as he said, had resulted, and all on false pretences. All that remained was a fiction: 'We have the empire in name, but the pope has our property, honour, body, life, soul and everything we own.' Or more tersely: 'While the pope devours the kernel we play with the empty husk.'

Luther ended his booklet, as he had begun it, almost light-heartedly: 'Very well then, I know yet another little song about Rome and these people; if their ears are itching I will sing it to them and pitch it as high as I can. You know quite well what I mean, my dear Rome.'

It is easy to be misled by the lightness of his tone, the bluntness of his sallies, the diversity of the questions he raises, many of which he only touches on. It was the heaviest blow ever dealt against Rome. The very ease with which Luther blew down the three walls with his trumpet merely confirmed the long-held impression that they were made of nothing more than 'paper and straw'. The most important scrap of paper, the terror of emperors and kings, was a forgery and worthless! The patriotic appeal to the Germans, who for so long had 'allowed themselves to be mocked and made fools of,' caught hold. The practical proposals commanded respect; they were not just complaints and curses and hopes pinned on vague promises of negotiations. As with all Luther's calls to action each individual took from it what most affected him and his purse. He had in truth addressed 'every estate'. The pamphlet did not contain a programme, or even a developed system, but it fitted into every programme, or rather, since no one in Germany had a programme, it corresponded to all the vague hopes and desires in people's minds. 'Aha, he has come!', someone had exclaimed on first hearing of Luther, and this uncouth 'Aha!' was soon echoed back at him from all sides. He found readers in ecclesiastical circles at all levels as well as among the princes and the citizenry; the peasants heard of the pamphlet even though, like the Frankish kings, they could not read.

Four thousand copies of *On Improving the Christian Estate* were sold in a few weeks; to translate this figure into its modern equivalent we must multiply it by at least ten. Pirated editions appeared at once. Luther's close friends grew nervous; had they not advised him to withhold the pamphlet? Quite unperturbed he wrote to his friend Link: surely people must realize he was not out to win praise and fame. Everyone, from his friends to high Church dignitaries, condemned his strong language. In a phrase that remains eternally true for every revolutionary he said: 'I notice that those in our day who write quiet tracts are quickly forgotten: nobody pays any attention to them.'

Satirical woodcut by Lucas Cranach – the pope receiving indulgence money

Whatever else it was, his tract was not 'quiet'. The people of 'exceptional intellect', whom at the start Luther had brushed aside with a wave of his hand, remained dubious; they have had their successors down the years. There is much that can be said against this little work – it comprises scarcely more than sixty pages – and every objection that can be raised against it has been raised. Albrecht of Mainz wrote to Luther pointing out that such difficult questions as the primacy of the pope and free will were really 'figments of the mind' and of no concern to Christians; they might, perhaps, be discussed some day among a small group of scholars, the public being excluded. This point of view, advanced by the archbishop with all the naïveté characteristic of this high prelate, was the one that prevailed among the rulers of the Church; in many respects it still does. What Luther did was to turn to the layman and speak to him in adult fashion about questions of religious belief; he was understood differently, with tragic consequences. People were now able to read and, Luther decided, it was time they read the Bible; there was the fountainhead of truth, not in papal decretals or other traditional documents.

Still further objections can be urged against Luther's pamphlet. He touched only fleetingly on the social question, which for us is the cardinal problem; a long time was to elapse before it was tackled seriously by anyone. His trust in the princes and the hopes he put in the young emperor were naïve and ingenuous; he lived to see how wrong he had been in this. At first Luther's pamphlet made itself felt only as a political manifesto. It was his 'straight ahead!', his 'buckle to!' that made the biggest impression. There was almost a feeling of spring in the lands of Germany, a feeling that things were on the move, and some sensed apocalyptic undercurrents. The Cassandras were to be proved right all too soon.

Luther immediately followed this first 'breakthrough pamphlet' with a second treatise, his 'new song'. He wrote it in Latin, in the Church mode. But this one, too, was intended only as a prelude; he had more up his sleeve. With the uncanny logic – it amounted almost to a method – that marked his advance from each position to the next, and was in such strong contrast to the easy way in which he threw out his proposals, he now stormed, not the outworks of the institution of the Church of Rome, but the citadel itself. His treatise, a book longer than the first pamphlet, was addressed to the world of learning, to the theologians. He called it *On the Babylonian Captivity of the Church of God*; it put the final seal on his break with Rome. Even among the dignitaries of the Church there were many who forgave, or indeed welcomed, the treatise addressed to the nobility; complaints and reproaches against Rome were a commonplace, and in a popular brochure it was permissible to go a little too far. But this book was unforgivable, and during the attempts to settle the quarrel Luther was urged to deny it and declare it spurious, the work of another. Nothing would induce him to do so. In writing it he had, in fact, been helped by someone else, to whom the more systematic treatment that characterizes the work must in part be ascribed.

The young Melanchthon had now joined Luther as the second reformer; the fact that he always remained the second does not lessen his importance. A humanist, he was an enthusiastic disciple of Erasmus, against whom he would never hear a word of criticism, even when Luther raged furiously at the cautious old man; Greek and his knowledge of the sources were his strong points, and Luther subordinated himself to him with touching modesty where these were concerned. Especially during the early days of their relationship Luther would mention occasionally that he might have to go 'somewhere under heaven', or even to the stake; in such an eventuality 'Master Philipp' would carry on his work and perhaps do it better than he did. Melanchthon never believed in such a possibility. He was a man of compromise, like his master Erasmus; he believed in negotiation and later brought on himself the deep suspicion of his fellow Protestants because he contemplated yielding on certain points. He was well aware of what he lacked in comparison with Luther. His piety was that of the Reuchlin circle in which he had grown up; gentle, modest and placid, he was given neither to extreme exaltation nor to passionate raptures. His family came from the higher grade of craftsmen. His father, an armourer, died young and the boy was brought up by his grandmother, Reuchlin's sister; his great-uncle introduced him into the humanist world. His gift for learning developed very early and he always remained a scholar. His delicate, lean head, with its almost exaggeratedly large eyes, was in the strongest contrast to Luther's hard, peasant skull. But Melanchthon was neither weak nor timid, though some of his contemporaries thought him so. Drawing on all the knife-edged sharpness of the scholar who sees his system endangered, he could be harder and more pitiless than Luther. His first aim, as he announced immediately after his appointment to Wittenberg, was to 'reform the curriculum'. He won lasting fame as *praeceptor Germaniae*, as creator of the *humanistisches Gymnasium* (approximately equivalent to the English grammar school), as teacher and commentator. Scarcely less significant, however, was the part he played in formulating a doctrine for the Protestant Church and creating a new ecclesiastical structure; it was he who wrote the first basic summaries of the new teaching and the no less momentous ones of the Confession of Augsburg. While never failing to keep to his place as Luther's subordinate or assistant he always preserved an independent mind, which was cooler and better able to 'think'. He was anxious to reconcile the philosophic conquests of humanism with theology: philology was necessary for a true understanding of the Bible as was also a knowledge of historical factors. In all this he acted as Luther's counterpart and often as his opponent. Luther was a prophet, a preacher proclaiming his prophecies; Melanchthon admired Luther's 'innate, passionate, sublime and burning courage', as he put it in his funeral oration for his friend. His own courage was of a different kind; he had the courage to give way, a quality odious to all absolutists.

This new colleague worked in secret with Luther on the latter's book on the Babylonian captivity. Its theme was that contemporary Christians were as captive as the Jews had been in Babylon; these captives were the true Christians; Antichrist, who ruled over the 'whore of Babylon', had cast them into chains. There was nothing especially new in these trumpet blasts. Rome had often been called the whore of Babylon. What was new was that Luther questioned the sacramental doctrines and in so doing attacked fundamental dogmas of the Church. Once again the Bible was his basis and sole authority; everything not contained in it was the work of man and a later addition. In the Bible he could find only one sacrament, the Word of God, and only three sacramental 'signs': baptism, penance and the Lord's Supper. To these the Church had added four others: confirmation, marriage, ordination of priests and extreme unction—none of them contained in the Holy Scriptures and hence, for him, invalid. But even the first three had been changed in the course of time, by canonic decree, and needed to be given back their original meaning. This meaning was that faith, and faith alone, was decisive and efficacious, and not simply the sacramental procedure. If a man had faith he could go to heaven even without the sacraments.

This cast doubt on the whole edifice of the Church, which was founded on the administration of the sacraments by ordained priests. Luther's most menacing attack was directed against the Mass, as the chief religious rite. It was not a 'sacrifice', not a mere 'object of faith, as they say', by means of which Christ, as it were, became the 'sacrificial victim', a sacrifice which the priest alone could perform. Luther demanded the direct participation of the communicant who believed in the promised Word; only then would the Word be effective. Mere presence without this active participation was not sufficient; the Mass was worthless if merely 'accepted', or celebrated in the absence of the believer by a priest who said Masses which had been endowed for the dead. Luther rejected the whole ceremonial of the Church chapter by chapter, taking all seven sacraments in turn.

His presentation was 'historical'; what he wanted to see was the old, not something new, the old as it had been announced in the Scriptures, not the new which had been added by decretals and ecclesiastical authorities. The old was to be reinstated in its primitive, original entirety. The Church had no right to claim authority to exceed the words of the Scriptures, invent new teachings and practices, and then declare them binding. It could not create new sacraments; to do so would set it above the Word of God. Luther's real desire was to restore. He was a revolutionary.

His interpretation meant the destruction of the whole body of religious rites built up in the course of centuries; these implications were realized immediately, in their full magnitude, and the book aroused incomparably more indignation than the first pamphlet. The very reduction of the seven sacraments to three, and to Luther's three in particular, was considered a sacrilege of unimaginable wickedness. Luther had asked, with historical justification, when mention had first been made of seven sacraments. The only authority he had been able to find was Dionysius, a Greek whom Paul had converted and to whom the Middle Ages ascribed a series of much later writings. Luther was unaware of this mistake, but his sure instinct and acuteness led him to mistrust this leading representative of Christian mysticism and declare, as it were by divination, that he was a Platonist rather than a Christian: 'Let us listen rather to Paul!' These were specialized questions for professional theologians. But to cast doubt in this way on the time-honoured sanctity of the seven sacraments caused enormous upheaval among the laity as well. King Henry VIII of England immediately sat down and wrote the first of his scathing and abusive polemics against Luther, who replied in similar vein and extremely disrespectful terms. King 'Heinz', as Luther called him, was rewarded by the pope with the honorary title *Defensor Fidei*, which the kings of England still retained after they had been anathematized and excommunicated as apostates. Of greater importance is the fact that when Henry VIII broke with Rome, and established his own state church, he clung resolutely to the seven sacraments. Alterations in forms of worship have always provoked much stronger reactions than changes in dogma. The battle over giving the laity wine as well as bread at Communion, the Lord's Supper in both kinds, had been the cause of the Hussite quarrel and continued to be a main point of disagreement throughout the whole period of the Reformation. To take the Communion cup meant defection from the Church of Rome, even if the person concerned remained a 'faithful believer' in other respects and complied with all the remaining practices and regulations. Luther himself hesitated a long time before he ventured to change the traditional form of the Mass; this gave rise to severe conflicts. Ceremonial and custom exercise a mysterious power, and the more cryptic the mysteries they symbolize the greater the power. Luther still had to learn this.

For the moment the matter did not concern him. He strode boldly on to this next position, using the international language of scholarship to make the most audacious proposals. Not only did he reject the sacraments as administered by the Church, and the privileged position of the priest, he repudiated monasticism in principle – again on the basis of his fundamental attitude that in comparison with faith mere 'good works' or praiseworthy acts were of no account. The monk's renunciation was no more estimable 'than the work of a peasant in tilling his fields or a woman looking after her household'; indeed the activities of a manservant or maidservant were more pleasing to God 'than all the fasting and toils of a monk or priest, if faith is lacking.' He condemned celibacy and praised marriage. He rejected the Church's jurisdiction, especially in marital conflicts and dispensations; this, one of the Curia's great means of exercising its authority, extended into the higher, and indeed into the highest, levels of international politics and led to the historic break with England. 'In such matters some scholars and lay citizens are more skilled than popes, bishops and councils.'

The book is much more penetrating and much more penetratingly thought out than the first polemic; the emperor's father confessor, who had read Luther's earlier publications with a measure of approval, declared that on reading it he felt as if someone were whipping him from head to foot all over his body. With a single blow Luther split the whole existing outlook on life and the world into two, into the new faith and the old.

He followed these two works with a third in the same year, the real year of his calling: *On the Liberty of a Christian Man*. The shortest of the three treatises, it is little more than sixteen pages long and was written in two or three days as a final attempt to come to terms with the Church. The title has led to a great deal of misunderstanding: the work is no polemic – it is much more like an about-turn, though basically it is a Utopia. The misunderstanding has been caused by the opening sentence: 'A Christian man is a free lord over everything and subject to no one.' It became a slogan. However, it was followed immediately by the sentence: 'A Christian man is an obedient servant in everything and subject to everyone.' This second statement was ignored; no one wanted to hear it. The public figure and revolutionary had withdrawn completely into his little room, not to rage and roar but to meditate. The tiny work constitutes an important facet of the complete portrait of Luther; he was both a solitary and a man of wide influence, and every attempt to tie him down to a narrow formula is idle. He had stormed and raged and, as Erasmus with his incomparable gift for epigram put it, made himself hated by 'seizing the pope by his tiara and the monks by their paunches'. But now he spoke directly to the heart. Much of the power he exercised over people came from this many-sidedness of his nature, and many were convinced that he was the apostle they were waiting for just becaue he not only raged and threatened but could also speak so 'simply' and movingly. He was a monk who sought nothing for himself, not money, not a great post in the Church, not an influential position as leader of a movement – this is how people, or at any rate the 'quiet ones in the land', saw him at this time.

It was to the 'quiet ones' that he now turned, and they were a great force, distributed widely in small groups and cells of which the ordinary person was scarcely aware. German mysticism had already led to the establishment of such groups and Luther now spoke, just as they had done, of the inner and outer man. He was concerned exclusively with the inner man; what appeared outside was simply an adjunct. The inner man was free; the outer man was bound, captive, 'sick and tired, hungry, thirsty and suffering', but none of this touched the soul. In faith the soul had honour and dignity, a kingdom. Faith was the dowry; Luther still made use of the old metaphor of the bride and bridegroom: 'Is it not a cheerful, happy household in which the rich, noble, devout bridegroom, the Christ, takes in marriage the poor, despised and wicked harlot, frees her from all that is evil and adorns her with all that is good?' Sin was 'swallowed up' in Christ, and man was thereby justified. This, however, was not enough; he continued as a bodily existence 'and must govern his own body and mix with people'. Luther turned his back completely on mysticism, which recognized only the individual man, whose purpose was to perfect himself and himself alone. Man had to do good works, only he must not imagine that good works such as fasting and mortification were enough: he must work as Adam did and not be idle. Here we can already see the Protestant 'ethics of work' proclaimed. Luther issued a warning: good, devout works do not make a good, devout man but a good, devout man does good works; a good carpenter builds a good house. We must 'look within a person to see what makes him devout'; he is not made devout by works but by faith. Good works should not serve merely selfish ends but one's fellow men. Just as Christ did all that he did for mankind 'without reward', so man likewise should serve his fellow men 'freely, cheerfully and without reward'. This was Christian living, 'which, alas, was not only ailing throughout the world but was no longer either recognized or preached.'

This pamphlet was a sermon, and it is not easy to understand why, apart from some remarks directed against 'stark hypocrisy', it was

considered so insidious. In fact Luther went very far in his willingness
to comply with (or compromise with) the authorities whom he had just
attacked so mercilessly: man should be subject to the higher powers, as
Paul said in his Epistle to the Romans – for Luther this was a key
passage in respect of everything connected with the outward life. If
this were really understood, he said, it was possible to adapt onself even
to the 'innumerable commands and laws of the pope, monasteries,
religious foundations, princes and rulers', although these had been
carried to such a pitch by some 'mad prelates' as to seem necessary for
salvation. A free Christian could comply with all this, not as a means of
going to heaven, but to set an example to the pope, the bishop, the
community or his comrades. He should suffer, as Christ suffered, for
greater things. 'And though the tyrants do wrong in making such
demands, they do me no harm provided they are not against God.' He
did not put the pope on the same footing as princes and rulers by accident; for him the pope was simply 'an authority', one of many, something external. His authority did not reach as far as the soul, which
Luther reserved strictly to himself; it was free. And so even this quietest
of his three writings was a declaration of war. At the same time it is
worth remarking how frequently the word '*fröhlich*', cheerful, occurs in
it, but appealing to the mind and the sentiments rather than jocularly
to the senses as it did in the pamphlet addressed to the nobility.

The effectiveness of this trio of writings lay in the practical, statesman-
like proposals contained in the chords in the middle register and in the
soft *cantus firmus* of an unshakeable conviction. Much was only hinted at,
not a little was later withdrawn or in some cases intensified (Luther was
never 'finished' either with himself or his task); a great deal passed un-
noticed. But this was the breakthrough. It marked the end of the
fundamental medieval doctrine of two different races, the clergy and
the laity, both of whom were needed to create a unity, a unity that had
always been purely theoretical, 'reality consisting in endless strife
between the two 'races'. Pope Boniface VIII had categorized the laity
as 'the enemy'. The powerful monk Hildebrand, Pope Gregory VII, the
originator of the theory of the papacy's absolute primacy over all
secular rulers, had already propounded the thesis that the lay world
represented only a communion of the devil, ruled by the prince of this
world, Satan, and by earthly lords who sought to govern only by 'lust
for power, robbery, murder, in short by almost every crime against
mankind'; to them could be applied the saying of Jeremiah, which
he himself used almost as his motto: 'Cursed be he that keepeth back his
sword from blood.' The 'endless shedding of blood', to which Luther
referred from his very inadequate knowledge of medieval history, was
no mere theory. And whatever may be said of supposed periods of

unity – and generally speaking these are relegated to increasingly remote and unfamiliar eras – there is no doubt whatever that in Luther's day a point had been reached when the old ideas had lost their force. He implemented a historical process which had commenced long before his time and which had now reached its peak. It is possible to see in him only the 'trigger', the catalyst, which set off a host of different forces and 'reactions', but this is to do him an injustice. He stamped his image on an age.

# 18

# Ulrich von Hutten

LUTHER's great polemical writings of 1520 had made him a popular hero; boundless hopes were placed in him. Prior to this his name, for many people, had signified no more than an 'interesting case', a sequel to the Reuchlin affair; this, at any rate, was how humanist circles had regarded him. The young Hutten, as we have seen, had also considered the whole business at its inception as nothing but a 'monks' squabble' between the Dominicans and Augustinians. But now that the matter was assuming wider importance, the knight decided to range himself on the side of the monk who clearly was the 'new man', the man for whom they had been hoping and whose advent had long been prophesied. Hutten never had any real grasp of Luther's religious intentions, let alone of his doubts and anxieties; it was enough that Luther was the champion of a great national cause: the fight against Rome, against 'Rome's foreign domination'. And since Hutten was, or wanted to be, a political force, he now intervened with his scathing pen: a new and freer Germany was to arise. Scholarship was already in the process of freeing itself from centuries of patronage. Now the empire was also to become strong again, as it had been in its glorious past, under a great emperor comparable to Charlemagne. Did not the young Charles, untried though he was as yet, bear the same auspicious name? Brimming over with hope, and throwing caution to the winds, Hutten expressed his joy and exaltation in a celebrated letter to the Nuremberg patrician, Willibald Pirckheimer, the friend of Albrecht Dürer and leader of the Nuremberg humanists: 'Oh century! Oh scholarship! What a joy it is to live at this moment – and not to retire into inactivity, my Willibald! Intellectual pursuits thrive, the human mind is astir! But as for you, barbarism, you can get yourself a piece of rope and go into exile ...'

Hutten was not the only one to indulge in joy and hope. Even the habitually cautious Erasmus had dreams of a new golden age; he saw Pope Leo x as the Maecenas who would bring it about, and in one of his extravagantly flattering letters, which secretly amused him, he announced the fact to Leo himself. The effects of this letter were far-reaching. A letter written by the great Erasmus was always an event: shared, copied and printed, it was regarded as a literary accolade, a great intellectual occurrence; no other pen has ever exerted such an influence throughout Europe. The few lines of recommendation he wrote for the young Hutten were the most valuable and important credential to which the latter could aspire; armed with them he fancied himself in a position to take the Habsburg court in Brussels by storm and sway the course of international politics. There was no limit to people's hopes during these years; the naïveté and unawareness of the brutal realities of life is almost touching. Disillusion soon followed, turning to despair, self-abasement and self-humiliation. Hutten was an example of this. He died at the age of thirty-five on the small island of Ufenau in Lake Zurich, lonely, exiled, forsaken by almost everyone, exhausted by his failures and ravaged by the illness which had dogged him since he was twenty.

For a few brief years, however, he stood and fought at Luther's side in the full glare of the international spotlight; he too was a master of language, he too was wild and reckless, one-sided, given to violent anger. 'I dared' was his motto, and he dared much. A lone wolf like Luther, without following or connections, he was poor and, to make matters worse, ill; small and plain, he had fair hair and, beneath his prematurely lined face, a thin black beard. This contrast was repeated within his own nature, which was compounded of noble and frankly dubious qualities. It was always easy for his opponents to score him off. Look at him, they said, he wants to be independent and then goes and sells his liberty to every potentate who comes along, ecclesiastical and secular alike! He paraded his noble lineage and yet remained nothing more than a wretched, impecunious scribbler; his fellow nobles turned their backs on him. He preached health because his own was bad, abstinence because wine no longer agreed with him. Finally his end proved how little there was to him: the emperor, whom he had praised so highly, dropped him, his great friend Erasmus, the prince of the mind, did likewise, and even Luther, on whose behalf he had entered the lists, wanted nothing more to do with him. He died utterly alone; a divine judgment.

We know more to his discredit than his contemporaries did, and his story contains elements both grotesque and moving. Perhaps the most serious charge against him is that he completely failed to appreciate the political and social realities of his day, although his court activities and diplomatic missions should have equipped him far better to do so than the monk Luther sitting in his cell.

Ulrich von Hutten came of an old Franconian noble family with

231

many and widespread branches; its members were to be found in numerous castles and in influential positions at court. His branch of the family was poor, owning little more than Steckelburg Castle, a woe-begone robber stronghold deep in the forest. His grandfather had tried to form a sort of joint-stock company composed of thirty-two robber knights like himself who, for a fixed share, would be able to use Steckelburg as a base for their raids against the scoundrelly merchant riff-raff; but the project came to nothing. The towns had grown too strong, their convoys were too well protected. Hutten's father wanted his small, unprepossessing son, who seemed ill-fitted for a soldier's life, to enter the Church, but Ulrich very quickly disappeared from his monastery. He was to become a lawyer, the profession Luther's father had chosen for his son, but Ulrich escaped into *belles-lettres*, an occupation in which there was no money and which was tantamount to begging. Many were the high roads which Hutten travelled from one end of Europe to the other, on foot or on horseback, always short of money, adrift, occasionally being given a meal or invited to dinner. Some angry poems written in revenge against one of his hosts, who had had him thrown out and beaten by his servants, were the first literary productions of the young man of letters. But he earned wide fame, even abroad, with a small volume of hexameters designed to teach the diffi-cult art of writing elegant Latin verse. The humanists took this art very seriously; the syllables had to be counted, their quantity known, the metre mastered. For many years Hutten's work was used as a textbook, and today its numerous editions would have brought the author a good income; all Hutten gained from it was the honour of being known and published, even in Paris.

He made friends and quarrelled with them. A secure post evaded him. While in Italy he had to serve at times as a common soldier, and it was as a soldier wielding his pen that he wandered from place to place. His poems extolling as a patriotic act the Emperor Maximilian's attempts to seize Venice were his first incursion into political pamphlet-eering; they brought him no financial gain, but the emperor bestowed on him the title of poet laureate, and his portraits from this time show the thin, bitter, keen-eyed face crowned by a laurel wreath. A whole literature of polemic and inflammatory political writings now started to make its appearance everywhere: with Hutten the German eagle began to stretch its wings, while in France Le Maire perched the Gallic cock on the battlements. Age-old claims were aired and reasserted. In its first crude outlines every method of modern political publicity was tried.

Before entering this arena, in which he was to achieve his greatest successes, Hutten had to fight out a family feud of his own, which very

soon developed wider political repercussions. The feud had started
when Hans Hutten, Master of the Horse, was slain by his lord Duke
Ulrich of Württemberg. Ulrich, or Utz, of Württemberg was perhaps
the most picturesque of all the wild and dissolute petty German princes.
Pronounced of age when still almost a child by his uncle Maximilian, he
at once proceeded to mismanage his affairs with such abandon that
the peasants rose in one of the earliest peasant revolts; it was suppressed
ruthlessly. Utz's love affair with the beautiful Ursula, whom he had
visited when she was still a girl in the women's apartments of her
father's castle, also came to a bloody end; she had been quickly married
off to the master of the horse, a cousin of Hutten's, and the Emperor
Maximilian immediately placed his ward and nephew in the marital
care of a hard Bavarian virago. The duke did not relinquish his love; in
fact—and at this point the story resembles some old folk song – he fell
on his knees at the feet of his master of the horse and implored him:
Leave her to me, Hans, leave me my Ursula; I cannot, will not and do
not know how to give her up!

When the Huttens started to spread the tale, the proud Utz flew
into a rage and killed his master of the horse when out hunting, from
behind according to the Huttens, from the front, in a duel, according
to the duke. The Huttens, who were a large clan, were stirred to action;
the duke had made enemies enough and to add to the confusion his
formidable wife fled to her brothers in Bavaria. She claimed that her
husband had made inhuman and 'outlandish' demands of her in bed;
the lovely widow of the master of the horse thought otherwise, since she
stayed with her Utz, though cursed by the Hutten family as the
Swabian Helen of Troy. Ulrich von Hutten published long and detailed
accounts in defence of his family cause, indicting the 'Württemberg
executioner' before the whole world.

It was a family feud, but it soon proliferated, becoming a touchstone
for conditions in the empire. The Emperor Maximilian stood steadfastly by his wild protégé, although the latter went on to perpetrate
further excesses, among which was a daring raid on one of the free
imperial cities that had helped him to suppress the peasants' revolt.
Finally the new Emperor Charles intervened in the interests of the
Habsburg dynasty, annexing a large and beautiful territory important
as a bridge between the patrimonial lands in Austria and Burgundy.
German politics were poisoned for decades by the 'Württemberg
question'. From the outset of Charles v's reign it became abundantly
clear that far from being the German emperor people had hoped for, he
would always put first the dynastic interests of his house.

Hutten experienced his first great disappointment and saw his hopes
of a new empire vanish into thin air. Maximilian, whose praises he had

sung so ardently, had failed him; his only chance now was to guide the young Charles into better ways. He tried to rouse the nation with his polemics and dialogues; such passionately 'engaged' writings had rarely been seen in Germany. At first he wrote in Latin and found a wide, international public; then, under Luther's influence, he also used German, speaking directly to the people. His starting-point was always his own highly personal experience and suffering; and his sufferings were considerable. He was tormented by syphilis, which had quickly spread through Europe at the beginning of the sixteenth century and begun to cause universal and fearful havoc. There was no cure; poultices were used, as well as baths and applications of quicksilver, which even in the Middle Ages had been known as a remedy for skin diseases. Hutten describes in the minutest detail the eleven different cures he underwent: ointments containing a mixture of salt, red lead, rust and verdigris, powdered worms, starvation, incarceration in a fiercely overheated room for three weeks. His teeth became loose and he put a piece of alum in his mouth to harden the gums a little; he was racked by thirst but his stomach refused any form of liquid. He lived on and, in the intervals between his eleven cures, continued to write.

Hutten does not correspond to our image of the knightly hero, and in one of his dialogues he portrayed himself and others of his type. Describing the Diet of Augsburg, at which Luther faced Cajetan, he castigated his fellow Germans. Did they engage in discussions? Did they take the empire's fate seriously to heart? They drank, their tippling knew no bounds, the diet was nothing but one long drinking bout; enormous men were to be seen in magnificently embroidered doublets, their hair beautifully curled, gold chains hung around their necks – and all drunk. He caught sight of only a few sober men among them, undersized dwarfs compared with the great, hulking giants, but with plenty of brains and very shrewd: 'May the gods protect the great little men!' he exclaimed. In the picture he painted the role of the 'intellectual' in the assemblies of the mighty was already memorably drawn.

The great little man fought his battle single-handed. His fever continued and to it he dedicated his first two fighting dialogues, 'the first fever' and 'the second fever'. He spoke to the disease, telling the fever to move off and find someone else; he suggested Cardinal Cajetan, a rich Roman prelate on whom it could really regale itself, but the fever rejected the dried-up Italian. How about the fat monks and well-fed canons? Or the Fuggers, the merchants, the doctors, the emperor's plump scribes and secretaries? There was no trace of fever, however, in the way in which Hutten expounded his thoughts on reform. They were hard-hitting and found their targets, the universally deplored evils of the day: down with all the lazy loafers, the benefices, the idle life of pleasure! Let these drones do some work for a change and till the fields by the sweat of their brows like other people! It was high time the Germans pulled themselves together; things could not go on as they were. Rome was the target to aim at, it was the source of all the evils.

Ulrich von Hutten

In his next work, *On the Roman Trinity*, Hutten attacked Rome directly. Drawing on what he had seen and heard in Italy, he touched a sensitive nerve by remarking on the contemptuous way in which people in Rome dismissed the Germans as good-natured simpletons, whose mission in life was merely to pay and go on paying. In Rome stood the vast barn and granary into which the spoils from every country were shovelled: 'And in the midst of it sits the insatiable corn weevil polishing off huge stacks of corn, surrounded by countless other fellow gorgers. They have sucked our blood and gnawed our flesh until they have reached the marrow, and they will go on to break the bones and grind the whole body to pieces.' He called the nation to arms against the plunderers who lived off the blood and sweat of the German people. What did they do with their gold? They got themselves mules, they kept women and boys for their amusement, they built marble palaces, and if they were not flattered and fawned upon they threatened violence and terror. When would the Germans finally learn some sense and avenge the shame? 'Formerly religious considerations and reservations of piety may have held us back; now we are driven by sheer necessity!'

No one had attacked Rome like this before; even Luther's most scathing diatribes pale before it. Hutten hammered his slogans home with triple repetitions. In Rome everything went in threes: its reputation was based on the pope, worship of saints and the indulgences, but the triad of simplicity, moderation and piety was outlawed; whores, priests and scribes existed in profusion while the Council, reform of the priesthood and the German awakening were odious.

Hutten voiced the three watchwords that were on everybody's lips. Discontinuation of payments to Rome was one of his ideas; the pope might remain, but he was to live modestly and get rid of the idlers. The huge priestly population in every country was to be reduced and the posts filled with good, well-informed men instead of with wretched, uneducated substitutes; priests must also be allowed to marry, in order to put an end to the mischief of concubinage. The need was for reform. Hutten saw clearly that this would not be easy. Their opponents should not be underrated, declared his partner in the dialogue, just back from Rome. 'No great deed can be accomplished without danger,' replied Hutten, 'and even if the cause itself is unsuccessful, the attempt is worth making.' – 'Will you persuade the Germans to do this?' – 'I shall try.' – 'Will you speak the truth?' – 'I shall speak it even if they threaten me with death.'

These were no empty words; the first list of excommunications, headed by the name of Luther, also contained that of Hutten. Compelled to go into hiding, he sought refuge with his friend and patron the great condottiere Franz von Sickingen, whose castle of Ebernburg he called the 'Refuge of Justice'. He went on writing; later he wrote in German, which was clumsy at first, because he was new to it, and never achieved the smooth polish of his Latin.

In the best known of his German songs Hutten wrote: 'I've proved, in word, my daring: good landsknecht, brave horseman, rise, and let not Hutten perish!' The good landsknechts had better things to do than rush to the colours of a lone, vagabond knight; they sold their services to ruling princes, who won the victories. Hutten believed in a 'third force', the lesser nobility from which he came, but it was now no more than a figment of the imagination; he envisaged it still playing its long extinct, medieval role. He carried on a stubborn fight against the rising power of the princes and at the end even hoped to win over the cities, at whose commercial souls he had scoffed and jeered, to an alliance with the nobility. He commended the war against the priesthood as a means of throwing off the yoke of Rome, and he always retained his supreme hope in the emperor, without whom no one in those days, not even the peasants, could imagine a new order.

One after another these illusions were shattered. In the very first lines of the letter he wrote to Luther, offering himself as an ally, he wrote: 'You could not help being moved by compassion were you to see the difficulties I have to contend with here – so fickle is human loyalty. While I am recruiting new auxiliaries the old ones leave me. Everyone has his fears and pretexts. Above everything looms the delusion on which they were suckled: that it is an inexpiable crime to rebel against the pope, even against the unworthiest and most criminal pope. I do what I can and yield to no misfortune'. Public opinion of a kind already existed, and it was this to which Hutten appealed; but it was indeterminate, was nowhere crystallized and lacked even the smallest of definable groups. Hutten's own friends continually vacillated. His one and only protector, the condottiere Sickingen, was about to join the emperor as commander-in-chief. Hutten visited the court at Brussels, but his journey was both fruitless and pathetic; with Charles still in Spain, only his younger brother Ferdinand was in residence, and Hutten was refused permission to see even him. The tasks he undertook, or said he would undertake, became more and more distressing. Encouraged by his friends he wanted to abduct the papal legates; when nothing came of it he was derided. Then he became involved in a number of petty and grotesque affairs: a personal feud against an abbot who had used Hutten's widely circulated portrait 'to clean unclean parts of his body' and from whom he demanded a large cash indemnity; attacks on other abbots, in one of which a servant of Hutten's was seized and hanged. The great war against the priesthood degenerated into Sickingen's senseless raid on Trier and ended with the death of Hutten's only protector. Hutten had to flee. In Basle he hoped to get help and encouragement from Erasmus, but the cautious old man refused to let him cross his doorstep and turned him away. Hutten's last piece of writing was a bitter indictment of the humanist intellectual élite, whom, in the most biting words the pampered Erasmus had ever heard, he accused of cowardice and betrayal of the cause. The latter's answer, under the apparently innocuous title *Sponge*, and ostensibly intended to mop up the 'splashes' made by Hutten, was in fact stinging and malicious and aimed at Hutten's most vulnerable spots; it seems never to have reached the dying man. The Zurich reformer Zwingli was the only one to show compassion for the hounded man and persuaded the Zurich city council to give him sanctuary on the island of Ufenau. There the knight died, in conditions amounting to solitary confinement, cared for, as a final irony, by a few kindly friars and a medically trained priest, who, however, could do nothing to help him. But Erasmus, the great champion of gentleness and humanity, the great advocate of reconciliation, had not hesitated to incite the Zurich city council to expel the persecuted man. Hutten, he wrote, will 'abuse your kindness with his salacious and mischievous writings' and Zurich would suffer severely as a result of his 'unbridled wickedness'; to this Erasmus, who had long ago bid farewell to the Reformation and all it stood for, added that Hutten's activities could 'exceedingly damage evangelical affairs', as well as the noble arts and morals in general. This lamentable denunciation was the end of the humanist dream, with its hopes of a brotherhood of free minds, and of all Hutten's other dreams.

As can be imagined, his estate consisted of debts. Important to us, as well as to his contemporaries, would have been the great collection of two thousand letters from princes, priests and scholars of every country, who assured Hutten of their sympathy, admired his fight and then prudently withdrew. The letters disappeared very quickly because they contained too much compromising material. This is the verdict on his fellows who were unwilling to 'dare' anything, and welcomed Hutten's bold conduct only so long as it suited their plans or they could admire it from a safe distance. Luther's letters to him have also been destroyed, but for other reasons. It may well be that the peasant in Luther did not find the knight overly sympathetic, even if at times he welcomed Hutten's fanfares. Luther refused to have anything to do with the war against the priesthood: 'I do not want force and homicide used on behalf of the Gospel,' he wrote on receiving one of Hutten's letters; 'the Word has conquered the world, the Word has sustained the Church, and through the Word the Church will be re-established.'

The woodcut by Hans Baldung Grien on the title page of the German edition of Hutten's polemic writings shows Luther and Hutten side by side: the monk meditating on truth, as the caption tells us, and the knight accompanied by his saying, which became a watchword, 'We shall prevail'; underneath a warlike band of knights on horseback, with landsknechts carrying long pikes, scatter the frightened crowd of popes, cardinals, abbots and monks. For a short time Hutten took his place at Luther's side, or rather fought simultaneously in his own way and with his own means: 'I do what I can, and yield to no misfortune.' Hutten did not prevail; he was swept away by forces mightier than the pen. In a postscript to his last letter, written from his little island in a hand that was already shaky, to a friend, Hutten asked for some books because he wanted to devote himself once more to study; one of his requests was for a 'little book on how to make fireworks'. This is characteristic of the man. His writings, conceived as fiery darts and deadly missiles, turned out to be little more than fireworks displays. Still, he commands our respect. In the same dying breath he wrote to another friend: 'I do not give up hope that a time will come when God will once again gather together men of courage who are now dispersed; you must not give up this hope either.'

# 19

# The Bull of Excommunication

LUTHER had dedicated his work *On the Liberty of a Christian Man* to Pope Leo and accompanied it with a detailed explanatory letter to the Holy Father; the pamphlet was a further outcome of the talks with the peripatetic Miltitz and was intended as a final attempt at reconciliation. Luther, it must be admitted, had a peculiar notion of tractability, and his letter to the pope reads more like a monstrously defiant refusal. Showing what to Roman eyes seemed reckless temerity, he even declared that it would be better for the pope to confine himself to a benefice or his patrimony, in other words to resign and withdraw, than to remain a 'sheep among wolves': for 'the See of Rome is finished. God has never ceased to vent his wrath on it. It is hostile to the General Council, it will submit to neither instruction nor reform.' Reform, he said, should be the work of the cardinals, but they did nothing either; there might be three or four willing men among them, but they could not get their point of view accepted – 'the disease is making a fool of medicine, horse and carriage ignore the driver.' Luther saw his opponent Eck as the instigator of the whole process against him; 'with his lies, open letters and secret machinations [he has] brought bitterness and confusion into the whole affair.' The pope had only to order peace, and all the discord would be eradicated. 'But for me to withdraw my teaching would accomplish nothing . . . because the Word of God, which teaches freedom, should not and must not be imprisoned.' The pope never received this letter. Luther's conjecture that Eck was behind the whole affair was correct. Eck, as victor in the Leipzig disputation, had been summoned to Rome, where he began to display great energy. In his opinion everything done so far had been too tame and formal; a bull of excommunication should be published at once. The action for heresy, so long adjourned, was re-opened – for political reasons.

Leo, true to the example set by his predecessors, was forever trying to play off one power against another; it was the Curia's sole panacea. The policy had often been successful in the past, but its day was now over; countries and their leaders, very conscious that things had changed, now acted with a wholly new self-assurance. France already had an established Church, and it was to a large extent independent. In England Cardinal Wolsey reigned like a second pope, with unprecedented powers. The King of Spain also exercised great independence, in addition to which he was able to exert severe pressure on Rome through his kingdom of Naples; for centuries the Curia had regarded this threat of 'encirclement' as the gravest danger, using every means in its power to hold it in check. Germany was the only nation in which the Curia could still hope to maintain its traditional dominant position; it could count on stronger support there than in other nations where no reigning potentates were princes of the Church. The prevailing view in Rome was – and here the bitter polemics of Hutten and others were entirely justified – that in the Germans they were dealing with a simple, rather obtuse people, who like everybody else protested at times but toed the line when they saw that Rome meant business. One cannot attach much importance to expressions of national hostility and antagonism when these are open to manipulation; nevertheless it seems clear that the sense of superiority of the Romans was a very material factor in the ensuing catastrophe. Pope Leo had some reason to feel proud; lamentable as were his international politics, Rome, during his papacy, stood magnificently before the world as the centre of the arts, as a setting for great buildings and festivities, for Latinity at its finest. His rhymesters, rewarded with princely fees, extolled this splendour, while true poets, like Ariosto, occasionally added their voices and produced brilliant comedies for the papal court. That the great new Church of St Peter, which was again to symbolize, down to the smallest details of its design, the central idea of the papacy, had been held up by the untimely intervention of a barbaric monk and his fight against the indulgence system, was a threat to papal prestige. But Leo continued to hesitate, and not on political grounds alone. It was as if some vague premonition had warned him that a great decision was imminent. Perhaps this is overrating him, but he was no fool; he was simply a gambler incapable of decisive action.

In January 1520 it was decided to re-open the case and extend the proceedings to include the elector. A committee of cardinals and vicars-general of the orders was then appointed to work out the text of a bull of excommunication. They took their task lightly; the Dominicans in Cologne and Louvain had already extracted and condemned passages from the collected edition of Luther's works published in Basle, and the committee merely voted on these.

But now someone else's prestige was threatened, that of Cardinal

Cajetan, who was a member of the committee. This experienced theologian and expert on canon law considered the proceedings too cursory; he alone seems to have had any clear idea of what was at stake. He persuaded the committee to accept his proposal that ten more theologians be co-opted – cardinals in his view being inadequately trained in theology; he was anxious to make a clearer distinction between those of Luther's utterances that were out-and-out heresy and those that were merely 'aggravating', 'offensive' or calculated to unsettle people. But Cajetan was a sick man – he had to be carried to the meetings in a litter – and Eck, who was in robust health and considered all this excessively cautious, went into action. He prevailed on the pope to drop Cajetan's proposals. Another committee was appointed, this time with only four members and with Eck as its head. Things now progressed rapidly; only the text of the condemnation still had to be written. Leo signed it at his hunting lodge at Magliano. He also was a sick man and died in November the following year, aged forty-six. Already ill when elected, as one of the youngest of the popes, to the holy see at the age of thirty-eight, he had been operated on for a stercoral fistula in the middle of the electoral deliberations; he was very near-sighted and his small eyes, set in a puffy face that not even Raphael in his famous portrait could ennoble, were able to enjoy the constant pleasures that marked his tenure of office only through a lorgnette. There was a desperate, hectic quality about his insatiable desire for pleasure. He thought he could prolong his life by gaiety, and spent money lavishly in order to surround himself with cheerful and contented people; as he lay dying, his last words were: 'Pray for me, I want to make you all happy!' There was no time to administer the sacraments and extreme unction, the extreme unction which Luther, in his *Babylonian Captivity*, had wanted to delete from the list of sacraments hallowed by the Church.

Strictly speaking, and in accordance with the legal practice of the Curia, the document signed by the pope at Magliano was not the final Bull of Excommunication, but only a threat of excommunication in case Luther failed to recant within the given time-limit. The excommunication was not completed until the beginning of the following year when a further bull, introduced by the words '*Decet Romanum Pontificem*', was promulgated; but scarcely any attention was paid to it, because it was merely the formal conclusion of a process that had been constantly postponed for political reasons. The first bull was the historic and decisive step and has always been understood as such: 'Rome has spoken; the case is now closed' – in the words of the traditional phrase that went back to the time of St Augustine.

Eck took good care that the document, over which there had been

Title-page of Pope Leo x's Bull of Excommunication against Luther

such procrastination, was published quickly, and once again it is a sign of the casual, irresponsible way in which the whole proceedings were conducted that later, when the consequences became apparent, he, the principal actor, coolly complained that several of the condemned passages were incomprehensible even to very learned men and that he himself found them quite unimportant. No attempt had been made, he said, to refute Luther's theses, although a thorough refutation should have been undertaken; moreover the bull contained nothing whatever from the Gospels, and no one in Rome really knew what the heretic's errors were. This was, in fact, the distinguishing feature of the fairly comprehensive decree, headed by the Medici arms and universally distributed.

It began, in the oldest Curia style, with ringing, solemn phrases reminiscent of certain verses in the Psalms in which God is also called upon to rise against his adversaries: 'Rise, O Lord', *exurge Domine* – and this is the name by which the bull is known. The Lord was asked to listen to the pope's entreaty, foxes had appeared, intent on despoiling the vineyard, a wild boar, a beast, had broken in; immediately after this, however, vigorous stress was laid once more on the traditional significance of the papacy: 'When thou didst ascend unto the Father, O Lord, thou didst entrust Peter, as its head and thy representative, and his successors, with the care of this vineyard, its government and management.' Peter, too, was therefore called upon to rise, together with Paul and all the saints, and finally the whole Church; for their true interpretation of the Holy Scriptures was being falsely perverted by certain people whom Satan had blinded, as had been done by heretics from time immemorial 'for reasons of ambition and in order to catch the ear of the people' – of the German people, on whom the popes had always bestowed such especial love and to whom they had also assigned the empire. The political hint is clear. The long hesitation was explained as forbearance and paternal love: the guilty man had been treated leniently and had even been offered the cost of his journey to Rome in order to defend himself there. Even now he was being given sixty days' grace. If by that time he did not recant the punishment would take effect. What he had to recant was itemized in forty-one clauses, which included, among other things, Luther's assertion: 'To burn heretics is contrary to the Holy Spirit.'

Passages of Luther's were cited which, according to the prevailing canon law, were indeed heretical, and if the bull had had the careful preparation Cajetan proposed an impressive list might have been compiled. But those of Luther's writings which presaged his break with the Church had not been considered at all. The authors had been content to accept the verdicts of the Dominicans in Cologne and

Louvain who, in their turn, had proceeded in a more or less arbitrary manner, taking some passages out of their contexts and re-wording others. Luther could protest that these were not his teachings. The bull ended by condemning all forty-one clauses in their entirety, forbidding anyone, including the emperor and the princes, to defend or promote them, and ordering Luther's writings to be burned.

To sum up: the entire affair had lasted three years, from January 1518 to January 1521, when the bull came into force. It had begun with the denunciation of the Dominicans at Tetzel's instigation, as a result of which Mazzolini submitted his report and Luther was summoned to Rome; he did not go, and demanded a hearing in Germany. The institution of formal proceedings for heresy was occasioned by the Emperor Maximilian's letter. The pope issued instructions that Luther was to be apprehended and brought to Rome; nothing came of this, owing to the political moves attendant on the emperor's election. Not until the beginning of 1520, that is after a period of two years, was the matter taken up seriously, and even then it dragged on for a further twelve months. The legal basis of the bull was extremely weak; the fact that in the meantime Luther had broken with the Church was a different matter. The Curia's position in relation to this fateful document would have been a much worthier one if it had adopted Cajetan's proposals; had it done so there is no doubt that Luther would also have been convicted, but on much better grounds.

There still remains the question how much there was to the charge of heresy. Who decided if someone was a heretic or if his teaching was heretical? In the early centuries this had been the prerogative of the Councils, and in the Middle Ages it was also primarily the great synods that had made the decisions; in the first thousand years of the Church's existence relatively few cases had arisen. The great age of the persecution of heretics began only in the twelfth century, as a measure against the popular uprisings of the Bogomils, Waldenses and Albigenses. For the first time it was not merely single individuals or small groups that were involved but whole regions, which had developed their own church organizations. Massive counter-measures were taken, not only by the Church but by the state as well. The Hohenstaufen Emperor Frederick II, later acclaimed by unsuspecting romantics as a 'broad-minded', 'enlightened' man, issued an imperial decree solemnly declaring that proceedings against heretics were a matter for the state; a heretic was not only an 'enemy of God' but an enemy of the emperor too, a public enemy and as such to be exterminated. The decree stated with biting irony that heretics, yearning as they did for the Passion, 'shall suffer the death for which they long; they are to be burned alive in full view of everyone and incur the judgment of fire, whereby we are caused no distress, for in so acting we are merely conforming to their wishes.' It was only with this decree, and as the result of joint moves by an emperor and pope who condemned each other as heretics and sought to exterminate one another, that the concerted action of Church and state was firmly established: the Church took over the investigation and conviction, the secular arm the execution. Frederick II found a worthy successor in Charles V; in his Spanish territories the Inquisition was first and foremost an instrument of the state and only secondarily of the Church. He too saw in Luther a 'public enemy', a rebel and inciter, and reserved exclusively to himself the right to outlaw him.

As the pope's representatives the Dominicans had been appointed inquisitors. In Germany they had soon made themselves hated and had to tread warily; but there was no dreaded Office of the Holy Inquisition as there was in Spain, nor was there in Italy, where it was introduced only in the middle of the sixteenth century. Nevertheless, the Dominicans were always at great pains to fulfil their task as 'watchmen', and not least in the case of Luther. But what counted as heresy? Opinions on this varied greatly from century to century. Furious battles were fought over questions which later were almost forgotten and whose importance it is not easy to grasp: whether the dead, for example, even if saints, could see God face to face the moment they entered heaven, or only at the Last Judgment. Charges and counter-charges flew back and forth; popes and antipopes execrated each other as heretics. Here inflation set in; the constantly developing juridical system of the Church brought in its wake a constant increase in the number of cases. To cover sorcery and witchcraft the Dominicans in Cologne compiled their textbook *The Witches' Hammer*, and the first papal bulls on the subject were issued at the time of Luther's birth. The famous example always cited in Luther's case was Hus. Hus and his predecessor Wyclif were the two names still remembered by Luther's contemporaries; the Maid of Orleans had been forgotten. Also important for the charge of heresy brought against Luther was the fact that, to an increasing extent, any question that touched even slightly on the institutional apparatus of the Church could be regarded as an offence. Admittedly, opinions on this were divided. Erasmus ridiculed the fact that even the study of languages or philosophical viewpoints was denounced as heresy. Such denunciation had become almost completely arbitrary. Since the papal imprisonment in Avignon no pope had dared to condemn or excommunicate a great sovereign, no matter how offensive he might be; lesser opponents were subjected to more rigorous action.

Luther had pleaded that he had attacked only 'viewpoints', never dogmas or officially promulgated doctrines. The infallibility of the pope on doctrinal questions was not established as dogma until 1870, and even then there were violent repercussions in the Catholic Church. In Luther's day canonists held the view that even a pope could also be an apostate; in fact canon law made allowance for this, although it was less precise on what should be done about it. There were arguments over which of the popes had been heretics, with even the Church admitting to certain cases – that of Pope Honorius, for example, whose case was debated from the seventh to the nineteenth century. Still more controversial was the question of the supreme authority of the Council, which in the early days had decided all important problems; the experiences of the great schism, which came to an end only at the Council of Constance, had shown that there were times when a final court of appeal of this kind was essential. Almost every ruling monarch used the threat of a Council as a means of applying political pressure; public opinion throughout Europe saw in the Council the hope and solution for all difficulties, and even in high Church circles, and among the cardinals, the demand found considerable sympathy. As a defensive measure the Curia had developed the thesis that only the pope could convene a Council, and that his consent was necessary to give validity to its decisions. By disputing this thesis Luther put his finger on the hierarchy's most sensitive spot; it was no longer a question of religious belief but of power. Nor were these problems exclusively German, they concerned the whole of Europe. The fact that Luther had broached this controversial subject was not the least reason for his rapid and widespread international influence. From the purely political point of view his most disastrous mistake was that, in the heat of forging ahead, and riled by the charge that he was a second Hus, he disputed the supreme authority of the Councils as well. This meant the end of any appeal to a tangible authority; for him the Scriptures were the only authority, but to many people they seemed elusive and to need interpretation. Here the Church was on surer ground and could appeal in its turn to public opinion: it was not self-evident to everybody that Doctor Martin Luther alone was in a position to interpret the Bible. Later, when others appeared by his side, and in his wake, and put forward their own divergent interpretations, this issue was to acquire still greater significance, enabling the Church to recapture its strongest position: it reasserted its reliance on tradition, on a secret and invisible 'Super-Council', comprising virtually all the great Doctors of the Church, which could lay claim to greater authority than any temporary assembly of distinguished prelates mixed, possibly, with members of the laity.

It is clear that, in his advance from one position to the next, Luther had broken quite consciously with 'Rome'. What is less clear is whether he had broken with the 'Church', or had even wanted to do so. Some churches diverged widely from the views of Rome, Bohemia being a case in point. The Curia had been forced to let it retain Communion of both kinds, and also to condone its secularization of much Church property. The 'heretic country' remained within the Church of Rome because Rome did not want to lose it – to the Greek Church, for example, with which the Bohemians had entered into discussions. The Greek Church was also regarded as heretical; in Leipzig Luther had protested strongly against this view and there had been constant talks, with varying success, in an attempt to bring about a union. At the time of his condemnation Luther called for a reform of the existing Church, but reform far more radical than any of the earlier reformers had envisaged. The Councils had failed because high ecclesiastical dignitaries had no intention of seeing their own positions weakened. Luther was confident that he could carry through a reform, if necessary, without a Council and also without the Curia. He appealed to the laity. This was the unforgivable offence, the real heresy, though it was hardly touched on in the Bull of Excommunication.

The bull was drawn up and approved by the cardinals; but if the text had been compiled carelessly, what happened next was more slapdash still. The authorities in Rome seem not to have had the remotest idea of the conditions and mood in Germany, and in order to settle the matter as quickly as possible Eck, as the most active participant to date, was appointed nuncio and entrusted with publishing the ban and implementing it. The papal librarian, Aleander, also appointed nuncio, was dispatched with the same mission to the Netherlands and the Rhineland. It turned out that the excommunication, fearful though it sounded, had very little force. Eck's authority was more sweeping than that of Aleander; he was empowered to add further names to the bull at his own discretion. Without any undue scruple he added the names of the Nuremberg patrician Pirckheimer, whom he presumed to be the author of the sarcastic pamphlet *Eckius Dedolatus*, Spengler the town syndic, another respected citizen of Nuremberg, and a canon in Augsburg – all personal enemies of his. The procedure was the more improper since in actions of heresy, and even before the Court of the Inquisition, the accused had the right to refuse biased judges, provided he could prove they were personal enemies. Nevertheless, Eck had the satisfaction of seeing the three accused submit with considerable self-abasement and sign declarations of repentance. But his visit to Saxony was a total failure. Only in a few places, such as Meissen and Merseburg, was he able to get the bull publicly posted; he failed even in Leipzig, where he had been so fêted the year before. His journey turned almost into a rout. He was threatened, and became the subject of satirical songs; as for Wittenberg, he dared not even go near it. It was evident that the Luther case had become a matter of national importance.

This was also clear from the mission of Aleander. He was successful in the territories of the Netherlands, where he could count for support on the authority of Charles v, the reigning monarch; but in the Rhineland he had difficulties. He was threatened in Cologne, the headquarters of the Dominicans, which hitherto had taken a leading part in the battle against heresy. In Mainz a stake was erected – but instead of bringing Luther's writings the students brought those of his enemies. Very soon Aleander, whose early reports to Rome had been so confident, had to admit his mistake and write in bewilderment that almost nine-tenths of Germany consisted of Lutheran heretics and rebels.

The arch-rebel himself was perfectly calm. The elector had suggested to him, through Spalatin, that he write personally to the princes and state his case. Luther turned to the public; 'Put not thy trust in princes', he wrote to Spalatin. He went ahead on his own and circulated a printed counter-proclamation: the bull, if indeed it was genuine, which was open to doubt, was a 'sacrilegious heresy'. He further addressed a notice, in both Latin and German, to 'Emperor and Empire', to the princes, towns and communes, requesting them to support his appeal for an independent Council and not to obey the bull. He demanded a hearing before unprejudiced judges, a demand that brought him widespread sympathy. The permanently smouldering antagonism between Rome and the German lands ignited over this issue and burned with totally unexpected fury.

Luther now took the step which more than any written word announced to the world that he had broken with the Church: he burned the Bull of Excommunication. And in an act so radical as to be unparalleled he first, and far more significantly, burned the decretals, the foundation of the papacy and the institutional Church. His contemporaries rightly regarded this as his most daring action; the burning of the bull was secondary, and is not even mentioned in the reports. Luther's burning of the entire body of law built up through the centuries meant the end of the medieval ascendancy of the Church, which saw itself embodied in this collection of statutes. It also meant divorce from Rome, and not merely from the Curia and the papacy. The canon law had grown out of the Latin thought of ancient Rome, out of the tradition of the Roman emperors; it was the continuation of imperial Rome, whose heritage the Church had assumed. The jurists had created Roman law; the popes, who in conjunction with the great legal experts of the University of Bologna had erected this monument year by year in carefully assembled tiers, were jurists. To us the phrase *Corpus juris canonici* has only a feeble ring, the distant sound of something that concerns the most recondite specialists. To the Middle Ages, and up to Luther's time, it was 'thunder and lightning', a power that insinuated its countless tentacles into every aspect of daily life; only if we bear this in mind can we appreciate Luther's audacity.

Canon law had a unique advantage over all other systems of law: it was not a codification of established legal practices, it constantly created new laws. With every claim of the papacy, however revolutionary, new decretals were added, which henceforth had juridical validity. It was international and thus had its own title over the whole of the west. It took precedence over all other law. From this code issued the mighty thunderbolts which shattered emperors and kings. The first basic books of decretals – termed then 'official' – appeared in the stormy atmosphere of the Hohenstaufen era. The main body of the collection bore the names of the Caesarean Popes Gregory IX and Boniface VIII. The Avignon Popes Clement V and John XII added further books to the great codex; supplements continued to be added until the beginning of the sixteenth century. The agitated reports sent to the emperor said that Luther had 'burnt the Clementine Decretals'. Few people in Luther's day knew anything about Clement V or what his decretals said, but everyone knew that the Clementine Decretals represented an important and operative code of law. Luther himself had only a very imperfect knowledge of the vast work, but his instinct had led him to stress those points that were felt most acutely in the life of the people. It made him furious that the pope used canon law to annul any oath, however solemn. Yet this had been one of the most powerful weapons in the political war: by annulling the oath of allegiance the popes, in their conflicts with the emperors, had forced their opponents to their knees more effectively than by the weapon of excommunication which often rebounded; there were always plenty of German princes only waiting for this 'legal' permission to defect and rebel. Until quite recently, the legal power over marriage had been exercised no less ruthlessly. Economic life was controlled, in so far as it is possible to speak of control at all, by the canonical ban on interest; it was continually side-stepped and by no one so blatantly as by the Curia and its bankers. In practice the whole legal system had become a complex of exceptions, whether the point at issue was the 'canonical age' for bishops, archbishops and cardinals – who in practice were often appointed as children or boys – or pluralism and simony. The secular powers had started to develop their own law, and for this purpose the ancient Roman law, which was enjoying a revival, offered a very effective basis. The law of ancient Rome triumphed over the

Roman law of the Curia, Justinian over Gratian, the first compiler of the decretals. Here too, in eliminating canon law, Luther was fulfilling a historic mission, although he was unaware of it. For him it was first and foremost a question of conscience. He committed the book to the flames because the pope had placed himself above the Scriptures, the Word of God, because he had to account to no one, being considered infallible and irremovable, however great his 'offence'.

Luther chose his moment very carefully. The sixty days' grace allowed him in the bull had just expired; according to legal custom, to which he adhered, they dated not from the day of issue of the bull but from the day on which it had been posted up and thus 'served' on him. Early on the cold winter's morning of 10 December 1520 he proceeded with a group of companions and students to a point outside the Wittenberg town gate. In a notice, which he nailed to the door of the parish church, he had called on 'all friends of evangelical truth' to assist in burning the 'godless books of papal law and scholastic theology'. A copy of the decretals had been procured, as well as a manual on questions of conscience for father confessors; with the classics of scholasticism he had been less fortunate – no one had been willing to hand over his copy of Thomas Aquinas or Duns Scotus. The procession made its way to the place of execution, a knacker's yard outside the walls on the banks of the Elbe. A master of arts lit the wood round the stake and threw the three volumes of the canon law into the flames; in view of the thick paper used in those days, they must have burnt slowly. Only after this did Luther step forward and, scarcely noticed by most of the onlookers, add the small volume containing the printed text of the bull of excommunication, pronouncing a few words of Latin in an undertone as he did so; these are said to have been: 'May this fire destroy you, because you have obstructed God's truth.' He went quickly back to his room and composed a short letter to Spalatin, telling him what had been done, so that he could inform the elector. But this peaceful procedure did not satisfy the students, who, after they had breakfasted, celebrated the great day by holding a carnival procession. Having decked out a carriage with placards and inscriptions attacking the pope, they drove through the streets collecting more fuel for the fire and writings by Luther's opponents. In the front of the carriage – because anti-Jewish jokes were popular and could not be left out – sat four boys in fancy dress who were supposed to represent the vanquished 'Synagogue', as the counterpart of Rome, and whose task was bitterly to lament the misfortune. A trumpeter blew discordant blasts. When they reached the stake they burned the other writings, to the accompaniment of speeches, recitals of their contents and laughter. It was this procession which first attracted onlookers in number.

Luther was not at all pleased when he heard that his action had been followed by these discordant notes. The following day he addressed the students in the lecture room; his lectures now attracted between three and four hundred people. Quite against custom – because Latin was strictly prescribed – he spoke in German. He made it clear that no students' prank had been intended; the matter was extremely serious, presenting the alternatives of martyrdom or hell. Martyrdom, he told them, could be expected by all ready to join in the fight against the papacy; hell would be the lot of those who persisted in their adherence to the Antichrist. He himself had been left no choice. He had not decided to take this step for 'worldly reasons' but in order to save his fellow men from eternal perdition. To burn the books was not enough, the papal see must be consigned to the flames.

On the effect produced by this address we have very little information, just as we have very few reports of any kind from Luther's immediate circle. No one mentioned the burning of the bull; we know of it only from Luther's letter and from a later statement by Agricola, the MA who set fire to the faggots round the stake. Luther's university colleagues remained silent and alarmed, except for the jurist Goede who exploded in a fury: 'How does he have the nerve, the mangy monk!'; he saw the whole basis of his work go up in flames with the canon law. Luther, however, at once wrote a popular justification: *Why the Books of the Pope and His Disciples Have Been Burnt*, dedicated to 'all lovers of Christian truth'. He enjoined 'all and sundry to take notice' of what had happened at his instigation. All he had done was to carry out an ancient custom; the history of the apostles told how they had 'burned five thousand pence worth of pernicious books, obeying the teachings of St Paul.' He was a 'sworn Doctor of the Holy Scriptures' – a solemn affirmation of his mission that from now on he emphasized constantly – and a 'daily preacher' who, as such, was in duty bound to oppose false doctrines. He referred to the fact that his books had been the first to be burned; that in response to the great confusion this had caused among the people, he had now burned the pope's books in his turn. He did not mention the bull of excommunication. Next he went on to list the 'main articles' of the canon law in thirty items, of which the tenth was the most important: though no one was entitled to judge the pope, he was 'entitled to judge all men on earth'; this, he said, was laid down in the decretals. 'If this article stands, Christ and his Word fall to the ground – but if it does not stand, the whole ecclesiastical law, together with the pope and the see of Rome, falls to the ground.' In closing, he admonished the reader to reflect on what he had said. 'What concerns me most is that the pope has never once drawn on the Holy Scriptures or on reason to refute anyone who has spoken, written or acted against him.' As all the histories told, he had 'exiled, burnt or otherwise choked' his opponents by resorting to force and excommunication, through the agency of kings, princes and other followers. The pope had never accepted a court of law or a verdict, he had merely declared himself to be 'above any Scripture, court of law and power'.

Luther's demand to be heard before unprejudiced judges and on German soil found the widest response; the fact that the Curia thought of wielding its power more ruthlessly in the empire than elsewhere had caused universal bitterness. In woodcuts, broadsheets and polemical writings Luther's portrait now appeared surrounded by a halo and sometimes also surmounted by the Holy Ghost in the form of a dove. Whether it was to be the halo of a martyr, or of the hero for which everyone was waiting, still remained to be seen. That the pope's sentence alone was inadequate had been clearly demonstrated. Luther had appealed to the emperor and the empire. The young emperor was on his way up the Rhine. In his hands lay the fate of the monk.

20

# Summons before the Emperor

IN HIS slow and guarded way the Elector Frederick had already considered the idea of taking his Doctor Luther with him to the next
meeting of the diet. He was still careful to dissociate himself explicitly
from Luther's teachings, deliberately emphasizing his neutrality. But
for him the affair had developed into a question of honour; it had also
become dangerous – he, too, had been threatened with excommunication. Letters passed to and fro between Saxony and the imperial
court; his plan was approved and then rejected again. Imperial policy
had not yet been formulated; it was dependent on the attitude of the
Curia, which, in turn, veered between France and the emperor.
Aleander, however, was indefatigable. Among the large number of
nuncios and legates active in Germany on the pope's behalf he was
actually only a secondary figure; another legate, Caracciolo, was in
charge of negotiating questions of a highly political nature. But
Aleander intended to play the chief role and thus earn immortal fame;
and for a time, like Tetzel and Eck before him, he took his place on
the contemporary stage. Each of the three men represented a perennial
type: the simple soldier or fighter, the learned advocate brought in as
an auxiliary, and the diplomat acting on behalf of the supreme general
staff. Each represented a distinct category of the Church Militant of the
day, and each received his due reward: Tetzel, the 'foot soldier', was
left to die at his post when, no longer tenable, it was abandoned; Eck
got his small benefice; Aleander was given the titles and emoluments
of archbishop and cardinal, the usual reward for senior officers.
Erasmus, the friend of his early years but later his enemy, wrote of
him in 1533: 'He now lives in Venice, quite the epicurean – but he
behaves with decency.'

Their friendship dated from the years when life had been pleasant
and full of hope, when they had both been up-and-coming humanists,
ambitious, gifted and poor. In 1506 Erasmus had gone to Italy, the
promised land of the new humanities, and to Venice, their source.
There, from among the small group of Greeks who had fled from

Constantinople, there still lived men who knew the ancient language and could pass on their knowledge; and, most important of all, a great publisher had emerged there in the person of Aldus Manutius, perhaps the greatest his profession has ever known. He printed his classics in small 'pocket editions' that were easy to handle, and in the elegant Italian italic type, thus assuring the new learning the widest distribution in a style and format that made clear at a glance the difference between this bright, new, intellectual world and the ponderous folios of the old school with their elaborate Gothic lettering. Aldus realized at once the calibre of this small, frail man from the Netherlands: he published the New Testament in the original Greek, and we have already seen how important this was for Luther; he also published the *Adagia* of Erasmus, a collection of choice Latin passages which provided a whole generation with models and usable formulae, and did so, to the author's delight, in his 'most beautiful small lettering, the tiniest of all.' Aldus also found the young scholar board and lodging with his father-in-law, where, as was customary for people without means, he shared a bed with the young and equally poor Hieronymus Aleander, a doctor's son from Friuli. Aldus introduced the two of them to the circle of his Greek friends, who formed a sort of academy where Plato and Pindar were read in the original; at the same time he enlisted the aid of the two students in his firm, where they helped as readers. Erasmus retained a liking for printer's ink all his life; his works were written in the printing room – where he sat at a table directly facing the type-case – often from memory and in such a hurry that he scarcely had time 'to scratch his ears', as he put it. But the ways of the two young friends parted. For Erasmus the humanities were the whole purpose of life, for Aleander they were only a springboard. The latter advanced rapidly, the first rung in the ladder being the well-paid post of cathedral canon in Liège; here, at a focal point of the political tricks and stratagems of the high prelacy, he gained experience of the demands, bribes, threats and favours that characterized the upper reaches of the ecclesiastical life of the day. He also claimed to have gained an insight into conditions in Germany while he was in Liège and, on being called to Rome as Vatican librarian, was considered to be especially well informed on questions touching the empire, of which so little was known in that city; this was why he was sent there. His sharp features were now to be seen everywhere. When he was young it seemed as if he would develop a fine scholar's head, but his face soon became fleshy, heavy-lidded eyes surmounting a large nose, because of which he was suspected of Jewish origin. Even Erasmus – who was by no means above making such asides in his letters – spread this story: 'He is a man who can speak three languages, but everyone says he is a Jew' – after which he hastened to add that all the evidence showed him to be an admirable man. When they met again their early friendship came to an abrupt end. Erasmus soon felt himself to be in as great danger as Luther, and was convinced that Aleander was intriguing against him everywhere: 'It is as though he were tearing my work to shreds; he is pompous, impertinent and touchy, and his desire for fame and profit is insatiable'; in conversation he still continued to profess himself Aleander's best friend. He claimed that, through his agent in Rome, Aleander had submitted to Pope Leo a list of 'six thousand' heresies in his works. Erasmus had already enlarged on this in a letter to Archbishop Albrecht of Mainz. Once upon a time, he wrote, heretics had been given a respectful hearing and, as punishment, simply been excluded from Communion;

Erasmus of Rotterdam (woodcut after Holbein)

now things were quite different, and the cry of heresy was raised over the most trivial matters. Formerly a heretic had been someone who repudiated the Gospels, the articles of faith, or some other authority of equal standing; nowadays anyone was a heretic who deviated in some point from Thomas Aquinas or from a fabricated argument 'thought up yesterday by some sophist of the schools'; even to understand Greek or express oneself elegantly was heresy. Erasmus saw his branch of learning, and the peaceful élite of scholars, threatened. And it was Aleander he blamed when he had hurriedly to leave Louvain, where he had first won fame, and go to Basle, the next stage on his life's journey; here once again a great publisher and printer awaited him in the person of Froben. Throughout his life his patrons were the printing magnates, not the secular potentates.

What Erasmus said about Aleander was biased. The great master of compromise and gentleness was also capable of hatred and malice; he was also a frequent victim of morbid persecution mania. He was right, however, in suspecting that behind the nuncio were manœuvres antagonistic not merely to him personally but to the 'Erasmic trend'. Aleander circulated the dangerous epigram that Erasmus had simply 'laid the egg which Luther hatched'. It was a remark that showed his grasp of the circumstances: the much gentler and more conciliatory teachings of Erasmus constituted an even greater threat than the angry polemics of the monk. They were starting to penetrate as far as Spain; followers of Erasmus were to be found in the hig est places, including the imperial court. With its cry of 'back to the sources', its rejection of scholasticism, and not least its wit and irony, in which Erasmus excelled, the whole humanist movement had already severely shaken the position of the hierarchy before Luther came on the scene. Aleander, having once been a humanist, knew his former colleagues; he himself resorted to irony in his secret dispatches to Rome and could not refrain from quoting Ovid, even when speaking of the arch-heretic Luther. These writings were not intended 'for the people' or for publication; as the immortal formula expressed it, religion had to be 'preserved' for the people.

The people now opposed Aleander. He was dumbfounded. The pope had spoken; the excommunication had been issued at the highest level. The official secular authorities conformed, at least in the Netherlands; the bishop of Liège, under whom Aleander had once served, hastened to burn the heretic's books, which contained so much that was identical with what he himself had stated in his memorandum to the Diet of Augsburg. The University of Louvain obeyed the order and later became the most zealous champion of papal authority. But from Germany Aleander was beset by a deafening clamour from writings that had cast all restraint to the winds by threats against his person, by open declaration of war against the priesthood, this last, to make matters worse, emanating from the court of Archbishop Albrecht of Mainz, the primate and lord high chancellor of the empire. He had set out with complete confidence in the familiar and hitherto invariably effective means and methods, his luggage consisting of a plentiful stock of 'expectancies' of great and lucrative benefices, abbacies and bishoprics as well as ready cash; it also contained full powers to disappoint expectations or at best to encourage hopes of reward for good behaviour. None of it worked. What had happened to the great princes of the Church? The archbishop of Mainz, who had been showered with honours, turned out to be the least dependable of them all. He had even been offered a position, similar to that of Wolsey in England, as head of an established German Church with its own permanent legates. The archbishop of Trier, a friend of the elector of Saxony, appeared to be openly sympathetic to the heretic, while the archbishop of Cologne was at the very least lukewarm. In Würzburg and Bamberg sympathy with the monk was so strong that people invited him to their houses; even the emperor's father confessor was said to have spoken kindly of the rebel. What had come over this good and patient people? 'This is no longer the Catholic Germany of old,' he wrote in consternation to Rome; nine-tenths had the battle-cry 'Luther' on their lips, the rest were shouting 'Death to the Roman Curia.' And, worst of all, they were all unanimous in their repeated demands for a Council, and moreover a Council on German soil.

Since Constance a Council had been the Curia's nightmare: it might result in the deposition of the pope; this had happened at Constance and had recently been attempted again, under France's leadership, at Pisa – sovereignty over the pope was a slogan that had always found adherents, even among the cardinals. It was possible that the new emperor might make use of it if too much pressure were put on him. The monk from Wittenberg had chosen a highly inopportune moment to enter the scene and make his appeal; there was a danger that the emperor might use him to force the Curia's hand, as the king of France had once used Savonarola. Savonarola had been burnt at the stake, and the revolt had subsided with gratifying rapidity. Quick action against the Wittenberg monk would have the same result; the essential thing was speed and careful attention to detail. Aleander set to work, indefatigably and doggedly, with the petty weapons of bribery and cultivation of 'important people'. He always remained a 'pocket-sized' man.

Luther's blunt strategy soon cost him the sympathy of Erasmus and many of the humanists; and yet the great master, with his widespread fame, was of the highest importance to him at this crucial period. Aleander and many others regarded Erasmus as Luther's confederate, and because of this he also was victimized. In a carefully composed letter Luther had tried to win him as an ally; though habitually vacillating, Erasmus, who was courted by everyone including kings and popes, was adamant on one point: 'I wish to be a citizen of the world,' he declared, 'making common cause with all or, still better, remaining aloof from all.' Or yet more clearly: 'I have always wished to stand alone and hate nothing so much as sworn partisans.' For this reason he had answered Luther very guardedly; subsequently he behaved with still greater caution. To the blunt and insistent demands to join the cause he reacted with increasing irritation. All around him he saw growing threats to his ideal of a scholar's peaceful pursuits, to an education aiming at the path of reasoned moderation, to the practice of the virtues of tolerance and gentleness, from which he himself often deviated. Terminus, the Roman god of boundaries, became his device and symbol, signifying not only the limitation of all things and death but also the rational, orderly demarcation of boundaries in life and on earth. Nothing was more intolerable than violence and ferocity; everything Dionysiac was alien to him. He never married, but he wrote on marriage; he was childless, but he wrote on the education of children with remarkable wisdom. Like Luther, he never forgot the constant beatings he suffered as a boy; he advocated affectionate consideration for the child's 'nature', careful sowing and planting of what would later become second nature. He planned a great trilogy, the first part of which was to have been his satire *In Praise of Folly*, the second *In Praise of Nature* and the third *On Grace*, a subject on which his views would certainly have differed widely from those of Luther. The work was never completed. The times were not in tune with the quieter sonorities of Erasmus; they called for trumpets and trombones. Even the thoughts on religious reform which he developed in his *A Christian Fighter's Manual* were too gentle for them – a fighter's job was to go out and fight, to use his weapon to punish and chastise. Dürer had met and drawn Erasmus in Brussels and when, on returning from the Netherlands, he heard of the sentence passed on Luther at the Diet of Worms, and his subsequent disappearance, he wrote in his diary: 'O Erasmus of Rotterdam, where are you going to take your stand? Listen, you Knight of Christ, ride forth at the side of our Lord Christ, defend the truth, win the martyr's crown – else you are just a useless old man. I have heard that you have given yourself only another two years in which to achieve something. Make good use of them in the cause of the Gospel and the true Christian faith ...' Erasmus was neither knight nor horseman; he went on foot, carefully watching his steps, and it was thus that he now made ready for a last attempt at reconciliation in the by now hopeless Luther case.

Those with natures similar to his have always been attracted, and indeed roused to enthusiasm, by his ideals, by his vision of mutual understanding, compromise and conciliation, even in questions of religious belief. But his eyes were the eyes of a scholar, and what they saw was further confused because he mistook his immense fame for influence. His insight into the folly by which mankind is constantly governed produced his most powerful work; it was not by accident that the other two parts of his trilogy were never written. He himself fell victim to the goddess of folly: he had no idea of the 'nature' of power.

He believed that it needed only a few rational men, and in the last resort a single one, himself, to coax the great rulers into giving up their frivolous activities. He believed in a small élite who, in the humanities, had found the philosophers' stone and with it power over the great ones of this world. Like everyone else – and in this he showed himself no more perceptive than the common people – he pinned his faith on a good emperor, a good pope and a good Church, cleansed of all aberrations by the intelligent reforms of enlightened men. He believed in a unity, based on Latin, under the dual banner of the great classics, which he had published, and the pure, original text of the Bible, which he had brought to light – in other words in the possibility of reconciling ancient philosophy with the Gospel.

Erasmus had set out from Louvain to go to nearby Cologne where the electors, among them Luther's Frederick, had gathered for preliminary talks on the coronation of the emperor who, long awaited and long delayed, was at last expected from Spain. Erasmus ventured as far as the fringe of the diet and its associated events, but no further; he wanted to remain in the background, to advise and coax and so avert, if possible, the catastrophe whose approach he saw more clearly than most. His concern was still the 'study of languages', the humanities: 'It was through hatred for these and the stupidity of the monks that the whole tragedy arose in the first place.' He did not want to take any direct part himself although, as he could not resist saying, a bishopric would have been his had he been willing publicly to oppose Luther. This was no empty boasting; later, after he had actually written against Luther, he was offered a cardinalate. Erasmus refused all such honours; he wanted to remain independent. In any case his intention now was to act as arbitrator between the parties; it never occurred to him that his presence was not required for this, that what was wanted was his name and nothing more.

Nevertheless he still made one further contribution to events, although it was only a modest one. The Elector Frederick, being excessively shy, did not want to see anyone – in this respect he outdid even Erasmus. Aleander tried to see him but was turned away, the elector informing him through his councillors that Luther must be heard before judges who were above suspicion and that he should be sentenced only if convicted of the wrong of which he was accused.

This is what Luther himself had proposed in a published 'offer'. Frederick, still hesitating whether to identify himself with this offer, had spoken about it to Erasmus, after the latter had urgently requested an audience. The meeting between the two ultra-cautious 'neutralists' must have been a tedious affair, especially as Erasmus did not speak a word of German and the elector only a little Latin; Spalatin, the court chaplain, had to act as interpreter. Erasmus talked mainly about his own problem, the humanities. They were in danger; the whole conflict had arisen out of ignorant hostility to learning. Scholarship would be threatened if, as a result of too severe measures, the ignorant and those with a thirst for power were to gain the upper hand; the punishment clauses in the Bull of Excommunication had caused nothing but indignation, and in any case Luther had been condemned only by two universities, those at Cologne and Louvain. He agreed with Luther's 'offer', a copy of which he had seen displayed. It was right that Luther should be examined, but it must be before experts and impartial judges.

The conversation was hardly a triumph for Erasmus but, because of the great authority of the world-famous man, it may well have strengthened the elector in his adherence to Luther and his proposal; he was certainly in need of encouragement and advice. Erasmus, afraid of misunderstandings, set out the main points of the interview under twenty-two headings and sent them to the elector. That they were immediately published – every line Erasmus wrote was published – caused him considerable annoyance, because he had no wish to be involved in the affair.

He intended to intervene only from a distance, preferably anonymously or through intermediaries. Another work then appeared and was widely circulated; everyone assumed it to be by Erasmus, although in fact its author was a highly respected Dominican prior in Augsburg named Faber. In the Dominican Order too, as in all the other orders, there were tensions and sharp antagonisms, both internal and directed against Rome; even among the ranks of the official inquisitors there were followers of Erasmus and the new 'humanities'. The old prior was one of these; he also considered that he and his monastery had been badly treated, and he had had serious differences of opinion with Cardinal Cajetan. All this is worth mentioning only because it shows how disunited the various fronts were up to this time and how much sympathy for Luther's cause existed even in very 'conservative' Church circles. And so there appeared, in both German and Latin editions, the prior's heartfelt advice that the see of Rome be honoured but that, at the same time, peace should be preserved in Christendom. Erasmus was clearly the inspiration of much contained in this work, but there were other things for which the prior himself was responsible. Luther was appraised very sympathetically. The quarrel was the fault of the enemies of learning, and above all of those who had expressed views on indulgences and the power of the pope that were intolerable to all devout and learned people. The cry of heresy was condemned, as was the severity of the Bull of Excommunication, which did not accord with

Pope Leo's gentle nature. Luther should have been admonished in a brotherly way and then refuted; to burn his writings was pointless, because 'his opinions remain fixed in the hearts of many people, who cannot see that he has been refuted.' The work gave the impression of a final plea for reason. It even mooted the idea of a court of arbitration.

But the events surrounding Erasmus and his followers, and all ideas

The Emperor Charles v as a youth

of a court of arbitration, had long been superseded. The emperor, Luther's lifelong and greatest opponent, now arrived. News of his election had reached him in Barcelona, where he had been detained by affairs in Spain; much that had happened there was extremely unnerving. The country was rent by revolt, and he had been forced to leave almost as a fugitive; his position as ruler, insecurely founded from the beginning, was highly precarious. Just how precarious the position of the new monarch was would scarcely have reached the ears of the German princes, who received only scant and contradictory reports from the peninsula; for long considered a remote province, it was only very recently that, to the great surprise of the old-established powers, Spain had proved itself to be a full, and indeed dangerously powerful, member of the European community. The twenty-year-old ruler was the object of great curiosity. He was an excellent horseman and, despite his not very imposing figure, skilled in tilting and jousting; his hair, falling in long, pale strands, framed a thin, boyish face; his mouth, because it was always open, gave him a slightly stupid expression. He spoke little, his councillors doing the talking; rumour had it that they completely dominated him. It was they with whom one had to maintain contact; Charles himself was hardly ever to be seen. There were some who doubted whether he had a will of his own at all, and this was precisely what many of the German princes wanted. Others pointed out that his mother, Joanna the Mad, was kept in strict custody in Tordesillas Castle; according to another version this imprisonment may have had political reasons, because Joanna was in fact the lawful queen, the realm having been left to her by her father, Ferdinand the Catholic. Charles was in fact only co-regent and, had his mother recovered, he might conceivably have been forced from power.

Today we see Charles v as the sovereign 'on whose empire the sun never set', as the last emperor of a truly world-wide domain. We see him with the regal features of a cynic and conqueror, as Titian painted him. We shall meet him again at various stages of his development, but here in Cologne, Aix-la-Chapelle and Worms we are concerned with the young man of twenty, a youth of uncertain health and future. He was welcomed hopefully as 'a young nobleman of ancient German lineage' and played off against Francis i of France. In spite of the great importance attached at this time to family trees, it had entered no one's head to enquire a little more carefully into his origins: barely one-twentieth of his ancestral heritage was German; fourteen close Spanish or Portuguese ancestors have been counted, three French, two Plantagenet and one each from the Netherlands, Italy, Poland, Lithuania and Germany. He was brought up in the Netherlands as a Frenchman, by Adrian of Utrecht, later Pope Hadrian; subsequently he became Spanish in speech, dress and way of life. Although his life is extraordinarily fully documented, we know relatively little about his early years. His education was of the scantiest and included neither languages nor history; for him history was built round the legend of a mighty Burgundy, which Charles the Bold had raised almost to the status of a great European power before, in company with his heavily armoured knights, he was dragged from his horse by the contemptible Swiss peasants and slain. A romance telling of the glorious deeds of this ancestor by Olivier de la Marche, master of ceremonies and director of festivities at the Burgundian court, was Charles's favourite book when he was a boy. Ceremonial, one of the great creations of the Burgundian court, took on a virtually ritual importance for Charles. In the Netherlands it was already known during his lifetime as '*la nouvelle religion*' and, following its introduction into the world-wide Spanish Empire, dominated Europe under the name of 'Spanish etiquette'; it spread far beyond the sphere of influence of the Habsburgs, who retained its style until 1918. Having been brought up by Adrian of Utrecht as a strict Catholic, he remained one. Later he appointed his tutor grand inquisitor of Spain, where the Inquisition was an instrument of political power; in Charles's eyes, as in those of the Emperor Frederick II, a heretic was first and foremost an enemy of the state who threatened the divinely ordained order of things. Strict observance of the prescribed religious rites was as important to Charles as court ceremonial. He held very concrete and precise notions, too, of the supreme importance of his position as ruler; in this field Charles, the Church's most obedient son, would tolerate no supremacy on the part of the pope. The fact is often overlooked that, until after his death, the so-called Reformation era was one of incessant fighting between the Spanish kings and Rome.

Burgundy, the old heart of Burgundy that had become a part of France, remained the political dream of his life. To win back Bourgogne was his life's aim, and he pursued it blindly; the rich Netherlands, that went by the name of Burgundy, never satisfied him, and from this insatiability arose his antagonism towards France – the other constant in these constantly changing times. In the young man of twenty all this was only in its initial, preparatory stage, but he never deviated from it. He became an old man very early in life; he never tasted the 'joys of life', and the three bastard children he left were the offspring of merely fleeting associations. No trace of fun or humour is discernible in him. Music alone was capable of bringing some solace to his gloomy spirit, the exceedingly elaborate polyphonic music of the great Netherlands school. His band of musicians was among the best of the day. We can reconstruct, though we cannot hear in full contrapuntal detail, the compositions of the great masters and above all of Josquin Deprès; it is 'abstract music' and it is only in terms of abstractions that we can hazard a guess at what it meant to Charles. Probably it was closely connected with his love for mechanical toys and clocks, a love that also accompanied him to Yuste where, in his beautiful villa, he had a large collection of timepieces with a specialist to look after them. It was symbolic of the tragedy of his life that he was never able to bring his collection of clocks into perfect order and synchronize them.

Order – symbolized in ceremonial – was his aim, yet his youth had been spent in chaotic conditions. His grandparents had quarrelled over him with a total lack of restraint. All conceivable European combinations were tried in the jumble of the ten engagements that were concluded in the name first of the infant and later of the boy. Marriages were the Habsburgs' main road to power: Maximilian had acquired Burgundy by marriage, his son Philip Spain. Marriage politics, carried to a pitch of brutality that could force a twelve-year-old girl into bed with a brute known to be a drunkard, remained Charles's practice. His earliest years were spent in the midst of the fight that raged between his pleasure-loving, amorous father and the highly-strung Joanna, who was beaten, locked up, and so tortured by her fanatical jealousy that she went mad, or at any rate could be declared mad. Charles retained a lifelong, and almost equally fanatical, hatred of 'woman'; for a long time he hesitated to marry at all – urgently though this was desired – and on his arrival in Cologne word immediately spread among the princes and ambassadors that the twenty-year-old emperor was still a virgin. This was not just a piece of piquant gossip; in view of the engagements still under discussion, each of which could be a matter of war or peace, it was a political fact of the first magnitude. Charles's boyhood development had been exposed to a yet greater danger: the death of his father, whom Ferdinand the Catholic had vainly tried to exclude from the Spanish succession, created the possibility of a struggle over the inheritance won by marriage. Not until six prior claimants had died was the way freed for the boy in Brussels. In all this Charles could not but see the finger of God pointing to him. When he was fifteen Maximilian, his grandfather, had declared him of age; this was a stratagem directed against the boy's aunt Margaret, the powerful and self-willed regent of the Netherlands, and engineered and encouraged by the leading figures in Burgundy, who thereby got hold of the reins of government.

Encircled by this high aristocracy, Charles entered into his contested Spanish inheritance. The Spaniards wanted his younger brother Ferdinand as their king; he had been brought up in the country from birth and the Spanish grandees intended to dominate him as their peers in the Netherlands had dominated Charles. Ferdinand had to be banished to Brussels before Charles could accede to power. Savage risings were the result. The towns rose against the aristocracy; in Valencia a people's government was formed. Other risings followed, and in many ways this Spanish civil war was a bloody curtain-raiser to the German Peasants' War of 1525. As in Germany the revolts, which for a time were very successful, collapsed because of particularism and lack of unity and discipline among the rebels; the aristocracy was victorious. But when Charles made his hurried departure from Spain in order to show himself in Germany at last, the outcome was still far

from clear; indeed the news he received in the course of his journey
was disquieting in the extreme: a 'Holy Junta' had been formed with
the object of placing his mother at the head of affairs. Fortunately the
woman, in her melancholy frame of mind, was unable to come to a
decision. Ecclesiastical dignitaries also took part, and the bishop of
Zamora, at the head of a large body of men, went about plundering
the churches and monasteries and preaching rebellion. The emperor's
councillors appealed to the pope, who, however, took no action; in
Rome, it is true, there was talk of a 'second Luther', but he was considered to be serving a useful purpose and there was no thought of
excommunicating him like the first Luther. France intervened on the
border, pursuing its old struggle for Navarre; this provoked the incalculable danger that the rebels might side with France.

Thus, harried on all sides and in a hurry – he had to return to Spain
as soon as possible to avoid losing his possessions there – Charles
arrived in Cologne and Aix-la-Chapelle. His business in Germany,
including the tiresome Luther case, was to be concluded with all
possible speed, and Charles quickly put his name to the electoral
capitulations, not one of which he had the slightest intention of keeping.
In complete ignorance of conditions in Germany a few cursory measures
were taken through his councillors. Most important of all Sickingen,
the great condottiere, was secured as the emperor's commander-in-
chief – this in spite of the fact that Sickingen had turned his castle of
Ebernburg into a 'refuge of justice' for the Lutheran rebels; apart from
some grooms and bodyguards Charles disposed of no armed forces.
Attempts were made to eliminate the heretic Luther by means of
private, unofficial talks, Sickingen lending Ebernburg castle for the
purpose.

The emperor's father confessor, the Franciscan Glapion, now
appeared on the scene – one of the first 'grey eminences' in the long
line of great father confessors. Erasmus, who corresponded with him,
declared him to be so opaque that even after ten years' intimate
association one would never be able to see through him. In any case he
was said to exert great influence over the young emperor; history has
been unable to establish much beyond this. Whether on this occasion
he spoke as a diplomat, or as a man honestly concerned to bring about
a settlement, nothing came of his attempt at mediation. He seems to
have gone very far and to have spoken sympathetically of Luther to
Brück, chancellor to the elector of Saxony, who took part in the talks:
the only shocking work, he said, was the treatise *On the Babylonian
Captivity of the Church of God*; the monk would have to retract or deny
this – Luther could simply say the work had been falsely attributed to
him. But the proposal for a court of arbitration also met with Glapion's

approval; during the Diet of Worms, and during Luther's presence there, he endeavoured to find a way to settle the affair 'with the public excluded' but finally gave up, announcing with a sigh that he had honestly done his best. In Rome it was apparently thought he had done too much because he was recalled from the emperor's court, ostensibly to be sent to America to take charge of the new province of the order; but he died in Spain on his way there.

These steps were all designed to keep Luther at a distance and prevent him appearing before the public, which was already in a state of excitement. The individual stages in the advance and retreat of the imperial court were determined by international politics; when the Curia was difficult there were threats to produce Luther, when Rome gave way attempts were made to put him on one side. Only when it became all too clear that the pope was negotiating with France, and his intrigues in the Spanish disorders became blatant, was it decided to summon Luther to Worms. In order to make a still deeper impression on the nuncio Aleander, who protested in great agitation against this action, the emperor's summons was couched in courteous terms; the heretic was addressed with full decorum as 'Dearly beloved'. As a further sign of the new attitude at court the imperial herald was sent in person, with his attendant, to fetch Luther and accompany him.

But in order to afford the desperate nuncio some consolation an imperial edict was hurriedly drawn up ordering the seizure of all Luther's books and – which was more significant – stating that Luther had been summoned to Worms only to recant. As he travelled to Worms the monk saw the edict posted up along his route. On this occasion Luther travelled in a small carriage, placed at his disposal by the Wittenberg town council at the request of Luther's friend Lucas Cranach. In conformity with the regulations of his order he was accompanied by a fellow Augustinian, as well as by a student and by Nikolaus von Amsdorf, his colleague at the university; the town of Wittenberg had also given the penniless monk money for the journey. The edict impressed and alarmed even Luther. His friends warned him, pointing to Hus and Savonarola, but he kept to his decision, and the reception given to him almost everywhere confirmed him in his attitude. The imperial herald reported to Worms that wherever they went the people ran out to greet Doctor Luther – there was nothing he could do to stop it. The town councils made the heretic the traditional gifts of wine offered to distinguished travellers. In some places he was invited to preach, and in Frankfurt, as the nuncio's informants told him, something quite scandalous happened: Luther was seen in his room 'playing brazenly on the lute'. But there were also reports of severe attacks of illness during the journey. From Frankfurt Luther notified the elector and his councillors of his imminent arrival. Frederick was aghast. Up till the very last moment he had hoped that his doctor would turn back, or at least stay outside the town until a decision had been taken in his case. Luther wrote a few brief lines to Spalatin, telling him of his attacks of illness and announcing: 'We shall enter Worms in spite of all the gates of hell and powers of darkness ... Find me somewhere to stay.' Spalatin obeyed.

Luther was thirty-eight, a ripe age by the standards of those days, when a man was on the verge of old age at forty and not many survived the fifties. The Emperor Charles was twenty-one; in the portraits painted of him at the time he looks younger. Until this moment he had done nothing on his own, nor had he shown any signs of will-power. The world knew only of the long list of titles and honours that had been heaped upon him. His official title, occupying almost half a page and worded after careful deliberation by his councillors, ran: 'Roman Emperor by the Grace of God, Augmenter at all times of the Empire; King of Germany, Spain, the two Sicilies, Jerusalem, Hungary, Dalmatia, Croatia, etc., Archduke of Austria and Duke of Burgundy, Count of Habsburg, Flanders and Tyrol.' The list continued and included even the little castle of Pfirt in Alsace; as a finishing touch Charles was given the title of 'Lord of Africa and Asia'. America, however, which the intrepid Spanish pirates Cortez and Pizarro were in the process of conquering for him, was not mentioned. These two men, the Emperor Charles and Luther the monk, now came face to face. As motto for his coat-of-arms Charles had chosen '*Nondum*' – not yet.

## 21

# The Diet of Worms

'HERE I stand. I can do no other. So help me God. Amen.' These are the famous words that Luther is said to have spoken before the Diet of Worms. In all probability he said only 'So help me God', the usual form of affirmation of an oath, but broadsheets printed immediately after the event already contained the defiant 'Here I stand', thus evoking the monk's attitude with the matchless brevity that turns a saying into a legend. The detailed reports vary. There was shouting, Luther was the centre of a wild throng of people, the meeting broke up, the emperor rose to his feet, it was hot in the low-ceilinged hall, it was late and the scene was lit only by the flickering light of torches. What is certain, however, is that Luther stood there and, to the demand to recant, answered 'No'.

Scarcely anyone was aware of the historic importance of the moment, least of all the young emperor whose task it was to decide this case of a rebellious lecturer in a small university, of which he had never heard, in the electorate of Saxony. He had other things on his mind: troubles in Spain, plans for war in Italy, dreams of Bourgogne, and above all severe monetary worries, from which he was never free all his life. He found these German matters irksome in the extreme; he intended to turn his back on them without delay – they interfered with his global designs. The very appearance of the monk, whose name he was not even sure of, he found repellent – in the reports in front of him he was referred to as 'a certain Brother Martin'; he knew only that he was a rebellious, gaunt, fanatic monk, a Bohemian, a Hussite, not willing to accept any authority, whether that of the holy see or that of the emperor, whose majesty was certainly no less sacred. He hoped to settle this affair, which had already caused far too great a disturbance, with a short, sharp edict.

In the emperor's opinion the case was a '*querelle Allemande*', French being the only language he knew. He was concerned with entirely different things; the meeting in Worms was not so much a German Diet as an international summit conference. In addition to his

269

Burgundian councillors, the emperor was attended by Spanish grandees, the two Italian nuncios, representatives from Savoy, and by Venetians, Danes, Poles and Hungarians. There was a French envoy present, who carried his king's declaration of war in his pocket; the English ambassador was armed with a project for an alliance and marriage. There was great confusion of languages. The Germans were also represented, but thrust very much into second and third places. An Austrian from the emperor's patrimonial lands wrote home: 'The court is so utterly parlous and wretched that no one who has not seen it would believe it. The emperor is a child; he takes no action on his own but is under the thumb of some Netherlanders who concede to us Germans neither honour nor any good quality. And any German matters that are raised are all referred to the commissioners, from whom nobody can get either an answer or a decision; everyone cries out against them ... It is all knavery ...'

The ingenuous tone should not blind us to the fact that most of what the Germans had been planning and negotiating, during the four months before Luther was allowed to appear, was also knavery. Each had his special interests, which he furthered with a great air of respect before the new young ruler, who quite certainly had not been elected to prove his ability to rule. Grey-haired councillors from the days of Maximilian hastened to chalk up some success in the game of intrigue before they were forced to retire. Not a few of the princes furthered the interests of France, whose role had by no means been brought to an end with its electoral defeat. Princes, as coarse and uncouth as landsknechts, paraded their powerful limbs in colourful tunics festooned with weapons; they held no definite opinions of any kind. They saw a diet as an opportunity for merry-making, drinking, whoring and breaking a few lances. 'There is racing and jousting almost every day,' Luther's elector wrote to his brother; 'otherwise everything makes very slow progress.'

The matters with which they were supposed to deal were, in fact, very pressing: an imperial government was to be set up; the emperor wanted to leave Germany immediately after the meeting – he was to stay away nearly ten years. Who was to take charge of affairs during his absence? Following the electoral capitulation a government of sorts by the estates, with the voices of the electors predominating, had been envisaged. The emperor lost no time in making it clear that he did not intend to keep his promises; he would appoint a regent, and the man he had in mind for the post was his brother Ferdinand. The princes found this extremely inconvenient and finally a compromise was agreed on – the regular practice of the imperial diet. In order to calm ruffled tempers, the emperor broached the subject of the expedition to Rome for his coronation; traditionally this was necessary to bestow full authority on the emperor, who up till this moment was merely the emperor 'elect'. But to travel to Italy also meant reasserting the empire's old claims over all the lost territories in Italy; it also meant war with France, which was in possession of Milan. The leading advocate of this policy was the emperor's chancellor, Gattinara, who had replaced as councillor the ageing Burgundian Chièvres, duke of Croy. Gattinara, an Italian from Piedmont, a jurist and man of simple background, represented the new type of minister-civil servant, whereas Chièvres had been the old type of Burgundian lord with a princely fortune of his own, which he had doubled or trebled during his tenure of office as tutor and governor to the young Charles. Gattinara could not aspire to emulate the Croys and build up a family dynasty; he wanted only to be his master's servant, his 'minister', but he intended to guide him and had gigantic imperialist plans for him. Among these Italy occupied first place, and there were many who heard this news with pleasure; Italian campaigns had always provided opportunities for individual gain. But money was needed to wage war in an age of hired troops, landsknechts, and Swiss mercenaries, and money was desperately short. In its anxiety the banking house of Fugger, which had been financier-in-chief of the emperor's election, had already covered itself by taking over the Austrian mines as security. Spain was exhausted and in the throes of a fierce civil war; the great Spanish nobles attending the congress complained bitterly that they could not even appear in public as befitted their rank. The Germans would have to pay, and they grumbled about the ruptured state of the empire, the high cost of living, the low level of health, the disorder. And if it was a question of payments, the 'gravamina' against Rome and the everlasting 'ecclesiastical' tributes could be brought up again. Under such circumstances an appeal could also be made to the 'common man', and in this connection even the Wittenberg monk was not unwelcome.

The emperor's councillors did all they could to enlist sympathy for the Rome expedition. They had no qualms about giving permission to preach in Worms Cathedral to Faber, the venerable Dominican prior who had written the 'Advice' on how to preserve peace on the lines advocated by Erasmus. But instead of preaching peace, Faber preached war. The occasion was a death: the twenty-three-year-old brother of the duke of Croy, to whose other benefices had just been added Toledo, Spain's richest archbishopric, had fallen from his horse while out hunting and died in agony. All persons of rank attended his funeral. But Rome received horrified reports of the sermon; instead of pious reflections on death and the transitory nature of human life, Faber had

271

delivered an inflammatory political speech. He had spoken of Luther, saying that his machinations must not be tolerated. But who should intervene, in the opinion of the prior? Not the pope but the emperor! To make matters worse he had also added: 'If the pope has failed in his duty, it is up to you as emperor to rise and punish him.' 'Italy, Italy!' the monk had cried with 'unbelievable insolence'. And turning to the princes he had said: 'While you wage war among yourselves and against the emperor, the pope, Venice, France and the rest of them have been opposing the emperor. Therefore unite now and assault them!'

This was not irresponsible baiting of the Wittenberg monk, but a carefully considered move on the part of the imperial Government; the nuncios were to have many further occasions to send agitated reports to Rome. After a long search and repeated refusals Aleander, who, not without justification, considered himself the most important person attending the diet, had been able to find no better quarters in the town than a sort of garret, unheated and dirty; he shuddered, not merely with cold but at the threats he encountered. 'I feel less safe in these German towns than in the Campagna,' he wrote in his dispatches, and that meant a great deal to anyone familiar with conditions on the outskirts of Rome. Worms was cramped and every room taken, not only in the town but far beyond the walls. The emperor himself shared a room with the aged Chièvres, who wanted to keep an eye on his pupil as long as possible. In the inns there were five to eight knights in a room, while a dozen grooms had to share a single bundle of straw. Among the lower orders brawls between the various nationalities were as much a daily occurrence as the clashes between the nobility; at one sitting swords were drawn and it almost came to a fight when the elector of Brandenburg quarrelled with his enemy the Elector Frederick. Attendance at church was accompanied by disputes over etiquette. Queens had wrangled over questions of precedence on the steps of Worms Cathedral in the forgotten days of the Nibelungs; now nobles fought for their rightful places at Mass, and some strode majestically out rather than accept a humbler position.

A storm of rumours rent the town. Broadsheets drifted in, although they were forbidden. Pamphlets by the heretic were displayed; the Spaniards tore them up and were called to account for doing so. A Spanish horseman pursued a citizen with drawn sword, but the quarry escaped through a doorway, the Spaniard falling with his mount: 'Many Germans were standing round but none dared to raise so much as a finger against the Spaniard', a friend wrote to Hutten. Ordinances were posted; other posters carried anonymous threats. Pictures of the heretic were on view as well as caricatures of the nuncio hanging head down from a gallows – imperial policy by no means scorned such storm signals when the moment seemed opportune. Chièvres told the Venetian envoy that the Wittenberg monk was prepared to supply the emperor with a hundred thousand men if Charles would march into Italy and reform the Church. Obviously he regarded Luther as a cleric of the stamp of the versatile Swiss, Schiner, bishop of Sitten, who sold his bellicose countrymen to all and sundry; he sold them to the pope, who had rewarded him with a cardinalate, and was prepared to sell them to the emperor as well, provided he could pay the price. The threat of war was in the air. It was already being waged on the Nether- lands border by partisans of France, the duke of Geldern and the brother of the bishop of Liège who, known as 'the boar of the Ardennes', was leading an attack from Bouillon and Sedan. War had been declared in Italy. In the Balkans the Turks were threatening Belgrade. A bloody civil war was being fought between Denmark and Sweden. Hutten had called for a rising against the priesthood. A peasants' war was no empty threat; there had already been serious riots.

The talks had already been going on for four months when on 16 April 1521 Luther and his companions arrived in Worms. Aleander had renewed cause to feel indignant: it was quite improper for a man under ban to arrive as it were in procession. People, their curiosity aroused, had ridden out to meet the heretic; the imperial herald, his cloak emblazoned with the emperor's coat-of-arms thrown over his arm, preceded him to let everyone know that Luther was travelling under protection of the emperor's safe conduct. The streets filled with people. The procession had difficulty in making its way to the hospice of the Knights of St John, where Luther was to stay; it was near the Swan Inn, where the elector of Saxony had his lodgings. The heretic took his midday lunch with ten or twelve other people; his room was never free of visitors who came to encourage him, frighten him, or merely to see him.

Although his experiences on the journey had prepared him for the situation, Luther now became confused. He received advice from all sides. The elector, who remained carefully in the background, sent his councillors. Schurff, the Wittenberg jurist, briefed him. Luther, we may assume, was nervous, like all brave men before a great battle. He had little fear of the stake but was afraid of appearing before his emperor, 'the young nobleman of ancient German lineage'. This respect, which all his unpleasant experiences never quite succeeded in destroying, he retained throughout his life; whatever his conduct, an emperor was a God-given figure. Luther also had other, deeper fears. He knew far better than anyone else what it meant for a man on his own like himself, relying solely on his conscience, to face the massed authority of the entire world. He also feared the hubbub, the large numbers of people all making their individual and very different demands on him. He had already had doubts when Hutten and Sickingen had tried to win him as an ally; he was concerned with something other than a war against the priesthood. Victory had to be won by the Word, not by force of arms.

The advice, the persuasive talk, must have continued far into the night; he shared a room with two of his companions. The following morning he was summoned to appear. Etiquette was observed, to a very exaggerated degree in the nuncio's opinion. The imperial marshal came to the hospice of the Knights of St John and delivered the order: Luther was to appear at four o'clock that afternoon before the emperor and estates.

He was fetched and once again given a formal escort. The streets were so packed that, as a precaution, he was taken by a circuitous route through gardens and backyards, and entered the council chamber by a side door. An uproar broke out in front of the main entrance when the crowd saw what was happening. The guards made strenuous efforts to prevent unauthorized people from entering the building. Many climbed on to the roofs to gaze across at the roof of the bishop's palace.

The scene in the chamber itself bore no resemblance to the bleak and solemn settings of later times. Seats with canopies had been provided for the emperor and some of the most exalted personages; stone benches ran along the walls down the length of the room. Most of those present stood, crowding forward in order to see and hear better. Luther and his companions had to force their way to the front. The monk, catching sight of the familiar face of his former host in Augsburg, greeted him delightedly. The imperial marshal called him to order at once; he was not to speak until invited to. The nuncio, who was unable to be present at the examination of the excommunicated monk, received a report that the heretic looked about him insolently in every direction: 'Despite the presence of the emperor, he moved his head this way and that, up and down.'

Luther's writings lay heaped on a bench. The examination began. The official of the archbishop of Trier, a tall man with a very carrying voice, read a statement that had been agreed with the nuncio. Luther had been summoned by the emperor to answer two questions: 'Firstly, do you here and publicly acknowledge the books that have been circulating under your name? Secondly, do you wish to uphold their contents or recant anything they contain?'

Luther's legal adviser called out: 'Read out the titles!' He was afraid the pile of books might contain writings that were not Luther's. The titles were read out; Luther acknowledged them. He began to speak. He spoke slowly and seemed ill at ease. His supporters were disappointed, his opponents pleased – they assumed he was frightened and despondent. The distinguished audience found him lacking in dignity and decorum and was unable to understand how this sorry figure could have caused such a stir. Some noticed how low his tonsure had been cut, others claimed to have been struck by the 'demoniacally sparkling eyes' in the bony face. The man was unsure of himself; he had been instructed to bend his knee before the emperor, so he pushed it out from beneath his heavy black habit, not quite certain whether he was supposed to do it once or several times. In speaking he used quotations from the Bible, most of them not very familiar. He cited Christ's words: 'Whosoever shall deny me before men, him will I also deny before my Father which is in heaven.' Then he asked for time to consider the second question; he needed to think over his answer very carefully.

The emperor, who had been given a précis of the monk's remarks, reacted impatiently, but his councillors and the princes considered the request reasonable. The official announced their decision: Luther was given time to reflect, but only briefly; he must appear again the following day. Moreover his answer must be given orally and extempore, it must not be written or read. Murmurs and questions filled the room, many of those present scarcely knowing what had been said. The heretic was led away and taken back to his hospice. It had been not an impressive appearance, though it was the prelude to one; he may have behaved as he did because of suggestions put to him by the elector's councillors, or he may really have felt ill at ease.

Once back in the hospice he was subjected to further persuasion and advice; Spalatin, in his capacity as court chaplain, instructed him how to address the emperor and princes. Luther sat down at his table and wrote. In a letter to the Viennese historian Cuspinian he gave a report of the meeting 'direct from the bustle and excitement' and declared he would not recant a single word. He took another sheet of paper – it still exists – and began to sketch out his address for the following day, noting the obsequious flowers of speech he had been enjoined to use. At the second question, concerning his recantation, he came to a stop. In the oral answer demanded, he wrote, he might say something 'unguarded', 'too much or too little, to the injury of my conscience ...' He broke off in the middle of a sentence: 'And although certain things have slipped into the speech, such as ...'

Probably he was disturbed; his room was never free of visitors. The handwriting is perfectly composed. It is possible that he already knew exactly what he wanted to say. On the next day he made his great appearance, though once more not until late afternoon, because the noble lords had a great deal to discuss first. The hall was even fuller than before. Some people had been standing since early morning to make sure of getting a place, others made their way into the low-ceilinged room by force. Torches were already needed. This time Luther spoke in a loud voice, and his words were carefully chosen. The official had asked him again if he wished to recant, adding some admonitory remarks to the effect that the extra time for reflection had been unnecessary because Luther had known perfectly well why he had been summoned. In questions of faith, he declared, everyone, and above all a distinguished teacher of theology, ought to be able to answer for his opinions whenever he was required to do so.

Luther started very correctly by addressing the emperor and princes in the prescribed manner; in the crush he had been thrust forward until he stood close to these eminent nobles. Then he apologized in case he had failed to give anyone his proper title: 'My life has been spent in a monk's cell, not at court.' He repeated that he acknowledged the books exhibited unless, he added, alterations of which he knew nothing had been made to the texts – the editions were not his own but reprints published in Basle and elsewhere; he could accept responsibility only for what he had written.

He now proceeded very methodically. As though he were lecturing, he divided his writings into three categories – they were not all alike, he said. At first his writings had been of a purely edifying nature; even his enemies could find nothing harmful in these. Therefore he could not possibly withdraw them; they contained universally acknowledged truths. The second category, he went on, comprised his writings against the papacy. Here his remarks became highly political and dangerous. 'Everyone,' he said, 'is witness to the fact that the laws promulgated by the pope and the doctrines made by men ensnare, harass and torture the consciences of believers in the most woeful manner.' Amidst lively murmurs and half-suppressed agreement he spoke of the tyranny of Rome, of the goods and chattels of the Germans which were being swallowed up. These writings he could not withdraw either. The people, who were at the mercy of this unbridled wickedness, would not understand if he did so, above all if it were to be done at the request of the emperor. The third category encompassed his writings against personal opponents. Here, he had to confess, he had often written with greater vehemence than was seemly for a member of a holy order. But these he could not withdraw either, because were he to do so there would be danger of even greater suppression of conscience than existed already.

The threefold refusal to withdraw was strong enough in itself, because it had been fully expected that he would comply with the order; but Luther now went on to speak for the first time of the subject which for him was the most important of all – the authority of the Scriptures. 'If

I have spoken evil, bear witness of the evil,' he quoted from St John's Gospel. 'If Christ Himself, who knew He could not err, did not scorn to hear testimony against his teaching even from the humblest servant, how much more must I, who am a servant subject to error in all I do, ask that someone bring testimony against my teaching ... Bring testimony, convict me of my error, from the Prophets and the Gospels! Correct me from these and I will gladly recant and be the first to cast my writings into the fire.'

This was understood by many to mean that the monk was, after all, prepared to give way. But, again quoting the Bible, he proceeded to speak of the controversy his teachings had caused, declaring boldly: 'To me this controversy over the Word of God is the most welcome thing in the world ... Did not Christ say: "I came not to bring peace but a sword. For I am come to set a man at variance against his father."' Phrases like these went home, even in the short précis handed to the emperor. Luther continued: 'Consider the wonderful and fearful ways of God! In order to compose this quarrel, are we going first to condemn His Word? Would that not bring on us a flood of evil greater than we could bear? Would that not be a bad beginning to the reign of the young emperor, on whom, next to God, we set such high hopes?'

The young emperor had long since made up his mind. The fact that the monk had spoken of the sword – this much Charles had gathered from the phrases whispered to him – of sons rising against their fathers, of floods and fearful evils, had only confirmed him in his view that the man was a rebel and a fire-brand.

Luther produced still more evidence from the Bible. Menacingly he cited Pharaoh, the king of Babylon and the kings of Israel: 'They all prove how they undermined the strength of their kingdoms, trying to safeguard them by plans that were too clever. God traps the crafty in their own snares! He moves mountains without our noticing it. Therefore we have to fear him.'

This was more like a passionate exhortation to repentance than a defence. In the existing situation it was almost tantamount to suicide, especially in front of the young emperor who had no particular desire to hear of Nebuchadnezzar's fate, of the downfall of kingdoms – having just succeeded to his own – or of too clever plans which could result in one's being caught in one's own snare. The monk ended, as he had been instructed, by bending his knee and excusing himself: he had no intention of trying to teach such exalted rulers, he wanted only to render a service to his country. 'And so I commend myself to Your Sacred Majesty and Your Highnesses, and humbly beg that I be not allowed to fall into disgrace as a result of the machinations of my adversaries. I have finished.'

There was shouting, both friendly and hostile. The many foreigners present requested a Latin translation. A nobleman standing close to Luther remarked: 'Even if you can do no more, you have done enough, Doctor'; he alone had seen that the monk was exhausted. Luther repeated his speech in Latin. To us his words seem clear enough; they were far from clear to his listeners. They thought they detected willingness to recant. The princes and the emperor's councillors withdrew to an upper room to discuss the situation. It was decided that the official should ask Luther to state unequivocally whether he recanted or not.

They returned to the council chamber. The official also wanted to have his say on this great day. He reproved Luther for his lack of modesty, but on a sign from his master, the archbishop, slipped in a discreetly conciliatory phrase: 'If there is good in your writings, Martin, you are in no danger on that account. The emperor will take a lenient view as soon as you alter your decision.' The first thing, however, was to recant in words that left no room for doubt; if he refused, the answer would be 'destruction and everlasting oblivion'.

Luther gave his answer, 'without horns and teeth', as he put it: 'Unless I am convinced by testimony from the Holy Scriptures and clear proofs based on reason – because, since it is notorious that they have erred and contradicted themselves, I cannot believe either the pope or the Council alone – I am bound by my conscience and the Word of God. Therefore I can and will recant nothing, because to act against one's conscience is neither safe nor salutary. So help me God.'

Great commotion answered this speech. The emperor was on the point of rising. He had heard enough: the monk would not recant, he remained obdurate. The official, exceeding his instructions in his zeal, urged Luther excitedly: 'Abandon your conscience, Martin!' What had provoked him most had been Luther's rejection of the authority of the Councils. 'You will never be able to prove that the Councils have erred,' he cried, 'even though it be admitted that mistakes have been made over questions of Church discipline.' Luther retorted: 'I can prove it.' The emperor, now on his feet, brought the proceedings abruptly to an end. No more arguing! Take the man away! He gave a sign to the herald and hurriedly left the chamber.

Wild disorder and shouting followed. Many thought that Luther was to be taken off to prison. People flocked round him; almost all were armed. The herald came up; Luther quietened them down: they could see he had an escort. He was thrust out of the hall as quickly as possible. The emperor's Spanish grooms outside the door shouted some words after the procession, but luckily they were not understood; '*Al fuego! Al fuego!*' they cried – to the flames with him. The babel of tongues prevented a bloody fight, at least then and there. Back in his room Luther threw both his arms in the air, crying 'It is over!'

Many years later there was a sequel to the cry to send him to the stake. After a lifetime spent warring against France, the popes, the heretics and the Turks, the Emperor Charles had abdicated and installed himself in his beautiful villa near the monastery of Yuste. From time to time he talked with the monks. In spite of the sharpest surveillance on the part of the Inquisition, some centres of heresy had just been discovered in strictly orthodox Spain. They must be ruthlessly pursued, said the emperor: Burn them! Show them no mercy! Even repentance must not be accepted. 'I did wrong,' he mused, 'in not killing Luther at the time. I was under no obligation to keep my word.' For the heretic, he argued, sinned against a greater master than the emperor, he sinned against God. 'I did not kill him, and as a result this mistake of mine assumed gigantic proportions. I could have prevented this ...'

He continued to muse aloud to the monks, who have handed down to us what he said: One should never talk to heretics, argue with them, or even listen to them. 'They argue so strikingly and logically that one easily becomes confused. And suppose a false argument had become embedded in my mind? Who would have had the strength to prise it out of my soul again?'

Luther, too, often wished to see his enemies dead; he enjoyed an unholy triumph when one of them died in misery, or was killed like Zwingli. But he trusted in the Word, and it can hardly be said of him that his soul lacked the strength to stand firm against the arguments of his enemies. The emperor, as the embodiment of authority, put his trust in power; it was the only proof he knew. His faith, secure though he felt himself in it, could be shaken. It was Charles's tragedy that he lived to see the failure of this greatest, and in reality the only, argument of his: the appeal to power. The far greater tragedy was that the population of half the world was split into two in the process.

# 22

# To the Wartburg

IT WAS not 'over' for Luther; his great appearance before the emperor and empire was not the end. For the first time in his life the Emperor Charles now also had a great day, making it clear that he was no longer the obedient pupil and adolescent boy for whom everyone, including Luther, had taken him. Some years later Luther wrote of Worms: 'You did something to me there that is written with the point of a diamond, something that will never be erased and will not even be silenced until you are all dust blown with the wind. You sat there like masks and idols round that tender youth, the Emperor Charles, who was not versed in such things and was bound to do your bidding, and you condemned me unheard and uncomprehended and, as your consciences are my witnesses, wholly unjustly.'

This was addressed to the archbishops and princes. They for their part sat around in Worms like blockheads, not knowing what to do. To put off unpleasant things, to think over and postpone them, had been their tactics since time immemorial; mistrust was their most prominent characteristic and strongest weapon. Luther's elector was also uncertain; although he sent word to his doctor that he was satisfied with the manner in which he had conducted himself, he said to those close to him that the monk had been 'far too bold'. The emperor summoned the princes, as the highest ranking body, and asked them what was to be done. Craftily, and with great respect, they murmured indefinite answers, and were considerably taken aback when the young sovereign produced a page of notes he had taken down himself – a practice he continued to follow later. He spoke badly, hampered by his protruding chin and laborious adenoidal breathing. Apart from this, however, he showed no trace of uncertainty. '*Eh bien,*' he declared in French, 'in that case I will tell you what I think.' His statement was read in a German translation. It was both Charles's first public expression of opinion and a sort of testament; to the end of his life his views and convictions never changed. He was slow, being one of the greatest temporizers in history, and stubborn; a melancholic, he was subject to

1 and 2  Luther's parents, Hans and Margarethe, in 1527

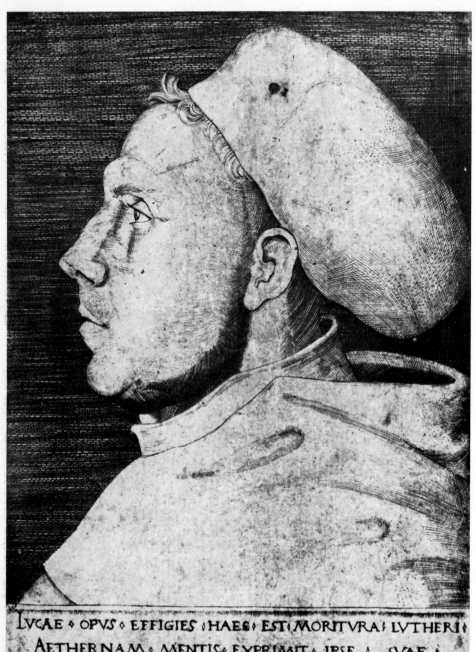

LVCAE ✦ OPVS ✦ EFFIGIES ✦ HAEC ✦ EST ✦ MORITVRA ✦ LVTHERI
AETHERNAM ✦ MENTIS ✦ EXPRIMIT ✦ IPSE ✦ SVAE ✦
. M D X X I .

**3**   Martin Luther in 1521

# Supplementū Celifodine.

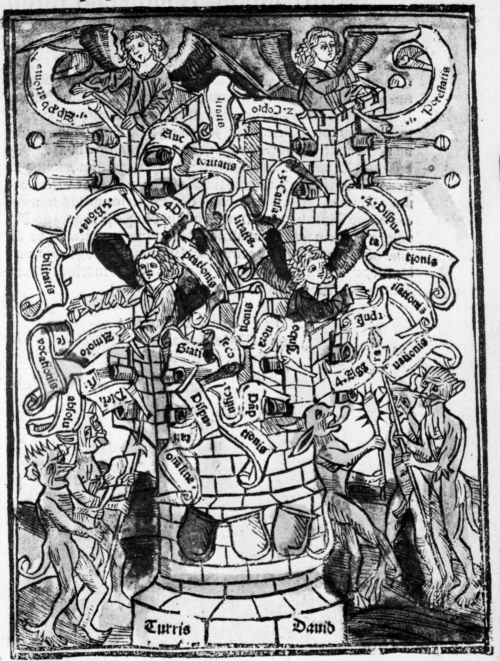

4  The 'Feste Burg' (woodcut from Johann Paltz's *Celestial Storehouse*, 1511)

5 'The Church Triumphant': Thomas Aquinas confounds the heretics (detail from a fresco by Andrea of Florence, *c*. 1365)

6  Philipp Melanchthon

7  Albrecht of Branden-
burg, Archbishop of
Mainz

8  Pope Clement VII

9  (*below left*) The Emperor Charles V
10  (*below right*) Pope Leo X

11 Katharina von Bora in 1526

12 Luther in 1533

13   The Elector John Frederick of Saxony

14   Landgrave Philip of Hesse

the sudden outbursts characteristic of this type. Perpetually obsessed with death, even at an early age, he was for ever drawing up new and detailed wills in which his burial place played a decisive role. He never considered Germany in this connection: Burgundy was where he wanted to be buried, in the true Burgundy of Bourgogne which he planned to win back from France; later, when he had become a Spaniard, it was Spain. His ancestors, his family tree, his genealogy – these were what he clung to and believed in; they determined his religious faith. What his ancestors had believed in he had to believe in too, and with him the whole world, whose very existence depended on this hierarchic system.

And so now he called to witness the long line of his ancestors, the Most Christian German Emperors, the Kings of Spain, the Archdukes of Austria and the Dukes of Burgundy: 'They were all true sons of the Church of Rome until they died, constant defenders of the Christian faith, the hallowed ceremonials, the decretals, ordinances and sacred practices.' This, at least, is how he saw them. His knowledge of history was meagre in the extreme; he had been brought up on the courtly romances of Burgundy, in which no mention was made of the centuries-long battles of emperors and kings over the 'decretals and ordinances' of the Church. But let us not interrupt him. 'They have left us as our natural heritage the duty to fulfil these sacred Christian duties, and it is as a true successor to these ancestors that, with God's grace, we have lived until now. Therefore I am determined to uphold what my ancestors and I have observed until this present time.' He went on: 'An individual monk is certainly wrong when he opposes his view to that of the whole thousand years of Christendom – such a view implies that Christendom may have been wrong at any and every period ...' He solemnly undertook that he, the empire and its rulers, and his friends would do everything in their power to ensure that nothing was changed. Then, turning abruptly to the matter in hand, he said: 'Having heard the answer which Luther gave yesterday in the presence of us all, I declare that I regret having put off for so long the proceedings against him and his false doctrine. I am determined to listen to nothing further from him. On the contrary I intend to send him back immediately under protection of an escort, but on condition that he does not preach, instruct the people in his wicked doctrine, or incite revolt. As I have already said I am determined to proceed against him as a notorious heretic and I call upon you to prove yourselves good Christians in this matter, in accordance with your duty and your promise to me.'

Many of the princes went as white as a sheet, as the nuncio reported delightedly and no doubt accurately. This was a completely new way of speaking, clear, frank, highly personal, and without a word about councillors or compromises. It was an order from the emperor to his subjects. These words were pithy, and in spite of their impressive bodies and powerful shoulders, their broadswords and long poniards, there was little sign of pith in the princes; of the princely liberty which was their leading article of faith, there had not been so much as a hint. They assembled, and, experiencing a certain sense of security in numbers, began to deliberate.

The elector of Saxony, Luther's protector, had already withdrawn. The elector of the Palatinate had also slunk away. This meant that the electors' assembly was no longer competent to reach a decision, which was what the two wary rulers had intended. The others were not merely alarmed by the emperor's order; the elector of Mainz, a nervous individual at the best of times, was actually trembling. Not that he would have been disturbed by the fact that in the last resort it was he, with his electoral and indulgence activities, who had set the whole affair in motion; he was trembling at the thought of the people's anger, of the threat to himself. He had been handed broadsheets in which his name was specifically mentioned and which stated that four hundred knights had sworn to stand by Luther; furthermore they contained the words: 'I write simply, I consider a great wrong has been done; I will fight with eight thousand men,' and beneath them the dreaded slogan of the rebellious peasants, '*Bundschuh! Bundschuh! Bundschuh!*' (A *Bundschuh* was the peasant's leather shoe, tied at the ankle with a leather strap, and the watchword of the peasants' revolt.) He saw this as no idle threat. The first risings had occurred on his own doorstep and had been put down only with great difficulty; they could flare up again at any moment. Where was help to come from? What troops did this emperor possess, who had spoken with such severity? Court officials, bodyguards, a few Spanish grooms – 'barely four crocks in all', as Aleander, who felt equally persecuted and threatened, had complained.

Albrecht, who had been brought the inflammatory leaflets during the night, had them delivered to the emperor before dawn. The latter did not take them seriously. Was it courage, or was he merely casual and uninformed? Albrecht enlisted the help of his brother, the elector of Brandenburg, who suggested to the emperor that Luther be examined again by scholars in the presence of some of the princes. The elector of Brandenburg was actually one of the monk's bitterest opponents and above all a sworn enemy of his protector, the elector of Saxony; but he, too, was a staunch supporter of princely liberty and regarded the emperor's attitude as uncomfortably menacing. Charles rejected the proposal out of hand. He made it clear that he did not intend to alter a single syllable of his declaration. The electors, or rather those of them who remained, submitted a petition.

Calling themselves obedient subjects, they addressed Charles as His Most Sacred Majesty and 'invincible Emperor'; with frequent protestations of loyalty, they said what a pleasure it had been to hear his views. Then came their new proposal for a further hearing. Luther had stressed that if someone were to instruct him he would admit his error. It would be dangerous, they pointed out, to give the people, who were unfamiliar with the facts of the case, an opportunity to say he had been condemned without a hearing. It would be better if he were set on the path of truth once more. Therefore, theologians of repute should be appointed to explain to him what was questionable in his writings and so induce him to recant.

All these princes were opponents both of innovation and of Luther; they were also opponents of the innovations they scented in the emperor's attitude. In paragraph 24 of his electoral capitulation Charles had sworn that no German, whether of high or low estate, would be condemned without a hearing. Charles had sworn to a great number of other things, and the princes were to have further occasion to recognize the worthlessness of such election promises, whether made under oath or not. The princes chose Luther's case in order to 'uphold their rights' in a relatively harmless fashion. In doing so they also took into account public opinion, which quite clearly might become threatening. So a committee was formed, the time-honoured device of such bodies. The emperor gave his consent to an examination to be conducted under the direction of a jurist, the chancellor of Baden. In the meantime some days had passed, during which Luther had been besieged by visitors, and others who were merely inquisitive.

The examination passed off surprisingly quietly. The main endeavour was to find a compromise formula. The chancellor of Baden spoke compellingly of brotherly unity and the unity of the Church. He also mentioned the Councils, the main point at issue, because characteristically the question of the pope and his authority had been put almost entirely on one side; but that Luther also wanted to dispute the position of the Councils as Christendom's supreme authority was, in the eyes of both emperor and princes, his real heresy and something quite unthinkable. The Council represented the last chance to bring unity into the already disintegrating situation. The chancellor went a long way in his desire to reach a settlement. Certainly, he admitted, even Councils had been mistaken, and this was all Luther had asserted; but this did not mean that one might scorn their power and authority. As a jurist he went on to draw fine distinctions: the Councils' decisions had not been '*contraria*', or self-contradictory, but '*diversa*', or divergent; they had also done a lot of good, he added. He then turned to the question of Luther's conscience and quoted St Bernard. Was one really entitled to appeal solely to one's 'own understanding'? The chancellor praised much that Luther had written. If he acted reasonably the emperor would see that the 'good books' were preserved.

They talked for two hours. Luther was respectful but stuck obstinately to his view that he could be induced to recant only if he were refuted from the Bible. The committee dismissed him as a hopeless case. But this was not the end of the efforts to reach a settlement. The archbishop of Trier, with his official, took Luther aside. A whole series of private talks followed. The archbishop offered him a priorate in his vicinity and a seat at his table if he was willing to recant but, because of that, did not feel able to return to Wittenberg. The committee of princes also came back with a new proposal: might not the decision be left to a future Council? One is constantly aware of the strenuous efforts to keep the affair out of the hands of the Curia. This way out almost led to an agreement; Luther consented, provided the Council were to take place soon and the articles to be submitted to it were shown to him first. The archbishop was informed and sent for Luther again. And now, at the last moment, the outcome was finally decided. Luther left the archbishop in no doubt that he would not comply unconditionally with the findings of a Council. What would he do, the archbishop asked, if certain theses from his writings were made the subject of inquiry by the Council? Luther said he could not remain silent even if it cost him his life; he could not deviate from God's Word. Quoting the Acts of the Apostles, he said: 'If this counsel or this work be of men, it will come to nought: But if it be of God, ye cannot overthrow it ...' If God did not approve his attitude, it was certain that he would be completely finished within a few years. The archbishop dismissed him, not unkindly, and with an assurance that he would see that the emperor granted him safe-conduct.

Luther was told he still had twenty-one days' safe-conduct. He left Worms after lunch on 26 April, with two carriages, but this time without the herald. Through his councillors the elector of Saxony had informed Luther that he was to be taken to safety in the greatest secrecy, to a place of which even the elector must not know, so that he could assure the emperor and diet with a good conscience that he knew nothing.

A small troop of horsemen joined him outside the gates. There was general fear of an attack or an attempt on his life. At Oppenheim the imperial herald joined the party after all with the little waggon; he accompanied it for a while until Luther told him he no longer needed his protection. At his next stopping place he sat down and wrote. To the emperor he addressed a lengthy and detailed letter, which was intended for publication and which recapitulated events. He reiterated that he was ready to place himself before 'ecclesiastical and lay judges, who are above suspicion, scholarly and free, and to accept instruction ... without exception, provided recourse is had to the manifest, clear, free Word of God.'

He wrote to his friend Lucas Cranach: 'My view was that His Imperial Majesty should have assembled doctors, one or fifty of them, and honestly vanquished the monk. But all that happened was: Are the books yours? – Yes. – Are you willing to retract them or not? – No. – Then go. – Oh, we blind Germans, how childishly we behave and how we let ourselves be so abominably mocked and duped by the Romanist Scholars.' He also told him that for a time he would be 'shut up' on the advice of good people.

In defiance of the emperor's order he preached, and in flagrant defiance of it he was given a ceremonial reception in a number of places, where he was conducted in procession and entertained, although he himself was afraid that these reckless people might be called to account for their behaviour. The cautious ones attested before a notary that they permitted him to use the pulpit only under protest. Near Gotha his legal adviser parted from him and Luther continued his journey on a side road, alone save for two companions. Of these only one knew what had been planned, the other, Luther's fellow monk Petzensteiner, having been deliberately kept in ignorance.

A small troop of armed horsemen fell upon the carriage, brandishing their weapons. Brother Petzensteiner jumped clear and ran off through the woods; the driver, as the other witness, was asked at the point of a drawn bow whether he had Luther with him and at once answered yes. To the accompaniment of curses Luther was dragged out and made to stumble along in harness beside the horses for some distance; then he was put on a horse. The small cavalcade rode this way and that through the woods for a few hours, then it set off for the Wartburg. The drawbridge was lowered and Luther was received by the captain of the castle, Hans von Berlepsch, but without ceremony because even the castle garrison was to know nothing of the new guest. Luther's case was, after all, more than a jolly escapade on horseback; it was an insurrection against emperor and empire and, above all, the elector and the land of Saxony had to be safeguarded from what could be extremely serious consequences. Luther was taken up to two small rooms entered by a ladder, which could be drawn up at night. Thus he was guarded by two drawbridges. He was ordered to stop wearing his habit immediately, to dress as a knight, to let the hair grow over his tonsure and grow a beard; only after this had been done would he be allowed to appear before the occupants of the castle. He would be introduced as Junker Jörg, a guest of the captain of the castle. Lucas Cranach did a painting and also a woodcut of him as Junker Jörg, showing him with a long, turned-up moustache, a thick growth of beard covering his chin, and a full head of hair. Underneath his habit Luther had brought with him a Hebrew Bible and the Greek New Testament, so that he would have something to read during his confinement. He put them on the small table in his sitting-room. He was provided with an ink horn attached to the side of the table. He did not have an extensive view over the countryside; the windows were small and glazed, with bull's-eye panes. He was alone with his Bible, on which he had taken his stand in Worms. The Wartburg was both a prison and a sanctuary.

# 23

# The Edict

In Worms no one knew where Luther had vanished to, and the news of the carefully prepared attack arrived only weeks later; people continued for a long time to puzzle over what had happened. Wild rumours went the rounds. He had been killed by the nuncios, or he had been found, his body, run through, in a mine; others, and in particular Aleander, surmised more accurately that he had been conveyed to safety somewhere. The Elector Frederick solemnly declared before the diet that he could swear any oath that he knew nothing. Aside from this, however, he took no part in the discussions; as before he remained meticulously aloof, and when a crisis gathered, he left. The Elector Palatine, no less cautious, followed suit.

The time had now come to issue an edict concerning this troublesome affair, as the emperor had announced would be done. For him the matter was very pressing; affairs incomparably more important than the case of Brother Martin awaited his attention. The war with France had already begun, with an attack across the Pyrenees into Navarre, although it was still undeclared. The question of the expedition into Italy was still unsettled. To the best of his knowledge the war of the *comuneros*, the rebellious town communities, under the leadership of the bishop of Zamora, continued to rage in Spain; the emperor's ambassador reported from Rome that Pope Leo had called the bishop a 'second Luther'. One can understand the emperor's impatience with the slow-moving German princes, who requested time to think over every question, whispered among themselves, drank prodigiously in the intervals, and at the end of it all were never prepared to give a clear answer. From what he gathered war with France was not unpopular, provided the emperor waged it himself and as far as possible with his own resources. The pope was highly unpopular. The estates had just submitted once more, in a hundred detailed points, their perpetual grievances against Rome; these did not seem to be very different from the things the 'first Luther', the Wittenberg monk, had been saying in popular language. And the emperor himself, who was in the process of rendering the pope a great service, also had reason to be annoyed with Rome. For what did his ambassador report from the Curia? Pope Leo was negotiating with France at the very moment when the alliance with him against France was under active and detailed discussion, and the holy father had waxed indignant because the young emperor was not showing greater energy in mounting the offensive. The most infuriating thing of all was that he clearly did not take the 'boy Charles' quite seriously; in his light-hearted way he had referred to that 'good child, the emperor', that well-behaved child whose proper course was to turn trustingly to the proved guidance of a vastly experienced and superior leadership such as that of the pope. This touched Charles's honour, the most sensitive point in his nature. Furthermore, the Curia was even speculating on the possibility of attacking Naples, Charles's second kingdom, using hastily commissioned Swiss mercenaries. It seems fantastic that, faced with the appalling danger represented by Luther, the pope had nothing better to do than threaten and embarrass the emperor, his most devoted standard-bearer. The true task of the holy father should have been to extinguish rather than to create fires. It was not Luther who toppled the papacy off its pinnacle; seriously undermined for a long time, it actively contributed to its own downfall.

The two-faced policies of the Medici pope found clear expression in the two nuncios whom he had sent to the emperor: Caracciolo, whose province was high politics with all its wire-pulling; Aleander, whose simpler task was removal of the heretic. Charles's mind was made up, and Aleander, who had so often been close to despair in the preceding months, had his great day too: he was commissioned to draw up the edict promulgating the empire's ban on Luther. According to the constitution – if one may optimistically give that name to the loose threads that still held the empire together – the estates meeting in the imperial diet had to discuss and agree to this. But Charles was determined to prove that he was the emperor and no longer a 'good child'. He had already shown his claws when he addressed the princes; he now bared them still further. There was no longer any talk of government by the estates, as he had promised in his electoral capitulation; his regent would govern, and for this post he had in mind his equally youthful brother Ferdinand. It was of no account that this youth, who had been born in Alcalá and had lived there ever since, understood not one word of German and had no clear idea of what territories composed this Holy Roman Empire. There would be no more discussion of the edict; it would be read out, and the electors, princes and any other interested persons would give their consent. And so it happened.

In any case attendance at the diet had dwindled considerably; officially it was incompetent to take decisions, since there was no longer a quorum. Many of its members found Worms very expensive for any length of time, and unhealthy into the bargain. In addition to the sordid intrigues which pervaded the absurdly overcrowded little town, its streets, in every corner of which grooms, servants and knights urinated, were the breeding grounds of a foul epidemic. In the unsettled spring weather it flared up, claiming victims among the most important people. Whether it was typhoid or one of the other recurrent epidemics, all of which went by the name of plague, people died of it in hundreds; the Spaniards, unused to the German climate, were particularly stricken. The death of his old governor and adviser Chièvres, duke of Croy, was a severe blow to the emperor. Now he was left to face the great decisions alone. Until late in life, when he could find no way out of the everlasting wars with France, he often regretted that the wise and crafty old man was no longer at his side. 'He managed me, but he gave me good advice,' he used to say sorrowfully. The city chronicler of Worms, on the other hand, naïvely recorded another current story in his notes on the diet: the emperor had had the distinguished lord and his brother – the young cardinal who fell from his horse – poisoned as dastardly traitors. In higher circles greater interest was shown in the ultimate fate of the huge spoils left by the dead man. According to one of the envoys, the emperor immediately seized half a million gold ducats for himself.

It was in this fetid atmosphere that the diet drew to a close and the edict against Luther was issued, a fateful document for the Holy Roman Empire of the German Nation. The nuncio Aleander now came into his own; his edict, a lengthy missive, was drawn up and immediately published.

When the edict was read out to those of the estates who were still in session in Worms, the elector of Brandenburg assumed the role of speaker of the rump diet. He announced briefly that it represented the opinion and decision of all the estates of the empire and that therefore it would now be released without the change of a single word. This was intended as a severe blow against his chief opponent, the elector of Saxony, Luther's protector, and at the same time to affirm his own position as the electors' leader.

In order to increase the solemnity of the occasion, the edict was signed in church, following the sermon and High Mass. The nuncio reported that during the ceremony the emperor looked content, indeed pleased, adding that Charles had said to him with a smile: 'You are satisfied now, are you not?' Aleander assured him that His Holiness and the whole of Christendom must feel still greater satisfaction that God had given them an emperor of such goodness, nay of such sanctity – and so on with similar phrases. He expressed himself less ceremoniously in a letter to Cardinal Medici, saying he could not help thinking of that old and cultured humanist Ovid, whose writings he had studied as a boy and remembered well; there was a passage in the *Art of Love* where Ovid spoke of a different sort of chase:

> When the song of victory with its I-o, I-o sounded, my friends,
> And the game I so desired as prey fell into my net.

After which he quickly added: 'But I must pull myself together; after all we are discussing the sacred subject of religion. So let us put such childishness aside and exclaim on this day: praised be the holy, un-divided Trinity.'

Far from being the polished work of a humanist, his edict could more accurately be described as coarse and blunt, as seemed to him fitting for the coarse and blunt Germans. They, and their princes too, of whom Aleander had no better opinion, needed simple, straightforward arguments, so he used diction that did not come naturally to a polished diplomat. Luther, this 'devil' who had 'assumed the likeness of a monk', had gathered his whole accursed doctrine into one 'stinking puddle'. He preached a 'free, self-willed life, beyond the reach of any law, and wholly bestial'; he 'shamefully defiled' the 'indestructible laws of marriage'. The entire teaching of this Satanic emissary from hell was aimed at preaching 'insurrection, schism, war, death, robbery and incendiarism' – a remark addressed mainly to the princes. Not only had he brazenly committed the decretals and spiritual laws of the Church to the flames, and incited the people to wash their hands 'in the blood of the priests', he had done still greater harm to 'temporal power and justice'. Luther was repeatedly and effectively described as successor to Hus, the Bohemian heretic, as a man who poured contempt on the most sacred Council of Constance, which had so opportunely burned the heretic of its day and become a glory of the German nation. Had not Luther gone so far as to boast that if Hus was a heretic, he was a tenfold heretic? This tenfold heretic, following his previous condemnation by the pope, had now been placed under the ban of the empire. Therefore everyone, under threat of punishment for *lèse-majesté*, was commanded to give Luther no shelter, food, drink, nor any kind of assistance. On the contrary, he was to be seized and handed over. For this sacred task a reward was offered; those, princes and towns alike, who contravened the ban were threatened with loss of all imperial fiefs, benefits and liberties. All 'associated with him, all disciples, patrons or successors', were likewise threatened with the loss of their 'movable and immovable goods'; any person willing or able to do so was authorized to 'overpower and seize' them and confiscate their goods for his own use – a provision which, had it been acted upon, would inevitably have led to endless civil war. Finally came the regulations stipulating the penalties imposed on the heretic's writings. Not content with these, the emperor imposed a general censorship. With the experience of so many indecisive negotiations behind him, he was not going to compromise: not only Luther's writings but all books, pamphlets and printed matter of whatever kind were to be placed under strict censorship by the bishops. 'Leaflets, copies', and even woodcuts and pictures harmful to pope, prelate, prince, university or other 'respectable persons', were also forbidden. No one was any longer to 'compose, write, print, sell, buy, or secretly or openly keep' such productions or – to leave no loophole – 'anything else that may be thought up'. It was the first and most thorough restrictive edict and censorship measure of the dawning age of modern times; it ended with the familiar phrase: let each and everyone act accordingly.

It was obeyed even less than the decree about the ban. The whole document bore the mark of impatience and haste; the emperor's one idea was to turn his back on this troublesome empire. He left, travelling down the Rhine and leaving behind him disappointment and disillussion. This was not the young man the princes had pictured when they elected him; they had been led to believe he was docile and tractable and not very robust in health. Neither did he correspond to the people's idea of the 'young nobleman of ancient German lineage'. Nor, indeed, was he the emperor the Curia had counted on; they thanked him in meaningless eulogies for the service he had rendered but, at the same time, made it clear that this necessary enactment was not on the level of the great questions of high policy.

Nevertheless Rome now felt inclined to conclude an alliance with Charles. As he journeyed down the Rhine it was not only the curses and angry shouts of 'dissatisfied Germans' that accompanied him, though this was how it appeared to him and his entourage. From Spain came the good news that the insurgent *comuneros* had been decisively beaten and the bishop of Zamora, the 'second Luther', taken prisoner. For the moment, at any rate, the Curia had adopted a conciliatory attitude, an incalculable advantage for the Italian war. Sickingen and his mercenaries had entered the emperor's service and were already fighting on his behalf on the French border – this in spite of the condottiere's well-known sympathy with the Wittenberg heretic, which was not taken too seriously.

Great marriage plans were again afoot; it was the tenth betrothal of this world ruler who, since the day of his birth, had been so often and so variously promised. This time it was to the English Mary, one day to be known as 'Bloody Mary' but now only a child of five; the marriage was to cement the alliance with her father, Henry VIII. How remote the Holy Roman Empire of the German Nation seemed as he thought over all these moves in Brussels! He had placed the empire in the hands of his brother Ferdinand, making over to him the patrimonial lands in Austria as compensation. While in his home town of Brussels, surrounded by the wealth and splendour of his Burgundian court, he received news that the imperial troops had entered Milan, forcing the French to withdraw. Charles spent a few weeks encamped near Audenarde, facing the French enemy. In high spirits, and conscious of his new status as man and warrior, he now broke – apparently for the first time – the celibacy which hitherto he had guarded so carefully and which, in a dynastic figure of such vast importance, had caused observers no little uneasiness. He formed a fleeting association in his field quarters with a Flemish girl named Joan van der Gheenst, who bore him a daughter. But, unlike her mother, this daughter was far from being a passing interest; every drop of dynastic Burgundian blood was precious. His ancestors before him had distributed the leading bishoprics in Burgundy among their bastards; Charles's daughter was entrusted to the care of her aunt Margaret, regent of the Netherlands, and received her name. Later, when still little more than a child, she was married to Alessandro Medici, the pope's nephew, and Florence had to forfeit its freedom in bloody fighting in order to provide a dukedom for the couple. Alessandro was murdered and the girl, now fifteen, was immediately found another husband; this time it was Ottavio Farnese, the grandson of Pope Paul III, with whom she led an unhappy life. The emperor also named her as regent of the Netherlands in succession to her aunt, and as Margaret of Parma her name was linked with the outbreak of the fearful battles for Holland's independence.

How completely the emperor had put Germany out of his mind may be seen from the way in which he reacted to news and inquiries from this quarter. He never answered. He had left behind him a so-called 'imperial government', whose first task had been to nominate someone to represent the emperor's representative, his younger brother Ferdinand; the choice fell on the elector of the Palatinate, an amiable but colourless figure. The estates also appointed delegates to represent them, but for a long time to come it was impossible to speak of a government in Germany worthy of the name. This was to have the greatest significance for the fate of both the Reformation and the revolution that was then beginning. What purported, under the guise of high-sounding phrases, to be the leadership of the Holy Roman Empire borders on the grotesque. At the beginning the princes could not even make up their minds whether the emperor should be looked upon as 'absent', thereby enabling the imperial government to assume responsibility; he was in the Netherlands, which supposedly belonged to the 'administrative district of Burgundy' and therefore to the empire. Two circumstances settled the matter: in the first place the emperor simply ignored the questions that were put to him and, in the second, he left Brussels shortly afterwards and went to Spain. In fact he always ruled Germany as an 'absent' monarch. Next, the delegates could not agree on the contributions to be made towards maintaining the 'imperial government' – in any case they were bound to be pitifully small; the result was that most contributors paid nothing at all. The imperial high court of justice moved to Nuremberg, taking with it waggonloads of documents relating to three thousand five hundred unsettled cases.

The two edicts proved to be so much waste paper, especially the one imposing censorship. No one was to 'compose, write, print, paint, sell or buy' anything that could give offence to anyone: more was published, and more woodcuts were made and sold, than ever before. Illustrations proved at least as effective as tracts or the newly popular dialogues, these last taken over from the humanists, remodelled and used as vehicles for striking arguments. The slogan entered a golden age, which is not yet over; even today certain slogans of this period can be turned to profitable account. Those championing the new doctrines clearly had the upper hand; the champions of the old Church complained pathetically that they could find hardly a single printer to take what they wrote. Eck, Cochläus and others, who volunteered to enter the lists against Luther, were for ever lamenting that they had to publish their writings at their own expense; they expected to be repaid by the Curia, but in most cases got nothing. Most important of all, however, they did not understand the language of the people. They wrote thick tracts containing numerous quotations from established authorities, and kept on appealing to tradition; no one read them.

Their opponents looked 'the man in the street in the mouth' – it was not only Luther who did this. They wrote bluntly and arrestingly, and they preached in the same way, because the spoken word still greatly predominated. They sang too; the coming storm was ushered in everywhere by songs. The church where people sang, as opposed to the church in which Mass was celebrated solemnly in Latin, became the distinguishing feature of the movement for reform. And the songs they sang were not the hymns and chorales that were soon to become a tradition, they were German *Marseillaises*. The authors, however, were rarely men of the people, more often they were students and men of letters; even the knight Hutten, who prided himself on his elegant, humanist Latin, now wrote in German, still somewhat haltingly but with great power. The songs put into words what the people thought, felt and wanted. Things were going to be different, utterly different. As to precisely what was going to be different opinions varied widely, and it was still far from clear how the revolution was going to be accomplished. 'Freedom from the yoke of Rome' was the cry. For some this meant cessation of the payments to the Curia, reform of the church services, sermons in German; for others, like Hutten, it meant national uprising and destruction of the ecclesiastical principalities, with vigorous assistance from the lesser nobility. But to the peasants it was a yoke of a different kind that had to be shaken off, while to the smaller townspeople and journeymen the enemies were the patricians, with whom they had been at daggers drawn for centuries. The national peace, so often proclaimed, had never become a reality. Not only did the robber knights continue their raids unhindered, and robber princes their feuding expeditions that laid waste whole districts, but so-called princes of the empire and their troops were fighting for France on the Netherlands border. The ancient Westphalian vehmic court was revived and dispatched its secret envoys far into southern Germany where, in execution of a secret sentence, men were hanged, not always without cause but equally often from motives of personal vengeance.

This anarchy was reflected in the furious output of pamphlets, news sheets, ballads, which were often vehicles for personal feuds and local quarrels fought with appalling bitterness. God was unceasingly invoked, even in aid of the brewing rights of a monastery which was competing with a town brewer. The imminent end of the world, based on the ancient prophecies of the abbot Joachim in Hohenstaufen times, was constantly foretold. It was not simply random comment when Aleander's edict spoke of the 'insurrection, schism, war and death' said to have been preached by Luther; these scourges had been gathering momentum for a long time: insurrection on the part of the princes, schism between the supreme powers of the west, wars and preparations for wars everywhere, and death in countless individual actions. In Germany the waves of the mighty social tide of the peasantry now beat against the very gates of the ecclesiastical and secular principalities.

The emperor was in Brussels; Luther was in the Wartburg, the prisoner of his elector. The emperor's mind was on the war with France, which was just beginning, on Italy, and on the disorders in Spain. Of all this Luther knew next to nothing. The edict had forbidden him to 'write and publish'; there was no appeal against this verdict. He eventually appealed to a higher court, to the people. In Worms he had put his reliance on the Bible, the only authority he felt able to acknowledge. He now gave himself to writing. He translated the New Testament into German; it was his greatest and most lasting work.

# 24

# The German Bible

IT WAS in the Wartburg that Luther struggled with the devil and threw his inkpot at him – popular imagination retains this as the chief memory of those days. But while he was there Luther also started to translate the Bible into German, and this was by far the more important outcome of this incarceration. Let us first dispose of the devil.

Luther very often felt himself to be in the presence of the devil as an 'incarnate' form. But he never described the devil's physical characteristics in the usual terms, never referred to him as having horns or a club foot, or as appearing in the guise of a hunter or junker; this was left to his enemies, who were soon spreading the story that Satan had secretly visited Luther's mother in the guise of a fine gentleman and sired this son. Luther was under the impression that his every step was dogged by the devil; he was especially plagued by him at night. He saw the devil as the 'spirit of melancholy', like Saul whose evil spirit David had to drive away by playing on the harp. It was the devil who enticed people to commit suicide; Luther forgave the suicides, although in his day those who failed in the attempt were severely punished. This was wrong, he said, because they had not taken the step voluntarily but had been coerced into it by the power of the devil, like 'someone who is murdered in the forest by a robber'. Even today Luther's use of the word devil, or as we should say 'devilry', to explain the engines of war, for example, will not seem unduly far-fetched, just as many of his contemporaries, in their enthusiasm for the new weapons, had no compunction about inscribing the names of the apostles on their cannon. 'I regard them as Satan's very own invention,' Luther declared; of the soldier, who had to fight against invisible forces operating at an incalculable distance, he said: 'He is dead before he is seen.' Money he also described as the devil's means of achieving his ends, whereas God acted through his Word. He never had any time for the subtleties of the new economic doctrines then being introduced or for the practices of capitalism.

To Luther, however, the devil was above all the great adversary who engaged in disputes with him, using the methods of scholasticism which Luther had been taught at the university; he advanced all his enemies' arguments, as well as those with which Luther was forced to torment himself. 'I have one or two devils who keep a close watch on me and are very purposeful devils. And when they can make no headway with my heart, they attack my mind and torment me that way.' His heart was safe from their attacks, his mind less so. Luther had to summon to his aid his whole newly-won creed before he could vanquish his opponent. The latter, for instance, demanded to know who he, Martin Luther, was to presume to conduct a campaign against the pope and the whole body of religious orders. The devil's supreme skill lay in the fact that he, too, could quote the Gospel; when he did this only one thing helped: the Word could be variously understood – 'to one person [it is] terrifying, to another comforting.' What mattered was consolation, grace. 'To this Satan objects: but God has said thou art cursed if thou dost not obey my law. I reply: but God has also said that I should live.'

If disputing did not help, Luther, with all the vividness of which he was master, recommended his pupils to use the well-tried domestic remedy of simply presenting their backsides to the devil and answering stink with stink: 'Then he will stop. Otherwise one can't get rid of him.' His pupils faithfully wrote this down, as indeed they wrote down in their notebooks every slightest word spoken by the eminent Doctor, even at table. Analytical psychology has applied itself enthusiastically to this reverse side of his nature.

Luther's recollections of the devil's 'corporeal' activities stem mostly from his later years when, in physical distress and grown heavy through too much and too hurried eating and drinking, he became increasingly a prey to the demonism instilled in him in his parents' home. According to this the devil was a poltergeist who threw pots and pans at the local pastor's head; one should say to him: 'Off with you, Satan! I am master in this house, not you.' The devil always remained invisible. Luther's view was that he would see him for the first time on the Day of Judgment, both him and his 'fiery darts', which rebounded from the shield of faith, as Paul told the Ephesians; in the Wartburg, too, the devil remained invisible and out of reach of inkpots. 'I was remote from everyone there', Luther said in the last years of his life, 'and no one could get to me except two pages, who brought me food and drink twice a day. Once they bought a sack of walnuts for me, which I ate from time to time and kept in a chest. When I went to bed at night I undressed in the living-room, put the light out, went into the bedroom and got into bed. Then it was as if someone began cracking the nuts with a loud noise on the beams, one after the other, and shaking my bed; but I took no notice. Just as I started to fall asleep, a din broke out on the ladder as if a whole lot of barrels were being hurled down it, although I knew quite well that it was firmly secured with chains and irons so that no one could come up; but quantities of barrels still seemed to be falling. Getting out of bed I went across to see what was up – the ladder was fast. Then I said: if it is you, so be it! And I commended myself to the Lord Christ and went back to bed.'

The story is of less interest to us for the harmless poltergeist than for the description of Luther's lodgings: the two rooms, living-room and bedroom, and the drawbridge, operated by chains, intended to protect him from any intruder. Hans von Berlepsch, the captain of the castle, was very concerned that Luther's presence should be kept secret from the outside world, and it was certainly kept secret from his enemies. This was made more difficult by the fact that Luther would submit to almost no restraint. He went down to Eisenach and borrowed books from the Franciscans. He wrote and received letters constantly, and from very far afield, and was always sending manuscripts to Wittenberg. He also went out riding, but before he did so the groom assigned to him by the captain had to teach him how to behave when they met people: 'In the way of the nobility, gesturing, stroking one's beard, and with one's hand on one's sword.' 'But Luther could not break himself of the habit of picking up and examining every book he saw. The groom rebuked him for this, telling him to give up the practice because it was not aristocratic, and riding and writing went badly together.'

He continued to write; the ink horn was in constant need of refilling. Luther wrote just as many works in his prison room in the Wartburg as he did in his little study in Wittenberg. His sedentary life, food to which he was unaccustomed and, in all probability, the after-effects of his excitement during the diet produced severe disturbances; there are constant references to them in the letters he wrote during the first six months of his incarceration. He slept badly and had little peace. The captain of the castle wanted to cheer up the junker, whom the personnel of the castle assumed to be some aristocratic prisoner of the elector's, and took him out hunting. But here again the monk was quite unable to behave in a way fitting his rank: gingerly picking up a hunted hare, he tried to hide it under his cloak, but the hounds scented their prey, seized it from him and tore the animal to pieces. This caused him to 'theologize' over the incident and see the hounds as his persecutors, a train of thought not unconnected with the Dominicans as the 'Hounds of God'. He headed his letters 'The hermitage' or 'Above the birds', and ravens, screech-owls and bats appeared as similes in his writings. Enthusiasm for the countryside was virtually unknown in Luther's day; at the most this peasant's son would have looked with pleasure on the meadows, the state of the grass or the harvesting of the hay. He was the monk again, and his days in the Wartburg were the last he spent in the seclusion of a cell. All the monastic ideas he had held, and with which he had done battle, had to be fought out afresh. But a new element had been added as a result of his emergence into the world: an enemy, an opponent, a multitude of opponents. They were the real Satans and demons who kept watch on him, and when he uses these terms it is almost impossible to tell whether he means the 'devil' and his retinue, or the pope and his followers.

Luther's almost nonchalant lack of concern over his fate is a sign of his courage, which went hand in hand with a deep-rooted propensity to martyrdom, to the very German preoccupation with death. The stake still loomed very near. The Edict of Worms had proved to a large extent ineffective, but it existed. He had been outlawed, and this meant that anyone was free to capture him, deliver him to his enemies, or kill him; to do this would not only please God – it had been made legal by imperial decree. To what extent the elector would protect him was still an open question. The Saxon court, including his friend Spalatin, was steering a middle course; it had to move cautiously, since it was by no means certain that the ban would not be extended to include the whole country. It would have given the neighbouring Hohenzollerns great pleasure to deal their rival this new blow. Luther, therefore, received continual warnings that it was advisable to remain quiet or at least behave more circumspectly. He had become such a power in his own right that people were forced to respect him. Spalatin did his best to withhold the manuscripts, with their wild invective, which were sent him by messenger, but when Luther started to insist menacingly that they must go to the printer he dared not suppress them entirely. In this matter Luther feared no one, nor did he show any humility towards the prince who had been his sole protector. He also threatened to leave and not return to Wittenberg, which in only a few years he had made famous. Where would he go?

Paris, which he had once considered so seriously, was already ruled out; the faculty of theology there, like that at Cologne and Louvain, had condemned his writings, and his friend Melanchthon had to assume the task of composing an answer. Hutten and Sickingen had offered Luther their protection; they claimed to have the support of the knights of the empire, but they were an unknown quantity and Luther, with his sure instinct, deeply mistrusted them. Events were very soon to show how right he was. He now had a European reputation as a 'second Hus', and it was widely presumed that he would go to Bohemia, the country of the heretics; but Luther had reservations about the Bohemians too, and here again he was right. Their great days of extremist popular risings were over, and it was in vain that Hutten, in one of his writings, evoked the example of Ziska, the great Hussite leader. Hutten's friend Sickingen was no Ziska; he wanted to carve a principality for himself out of the lands belonging to the priesthood. Rebellion was surreptitiously active everywhere; the masses of the people were in ferment. Luther mistrusted them as well. He did not believe *Herr Omnes* capable of governing, and he had only a limited sympathy with the peasants, although he himself came from peasant stock. He was no popular leader. He had no great gift for organization, and, moreover, it is questionable to what extent these masses could be organized; this, with all its consequences, was to be made clear in the Peasants' War. He had no political programme. He could count only on individual followers, who were widely dispersed and very much at odds among themselves; the first repercussions of the disputes that broke out among them reached Luther in the Wartburg. The first 'fanatics', as he called them, were already on the move in Zwickau, where Thomas Müntzer was active. In Wittenberg his colleague Karlstadt, who wanted to go his own way, was causing him concern. The young Melanchthon was the only reliable one, and even he at times aroused Luther's displeasure. In reality Luther was alone.

'Many and wicked and cunning demons' tormented him, as he wrote to Spalatin. Even to his dearly beloved Melanchthon he once snapped: 'Your letters displease me greatly! As usual you give way far too much to your feelings in putting me on a pedestal, as if I were the only one fighting in the cause of God and the Church. You are entirely wrong; I sit here idly and heave no sighs for the Church. It is my unruly flesh that burns so fiercely. Instead of worrying about the spirit, as I ought, my thoughts are centred on the flesh.' He reels off all the old monastic vices and 'deadly sins', lust, sloth, idleness, lethargy, and asks Melanchthon to pray for him; then he adds tenderly: 'You will take my place, your gifts are greater than mine and more blessed of God.' Self-accusations such as these, which were all part of the monastic tradition, have very misguidedly been used to draw conclusions about 'sensual excesses' and sins, and indeed they lend themselves to this interpretation if they are taken out of their context. Because immediately after this passage, in the same letter, Luther complains that he has written nothing for eight whole days; and the temptations of the flesh are quite adequately explained by his constipation, which later on forced him to consult a doctor. In saying that he had written nothing for eight days, Luther exaggerated absurdly. 'I sit here thoroughly lazy and very busy,' he wrote on another occasion, or again 'I sit here all day long, the idlest and most wretched of men. I read the Bible in Greek and Hebrew.'

He began to translate it – without proper auxiliary means – and so to create his greatest work.

Before starting on his translation he felt the need of a period of inner preparation, though even this was not spent doing nothing. Tracts and pamphlets, long letters that grew into dissertations, short notes and voluminous collections of homilies made their way out of the Wartburg; Spalatin was instructed to take them to the printer at once. Luther paid great attention to printing, paper and choice of type. The Wittenberg printer Grunenberg was given a thorough dressing down: 'Dirty, slovenly, muddled printing! Bad type, different kinds of paper! Hack work from beginning to end!' Lotter, the other printer, was praised. Luther wrote to Strasbourg and to Mainz, where Archbishop Albrecht, his first opponent over the traffic in indulgences, was by no means ill-disposed towards him; the ambitious Hohenzollern still had his eye on the post of primate and leader of the German Church. But being in constant need of money to maintain his court in its accustomed luxury, he had announced a new indulgence for the city of Halle, based on new relics and blessings of almost unheard-of potency. The printed prospectus of the relics, which is still extant, includes the basin in which Pilate washed his hands, St Christopher's shoulder blade, a piece of the earth from which Adam was created, some of the manna in the wilderness, twigs from the burning bush; Charlemagne, as the saint not the emperor, and Thomas à Becket were also represented. The collection was considerably more extensive than that in the Schloss-kirche at Wittenberg, which the Elector Frederick had spent a lifetime amassing at great cost from all over the world. The catalogue promised: 'Summa Summarum, 8993 "particles" and 42 complete bodies of saints'; the indulgence was calculated at 39,245,120 years and 220 days – 'blessed are those who avail themselves of it.' Luther heard of it and at once decided to write an attack on the 'Idol of Halle'; his intention became known in Mainz and the archbishop's intermediary, Capito, urged him not to carry it out. Luther replied with a thunderbolt addressed to the archbishop himself. He should leave the poor people alone and not mislead and rob them; he should remember how it all began and 'what a ghastly fire had grown out of the despised little spark.' The cardinal should also leave in peace those priests who wished to marry in order to keep from living unchaste lives; if he did not do so the cry might be raised that it would be more seemly for the bishops 'first to drive out their whores before they separated devout wives from their husbands.' The excommunicated and outlawed monk demanded an answer within fourteen days.

It came back by return – 'Dear and greatly respected Doctor'. The cardinal had received his letter graciously and in a friendly spirit; he was under the impression that the cause of the trouble had been eradicated long ago, and humbly promised to conduct himself as befitted a devout prince of the Church. 'I am prepared to endure brotherly and Christian punishment.' May God grant patience. '*Albertus manu propria.*'

If Luther had had the slightest gift for diplomacy, a conciliatory gesture of his might have made an ally of this powerful ecclesiastical dignitary. But such a move never entered his head. He doubted, and perhaps not wholly without justification, whether the letter was sincere. He roundly berated the intermediary, Capito; his letter was immediately published. To the Saxon court, where eyes were already turning hopefully to the new ally in Mainz, he wrote recklessly: 'So I am not to write attacks on the archbishop, or anything else that might disturb the public peace? I would rather lose you, Spalatin, or the prince himself'. It was not the public peace but God's peace that was at stake and threatened by the pope and his puppet, the cardinal. 'Such a thing is not possible, Spalatin. It is not possible, my Prince.' The fight had to go on. 'Are we to argue on and on and never do anything?' On another occasion he declared curtly: 'I intend what I write to be printed; if not in Wittenberg, then elsewhere.'

And printed it was, all of it, in Wittenberg and elsewhere. The only exception was the tract *The Idol of Halle*; the archbishop had felt constrained to put a stop to the issue of this indulgence in order to avoid infuriating this fearful monk still further, whose whereabouts he did not even know. Apart from this, everything Luther wrote was published, including the longer letters. The Bull of Excommunication, *Exurge Domine*, had opened with a quotation from the 68th Psalm; Luther looked this up and wrote a paraphrase. David's curse on God's enemies – 'As smoke is driven away, so drive them away' – was turned by Luther into 'The smoke curls, rises of its own accord into the air and makes as if to blind the sun and take the heavens by storm. But what happens? A puff of wind and the smoke in all its splendour writhes and vanishes, and no one can tell where it has gone. So it is with all the enemies of truth ...' He was told that a new edict was to be issued mobilizing the obligation of confession against him: priests would be instructed to ask their penitents whether they possessed any of the heretic's writings. Luther wrote on confession, not rejecting it but wanting it to be free, without constraint. And so he took another step forward: of the three sacraments he had retained, only two were now left. As if it were a minor work, he wrote an extensive *Collection of Homilies for the Church and the Home*; it was published in instalments and long remained the pastors' chief standby in explaining the Bible passages selected for Sunday services.

As a monk Luther still had a very real veneration for the Virgin Mary. In the middle of all the turmoil surrounding his summons to Worms, he had begun to expound the Magnificat, the Virgin Mary's hymn. He now finished the work. This was an entirely different Luther. He neither thundered nor raged; he painted his pictures lovingly and

Luther as a monk

in muted colours, like the painters of his day. He pictured Mary in the dress and surroundings he knew, a 'lowly, poor little thing', no better than a serving girl, who remained humble even when the angel brought her the tidings; she 'does not announce that she has become the mother of God or claim any honour, she goes about her housework as before, milks the cows, cooks, washes dishes, sweeps and dusts, and performs the small, menial tasks as a servant or mistress of the house should.' Bach too, when he composed his Magnificat for the Thomaskirche in

Leipzig, represented the lowliness of the maid by means of a distinctive and charming musical figure. It is worth reflecting that, in spite of all the conflicts over creeds, this cornerstone of Catholic worship survived until Bach's day, even the medieval practice of 'rocking the infant' in mime being retained; it was performed at evensong on Christmas Eve. In this work Luther still kept very much to the old faith, although he could not refrain from alluding to his new teaching. But primarily he was speaking to simple people; referring to his word-pictures he stated expressly 'that for simplicity's sake we are fashioning it for the eyes.' He explained the Latin words they had heard so often and only partially understood, and altogether the little work is like a preliminary study for his task of translating.

For him, however, there was something bigger at issue; at the very outset he stressed the fact that when Mary praised God she was speaking 'from personal experience': 'For no one can understand God or God's Word correctly unless he receives it direct from the Holy Ghost. But no one can receive it from the Holy Ghost unless he experiences it, puts it to the test and feels it.' The whole treatise was an exhortation to be humble, an appeal to the poor and lowly; when he used stronger language it was directed against the rich and the proud, against the proud scholars too, who secretly thought only of how to increase their own importance. He preached tractability and understanding as the chief virtues and, in startling contrast to his later attitude, maintained that one should be friendly also to the Jews – there might be future Christians among them. Moreover the Bible promise was made to them, 'to them alone and not to us heathens'; they were Abraham's seed and Mary also came of this seed. 'Our cause rests on grace alone, we have not God's promise, and who knows the how and the when; to live like Christians and bring them to Christ with kindness is surely the right way.' To which he added: 'Who will want to become a Christian if he sees Christians treating people in so unchristian a manner? Not thus, beloved Christians, but tell them the truth kindly; if they refuse, let them go their ways. How many Christians pay no attention to Christ and do not hear his words; they are worse than the heathen and Jews. Let us abide by this for now.' Unfortunately in his later years Luther did not abide by this conciliatory attitude.

His explanations of the hallowed text often seem like a soliloquy during his work on the translation. He wanted to make 'the Word' available to his countrymen, and in one of his letters wrote the phrase which has since become famous: 'I was born for my fellow Germans, it is them I wish to serve'; he wrote it in Latin, not as a solemn pronouncement but in parenthesis, as though it were self-evident – at the time he was not thinking of his Bible translation. But already he saw his main task to be that of making the Word known to the people, clearly and in their own tongue; it was not enough for them to listen to the sound of the Latin. What did *Magnificat* mean? It meant 'to magnify, to praise, to set great store by God'; it was like the title of a book that told of great deeds and works done by God, 'to strengthen our faith, to comfort all the lowly and to frighten all the mighty ones of the earth.' God had done great things, how could one picture this to oneself? 'As the words flowing of their own accord – not thought-up or composed – and breaking forth, as if it were the Spirit gushing forth so that the words come to life and gain substance, yes, so that the whole body and everything comes to life and every limb wants to speak, that is to praise God in spirit and in truth – then the words are pure fire, light and life.' Luther's gift for translation cannot be better defined than in his own words.

Luther now arrived quite logically at the composition of his master-piece. Secretly, and very much against the wishes of his elector, he had been to Wittenberg, where his friends, the 'little handful' as he called them in the dedication of one of his polemic writings, encouraged him; during his final months in the Wartburg he set about translating the New Testament. It was a Herculean task for a man on his own, with only the scantiest auxiliary means: these were the Greek original, which for the first time he now used as his basis; the Latin Vulgate, on which he had been brought up in the monastery and which he knew virtually by heart; and possibly also one of the existing German translations, which had been done from the Vulgate in ponderous, self-conscious, though not undignified German. He had no dictionaries or commentaries, no assistants to help him – it was only later that he was able to make free use of these – and only a very imperfect knowledge of Greek. He did not venture on the Old Testament at this time, because he knew his knowledge of Hebrew was inadequate; subsequently this translation became the task of a whole group of friends in Wittenberg and was the result of many years of laborious work. It took him about ten weeks to translate the New Testament – a copyist would have been hard put to it to copy the text from an existing original in this time. We hear nothing during these weeks of bodily ailments, and nothing of the devil or demons. But we hear of the disturbances in Wittenberg and elsewhere, which Luther could not afford to ignore; he already sensed that his mission was being threatened, obscured and undermined by extremist reformers and know-alls as well as by those who were half-hearted or undecided, and those who were easily led astray, among whom, it seemed to him, was his friend and disciple Melanchthon. All of which rendered it doubly important to make the Word available. Further-more Luther had already made up his mind to break out of his prison, his 'wilderness', and mix with people again, and before he did this, in a few weeks' time, the work had to be finished.

And finished it was, although when he got back to Wittenberg he improved it, with the help of Melanchthon, the great Greek scholar. *Das Newe Testament Deutzsch, Vuittemberg* appeared in September 1522, printed by Melchior Lotter, whose superior work had recommended him to Luther. It was, in fact, very carefully produced, the list of *errata* at the end comprising only eight items; this also was an astonishing achievement, especially as the printing had to be done on three presses simultaneously. Lucas Cranach's enterprising studio had supplied twenty-one large woodcuts for the Book of Revelation; there were no illustrations to the other books. By December a new edition was needed; pirated editions followed immediately, including plagiarisms by Luther's enemies, who published his text as their own work. Reprints still appear today.

It is impossible to trace here the history of Luther's Bible, but we shall take a look at the history which led up to it. It is quite untrue that the Bible before Luther's translation 'was to all intents and purposes unknown,' as Luther's followers claimed. German translations, mostly based on the same original, already existed in more than a dozen editions; there were also versions in Low German. Some of these, the Lübeck Bible in particular, were beautifully illustrated with woodcuts; the illustrations in the Nuremberg Bible, published by the great printer Koberger, served Dürer as the model for his *Apocalypse*. But these were sumptuous and expensive editions for the rich; they were intended to replace the still more sumptuous manuscript Bibles, which had been so beautifully copied – the famous Gutenberg Bible, for instance, the first monument to the printer's art – that the costly early printings could be sold to those who did not know better as 'hand written'. For the people, the 'uninitiated', the 'Gospels and Epistles in German' were read aloud at Mass from books of pericopes, or selected texts, with notes and commentaries, compiled for the purpose; these were later superseded by collections of homilies, for which Luther had just compiled the prototype at the Wartburg. The Bible in its entirety, the complete text, was reserved strictly for scholars; we have seen how, in Luther's monastery, only the *patres*, not the common friars, were allowed to handle the Bible, and even they were given only the Latin version to read, and above all to study with the aid of the approved commentaries.

The struggle to make the Bible available to the laity had continued down the centuries, following the course of the great heretical movements; the Waldenses and Albigenses already had their own translations, which had been completely exterminated together with those who read them. The next stages are linked with the names of the great heretics Wyclif and Hus, which even in Luther's day were still mentioned with either horror or secret admiration.

With the help of his students, by the end of the fourteenth century, Wyclif had produced a complete English Bible written in a language that was still inflexible and dry; English was just beginning to supplant the Norman French of the upper classes. Luther knew the name Wyclif only as that of a heretic who had been condemned by the Council of Constance and whose corpse, since the man had evaded capture during his lifetime, had been exhumed and destroyed forty-four years after his death. Of the life of this predecessor, which in many respects had been so like his own, Luther knew nothing. Wyclif had also protested against the financial supremacy of the Church and referred to the pope as 'Antichrist'; he, too, had had his princely protector who sheltered him from the final extremity and allowed him to die in peace in a small parish, although the archbishop's court had convicted him. Wyclif also had addressed himself emphatically to the laity, sending out his 'poor priests' to spread his teaching. His translation of the Bible stemmed from this opposition to the hierarchical Church; the simple people, he taught, understood the Word of God very well, better perhaps than the mighty and the scholars, who wanted to reserve it to themselves: 'Christ did not write his teachings on tablets of stone or on the skins of animals [parchment], but in the hearts of men.' He too, and in this he was far ahead of his time, stressed the fact that selected passages and phrases were not enough, and insisted that the Scriptures must be made known in their entirety. His translation could be circulated only in copies, but one hundred and seventy manuscripts have survived; very many more must have existed. His influence ended with his death, his followers being ruthlessly suppressed; in this Wat Tyler's peasant revolt played a decisive part, as if to parallel Luther's fate. His ideas continued to live in the underground movement of the Lollards, but greatly extended and combined with social demands.

Hus was his greatest disciple and translated Wyclif's writings; it was only in this form that Luther gained some knowledge of them. Hus also made use of the language of the people and, like Luther, wrote a collection of homilies and through his writings became the founder of the modern written Czech language. The Czech movements, which, in Hus and the Hussites, rocked the whole of Europe, originated in small groups of Waldenses who, in spite of all the persecutions, had remained in existence hidden in the Bohemian forests. For the first time a popular movement, having made its appearance, remained victorious; none of the countless revolts in all the other countries had ever succeeded in doing this. The vernacular, the *Lied*, the battle song, the Bible for everyone, the Communion cup for everyone – this was the great precedent set by the Bohemians. Its effects were still felt in Luther's time. The Bohemians and the Swiss were the nightmare of every ruling prince; that Germany might turn 'Bohemian and Swiss' was the fear of all administrations and ecclesiastical chancelleries. It was in Bohemia too, where at this time the Czechs and the German minority, later to become such bitter enemies, still lived peaceably together, that the first German translations of the Bible came into existence.

Each of these translations exudes the smell of burning that was the lot of heretics, each stands for political history and social upheaval, for bitter strife, for brutal intervention from above, as well as for a silent influence that extended into the highest circles; King Wenceslas's sister, Queen Anne of England, protected Wyclif, just as her brother, in the course of his political switches, many of which were highly questionable, came forward as the defender of Hus.

Yet another clue to the linguistic foundations that were of importance for Luther's work leads to Bohemia. Wenceslas's father, the Emperor Charles IV, had made Prague the capital of the Holy Roman Empire and the most beautiful European city of its day; he gave it a university, and his court was the first home of early humanism. This circle, under the auspices of the chancellor, Johann von Neumarkt, was responsible for making the first attempt to create a new standard German language which would be compulsory for everyone; while it was intended, in the first instance, for use in the imperial chancellery, it was also to be used for translations, prayers and transcriptions of texts by the Fathers of the Church – things in which the chancellor took an interest. The example was followed in the neighbouring state of Saxony, where it was developed further. It was in this language, which transcended the limitations of local dialects, that Luther wrote. 'I speak the language of the Saxon chancellery, which is that of every prince and king in Germany and of all the free cities of the empire,' was his defence when he was attacked; 'I have no special, personal language of my own.' He wanted to be understood by everyone, and he was. The remark was made in self-defence, because he was immediately accused of trying to impose on people his own highly personal style and interpretation. The language he spoke was certainly not the German of the chancelleries. He rounded angrily on the 'Chancellery gentlemen, numskull preachers and puppet writers who imagine they have power to change the German language and daily present us with new words.' His own recipe, stated in his *Epistle on Translation*, was different: 'It is no use asking the letters of the Latin language how to speak German, as these fools do; it is the mothers in their homes we must ask, the children in the streets, the common man in the market place, and we must look them in the mouth and see how they speak, and translate accordingly. Then they will understand and realize that we are speaking to them in German.'

The passage has become famous, but it makes it easy for us to overlook how much painstaking work and effort went into every single word of Luther's translation. Nor did he only 'look the common man in the mouth', although it was from him that he got the richness and directness of his language. Luther was not a humanist in the ordinary sense but he was so in the sense that, very much the offspring of the great scholarly movement, he wished to go 'back to the sources'. He translated from the original Greek, and later from the Hebrew, a thing that hitherto had been attempted only on a very limited scale. In doing so he immediately found himself once more in conflict with the Church. The Latin Vulgate had become 'canonical'; countless lines in it had been used by the Church as the basis of binding interpretations, laws, and even claims to power. Far from welcoming a translation of the Bible, the Church was horrified at any such undertaking and did everything it could to prevent it. No translation of the Bible is known which was encouraged or even welcomed by the Curia; the commentaries alone were recognized and these only after a thoroughgoing selection had been made. That so many translations were attempted, however, shows how strong and how general was the desire for them. If we plot these attempts, the map shows every imaginable place in Bohemia, England and elsewhere – only Rome, in the centre, remains blank; there was no Roman translation. Strangest of all, not even the text of the hallowed Vulgate, the only version recognized, was definitively established, although it was supposed to be 'canonical'. Only under the influence of the great arguments at the time of the Reformation, and following the Council of Trent, was a start made at producing a radically revised Vulgate, and then the work went on for fifty years and required the efforts of large committees. It was not only theologically that the Church entered its greatest battle ill-equipped; it was equally unprepared in the biblical sphere. The Renaissance popes were great patrons of the Italian humanists, they collected the finest manuscripts, they had themselves painted, like Leo x, holding a breviary sumptuously embellished with miniatures; but to the text of the Bible they paid little attention, indeed there is scant evidence that they read it at all. They were satisfied with the 'selected passages', returning above all to those which seemed to confirm them in their office.

Luther was breaking new ground. We can appreciate the magnitude of his achievement only if we contrast it, the work of a single individual, with the efforts of whole bodies of learned men, who needed decades merely to revise the existing Latin text. He believed that 'God does no great work *nisi per impetum*', and in his table-talk he referred to the same subject still more simply when he said that everything had to be done with a swing, headlong, almost as if in a state of intoxication. He had approached the teaching profession in the same way: 'Had I known what I know now, ten horses could not have dragged me into it.' He pointed out that St Jerome, his predecessor in Bible translation, had also gone about it in the same way, deceived as to the magnitude of his task.

His translation was immediately criticized; the critics of his day, like those of our own, had a predilection for details, and it was in details that they tried to prove him wrong. Mistakes were inevitable, but in those days they had the added, and possibly fatal, significance that they could be denounced as heresy and as an attack on the hallowed, established order of the Church. He translated a passage in Paul's Epistle to the Romans as 'Thus we hold that man is justified by faith alone, without the agency of the law.' For him it was a cardinal passage; 'by faith alone', *sola fide*, became one of the fundamental theses of his teaching. Bitter wrangling over this developed at once. Luther defended himself: he was well aware that the word *sola*, alone, was not in the original, but he was speaking German, not Latin or Greek; it was like saying 'the peasant brings no money but corn alone'. He cited Ambrose and Augustine as authorities, and could even have added Thomas Aquinas had he read him more carefully. More criticisms of the same kind, but attacking far less important lines, rained down on him. It is not surprising that Luther became annoyed, more especially as his enemies were pirating his work so shamelessly. 'Now that it is put into German and finished, anyone can read and master it, anyone can now run his eye over three or four pages without stumbling once. He will not be aware of the rocks and boulders, because he will now pass over them as over a well-planed board ... It is easy to plough a field that has been cleared. But no one wants to uproot the forest and tree trunks and put the field in order.' It is the eternal complaint of the pioneer, and in this field he was a pioneer. When his academic qualifications were called in question he answered angrily and very sure of himself: 'You are doctors? So am I ... You are theologians? So am I. You write books? So do I.' But then he went on: 'I can expound the Psalms and the prophets. You cannot do this. I can translate. You cannot do this ...'

Luther could translate. He was at the height of his powers during these years. Words and ideas crowded in upon him; people flocked round him, coming from further and further afield. His Bible embraced the whole range of the German language; its influence went beyond it.

All the Bibles of those days, and they were produced in a very wide variety of languages, were modelled on his, and often enough used his text. But for Germans he had created 'the Book', which for the next two or three hundred years was to mould their language. It is possible to criticize certain things in it, things of a geographical, philological, textual or theological nature, but this only touches the surface. German

Wuittemberg.

Title-page of Luther's first translation of the New Testament, 1522

classic literature itself is unthinkable without Luther's German. His Bible exerted an influence on all strata of society, except perhaps the uppermost class, which either never read at all or else understood German only imperfectly; very soon this trend reached a point where foreign languages were spoken exclusively. It also reached the illiterate because it was read aloud. Countless phrases from Luther's translation found their way into everyday speech and are still current today. They came from his Bible, although they may not all have been his; he protested strongly that he did not 'coin or invent' anything. But they bore his impress; they 'took wing' from the rhythm of his speech and language.

He wrote spoken German, not bookish German. Before passing his phrases he tested them with his ear, not his eye. The cadence of his language was his greatest strength, and no revision of his text has been able to impugn it; wherever such a thing has been tried, it has only weakened the effect. He also listened very attentively to the rhythm of foreign languages; he had been familiar with Latin since boyhood, though next to his native German he believed Greek was closest to him, but he was not prejudiced in its favour. He had a high opinion of the power of Hebrew too, and indicated clearly those passages in which he had found it impossible to match the original. He manifested pride in his work when it was attacked by wiseacres; he was extraordinarily modest when it came to improving it, and this was to be his greatest achievement in the coming years, when the shadows fell ever deeper over the rest of his work.

In 1534 the complete Bible, containing both the Old and New Testaments, appeared; starting in 1539 a major revision was undertaken, with a large team of assistants under Luther's chairmanship – a strict record of their meetings was kept. Each assistant brought his own special knowledge to the task; the whole literature then available was consulted, including the rabbinical commentaries and, in addition to the Hebraic, the Chaldean Bible. Luther would propose a text and pass it round for comment, listening to what each had to say from the point of view of language or the old Doctors' interpretations; there were times when he despaired of finding a correct and satisfactory version. In one letter he wrote: 'We are now working on the Prophets; great heavens, what a huge and wearisome task it is to make the Hebrew writers speak German. How they dig their toes in, and how unwilling they are to leave their Hebrew ways and follow the coarse German ones; it is like asking a nightingale to abandon its sweet melody and imitate a cuckoo.' Of the building of Solomon's temple he said: 'We shall have our work cut out with this beastly building ... How I dislike building Solomon's temple!' But he did not relax. He visited craftsmen in their workshops to get them to explain their tools to him, like Diderot when he was preparing his encyclopaedia. He had a butcher cut up a sheep, so that he could get a better knowledge of its entrails. When they came to the 'new Jerusalem', in Revelation, with its appointments of precious jewels, all of which were unfamiliar to him, he sent to court for precious stones from the elector's collection, with explanations of their names. He endeavoured to put the Bible into 'pure and clear German, and it often happened that we sought and enquired after a single word for a fortnight, or three or four weeks, and sometimes even then we did not find it ...' A final revision appeared the year before he died; a year later an absolutely final one came out, based on posthumous corrections.

We can do no more than estimate the number of copies that were printed. A figure of a hundred thousand has been accepted for Luther's main publisher Hans Lufft, who replaced Lotter. Along with Lucas Cranach, Lufft became one of the three richest men in Wittenberg. Not even as a translator did Luther take a fee. The total output, including the numerous pirated editions printed elsewhere, may have reached a million. The most eloquent testimony to the book's influence, however, is that it was not only bought but read and constantly re-read. Only a very few surviving copies are as undamaged and in such excellent condition as the sumptuous volumes of the previous translations. A contemporary Luther Bible, when it has survived at all, has almost inevitably been read until it is falling to pieces.

The whole Bible, the complete text, was now available, 'the words flowing of their own accord ... as if it were the Spirit gushing forth so that the words come to life and gain substance ... then the words are pure fire, light and life.' But these words have unintentional, sinister implications. The Spirit welled over. The Scriptures gained substance. The Word took fire. In modern terminology the circulation of the Bible through the newly discovered art of printing was the first example of a mass medium infiltrating into the social order of the times. Everyone read it or listened to someone else reading it; everyone disputed, interpreted and took his precepts from the Bible. 'The Book' became not only a distant pronouncement whose main accent was on the life to come – which is what the Church had made it – but a present reality. Its mission was not only to teach man how to die if he wanted to go to heaven, it became a battle-cry, a social demand; every trend of the day, including, and quite particularly, those we now regard as forerunners of socialism and communism, was determined by the Bible and inspired by the Scriptures. The 'clear, transparent Word', which to Luther was unambiguous, could actually be obscure or diversely interpreted. The complete text of the Bible was very varied and often contradictory, and the selections made from it were arbitrary.

Luther himself had gone about his task in a very individual way, although he had done so with a good conscience and to the best of his knowledge, and the scholar and theologian in him had subjected the text to careful scrutiny. He transposed parts of the text and rearranged it; he had his own views as to which were 'the true and noblest books of the New Testament', and in his preface addressed his readers quite frankly on the subject. Of certain books he had a lower opinion, calling the Epistle of James, for example, a 'thoroughly insipid epistle', from which it was impossible to extract any real grains of truth. Very perceptively he considered that the Epistle to the Hebrews was not by Paul himself but the work of one of his disciples – a view that has been confirmed by later textual research. He mistrusted Revelation – which was to become the mainstay of all those who concerned themselves with apocalyptic prophecies – and included it, along with other passages, in a special section at the end, in order to leave each reader free to make what he could out of it. He had no use for visions, declaring that 'the apostles have no truck with visions but prophesy in clear words'; that John 'issued such harsh commands and threats' was also too much for him. But it was precisely the harsh commands and threats that appealed to the radicals' uncompromising frame of mind. Luther himself was uncompromising enough over the few points which he regarded as crucial for his teaching; otherwise he treated the Bible with a freedom and generous composure never again equalled by those who followed him. In this attitude he was completely naïve. He did not consider the consequences.

In assessing Luther's accomplishment we shall do well for the moment to ignore these historical consequences. He undertook the work, knowing quite well that it was 'beyond' him, because no one else had the courage to tackle it. It had to be done, people everywhere yearned for it to be done, but the Church did nothing to satisfy this desire. Luther went about the task 'cheerfully'. As he stressed in his preface, the Gospel was 'good tidings, good news, a new message of good ... of which a man sings and speaks and is glad'. The message was 'dear and sweet'; 'when one believes it to be true' the heart must 'laugh from its depths and be glad'. Christ did not 'exert pressure' or force, did not threaten or punish; instead He 'beckons us kindly and says *blessed are the poor*. And the Apostles, in saying *I exhort, I beseech, I beg*, tell men everywhere that the Gospel is not a code of law but only a sermon on Christ's merits, delivered and given to each one of us for himself.' Faith's commandment was that man should not think only of himself: 'He will prove himself, break away, and confess and teach this Gospel before the people, risking his life for it. All that he lives and does will be for his neighbour, to help him ... This is what Christ meant too, when at the last He gave no other commandment than to love.'

This was Luther's final decision. There was to be no dogma, no hard and fast doctrine; only preaching. Luther's period of incarceration was the last in his life in which he was able to see things so simply and confidently. In 1522, in uncertain March weather and still disguised as a knight, he rode down from the Wartburg and made his way, through the territory of his enemy Duke George, to Wittenberg. He found a changed world in which people talked not of love but of pressures, force and threats, and of the sombre prophecies of the Book of Revelation.

# 25

# Unrest in Wittenberg and beyond

LUTHER's break-out from his prison in the Wartburg did not have the same dramatic quality as the other turning-points of his life, as the posting of the ninety-five theses, the burning of the Bull of Excommunication, his appearance at Worms, and his capture; the legend has passed this episode by. And yet it was the most courageous act of his career, foolhardy almost to the point of insanity. His early biographers dismissed it in a few bleak words; they also treated as perfunctorily as possible the period that followed shortly afterwards, which they found distasteful. It is true that the letters and documents we have today were not available to them. They knew only that there was unrest in Wittenberg; '*Schwarmgeister*', as Luther called them, had arisen and were threatening the master's work. These *Schwarmgeister* were radical, even fanatical groups which had appeared everywhere and threatened to disrupt Luther's achievement. The word, which has a dual meaning, indicates on the one hand the spiritual sense, and the over-enthusiastic, ecstatic ideas of some of these sectarians, and on the other a swarm of insects buzzing round Luther's head; it was this second meaning that was uppermost in the minds both of himself and his readers. Luther had appeared among the *Schwarmgeister* and restored order – it was as simple as that.

Luther was in the honourable protective custody of his prince, whose only means this was of saving him from the consequences of the Edict of Worms. Frederick, following his usual tactics of procrastination and evasion, hoped the storm would blow over and that he would then be able to bring Luther's case once more before the diet; the emperor, who was the chief antagonist, was hundreds of miles away in Spain and barely replied even to the imperial government's most urgent questions. The German princes were left to their own devices, and the old ruler was confident he could find some way of dealing with his peers. He agreed with them that government by the estates, in other words by the princes, should now be made a reality; all his life, even under Maximilian, he had worked towards this, and it was his quiet, stubborn opposition to a strong central power that had earned him the considerable respect in which he was held by the other rulers, both temporal and ecclesiastical. This 'particularism' was nothing new, it was a German singularity of long standing; none of the emperors had been able to conclude a lasting peace with the racial groups and their dukes. The concept of a nation, passionately though it was advanced, had established no firm roots in the widely scattered territories that comprised the Holy Roman Empire. The people were Saxons or Thuringians, natives of Nuremberg, Cologne or Lübeck, not only speaking different dialects but belonging to entirely different spheres of influence: the west looking to the west, the north to the north, the east to the east. In Wittenberg this was to be seen exceptionally clearly, as Luther was constantly accused of having 'Bohemian' ideas, of Hussite heresy. These ideas were now adopted by some among his little handful of followers and caused serious complications.

The 'common man' in the towns and in the flat countryside was on the move, the first bloody revolts had started to break out. But here again there was a lack of cohesion. The lower orders in the towns were engaged in a centuries-old struggle within the confines of each town, the journeymen against the master-craftsmen, the guilds against the town councils, and all of them against the ecclesiastical overlords. The peasants in neighbouring districts, and often in neighbouring villages, were rivals rather than allies; the gibes they levelled at one another were scarcely less spiteful than those which town dwellers of every class levelled at the stupid, boorish, 'sly' villagers. To add still further to the confusion, the strong ties afforded by the Church's jurisdiction, services and discipline, which created a certain cohesion, had been, or were in the process of being, severed. Here the revolution followed widely divergent courses; for a revolution it was and one, moreover, that, extending far beyond the sphere of religion, made an impact on living conditions everywhere. Monks of every order were leaving their monasteries by the hundreds; what was to become of the monastic possessions and religious endowments, many of them centuries old, and of their rents and revenues? Priests started to marry, and the whole privileged position of the priesthood, as well as the material advantages that went with it, began to totter. The Mass as the principal act of worship, in its form of the 'propitiatory Mass', which could also be said for the dead and the absent, had been declared untenable by Luther. But important family rights and bequests were attached to it, as well as the livelihood of the priests. What was to happen to the countless benefices? They were the customary means of providing for the sons of the nobility, who always disposed of one of their eight or ten sons in this way. Pilgrimages, which meant their means of existence to the places concerned, became unpopular. Here and there iconoclasm was already beginning, the objects to suffer being the 'idols', the pictures of saints, and the magnificent, expensively carved choir stalls for the canons with which the churches were furnished. To every ecclesiastical question was attached a social problem. Every time one of the old forms was abolished or overthrown a new problem was created. Every attempt to preserve the old led to conflict, opposition and revolt, yet there was no plan for the new nor even any clear concept of it; everyone took a hand according to his own ideas. The defence was just as haphazard and was conducted with the severity and cruelty typical of the day; men were beheaded, quartered, burned alive and driven out with a nonchalance only exceeded in our own time. Of still greater significance, however, was the indecision: with very few exceptions, of whom the energetic Duke George of Saxony was one, the ruling princes had not the slightest idea what attitude to adopt. The most completely at sea were the princes of the Church. Frequently toying, like the archbishop of Mainz, with their own revolutionary plans, they had bad consciences. To most of them religious questions were a matter of almost complete indifference; they were interested only in retaining, and if possible extending, their temporal authority, and hoped the general confusion would assist them in furthering this end.

The Elector Frederick, Luther's one and only protector, was perhaps more at sea than anybody else. To his dying day he remained loyal to his old faith and to his beloved saints and religious foundations in Wittenberg; at his court, in which Luther's adherents were in a majority, Mass was said in the traditional form. He had a high opinion of his Doctor Luther and was anxious that no harm should come to him, this being something that neither his human decency, nor his position as one of the most important princes within the empire, would permit. He also had great scruples about imposing his rule too harshly; in this he showed himself to be a true representative of the old patriarchal days, although his proverbial shyness and tendency to procrastinate also played their part. He wanted everything to develop slowly, 'organically'. But the currents of the day moved fast, forcing him along. Luther was forcing him too, and without showing him the slightest consideration.

None of Luther's correspondence is more astonishing than his exchange of letters, or 'notes', with his prince. The outlaw, in safekeeping at the Wartburg, confronted his protector like an independent power. Not a word of thanks went to Frederick for saving his life. On the contrary he reproached him for having taken him to safety; he did not want safety. He reproached the Duke for keeping him on tenterhooks, referring to the diet, of which Luther had no hopes at all, and trying to establish ties with such questionable princes of the Church as the archbishops of Mainz or Trier. And meanwhile things were being allowed to drift in the one sphere that was of importance to Luther – that of faith.

In Wittenberg complete anarchy reigned. Only a few reports reached Luther in his Wartburg refuge and, at first, he did not take them very seriously. The monasteries were emptying, the exodus led by members of his own Augustinian Order; scarcely a friar remained in the Black Monastery. Priests and monks were starting to marry – so far so good, he himself had fiercely condemned celibacy; the Mass, which he had criticized often enough as idolatry, was being changed. But what was the meaning of the new and improvised forms they were trying to introduce in Wittenberg? It was not only his conservative nature that was outraged when his colleague Karlstadt and others suddenly began passing the Communion cup, as was done in Bohemia, and instead of the host being held by the priest high above the heads of the congregation and then placed on the communicant's tongue, which was the customary procedure, it was handed to each member individually, who then put the wafer himself into his mouth – a practice that had been considered a deadly sin. What concerned Luther far more was that this handling of the host emphasized the purely material aspect of the sacrament, which he wanted to replace by a more spiritual concept. Above all he did not want the 'weak', who still clung to the old ritual, to be coerced. To him all these externals were unimportant. What mattered, indeed all that mattered, was the change within: the Word was now made accessible, and if it were preached correctly people would change as he had changed, and as a result the old forms would also change automatically. He completely underestimated the great power exercised by the form of divine worship, by ritual. He overestimated the Word; having experienced its power himself, he expected others to experience the same power. As he wrote in the preface to his New Testament, he wanted to 'exhort, beseech and plead', not to threaten, force and punish. He also grossly and dangerously overestimated the men with whom he had to deal, and this led inevitably to tragedy.

At the time when he left the Wartburg, however, he was still in good heart. He had paid a short, secret visit to Wittenberg in 1521; this had also been an act of defiance and caused much ill-feeling at court when news of it leaked out later. He wanted to speak with Melanchthon, who had shown signs of faltering as a result of the excessive demands made on him. Melanchthon was a scholar, with a systematic mind, and, in his *Loci communes*, had just compiled a first, carefully thought-out synopsis of the new teaching which, written in Latin, had won Luther's admiration; without a trace of jealousy, the master recognized in it gifts which he himself did not possess. But Melanchthon was young, still developing, gentle, compliant, easily influenced; so long as Luther had been at his side, the older man's stronger character had completely dominated him. Now he was almost entirely alone among the 'little handful', and he was at a loss. Wittenberg was no longer what it had been when he gave his first lectures and announced a reform in the study of Latin and Greek. It had become a centre to which emissaries came from every country: students from Bohemia, Scandinavia and Poland, many of them wild and all of them armed, all ready to demonstrate and take action against unpopular teachers, the town council if it tried to interfere, the citizens, monks and priests. Other emissaries, artisans, clothiers, weavers, who knew the Word of God by heart, came from Zwickau, where unrest was rife; brooding and introspective, they were gaunt men with deep-set eyes who pinned their faith on inner light and on their visions and revelations. During this visit Luther was still calm, enjoying the pleasantest conversations with his friends and not taking their misgivings too seriously. But after he returned to the Wartburg, fresh reports began to reach him; he heard of members of his old order leaving their monastery in Erfurt and of the trouble this was causing there, and he heard rumours of a great popular uprising.

In the middle of his work on the Bible he wrote a short pamphlet, *Sincere Exhortation to Beware of Revolt and Insurrection*. In many respects it already contained the quintessence of his political views – unfortunately they were not really political. As always, Luther took as his starting-point his own experience: through his agency the Word had been made effective beyond all expectations; the Word was all that mattered, it was the Word that would triumph, not force of arms. 'Look what I have done! Have I not done more damage to the pope, bishops, priests and monks with my tongue alone, without one stroke of the sword, than all the emperors and kings with all their might?' If the Word of Christ was preached correctly, if everyone led a Christian life in obedience to it, the great change would come about at once. He added some practical instructions: Let there be an end to monastic life and let the monks and nuns leave their monasteries and convents, let no more money be paid out for indulgences, candles or the baptism of bells, 'and let us persevere with this for two more years, and you will see what has happened to pope, bishop, cardinal ... habits, cowls, rules, statutes and the whole crawling mess of papal government.' But if Christian living was not taught in faith and love, a thousand revolts would not help.

These were very simple instructions – for him but not for the people. As soon as Luther touched on the 'outward life', he was always liable to be misunderstood. They were to preach that 'man-made law is nothing', he said in his list of measures to be adopted, having in mind the man-made papal laws that were to be set aside; but the people took this to include other man-made laws, that touched and oppressed them in far more sensitive spots. When they thought of 'rules and statutes' they did not think only of ecclesiastical law. There was to be no resistance – and yet the Wittenberg monk had just sent out a fire signal which proved that words were not enough. He had rebelled against the highest authorities, against the pope and the emperor; he was also in rebellion against his own prince. When he now took his stand on the Scriptures and Paul's 'be subject unto the higher powers', the people found it hard to make distinctions that to him seemed obvious. The pope and the Church continued to be 'powers' – if their authority was no longer to be valid, it was difficult to see why that of the temporal authorities should remain inviolate; they also, like the pope, claimed to rule 'by the Grace of God'. There was a real conflict here, and it was to disrupt Luther's whole life and turn it into tragedy.

He expressed this conflict in his notion of the 'two kingdoms', the inner kingdom of the soul, of faith, which for him was the only one that mattered, and which was free and subject to no interference from without, and the 'merely external' kingdom, which might be the Holy Roman Empire, the electorate of Saxony or a free city of the empire, with all the imperfections God had ordained for this life on earth. Luther, utterly uncompromising and utterly certain as he was, was never able to extricate himself from this conflict. In this he remained the monk. He also held to the ways of thought of the old faith: God's kingdom, which could become reality only in the life beyond, was infinitely higher and purer than the lesser world of this earthly kingdom, which was always sinful; the earthly kingdom was the kingdom of reason – here Luther followed the teachings of Ockham – and faith had nothing to do with reason. 'In the earthly kingdom we have to act from the standpoint of reason, because God has made this temporal government and bodily existence subject to reason,' he taught later; the Scriptures contained no instructions on building houses, on marriage, on warfare or on navigation, for all of which the 'light of nature' sufficed. But the heavenly light was something quite different. He went so far as to declare that God had no need whatever of true Christians for earthly government; after all God even maintained a kingdom of the Turks, where Christians also lived and were able to preserve their 'inner kingdom'.

Luther had taken his stand on his faith, his inner light, and his interpretation of the Bible based on those passages which seemed to him to constitute its true essence. Thus the way was opened: others also read the Bible and they also had their inspirations, only they selected different passages and prophesied according to their lights. They called themselves the 'heavenly prophets', a name by which Luther also referred to them. So far as they were concerned it had never been established that God had appointed Martin Luther alone to proclaim his Word; they considered themselves equally capable of doing this. And so began the hardest battle of Luther's life, a battle he was never to win. In his great polemical writings he had announced man's coming of age. Those who had not yet come of age now raised their voices. They spoke with great cogency and found many adherents. Melanchthon listened to them and found much of what they said worth serious consideration. Professor Karlstadt, who had been Luther's sponsor when he took his doctor's degree and had been regarded as Wittenberg University's leading light at the Leipzig disputation, became caught up in the new movement. A sort of primitivism grew up and people were urged to leave textbooks, scholasticism and commentaries and return to the simplest primal causes; in the last resort this meant leaving the Bible too, in favour of direct, immediate inspiration, and this, it was believed, was more fit for the mouths of the untutored than for those of established teachers. Karlstadt went from house to house getting artisans and citizens to expound the Scriptures to him. Itinerant preachers appeared everywhere; they were called 'predicants' to distinguish them from the official preachers, who had been appointed to their office. The conflict between predicants and preachers was to continue for decades to come.

The ranks of the predicants contained former university students, ex-monks, experienced Bible scholars like Thomas Müntzer, social agitators; Bible texts and political or social demands became indistinguishable. 'At baptisms, at feasts, in inns, in common taprooms … through his honeyed, pleasing, heartfelt public sermons,' one of the Zwickau prophets had seduced the people, said a report on a clothier named Storch, who went about in a long, close-fitting grey robe and a wide-brimmed hat; he had flattered the common people and told them that they should now 'carry the blood-red banner against all authority, both ecclesiastical and secular, and take and bear in their hands the golden sceptre before which men must bend the knee, bow and doff their hats.' By acts such as this, the report went on, these people had 'helped to fan the flames and scatter the powder so that in a trice the thing had caught, spread, and gained the upper hand, not only in Thuringia but in Upper and Lower Germany as well.' And it was not only the simple people whom they had taken by storm but also 'especially the wealthy in the towns and villages'; they were secretly bringing men and women 'into their league and religious society', holding conventicles and fraternal meetings in their houses, and enrolling these people in their registers. The report was 'party propaganda', a denunciation.

What might loosely be called 'parties', in fact, now began to make their appearance. Neither the authorities nor the princes formed 'parties'. They had their class interests and those of their estate and sometimes they joined forces, very locally, to form a temporary alliance or take common action; much more often they quarrelled among themselves, and even made use of the peasants and plebeians to pick a quarrel with some hostile peer. The terms 'league' and 'conventicle' were the current expressions of the day. The league, in the form of a secret association of small groups of 'chosen' people to whom the revelations of the Holy Ghost were communicated, corresponds most nearly to our present-day ideas of cells and bases for underground propaganda; Thomas Müntzer was the master of these tactics, and in him it is already possible to discover political and social portents that can be interpreted as socialism. The conventicles were something else; lacking any kind of 'programme', they were the successors of the Waldensian and Hussite heretics and also of the 'quiet ones in the land', the successors of the old German mystics. They desired no contact with the sinful, lost world but wanted to be entirely separate. They actually welcomed the poverty, persecution and derision which were their lot, as a sign that they were the chosen ones; when they spoke of the need for the brothers and sisters of their immediate circle to share everything in common, it was their poverty to which they referred and it was often dire. They regarded re-baptism as the most important point in their otherwise not very precisely formulated teaching, some aspects of which we know only from their opponents' calumniations. Baptism of children at birth did not satisfy them, because the infant was unaware of its significance. One had to 'opt' to join the community; only then was baptism efficacious as a sign of grace. This choice inevitably meant poverty, distress, opposition to the world, which was rejected in all its manifestations. Even very quiet and withdrawn conventicles could sometimes break out in wild rebellion. It was the anabaptists who later attempted to establish in Münster a Kingdom of God on earth, instead of waiting for Judgment Day, which most of these groups proclaimed to be imminent.

All this was in its early stages when Luther, in the Wartburg, heard of what was happening in Wittenberg and Zwickau. His elector's attitude seemed to him both timid and disastrous; in his *Sincere Exhortation* Luther had reminded the princes of their duty to see that order was maintained. The electorate was in great disorder. Frederick had the gravest misgivings about intervening in any way at all; he respected the 'ancient rights' which existed in great diversity throughout his scattered lands. Moreover his means of enforcing his authority were negligible: he had no army, no police force and no significant government machinery; a few councillors at court, a small chancellery, officials here and there about the country were all he could draw on. Everything had to be transacted in writing. He listened to every complaint, thought it over conscientiously, and waited as long as possible before giving his answer; he proceeded with particular caution over questions of religious belief, trying to weigh up every aspect of them. Even Thomas Müntzer, the violent revolutionary, turned to him, thinking he might win him for his cause; during the Peasants' War he was the only ruling prince in whom the insurgents set any hope. He gave his Doctor Luther a free hand and suffered many things from him that no other ruler would have tolerated; but the man was 'much too bold' for his liking, as he had already remarked in Worms. And so in March 1522 he wrote to Oswald, his representative in Eisenach, telling him to make sure that Luther behaved quietly and peaceably in the Wartburg.

In a short and almost insolent letter Luther had told him that he had heard enough of what was happening in Wittenberg. He even made a derisive reference to Frederick's collection of relics: his prince now had a new relic free of charge, a genuine cross complete with nails and scourges. The closing lines of his letter showed scant respect: 'My pen has been forced to run at a great speed; I have no more time, God willing I shall soon be with you myself. Your Royal Highness must not assume responsibility for me.' He set out at once, without waiting for an answer; the 'be subject unto the higher powers', which he had just been preaching, did not apply to him and this emergency. The elector's letter to Oswald he read only after starting on his journey; he replied to it with a letter the like of which no fugitive ever wrote to his sole protector. What had happened in Wittenberg, he wrote, was a disgrace to the Gospel: 'All the harm previously done me in this cause has been a joke, a mere nothing. Had it been possible I would willingly have given my life to prevent it. For we can justify what has been done neither before God nor before the world.' But he had been humble far too long; he had allowed himself to be shut up in the Wartburg for a whole year to please the elector, not because he was afraid. Now had he had enough of it, he did not need protection any longer; 'I am coming to Wittenberg under a far higher protection than that of the elector'. He even said he was going to offer Frederick 'more protection than you can offer me'; and then still more pointedly, because he sensed that the elector's faith was still weak, he added: 'Under no circumstances can I regard Your Royal Highness as the man who would be able to protect or save me.' Should he be 'captured or killed', the elector would have sufficient excuse, he only had to point out that Luther was in Wittenberg against his orders.

Luther, still disguised as a junker, left the Wartburg in rainy March weather in the year 1522. The journey was hazardous because there was no way by which he could quite avoid passing through territory

Luther disguised as Junker Jörg at the Wartburg

belonging to his enemy Duke George. Two young Swiss students met Luther at a small inn, *The Black Bear*, in Jena; one of them has described the meeting. Sitting at the table was a knight wearing a red cap that hung far down over one side of his face, close-fitting breeches and a thick doublet; at his side was a sword, on the hilt of which he kept his hand in the manner of the nobility taught him by the groom. On the table in front of him lay a little book. The students, soaked to the skin and their boots dirty from their long tramp over the sodden ground, huddled modestly on a bench near the door; but the junker invited them pleasantly to join him at the table. Having seen that they were Swiss, he asked them which part of Switzerland they came from. From St Gallen. And where were they going? To Wittenberg. The man they most wanted to see was Doctor Luther; could the junker tell them where he was? Not in Wittenberg, was the answer, though he might soon be going there. The junker referred them to Melanchthon, who would be able to teach them Greek. He also spoke of Erasmus, and the students' astonishment at this knight, who interspersed his talk with words of Latin, grew and grew. He went on to ask: 'What do people in Switzerland think of Luther, my friends?' Opinions were divided, they told him; some could not speak highly enough of him, others condemned him as an insufferable heretic. Meanwhile the second student, having lost a little of his shyness, had furtively picked up the little book on the table and opened it – it was in Hebrew! Hurriedly replacing it, he said by way of apology: 'I would give a finger off my hand to be able to understand that language.' The knight told him there was no reason he should not do so if he worked hard; they taught Hebrew too in Wittenberg.

The students asked the landlord who the strange knight was and he indicated that it might well be Luther himself. Not being familiar with the Thuringian dialect, they thought the name he mentioned sounded more like Hutten, and they were still taken in by the knight's disguise. In the evening some travelling merchants joined them at supper. They began to talk of the diet in Nuremberg, and the junker came out of his shell a little: what would the princes accomplish there, he asked, in these difficult times? 'Nothing but jousting, sleigh-riding, whoring and feasting – but that is our Christian princes all over!'

The next morning Junker Jörg rode off, an outlaw and in constant danger. He entered Wittenberg with a group of other horsemen whom he had met on the way. The atmosphere in Wittenberg was far from pleasant and homely. His congregation was profoundly disturbed and the university in a state of semi-dissolution, many students having been called home by their worried parents; Karlstadt had gained control over both university and town. His ideas, more radical than those of Luther, were partly sensible and practical, and partly rabidly primitive and based on notions of early Christianity. After the iconoclasm, which he had organized, he immediately used the wealth of the disbanded religious brotherhoods and foundations to set up a 'community chest', a provident fund for the poor, from which cheap loans could also be made to small tradespeople. It was a very practical idea; all it needed was wise management and a firm hand. But these were qualities Karlstadt lacked. The small, passionate man was a receptacle for any ideas that were going the rounds, social, religious and pedagogic notions all becoming churned up together inside him; he seethed inside, but everything was tossed out half-digested. Nothing went quickly enough for him, he wanted to see each of his many ideas realized at once. Having read in the Bible that God had driven Adam out of the Garden of Eden to till the ground by the sweat of his brow, he told his students to leave the lecture room and go back to the land, to take up the pick and the hoe instead of their textbooks. The true estate was that of the husbandman, not that of the scholar or theologian; the other professors, unable to subscribe wholeheartedly to this doctrine, remained dejectedly in their rooms. The Latin school was transformed into a food distribution centre. Reports reached the court. The elderly elector declared: 'This is a great and important matter which I, as a layman, do not understand.'

Luther went to work. His first actions were significant: the junker disguise, the beard, the red hat, the doublet all went. He put on his black Augustinian habit again; as domicile he chose his old Augustinian monastery. He mounted the pulpit, because above all else he wanted to speak to his congregation as their old pastor. For a whole week Luther preached, powerfully, urgently; he did not thunder, but handled the mischief-makers with a forbearance and consideration they certainly would not have shown to him. As always he put his trust in the Word, and again it proved powerful beyond all expectation. Luther's immediate effect on people was never greater than during these few days in the little town of Wittenberg with its three thousand inhabitants; he was in surroundings he knew and of which he could take stock. He ranged himself firmly on the side of the 'weak'. There must be no useless compulsion, no innovations that might hurt or shock people, no haste, no impatience. Those who wanted to observe Communion in the old way were to do so; those who felt a need for the Communion cup were to have it. Those who still had the sound of the familiar Latin in their ears should continue to hear it. There must be no persecution of those who thought differently. He had already sent a letter to the court urging that no violent action be taken against the *Schwarmgeister*; it was up to Spalatin to persuade the prince. In any case there was to be no bloodshed.

Luther was still calm and composed. It did not matter to him that some people grumbled at his measures and saw in them a backward step. He was lenient to Karlstadt who, forced to relinquish his position as leader, sat in his room brooding fiercely over how he might attack Luther with his pen. Another difficult individual, a former monk named

Zwilling, who came from Bohemia and had been preaching Hussite doctrines with enthusiasm and success to large audiences, received a friendly rebuke from Luther and gave way. Patience was a keynote of Luther's sermons: 'My friends, each must not act according to his rights but must see how he can help and benefit his brother. Thus we should associate with our weaker brothers, be patient with them, not browbeat them cruelly but treat them in a kind and friendly way, instructing them gently.' They should adopt the same attitude towards the rites of the Church; it would be better to retain the externals of the Mass and the images of the saints until people had changed sufficiently – it was common knowledge that these things had been abused. '*Summa summarum*: I shall preach, I shall speak, I shall write, but I shall compel or forcibly persuade no one.' He also gave a political warning: hitherto the Word had accomplished everything; 'if I had wanted to make trouble, I could have caused great bloodshed in Germany, and I could have started something in Worms that would have shaken the position of the emperor himself. But what would have been the outcome? It would have been madness and would have corrupted both body and soul.'

Luther proceeded one step at a time, not because he was methodical but by instinct. He was advancing sufficiently fast and was not unjustified in complaining angrily that many for whom he had cleared the way now found him too slow and imagined themselves capable of charging ahead on their own. Here, in the troubled town of Wittenberg, he put things to the test for the first time and triumphed. For a week he spoke from the pulpit; the town quietened down, the students returned to the lecture rooms.

Luther would have nothing to do with laws, even in his own sphere of preaching the Word. The Church hierarchy had constructed its edifice by incessant decrees. He had no desire to see the process repeated by his followers. He enlarged upon this in one of his sermons: the Fathers of the Church in their day had quarrelled over the repeal of ancient laws; 'after them came the popes who in turn wanted to add something of their own and also made laws, and out of the repeal of one law grew a thousand new laws, so that they have completely overwhelmed us with laws; and here it will be the same, one law will become two, two will become three and so on.' He cited the quarrel between emperor and pope over the question of abolishing images: 'They wanted to make freedom a command. God cannot suffer that ...'

A fine thing to say, but dangerous. During these weeks Luther showed himself as a pure idealist, a utopian, practically and effectively though he was able to intervene in his immediate circle. He ignored the fact that most people did not want the freedom to make their own decisions, that what they wanted were laws, leadership and direction. He also failed to see that he himself would become the victim of compulsion. The Swiss student has described his appearance as that of a man who had grown rather stout but held himself well; he often leaned his head slightly backwards, gazing up like a visionary, but people winced when he turned his piercing brown eyes on them. They did what he wanted, not because he gave them a free choice but because he said: this is how it is going to be. The town council, grateful and relieved, had a new habit made for him, because his old one had become too shabby.

As he had said in his *Sincere Exhortation*, Luther thought that after only another two years everything would run of its own accord and the 'crawling mass' of the papal bureaucracy would have disappeared. Exactly two years were left him to maintain this calm hope.

# 26

# False Spring

WITTENBERG was not the world nor was the electorate of Saxony Germany, but even in this little half-state, which had no clearly defined forms of government or national boundaries, there was an astonishing variety of customs, rights and institutions. Under Luther's very eyes stood the Schlosskirche, with its great collection of relics, and its pre-bendaries who clung to every tenet of the old faith; from time to time the elector reminded them that his costly relics must be displayed at least on the namedays of those saints of whom his collection contained portions or 'particles'. In the parish church Luther preached his new doctrine, but with moderation; other preachers were sometimes less cautious. The university professors were a by no means homogeneous body, while the students, who came from many countries, were far less so. And in the surrounding villages, market hamlets and other Saxon towns there reigned what to us seems like utter confusion. Some monasteries had been abandoned, others still adhered to the rules; in many places the old forms of worship continued as they had done from time immemorial. Professor Karlstadt, who had laid aside his clerical dress, withdrew embittered to one of the villages, where he owned some property, and put into practice his slogan 'back to the land'. He made the peasants call him 'neighbour Andres' and instead of his simple townsman's coat wore the grey smock of the peasants; he also foreshadowed the 'cult of the proletariat', continuing busily to write his pamphlets instead of taking up his hoe and tilling his ground. Thomas Müntzer, driven out of Zwickau, found refuge in the little town of Allstedt in Thuringia, engaging in an extensive and successful policy of agitation through his secret messengers. In the other half of Saxony Duke George, his huge, waist-long beard now turning white, displayed great energy in persecuting every new teaching; he also thought of attacking his cousin Frederick's territory, under instructions from the imperial government, and wresting the electorate from him. Such was the treacherous, unstable ground on which Luther stood and announced that the Word alone would be victorious.

It was not victorious, but it spread in a quite unexpected way. This was due to no organization on the part of Luther, who did not send out any secret messengers and who, if anything, was inclined to temporize; often too he was suspicious, and sometimes turned visitors brusquely away, probably not without good reason. Informers, spies and crackpots flocked to see him; his every word was reported, repeated, distorted, exaggerated, modified or used for purposes other than those for which it was intended. Neither Luther's writings nor those of his opponents give any adequate idea of the excitement and confusion of the period; of greater significance are the single sentences, catchwords and slogans which contemporaries extracted from them. The sermon became the great weapon; it was no cosy sabbath-day message or pious exhortation containing possibly a hint or two at the stirring events of the day. Unfortunately there is very little surviving evidence – and most of what we have has been revised for publication – of the fire and fury of these pronouncements, which were delivered from the pulpit, beneath the village lime-tree, in the market place, from the tops of cemetery walls, in inns and taverns. It is almost impossible to translate into twentieth-century language the importance attached in those days to Bible texts and quotations, or to the gloomy prophecies foretelling the imminent end of the world; only with the danger of the atom bomb have comparable apocalyptic attitudes been revived and lay-preachers been heard side by side with the professionals. The Bible, and above all the Old Testament, was consulted about everything, in every situation; the great urge was to go back beyond the earliest days of Christianity to the primeval age of the Jewish patriarchs. Such a return to the original, God-given order of things was not new; the prophecies of Daniel had always caught men's imaginations and had been used to rouse their emotions. Now, however, the old Bible texts were known to all; in slim volumes and pamphlets they spread throughout the countries of Germany, animating broadsheets, dialogues, appeals and proclamations with the wrath of God and news of the birth of a new era.

The world now came to Wittenberg. Luther was overwhelmed with inquiries, requests and demands for his opinion. He had only a small band of helpers. Melanchthon proved increasingly to be a colleague who in many ways was Luther's equal, or indeed his superior. Above all it was thanks to him that the university started to prosper again, his gift for teaching bringing both him and it great renown; everywhere, even beyond the frontiers of the empire, the first reformers were recruited from men who had studied in Wittenberg. They were joined by others. Justus Jonas, Bugenhagen and others, who formed Luther's intimate circle, were not towering figures, but they were able men, hard-working, energetic and possessing many qualities that Luther lacked.

Bugenhagen, a native of Pomerania, became the most successful organizer of the new teaching in the whole of northern Germany and Denmark; the story of the Reformation in these territories is the story of Bugenhagen. As a theological teacher, he had thrown Luther's *On the Babylonian Captivity* angrily to the floor, but on picking it up again had studied it keenly and found it to be a revelation; he became one of Luther's most important assistants. He was not always gentle and considerate; he was tough and had tough opponents to contend with. A tall man – a 'commanding' appearance was a great asset in lecturing and preaching and a still greater one in dealing with city councils and princes – he had an excellent memory, which he also used to remember his enemies. He had a solid humanist education together with a good knowledge of history – this latter still a rare thing in those days – and had distinguished himself as a headmaster before going to Wittenberg. His sermons were powerful and 'concentrated', a quality Luther particularly admired in them. Luther once said there was a need for men who could present a 'tough hide' to the devil and take 'hard knocks'; among these Bugenhagen held first place. He became Luther's father confessor, or rather his partner in confession, a position he held till Luther's death. In his many temptations and breakdowns Luther turned for solace to the impassive 'Dr Pomeranus'. Bugenhagen would give him a good scolding, asking him what he meant by saying he was the victim of God's wrath – of course God was angry with him; He said to Himself: 'What am I to do with this man? I have bestowed so many excellent gifts on him, and yet he insists on despairing of My grace!' Luther said this had been a great comfort to him, the voice of an angel over which he had continued to ponder for a long time; ever since his monastery days his gratitude for the slightest consolation and encouragement had been one of his most endearing traits. Bugenhagen replaced Staupitz, who had acted as 'father' to Luther during his years as a monk. The two men were sharply contrasted: Staupitz, the aristocrat and diplomat, who imparted quiet thoughts in the tradition of the mystics; Bugenhagen, the commoner's son, immensely energetic and not over-scrupulous, happily married to one of Dr Schurff's servants, the representative of a new era to which Staupitz could not reconcile himself.

Luther continued to respect Staupitz even when his old mentor thought it wiser to part company with his protégé. Staupitz had not waited for the order which he led to be dissolved; he resigned his office before this happened and, leaving the Augustinians for the Benedictines, found a new post in Salzburg as abbot of the Benedictine monastery of

St Peter. He conformed. Luther had vainly tried to persuade him 'to shoulder the cross', at the same time clearly underlining the difference between them: 'You are too humble, I am too proud.' He would not condemn Staupitz, he said, for the step he had taken, the matter was too serious, but 'I shall not remain silent.' His last letter to Staupitz was addressed to his 'Superior in the Lord, my father and teacher' and signed 'Your son Martin'. The abbot replied to his 'dearest Martin' and assured him that he continued to love him steadfastly, adding, in allusion to David and Jonathan: 'I am distressed for thee, my brother Jonathan: very pleasant hast thou been unto me: thy love to me was wonderful, passing the love of women.' Staupitz quoted another example from the Bible, the parable of the prodigal son: Luther had led the people from the empty husks of the grapes, which the prodigal in his extremity had shared with the swine, and brought them once more to the 'pastures of life'. The debt owed to him was great. But he warned Luther not to disturb the hearts of the simple people; he begged his 'beloved friend' to think of the 'little people' and not unsettle their consciences. He prayed for the 'neutrals', who persisted in their honest faith – Luther should not condemn them (it was already evident how many were abusing the Gospel for the sake of the 'freedom of the flesh'). Perhaps, he declared resignedly, his spirit was too hesitant or timid, and Luther must understand if he wrapped himself in silence.

And so this friendship ended in silence and tranquillity, without any rupture; shortly afterwards Staupitz died. The friars of the monastery burned his books in the courtyard, but they hung his portrait in the refectory, among the long line of abbots; it is the portrait of a refined, cautious, thoughtful pedagogue, who knew how to lead those round him but was out of his depth when faced by larger problems. None of his more recent attempts at mediation had been successful; he was a man caught between two epochs. Like Erasmus – to whose generation he belonged and whose mental attitude he shared, although he was no humanist – he felt a sense of chill, and his eyes could not bear the harsh light that now burst upon the scene. His strength lay in quiet conversation, such as he had held with Luther beneath the pear tree, not in fighting.

But fighting was the order of the day. It broke out everywhere, without Luther and the 'Wittenbergers' needing to lift a finger to further it. There were still no clearly defined fronts and, in fact, almost up until the time of Luther's death these were far less definite than was often assumed in retrospect. The notion of 'true Catholic' or 'convinced Protestant' pioneers, of whom a few existed, easily blinds us to the fact that the great majority had still reached no decision, religious or political. Men who later became whole-hearted champions of the

Reformation, even princes like Philip, landgrave of Hesse, at first ranged themselves on the side of the old authorities; large numbers of scholars who, during the battle over Reuchlin, had been among the severest critics of the Church, subsequently made their peace with Rome. Between 1520 and 1525 the decisions were taken that moulded Europe for centuries to come. The thrusts and breakthroughs are visible in the foreground, and there is something breathtaking about them; the moderating forces are harder to see at first, the inertia of large masses of the population who desired not even to be 'neutral' but simply to go on living unmolested as before.

At the outset Luther's cause advanced by leaps and bounds. A false spring broke out; an intellectual and spiritual awakening was apparent everywhere. The humanists, loosening the ground under the feet of the intellectuals and at the universities, had formed the first wave. Now they withdrew, most of them, like Erasmus, disillusioned because very different forces and groups had taken over from the quiet scholars who had fenced so shrewdly and intelligently among themselves. The powerful weapon of irony had been devised for free and sceptical minds able to smile at the eternal foolishness of the world. Far tougher natures were now shouldering their way to the front. They did not want to smile but to laugh aloud; their weapon was not the subtle taunt but the flail. The public had changed. A sort of public opinion already existed, and it could be influenced only by the crudest means; the language used by almost all writers became increasingly coarse. The devil turned out to be the most popular figure of all. Books about devils were the booksellers' best line; they were often fairly harmless devils, like the trouser devil, the dance devil, the devils of whoredom and worry, the devil in female form, the melancholic and brooding devils, but some, like the junker devil or the devils of avarice and usury, had to be taken more seriously. Finally one Jodokus Hocker hit on the last word in devils and wrote a small book called *The Devil in Person*. Nevertheless both Luther and his opponents were convinced that Satan himself was behind every dissenting opinion. His name was invoked almost or just as often as that of God. There was only black or white, hot or cold; to call someone 'lukewarm' was Luther's sternest rebuke. The black-and-white woodcuts supplemented this literature in the most effective way, providing pictorial propaganda for those who could not read.

The crudeness of the literature of this time renders it indigestible to us. We find the repetitions wearisome; the same catchwords and images recur over and over again. What cannot be denied, however, is that this was the only period when Germany possessed a truly popular literature that appealed equally to all classes of the population. It is usually hard to discover the identity of the authors; they had to remain anonymous if they did not want to find themselves in prison or in a still worse predicament. The fact that the peasant was so often quoted does not mean that the peasant himself received a hearing, but simply that he was regarded as the chosen spokesman of the German nation; the authors were mostly students and men of letters, but there were also professional scribes and preachers among them. The 'common man' was looked upon as the person who knew where the shoe pinched better than 'those at the top'.

The shoemaker Hans Sachs, the greatest talent ever produced from the ranks of the craftsmen, and a popular poet of remarkable gifts, immediately placed his indefatigable pen at the service of the cause. His song of Luther as the 'Wittenberg nightingale whose voice is now heard everywhere' heralded the arrival of the dawn after a long spell of pallid moonlight; 'the Wittenberg nightingale' became a household phrase. Hans Sachs owned an extensive collection of Luther's writings as well as an astonishingly well-stocked library for a master craftsman, although admittedly he was no mere cobbler but a man who had a very comfortable home, a whole bevy of apprentices and a respected position in the town; for these reasons he was very anxious for the old class system to be preserved. But in his poems and extremely vivid prose dialogues he took up the cause of the new teaching with wit and humour. In one of these he himself, as a cobbler, argues with a rich canon and routs his clerical opponent with well-chosen quotations from Luther and the Bible. The priest, naturally, has only a very vague knowledge of these things; he knows the papal decretals, and he knows that heretics should be burned, but when the cobbler begins to speak of passages from the Scriptures he is completely at sea. The apostles held a council in Jerusalem, states the cobbler. Really, replies the canon, did they? Cobbler: 'Yes. Have you a Bible?' Canon: 'Yes. Cook, bring us that big old book.' Cook: 'Is this it, sir?' Canon: 'Heavens no, that's the decretals. Be careful how you treat it!' Cook: 'Is this it, sir?' Canon: 'Yes, devil take you! Dust it off. Now then, Master Hans, where is it?' The cobbler gives him the reference in the Acts of the Apostles, but the canon says irritably: 'Look it up yourself, I don't know my way about the book very well; I have better things to read.' And he flies into a rage about the laity in general, who now give themselves such airs: 'It is time you had this nonsense beaten out of you, there is no other answer. Many a man who is now shouting his head off will be reduced to silence!' After the cobbler leaves he tells his cook that in future he will use another cobbler, Hans Zobel: 'He's a good, simple fellow who is not forever holding forth about the Holy Scriptures and Lutheran heresy.' And now she must get dinner ready; there will be fieldfares because 'My Gracious Lord the Chaplain is coming with some other gentleman and we shall have a banquet. Remove the Bible from the parlour, and see that the pieces and dice are ready on the playing board, and that we have one or two clean packs of cards ...'

In the dialogue *The New Peasantry*, a peasant pours out his troubles to the knight Sickingen: 'Junker, I have a young horse, he is a very pretty animal and I am very fond of him; because of this, when I take him from his stall I often stroke and make a fuss of him and sometimes kiss him on the head.' The priest had immediately declared this to be a sin and imposed a fine of twenty guilders; the peasant could not pay it, or even the twelve guilders to which the priest eventually reduced it. He had given him six and begged him for pity's sake to wait until the harvest, until 'I had threshed my corn and sold some fruit; but he was not to be moved, and the following Sunday announced that I had been excommunicated.' The peasant turns confidently to the great con-dottiere, who promises redress, but then has to give his attention to more important matters. The dialogue follows the peasant's trusting hope in the knight and his fellow nobles with a list of thirty clauses that already reflect the fiery glow of the Peasants' War. These announce that all priests are rogues, not another penny is to be given for religious founda-tions, pilgrimages or indulgences, those who support the papal court are 'mad dogs', 'whom it is right to beat, seize, strangle and kill.' Clauses urging piety and gentleness are interspersed with talk of cutting off people's ears and gouging out their eyes. Pastors should preach the Gospel and live respectable lives. Idols must be removed, whether made of stone, wood, gold or silver; God alone is to be worshipped, in spirit. The merchants who deal in relics should be relieved of their horses and money-bags and then allowed to continue on their way with their relics. On the subject of auricular confession people should consult Luther and other experts. Friends are to pledge their persons and possessions to stand by these clauses; in doing so they will be seeking 'no selfish aims but divine truth, Christian faith and the welfare of our common fatherland.'

Restraint was often urged. People still pinned naïve hopes on the emperor or on some discerning move by those in authority. The ener-getic Eberlin, a former Franciscan monk, could not refrain from lamenting in one of his hard-hitting pamphlets: 'Merciful Heavens, the Emperor and his brother are young and devout masters, trust in them and do not start accusing the youngsters of duplicity yet, God will soon open their eyes.' The perennial excuse that everything that is wrong is the fault of a few 'false counsellors' or a single leader has been a source of confusion throughout the ages. Only immediate objectives were now unambiguous; the hierarchy was to be fought and its posi-tions stormed. The defenders of the old order had a difficult task.

Complaining as loudly as their opponents of the worldliness of the clergy and other abuses, they set their hopes on a good pope who would put everything right.

Among the champions of the old faith, who in general were a poor lot, the only one who advanced his cause with any talent or verve was the Franciscan Thomas Murner from Alsace. He had started by writing satires on the immorality of the age, lustily denouncing the vices of every rank and class, including those of his fellow monks. Then he attacked Luther for destroying the law and order he had just been richly and colourfully portraying in all its disorder. He began his poem *The Great Lutheran Fool* cautiously, careful not to invoke Luther personally at all; he intended only to ridicule his countless hangers-on, whom he condensed into one enormous, bloated fool. But he quickly forgot his intention. The poem became a a Shrovetide play in which Luther himself appears; the characters argue, Luther counsels peace and, as a token of reconciliation, offers Murner his daughter in marriage – at the time the piece was written Luther had not contemplated marriage. Murner greets his bride with a serenade and after the marriage feast, which consists of the gift of a pair of underpants liberally sprinkled with pepper, the pair make their way to the bridal chamber. Here, when the girl takes off her veil and headdress, it transpires that she suffers from favus, with pustules three fingers wide on her forehead, and that her hair is matted. The bridegroom whips the 'monk's whore', the living embodiment of the favus or sinner's itch from which the Lutherans suffer, out of the house. The frivolous wedding was meant to show what would become of marriage if it were solemnized according to Luther's teaching, and without the hallowed sacrament. Finally Luther dies without receiving the sacrament of extreme unction; the end is brief: 'To the shit-house with the man who seeks the sacrament to ban,' the descent into the latrine being accompanied by the screaming of cats.

This same Murner wrote the most tender hymns in praise of the Blessed Virgin; he described the plight of the peasant in moving language, pointing his finger at Luther as the secret leader of the Bundschuh. On the title page of his works he called himself proudly the 'most learned Dr Murner' and had, in fact, studied in Paris, Cracow, Prague and Freiburg, and been appointed poet laureate by the Emperor Maximilian. He wrote German without flowers of speech and more powerfully than most of his contemporaries. As an honest champion of the Church and the authorities he had every reason to expect some reward and assistance, but he became a homeless fugitive, wandering from place to place, turned out by the authorities wherever he went; heresy was making frightening headway. Murner wrote sadly: 'The shepherd's put to rout./The sheep have gone astray,/The pope's been driven out ...' And when the iconoclasm began, he prayed: 'If, pious Christian members,/You want your saints no more,/Keep one, just one, among them/Keep Mary, I implore.'

The iconoclasm became a general signal to attack. Karlstadt had made the first move in Wittenberg; the title-page of his pamphlet *On the Abolition of Images* showed two naked figures, Adam and Eve, supporting with their hands the vault of the new era – there is something disarming in the fact that the worship of images could not be abolished without imagery. The decorated borders and initials of the day were often at variance with the text, or else pursued a life of their own, embellishing grimly theological tracts with uninhibited *putti* turning somersaults, hunting scenes, satyrs and nymphs, and totally fruitless pages with luxuriant garlands of fruit. In one publication by Luther's sworn enemy, the Dominican Prierias-Mazzolini, a pair of lovers are sitting on the grass fondling one another under the letter D; elsewhere one finds monks taking their trousers down and relieving themselves, although the book is supposedly a missal. This aspect of the taste of the day deserves mention because it provides the setting for the bitter fight over dogmas.

But the iconoclasm was serious. In the eighth century it had almost brought about the downfall of the Byzantine Empire and had started the disastrous split between the Eastern and Western Churches.

Interpretation of the Bible had always been the great bone of contention. The Old Testament severely condemned the worship of images and contained constant warnings against idolatry. From its earliest days the Byzantine Church had refused to allow plastic representations and had often been content merely with symbols, such as a fish or a letter. When, in spite of this, pictorial imagery was adopted special care was taken to see that the Deity and saints were portrayed in a very dignified manner, in order to obviate all human comparisons; they were placed high up in domes or on walls, and done in mosaic on a gold background to indicate eternity, and given expressionless faces. Through the centuries this art remained 'stiff' and hieratic. One Byzantine emperor, on sanctioning the images again, stipulated very significantly that they must be placed 'high up on the wall'. Everything that smacked of homeliness and familiarity was forbidden, and to touch an image 'with the hands' was regarded as sacrilege. The contrast between this concept and art as it developed in the west was well expressed in the horrified remark of a Russian priest on seeing a painting of the Virgin by Titian in Venice: 'That is no way to paint the Virgin Mary.'

But this was how she was painted in the west. The Russian would have had far greater cause to be indignant if he had seen Jean Fouquet's

beautiful Madonna of Melun, for which Agnes Sorel, known by everyone at the time to be the king's mistress, had displayed to the world her
breasts in all their naked glory. We find aesthetic pleasure in the
realism and naturalism of the Netherlandish and German painters and
find it hard to reconcile ourselves to the iconoclasts who destroyed so
much of this splendour. But we must not allow our view of history to be
determined by aesthetics, which in any case provides a very inconstant
standard; it can veer from the cult of the representational to that of the
abstract. The idea of abstraction, in fact, lay behind the fight against
images. What was incomprehensible and intangible should not be
portrayed in so tangible and realistic a fashion that one could go up to a
picture and feel the velvet and satin of the draperies with one's finger-
tips, which was what the painters enabled one to do.

The cult of images had undeniably become secularized. The man
who commissioned the picture came increasingly to the fore, as an
imposing and sumptuously, even ostentatiously, dressed person; having
commissioned the work and paid for it, he demanded that the saint, or
Madonna, bless him. This is brought out dramatically in Jan van
Eyck's famous painting of the Chancellor Rolin, a great financier and
political *arriviste*; the patron and no one else matters here. In the
Holbein Madonna commissioned by Burgomaster Meyer all the
members of the numerous family cluster round the Virgin, who is
shown in the bosom of the family wrapping her cloak about the
shoulders of the great councillor and his wife. The cult of the saint had
been turned into private worship (which could, of course, include true
piety).

Images had become material objects. Luther and the iconoclasts,
who smashed the images not only independently of him but against his
wishes, called them '*Ölgötzen*'; according to Agricola, collector of
proverbs and sayings, an *Ölgötze* is a 'stick or piece of wood' which has
been soaked in oil as a means of preserving colour – 'a likeness without
life and without soul'. Etymologically this contemporary definition is
open to question, but it applies in a higher sense: the spirit, the life, had
gone out of the figures, perhaps just because they were 'lifelike' and
realistic. The inflation in saints and images had reached a peak and had
already begun to pass into the stage in which every believer had 'his'
saint or his personal guardian angel. Miraculous images, which in the
early Middle Ages had been rare and consequently the objects of long
pilgrimages – to the distant Compostella in Spain, for instance – had
now multiplied a thousandfold. Every town, almost every village,
insisted on having a shrine of its own, and the Church authorities themselves were often very suspicious of the claims of these. The multiplica-
tion of blessings and the increase in their potency was turned into a

business pure and simple and, as in the case of indulgences for example, was seen and criticized as such; for years the pilgrimages and their dangers had been a theme of all who preached repentance. In practice no attempt was made any longer to observe the theological distinctions between 'reverence' and 'worship'. The saint was no longer the 'mere intercessor', as in theory he should have been. This was the point at which Luther rebelled, although he himself had prayed to St Anne at the moment of his conversion, when he decided to become a monk. A form of specialization had set in, a particular saint, like a medical specialist, being appointed for every case that arose: St Apollonia for toothache, because at her martyrdom her teeth had been pulled out; St Rochus for the plague and diseases of the skin, because he suffered from plague-ulcers; St Anthony for epilepsy. They rarely helped, and so the patient resorted to baths or doctors in any case. This was the age that saw the first clear outlines of the modern sciences. The images, and the practices that had become attached to them, were now seen as superstition and idolatry. The Word alone was to have validity, not the image; the Bible was to show the way, not the calendar of saints or the passional. The Bible forbade man to worship images.

We possess the testimony of a contemporary, the Swiss student Kessler who had met Luther when he was travelling to Wittenberg disguised as Junker Jörg. He came from St Gallen, long famous as a centre of great artistic achievement, where the iconoclasts had done thorough work. As in the case of the Byzantine emperor's fight with the monks, who were guardians of the images and antagonistic to the sovereign, the struggle always had its political aspect. For a long time the city council had been engaged in a feud with the abbot of the great and wealthy abbey, which formed an enclave with its own rights and privileges in the middle of the city; the abbot still considered himself a prince of the empire, whereas the towns were independent members of the confederation. To complicate things still further, the wide tract of land surrounding the town and reaching as far as Lake Constance belonged to the abbot; it was a truly princely possession. Thus there were three interrelated concentric circles: first the abbey, beyond it the city, and beyond that again the territory of the prince-abbot. The townspeople supported the new teaching, the abbot defended his privileges and the old faith. There were discussions; the people issued threats and banded together, demanding that the abbey 'discard the innumerable idols and the celebration of the Mass.' The abbot fled to his castle on Lake Constance. The city council assured the monks that no harm would come either to them or to their property. Then the city gates were shut. The mayor, at the head of a large crowd of people, entered the church: 'The idols, and nothing else, were to be seized, taken away and burnt' – there was to be no plundering. 'And lo and behold, no sooner were the words out of his mouth than everyone fell upon the idols. They were torn from altars, walls and pillars. The altars were smashed, the idols hacked to pieces with axes or battered to smithereens with hammers; you might have thought it was a pitched battle. You have never seen such chaos! Such a fury of noise and destruction as there was within the high dome! An hour later there was nothing left undamaged and in its proper place. No load was too heavy to lift, no one hesitated to climb to dizzy heights after the idols; in my heart I kept on thinking: what a miracle, is no one going to be hurt today in this onslaught? The heavy stone and wooden idols, with their casings and surrounds, fell forwards, backwards and sideways to the ground, where many of them shattered to fragments. What exquisite, what subtle art and workmanship was reduced to rubble! The panels in the choir, commissioned by the Abbot Franciscus, had cost 1,500 guilders and taken ten years to paint, the carving as much again or even more.'

The operation ended with a great fire: it 'was amazing the number of idols that were smashed and burnt; could the heathen Pantheon in Rome have contained more?' The mayor, the former mayor, the steward of the abbey and the abbey's architect kept watch to see that no one made off with anything. The number of altars demolished was specified as thirty-three. The following Sunday the city's lay preachers went to the church and preached according to the new teaching. The writer added a prayer of his own: 'I also beseech Thee, O Lord and Merciful Father, that, as we have destroyed and uprooted our handiwork with our own hands to please Thee, Thou also, through Thy Holy Spirit, wilt uproot and wipe from our hearts all spiritual idolatry and prepare and dedicate within us a clean temple for Thee, through Thy beloved only begotten son Jesus Christ, our Lord and only Saviour. Amen.'

It is not without significance that the cost of the painted panels, which Kessler quotes with such distress, was less than that of the carved frames, the 'casing'. The casing had become more important than the contents. We feel little sympathy for those who destroyed either the panels or the carving, but we cannot regard this destruction solely with the eyes of admirers of late Gothic painting; the following centuries did not do so and had no hesitation in destroying most of what was left. At the very moment when the iconoclasts were going about their work, Pope Hadrian in Rome was proposing to have the ceiling of the Sistine Chapel whitewashed, because Michelangelo's 'heathen' figures offended his sense of piety; only his early death prevented the realization of his plan. His successor contented himself with having *The Last Judgment* painted over, because he found its naked figures unseemly – 'as if they were in the bathroom'.

Elsewhere things did not always proceed under the supervision of the authorities and in the same, almost orderly way as at St Gallen. There was often bitter fighting, and most authorities considered it extremely dangerous for the 'rabble' to go into action with axes and hammers. Some of the more wary city councillors pleaded that the images, since they had cost so much money, should be sold in other districts where they would still find fanciers. But a strong tendency was unmistakably emerging, a tendency that was later to find its most powerful and clear-cut expression in the Puritans. The vigorous rejection of every form of luxury whether within the Church or without, the closing of the brothels (in most cases one of the first items on the programmes of the wreckers and innovators), the reduction of the huge numbers of holidays, and the demand that daily work should become a hallowed activity were all to be seen again in the Puritan movement. Mendicancy was to be abolished; to this end the great charitable foundations were taken over and administered by the community. Aid was not to be given on an arbitrary basis but according to merit and deserts, and only after the circumstances had been examined; the chronicles are full of complaints that the hordes of beggars who roved the countryside and besieged the monasteries had become a national menace. All these individual activities also touched on social problems and involved serious attacks on the structure of the Church. They were not carried out consistently and systematically but in widely divergent ways, according to local conditions. A single preacher, if he was allowed to, could revolutionize the situation in a few weeks; in other localities he might be driven out, banished or executed.

The beheadings, drownings and burnings began early but, in the eyes of those who advocated vigorous action, too late; they were almost totally ineffective. On the contrary, the martyrs of the new teaching now replaced the ancient, legendary martyrs of the Church. People had not read in vain of the steadfastness with which the witnesses to truth had faced every kind of torture. The brutality of the punishments was no deterrent; the population had grown accustomed to it as a result of the increasingly bloodthirsty forms of execution practised by the secular authorities. The illustrations in contemporary law books, showing mutilation by stages and the ground strewn with severed limbs, are the exact counterpart of the portraits of the saints. One could even say that the legends, depicting in great detail methods of execution most of which were unknown to antiquity, contributed to the brutalizing of people's minds; at any rate what they reproduced was contemporary practice. Torture was the generally accepted instrument both of the administration of secular justice and of the Inquisition. A confession of the alleged crime, obtained from the victim under torture by thumbscrew, rack or burning by torches, was accepted as irrefutable. People had strong nerves; armed with plenty of food and drink the menfolk would take their wives and children to watch someone being executed on the wheel – a very long-drawn-out process. In Spain, and in other countries too, a public holiday was proclaimed when a man was to be burned at the stake. The scorn and derision to which the condemned was subjected was an integral part of the entertainment. The manner in which the unfortunate victim bore the agony was carefully noted and criticized, as though it were a gladiatorial contest. An Italian humanist has described in elegant prose the burning of Hieronymus of Prague, the companion of Jan Hus; he admired the way in which the heretic maintained the heroic dignity of an ancient hero. Another eyewitness, employing a less literary style, remarked how long the tall, powerful man, who was much more strongly built than Hus, battled with the flames and how hideously he screamed.

These screams are always ignored by later ages. The stories of the martyrs tell only of steadfast endurance and unshakeable conviction. Such qualities were not rare. Burning and execution were easier to bear than the agonies of prison, which meant a torture chamber and could crush the staunchest character. A short note in the records that an individual had finally recanted after a year of imprisonment or more, or had 'died' impenitent, was usually the only information it was thought necessary to give. These silent tragedies form the background to the raucous events of the time. The many lone voices of these forgotten men unite to form a muffled choir heard only by those who have ears to hear. The abundance of similar fates in our own day should not be allowed to tempt us to calculate how great, in purely numerical terms, the sacrifice was and then make comparisons. There were many who screamed. No more need be said.

The shouts of victory, however, were louder. The new teaching was forging ahead everywhere, even in countries like Bavaria and Austria which later were to become pillars of the old Church again. Ranke, in his *German History at the time of the Reformation*, has left a sanguine description of this emergent mood: 'No preparations were necessary, no plans, no missionary work. Just as at the first touch of spring sunshine on the tilled fields the seed shoots up everywhere, so throughout the territories where German was spoken the new convictions, brought to the point of readiness by all that people had experienced and heard, thrust into the light almost of their own accord or at the slightest provocation.'

Sometimes the provocation was slight indeed; it could even be banal and grotesque. In Zurich a sausage feast, staged at Easter 1522 as a protest against the Church's rule of fasting, set in motion the first stirrings of the Reformation. The printer and publisher Froschauer had invited some friends to the meal, all present eating a small quantity in spite of the Lenten fast; the only guest to refrain from committing the sin was Ulrich Zwingli, a pastor from the great minster. An investigation was ordered at once. The ecclesiastical overlord, the Bishop of Constance, caused trouble by sending envoys to Zurich expressly for the purpose. Constance was within the empire while Zurich was one of the leading cities of the Swiss Confederation and proud of its independence; long ago ecclesiastical boundaries had been superimposed on the secular boundaries and, as in the case of St Gallen, this had not been without its consequences. The people of Zurich were furious: what did the bishop 'over there in the empire' mean by interfering in their Swiss affairs? There were excited rumours that he intended to arrest Zwingli and carry him off to face a charge of heresy. The city council decided that the printer must pay a fine, Froschauer protesting in vain that he had needed to fortify himself with meat in order to deliver a pious tract in time for Easter: 'I have to work day and night, holy days and working-days, in order to finish it.' Many Zurich citizens found this hard-working and successful man, who had already printed various works by Luther, more sympathetic than the 'lazy priests', who were interested only in collecting their dues and issuing threats of punishment. Zwingli, who now published a sermon on the 'freedom of eating' – the first of his Reformation writings – found even greater support: 'If you wish to fast, do so. If you prefer not to eat meat, do not eat it. Leave the Christian free to do as he wants!' Everyone should act according to his own conviction, but not under compulsion and fear of punishment. In Basle the 'provocation' was the serving of a sucking pig; revolt against the restrictions on eating was frequently the first sign of resistance to Church discipline. In themselves the 'provocations' might be quite trivial, but a great deal had built up behind them; the spark fell on tinder that had been accumulating for centuries.

All the old grievances now came to a head, all the 'ancient rights' were called in question, and it was sometimes very hard to say where they had originated or whether they were not already obsolete. The bishops and abbots produced the relevant documents, but the time had passed when this was enough. The councillors and syndics examined them; they could now read and in fact were often better instructed than the clergy. If a document as basic as the alleged gift of the whole of the west to Pope Sylvester had been proved to be a forgery – and news of this had already spread – might not other documents also be dubious? Just how many such monastic and episcopal documents were forgeries has never been established, although the number is known to have been very considerable. But precisely what had been regarded as 'rights' in former centuries, and precisely why donors had made over large tracts of land to the Church, no one, with the knowledge then available, could determine. People were governed by existing conditions. The gifts had been made for devout purposes, to ensure eternal salvation for the donors and their families. If the bishops and abbots were now using these gifts to maintain luxurious households, and if the Masses for the dead were no longer being said or were being said perfunctorily by ill-paid substitutes, it appeared that the rights enjoyed by such religious foundations were no longer valid. Still graver doubts were entertained as to whether any devout purpose was served by the tax-free businesses carried on by religious institutions – by brewing and milling, by the retail sale of beer and wine, and by the sale of woven materials. These questions were much more hotly and universally disputed than questions of religious belief. The Church's position was hopeless.

The new movement everywhere, both in the free cities of the empire and in the courts of the princes, was drawing its legal experts and pioneers from the ranks of the councillors, syndics and city scribes; this was true even in those countries whose rulers remained loyal to the old Church. They refused to be fobbed off with appeals to tradition, with the old formula 'from time immemorial'. They established still older rights or invoked natural law. Whereas their rulers had been easily sidetracked by the extension of benefices or else, absorbed in their drinking and jousting, simply forgot what it was they intended to demand, these men scrutinized every detail and were tough negotiators. Frequently incorruptible, unlike the old-style aristocratic advisers, they had hard bourgeois heads and were 'niggling' – they kept and checked accounts. The once unique and all-powerful bureaucracy of the Church now found itself confronted by large numbers of other, equally efficient, bureaucracies representing the interests of their towns, their countries and their people. The appeal to the 'unity of Christendom' was no longer effective; it had been used too often for the sole purpose of filling the coffers of the Curia. The complaints of the papal nuncios were typical, involving always and above all the wicked councillors who were responsible for all the mischief; the princes were much easier to deal with. A single councillor was in fact often of greater importance to the new cause than an assembly of high-ranking nobles, who spent most of their time haggling over questions of precedence, marriage prospects, family claims going back to the time of the Crusades, or staggering about drunk and vomiting. Their insatiable gorging, gambling and whoring infuriated Luther, who was forever talking of 'we drunken Germans'. The Italians representing the Church and the Spaniards representing the emperor were their superiors, if only because they were reserved and abstemious; not infrequently they owed a success simply to the fact that they remained sober. It was only in the equally sober councillors and city scribes that they met their match.

Luther's doctrine that all the legislation introduced by the papacy in the course of the centuries was a 'human institution' proved to be one of the most effective weapons. It was difficult to refute, and an appeal to history compounded the difficulty. The historians, who now made their appearance alongside the jurists, supported the new faith almost to a man. They were constantly producing new material on the conflicts between the emperors and the popes, the disputes of the Councils, the popes and antipopes, the fearful charges of corruption against the clergy in every century. Hitherto history had meant Church history or history written by priests. Now laymen began to write history, and although they wrote in the style of the old chroniclers they wrote from a higher standpoint; examples were Aventin, a Bavarian of great ability, or Sebastian Franck who, very independent in his viewpoint and critique of human activity, wrote a German which in its power can stand comparison with that of Luther. Franck's ambition was to 'raise a forest of the finest and most memorable history in this my German country'; he deplored the fact that 'the Germans know more of Indians than they do of Germans,' but he was no hidebound nationalist and gave every nation its due. He wanted 'rational, worldly wisdom, which is also a gift of God,' to be given a hearing; he did not presume to judge 'what is right or wrong, divine or un-Christian but, as a historian, good and evil as fact and history show them to exist. I am a writer, not a censor of what others do and say'; above all he wanted to extract from the multiplicity of events their 'inner core and binding thongs'.

What were the binding thongs that held all this multiplicity of phenomena together? Even Sebastian Franck could not answer this. He had been a priest, was at first attracted to Luther and then rejected him; he became an artisan, printer, man of letters, writer of books, solitary, brooding mystic and spiritualist. He followed none of the trends. There were many like him. There was much talk of alliances, and Eberlin wrote of 'fifteen allies'; but no party was formed, no clearly defined front existed – which makes this movement of the early years the more astonishing. There was no one 'behind' the preachers or those who wrote the broadsheets and pamphlets; everything lay ahead of them. The defenders of the old doctrines looked on in amazement as they saw the heresy spread 'as though of its own volition'. The heretical writings were read, the defence tracts remained unread. The lay preachers gained ground everywhere, and discovered new, undefended territory. The pitiful proletariat of half-educated or quite uneducated priests which formed the broad substructure of the Church had little desire to apply itself energetically on behalf of its bishops; at any rate it had scarcely any even tolerably convincing arguments with which to defend itself. The religious orders, on whom the Church mainly depended for its preaching and propaganda, supplied the new teaching with its staunchest champions, although many who left the monasteries did so only to marry or escape the discipline. But it was the better and more serious among them who turned rebels and revolutionaries; they were masters of dialectic and the technique of speaking, which they had learned in the schools of their orders, and in addition had a burning zeal for which there had been no outlet in their previous sphere of activity. The Augustinian orders were almost completely disbanded, many priors sending their best monks to study in Wittenberg; even in the Netherlands, on which Charles v's government kept so strict a watch, the Augustinian monasteries provided the new teaching with its first footholds and supplied its first martyrs. But reinforcements came from other orders too, from the Franciscans and Dominicans for example. Argument had long ago left the specialized sphere to which belonged questions such as indulgences, reform of the Mass, the supremacy of the pope, or even, as Luther believed, simply the 'clear, shining Word'. Every question, all the longings, hopes and problems of the day, had been activated. Every class was involved, including the lowest.

At the beginning of 1523 Archduke Ferdinand, his brother Charles v's viceroy, sent one of his reports to distant Madrid, where Germany was regarded merely as a secondary theatre of affairs; in it he wrote: 'Luther's teaching has taken such root throughout the whole empire that today not one person in a thousand remains untouched by it; things could not be worse.' And towards the end of the year he wrote still more despondently: 'The Luther sect holds such a dominating position in this whole country that the good Christians are afraid to oppose it.'

The young archduke was exaggerating a little because he needed help. He was hard pressed by his own subjects in Austria, by the princes of the empire and by neighbouring Bavaria, while from the Balkans, on which the Sultan Suleiman was continually advancing, arose the Turkish threat. No help of any kind came. Charles was at war with France, which he wanted to divide between himself and his English allies; by this means he hoped to win Bourgogne, the country of his dreams. In Spain he had an uphill struggle to keep his position. He had no army and no fixed income; his most valuable possessions had been mortgaged to the Fuggers ever since his election. The only empire over which he held undisputed sway was in his own imagination, and this had no boundaries. Following medieval tradition he wanted, in conjunction with the pope, to rule the whole of the west, as well as the New World, large parts of which were being laid at his feet by brave and rebellious pirates like Cortez and Pizarro. He was dependent on strokes of luck, which he invariably attributed to the will of God. It was a stroke of luck when Leo x, on whom he had never been able to count, died and Charles's old teacher, Adrian Dedel Floriszoon of Utrecht, became pope, taking the name of Hadrian vi. The first Pope Hadrian had summoned Charlemagne to his aid, and with his help had put an end to the Langobard domination of Italy; those close to the emperor hoped that the new Hadrian would co-operate in a similar manner with the new world ruler. It was only a question of subduing the new Lango-bards – or Goths – in Germany; religious unity would then be restored and the way freed to establish a universal monarchy, to which France, England and the other nations would have to submit. Gattinara, Charles's chancellor, was the architect of this imperial design; he also had visions of becoming pope and had already acquired the title of cardinal.

Charles, still only twenty-three but with the features of a man of forty, was growing into his role of emperor. Having frittered away so much of his time on expensive court ceremonies, festivities and hunting, he now started to work. He learned Spanish, and this became his main language; 'God speaks Spanish to mankind', he used to say. He was a slow worker and put everything on paper before confronting his advisers. The only thing that worried those close to him was that he showed no intention of marrying, and indulged in none of the royal love affairs considered proper to a king and a gratifying sign of his manly nature. His conduct was strict, almost monastic. He was punc-tilious in fulfilling his obligations to the Church, and his father con-fessor's only complaint concerned the unseemly and dangerous gluttony of his penitent, who bolted his large and heavy meals in greedy silence, washing down the mouthfuls with cold beer. His physicians, who early on found he had a tendency to gout, were worried. No one had any influence over him. He did not have a single friend. Only the members of his own family, with whom he carried on an endless correspondence, were at all close to him; even they had to bow to his will however, being unscrupulously exploited for his own purposes or, as later in the case of his younger daughters, moved around ruthlessly on the inter-national chessboard. His cold aloofness made an enormous impression in an age when most other ruling princes mixed so freely with their sub-jects, drinking, chatting and going to bed with them, conversing with them in their own language and participating freely in all their curses, obscenities and coarse jokes.

Basically Charles's mind worked only in a single groove, that of the Imperator. An empire greater than that of the Roman emperors lay before him, almost within his grasp; God had appointed him to turn this vision into a reality. He must have found it exasperating, and a little grotesque, that in a minute town called Wittenberg, in the half-state belonging to his 'good uncle' Frederick, there was a monk who presumed to upset his universal designs. For this very reason, however, he saw no need to pay any attention to his brother's call for help or to give serious consideration to the questions put to him by the provisional imperial government, which was not a government at all but merely a government commission with no executive authority. To the Imperator these questions seemed petty and trifling, as only too often they were; he handed them over to his 'German Aulic Council', an institution of minor importance that had been created at his court. Perhaps nothing else demonstrates so clearly how little attention the Imperator paid to the empire. The chief councillors were two active and ambitious Burgundian notables, who pursued the interests of the House of Habsburg-Burgundy with great energy; added to these were a Hohenzollern prince, bent on making an important Spanish marriage and successful in this ambition, Charles's boyhood playmate the count of Nassau, and finally a minor German provost named Märklin, from Waldkirchen, whose task was to conduct the verbal negotiations, probably because he was the only member of the council able to speak German fluently. The feudal disorder characteristic of the late Middle Ages was carried to an extreme at the court of the Emperor Charles, at any rate so far as the interests of the empire, whose title he bore, were concerned. The anarchy which prevailed in the territories of Germany, and which alone made possible the advance of the new teaching, had its counterpart at the summit. Such were the arbiters of Germany's fate, and of Luther's.

The fate of the Church lay in the hands of a sixty-three-year-old scholar, who reluctantly and slowly now set out on the long journey to Italy to take over the holy see.

# 27

# A Dutchman as pope

'WE ARE aware that for many years great abuses have grown up around the holy see ... it is no wonder that the sickness has spread from the head to the limbs, from the popes down to the humblest prelates. We prelates and clergy have all gone our own ways. For a long time no one, not a single one, has done anything good.' This confession of sins, altered by Hadrian VI, was proffered with full solemnity by the papal nuncio at the Diet of Nuremberg. The pope promised a thoroughgoing reform of his court at Rome from which, as he said, it was possible that all the evils had emanated and spread; he further admitted that the whole world demanded a return to a healthier state of affairs. On his way to Rome Hadrian had already dispatched threatening messages; he intended to do away with the customary bestowal of benefices, 'expectancies' and other gifts which, on the election of every new pope, had been distributed as blessings and favours among the flocks of hungry aspirants.

This was unprecedented news. Who was this Pope Hadrian, who had also inappropriately selected his own name for his pontificate instead of following the usual custom and sensibly choosing a fore-runner as godfather? To the Romans he was an 'Olandese', a Nether-lander, and this was tantamount to saying 'almost a German', which would have been totally unacceptable. Since the end of the exile of the popes in Avignon it had been virtually an unwritten law that only an Italian could be considered an aspirant to the highest office; even the Borgias had been accepted only because they were half Italian. Hadrian was the last to interrupt for one short year the unbroken succession of Italian popes. How had the choice of a foreigner come about at all? What were the cardinals thinking of when they chose a sixty-three-year-old scholar to bring Peter's ship, battling hard against heavy seas as it was, into port? A number of explanations went the rounds. During the fifteenth and sixteenth centuries the papal elections were secret only in name. It is true that the cardinals were locked in conclave in the Vatican, where they had their wooden 'cells', erected specially for

348

the purpose, and observed a solemn protocol; but the envoys of the great powers were pretty accurately informed about everything. They sent full and detailed reports to their masters, recording in plain figures the bribes that were demanded and paid, as well as the promises of benefices and honours, which were in fact the most important means of influencing the election. It had long been accepted as a foregone conclusion that great pressure would be brought to bear by the emperor, the King of France and the King of England; the internal situation in Italy also always played a leading role. This election was no exception. To continue unbroken the rule of the House of Medici was regarded by many as inopportune, though for a long time the most likely candidate was thought to be Cardinal Medici, the late Pope Leo's cousin and a diplomat of great experience, thanks to the many years he had spent as the Curia's secretary of state. During the eleven ballots it took to arrive at a decision, he came near to achieving his goal; a year later, as Clement VII, he continued and brought to an end the 'Medici era' of the papacy. But he was strongly opposed by the French faction.

A glance at the cardinals is now desirable since they were the embodiment of the hierarchy, and it is wrong to let the light fall exclusively on the wearers of the tiara who, in any case, often reigned only for a few years and sometimes only for a few months. This rapid succession of elections entered into the calculations of the cardinals; not infrequently they had placed a man who was almost dying on the papal chair or, as in the case of Leo X, had allowed themselves to be guided by indications of a candidate's poor state of health. A long reign was regarded *ipso facto* as undesirable, or as a misfortune when it occurred contrary to expectations. In this the people of Rome agreed wholeheartedly with the high princes of the Church, and when a pontificate, however satisfactory it might be, lasted too long for their liking they sometimes rebelled in the most merciless way.

Leo X had appointed thirty-one cardinals at a single stroke, his reason, as everybody knew, being need for money; the move brought him in half a million ducats, enough to cover the most pressing requirements of his court. Among the thirty-one were a few who could be considered worthy of their high office; two or three made names for themselves. The others consisted partly of very young nobles whose activities were a source of amusement both to pleasure-loving Roman society and to the Roman people; some among them were extremely young, the sons of princes in countries where the great archbishoprics went by hereditary right to the sons and bastard sons of the ruling houses. 'Secularization', a word that was used with such emphasis to describe the temporal powers' outrageous designs on the Church, had long ago become the tacitly accepted practice when diplomatic considerations made it seem advisable. In Portugal Pope Leo had made the king's nine-year-old son a cardinal, an appointment that also carried with it four of the main bishoprics; the Portuguese royal house already had almost complete control of the Church revenues. In Lorraine a comparable situation existed: the red hat was bestowed on a small boy, Jean, whose father, the duke, took good care to see that some of the ten important bishoprics accruing to his son – Verdun and Rheims for example – were passed on to his nephews, boys of a similar tender age. In Naples the highest ecclesiastical post belonged by a century-old tradition to the Caraffa family; the Italian cardinals made similar use of a custom which although not 'canonical' had become accepted practice in order to ensure that their nephews benefited from the abundance of great sees. Nepotism, the hereditary curse of the papacy, was by no means confined to the families of the popes and their legitimate or illegitimate offspring. Hence there was always marked tension in the College of Cardinals between the 'young' and the 'old' cardinals, among the latter of whom some papal progeny were invariably to be found. Thus before Hadrian's election the candidate who at first seemed to have the best chance was Cardinal San Giorgio; a Riario, and already well on in years, he was known as the great-nephew of Pope Sixtus della Rovere, although in fact he was his grandson and a member of a clan whose astonishing activities can well bear comparison with those of the Borgias.

Riario died unexpectedly the day before his enemy Leo. The half-consumed stumps of the wax candles used at his funeral had to be used again at the solemn service held for Leo, a circumstance that was seen as a bad omen. The papal treasury was completely empty; Leo's debts amounted to almost a million ducats. The treasury officials managed, with some difficulty, to borrow a few thousand ducats from Chigi, the great papal banker, in order at least to be able to pay the Swiss Guards. It was feared that the mob might indulge in its traditional rioting and loot the cardinals', and even the pope's, palaces. The wealthier cardinals had paid troops of their own. Riario had always been able to avoid arrest, thanks to his personal guard of four hundred heavily armed men; a number of the less affluent cardinals also enjoyed his protection. Others like Cardinal Colonna, a condottiere rather than a prince of the Church, had small armies at their disposal, of which they made energetic use; Colonna had used his during the insurrection against Julius II, and later did so again, and to good purpose, under the papacy of Clement VII. At the time of the conclave these private troops were stationed in readiness at selected vantage points, while from farther away came threats of intervention by the emperor's mercenaries.

The obvious solution was a man with diplomatic experience conversant with the tricks and stratagems of high politics. Thus for a time Cardinal Medici received the majority of votes, but never enough; a whole string of candidates was then considered, under strong pressure from outside. Cardinal Farnese's name came up; the banks, who had wagered large sums on the election, supported him strongly. This brought Cardinal Egidio, from Viterbo, into action; vicar-general of the Augustinian Order, he was one of the two or three members of the electoral body prepared to sanction reform. Preferring the most serious charges against Cardinal Farnese, he tore his reputation to shreds. He had no need to remind the cardinals that Farnese owed his red hat solely to the intervention of his sister, the lovely Giulia, who, as Alexander Borgia's mistress, was taking care of the interests of her family; it was also well known that he had been released from prison, where he had been put for counterfeiting, only on the insistence of Pope Alexander. The people of Rome called him in good-natured fun the 'petticoat cardinal'. Egidio made it clear that to elect a man with such a past would put an end to every hope of resolving the conflict which was splitting Christendom. Farnese was forced to withdraw and had to wait twelve years until he was in the running again.

Whatever the reason, whether after so many fruitless attempts exhaustion played a part, or whether the darkness was responsible – the general lack of money meant that there were no candles for the conclave either – or whether supporters of the emperor brought strong pressure to bear, the Dutchman Hadrian, son of a ship's carpenter from Utrecht, was elected. No one had anything against him on personal grounds; he led an exemplary life and was well-known as a scholar and luminary of the dependably orthodox University of Louvain. As grand inquisitor in Spain he had won a reputation in the fight against heresy; as Charles's former tutor and the emperor's governor in Spain he was credited with a knowledge of the great world and high politics. He was not present. He received the news of his election in Spain and was asked to assume office as soon as possible.

The choice of a foreigner came as a surprise. The Romans were furious: a Dutchman, a barbarian, who did not understand a word of Italian. The cardinals themselves soon began to have second thoughts, especially when the first messages from their new master started to arrive. Their defence was that the choice had been inspired by the Holy Ghost, there was no other way to explain it. On this Guicciardini, the papal statesman, and in his acuteness and insight the leading chronicler of contemporary events, made the following comment: 'As if the Holy Ghost, who loves men of a pure heart, would stoop to the level of people such as these, who are eaten up with worldly ambition, avarice beyond belief and lust for pleasure – to put it no more strongly.'

It was into this circle that Hadrian now entered, with the best intentions and the total innocence of a bookman. His tenure of high office in Spain had been characterized by one long string of failures. He had failed on virtually every occasion, partly because he did not understand the conditions of violence prevailing in Spain, and partly because he was a doctrinarian and theoretician, accustomed to the clear-cut, dialectical categories of the lecture room, which no more needed to

Pope Hadrian VI

coincide with reality than did the ideas of his master, Thomas Aquinas, on the omnipotence of the pope. He thought he had only to issue orders, in the same way that he had told his students in Louvain what they must read and know. He treated the cardinals like schoolboys, the disturbed land of Germany he saw as an unruly class; Rome, which he had never seen before, was a sink of iniquity that he would transform into a clean place to live in merely by issuing a few decrees. His attitude to his former pupil, the Emperor Charles, who in the meantime had become lord of a great empire, and to the emperor's advisers, who saw in Hadrian merely the puppet of their choice and their plans, was that of the former teacher.

During the six months of the interregnum the thin veneer of brilliant 'Renaissance culture', which to posterity represents the Rome of those days, had split down every seam. Only a ruthless tyrant like Julius II could keep the populace under control; to a quite disproportionate extent it consisted of beggars – in every income bracket – buffoons, satellites of the cardinals, and those who made their living out of the papal court, the many other courts, the pilgrims and the visitors. On the outskirts of the city the robber bands held almost undisputed sway and were strongly represented in Rome itself. People hired assassins as they hired bearers and muleteers, and the countless rights of sanctuary made it almost impossible to catch the murderers; in addition to the churches, all of which offered sanctuary, the right was also claimed by every cardinal for his palace or his territory, which might comprise several buildings or half a city sector. One of the first measures Hadrian announced was a very sensible decree to deprive the bellicose cardinals of this privilege. This measure immediately caused serious discord, being seen as a grossly improper infringement of hallowed rights.

The veneer of faith, so impressive to the devout pilgrim, was equally thin. As so often, there was a threat of plague; instead of congregating in the churches the populace flocked to the Colosseum where a sorcerer, rumoured to be a Greek, solemnly slaughtered a black bull to propitiate the demonic powers that threatened Rome – a survival of the cult of Mithras. When the new pope, who had forbidden the erection of any archaic triumphal arches decorated with figures of Minerva and Hercules, entered the city he was greeted by a horde of half-savage, naked children who flogged each other till they were raw. It was hard to tell whether the shouts and yells that accompanied the Dutchman's entry were mournful lamentations or maledictions. Everybody had been seized by fear: fear of the plague, fear of the new regime, and fear of the Turks, who had just conquered Rhodes, the last bastion of the Knights of St John, and threatened very soon to turn against Italy, as they had done once before.

And so, once he had installed himself laboriously in the Vatican, Hadrian's principal concern and watchword was a crusade against the Turks. He preached it unremittingly, to his pupil Charles as well, who refused to listen, the pope's remarks becoming more insistent and more biting until they became abusive. The unity of emperor and pope was on a very insecure footing; Hadrian's rule in Rome was even less firmly based. He asked Cardinal Egidio of Viterbo to submit to him a detailed memorandum on the necessary reforms, and there is something stirring in the similarity of the vicar-general's ideas to those of the Wittenberg monk; he censured the unlimited conferment of benefices, the Curia's blood-sucking dataries, the system of indulgences –

'Unlimited conferment breeds a limitless desire to sin,' he wrote. Egidio, however, took it for granted that reform must come from above. Hadrian went to work in earnest, beginning with himself. He moved into a small study within the vast halls of the Vatican, an old Flemish servant was given charge of the kitchen; every evening, to the huge amusement of the Romans, the pope took a ducat out of his pocket and handed it to the major-domo to cover the next day's housekeeping for the whole palace. The swarm of writers, entertainers, musicians and jesters was driven out and at once took its revenge by writing squibs attacking the barbarian 'skinflint'; Hadrian threatened to have Pasquino, on whom the blame for the scurrilous verses was pinned, thrown into the Tiber. The Belvedere, with its heathen abominations in the form of antique statues, was closed, and Hadrian considered whitewashing the Sistine Chapel. He rose early, prayed, studied, and continued to work on a scholarly treatise he was writing, although his official business alone was too much for him. He gave orders that the sale of offices, the surest and most direct source of income, was to cease. The minister of finance drew his attention to the fact that Leo's debts had to be paid. The interest on these was reaching vast sums, and no banker with whom the Curia dealt observed the Church's ban on usury; Leo had unhesitatingly agreed to semi-annual interest rates of up to twenty-five per cent. He had created over thirteen hundred new offices, in addition to those already in existence, and each aspirant had to pay for his nomination. Hadrian intended to abolish all this. He became suspicious. There was no one he could depend on, apart from a few assistants whom he had brought with him from the Netherlands and who understood no Italian. The cardinals even scoffed at his pronunciation of Latin, which they could not understand and regarded as 'Gothic'. The strictly monastic Hadrian, whose furrowed face beneath the close-fitting cap seems to belong to an earlier century, rode roughshod over the young cardinals, issuing orders about their clothes and hair styles; most of them went about in secular dress and sported the fashionable, perfumed, well-groomed beard of the free man – they were ordered to shave their faces clean immediately.

He did not understand the quarrel between France and the emperor – both were loyal sons of the true faith. He planned to terminate Leo's treaty of alliance with the emperor, which in any case had been concluded only with numerous reservations, and replace it by a policy of co-existence. The French faction, with Cardinal Soderini as France's secret *chargé d'affaires*, opposed and intrigued against this with the utmost vehemence; when Hadrian was shown highly compromising letters, which had been intercepted, he had Soderini arrested and imprisoned in the Castle of St Angelo, where so many cardinals had been housed. The king of France, furious at this treatment of his delegate, retaliated with a threat recalling the worst defeat suffered by the papacy in its heyday, the seizure of Pope Boniface by French emissaries in Anagni. Francis I hinted at a similar fate for Hadrian. The pope issued a solemn decree proclaiming a three-year truce. No one paid any attention to it. In northern France the imperial forces and their English allies swept over the countryside taking revenge for their inability to attack the strongly fortified towns by ravaging villages and small townships: 'When we have burned Dorlans, Corbie, Ancre, Bray and the districts surrounding them to the ground, which will take about three weeks, I do not see what more we can do,' the English commander wrote to Cardinal Wolsey. The poorly planned campaign was brought to a standstill by rain, reinforcements from the Netherlands failed to turn up, and as usual the allies started to indulge in mutual recriminations. The French king refused to allow the monies destined for the Curia to leave France. Hadrian complained: 'I do not wish to declare myself opposed to France, because on the day that I did so the monies from there, on which my court mainly depends, would dry up. I also know from a reliable source that the King of France would foster Luther's heresy and readjust the affairs of the Church in his own country.' It was one of the few occasions on which Hadrian mentioned Luther's name; in his extensive correspondence with the Emperor Charles it hardly appears. All the same he was forced to yield to pressure from the emperor; the truce plan was allowed quietly to lapse, Hadrian joining the grand coalition consisting of the emperor, England, Venice, Florence Genoa, Siena and Lucca, whose intention was to crush France once and for all.

In the middle of the worries caused him by his alliance, which he concluded against his better judgment and which reduced him to the level of his predecessor Leo, Hadrian died. He had spent barely six months in Rome as pope. Whether he was poisoned, as many Romans believed – a notice saying 'To the saviour of his country' was stuck on his physician's door – we have no means of knowing. He was buried in the German national church of Santa Maria dell'Anima. The inscription on his tombstone reads: 'How much depends on the age in which the work even of the most admirable man is done!' Round the sarcophagus stand the figures of Giustizia, Prudenza, Forza and Temperanza; of these Forza is wholly out of place and even Prudenza can be justified only by the exercise of considerable goodwill.

We have seen the disunity of the Church under Hadrian. The picture of the empire that emerges from the assemblies known as 'imperial diets' does not convey even the hope of any future concentration of forces. In fact there had been a widespread tendency to split and break up into individual countries long before the religious question arose and was seized as a welcome opportunity to intensify the schisms. Taking advantage of the emperor's absence for years on end, the old plan of government by the estates had been resurrected and half-heartedly put into practice – everything in politics was done half-heartedly. The electors wanted the government in their own hands; they formed the committee, with its high-sounding title of Imperial Government, which was supposed to execute state business but which, owing to lack of funds, never went beyond fractional measures. The princes' councillors had hatched a grand design for the creation of a single, integrated customs area with an imperial customs tariff to be levied at the frontier: this frontier, incidentally, was to include half the Netherlands. The towns, however, and above all the great banking houses and merchant companies, saw in this plan a serious threat to their interests and wrecked it. The princes had also broached the question of the great monopolies, and passed resolutions limiting drastically the powers of the finance companies; on appeal to the emperor in Spain this project also came to nothing, if only because the Fuggers, to whom the emperor was deeply in debt, would not permit it. Another plan provided for the imperial government to be financed by a comprehensive tax on Jews; this collapsed on the objection of the towns, which had purchased from the emperors, and at considerable expense, the right to tax the Jews in their areas. The princes, who had offered their services to the imperial government in rotation – a new one taking over the management of affairs each quarter – lost interest. The proud imperial government after carrying on for decades with the special support of the Elector Frederick came to an inglorious end. Only a rump was left, and this withdrew from the free imperial city of Nuremberg to the little Württemberg town of Esslingen.

There remained the imperial diets whose comprehensive 'ordinances', couched in the most ponderous official language and formulated as imprecisely as possible, provided the last shreds of any mandatory legislation. The Edict of Worms, which outlawed Luther and his followers, though conceived as a piece of imperial legislation, was rendered virtually powerless by its vague if strong wording. The edict was opposed on the ground that it would appear as an 'intention to suppress evangelical truth by tyrannical means and uphold un-Christian abuses'; this could lead only to 'opposition to authority, indignation and defection'. The way was thus freed *de facto* for Luther and the Reformation, and this is how it was understood. It was to the Nuremberg meeting of 1522, at which this momentous decision was taken, that Chieregati, the papal legate, brought Hadrian's confession of sins.

Once again it was made clear how inadequately Rome was informed on conditions in Germany. On his arrival the legate experienced the most unpleasant surprises: because 'the times were not propitious', the city council refused him the ceremonial entry, on a white charger caparisoned in purple, that Cajetan had claimed and received in Augsburg. In the churches lay preachers were preaching the new doctrine. The legate demanded their arrest; the city council refused because it might cause indignation among the people. Luther's writings were openly displayed; the council deputed some of its members to see that they disappeared during the legate's visit, a commission that was somewhat negligently carried out. There were noisy arguments on the subject in the College of Princes. The Archduke Ferdinand, who had just assumed his duties as the emperor's viceroy, stressed the fact that he represented His Majesty. The envoy from the electorate of Saxony replied: 'Agreed, but in conjunction with the Imperial Government and in conformity with the Statutes of the Empire!' It was known how weak the position of the young ruler was; he was only just beginning to learn German, and governed his patrimonial lands through his Spanish confidant Salamanca, a situation that had already almost led to civil war.

The legate found himself confronted by a group of bearded princely figures, and some very alert young councillors, all of whom seemed to him to be Lutherans, even when they represented powerful bishops. What he had to say was listened to with suspicion: the Edict of Worms would have to be carried out to the letter before the desired measures of reform could be undertaken. Hadrian had made a solemn pronouncement on the subject, quoting Biblical precedents: God Himself had killed Dathan and Abiram, as had the early emperors the heretics Jovinian and Priscillus; Hus had been burned by the ancestors of the assembled princes. The princes had no use for Dathan and Abiram; they were interested in the redressing of the hundred 'gravamina'; once the complaints against the see of Rome were remedied, Luther's following would disperse by itself. They took due note of Hadrian's confession – all it showed was how urgent the need for reform was; a start must be made, they insisted. New in the proceedings was a clearly formulated threat: should the complaints not be remedied, and remedied within a specified period of time, the German estates would 'of their own accord devise means of ridding and divesting themselves of this affliction and burden imposed by the priesthood.' The Council was the proper solution to the problem: it must be called at once, within a year; the emperor and pope together were to convene it, and it was to be held in a German city. The most important and unprecedented request was that the laity were to be represented alongside the prelates and have the right to vote.

Finally, freedom of ideas and discussion was demanded; no one taking part was to be bound by predetermined obligations. Everyone must be free to express his opinion on what should be done in 'divine, evangelical and other matters of common benefit'.

One might pause to admire this proposal and speculate on what would have happened had such a league of nations or national council come into existence; but it never even reached the preliminary stages. The grievances were not remedied. The princes continued to pursue their territorial policies; the nobility made ready for war against the clergy, and here and there the peasantry was already beginning to rise in revolt. The rich and powerful cities, which held the key to the situation, closed their gates and devoted themselves energetically to trade and the interests of their communities. The knights of the empire were the first to break loose.

# 28

# Sickingen and the end of the knights

LUTHER trusted in the Word, and it had proved mighty beyond expectations. The knights relied on their 'trusty swords'; the princes counted on their 'devout landsknechts' and on the money needed to pay them. Franz von Sickingen, the leader of the lesser nobility, took an intermediate stand. His main wish, which he believed within his grasp, was to found a principality of his own. But he had even more ambitious plans. The centre of hopes and aspirations from many quarters, he was sometimes called the 'King of the Rhine', either in awe or in derision, and it did not strike him as beyond the bounds of possibility that the throne itself might fall to him. At the moment there was no German king. The emperor was in Spain and showed no signs of returning in the foreseeable future. The knights, reduced to poverty and driven from their leading position, still considered themselves as the great estate to whom, in the divine order of things, the most important role had been assigned. They were anxious to come into their own again and establish, or re-establish, their order; their enemies were the priests and the princes, the two offices frequently being combined in a single person, in as much as the priesthood had annexed the richest principalities. This, at any rate, is what the polemics of Ulrich von Hutten proclaimed. Sickingen had adopted a cautious attitude towards his friend and his rather indefinite plans; he had often disappointed the impetuous Hutten by his hesitation and dealings with the emperor. He was a knight but he was also a man of enterprise who by no means despised 'Italian practices', in other words those practices which people preferred to ascribe to the Latins. His troops had safeguarded Charles's election as emperor, and as the latter's commander-in-chief he was in charge of the campaign against Francis I, in whose service he had previously been. He had lent the young ruler twenty thousand urgently needed guilders before the election, without security or promissory note. The bankers showed greater caution in such matters, taking mines and estates as security on occasion. Sickingen hated the financiers too. A man with many enemies and many sympathizers, he had few real friends.

Old-style chivalry combined with modern traits to make him a representative figure. He was very far from scorning the Word, and above all Luther's word; whether there was any deeper insight into Luther's ideas is as doubtful in his case as in that of his friend Hutten. But throughout one long winter, in the customary pause between feuds and campaigns, he settled down with some of Luther's pupils in his castle at Ebernburg, listened to their readings from the master's works, thought them over and decided to throw in his lot with the new teaching. It is possible that he envisaged welcome support for his grandiose plans, but there seems no reason to credit less religious conviction to him than to his enemies, who looked to the old faith to strengthen their positions. When he heard that Luther could no longer remain in Wittenberg he offered him sanctuary. His castle became a 'refuge of justice', as Hutten called it, and a whole succession of persecuted preachers found safety there; among these were men who later played leading roles, such as the Alsatian Martin Bucer and the Swabian Johannes Hüssgen, who took the pompous name of Oekolampadius and became the reformer of Basle. A first evangelical service, with readings from the Bible in German, was held in the castle, thus anticipating even Wittenberg; Hutten's boldest polemics were printed there. The upshot was that the fortress belonging to the imperial councillor and commander-in-chief Sickingen became *'eine feste Burg'*, or safe stronghold, for the new teaching. The pension he drew from the emperor, as well as his contract, continued, or, more accurately, his contract continued – the imperial court was in arrears. The troops he commanded had been enlisted through his personal fame; he paid them with his own money and on his own credit. Sickingen was not the only creditor of the ruler of the world-wide empire.

Sickingen could not complain, he had to run the same risks as any other entrepreneur. He was modern, too, in not relying exclusively on the knight's mailed fist; anticipating the military leaders of the Thirty Years' War, he also made use of a new military force, the landsknechts. The money he needed to wage this kind of warfare had been raised by careful administration of the estates left him by his father; these were in the neighbourhood of Kreuznach where the soil was rich and where some of the best wine in Germany was made. He also had mining interests. Sickingen was of a different type from the petty highwaymen knights who with a few henchmen would set upon a small, badly defended column of merchants. His raids were more ambitious; they also brought him considerably greater spoils. At the head of seven thousand men he besieged the town of Worms and laid waste its territory – the threat of outlawry did not deter the condottiere for an instant. Then, at the instigation of a fellow knight, he turned his eyes on a richer prize: the duchy of Lorraine. In this enterprise he enjoyed the tacit connivance of the Emperor Maximilian, who clandestinely made over English subsidies to the man he had outlawed. This method of waging war while ostensibly at peace, by means of partisans who could be disowned or dropped, was a favourite one with all the powers. The duke, hard pressed, bought his freedom with annuities. The king of France, his attention drawn to this able military leader, received Sickingen graciously at Amboise and bought him from the emperor, who in any case, like his successor, paid very badly or not at all. Sickingen began to grow rich. He conducted further large-scale campaigns, made his peace with the emperor, and assumed the task of enforcing the imperial writ of execution against Ulrich of Württemberg, taking his own and his army's pay from the country and rounding off his estate. The powerful city of Metz was invested and paid ransom money; Frankfurt was threatened and the ambitious knight also turned his eyes on the rich city of Erfurt. His only miscalculation was a raid on the young Landgrave Philip of Hesse, who was in a state of conflict with his knights; the raid was successful, but Sickingen made an implacable enemy for the future. He also made a great name for himself among the knights by sharing the profits with them.

He was now a figure on whom many hopes were pinned; soldiers' songs celebrated his name, pamphlets lauded the noble Sickingen, who was also said to sympathize with the common man. Petitions were sent to him at Ebernburg and, when he thought it right or to his advantage, he took action. Prompted by Hutten, he went to the aid of Reuchlin, who was being victimized by the Dominicans in Cologne. The great man's threats were enough to bring the action for heresy against the elderly scholar to a speedy halt; the Dominicans even paid compensation when Sickingen shook his fist. He was feared by the towns and by the bankers too. In one of the dialogues printed in his honour he gave his views on the meaning of the terms 'finance' and 'financier': 'They call it finance when a lord cannot manage on what his income, interest, revenues and liens bring in, or for some other reason is unable to pay; when he then raises money by other means, promising much and returning little, this is called finance.'

The clergy quailed before him because it was from his castle that Hutten issued his calls for a ruthless war against the priesthood. At the same time Sickingen entertained intimate relations with Archbishop Albrecht of Mainz, who was sermonizing to his other ecclesiastical colleagues, especially his neighbour the archbishop of Trier. Sickingen took it for granted that the emperor would look on in silence if this archbishop-elector, well known to be a partisan of France and to have been heavily bribed by Francis I before the emperor's election, were humbled or even put out of the way. The idea was to create 'an opening for the Gospel' by attacking Trier, and the consequences would indeed have been incalculable had Sickingen been able to force a breach, here on the Rhine, in the 'Priests' Way', as Maximilian had called the Church's possessions in this area.

This plan, far from being kept secret, was zealously publicized. Sickingen felt sure of support from all sections of the knighthood and from as far away as the borders of northern Germany; his envoys travelled the countryside. A meeting of knights had been held in Landau and elected Sickingen their leader. Shortly before this Luther had published one of his fiercest polemics attacking the 'falsely so-called spiritual estate of the pope and bishops'; he had threatened the bishops: 'Because of the way you have treated me, may you not have your will until your iron brows and brazen necks have been broken either by grace or by disgrace.' He declared that all 'who contribute by pledging body, home and honour to see that the bishoprics are destroyed and the bishops' rule abolished' were God's beloved children and true Christians. He was entering that period of his life when he moved, or was dragged, into the world of everyday politics. No one could have been less suited to it. But he was carried away by his own words and his faith in the 'will of God'. God's hand had been clearly visible in all that had happened so far; if the knights were to rise and give a new turn to events this would also be God's will. He had no idea of the strength of the forces that were gathering on either side. When he spoke of the bishops it was because they were persecuting his Gospel instead of preaching it: 'What is a bishop who does not preach but a spring that gives no water or a cloud that gives no rain. His office is to preach and he does not do it, like a spring that produces nothing.' They were neglecting the souls entrusted to them. He cried out in a fury: 'It would be better for every bishop to be murdered and every religious foundation and monastery to be uprooted than for a single soul to be corrupted.' It was in vain for him to protest afterwards that remarks such as these were not to be taken in their literal meaning. The people could not possibly understand the glaring paradoxes that were part of his nature and way of writing. They were meant for the study and for learned theological discussions – it was another case of his education turning against him; the school of Ockham had indulged in still bolder dialectical paradoxes. But now he was speaking and writing for everyone and with unprecedented power.

In terms of intelligence, the knights were on a level with the ordinary people; their significance as an estate was soon to be revealed. The technique of war had passed them by. The massed assault of a concentration of mounted knights in armour grouped round a standard was already out of date when Charles the Bold had fought his battle against the Swiss. The infantry and artillery had taken over. That the knights did not grasp this seems less astonishing when we remember that their concept of attack and faith in cavalry as the decisive weapon dominated military thought until the First World War. It was only in jousting, the chief amusement of the nobility, that the knight in armour could still win honours; it was the age of profusely illustrated books on jousting, in which free scope was also given to knightly pride. To be 'good at jousting' was the true test of nobility; it was also a passport to the richly endowed posts in the great cathedral foundations. Commercial life had also passed the knights by; this accounts for their hatred of shop-keepers and merchants and their impotent jealousy of the townspeople, who lived in far greater comfort than the nobles in their excessively uncomfortable and cheerless castles and robber strongholds, who dressed in silk and satin and consumed expensive delicacies from all over the world, while in most cases the wife of a knight was little better off than a superior peasant woman. A few of the lesser nobility, recog-nizing the signs of the times, had gone off to seek posts as advisers in princely courts; but this involved study and some knowledge of books and the world. Public peace, proclaimed again and again with threats of severe penalties, existed only on paper. The decisions of the imperial high court of Justice were laughed at, and the knights in the various districts met to celebrate solemn 'unions' and alliances, drinking vastly and forging great plans. Sickingen, hitherto so successful, was their acknowledged leader; he had a reputation for caution and cun-ning and was known for his important connections at the emperor's court, his wealth, and his ability to obtain credit from the odious financiers, an accomplishment beyond the dreams of any of his brother knights. He had troops at his command, and this was important too because these nobles were already sufficiently conversant with the times to prefer to leave the actual fighting to paid soldiery while reserving to themselves the post of commander. The plan now was to carry out a raid on a truly grand scale, under Sickingen's leadership, against the wealthy city of Trier.

During the winter prior to this campaign Hutten had issued a whole string of manifestos from the castle of Ebernburg for the purpose of enlisting allies. A little late in the day he also thought of the philistines in the towns; they too would see the need to join the knights in fighting the princes, who were the real danger. A knight by the name of Hart-mut of Kronberg in the Taunus, who was related to Sickingen by marri-age, wrote some rather muddled tracts in which he came out in support of Luther, and appealed to the emperor, on whom people still continued to pin their hopes, begging him to make it clear to the pope that he was indeed Antichrist; he also sought to win the Bohemian nobles as allies. To Luther he wrote a long letter which immediately appeared in print, and one can well understand the outlaw's pleasure at this encouragement. For the knight's letter bore touchingly naïve witness to the way in which the new ideas were being taken up and to the trust people put in Luther personally. He addressed Luther as his 'dearest brother', remarking that he preferred to keep the word 'father' for Christ alone; he admired the courage 'with which you have undoubtedly accomplished the will of our Heavenly Father, in whom you so justly rejoice.' Titles and riches meant nothing, he went on, all a man needed as a child of God was faith; with his childlike faith Hartmut was also confident that 'the kind, merciful God will bestow His grace on our superiors and on us all.' He did not mention the war against the clergy and spoke only of the 'misery, distress and abominable corruption throughout the German nation' that was also Luther's concern. Now, however, thanks to the art of printing, 'first invented in German lands', Luther had brought the Bible to light and thus enabled the richest and poorest man alike to understand his salvation 'in good, clear German'. The art of printing also enabled Hartmut to append to the little volume his self-created 'appointment' as commander-in-chief not only of the troops in his pay but of 'every fighting soldier in the world'. He was one of the first to hurry to Sickingen's aid with his small body of men.

In spite of the widespread sympathy for Sickingen's cause the soldiers from far and near did not arrive. The campaign against Trier was badly planned. Sickingen had not been lucky in his campaign against France as the emperor's commander-in-chief: the weather had been bad – the perennial excuse for unsuccessful operations – the emperor's court had given him no support and ceased its payments, and Sickingen, having no wish to sink any more money of his own in the enterprise, had turned back. His troops had dispersed and his reputation had suffered a severe setback. This was not his least reason for wanting now to strike a major blow, at his own expense and on his own behalf. The prospects seemed favourable. Help had been promised him by his fellow knights on the Rhine as far as the Dutch border, by others in Westphalia and Brunswick and by many individuals; in Franconia the nobles banded together, but then pursued plans of their own. Sickingen had talks with the elector of Saxony, who made it clear that he wanted nothing to do with the scheme. He now hoped for support from Bohemia.

What materialized was not an army of knights but a body of men enlisted and paid by Sickingen. In August 1522 he sent his written challenge to the archbishop-elector of Trier; even raids like this had their formalities, which were meticulously observed. Manifestos were sent to the inhabitants of Trier: they were to be released from the 'grievous anti-Christian law of the popes' and introduced to evangelical freedom. The committee in Nuremberg – the so-called imperial government – urged peace. Sickingen replied proudly that he intended to establish a new order in the empire. Did they intend to summon him before the imperial supreme court? If they did, he had his own court, and it consisted of horsemen and cannon. He also hinted that the emperor approved what he was about to do and would not object if he punished the archbishop of Trier, who had been paid so many crowns by France, for his perfidy. His plan was to take the city of Trier by a surprise attack. A few of the smaller ruling princes also wanted to take part.

Archbishop Albrecht of Mainz arranged for safe passage across the Rhine within his territory. Sickingen had organized his expedition as a crusade: on their gaily coloured sleeves the horsemen bore the device 'Thy will be done, O Lord'; the watchword was 'Death or victory for the Gospel'. The commander issued instructions that the countryside and people were to be spared and the vines left untouched; it was a district of fine vineyards and to hack down the vines was a favourite means of waging war. At first his order was obeyed fairly well, the men contenting themselves with looting the abbeys and monasteries. Before Trier, however, the attacking forces came to an abrupt halt. Sickingen had dangerously underestimated his opponent. Archbishop Richard von Greiffenklau came from the old nobility, like himself, and his training had not been confined to prayers and religious processions. Torch in hand he rushed into the monastery of St Maximin, which might have served the enemy as a strong-point outside the city gates, and burned it to the ground; any tendency to come out in support of the attackers was held in check with an iron hand. He too had his mercenaries, who kept watch on the city walls. The nobility in the electorate, who were bound to the archbishopric by numerous family ties, had no intention of going over to Sickingen. The city was too large and too well defended to be taken by a force of a few thousand men. Discipline among the motley collection of troops, never very strict, broke down completely; plundering and burning the villages as they went, Sickingen's men, now reduced to an undisciplined rabble, withdrew. Many of them deserted because, instead of help and reinforcements, what arrived was bad news.

The archbishop's energies had also mobilized the friendly princes. The young landgrave of Hesse, still smarting under the indignity of Sickingen's raid on his territory, freely offered his allegiance. The Count Palatinate, Sickingen's former patron, also responded; he had long ago discovered that 'little Frankie had become Sir Francis', intent on overthrowing the courts of princes and aiming to become an elector himself. In marked contrast to Sickingen who, as if paralysed by his failure, returned to his castle and abandoned himself to gloomy meditation, the princes acted quickly and with vision. They had their own connections, and these functioned much more effectively than the rather vague affiliations of the attacker. Friendly potentates, as well as some less friendly, added their assistance, all united because a fundamental interest of their class was at stake. All reinforcements, whether of knights or troops, were stopped by threat or force of arms. A detachment of fifteen hundred recruits for Sickingen was on its way from Brunswick; the young landgrave of Hesse intercepted them and took them into his own service – so long as they were paid properly and punctually the landsknechts were prepared to fight under any flag. Showing admirable tactics, the princes did not attack Sickingen immediately but moved against his less powerful and widely scattered supporters. First to suffer for his relative was the naïve and indiscreet Hartmut von Kronberg; he lost both his castle and his possessions and went into exile, spreading discouragement wherever he passed. The small consortium of princes also found allies among the free cities of the empire. Castles were stormed everywhere, many old scores being settled. A leading part in these activities was taken by the Swabian League; the only political union in the fragmented empire to possess some degree of cohesion, it disposed of men, money and a brutal but able commander-in-chief in the person of George of Truchsess. The knights were forbidden to associate or band together in any way and, unlike the ineffective decrees issued by the imperial government, this order was backed by force of arms. The knights capitulated; there is no record of a single bold and daring action. Nor did Sickingen's own role and end do much to confirm his great reputation as a national hero, except that he died bravely among the ruins of his castle, instead of running away like most of his peers.

He had grown heavy and slow and, although only forty, already looked an old man; in the portrait done of him at this time the bold lines of his early years have given way to puffiness. He suffered from gout; the astrologers, who in his youth had prophesied great things, now tormented him with their gloomy predictions. He is said to have practised alchemy in his castle, having as protégé a 'second Faust' who busied himself with 'mystic things'. During his last winter he attempted only political alchemy: ties with France were planned, and with Bohemia. While round him everything collapsed, his plans grew more far-reaching and extravagant. He had lost all grasp of essentials. Instead of the powerful and famous fortress of Ebernburg, which housed all his treasures as well as his best artillery, he chose the stronghold of Landstuhl. Here he hurriedly and nervously added brickwork to the towers; three rows of thin palisades were constructed round the hill below the castle, although this was dominated by a neighbouring hill from where it was in full view. In April 1523, in changeable weather, he was looking from his tower, in the hope of seeing help from Lower Germany or Bohemia, when a troop of horsemen came in sight; Sickingen greeted them hopefully. They tethered their horses to trees, and shortly afterwards columns of waggons appeared with artillery; the hilltop was occupied. The landgrave of Hesse, now a young man of twenty and dressed in the uniform and baggy breeches of a landsknecht, insisted on personally training one of his large-bore cannon on the castle. The guns still had names, such as 'Lion of the Palatinate' or 'Wicked Elsa'. In Ebernburg Sickingen himself had the famous 'Nightingale', cast by Meister Stefan in Frankfurt and bearing the inscription 'Sweet and lovely is my song,/Hear it and your time is long'; it was a showpiece, over thirteen feet in length and weighing seventy-one hundredweight, but it had been left behind and did not fire a shot. The effectiveness of these pieces of heavy artillery, with their beautifully engraved inscriptions, was always considerably exaggerated in the records of the day; most of them fired only round stone balls and at very long intervals. Their moral effect may have been greater than their fire-power. The knights had felt safe in their impregnable fortresses for too long; they generally capitulated after only a few shots. Sickingen, however, fell victim to the new weapon. A well-aimed ball from a culverin on the dominating hill of the Geierfelsen struck the wall where he had gone to observe the bombardment; a beam was splintered and tore open his side. He had himself carried to a safe vault, where he listened to the 'unchristian shooting'; in a last letter to a friend he wrote: 'Although the ball grazed me slightly, it has done me no harm.' Gangrene set in. He capitulated. The princes entered the casemate and approached the dying man's bed. Sickingen doffed his cap to his old feudal lord and patron, the Count Palatinate, who brushed the gesture kindly aside. The landgrave was less considerate: 'Why did you overrun my country when I was still only a boy?' The archbishop of Trier asked: 'Franz, what reason can you give for that sudden attack on me and the poor people in my archbishopric?' – 'On that there is much to be said; nothing happens without a cause,' replied Sickingen defiantly. The chaplain elevated the Host; the princes bared their heads and said a Paternoster as their great adversary expired. The corpse was with difficulty forced into a chest and carried down the hillside to lie in state in the village church.

The princes did not linger. Sickingen's other castles, twenty-seven in all, were stormed and taken; Ebernburg Castle, which held out for a while, contained great booty. In order to prevent quarrelling three notaries were brought in to make a detailed catalogue of the treasure, which consisted of valuable costumes, tapestries, ammunition, cannon, weapons and money. The landgrave got the famous 'Nightingale'; the silver alone was valued at ten thousand guilders. The correspondence, a heavily mounted chest filled with material extremely compromising to many of the great ones in the land, was taken to safety and a great part of it destroyed. Letters from Luther, which would have done him great harm, were said to have been found; they have not survived.

Sickingen's death meant the beginning of the princes' domination in its more positive form. The small coalition of the three allies grew. The fear of the lesser nobility, and it had not been inconsiderable, disappeared; the mythical greatness of a still powerful knights' estate had proved to be an illusion. Landsknechts and large calibre cannon had put an end to the 'king of the Rhine' in a few days. Castles were now stormed wholesale and far beyond the limits of the Sickingen affair; the cities of Nuremberg and Augsburg took part, providing their excellent domestic artillery. The knights' strongholds were destroyed a great deal more effectively by breaching than by stone cannon balls, the breaching being done by the peasants who, rounded up for the purpose, co-operated willingly by tearing down the battlements and walls; in this way they acquired a skill in storming fortresses that they hoped soon to put to their own use. Many of the proud lords of these castles wandered the countryside as fugitives. We hear of one of them, Absberg by name, having escaped from his castle before it was burned to the ground, wandering the high roads for years with the dregs of society until the people of Nuremberg killed him while asleep in a thieves' doss-house.

Sickingen continued to stir people's imaginations for a long time, up to the nineteenth century. Most of his contemporaries took a detached and realistic view of him, but even they spoke in awe of what might happen were the knights to join forces with the peasants. The Bavarian chancellor, Leonhard von Eck, put these misgivings in a nutshell when he told his princes that if the peasants rose they would polish off the bishops for breakfast, the princes for lunch and swallow the knights by bedtime.

In the midst of these events and apprehensions Luther wrote a new treatise, *On Temporal Authority and the Extent to which It Should Be Obeyed*. It was written in the winter of 1522, a work of only passing significance that should not be cited, as it often is, to provide evidence of Luther's doctrines and views 'of the state'. He was without solidly based political opinion and had no knowledge whatever of any state. The historic moment at which he wrote the work is important because there were others, better qualified than he, who also had no clear conception whatever of the state or even of what was likely to happen from moment to moment. The imperial government was sitting in Nuremberg, but having outlawed Sickingen it soon began to have doubts whether it should proceed against him; it was receiving many appeals from people victimized by the league of the three princes. The heavy fine they extorted from the archbishop of Mainz for his tacit support of the condottiere was felt to be justified, but others were attacked on the most far fetched pretexts. The princes paid no more attention to the decrees of the imperial government than Sickingen; they simply continued his raids on a somewhat higher level. The Swabian League pursued its own interests. Both these groups possessed effective armies and weapons; the imperial government could only issue edicts, and even then its members were divided among themselves. The whole, loosely constructed government of the estates, which had been so laboriously built up, collapsed. The cities had sent a delegation to the emperor in Spain which, after spending two months on the journey, was coolly received; in the end it was decided that the emperor should send a commissioner, one of the high Burgundian nobles, to Germany to put matters right. The state as Luther saw it, if indeed he saw or understood it at all, consisted of an emperor in Madrid, who was represented in Germany by a commissioner; an imperial government in dissolution; ruling princes who united in various combinations to oppose the imperial government or else furthered their own interests exclusively; free cities of the empire, each of which pursued its own business interests; armies of landsknechts engaged in campaigns throughout the length and breadth of the country – and as a background to this anarchy the muffled anger and resentment of the great masses of peasants, who were already hammering out their scythes and turning them into pikes.

Since no one at this time had a clear idea of the state or of the German form of government, the Augustinian monk, who still wore his habit, could hardly be expected to know better. He exhorted the people to repentance; this was the method he knew and had mastered. True to his unruly nature he lay about him in all directions. His Gospel, the pure, clear Word of God, was threatened. His first target had been the bishops. The princes persecuted the Gospel, especially his enemy Duke George who ruled the other half of Saxony on his very doorstep. Now he raised his hand against them. He addressed the treatise to his elector's brother and co-regent Duke John – there was still no unified rule even in this electoral half-state. Frederick the Wise shilly-shallied and stuck to his old faith; his brother had allied himself more closely to Luther but, because his ponderous soul struggled dully for enlightenment, he listened to other prophets as well. There were many such prophets. But for Luther the Word was so clear and unambiguous that he had no doubts about its interpretation.

In his Epistle to the Romans Paul had said 'Be subject unto the higher powers'. Luther did not read this historically as the missionary's considered advice to his flock to submit to the laws of the Roman Empire, which was a state with powerful government machinery and an established judiciary, to whose privileges Paul himself laid claim when he cited his Roman citizenship and expected protection as a result. The Epistle was addressed to a small group of Christians in the world metropolis of Rome; to Luther it was God's Word, God's commandment, and was valid for any age and under any circumstance. He translated the Greek word *exusia* by 'authority', but the German authorities, which were very numerous and often very questionable, were quite different from those of ancient Rome: they were emperors, kings, princes, councils of the independent cities, as well as petty rulers and even landowners.

Luther's attitude to authority, which ranged from the emperor down through the princes to the junkers and landed gentry, was in no way humble, however. He used strong language to them: 'Your tyranny and mischief will not, cannot, shall not be tolerated for long. My dear princes and rulers, you must learn to accept the fact that God will not suffer it any more. The world is no longer as it used to be when you hunted and drove the people like game.' The bishops 'have become worldly princes ... they have engineered a subtle reversal: they are supposed to rule inwardly through the Word of God, but they rule outwardly over castles, towns, countries and peoples, and torture the souls by committing unspeakable murders.' Similarly the temporal rulers 'can no longer grind and squeeze their subjects, piling levy on levy, tax on tax, letting loose a bear here, a wolf there ...' Sentences of this kind were understood and assimilated. But it was too much to expect the ordinary people to grasp Luther's crucial and fundamental thesis of the two kingdoms, from which he never deviated. There had to be temporal authority, God had ordained it, but it concerned the outward life exclusively. Its task was to have evildoers punished, and it had been given the sword for this purpose; but when authority arrogated to itself power over the soul as well it became tyranny. Its power did not extend to the conscience. Christians were the voice of conscience. Basically Luther still saw them as Paul did, as a small flock in the midst of unbelievers. 'The world and the great mass of people are and remain unchristian, even though they are all baptized and call themselves Christians. But Christians are few and far between, as the saying goes.' Luther's reading of the Bible always took precedence over contemporary life and its problems. Christians were destined to be long-suffering and steadfast; this was what Paul had declared, at the same time promising his flock that they had but a short time to wait – God's new kingdom was at hand. When Luther wrote sentences of this kind they met with much less understanding. The peasants considered they had been long-suffering long enough.

Luther by no means overrated those in authority. He told the princes to their faces that most of them were rogues, or at best fools. A truly Christian government was not to be expected; to govern a whole country according to the Gospel 'is as if a shepherd were to put wolves, lions, eagles and sheep together into a fold ... telling them: now graze and live meekly and peaceably together, there is no gate to the fold' – the sheep would not live long.

'Therefore we must be at great pains to keep these two governments apart, letting them exist side by side, one to make us godly, the other to create outward peace and prevent evil works; neither is sufficient in the world without the other.' This sort of thinking was possible in a monk's cell or in a study, but Luther had stepped out into the world and found himself up against the borders of the kingdoms he was so intent on keeping apart. Was the true Christian also permitted to wield the sword? This was a burning question and has not been conclusively answered to this day. His view was: 'No Christian should wield or invoke the sword on his own behalf or that of his cause, but he both may and should wield and invoke it for another, in order that wickedness be checked and piety protected.' Who were these others and who were the wicked ones? Still more problematically he wrote: 'Question: May I not use the sword on behalf of myself and my cause, if I am of the belief that in so doing I am not seeking my own ends but punishing evil? Answer: Such a miracle is not impossible, but it is very rare and dangerous. Only if the Spirit is rich enough, can it come about.' This is the most dangerous passage in the treatise *On Temporal Authority*. Luther himself was thoroughly alarmed and turned to the Bible for guidance. Using the dialectical method in which he had been trained, he placed contradictory statements side by side. Samson said: 'As they [the Philistines] did unto me, so have I done unto them'; Solomon said: 'Say not, I will do so to him as he hath done to me.' Samson, in Luther's view, had been appointed by God to save the Children of Israel; thus he was not acting on his own behalf but in the service of others. 'But no one can follow this example unless he is a true Christian and filled with the Spirit. When reason tries to do likewise it will certainly claim that it is not seeking its own ends, but it will be wholly mistaken. Because without grace it cannot be done. Therefore first become like Samson and then you can do what Samson did.' Without a doubt he saw himself as Samson bringing down, by God's grace, the pillars of the Temple of Baal.

But he also spoke with the wisdom of Solomon, holding up to his duke a 'mirror for princes'. The two sides of his nature, the uncouth

371

giant and the prudent counsellor, were inseparably mixed; together they make the man Luther. As always with him, much of the treatise is a kind of soliloquy; then suddenly he remembers that he has been invited to speak on urgent problems of the day. He had not yet founded a new Church, and he was still outlawed as a heretic, but false prophets were abroad and they also threatened him and his newly proclaimed teaching. Luther was conciliatory, as he had been when he returned to Wittenberg. Only God could judge souls. 'Hence it is vain and impossible to order someone, or compel him by force, to believe this or that ... On what grounds does foolish worldly might presume to judge and control so secret, spiritual, hidden a thing as faith?' Such compulsion leads only to lies and dissimulation, 'for the proverb "thought is free" is true'. Although pleading his own cause he spoke not for himself alone but also for those others who had put forward heretical views: 'Heresy can never be put down by force. A different approach is needed; it is not a fight or a matter for the sword. The Word of God must fight and if this does not avail, no worldly power will avail, though it soak the world in blood. Heresy is a spiritual thing, it cannot be hewn down by an axe, consumed by fire or drowned by water.'

This again pleased many, who later cast it in his teeth when he spoke in a much less conciliatory manner. He extended his comments to include topical questions. The legally trained councillors at the Saxon and other courts were in fact his strongest advocates and supporters, but it never entered his head to spare them or try to win their support. Always suspicious of laws and privileges, he was still more so of the jurists with their manuals. In addressing Duke John he likened him to the head of a household with a family to look after: his attitude to his subjects should be that of a good paterfamilias, not thinking to himself, 'the country and its people are mine, I will do as I please, but I will do what benefits and helps them.' He warned him to be wary of trusting his advisers, those 'bigwigs', nor should he listen to the braggarts 'who hound and provoke him to start a war' over some castle or other. He should administer punishment, but prudently and leniently, 'lest in taking up a spoon he put his foot on a pitcher'. In judging he should be guided by common sense, and this applied to all human beings in their behaviour to one another; 'But if you lose sight of love and the law of nature you will never succeed in pleasing God, even though you have devoured all the law books and works of lawyers in the world. On the contrary, the more attention you give to them the further they will lead you astray. A good and true judgment can only be pronounced freely of one's own accord; it must never, and can never, be pronounced from books.'

Luther wrote the little treatise *On Temporal Authority* in the winter of

1522; it was published in the spring of 1523, when Sickingen's strong-hold was being forced by the princes. The collapse of the knights was the first severe blow suffered by Luther's cause. Say and write what he would, the rebellion was laid at his door. He had called for an assault on the first and highest authority of all – the Church. He had threatened the princes. These now turned to their own affairs, and they had little to do with Luther. The expectation was: 'The pseudo-emperor is dead, the pseudo-pope will soon be dead too.'

# 29

# Twilight

EVERY innovator, whatever his views, was now referred to as a disciple of the 'Lutheran sect', not only in Germany but in France, Italy, England and Spain as well. Luther protested against this: 'What is Luther? The teaching is not mine. . . . What have I done, poor, stinking sack of worms that I am, that Christ's children should be called by my unholy name? No, dear friends, let us have done with partisan names and call ourselves Christians, after Him whose teachings we have.' But 'Lutheran' had now become the label attached to heretics, having taken the place of the earlier and ominous sounding Waldensian, Picardian, Hussite and Bohemian. His followers were scattered; they included preachers, influential citizens and members of city councils, a number of princes, simple people who read his writings, and peasants who could not read but knew individual sentences out of them. Very different ideas – religious, political and social – were inferred from the things he said and wrote.

Outlawed by imperial edict, Luther had returned to Wittenberg against the wishes of his elector, although for the present he was allowed to reside there unmolested. He could preach and write. His pamphlets were printed and pirated; he neither received nor asked any payment for them. His income amounted to 'nine old *schock*', or rather less than nine guilders. He lived in a little room in his old Augustinian monastery, where he slept on a straw mattress with a blanket over him; after he was married he said laughingly that his bed had remained unmade for a whole year. For the time being he was not allowed to lecture at the university, because this might have been interpreted as a deliberate flouting of the Edict of Worms and thus made things difficult for the elector. His letters were delivered by messenger and 'on special occasions' by friends and pupils. It was easy to intercept or break them open; not a few vanished, others were forged. From time to time he received a modest present: a small keg of beer or wine, some game. He still wore the habit given him by the town council on his return to Wittenberg.

Round him he had a small group of helpers. Numerous fugitives turned up, preachers who had been thrown out, former monks, even nuns. At Easter 1523 a small party of nine nuns of noble birth, who had fled from the convent at Nimbschen, were set down outside Luther's front door and handed over to him by some citizens of Torgau who had helped them to escape. Among them were a sister of his 'father' Staupitz, two von Schönfeld sisters, two von Zeschau sisters, and a twenty-four-year-old girl named Katharina von Bora. Faced by these overawed nuns, still wearing their habits and completely without means, Luther felt more than a little helpless. 'I feel so sorry for them, they are a wretched little bunch,' he wrote to Spalatin, to whom he had to turn immediately for help, because their aristocratic families would have nothing to do with their prodigal daughters. They had placed their surplus children once and for all in the charitable institutions of their ancestors, and the requisite donations had been given; if the girls now chose to run away, their future was their own affair. Luther deplored the cruelty of the parents and relatives. He also had bitter things to say of his fellow citizens of Wittenberg: they now had the Word of God in abundance, but when a short time previously he had tried to raise ten guilders for a poor person, the money could not be found. He searched for people willing to have the nuns in their homes – he could not very well keep them in the monastery – but people were not exactly eager to do that particular act of kindness; a nun who had run away was still considered a disreputable person. They had no accomplishment beyond praying and singing, and knew nothing whatever about housekeeping; in all probability, or so it was said, all they were interested in was a quick marriage. Luther did his best to find husbands for them, if only to prevent a still greater scandal, recommending his wards by letter and word of mouth. It is unlikely that any of them were ravishing beauties, because a beautiful daughter was not put in a convent but kept at home to make a good match. And so, in addition to his preaching and writing, Luther now found himself involved in the everyday practical life of a small-town community, in problems of marriage, board, lodging, clothing. Luther was no longer young; in those days a man was on the verge of old age at forty and, if not a cleric, was usually already a grandfather. Many of his friends urged Luther to marry; others, like Melanchthon, felt uneasy and advised against it. He hesitated. Fear of what the world would think, let alone of the howls of his enemies, is unlikely to have played any part in this. He was slandered enough as it was, and the story of the escaped nuns was a godsend to his calumniators; that the apostate and his friends were living in sin with these women was taken for granted by all who had been raised on the old doctrine that human nature was uncontrollably sinful. There was no lack of informers in Wittenberg, and every step Luther took was watched. Apart from patently malicious pamphlets nothing has come to light that, judged by the standards of ordinary morality, can be used to denounce his way of life; and this despite the fact that Luther behaved with total unconcern for the opinions of others. He was kind, always ready to lend a helping hand, easily taken in and often landed in embarrassing situations by people anxious only to exploit these qualities. It was for this reason that the cautious Melanchthon was suspicious of the nobly born virgins and their marriage plans; he was afraid that one of them might ensnare his Doctor Luther. For the nimblest and most capable of them, Fräulein Katharina von Bora, Luther found a home in the house of his friend and neighbour Lucas Cranach, who ran a large and very comfortable household. She seemed a little haughty, Luther thought, and had her eyes on the students who came of good families; when she formed an attachment with a son of the great Nuremberg patrician family of Baumgärtner, Luther, his hopes aroused, did his utmost to foster it.

He himself was not thinking of marriage. He did not even know whether he would be able to remain in Wittenberg, because during the debates of the imperial government in Nuremberg the question of an imperial enforcement order against the Electorate of Saxony had again been mooted. The Saxon envoy tried to persuade Frederick the Wise, and not for the first time, that the difficult doctor should be spirited out of the country with all due decorum before even worse calamity befell the electorate. There seems to have been talk of a further spell of protective custody in some castle; it caused Luther to write to Spalatin, for transmission to the elector: 'Do not imagine that I am going to creep into a corner again.' The more uncertain and precarious the outlook became for him personally, the blunter and more reckless became his language to those in power. A letter to Duke George of Saxony, who had banned Luther's translation of the Bible in his country, began: 'Stop raging and storming against God and His Christ, instead of at the service I have rendered, most ungracious Prince and Sovereign!' The pamphlet in defence of the sevenfold sacrament written by, or on the instructions of, King Henry VIII of England and directed against Luther was not couched in delicate language either: 'The most ravenous wolf in hell took him by surprise and swallowed him, and now he lies in the nethermost part of his belly, half alive, half dead ... and out of this satanic wolf's filthy mouth he belches his foul blasphemies ...' Luther's reply to 'Heinz of England' was no gentler: 'If a king may shamelessly spit out his lies, I may be permitted joyfully to cram them down his throat again.' The point at issue, he claimed, was very simple: Henry wanted to know for how many centuries a doctrine had been practised by the Church, whereas he wanted to know if it was based on the Scriptures. For the rest, he had no more time to give to the question: 'I have the German translation of the Bible on my hands, as well as other matters, and cannot spend any longer rooting about in Heinz's excrement.' The sensitive humanist, Thomas More, replying for the king, adopted a similar tone. Writing from the court of the pleasure-loving Henry VIII he waxed indignant over the 'bacchanals' and festivities in Wittenberg, the 'excessive womanizing', the 'bridal pairs first sunk in deepest shame, then ruined by illness and privation, and finally taking up thieving to escape.'

Even among Luther's friends there were always some who were embarrassed by the coarseness and bluntness of his language, especially when directed at people of such eminence; no very substantial difference is discernible between Luther's uncouth German and the humanist's more elegant Latin. The only significant aspect of these pen battles is that the humanist faction, still very influential in high places in every country, began increasingly to turn its back on Luther; the leader of this trend was Erasmus who also, though in a more polished style, was unable to resist making painful references to the illness and distress of an adversary like Hutten. A quite disproportionate part of the whole literature of the time is filled with abuse, calumnies, insinuations about personal conduct, or those comparisons with the innocent animal world which intrude to this day into politicians' speeches. The more Luther confined himself to writing German, and the more he appealed directly to the masses, the less he was able to resist the use of coarse and ever coarser turns of phrase. It was precisely this that alienated the humanists, who derived their arrogance *vis-à-vis* the profane masses from their beloved Horace. They wanted to engage in dispute only with people of their own kind, using a somewhat choicer phraseology, though this, too, was a form of vulgarity. Generally speaking they disdained to use illustrations, posters or caricatures, relinquishing these media to very effective use in popular propaganda. Lucas Cranach's workshop issued a 'passional' that contrasted scenes from Christ's life of suffering with the splendour and magnificence of the court of Antichrist in Rome; a monster in the form of a monk was used by both sides to point dire morals. Luther's enemy Cochläus published a 'seven-headed Luther', who spoke with seven different voices, as monk, doctor, devil, bishop, and peasant agitator shouldering his club. Anything that promised success was published; the publishers and illustrators were not fastidious, nor did they adhere too strictly to party lines. Cranach, Luther's sponsor and friend, did not scruple to work for Archbishop Albrecht of Mainz or Duke George of Saxony. In a postscript to a malicious attack on Luther by Murner, the Strasbourg publisher Grünenberger excused himself thus to his fellow citizens: he had been urged not to touch this book but, as everyone would understand, he depended on his publishing business for his living and so had accepted this commission like any other.

Luther was now forced to tackle the subject of 'trading and usury'. The Fuggers had commissioned their protégé Dr Eck to take part in a disputation in Bologna and defend usury. According to canon law to accept any interest at all on a loan was usury; Eck was in wholehearted sympathy with an economic development that had long ago ceased to pay any attention to the ban on interest. He did not speak as a prescient political economist, however, but in defence of the practice of his employers, and of the Curia which had no scruples whatever about paying the highest interest rates on loans from its bankers while maintaining the principle of the ban on interest. Because of this Eck was violently attacked by Luther's supporters; the polemics of the day all contain references to the Bologna disputation.

As a monk Luther was totally ignorant of the matter, and the Bible gave him very little help. As usual, he illustrated from his own experience. Man's duty was to lend his neighbour a helping hand, to succour him when he was in need, with no thought of reward; this was his own way with his 'nine old *schock*', and later when his income became somewhat larger. One should give freely, he wrote, or at the most expect to recover the sum lent, but nothing beyond it. Still, he saw that the outside world acted differently. Once again he addressed himself to the few who 'understand the Gospel'; even among the merchants and financiers there ought to be some who would listen to him and the Word. The chief motto of all finance was: 'I want to sell my merchandise at the highest price I can ... is that not equivalent to saying "what do I care about my neighbour?"' This was not only contrary to the commandment to love one's neighbour as oneself, it was also contrary to 'natural law'; it was exploiting the needs of one's fellow man, 'for what is sold to him is not just the merchandise on its own. There is also the fact that he needs it.' One should not sell for the highest price obtainable but on the principle of the right price, of fairness. This was not Luther's own idea, it had long been a subject for discussion in scholastic inquiries. His tract *On Trading and Usury* was a sermon: 'Take heed that you do no harm to your neighbour, rather than seek to gain something for yourself.' Having said this, he at once asked: 'But where are such merchants to be found?'

He realized that it was hard to determine the price of an article when it depended on a great many factors, on transport, fluctuations in production, and business expenses. It was fair and right 'for a merchant to get sufficient to pay for his expenses, his trouble, his labour and his risk.' Even a farm labourer had to have food and reward for his work.

What he proposed was that the secular authorities should appoint reasonable and honest people to assess and fix the prices, as was already the practice in certain places; 'But we Germans have other things to do, we have to drink and dance, rather than attend to such governmental regulations.' Luther's naïve simplicity seems a little less naïve when one reflects that economically enlightened governments of later centuries, whatever their ideologies, have not progressed beyond the idea of official price regulation. But he was able to give no more definite advice than to follow the Bible: every man was worthy of his hire; how this worth was to be assessed only conscience could decide.

He had heard a great many stories of the tricks and wiles of merchants and financiers; he wrote of hoarding, stockpiling, monopolies. 'These are selfish practices, and countries and cities should not tolerate them; if princes and those in authority were to exercise their functions properly, they would forbid them. For such merchants behave exactly as if God's creatures and goods had been created and provided for them alone, as if they desired to take them from others and dispose of them according to their own mischievous designs.' Only strict laws and supervision could prevent this. 'These people are not worthy to be called human beings or live among men ... the secular authorities would do right to take from them all they have and drive them out of the country.' When Luther wrote in this vein he found widespread agreement, and not only among the ordinary people. We have already seen how, in a brief order, the emperor, the highest authority of all, put an end to ideas of this kind. The estates knuckled under.

His faith in the intervention of authority was not blind. The monopolies and large companies were the main evil; they raised prices and sucked everyone dry, every penny 'has to sink down their pipe and be washed away'. 'Kings and princes should look into this and strictly forbid such things by law. But I hear they are up to their necks in it, and the word of Isaiah is fulfilled: "Thy princes are companions of thieves." Meanwhile they hang thieves who have stolen a guilder or half a guilder and associate with those who rob all and sundry, stealing beyond all measure and proving the truth of the proverb: one law for the rich and another for the poor.'

Other problems confronted him. Luther always responded to specific situations; he wrote for the moment. He had condemned celibacy; now he had to express his views on marriage, and not merely in generalized statements about Adam and Eve. The canonic rules governing impediments to marriage, which had been piling up for centuries, were still universally operative; they had developed into an esoteric legal doctrine. A person who had unwittingly transgressed one of its clauses

379

could buy himself out of his predicament only with costly dispensations, or else had to expiate his sin by submitting to severe penalties. Luther resorted to polemics and simplification. First he issued a poster announcing which bans on marriage, in his opinion, should still be observed. This he immediately elaborated upon. He began his treatise *On Married Life* by saying: 'Although I am apprehensive and do not like to preach on married life, the fact that I carry through what I put my hand to is going to cause me and others a great deal of trouble ...' His surmise was correct; scarcely anything else he wrote led to such bitter arguments. Celibacy had been a controversial issue for centuries; it still is. Marriage and authority over marital problems constituted two of the Church's most essential positions; they enabled it to intrude deeply into everyday life.

Luther started by attacking the 'papal laws', which had established countless impediments to marriage; in this the Bible was once again his sole authority. It preached that man and woman were created by God to grow and multiply; this ruled out celibacy. The vows of chastity were 'composed of spiders' webs, or in other words of human laws, and sealed with iron locks and bars.' This contradicted God's will and work. But, said Luther, he had also been accused of destroying marriage; this he denied categorically. If anybody was tearing marriage to shreds it was the pope with his regulations on marriage impediments. Luther enumerated eighteen of these, including degrees of relationship down to the third and fourth generation; one was forbidden to marry one's god-child, the sister of one's deceased betrothed, and there were similar strange clauses. For Luther the main point was that dispensation could be bought: 'But if you have money you may do it.' At this time he could have had no inkling that discussions on dispensations, and the more far-fetched clauses of the canon law, would take their place in history and bring about England's severance from Rome.

At the moment Luther was concerned with the simpler problems he encountered among his penitents. What should a husband do when a wife refused to fulfil her 'conjugal duties'? He had started his treatise with a self-exhortation: 'Go to it with a will'; this is what he now did, without a great deal of thought. 'There are no doubt cases when a pig-headed, obstinate wife shows no concern even if her husband has ten lapses from chastity. Then it is time for the husband to say: if you won't someone else will; if my wife won't, I'll take the wench.' Scarcely any other of Luther's sayings has been seized upon with such relish to illustrate his morality; his contemporaries did so. He had no intention of being flippant. He advised the husband first to give his wife several warnings and then denounce her, 'so that her pig-headedness shall be known publicly and be rebuked before the community. If she still refuses, put her away, abandon Vashti and take an Esther as King Ahasueras did' in the Bible.

But Luther quickly tired of this question; he wanted 'to stop talking of conjugal duty', about which there had been so many insidious sermons preached, 'and let it be'. He intended soon to speak of higher things, because the runaway monk took an exalted view of marriage. He strongly opposed the practice of slandering women as merely a necessary evil – a favourite theme since the days of the pagan poets. Such thoughts were unchristian, 'moreover it is my opinion that if women wrote books they would write the same thing of men.' 'God said of Adam: "It is not good that the man should be alone; I will make him an help-meet for him." So, as you see, he calls woman good and a help.' He did not portray marriage as a bed of roses. The wife had to 'cradle the child, wash its napkins, make the bed, suffer vile smells, keep vigil at night, soothe its cries, heal its sores and pox'; the husband had to 'look after his wife, support her, work, endure worries here and worries there ...' It was these little tasks that one had to accept willingly to please God. Labour and an early death in childbirth were still the almost inevitable lot of the majority of women; 'Remember, Greta dear', one should say, 'that you are a woman and that this work that is fulfilled in you pleases God; take joyful comfort in His will and commit yourself to Him ... You are dying in a noble cause and in obedience to God.' There was more to be said about marriage, but of this he was still ignorant; he would only say: 'Of the further benefits and pleasures to be derived from this state when it is successful, when husband and wife love one another, are united, cherish each other and so on, I will say nothing, lest someone shuts me up and tells me I am talking of things of which I have no experience ... What I say is in accordance with the Scriptures, and for me these are more certain than any experience.'

There was no problem, from the worries of his parishioners to those of the imperial government in Nuremberg, on which Luther did not have to give his views. Although his position in Wittenberg was both insecure and provincially drab and insignificant, the influence of his words was far-reaching and constantly growing. The early history of the Reformation was local history, and its details must be sought in individual localities and countries; its progress varied greatly from place to place and often extended over many years. What becomes very clear is the fact that Luther had produced no hard and fast doctrine and was himself undergoing constant development. Individual points were singled out, abandonment of the old faith was revealed in individual symbolic actions, which sometimes were violent and accompanied by the destruction of images and the gutting of churches, and sometimes took the form of cautious, or even officially prescribed, changes in the ritual. Frequently the signal of revolt was the taking of the chalice by the layman (the 'Bohemian' form of Communion, as it was called). It was with the greatest horror and displeasure that the emperor and his brother Ferdinand learned that even their sister, Queen Isabella of Denmark, was accepting the Communion cup and that another sister, Queen Mary of Hungary, inclined towards the new teaching. In Sweden the first signs of a reformation came when the national movement demanded liberation from Danish sovereignty and the appointment of a Swedish noble, Gustav Vasa, as a national king. Denmark became the scene of new disturbances and new opposition to the emperor's plans for world power; Scandinavia had been included in his schemes. Political and religious questions were inextricably intertwined.

To have been in Wittenberg, to have studied with Melanchthon and been instructed by Luther, became regarded as the great qualification fitting a man spiritually and intellectually to return to his homeland and embark on reform. Bible translations in the vernacular and sermons in local dialects – even in idioms that had not yet developed a written language, such as the old Prussian spoken in the territory of the Order of Teutonic Knights, the Wendish spoken in Lusatia, and Finnish – became distinguishing features of the new teaching. The church service was celebrated differently everywhere. In some places, in Sweden, for example, the Church hierarchy remained intact with its bishops and archbishops; the confiscation and utilization of Church property, monasteries and religious establishments continued to present a motley picture for a long time to come. The Swede Olaus Petri and the Dane Hans Tausen were two of the Scandinavians who spread Luther's ideas actively in their own countries. But it is only in retrospect, and then only by dint of radical simplification, that one can identify a Protestant 'party'. People certainly protested and there were widespread reforms, but no cohesion existed between all these various movements. Luther was no legislator and had no desire whatever to be one. From the outset this was both the great weakness and the strength of the Reformation.

The adherents of the old Church were not united either. Bishops sympathized with the new teaching, while archbishop-electors tried to sever their ties with Rome or, like Archbishop Albrecht of Mainz, toyed with the idea of secularizing completely their already semi-secular sovereignty. The grand master of the Order of Teutonic Knights in Prussia – it is difficult to say to what extent this medieval survival was a religious order – had discussions with Luther in Wittenberg and then became the first to take the great step of turning his territory into a duchy. He married a Danish princess and paid homage, as his vassal, to the strictly orthodox king of Poland, for whom the extension of his power was more important than religious scruples. Here again political factors played a part, as well as strained relations with the emperor who, absorbed in his imperial plans and worries, had never shown the slightest interest in this outpost of the Holy Roman Empire. Wittenberg and the tiny room in which Luther wrote his tracts and pamphlets did in fact become an international focal point, in spite of the total unconcern of the reformer whose writings, not accidentally, were full of such phrases as 'let it take its course', 'however it turns out', 'we drunken Germans know no better'. 'But the Word must endure' – this was all that really mattered; and the Word was still proving very powerful.

It was not only the great lay figures and princes of the Church in Germany who were disunited. Confusion was compounded when the emperor and the pope fell out again. Relations between the two had never been of the best; so far they had observed a precarious truce. Religious matters were not in dispute; it was a question of power. Bitterly disappointed by his former teacher Hadrian, the Emperor Charles had pinned his hopes on the new Pope Clement vii, whose election he had furthered by every means and on whom he counted as a reliable supporter. The election had taken place under difficulties; the French faction was still powerful. Nevertheless, Leo's cousin had won in the final balloting; his diplomatic skill inspired confidence – as secretary of state he had managed the Curia's affairs for many years and he continued to run them on the same lines, as business transactions and negotiations, and by playing off one power group against another. He was industrious and circumspect, held his audiences punctually and fulfilled his ecclesiastical duties conscientiously, this last a cause of astonishment; his private life was unexceptionable, another unusual trait in a Renaissance pope. Well versed in philosophy and theology, he even had a knowledge of the applied arts. Clement was good-looking, with a longish face and finely chiselled features, probably somewhat stylized by his portraitist, Sebastiano del Piombo. He expressed himself fluently on highly complicated political issues and moved skilfully on the chessboard of world affairs. But at heart he was weak and insecure. The stigma of his birth made him fearful: he was the bastard son of Lorenzo the Magnificent's brother, who had been murdered in Florence Cathedral; according to canon law he should have been excluded from all high ecclesiastical office, but his cousin Leo had generously overlooked this. Now that he was pope, there were others who took a less lenient view. He never overcame the fear that his election might be challenged, possibly by a Council; it was a fear that his enemies of the moment nourished with constant threats.

He was, in any case, apprehensive and had good reason to be. A highly intelligent man, he knew better than those round him how weak the position of the papacy was and how dangerous the emperor's assumption of world power could become for him. Discounting completely the fact that Charles v was the Church's most loyal son, and in fact the only sovereign of the day on whom it could rely, he saw in the Spaniard only the man who ruled Naples and was now intent on grasping Upper Italy as well; if he succeeded he would surround the papal states on both sides – a nightmare of the territorially conscious papacy since the Middle Ages. As Clement saw it, his first task was to use all the arts of diplomacy to prevent this. France offered its assistance, and in playing France and the emperor off against each other he gambled away the position of the papacy. That in the course of this the greater part of Germany was also lost to the Church seemed to him of only secondary importance; he knew as little about the land beyond the Alps as other people in Rome. He was an Italian, with an Italian's pride in the intellectual standing of his people, in its art, which he continued to further as his cousin Leo had done, and above all in the great art of political manipulation. Looking ahead to the day when the papacy's unlimited authority would come to an end, he planned to assume the role of world arbiter. None of the great powers was prepared to see him in this role and they drove him from one end to the other of the small territory still left to him, until symbolically he ended up as a prisoner in his own castle of St Angelo, where Benvenuto Cellini removed the stones from his tiara and melted down its gold while the emperor's troops plundered the city and the Vatican more thoroughly than they had been plundered since the days of Alaric. This *Sacco di Roma* of 1527 is rightly considered the end of the High Renaissance in all its manifestations, its art included. We now give the name 'mannerism' to what followed it. In the sense that he attached more importance to the *maniera*, the style, of his diplomacy than to its content, Clement had been a political mannerist long before this catastrophe overtook him.

By contrast, the activities of the German princes and estates at their diets strike us as boorish and uncivilized; colourful as a fair, these meetings degenerated dangerously into scenes of wild fighting, like the peasant gatherings that took place simultaneously. The difference in class was evident only in the solemn modes of address and the expensive clothing; otherwise the pleasures of these princes and great lords were not far superior to those of their farm hands. Luther's everlasting complaints about his drunken countrymen were not chance outbursts, nor was he alone in making them. How many agreements, arrangements and alliances concerning matters of vital national importance were wrecked, simply because those taking part were no longer in a physical state to take in what was being said, is something that no history books or resolutions of the imperial diets tell us. The princes and nobles met, only to disperse in a fury; often they protested obtusely and stubbornly against perfectly reasonable measures that had been agreed to a moment before. Then something resembling a hangover descended on the august assemblies and the great men left again in despondent mood, having spent large sums of money, thus causing bitter complaints at home, not least in the country districts whose produce had to pay for the junketings.

Money always played a decisive role; everyone was short of it, the emperor himself, the princes, counts and knights. Only the cities were rich, and for this reason were hated and envied by all. But politically even they seemed to be paralysed. All their energies were devoted to trade and to the arts and crafts; it was their great age, and one of great prosperity, the greatest in the cultural history of the towns. The religious questions of the day were also discussed there with unprecedented fervour. Lay preachers preached and drew audiences beyond their dreams. Everyone engaged in discussions, the masters, the journeymen, the women, the serving maids; everyone knew the pros and cons of the catchwords and arguments. But in these prosperous communities there was hardly a man who realized the lateness of the hour, the urgent necessity for the strongest forces in the nation to unite and form a counterweight to the stubbornly advancing particularism of the princes.

The breach, which was only just becoming apparent, might possibly yet have been healed; reforms, energetically carried out, might yet have united those of good will among all shades of opinion. Reform of the Church, reform of the empire, as the result of a National Council held in a German city, was the order of the day. Agreement was reached at the Diet of Nuremberg, the Council was to meet in Speyer; the decision was almost unanimous, even the princes of the Church, who had their own grievances against Rome, attending. Once again hopes ran high. Were the nuncio to raise objections he could again be told of the dangerous ferment among the people: to enforce the Edict of Worms would lead to 'revolt, disobedience, death, bloodshed – to ruin and destruction everywhere.' As a compromise solution for their own use the princes agreed on a formula open to the widest interpretation: each estate would carry out the edict 'as far as possible'.

This 'as far as possible' embodies the whole policy of the imperial diets; it was not used for the last time at Nuremberg. A letter from the emperor in Madrid, delivered by his deputy Hannart, Vicomte de Lembeke, quickly put an end to the great plan for reform: it forbade the National Council, which did not take place. The empire was placed to some extent under the emperor's deputy, though even to say this is to say too much; the Vicomte acted rather as an observer, who sent accounts in Burgundian French to his distant master and was easily upset: 'Everyone wants the affairs of the Empire adjusted to his own taste; all call for government and justice, but no one is willing to subject his home or territory to either. Each wants to be master ...' And the Saxon envoy to the diet commented that not in centuries had the empire found itself in such strange straits.

This diet and the abandonment of the National Council, at a flick of the emperor's fingers, decided in 1524 the pattern of things for many years to come. Smaller, and increasingly hopeless, projects still continued to be discussed and likewise abandoned. If the emperor had no intention of appearing personally, perhaps it might be possible to elect a German king. But who should it be? Charles's brother Ferdinand hoped he might be chosen. But protests against the foreigner met this proposal at stormy meetings of the regional diets, revolts were threatened, and the archduke had even less money than his brother; the rich mines had long been in the hands of the Fuggers. Opposition also came from the emperor, whose brother's plans for kingship made him acutely uneasy. That Ferdinand had also cast his eyes on the electorate of Saxony caused him still further uneasiness; he did not wish to see too much power concentrated in his younger brother's hands. It was to this jealousy that Luther owed the fact that, for the moment at any rate, he was left in peace.

Duke George also had a mind to divest his cousin of his electoral privilege, on the pretext of carrying out the orders of the imperial government; the electors of Bavaria and Brandenburg both had their eyes on the kingship. The emperor took advantage of these overlapping ambitions. While he himself was growing into his role of emperor, he must have felt an increasing contempt for the princes as opponents. Always prone to be contemptuous of his fellow men, he now became unapproachable, a development which impressed his contemporaries enormously and was considered a sign of true majesty. His deliberateness – so marked as to amount to procrastination – which constantly drove those round him, and even his father confessor, to despair, often proved a source of strength. He forgot nothing and never lost sight of his goal, which was to make his dynasty great, greater than all the others. His frequently arbitrary behaviour only added to the fear and dismay he aroused in the vacillating princes. Addressing the elderly and now seriously ailing Elector Frederick in almost affectionate terms as his dear uncle, and adding that he now proposed to address him still more intimately as father, he proceeded to deal him a cruel blow by curtly refusing to sanction his sister's marriage to the Saxon prince elector, although the marriage had been agreed as compensation for the elector's assistance in the emperor's election. Frederick almost wept over this insult, which he had no option but to accept. Others who had helped in the election fared no better; not one received the promised bribe in full. They grumbled and started negotiating with France, which was more generous in money matters. These moves and countermoves, which had nothing to do with national questions and interests, and still less with religious ones, continued throughout Charles's reign. A French party was opposed by a Spanish one, but of an empire party there was no sign except in solemn and worthless resolutions and fine words. When he found it expedient the Catholic Francis I supported the German Protestants; when occasion offered the Protestant cities sought help from the Catholic emperor. The Curia took its allies wherever it could find them.

The papal nuncio Campeggio's first move was to organize a separatist league. In Nuremberg his keen eye had taken the measure of the princes. Only reluctantly had he allowed himself to be persuaded to undertake the mission, and his predecessor Aleander, after his unpleasant experiences in Worms, gave him explicit instructions how to handle the Germans: be careful, tread warily, avoid arrogance! Campeggio was so alarmed by Aleander's warnings that he refused to embark on the journey until he had made arrangements for his children's pensions. Soon he was to see that Aleander had not exaggerated. Nuremberg was a veritable hive of heretics: sermons against Rome were preached from the pulpits; in the Augustinian monastery thousands of believers received the Communion in both kinds, joined by the emperor's sister Isabella who lived in the castle; pamphlets were distributed. The city council's mandates, demanded by his predecessor in Worms, were forgotten. Campeggio observed the situation shrewdly, realizing better than previous legates that generalizations like 'the priesthood' or 'the temporal princes' would get him nowhere. Abandoning positions that were no longer tenable, he restricted himself to what was still feasible.

The nuncio presided at the coalition which met in Regensburg as a counter-measure to the National Assembly planned and convened for Speyer. The Archduke Ferdinand and the two Dukes William and Louis of Bavaria, who thereby withdrew their approval of the National Assembly, formed the nucleus of the coalition. Campeggio was not content with mere plans for a league. The Curia offered active support. The Bavarian bishops had to agree to divert a fifth of their revenues to the reigning Bavarian princes; in Austria the proportion was a quarter. Previously such a step would have been seen as an intolerable encroachment on the rights of the Church; now, however much they resented it, the bishops were forced to comply. The Curia ranged itself firmly behind the princes. They were given authority, in place of the bishops, to supervise the monasteries, and this meant a considerable increase in their power; the University of Ingolstadt was placed under their control. Stringent measures were taken to eradicate heresy. Other leading South German figures joined in, led by the archbishop of Salzburg, though not until he had negotiated in Rome a considerable increase in the size of his diocese. Germany was not yet split into a Catholic south and a Protestant north, but a beginning had been made. Some reforms were also agreed to. A mixed commission, consisting of both churchmen and laymen, was set up – this again an unheard-of step from the standpoint of the recent past; superfluous feast-days were to be abolished. An even more radical move was made to match Luther's innovations: a German translation of the Bible was to be prepared and a rejoinder to Melanchthon's *Loci communes* as a first dogmatic statement of the new faith.

It was a great diplomatic success for Campeggio; the dreaded National Council had been undermined even before the emperor issued his veto. A solid block of countries, whose rulers were loyal to the old Church, had been created, while simultaneously from other parts of the empire memoranda, full of bold proposals for reform, arrived for the meeting in Speyer. With true German thoroughness it was also suggested that first of all a comprehensive list of all previous documents dealing with complaints, questions in dispute and resolutions of the imperial diet should be compiled and published. Delegates from the cities actually held a meeting to discuss the motions to be submitted to the great National Assembly. When the emperor's veto arrived they hurriedly left Speyer and moved to Ulm, where they discussed counter-measures to the Regensburg coalition. They were joined by a number of counts and princes, of whom the most important was the young landgrave of Hesse; he had been won over to the new teaching in a talk with Melanchthon. What took place was little more than a conversation, the gist of which was that no one could hold aloof in such critical times.

The times were more critical than either of the opposing blocks – they were still very loosely knit – imagined. The serious threat of the fourth estate had often loomed over meetings of the imperial diet, but it had entered scarcely anyone's head that the peasants, who were not represented in any assembly of the estates, might take up arms and rise in revolt. Into the dispute over religious convictions, into the battle for reform, into the reorganization of spheres of sovereignty, into the total anarchy of existing political conditions, there now burst a new factor for which, as yet, there was no name: the social question. It was admitted that the peasant had been included in the class structure ordained by God, but his place was at the bottom of the scale as a servant or labourer, and the possibility that he might claim rights, or even betterment of his position, had never been voiced at any meeting of the diet. It was only in pamphlets that the peasant had occasionally been allowed his say, hoe in hand.

When Luther heard of the contradictory resolutions passed at Nuremberg, and the measures introduced by the emperor, he took up his pen again. Not without reason, he felt himself personally threatened: 'It seems, my dear princes and rulers, that you are in a great hurry to see me dead, poor, lone man that I am; and if you succeed, victory will be yours. If you had ears to hear, I would tell you a single thing. What if Luther's life meant so much in the eyes of God that, were he no longer alive, the life and reign of none of you would be safe, that Luther dead would bring misfortune on you all? God is not to be trifled with. Go ahead! Strangle and burn! I shall not weaken, please God. I am here and would kindly ask you, once you have killed me, not to waken me again and kill me a second time. I see that God has not given me rational people to deal with but, if I prove worthy, I am to be killed by German beasts exactly as if I had been torn to pieces by wolves or wild boar.' He was ready to die, he assured them, but in spite of all the edicts he was still alive. He quoted the two contradictory resolutions, with his comment. Then he threatened God's judgment on the insane and drunken German princes: 'What is it you want, gentlemen? God is too clever for you; He could easily make fools of you. He is also too powerful, He could easily make an end of you.' He quoted the Bible: 'He hurls the mighty from their seats – this applies to you, gentlemen, even if you have overlooked the fact.' He himself overlooked – or deliberately omitted – the second half of the Bible quotation: 'He lifts up those that are down.' His wrath was directed solely at the high and mighty who were responsible for these resolutions. He ended by asking all devout Christians to have pity on the 'insane, inane, puerile, imbecile fools', and pray with him: 'May God deliver us from them and in His mercy give us other rulers. Amen.'

Totally unversed in worldly matters, he had no idea where these better rulers were to come from or how God was going to deliver the countries of Germany from the old ones. He was completely dominated by the apocalyptical notion of a divine judgment that would break over the world like a tidal wave or some other manifestation of the inscrutable hand of God. Human hands were to play no part in it but simply to remain folded in prayer. But that his words would inevitably be understood as a call to revolt against the insane and imbecile rulers never occurred to him. He urged obedience to an authority which he represented as appointed by God and, almost in the same breath, as abandoned by God and the victims of His wrath. From all this the people drew the conclusion that it was now up to them to take God's wrath into their own hands and that they were not only permitted, but specifically directed, to do so.

It was in the midst of this pervading twilight that Luther entered the most momentous crisis of his life. He was unprepared. Up till this moment the Word, his word which he interpreted as the will of God, had proved superior to all other powers. The pope's domain in Germany lay half in ruins; the emperor had issued a powerless edict. Now for the first time the Word met stubborn resistance. Luther could not understand it. When he heard of the brutal persecution of his followers in the emperor's Netherlands, in Bavaria and Austria, he looked upon these martyrdoms, like the martyrdoms of old, simply as a sign that the good cause would soon be victorious. The speed of his advances had taken his breath away; in three years the world had been transformed. In a further two years, as he had announced in the Wartburg, the papacy would be finished finally and forever, while God, who had been so generous with His help, could get rid of the princes, who stood in the way of His Gospel, more rapidly still, at a single stroke. He did not think in historical or political terms but in biblical imagery. The Prophets, whom he was in the middle of translating, had been promised storms, rocks broke asunder for them, they were sent earthquakes and fire. Kings and rulers took council together against God's Word, but his favourite Psalm said: 'Thou shalt break them with a rod of iron; thou shalt dash them in pieces like a potter's vessel.' From the Wartburg he himself had written: 'The heavens are of iron, the earth of brass.' His words became reality; within a year the world, his world, was transformed again. He went to his great defeat like a blinded man; it meant the end of his irresistible assault and the collapse of all the varied hopes that had gathered round his name.

# 30

# The Battle of Pavia

AT THE beginning of 1525, the year of the great Peasants' War in Germany, which was the turning-point of the century, an event took place in Italy whose effect on the contemporary scene was no less significant. The Battle of Pavia, fought in the early hours of 24 February, was acclaimed in soldiers' songs, in magnificent tapestries and in highly coloured reports; contemporaries regarded it as one of the great feats of the age. Every nation, even as far away as Turkey, was affected by the outcome of the battle; in France it brought about a profound change in the whole life of the country. The emperor, who on the day of the battle was hundreds of miles away in Spain celebrating his birthday and deeply worried over the failure of his plans, was hailed as the victor. This success of his mercenaries raised him at one stroke to the pinnacle of his career; he seemed now to hold undisputed sway over a world empire. For Germany it meant the impending overthrow of every movement for reform, the peasants' risings, as it turned out, being bloodily crushed, with vital assistance from the landsknechts who had returned to their homeland from Pavia.

A word must be said about these landsknechts or mercenaries, because it was they, not the people, who fought the wars. The age to which the Reformation gave its name was a time of ceaseless wars and campaigns, interrupted only by insincere armistice agreements and peace treaties that were disregarded as soon as they were signed. Even those taking part in the campaigns scarcely knew what was going on. They frequently changed sides in the middle of a battle or else went home, only to fight at the next opportunity against the employer they had previously served. To speak of great national wars or religious wars is impossible, although national and religious antagonisms and moods were stressed loudly enough, and in certain countries, like France and Spain, were already beginning to dominate the scene.

The mercenaries, moreover, fought for money and booty. It is true that conscripted forces, militias, national contingents and contingents from the provinces and cities existed, but their importance was minimal. The landsknechts fought for the House of Habsburg-Burgundy, the House of Medici in Rome and other dynasties, provided these could raise the money. The mercenary system and the rising monetary economy were intimately connected, the great banking houses in Genoa and Augsburg playing a decisive role, because it was only rarely that the princes could finance their wars out of the grudgingly paid taxes. The campaigns were, or were intended to be, short; the bankers as a rule lent money only on quarterly terms, and even grants from the various estates, supposing they could be obtained at all, were always on a short-term basis. This accounts for the numerous campaigns that were broken off and only restarted a year later, and for others in which the inadequately paid mercenaries split up into robber hordes and ravaged the countryside, indifferent to whether it was enemy territory or friendly territory belonging to their employer.

Two main sources of manpower were available: the Swiss and the Germans. Thanks to the victories of their peasant armies over Austria and Burgundy, the Swiss, for half a century, were regarded as the most formidable soldiers; it was they who had set the seal on the superiority of infantry over mounted knights in armour. For a short period the confederation was courted by everyone and almost became a great power. High politics were pursued at the meetings of these simple peasants, who discussed bold and far-reaching plans, and for a time were able to contemplate the conquest of half, or all, of Lombardy. The pope, the emperor, France and German dukes all obtained their troops from Switzerland. The question of the 'pensions', in other words running bribes, offered by France played a very substantial part in the Swiss Reformation, as did that of the moneys paid out by the Curia; in the early days of his career the Zurich reformer Ulrich Zwingli received a papal pension in recognition of his support of the Swiss Cardinal Schiner, who looked after the Curia's interests among his fellow-countrymen with great skill and was rewarded with the red hat for his services.

Towards the beginning of the century, however, the German landsknechts had begun to challenge the supremacy of the Swiss. But the Emperor Maximilian, though hailed as their 'father', paid badly, being always short of money; hence the German soldiers also fought for France and England, in Italy, or wherever there were good prospects of pay and booty. The promises made by ruling princes being generally unreliable, landsknechts preferred to adhere to a proven leader with his own fighting unit, which he paid in advance and hired out to others. Sickingen had been a condottiere of this kind, and Georg von Frundsberg became famous as such, his name continuing to live on in songs for many years; there was also a Swabian by the name of Schertlin, whose booty brought him a title and a wealth of landed property and who, on one of his campaigns, was honoured by the emperor with the significant title 'Grand Marshal and Plunder Master'. The German landsknechts referred to themselves as an 'order', the Order of the Devout Landsknechts, and regarded themselves as an estate on their own, with their own code of honour, customs and conventions. Their uniform was extremely colourful and a great attraction to painters: the tunic was heavily cut, as if 'cut to shreds' in battle, instead of trousers they wore huge, baggy knee-breeches, which were not very practical for running away in, and from their heads waved plumes of ostrich feathers. The best illustrations of this colourful world were done by the Swiss mercenary Urs Graf, who signed his work with a dagger.

The colour and variety of their uniform and customs earned the landsknechts a surprisingly good 'press' that lasted for centuries. But their contemporary Sebastian Franck, in his *German Chronicle*, described them as one of the great scourges of the day – a scourge that made its appearance at the same time as the French pox, or syphilis – an irresponsible lot 'who, happy in the misfortunes of others, seek misfortune, wander needlessly through every country looking for war and leave wives, children and fatherland for the sake of huge monetary gain ... motivated not by obedience but by sheer wickedness, thirst for blood and wantonness ... and who grow rich by strangling, robbing and burning, and by corrupting women and orphans.' Very few became rich, apart from those in supreme command, who were not only brave soldiers, fighting pike in hand in the forefront of the battle, but able businessmen as well; they knew how to use the services of the banks for the purpose of depositing moneys gained from forced levies and booty, and had the wisdom to invest their takings in the security of landed property. The rank and file, who were anonymous nobodies, had no credit, served on a day-to-day basis and were subject to ruthless dismissal. The wandering landsknecht, mixing with the crowds of other wayfarers, was a stock character in all the tales, farces and chronicles of the time. Hans Sachs, using a palette very different from that of the painters, has described the life of these men, whom in his youth his friends had tried to persuade him to join. 'They lay in the slime, soaked in blood and grime, their clothes torn and tattered, filthy and battered'; with grey, haggard faces, their wet clothes crawling with lice, they gulped down their half-cooked food. Dysentery was rife in the camp, and the maimed were stumbling around everywhere; those who ran away were killed by the peasants, the survivors made their way wretchedly home. The young men paid no attention to the voice of an elderly, well-to-do citizen like Hans Sachs; there was never any lack of recruits at the recruiting centres. They were attracted by the colourful uniform and the free-and-easy life; death 'on the free and open heath' had no terror for them: 'The rat-tat-tat of the drum roll's call is ten times better than the pastor's drawl.' Soldiers' songs were popular, whether composed by those who knew the life or by a writer with a ready pen; some were written in a hotch-potch of languages picked up by the landsknechts on their campaigns all over Europe.

Panic and sudden retreat were common if the first onslaught of the tightly packed formation failed to break through. It was when the landsknechts took to flight that they suffered their greatest losses; they were butchered without mercy, and the numbers of their dead come near to exceeding those of the bloodiest wars of succeeding centuries. The Swiss had introduced this style of fighting, which the Italians called the 'mala guerra' or warfare without mercy. They really fought for their pay and did not spare themselves as the Italians had learned to do in the earlier campaigns, in which the condottieri, carefully husbanding their costly troops by clever manœuvring, had contented themselves with ruthlessly plundering the peasants, villages and small towns. The German landsknechts adopted this new style of fighting, and when they came up against their Swiss rivals the encounters were particularly savage; even when they found themselves on the same side there were serious brawls in camp, either between individuals or between whole gangs. Mutiny was a commonplace, and if pay and provisions were not forthcoming the men went on strike; it was not uncommon for a campaign to be brought to a halt by this, with victory round the corner. On such occasions the commander-in-chief had to intervene with the full force of his personality and financial credit; to help him he had a whole staff of jailers and jailers's assistants. There was an overseer in charge of the large number of harlots and women who, carrying their children and large leather bags for the booty, followed the campaign. The thieving rabble of hangers-on was far more dreaded than the fighting troops, both by the population and by the wounded and defeated on the losing side; no quarter was given. The peasants avenged themselves as best they could for countless outrages. Before a battle the commander would tell his men: 'Acquit yourselves well; if you don't beat the enemy, you won't escape the peasants!' The landsknechts' brutal treatment of the defeated revolutionaries in the German Peasants' War was only the climax of this whole brutalizing method of waging war; it had been learned and practised over many years.

The landsknechts have also earned another place in the history of warfare. They fought in close, well-organized formations and possessed a highly developed military hierarchy from the regimental commander at the top, down through the captains in charge of companies, to the common soldiers at the bottom under their sergeants and corporals. The rank and file landsknecht carried a long pike and a short sword; if he owned his own harquebus he also fought as a harquebusier. They paraded in their tactical formation, the square, whose forest of pikes in contemporary illustrations inspired artists to turn it into a compact square. The impact of this concentrated mass, reinforced by the pressure of those in the rear, was tremendous provided the terrain was suitable and it did not come up against artillery or a strongly fortified position. A spearhead was sent in front to breach the enemy position; if this was successful the main body, or striking force, followed up to deliver the knock-out blow. Before the battle the 'devout lands-knechts' knelt in prayer to ask God's blessing on their weapons. The engagement was sometimes preceded by individual actions and challenges. The battle was heralded by tremendous shouting and beat-ing of drums – the Swiss blowing their alpine horns. (In appealing to the peasants and mineworkers Thomas Müntzer also used the landsknechts' cry 'On, on, on!' as a slogan.) Landsknechts returned to the German lands from Italy and fighting in close formation under their captains and commanders defeated the straggling, badly led peasant forces. They were as indifferent to what they were fighting for as they had been at Pavia, where German mercenaries also fought on both sides, peasant fighting peasant or German peasants fighting Swiss alpine cowherds. War was a trade like any other.

The Emperor Charles had waged war against France with varying success. His late thrust into Provence from Italy had failed; his forces had to turn back and, not receiving any pay, dispersed in Lombardy where the greater part degenerated into plundering hordes. Francis I, having advanced again, now laid siege to Pavia, which was defended by Spanish and German troops. Charles's calls for help to his brother Ferdinand met with little response; the archduke was as deeply in debt as the emperor. All he could do was persuade the experienced leader Frundsberg to raise mercenaries on his own account and bring them to Italy, where he joined forces with Lannoy, the viceroy of Naples, who was coming up from the south. On the emperor's side were Spaniards, Germans, Neapolitans and north Italians; Francis I had his knights in armour – the flower of the French nobility – a strong contingent of Swiss mercenaries and five thousand German landsknechts. Those in command were more varied still: in the emperor's camp were the Bourbon Constable, the most powerful of the great figures of France, who was in revolt against his king, the Italian marquis of Pescara, the Burgundian Lannoy, Charles's former tilting partner and now viceroy of the Spanish stronghold of Naples; in addition to these were the German commanders of the landsknechts. Pope Clement had dispatched his legate, Aleander, to the king's camp while formally, though with many reservations, he was on the side of the emperor; he was sure the French would win.

The besieging forces of the French king were surrounded and besieged in turn by those of the emperor. Both sides were short of money, and there was the constant danger that the mercenaries would desert.

The opposing armies were in close proximity. It was winter, living conditions were bad and the food inadequate; February came, bringing still worse weather and still worse morale. At a council of war in the emperor's camp the view was expressed that the men could be held together for another three or four days, after which the situation would be hopeless. Frundsberg persuaded his men to stick it out a little longer; the lure of booty was strong, and the French king and his knights were rich.

They decided to attack at night. The main French position was in the Mirabello Park, the game preserve and hunting ground of the dukes of Milan; the fairly extensive stretch of woodland was surrounded by a strong wall. Spanish pioneers were to breach the wall, the landsknechts not being prepared to do that sort of job. The pioneers hacked away as quietly as they could at the hard wall, on which the French had posted hardly a sentry; the work went on until dawn was breaking and then the first imperial troops forced their way through the breach. In order to be able to recognize each other in the half-light they had put white paper shirts over their armour – their own underclothes presumably being too dark. The battle was fought in the park, on soft, rain-soaked ground, among trees, kennels for hunting dogs and huts used for falconry. It was misty, and conditions were chaotic; the reports are all confused. For a time the battle seemed to be going in favour of Francis I and his mounted knights, his well-placed artillery firing with great effect into the massed formations of the landsknechts. But this was not in accord with the knightly tournaments the king loved; refusing to cede the honour of victory to the artillery he despised, he advanced with his knights into the line of fire, thus forcing the cannon to stop shooting. After a further advance he brought his companions to a halt and received congratulations on his victory: 'At last I can really call myself Duke of Milan,' he shouted through his visor to his friends. The Spanish troops, already the best infantry in Europe, went into action; heavily armed with harquebuses, they were also trained to fight in small groups. The harquebusiers broke up the knights among the trees and glades of the park. There was no longer any possibility of a massed attack. The mounted knights galloped about singly; when their horses fell – and the harquebusiers knew that their first target must be the mount – they were helpless in their weighty armour, and were massacred. Each harquebusier was supplied with special weapons for breaking open the knights' armour and cutting their throats. 'As though in a fit of heroic intoxication, the French aristocracy met a joyful death,' is how an Italian eyewitness described the scene somewhat grandiloquently; at all events they fell, one after the other.

The list of great names among the fallen was long. One helmetless knight – the king's master of the horse – continued to ride round, held up by his armour, long after he had been killed, his body riddled by a dozen balls, his glazed eyes staring straight in front of him – an apparition from which the Spanish harquebusiers shrank back in horror. This picture of death in the saddle symbolizes the battle, which sounded the death knell of tournaments and knightly jousts. The harquebusiers were the 'moderns'. The king's horse fell too, but Francis was able to get to his feet because his costly armour, made by the finest armourers, was lighter than the heavy suits of his companions. The Spaniards, not knowing who he was, intended to finish him off like the others, but he had a stroke of luck. As they were quarrelling over his magnificent suit of armour Lannoy, the viceroy and Charles's jousting partner, came up. With great difficulty he managed to rescue the king from the predatory infantrymen, who continued to follow him and his prisoner; he had to summon his own men to his aid, and a number of people were killed before he reached safety. The king was half naked and, in the graphic words of an eyewitness, 'the long points of his iron foot-gear slithered in the mud.' Lannoy took this greatest prize of the day back to his quarters, as far from the scene of battle as possible, because the other commanders were as anxious as the Spanish infantrymen to lay their hands on the king.

Meanwhile the garrison had made a sortie. The Swiss mercenaries, thrown in too late and furiously engaged by Frundsberg's landsknechts, broke up and fled; on this difficult terrain the compact formations with their erect forests of pikes, so beautifully depicted in the woodcuts of the day, were impracticable. By half past nine, in the still uncertain morning light, the battle was over; it had lasted little more than an hour. The murdering and plundering went on for the rest of the day. So long as they had not been slaughtered in the initial blood bath, the officers of high standing, recognizable by the splendour of their turn-out – some wore their ladies' colours attached to their arms – had a chance of survival; they could be ransomed. The ordinary soldiers were massacred by the victors without pity, the Germans on the French side being slaughtered by Frundsberg's landsknechts. The Swiss tried to escape by swimming the Ticino, but most were drowned, weighed down by their heavy jerkins and baggy breeches; eyewitnesses claimed to have counted eight thousand bodies washed ashore at the next weir.

The epilogue – the sale of the bodies and the turning in of the booty – began that same evening and on the following day. Traders, money-changers and merchants always appeared on the scene of battle with astonishing rapidity. Armies were accompanied by huge numbers of camp followers; every member of the higher nobility took his secretaries with him, and some their mistresses as well. Servants, henchmen or friends bargained with the soldiers for their duke or count, whose body had to be taken home and buried in the family vault; the traders paid with credit on a great house or else stood surety. The flower of the French aristocracy was laid out in orderly rows, often pitifully muti-lated. The prices obtained were noted down in writing; if he was not satisfied, an enraged landsknecht would throw 'his body' into the river for the servants and leave.

Francis I, the hero of the great day, whose knightly bearing won him much admiration, was immediately clothed by Lannoy in royal vestments – a gesture intended to inspire respect for royalty. He received the hospitality due to his rank and was given permission to write to his mother in France the lines that have become famous: 'Madame, I wish to inform you how my ill-fortune ended: everything is lost save my honour and my life.' As he rode towards the fortress of Pizzighettone, where Lannoy took him to keep him out of reach of the other com-manders, he started to joke and tell hunting stories. The great tourna-ment had ended, and he had been unhorsed; he intended very soon to be in the saddle again. Lannoy respected and secretly sympathized with him; great princes and nobles quarrelled and went to war, but this did not affect the strong ties of common rank that bound them. Spiriting his valuable prisoner out of the fortress, he took him secretly to Genoa and from there by ship to Spain. Only then was his booty quite safe from the clutches of his fellow commanders.

But what was the state of the victorious army? In spite of the booty and ransom money, most of which had been frittered away in a few days of gambling, drinking and whoring, it now mutinied for the first time. The Emperor Charles attended a solemn thanksgiving service in Madrid, where his humility made a deep impression on the foreign envoys; he expressed his gratitude to God, but not to his commanders in the field, let alone the fighting soldiers. There were wild scenes in Pavia when it was learned that even after such a famous victory there was to be no pay at all; the fortress's defenders had had no pay for almost a year and a half and Frundsberg's landsknechts none for many months. They paraded in formation, but without officers, in the square in front of the castle, where the commanding officers had their quarters. Shots hit the windows. Frundsberg came out radiating goodwill but unable to promise any money; the men were unimpressed and, threatening to kill him, stormed into the passages and corridors. The marquis of Pescara, renowned as one of the ablest military leaders and severely wounded in the previous day's battle, hid in a cupboard; the viceroy took refuge in the loft. They were dragged out and taken down to the square for judgment to be pronounced. It ended without bloodshed. Wiser elements joined in, pointing out that no pay would be produced by killing them; it would be better to come to terms. The army commanders had to offer payment on their own, the marquis pledging his houses in Milan and the viceroy giving promissory notes that were honoured more promptly than those of his emperor.

But further service was out of the question. Many of the landsknechts made their way home, grouped together when possible for fear of attack by the infuriated peasants; others stayed in their army formations, dispersed throughout Lombardy and degenerated into robber hordes. The prisoners, such as remained, were set free; there was no chance of getting ransom money for ordinary soldiers, they could not be taken on because there was nothing to pay them with, and to evacuate them was out of the question. They wandered back. Many died or were killed on the way. Enough crossed the mountains to find new employment mowing down the German peasants, Frundsberg, his reputation still intact, drumming them up for this purpose.

The victory was no sooner won than the army commanders fell out among themselves, and the emperor did nothing to improve matters; his treatment of the marquis of Pescara and the constable was cold and high-handed. In the surprise victory he saw the blessing of the hand of God: the good cause had triumphed, the just war had been won. Pope Clement saw things in a different light; his legate was among the emperor's prisoners. For the time being he had no choice but to acknowledge Charles; at the same time, however, he concentrated his attention on finding some way to offset his authority. On no account must France become too weak.

France at once revealed its best side as a nation; instead of being listless and dispirited in defeat it pulled itself together. The king's mother, Louise of Savoy, acting as regent, took the reins firmly in her hands. Although reputed to be unusually grasping, she gave the torn and tattered returning soldiers their pay, an unheard-of action in those days. She handed over large sums of back pay to the Swiss and, the only reigning queen, she had the money to do it with: the country gave it to her, and this again seemed an almost incredible miracle. A sort of parliament met, admittedly not representative by later standards, but nonetheless capable of acting. The city of Paris floated loans, the citizens took them up. French diplomacy worked at fever pitch. Contact was established with Henry VIII who, like every other leading monarch, was alarmed at the emperor's sudden dominance. The alarm, which was general throughout Europe, became intensified when it was learned what conditions the victor intended to impose on his prisoner.

The twenty-five-year-old Charles, though no longer a dreamer, still clung to his ancestor-worship. Burgundy, old Burgundy, was to be ceded; this was the principal demand. Then in the intoxication of victory everyone, including his otherwise intelligent advisers, became ever greedier. The whole catalogue of ancient feudal rights was brought out again. Provence, once a fief of the empire, was to be returned to the emperor – it might perhaps be given in fief to the renegade Bourbon as the emperor's vassal. Flanders and Artois, hitherto fiefs of the French crown, were to be handed over once and for all to Charles; the list continued. The prisoner refused. He was prepared to pay the usual large ransom for a knight and to hand over his sons as hostages, but he could not agree to the dismemberment of his kingdom.

The negotiations continued back and forth for a long time. They ended in an act of trickery, the so-called Peace of Madrid, which was sworn with great solemnity and full religious ceremonial. Previously Francis had made a secret deposition in the presence of his entourage that he would swear an oath only under duress, and it would therefore not be binding. The emperor had devised a further safeguard, of whose efficacy he had no doubt: Francis was to give his word as a knight to honour the agreement – this would be more binding than any oath. Francis hesitated; then he gave his word of honour too. To bind him still further, and as a gesture of reconciliation, he was given the emperor's recently widowed sister, Eleanore, to wed.

He was released, Lannoy accompanying him to Paris; on reaching the frontier Francis swung himself into the saddle with a shout of joy: 'Now I am king again!' His word of honour was brushed aside; the oath was mentioned only in terms of his secret reservation. The only condition he had to fulfil was to hand over as hostages his two sons aged eight and seven, the elder of whom was to become Henry II; although the emperor was unable to make the slightest use of them, they were held for a long time.

After all he had been through the French king was no longer the gay cavalier. He is unlikely to have been bothered greatly by scruples over his broken oath; Pope Clement set his mind at rest, using his apostolic authority to annul the vow. His broken word of honour may have worried him more, but tournaments and chivalrous thoughts were over and done with. He became hard, cruel, suspicious and calculating. He reversed his previous liberal attitude towards freedom of thought and those who supported the new teachings, and in fact towards anything that might stand in the way of a strictly centralized government.

The story of the Reformation, which already had numerous supporters in France, was no longer the same after the Battle of Pavia; intellectual duels had as little place as jousting with lances.

The emperor was left as the sole representative of the old ideas of knighthood and chivalry, holding the king's worthless word of honour and dreaming his feudal dreams of old Burgundy and ancient feudal rights. He actually thought of challenging the king of France to a duel, but nothing came of it. At the height of his success the picture was still gloomy. He did not even have the money to pay his victorious troops and exploit his advantages in Italy; the greater part of his army had dispersed. French diplomacy was enjoying great success, supported by the pope who, though with the utmost caution, set about turning the victory of his one-time ally Charles into a defeat. Planning on this level left little time for dealing with Luther and the spread of heresy in Germany, if we except a few routine warnings attached to treaties and agreements. We could ignore the whole web of plots and intrigues spun by the great powers were it not that this alone explains how it was possible for the outlawed and excommunicated monk in Wittenberg to continue on his way through this maze of international politics as if it did not even exist. The great decisions of the day took place at different levels.

On the level of Curia politics Pope Clement had embarked on a particularly sly attempt to undermine the emperor's position in Italy. The affair has gone down in history as the 'Temptation of Pescara'. Pescara, celebrated as one of the most successful military commanders, was bitterly resentful at his treatment after the victory. In the kingdom of Naples he was a man of very high standing, and his wife Vittoria, well known as a poet and friend of Michelangelo, was a member of the great Colonna family. Suppose he could be persuaded to leave the ungrateful emperor? The bait was to be the throne of Naples which, as a fief of the Church, the pope thought he was free to offer. Discussions took place, discreetly and under a solemn oath of secrecy. Pescara did not reject the offer out of hand, but wanted it made legitimate by the Church at the highest level. Clement, having taken advice from his experts on canon and other law found he was not in a position to offer much more than the rather vague formula: obedience to the holy father takes precedence over any oath of obedience to the emperor. This did not satisfy Pescara, who was jealous of his good name and reputation. He was also an ill man, suffering from his wounds as well as from wounded pride and gastric ulcers, and knew he had not long to live; he suspected that this fact might have entered into the pope's calculations. On a sudden impulse he put the go-between, who was horrified at this breach of faith, into prison and gave a full report of the whole affair to the emperor – full, that is to say, in so far as it concerned Charles, since he had sworn not to betray anyone. He assured the emperor of his loyalty but added serious warnings, which were received very ungraciously in Madrid. He stressed the importance of making a quick and generous peace: 'The whole world fears you, no one loves you, your army has made itself loathed, you have not a friend in Italy, and those who serve you are tired and discouraged.' Shortly afterwards he died. The observers assigned to him by the emperor thought he had been poisoned by the papal faction. The whole affair is shrouded in the semi-darkness in which such intrigues are necessarily conducted.

No one in this period trod a straight and narrow path. This world of broken oaths and unscrupulous bargaining with peoples and scraps of territory is today either softened by the word Renaissance, which art has made synonymous with beauty, or else explained as 'Machiavellian'. Little was known at the time of the theses of the former secretary of the Republic of Florence, who lived in forced retirement on his small country estate bent over his books. If the conduct of kings and princes corresponded to that of a despot as defined by Machiavelli in his *Principe*, they were only following the examples of their ancestors who, throughout the Middle Ages, had pursued 'Machiavellian' policies. It had long been accepted that if one wanted to reach one's goal one had to proceed without regard for 'loyalty, mercy, humanity or religion'; two hundred years earlier Werner von Urslingen, one of the great condottieri, had had the motto, 'Enemy of God, pity and mercy', honestly and boldly engraved on the breastplate of his armour. All that was new was that such ideas were now elaborated into a system, fully argued and committed to paper in a polished style; holding up a brilliantly polished mirror to princes and their rule, the *Principe* found many more disciples than the pious addresses of father confessors.

Machiavelli was accused of paganism though this was far from his intention; religion was an essential part of his scheme of things: 'religion, laws, an established army' was the order in which he set out the main buttresses of a state. Religion was one of the means of statecraft, and for Machiavelli statecraft was an art; it could be practised only by someone who, like a great sculptor, possessed the 'virtu', or power, to strike hard and ruthlessly and transform the lifeless block of stone into the vision he saw in his imagination. His book, following the tortuous fashion of the day, was dedicated to the Medici, who had just reduced his native town once more to bondage and driven out the republican government of his former masters. He was motivated by thoughts of a united Italy, under a great prince who would unify the country and drive out the foreigner. At one time his hopes had been centred on the reckless Cesare Borgia, but he had already vanished ingloriously. It is highly improbable that Machiavelli credited Leo, Clement, or the ineffectual Medici nephew whom the pope had now installed in Florence with the force of character needed to be a great sovereign. A deep pessimism pervades his notes. He saw the dismemberment of Italy and the cowardice which prevailed. In the light of recent events he recommended the establishment of national armies to replace the mercenaries, on whom no one could ever rely. He called for the discipline that had made the Romans great, citing the victories it had brought them over the Spaniards, the Gauls, the Germans and the Swiss; the reference to his own times is unmistakable. The last opportunity to win back freedom had been ignominiously thrown away by the disunited, suspicious, would-be wise communes, republics, duchies, petty tyrants and the great Curia. The 'Spanish century' had dawned in Italy. Machiavelli's thoughts moved on the level of free thought, and this permitted the boldest combinations. Many people, however, took them to be practical instructions, and on this level they were more like a game in a sand-box, the sad and lonely amusement of a penetrating mind and ardent patriot, who had been excluded from playing a part in the destiny of his country.

He had proposed national armies, seeing these as a desirable instrument in the hands of an able and energetic leader; he had called for discipline but, as he was forced dejectedly to admit, discipline simply did not exist in Italy. In Germany the same dismemberment and disunity reigned, the result of jealousy between the princes and the city republics. In the year of the Battle of Pavia the people rose in revolt. The peasants rebelled, the artisans and journeymen in the towns rebelled, but it was a leaderless rebellion.

# 31

# The Peasants' War

'WHEN Adam delved and Eve span, who was then the gentleman?' was a cry that had echoed down the centuries; in England it had been heard at the time of Wyclif and his 'poor priests'. The underground movement of the Lollards, of those who 'murmured' of a new and better era of justice for all, continued, in spite of every persecution, to exist until Luther's day.

Throughout the whole of the Middle Ages there had been peasant and popular risings in every country, and they had often been ferocious and bloody in the extreme; they had always been crushed. The Hussites alone had succeeded in establishing themselves over a period of decades, spreading fear and terror throughout Europe, though particularly in Germany, until they committed national suicide at the Battle of Lipan in 1434, when the radicals were defeated by former comrades who had veered to the right, and by the nobles. Since then the frustrated hopes of the Czech people had found their only solace in the legend of the cave in Mount Blanik, where the defeated heroes of the revolution were said to be awaiting an opportunity to break out and re-establish the former days of greatness. The fact that during all the fighting at the time of the Reformation the Bohemians did not revolt and intervene decisively was a supreme disappointment to every rebel and revolutionary.

The second great disappointment was the Swiss, on whom far greater hopes had been placed; the first peasant revolts broke out on the borders of Switzerland, and many of them spread across the frontier into the confederation. The expectation that the well-armed Swiss peasants, who had made a great name for themselves fighting for France, or the pope, on so many battlefields in Italy, would come to the aid of their German brothers had played a very considerable role. They never came, a decisive reason being that the Swiss towns were spread out along the German border, while the true peasant cantons in the mountains opposed the towns, which had accepted the Reformation, and pursued individual policies of their own; later on this led to civil war in

Switzerland and to the country's division into Catholic and Protestant regions.

Another hope that was constantly disappointed was the belief in a great emperor, king or leader, whom even the peasants regarded as a necessity. Where he was to come from and in what form was never clear. Lamentably bad rulers, like the shifty Sigismund, who was for ever breaking his word, or even Frederick III, about whom no one had any clear notions, were credited with the intention of introducing great plans for reform. A still deeper impression was made by predictions of the millennium. Such predictions, which are always to be heard in troubled times, were rampant, and the fact that they claimed to be based on the prophecies in the Bible gave them an authority possessed by no other catchwords; short and to the point, they could be understood and passed on even by uneducated people. 'The last shall be first': God's judgment on the priests, the Church and all those in high places would be fearful. This had been proclaimed again and again; Luther was not the last to do so.

The word 'law' in those days still had very lofty overtones. Luther's own basic idea was that God was a judge before whom man had to justify himself. The 'ancient law', which those in power had repeatedly broken and whose reinstatement was regarded as essential, was one of the chief catchwords of the peasants, as was also 'divine right', which had been in desuetude still longer, since the days when Adam delved and Eve span, or the early Christians had united to form devout communities, sharing all they had and subject to no one but the Word, with its promise of a new life.

The itinerant preachers preached their sermons. Because frontiers and frontier controls did not exist, they could pass from country to country without let or hindrance. It was only in the towns, with their protecting walls and gatekeepers, that they met opposition from the authorities; they were constantly turned out. On the other hand they found helpers and allies among the lower classes in the towns, who were in constant conflict with the privileged upper classes. Another phenomenon of the day that also played its part was the arrival of the unknown traveller, the man from foreign parts, who stirred people up by the power of his language. His outward appearance contributed greatly to the effect he produced: he was almost always haggard and emaciated, and often in rags, whereas the citizens were well nourished. The description of obese priests, or members of the city council, brimming over with contentment was a stock formula of all polemic writings. It was a battle of the hungry and haggard against the fat, and in an age of excessive eating and drinking a huge girth was the almost inevitable hallmark of the well-to-do.

Whether in fact the peasants lived in poverty and squalor has always been debated, but with inadequately substantiated arguments. The privations and the amount of work that may be expected of a man, let alone justified, has never been established with any degree of certainty under any social order. The pictorial and literary evidence we have of those days has added to the confusion: it all originated with the educated classes; the peasant was silent, he could not write. In their jokes, farces and caricatures the former, with self-conscious superiority, represented the peasant as a lout with his buxom girl, for ever stuffing himself, much too opulently dressed, much too pretentious in every way, vulgar, stupid, spiteful and sly. Those who took a kinder view sometimes remarked in their more serious moments that, when all was said and done, it was the peasants off whom everyone else lived. Economic history has established cycles when the plight of the peasants was better or worse, but it has insufficient data to go on, and above all has to contend with the unparalleled fragmentation and variety of conditions in Germany. The differences and gradations between one district and another were enormous; in some areas the peasants were still free and proudly conscious of their standing, while in others the most flagrant slavery existed.

What is certain, however, is that in most regions the feudal form of overlordship had gradually and relentlessly demolished all that remained of the ancient protective rights, until these had vanished further and further into the remoteness of mythical antiquity. The written complaints of the peasants – the only peasant documents we possess – reflect this state of affairs in detail; they constitute an endless catalogue of small demands and abuses. The contemporary expression, which Luther also used, was 'Schinden und Schaben', or skinning and scraping; it meant the persistent, stubborn scraping away and removal of 'rights' which, inadequate and unjust though they were, were nonetheless accepted as having existed from time immemorial, in favour of new burdens. The tithe, the 'great' tithe that had to be paid from the corn crop, was a tax frequently accepted by the peasants themselves; to this had been added the 'living' tithe, an impost in the form of cattle, foals, calves and lambs, and the small or 'dead' tithe, which consisted of hay, hops and gathering strawberries and bilberries – the list was continually extended until one lady of the manor, a Countess von Lupfen, ordered her peasants to collect empty snail shells, which she needed for spinning yarn. It was the bitterness caused by this demand for snail shells that touched off the first peasant revolt in south Germany.

This by no means exhausts the list of impositions. The forced labour demanded was increased constantly. A peasant family was hit hardest of all when the head of the family died: the lord of the manor then claimed the 'heriot', the best cow or horse, which was led away by force if necessary; it could mean ruin to the poorer peasants. Little by little the peasants were also deprived of ancient rights and customs permitting them to catch fish or crayfish and kill an occasional hare or head of game. Of these the most fiercely contested were the hunting and shooting rights, which were regarded as the exclusive privilege of the nobility; one of the first demonstrations of revolt was the removal of all his fish from some nobleman's pond. The worst aspect was probably the uncertainty of the legal position, which left the peasants completely defenceless. The 'old traditions', which, if they had ever been firmly established at all, usually rested on a verbal basis, had been superseded by severer forms of exploitation, by agents, acting as tax collectors, and by stewards. The religious foundations and abbeys were the most expert at this kind of extortion, already possessing something akin to a civil service and bureaucratic apparatus, with deeds and records which the peasants could not read and to which new paragraphs were constantly and quite unscrupulously added; these were then used to reduce the copyholders to serfs, impose yet further burdens on the serfs, confiscate farms and increase twenty-fold the so-called protection money.

In the present writer's opinion the uncertainty of the legal position must be regarded as a main cause of the revolts. It is significant that the peasant insurrection was confined to those districts – Swabia and Franconia in particular – in which, owing to division of ownership and a concentration of dwarf territories and seats belonging to the impoverished nobility, this uncertainty was greatest. North Germany, with its larger estates or otherwise regulated conditions of ownership, remained unaffected, although it would be hard to prove that the peasants there had a higher standard of living. In any case the degree of squalor in which people live is not necessarily a reliable guide; in fact it is those with a greater sense of personal pride, rather than the helots eking out an utterly numbed and hopeless existence, who tend to be the first to take things into their own hands. The main areas of revolt were also those in which the great war leaders recruited their manpower and had their recruiting centres. Former landsknechts formed the backbone of the peasant forces, and such military successes as they had they owed to the advice of these experienced fighters. Following landsknecht custom, the peasants fell in in a ring and formed a closed phalanx; they also copied the landsknechts in making their prisoners run the gauntlet.

Joss Fritz was also a former soldier, who had played a leading role in revolts in the Breisgau at the beginning of the century; a tireless agitator and organizer, he always managed to escape arrest. In him we can already see the characteristic features of the revolutionary leader:

the creation of a whole staff of emissaries, among whom he also enlisted the powerful beggar guilds with their picturesque 'kings'; clever exploitation of his connections with knights, citizens in the towns and poor members of the priesthood; secret signs and meeting-places; a banner displaying the emblem of the *Bundschuh* – the rough peasant shoe made out of a single piece of leather and held in place by an ankle-strap, which symbolized poverty and unity.

The single uprisings which formed the prelude to the main uprising, though always localized and always short-lived, at least succeeded in creating a revolutionary tradition in south Germany. The slogans were nearly always very simple: an end to the burdens; no master but the emperor; free pasture, water and woodland; 'divine right'. The precise details of the various programmes are always vague, and almost impossible to be sure of, for the simple reason that the surviving evidence consists almost entirely either of records containing statements extracted under brutal torture from captured ringleaders or of biased town chronicles written by officials who naturally were anxious to deny any complicity on the parts of their communities – which in fact were often deeply involved – and put all the blame on the peasants. The participation of the town, however, was a further significant factor. Urban revolts, caused by the centuries-old feud between the privileged 'patricians' and the lower classes, played just as big a part as the peasant revolts in shaking the whole insecure structure of the empire. And it was not only 'horizontal' solidarities, such as the alliance between the plebeians in the towns and the peasants, that operated here but 'vertical' interests as well. It was by no means beneath the dignity of the upper class members of the city councils to join forces with the peasants in order to oppose the detested overlordship of a bishop; we have already seen this in the case of Erfurt, and it was repeated elsewhere. In addition, every class felt the pressure of the advancing monetary and capitalist economy. War against the usurers was a slogan with which in theory almost everyone was in sympathy, without knowing where usury began or ended or how the growing need for goods of all kinds was to be met.

Economic and social hardship was behind the risings in Württemberg; other regions of the empire were shaken by similar revolts. In 1514 there had been a great peasant war in Hungary; news-sheets spread reports of it throughout Germany, and for a time its terrible end had a paralysing effect. On the eve of the conquest of Hungary by the Turks, who were already on the banks of the Danube, a crusader army had been assembled; it was an act of remarkable irresponsibility on the part of the primate, Cardinal Bakócz. The intention was to capture Constantinople, and those taking part were promised land in the

Turkish Empire, in addition to the usual indulgence; many peasants sold all they had, serfs, promised their freedom, joined the ranks, and an army of 50,000 men was formed under the command of a Transylvanian named György Dózsa. The cardinal left for Rome to attend the election of the pope, having also announced himself as a candidate; lord of twenty-six benefices, he entered the city with a pomp that astonished even the Romans and returned home with the news that the crusade was now unnecessary because, in the meantime, the Curia had come to an agreement with the sultan. The crusaders rose in revolt, Dózsa taking command of the rebellious forces. In the opening campaigns they were successful. Members of the nobility and clergy were killed and monasteries burned, and for a short time it looked as if the whole of Hungary would fall into the hands of the rebels; people already began to speak of 'King Dózsa' but, though an able tactician, he proved to be a bad strategist. Splitting his army into five divisions he advanced on all fronts, hoping that the peasants everywhere would join him; the five forces were destroyed one by one, the last to succumb being that led by Dózsa himself. The victor was a fellow countryman, another Transylvanian named Zapolya who, elected by the aristocracy and protected by the sultan, then became king, and an ally much sought after by all the powers that were conspiring against the Habsburgs. The sentences passed on the rebels exceeded in cruelty even those imposed later on the German peasants; 'King Dózsa' was roasted alive on a red-hot iron throne – the story went that his followers were then forced to eat his charred flesh. Serfdom in its most ruthless form was the lot of the Hungarian peasants for centuries to come.

Simultaneously there had been serious disturbances in Carinthia and Carniola. In Spain the *comuneros* had dangerously threatened the young king's rule; here too for a time, especially in Valencia and the Balearics, the fourth estate joined the opposition, which had originally started in the towns. Victory inevitably went to the nobility and its hired troops; merciless punishment, and increased oppression for a long time afterwards, was always the lot of the peasants. The picture was the same everywhere: great initial successes which proved short-lived, because discipline was bad, because of the influx of 'undesirable elements' who wanted only to plunder and soon fell away when things got serious, and in the last resort because the hoped-for aid from the broad masses of the population in other districts did not materialize. This was also to be the fate of the peasant revolt in Germany.

The greatest misfortune of the Peasants' War was that it *almost* succeeded, a characteristic it shares with other abortive promises in German history. The German emperors in the Middle Ages were almost victorious, the Hanseatic League almost introduced a great era for the cities, there was almost a great reformation and reorganization of the empire – there is no need to prolong this list of near-victories and almost successful wars and revolutions. The upshot was that people were misled into dreaming and writing about the victories that might have been.

The leaders of the great German peasant uprising, in so far as their features are recognizable in the almost invariably biased accounts, were a mixed lot. There were virtually no peasants among them. The peasant was inarticulate; he could not write, and even when he wanted to make a complaint – and these complaints are all that has survived of the peasants – he needed the services of someone else to put on paper those troubles whose 'pettiness' and modesty cloaked the most atrocious oppression. Thus a former chancellor to Prince Hohenlohe, Wendelin Hipler, became one of the most influential ringleaders and, basing his ideas on early writings on reform, the only one to draw up an extensive plan for a new kind of government. The peasant could not make speeches, he could only groan and cry out bitterly; innkeepers with a ready tongue, accustomed to holding forth to their clients, took over leading roles. Priests and preachers formed an important section of the leadership. The movement's most serious shortage was in military experts, who had to be drawn from the ranks of either landsknecht officers or extremely unreliable knights like Götz von Berlichingen and the brave and forceful Florian Geyer with his 'black legion', which soon fell out with the irresolute main bodies of troops. At no time was there any sign of an integrated leadership or of adequate contact between the various areas of revolt. From the outset the great movement disintegrated into local enterprises, often so widely separated that they were hardly aware of each other's existence even by hearsay; it was united only in the fury of its anger and the common slogans this produced everywhere.

There was also a complete lack of uniformity in procedure. In some areas the peasants sent in humbly worded requests to be relieved of certain particularly intolerable burdens, accompanied by assurances that they would continue to pay the 'great' tithes; in others there was a curt demand for complete freedom. Religious slogans – free choice of pastors, preaching of the pure Gospel – were often given priority, economic and social demands taking second place. Appeals were made to 'ancient rights' and 'divine justice', as well as to local diets, courts of arbitration and the emperor who, resident in Spain, did not hear of the events until the fight was over. Frequently much valuable time was lost negotiating with the authorities, with abbots, lords of the manor, princes and city councils, every imaginable form of treachery and betrayal being used in the process: leaders were bribed, erstwhile allies grew nervous and defected, or opportunists who had been on the side of the peasants so long as their cause seemed to prosper, seeing the change of fortune, climbed on to the victorious bandwaggon while there was still time. Intermixed with all this were furious attacks on any objective that was easy to reach and vulnerable, such as monasteries, abbeys and seats of the nobility. These quick successes blinded the peasants, making them over-confident and careless; they thought they

Armed peasants during the Peasants' War

could go straight ahead and storm the strongest fortresses, and they came to grief in the attempt. The greatest and most successful revolt in Franconia was wrecked when the peasants, against the advice of experienced soldiers, tried to storm the fortress of Würzburg. As in all wars – even those fought by the well-drilled mercenary armies of the day – panic repeatedly played an important part, although in this case the risk was increased because the peasant troops were completely unused to discipline; since as a rule the fighting took place in the immediate vicinity of the men's villages, their first thought was to get home as quickly as possible. Even the seasons played a role; the up-risings began in the spring and the men had to be home for the harvest. Large detachments of peasants simply melted away when the corn was ripe; already prior to this large sections of the levies had been unwilling to commit themselves to more than a few weeks' service. Only the landsknechts remained permanently with the colours, so long, that is, as they got their pay and there was booty to be had. It was the lands-knechts in the service of the princes who decided the day and reaped the bloody harvest: contemporaries estimated the peasant dead at over a hundred thousand.

That in spite of their helplessness and disorganization the peasants were able, if only for a short time, to develop into a force of such power demonstrates better than all their complaints, and the subsequent investigations into their justification, how rotten the ground was from which the revolts sprang. The initial bewilderment of all those in power, their cowardice and indecision, remains perhaps the most memorable spectacle of the whole conflict; it was equalled only by the brutality with which they treated their defeated opponents, and by their total disregard of the treaties and agreements they had made when things were going badly.

The first revolts occurred in the autumn of 1524; they were very local affairs. The real uprising and war did not last much longer than the few weeks from spring to early summer 1525, although in the more distant regions of Salzburg, the Tyrol and Styria fighting continued until into 1526. The main war zone comprised the districts from Lake Constance and the Black Forest as far as Franconia; in the west the movement extended into Alsace, while in the north an independent revolt developed in Thuringia. These names indicate only the geo-graphical outlines of the four main centres. Simultaneously, and only loosely connected with the peasant risings, revolts took place in the towns, in Frankfurt, for example, in Mainz, Augsburg and elsewhere. Individual actions often took the form of concerted attacks by com-munities within a single valley on neighbouring monasteries and castles; they had no aims beyond this, and indeed sometimes these communities resisted the approach of 'outside' peasant forces engaged in larger campaigns.

The figures we have for the various armies, or *Haufen* (detachments) as they were called, are extremely unreliable and, like almost all statistics of past wars and battles, have to be greatly reduced. But the peasant hordes must have been imposing enough, especially when, persuaded by veteran landsknechts in their ranks, they were drawn up in the usual battle array, with storm troops in the vanguard and the closed phalanx of the main force in the rear. The larger detachments had an order of battle, with instructions for 'officers, junior officers, non-commissioned officers and all others in responsible positions', including the important officers in charge of fire-raising and booty. To find reliable men for these posts was difficult and caused a great deal of strife; such antagonisms were responsible in no small measure for the failure of the cause. In general the peasant forces were inadequately armed, especially as regards cannon, for which, unlike their opponents, they lacked trained artillerymen. Accounts of the effect of a salvo from the culverins of the princes' forces, which often ended a 'battle' before it had begun, can easily strike us as rather strange, in view of the inaccuracy of the guns – their barrels were often lined only with stout leather – and the fact that the cannon balls were made of stone. But in those days there was still something demoniacal about the new weapon, and it could decide an engagement even between experienced mercenaries in a few minutes. On the other hand the troops, under good leadership, were capable of skilful manœuvres, using fortified encampments and entrenchments on well-chosen sites, and of great bravery in storming enemy positions and scaling castle walls. By and large, however, the peasant armies merely followed the military tactics of the day: battle positions were taken up, the first clash decided the issue. This meant that from the outset the peasants, in spite of their great numerical superiority, were at a disadvantage against their disciplined opponents.

These opponents were the princes and some of the large cities. The lesser nobility, demoralized by Sickingen's defeat, offered only sporadic resistance, and the peasants, having already taken part in storming the knights' strongholds, now continued to do this on their own account and on a very large scale. Nothing is more significant of the decline of this estate, which only a short time previously had boastfully proclaimed its leadership in establishing a new order within the empire, than the way in which it permitted its castles and strongholds to be razed and burned to the ground without offering the slightest effective resistance. Not a few counts and lords of the manor bowed their heads to the *Bundschuh* banner, allowed themselves to be called 'brother Hohenlohe' or 'brother Löwenstein', and willingly took any and every oath, fully intending to break it at the first opportunity. Hopes of winning this estate for the good cause brought a great many wholly unreliable elements into the movement; at the beginning a number of the nobility thought that the blow was to be aimed only at ecclesiastical properties: 'So long as only priests and monasteries were involved it was fine, everyone laughed', wrote one of the chroniclers. The awakening, which then turned to sheer terror, came when the peasants started to attack the knights; in Weinsberg a dozen nobles were made to run the gauntlet. In the words of a popular song: 'The nobles assembled, they started to speak,/Said the peasants: come on, let us give them a tweak./ The nobles went home, they began to feel scared,/Said the peasants: come on, let us beat up the laird.'

Overwhelming initial victories have always been ominous in German history. In a few short weeks during the spring the various peasant forces had subdued and laid waste wide areas, burning hundreds of monasteries and overpowering castles. Some of the smaller towns joined them, others negotiated with them, dozens of knights attached themselves to them for the sake of the booty, only to declare later, like Götz of the iron hand and brazen effrontery, that they had done so under duress. A peasant detachment was a colourful sight: the leaders often wore the 'slashed' uniform of the landsknechts, silk banners waved, drums and fifes marched ahead and were followed by a long baggage train with waggons for the booty and women; on the edges of the battlefields money changers and dealers lurked. The atrocities committed by the peasant armies were given exaggerated and biased prominence only because they were committed by 'blind rabble' instead of by regular soldiers. To slaughter men without mercy, to burn and scorch, was normal practice in war; if anything, the peasants seem to have shown more restraint than the regulars, because they were unpractised in the art. Plundering the rich abbeys and monasteries led to vast carousals in the well-stocked cellars, but only after everything had been wrecked and smashed to pieces. Provosts were appointed, but they had no authority; the leaders' councils were riddled with suspicion and dissension. Many of the detachments roamed the countryside on their own, and were wiped out one by one.

It was only in south Germany, the main centre of revolt, that a loosely knit rule over a definable area was set up, with the establishment in Heilbronn of a sort of government, a peasant chancellery. It was from south Germany too that, as early as the beginning of the year, the most widely circulated programme had been issued, the complaint known as the *Twelve Articles*, the secular counterpart of Luther's ninety-five theses, and like them distributed within a very short space of time in a large number of printings. There were many such collections of articles of faith, some more radical, some more moderate, but these twelve were the 'basic and true leading articles' as the title claimed. Moderate enough in all conscience, they were a defence rather than an attack, and intended as an answer to opponents who said that the fruits of the Gospel were now evident: disobedience, atrocities, contempt for every form of authority. No, they declared, it was not the Gospel that was responsible but the devil, by suppressing the Word of God. Only after this preamble did the document proceed to the articles proper; they contained demands for freedom in the choice of pastors, removal of unjust burdens, abolition of serfdom, which 'is to be deplored in view of the fact that Christ has delivered and bought us all without exception with His precious blood, the shepherd as well as the highest in the land.' The constant, ever-recurring complaints were that 'new impositions' had been inflicted, more statutory labour demanded, more and more communal property, which had belonged to the peasants since time immemorial, was being expropriated by the lords of the manor. The general effect of the manifesto is so moderate that joint authorship has been alleged, a priest for its overall framework, a revolutionary for the articles themselves. But there is no need for such constructions; in those days the two sides, the 'radical demands' and the appeal to the Gospel as a source of enlightenment and inspiration, could very well co-exist in the same person. The demand for freedom for the Word was a demand to be freed from the burdens. Moreover these *Twelve Articles* were the 'vanguard'; they preceded the storm at a time when it was still widely thought that things could be settled by negotiation. More strongly worded articles and open letters followed, once the peasant armies started their victorious advances.

In April and May it looked as if the peasants would overrun the whole of south Germany. Free cities of the empire joined their ranks; lords of the manor, counts and princes doffed their plumed hats to them. The wildest hopes circulated; in Thuringia Thomas Müntzer announced that even foreign countries were already on the move. Then came the turning-point, caused more than anything else by the return from Italy of the landsknechts who, now that the emperor had ceased to pay them, were on the lookout for new employers. The princes had recovered from their initial paralysis. The Swabian League, the only institution that could claim some degree of cohesion, intervened; in Georg Truchsess, its military commander, it had a ruthless leader who earned a horrifying reputation as the 'peasant slayer'.

For a moment things remained in the balance. The 'peasant chancellor' in Heilbronn, Wendelin Hipler, appealed vainly to the scattered detachments to join forces. He opposed the desire of the peasants to return home after a few weeks and be replaced by fresh troops, who then had to receive at least some training before they could go into action. Above all Hipler wanted to enlist the landsknechts for the cause. They were offering their services; they were actually reluctant to fight for the princes, if it meant being used against their 'brothers'. This might have been the turning-point. The princes had no troops on whom they could call, and those they attempted to levy refused their services; mercenaries were their only hope. The peasants' war council agreed to Hipler's proposals, but the majority of individual detachments rejected them; spoilt by their early victories, they were afraid they would have to share their booty with the landsknechts. Irresponsible statements had been circulated that the whole world was already up in arms and that God would make three peasants victorious over a hundred thousand of the enemy – and they were believed. The end was the same everywhere. In what were somewhat grandiloquently called 'battles', thousands of peasants were mown down by hundreds of landsknechts; stubborn resistance by small groups of brave men led only to merciless slaughter. Many acts of treachery, which increased automatically as the scales began to turn, complete the picture. Truchsess, a well-schooled and cautious commander, was also a skilled negotiator. The knights who had joined the cause – under compulsion or for the booty – were the first to defect. The sole exception was Florian Geyer, who took to flight only when his 'black band' was cut to pieces; his cousin, another knight, had him murdered when the hunted man sought refuge in one of his castles. In March and April the peasants of south Germany and Thuringia had had the power in their hands; in May and June they were defeated, in Württemberg, in Thuringia, in Alsace, and finally in Franconia. The executioners went to work. The mercenaries devastated the countryside still more ruthlessly than the peasants; they were more thorough and better trained to the task. The forced contributions and levies imposed on the villages and smaller towns became permanent; serfdom lasted until the eighteenth century.

Only in one area, the alpine regions, did the revolts continue into 1526; it was the only area in which the peasants were successful against the mercenaries. It is significant that the peasants in Styria, the Tyrol and Salzburg were not among those most ruthlessly suppressed; in the Tyrol they were even represented in the diet. They had a skilful leader in Michael Gaismair, who came of a miner's family and for many years had been secretary to the governor of the Tyrol and the bishop of Brixen; his wider viewpoint gave him an intimate knowledge of conditions in the country. In these revolts the peasants were joined by a further very important class of the population – the miners in what were then the richest mining districts in Europe; their work had accustomed them to discipline and close co-operation. In his plan for reorganizing the country Gaismair recommended that the mining and smelting works, which were controlled by the Fuggers, Höchstetters and Paumgartners, be taken entirely out of their hands; it was an early attempt at socialization. The monopolies, he claimed, had forfeited their rights, they had 'burdened everyone with their unchristian usury and thereby amassed their princely fortunes; this state of affairs should be appropriately punished and redressed.' In other respects too this plan for reform – which had already been preceded by sixty-two articles issued by the

Tyrolese diet of peasants and townspeople – was more liberally conceived than the articles of the Swabian peasants; admittedly, however, it was conceived exclusively in terms of a peasant regime in the Tyrol. All the town walls were to come down and henceforth, in order to ensure 'complete equality', there were to be no more towns but only villages. Gaismair looked forward hopefully to the introduction of energetic measures for reclaiming marshlands and producing more bread-stuffs.

In this area, too, the princes, Archduke Ferdinand and the archbishop of Salzburg, emerged victorious but only after heavy defeats, in which the miners had played a decisive part. Vain attempts to storm the great fortresses of Salzburg and Trent once more proved fatal to the peasants. Gaismair, with the remnants of his supporters, had to flee over the border; in Switzerland and then in Italy, where Venice took him into its service, he remained a threat until the archduke hired an assassin to murder him.

Luther knew little of these distant happenings. For him nearby Thuringia was the main scene of action; even of the risings in Swabia and Franconia he heard hardly more than wild rumours of unprecedented atrocities committed by the peasants. Thuringia, the Schwarmgeister and Thomas Müntzer – so far as he was concerned, these constituted 'the Peasants' War'.

In Thomas Müntzer Luther saw the spirit of evil, Satan, which had led mankind astray; Müntzer returned the accusation, or rather charged Luther first and foremost with corruption, with having flattered the princes and delivered the Gospel's cause into their hands. In Müntzer's teaching the people, the peasants, were the 'elect'; to what extent his followers in Thuringia, a few thousands in all, understood his apocalyptic utterances is unlikely ever to be known. It also seems to us unnecessary to go into his faults, his short-sightedness, his failure at decisive moments or his utter unsuitability to play the part of military leader. He was no more a popular leader in action than Luther was a politician; he was a visionary, a prophet, an agitator, a man who sounded the alarm. He died under the executioner's sword at the age of thirty-five.

His image has been twisted this way and that, and been subjected to the most varied interpretations, from charges of heresy to hymns of praise. What we know of his life comes, for the most part, from his opponents and from biased chronicles; to this must be added his confessions under torture. Müntzer came from Stolberg in the Harz Mountains of parents who were not badly off; he studied and, at an early age, began a life of wandering. On Luther's recommendation he went to Zwickau where he came into contact with the local Schwarmgeister, with the clothier Storch and the 'Zwickau prophets', who visited

TOMAS MVNCER PREDIGER ZV ALSTET IN DVRINGEN.

Thomas Müntzer

THE PEASANTS' WAR

Luther in Wittenberg and brought him the first disquieting news of
new and radical teachings. Affirming the principle of 'inner enlightenment', they rejected the baptism of children and replaced the Bible by
spirit, by personal revelation – God could be experienced only in
visions. Müntzer was influenced by Hussite teachings from nearby
Bohemia, among them the cry of ruthless war against the 'godless' and
the dissenters. From Joachim de Fiore, whom he honoured as one of his
teachers, he adopted the chiliastic expectation of the imminence of
the 'last days', which would usher in the millennium; he was also
attracted by the ideas of the German mystics, especially Tauler. He
addressed himself to the 'humbled and abused', to the poor, and among
them he gained a hearing. In Zwickau his sermons to the clothiers and
artisans were followed by disorders, and he was ejected; this was his lot
wherever he went. He was bitter, but there was nothing new in this,
he had always been bitter; the 'Cross', the cup of bitterness, was his
watchword. Against nothing else did he inveigh so violently as against
the 'honeyed Christ', the easy-going, comfortable faith, of which he
saw Luther as the representative. In 1523 he was in the small Thuringian town of Allstedt, where his preaching won him an enthusiastic
following among the five hundred farming townspeople and artisans;
the pastor of the town and the steward of the castle also joined him. He
married a former nun, by whom he had a son. His sermons, none of
which has survived, made a wide appeal in Thuringia. He remodelled
the church service, introducing a German Mass even earlier than
Luther; he wrote his liturgical texts, made powerful translations of
Latin hymns, and drafted very careful regulations for his congregation,
admonishing them to strict discipline. At the same time, however, he
had a burning desire to spread his ideas; the word ambition, which can
be applied to every independent figure of significance, is too weak to
describe this driving force. Müntzer believed as strongly as Luther in the
immediate and universal efficacy of the Word.

Müntzer made loyal friends who carried his message for him; as in
the case of all underground movements, in which strict secrecy has to be
observed, we have no precise information about either where they went
or what influence they had. Luther became uneasy about the 'Allstedt
spirit', which he regarded as a sequel to the 'heavenly prophets' in
Zwickau. He corresponded with Müntzer, who sought to justify himself
and denied any connection with the clothier Storch; Luther warned
him against making fresh enemies. In his town of Allstedt Müntzer
felt himself to be an independent force, the 'Wittenberger's' equal and
his intellectual superior. The people of Allstedt, following Karlstadt's
example in Wittenberg, took visible action by destroying a chapel
containing a miraculous madonna, denouncing it as a 'house of the

419

devil'; the national authorities opened an investigation. All this, which took place a year before Müntzer's death, was still of only very local importance – Allstedt was a small centre of unrest in a country which, in any case, was torn by many cross-currents of opinion. Karlstadt had disseminated his ideas, in many respects very similar to those of Müntzer, in Orlamünde, but the people of Orlamünde refused to join forces with the people of Allstedt. In Eisenach a preacher named Strauss announced the restoration of the laws of Moses; in Weimar the court chaplain rallied to him.

The Elector Frederick and his brother and co-regent John listened to all these views; John was considerably impressed by the court chaplain's ideas. The two princes went to Allstedt, in order to hear Müntzer as well, who presented himself to the 'active, dear dukes', as he called them, in the role of prophet. He explained the prophecy of the four earthly kingdoms and the eternal kingdom of God with which Daniel had interpreted Nebuchadnezzar's dream; it is a learned piece of writing, containing innumerable Bible quotations that denote the widely read theologian. The quotations reveal Müntzer's rabid hatred of the 'scribes who like to eat succulent titbits at court', the 'godless hypocrites and flatterers'; and, although he does not mention Luther by name, it is unmistakably him to whom he is referring when he speaks of 'Brother Fattened Pig' and 'Brother Easy Life'. The end of the fifth kingdom of the world had come, 'Ah, My Lords, how nicely the Lord will lay about Him with His rod of iron among the old potter's vessels (Psalm 2). Therefore, most dearly beloved regents, learn to judge correctly out of the mouth of God, and do not let yourselves be misled by your hypocritical priests or hindered by fabricated patience and goodness! For the stone which was torn from the mountain has become great. The poor laymen and peasants see it far more clearly than you do.'

We have no information on how the dear regents took the sermon, nor do we know if it was given in the form in which Müntzer printed it; the dukes were accustomed to plain speaking. But now Luther became angry. He wrote a letter to the dukes 'about the rebellious spirit' who, having wandered round in vain, had now made a corner for himself in Allstedt, 'and intends to fight against us under cover of our peace, patronage and protection.' He sharply opposed the breaking of images and the burning of churches and chapels; strict instructions must be given to stop this. He distinguished between preaching and action: 'Let them preach confidently and frankly anything they can and against anyone they wish. Because, as I have said, sects must exist and the Word of God must be in the battle and fight ... If theirs is the right spirit it will not fear us and will remain in good heart. If ours is right it will fear neither them nor anyone else. Leave the spirits to clash and strike one another ...'

Luther had invited Müntzer to Wittenberg to discuss religion. Müntzer declined; he was willing to answer for his views only before a truly universal assembly. John, the co-regent, summoned him to Weimar, where a sort of interrogation took place, during which he was asked about his secret society. The people of Allstedt abandoned him; he fled and went to the free imperial city of Mühlhausen, the next stage of his journey. The city was already in the throes of an uprising led by another preacher, Heinrich Pfeiffer, who was the spokesman of the humbler citizens in their fight against the city council. Müntzer allied himself with him; the two men, ordered to leave the town, wandered round south Germany. In Nuremberg Müntzer published his defence against Luther; it was seized and most of the copies destroyed. On the title-page Luther was described as the 'mindless, soft-living piece of meat in Wittenberg who has perversely and quite contemptibly defiled poor Christendom by stealing the Holy Scriptures.' The sixteenth century was not fastidious in the matter of personal attacks, but we shall look a long way before we find another to compare with this pamphlet; in it Luther is referred to as a liar, an arrant fool, a spiteful raven, a godless rogue, Father Sneak, a cockatrice, the arch-heathen, an impertinent monk, an arrant knave, a 'poisonous little worm with your filthy humility', a 'fox who barks himself hoarse before daybreak.' 'Sweet dreams, dear flesh! I would rather smell you roasted by God's wrath ...'

In the early days of the Peasants' War in south Germany Müntzer was active and influential in a number of places; when the peasants rose in Thuringia he went back to Mühlhausen, where Heinrich Pfeiffer had also returned. The city council was overthrown and a new 'eternal council' appointed, but neither Müntzer nor Pfeiffer was a member. The four weeks of April 1525 were the period of Müntzer's last and most famous agitation. Luther, and many of his contemporaries, regarded him as the 'King and Imperator' of Mühlhausen and leader of the whole movement. But to a greater extent even than in south Germany, where large areas fell temporarily into the hands of the peasant forces, the battle in Thuringia degenerated into quite small local actions; peasants took up arms against their own lord of the manor, a town rose against its council, a county revolted. Here too several counts and nobles joined the peasants. The desire for booty had the same disastrous results as in Swabia and Franconia; contemporary accounts speak of columns of waggons laden with bacon, church property and wine from the monasteries, of attacks in districts where there was easy booty to be had, of the reluctance of individual detachments to join up with others or go to their aid. There was no sign whatever of any unified leadership. Müntzer was not in fact 'King and Imperator' at all; he was a preacher and an agitator, and in these capacities displayed feverish activity. He wrote here, there and everywhere, and distributed his pamphlets. He addressed the people of Allstedt: 'The whole German, French and Italian countryside is awake. The master wants to have a gamble, the scoundrels have to do his bidding ... Where there are only three of you, and you trust in God and seek only his name and honour, you will not fear a hundred thousand. On, on, on! The hour has struck. The scoundrels have lost heart like dogs ... They will turn to you, whimpering and entreating like children. Do not be moved to pity, as God has commanded us by Moses ... See that this letter reaches the mineworkers ... On, on while the fire is hot! Do not let your sword grow cold! Do not let it grow weak! Forge it with resounding clangs on Nimrod's anvil ...'

'On, on, on!' was the landsknechts' war-cry in hand-to-hand fighting. Thomas Müntzer signed his name 'with the hammer' or 'with the sword of Gideon'. He wrote to the counts of Mansfeld, to 'Brother Albrecht of Mansfeld' who had decided in favour of Luther's teaching: 'Did you not find in your Lutheran groats and your Wittenberg soup what Ezekiel prophesied in his thirty-seventh chapter? And wallowing in Martin's peasant filth were you also unable to taste what the same prophet went on to say, how God commanded every feathered fowl and every beast of the field to eat the flesh of the mighty and drink the blood of the princes?' And he also warned Albrecht's Catholic brother to submit if he did not want to be pursued and destroyed: 'We desire your answer by tonight ... I shall come for it.'

The 'I', which Müntzer used continually, is characteristic. He was convinced he had been appointed by God, that the destiny of the peasants had been placed in his hands; the proud 'I shall come for it' is no peasant phrase. Apart from a tiny group of ardent followers, few people paid any attention to him. The mineworkers did not come. His letters to neighbouring towns were answered with lame excuses, even Mülhausen, his headquarters, being disinclined to throw in its lot with him; he had already quarrelled with Pfeiffer. Only a small band of three hundred men set out when an appeal for help was received from a large detachment of peasants who had assembled in Frankenhausen, on the Kyffhäuser ridge. For in the meantime a consortium of princes had been formed and was approaching with troops; it consisted of Luther's enemy Duke George of Saxony, his patron Duke John, the landgrave of Hesse, who had crushed the revolt of Sickingen and his knights, and the two counts of Mansfeld. Their religious convictions, in so far as these played any part at all, were divided; they were united in their immediate goal, which was to defeat the peasants. In the process they were also anxious to collect some booty or, as they expressed it, to indemnify themselves for the trouble to which they had been put; on the way to Frankenhausen the landgrave of Hesse had already annexed the rich bishopric of Fulda, while the two dukes of Saxony had their eyes on the free imperial city of Mühlhausen. As Müntzer marched out of Mühlhausen with his men he had a drawn sword, signifying ruthless war against the godless, carried in front of him, as well as a large banner made of over twenty yards of white silk and painted with a rainbow to symbolize the 'new league' of the elect. Carried on carts were eight small cannon, for which there was no gunpowder. Müntzer accompanied the expedition as preacher.

The peasant forces in Frankenhausen had entrenched themselves behind a barricade of waggons, in the Hussite fashion; they comprised between six and eight thousand men, while the princes had about three thousand horsemen and foot soldiers, together with some artillery for which gunpowder was available. Negotiations took place; there seems to have been little unanimity in the peasants' camp. Müntzer advocated resolute action; on orders from him his followers put to death four emissaries whom the princes had sent into the camp. But on the day of the engagement itself the peasant majority addressed a letter to the princes: 'We are not here to harm anyone, but to obtain divine justice. Nor are we here to shed blood. If this is your wish also, we have no desire to harm you. Each side must hold to this.' The princes replied by demanding that Müntzer and his followers be handed over; the peasants refused. The result was the catastrophe of 15 May 1525, known as the Battle of Frankenhausen. The princes had drawn up their cannon on a commanding site overlooking the peasants' encampment, into which they proceeded to fire. At the very first shots the peasants broke up and fled; there were only a few isolated engagements. Frankenhausen, and with it the deserting peasant troops making their way into it, fell into the victors' hands; according to their reports five thousand peasants were killed, while their own casualties totalled five. The inhabitants of the town were massacred.

Mühlhausen also surrendered quickly. Its citizens sent their women and girls, wearing garlands of wormwood, into the camp to kneel before the victors. By making large payments the city saved itself from plunder, the princes dividing the overlordship and the money between them. The trials began. Müntzer had been taken prisoner in Frankenhausen, where he had hidden in a peasant's house; Pfeiffer was also brought in. Both men were severely tortured and their confessions written down. Then they were beheaded and their heads impaled on stakes outside the city.

To us today confessions obtained under torture are of extremely doubtful value. Pfeiffer seems to have been brief and honest: they had seen what he had done, there was nothing to deny, he declared. He refused confession and absolution. The orthodox Duke George reported with disappointment that he had not been as 'devout' as Müntzer, on whom God had bestowed the grace to confess his wrongs; he had 'only desired the unity of the Christian Churches and so received the holy, blessed Sacrament in the form of bread.' To his contemporaries Müntzer's confession of repentance was incomparably more important than the other points he conceded in various confessions. As it is unlikely that he was still able to write after being subjected to the thumb-screw, we cannot attach too much weight to his statements that 'he had provoked the rebellion in order that Christendom should be the same for all, and that those princes and rulers unwilling to support the Gospel should be driven out and killed,' or that 'everything should be held in common and distributed to each according to his need, as occasion arose.' Müntzer's 'communism', like that of many of the anabaptist groups, was highly individual; he claimed the Bible as his authority and lived and died believing that the millennium was imminent. Müntzer's writings contain scarcely any ideas for a comprehensive new social order and not a word on his concept of the New Kingdom. He saw himself as a prophet and was obsessed by a passionate hope for the poor and oppressed, the elect of God. As many have done since, he thought in terms of universal categories: the whole world would rise simultaneously and usher in the new era at a single stroke. In this one can regard him as foreshadowing world revolution. He has always been accused of a lack of proportion, a trait he shared with all prophets. His eyes were focused on heaven; it was from there that he awaited the thunderclap which would precede the rainbow. Perhaps his end is most movingly summed up in the opening words of his farewell letter to his congregation in Mühlhausen – in all probability it was a piece of hypocrisy composed and dictated by his enemies: 'Salvation and bliss through fear, but death and hell come first, dear brethren!'

A slender ray of light is thrown on the victors, and the proceedings following immediately on Müntzer's capture, in a letter to Luther from a Mansfeld councillor named Rühel. According to this they sat Müntzer on a bench. The princes went up and interrogated him, each asking the ordinary, simple questions that seemed to him most important at the time. Duke George 'sat down beside him and in conversation asked him his reason for having the four [emissaries] beheaded the previous Saturday. He said: Dear brother, I tell you, Cousin, it was not I who did it but divine justice.' Another duke went up to him: 'Tell me, are you also a prince like us? Of course you are and a fine one too, you have made a good start to your reign. What gave you the idea that a prince should have no more than eight horses and a count no more than four?' – these figures actually occur in one of Müntzer's letters. The young landgrave of Hesse, who did not hesitate to quote the Scriptures, 'got into a violent quarrel with Müntzer over it. Müntzer made use of the Old Testament, but the landgrave confined himself to the New, which he had with him and from which he read passages to refute Müntzer.' There is something almost ingenuous about this bench on which the princes sat with their prisoner arguing about the beheadings, the horses, the differences between various Old Testament prophecies and Paul's command 'be subject unto the higher powers'. In the background stood the executioner.

In this same letter Rühel, who was related by marriage to Luther, also raised an admonishing voice: 'Be this as it may, many who agree with you find it strange that you condone merciless killing and maintain that by its means men can become martyrs.' It was also frequently said that Luther was afraid for his own skin.

The hint was a reference to Luther's furious pamphlet *Against the Thieving and Murderous Gangs of Peasants*; it had appeared just as the battle in Thuringia ended. Its savagery – people were to 'belabour, strangle and stab' the peasants, 'this is a time for anger and the sword, it is not a time for mercy' – was really out of date; in any case the princes needed no encouragement from Luther. Luther's reply to his relative was quite uncompromising: 'They do not hear the Word and are foolish, therefore they must hear the muskets and it serves them right. We should pray for them, that they be obedient. If they are not, there is not much place for mercy. Let the muskets whistle about them, otherwise they will make things a thousand times worse ... Anyone who has seen Müntzer can say he has seen the devil incarnate in all his fury.'

It was an age of anger and apocalyptic expectations. Luther, like Müntzer, believed the end to be imminent. This does not excuse his raging and ranting, which cost him the sympathy not only of the peasants and other classes but of many of his supporters in the towns as well. The year 1525 was the great turning-point of his cause. From now on he was no longer the hero of the whole nation, on whom everyone's hopes were centred, but simply the head of a faction. And even as such his position was increasingly questioned and threatened by leaders of factions within his own camp. But of all the charges levelled against him by Müntzer the most absurd were certainly those of being a sneak and a soft liver. Nor was he afraid for his own skin. Lack of courage can hardly be counted among his failings. He was proud of his recklessness and constantly stressed the fact that it had been he and he alone who had risen against pope, emperor and empire, while all the others had only 'murmured' and held secret discussions. His word and his word alone had won the victory. Within two or three years, or so he believed, it would have won further victories, without the use of arms – the 'fist' – had not hotheads and madmen intervened. This was not a new attitude occasioned by the peasant risings; he had already warned Sickingen and Hutten, with their knights' revolt, not to resort to arms. He had no faith in the plans for a democracy of the nobility and none in the idea of peasant rule. In this he may have been guided unconsciously by his peasant instinct, his deep mistrust of 'immature movements' which could lead only to trouble; from a historic viewpoint he was right. In spite of the deep sympathy he felt for those who took part in the only great mass insurrection in German history, Friedrich Engels – in his work on the Peasants' War, published shortly after the unsuccessful revolution of 1848 – was forced to the conclusion that 'the whole movement was ruined by local and provincial fragmentation and by the local and provincial narrow-mindedness to which it led.' From the materialist viewpoint he was also quite logical in recognizing that Thomas Müntzer failed because his stand came 'too soon': 'Not only this movement, but his whole century, was unready to put into practice ideas of which he himself had no more than a dim presentiment.'

Discernment of this kind was foreign to Luther; indeed discernment played no part in his judgments, he judged emotionally. All he saw was his Gospel threatened by Schwarmgeister, and at the very moment when victory seemed within his grasp without a sword being drawn. He had been tireless in going from place to place fighting this threat, fighting his old friend Karlstadt and others, among whom he regarded Müntzer simply as the most dangerous. While engaged on this campaign he suffered his first bitter experiences. In Karlstadt's town of Orlamünde people had hurled curses at him, in another place he found a mutilated crucifix on the pulpit; he was greeted with suspicious glances or in sullen silence. The advance of his Reformation had suffered a crisis before the Peasants' War began; he had defended himself against the 'heavenly prophets' with angry outbursts and fierce defiance. He had declared Church ritual to be redundant; but now, because attempts were being made to turn this suggestion into a command, he opposed it: originally, he said, he had also intended to do away with the ritual but now he had changed his mind 'in order to defy and resist fanaticism for a little while longer' – he would not yield by so much as a 'hair's breadth'. He had shown the same intransigence towards the peasants when they submitted their *Twelve Articles* to him; the *Exhortation to Peace*, with which he replied, was incomprehensible to both sides in the quarrel. It contained an angry threat to the princes and rulers: the time had come to put an end to 'oppression and taxation'; the common man 'neither can nor will tolerate it any longer – the sword is already at your necks!' The peasants, on the other hand, had the Bible thrown in their teeth – 'He that killeth with the sword must perish by the sword'; they were exhorted to obey those in authority, even if they were unjust. He had not gone into all the articles, maintaining that some of them were matters for the legal experts, 'because it does not befit me, as an evangelist, to judge them. My task is to educate the conscience.' The matter should be settled peaceably by a committee: 'As I have told you, you are both of you wrong and wrong to fight.' Luther's tragedy was that it was no longer possible for him to be simply an evangelist and adviser on questions of conscience; as the people's mouthpiece he had been called upon to give his views on a pressing emergency, on a crying wrong that could be remedied neither by prayer nor by committee meetings.

To make matters still worse, this letter not only appeared in print when the war was almost over, it contained a frenzied call to treat the peasants as robbers: 'Stab, strike and strangle who can! ... If anyone thinks this too severe, let him reflect that rebellion is intolerable and that at any moment the world may be destroyed.' Even his friends were puzzled and did not know what to say to this juxtaposition. To the peasants the suggestion that they negotiate must have seemed like sheer mockery, since they had already thrown themselves on their opponents' mercy, only to discover what the victors understood by mercy. The princes remembered the sharp rebukes he had levelled at them. In order to justify himself, Luther followed this pamphlet in July with another, even more chaotic one. Pursuing his doctrine of the two kingdoms, he declared that the kingdom of this world was the kingdom of 'wrath and severity' and that its tool was 'not a garland of roses or a flower plucked from love, but a drawn sword.' Simultaneously, however, he stormed against the junkers who, after their victory, had 'treated the poor people with such excessive cruelty.' He had heard that after the fall of Mühlhausen one of the nobles had tried to rape Müntzer's widow; indignant at this 'chivalrous, noble deed' he remarked that the Bible called such people brutes. He distributed his censure quite impartially. Having previously said, 'If the peasants came to power the devil would be made an abbot, but if such tyrants gained control his mother would be made an abbess,' he now added: 'Very well, they will also have their reward, although no harm would be done were they to be murdered by the peasants ... unless they repent, their reward will be eternal hell.'

The letters were written down hurriedly and intended for the moment; they were not political essays or blueprints of a just social order, of which Luther had no notion whatsoever. They are, perhaps, best understood as evidence of an unruly, indeed reckless, temperament that found itself suddenly checked after a triumphal progress without parallel. He was beset on all sides by difficulties, which he called the devil. To the rest of the world it was Luther who was possessed by Satan, being held responsible for causing the war by his teachings. He was threatened as scarcely ever before, and this may also explain his agitation even if it does not justify it. The victorious princes were now thinking in all seriousness of implementing the Edict of Worms; only jealousy among the various claimants prevented occupation of the electorate of Saxony. In the middle of all the confusion caused by the war, the old elector, Frederick the Wise, died. Cautiously, if not very firmly, he had held a protecting hand over Luther until the end; in his patriarchal way he was wise and kindly. In April, when the consortium of princes to combat the revolt was in the process of formation, he wrote to his brother and co-regent, a man of a robuster nature who also took part in the expedition to Frankenhausen: 'To resort to force is a big thing to do. Perhaps the poor people have been given cause to rise up like this, especially for forbidding God's Word. There are many ways in which the poor are burdened by us secular and ecclesiastical authorities. May God turn his wrath from us. If it is God's will that the common man shall rule it will happen so.' Three weeks later he died. On his deathbed he received the communion in both its forms, having also put off making a decision on this matter of conscience until the last moment.

His brother, Duke John, who now took his place, was a man of limited intelligence compared to Frederick who, when all is said and done, had shown considerable prudence, indecisive though it always was. Great plans for reforming the empire, which his predecessor had entertained all his life, were wholly outside his range; he had no ambitions whatever beyond the internal policies of the electorate of Saxony. He recoiled even from entering into agreements with other princes, although this might have been useful to him; his councillors, who were not without ambition, had difficulty persuading him to conclude any alliances at all. He wanted only to be the father of his people, and as such he held firmly to his Doctor Luther, much more firmly than his brother had done. He frequently summoned Luther to his court, exchanged letters with him, and made a copy in his own hand of the 'shorter catechism', which more or less circumscribed his spiritual and intellectual horizon. In the shadow of this bloody and revolutionary year of 1525 the Reformation, which in its beginnings had been a worldwide conflagration, has the appearance of declining into a small-town, small-state affair. It always retained traces of this.

Luther, very keenly aware of the receding tide and the coolness which surrounded him, once again made a bold decision. He married.

## Part Three

# The Wittenberg Reformer

## 32

# Frau Doktor Luther

IN THE weeks following the suppression of the peasant revolt in Thuringia, Luther married Katharina von Bora. It was a step he had long been expected to take, and one that many of his fellow Augustinians had already taken; he had continued to wear his habit longer than anyone else, discarding it only in December 1524, seven years after posting his theses. In many of his writings he had condemned celibacy and praised marriage, though he himself remained a monk, but without obeying the rules of an order. Every step he took was subjected by his enemies to the closest scrutiny; no effort was spared to find evidence of the 'fall' to which he seemed predestined by his powerful physique and full-blooded nature. Had he not written: 'Grow and multiply. This is not a command but something more than a command, it is a work of God that is not for us to prevent or permit; it is as necessary as for me to be a man and more necessary than eating and drinking, sleeping and waking. It is in our nature, implanted in us, just as are the parts of the body essential to it'? He had also said that the vows of chastity, against which the monks and nuns protested in vain, only made a mockery of God's commandment; 'if they hamper it, you can be sure that they will not remain pure but will inevitably be defiled by secret sins or whoredom.' He had quoted medical grounds: 'Therefore the physicians do not argue amiss when they say that if we forcibly curb this work of nature it must react on the flesh and the blood and become poison.' Was it possible for Dr Luther to resist this temptation?

Very different temptations plagued him when he had eaten too much or drunk too quickly, as he often did in following the extremely unwholesome diet with which he tried to ward off his attacks of depression. While the severe mental disturbances from which he suffered are not to be explained entirely in this way, there is no doubt that his highly irregular way of life was an important contributory factor. Moreover, he slept badly on a wretched bed which no one kept in order for him. And on top of it all he worked tirelessly and heedless of his body, letting up only when his kidneys, or the gall-stones from which he suffered early in life, made a break imperative. Luther's medical history would fill a thick file; his tough constitution enabled him over and over again to surmount ailments of the most varied kinds and, in spite of all his exertions and paroxysms of anger and exhaustion, to reach the advanced age for those days of sixty-two. The fact that he had reached the age of forty-two before he married, and that prior to this there is not a shred of reliable evidence of any moral lapse, will seem remarkable only to those unfamiliar with the life stories of other comparable men of genius.

But even at the time, his marriage caused tremendous excitement. The runaway monk and the runaway nun – it was the accepted formula, and it was applied with indignation and relish. Verses circulated among the students, one of whom, a young man named Simon Lemnius, having been sent down from the university at Luther's instigation for writing malicious epigrams about well-known people, wrote his *Pornomachomachia*, on the 'battle between the monks and the whores', an early exercise in pornography. In humanist fashion it paraded the verb *futuere* in all its variants, and in the nineteenth century circulated in private editions as a sought-after piece of eroticism. The following is Lessing's version of the story: 'At first Luther, who, under promise of marriage, is said to have taken his pleasure of Käthe when she was still in the convent, does everything in his power to get rid of her. But just as he is doing his utmost to marry someone else, and is already within sight of his goal, his old flame from the convent flings herself round his neck and manages to hold him so tightly that he is forced to take her as his wife. His friends Jonas and Spalatin, seeing this and not wanting to leave him alone in his disgrace, each takes to himself one of the religious nymphs whom Käthe has brought with her from the convent. But as all three subsequently find their husbands more or less impotent, they are forced to look elsewhere for nourishment,' for which purpose the services of various Wittenberg students are enlisted.

This wretched production is worth mentioning at all only because it gives an idea of the level on which the matter was discussed in Wittenberg. Lemnius had kept his ears open, and it is true that Luther had originally thought of marrying someone else. It is also true that, as the pamphlet states, the moment chosen by Luther for his marriage was particularly resented: 'Everywhere the smoke still rises from the ravaged villages, thousands of peasants are being led away in chains, the rivers are red with the blood that has been shed.' But there is not one iota of evidence to support the story of 'bacchanals'; the way in which contemporaries grew indignant over what they heard of Wittenberg and Luther is nothing short of amusing. Even the great Erasmus had nothing better to do than spread the rumour in his letters that Käthe was expecting a child and for this reason had to get married in a hurry; when the boy arrived after the perfectly normal interval of a year he had to retract this. Melanchthon also complained, in a letter to a friend in Nuremberg, that Luther had failed to let both him and others into his confidence; had he done so he would have advised him strenuously against taking this step at such a difficult time. 'But the man is so easily handled! The nuns, who are well versed in all the arts, have got him under their thumbs. Luther is so nobleminded and generous that merely being with the nuns has emasculated him; he must also have been smitten by her. And so he seems to have fallen into the trap and made this very untimely change in his life.'

Probably very little harm would have been done if Luther had made a 'slip' like Zwingli, who admitted it quite frankly. The reproaches hurled at him from bishops' palaces and Rome, which crawled with bastards and mistresses, were grotesque. The charge that Luther had broken his vow came a little late too; he had ignored the orders imposed on him as a monk at a much earlier date and much more emphatically. But in all this excitement there was an involuntary recognition of the facts of the situation; it seemed that by taking this step Luther crowned his rebellion against the Church. Now he had burned all his bridges. Widely as it was disregarded in practice, celibacy still remained one of the most important positions of the Church of Rome. And celibacy, or its abolition, remained one of the main points of conflict until after Luther's death; it was primarily over this question that the negotiations over reuniting the churches broke down, although both the strictly orthodox emperor and his brother Ferdinand were in favour of abolition.

It was above all in this light that Luther saw his decision; he was up in arms, his mood was one of defiance and protest. To Spalatin he wrote: 'I hope the angels will laugh and all the demons cry; by marrying Katharina von Bora I have shut the mouths of the scandalmongers.' This step was his last great act of protest, but at the same time it also signified his resignation. His intervention in secular affairs had ended in disaster, a fact of which Luther himself was keenly aware. However much he might continue to rage against the stubborn and rebellious peasants, and on the other hand exhort the victors either to leniency or to vigorous use of their swords, he knew, and heard on all sides, that the days of his popularity were over. The peasants mistrusted him, the humanists turned their backs on him; the princes and other powerful figures remained very aloof – they had not forgotten his biting attacks on them. Luther was no longer the great prophet to whom almost all Germany had listened, the cynosure of limitless hopes. There were many prophets now and they drew devoted disciples. In many respects he had to start again from the beginning, among those round him and indeed among those closest to him. To his peasant way of thinking the family was the nucleus of the world order, the point of departure for everything; the 'state' was simply a family on a larger scale with, at its head, a patriarchal figure. Seen in this light his marriage was in the nature of a political act, although Luther may hardly have thought of it like that. He conceived it as a duty imposed on him by his teaching. To proclaim that marriage was ordained by God and to remain unmarried himself was not permissible; it was up to him now to set an example. Starting from this small but rapidly increasing family circle he tried, during the years that remained to him after the great disaster of the Peasants' War, to build up a small world.

It was a microcosm, a modest house within the walls of the old monastery overlooking the moat of the little town of Wittenberg, which, thanks to him, had now become famous; but it was still a wretched place with its thin beer and empty gossip, the latter even penetrating into the circle of Luther's closest friends and associates when he announced his marriage. There was nothing romantic about this marriage, except perhaps the story of the abduction of the nine nuns from their convent. Katharina von Bora was a quite unromantic figure, an unusually competent, quickwitted Saxon who had a ready tongue – soon to become famous; she could hold her own even with her Dr Luther. She had to suffer a great deal of ridicule. There is more to be said for her than the comments noted at table by the students and paying guests, who did not always agree with her bills for board and lodging. Wives of great men scarcely ever have an easy time, either during their lives or at the hands of posterity. If they fail to cope with all the difficulties imposed by a man of genius, they are inevitably traduced, or else attempts are made somehow to equate them with the hero and thus render acceptable a relationship which otherwise seems inexplicable. In Luther's time, the position of the wife and of women in general differed greatly from that in later centuries. The wife had virtually no rights but, provided she had it in her, she could make a position for herself as mistress of the house that many of her emancipated successors might have envied.

Luther's wife had a position of this kind; he referred to her even officially as '*domina*', the name formerly given to the abbess of her convent. She ruled both her household and her husband, a situation which the latter accepted resignedly, since he was totally incapable of organizing the affairs of even the smallest household. She brought order into his life and not always to his satisfaction. His Augustinian monastery became a pension, an inn at which even princes put up, a large business undertaking with stock-breeding and rented land; later it grew into a small estate, accommodating twenty to thirty people – guests, students, staff and children, including those of relations – breeding its own cattle and with its own brewery, storerooms, cellars, barn and vegetable garden. In those days the mistress of the house, though having almost no legal rights, was a businesswoman, the head of a concern that had to be self-supporting, and this was true not only in the case of Frau Käthe. The life of the little community was dependent on her ability; a good wife was a blessing, a bad one a dreadful misfortune, especially since only death could put an end to the misery, a plight celebrated in countless songs, poems and malicious jests. But where had this nun learned all these arts, which she understood so much better than those 'artifices of the nuns' so feared by Melanchthon?

Katharina von Bora came of an impoverished aristocratic family in the district of Meissen, a part of Saxony that in Luther's day belonged to Duke George. The name is Slavonic, the ancestral villages being called German-Bora and Wendish-Bora. If we can trust the portrait by Lucas Cranach – who showed a partiality for this type in other paintings of his later period – Katharina's face, with its high cheekbones and narrow, rather slanting eyes, exhibited marked Wendish characteristics. The girl was no beauty, with her longish head, high forehead, long nose and powerful chin, though she had a very finely drawn mouth; being poor as well, her family put her, while still a child, into the convent where other relatives had also found a home. The Cistercian Convent of Nimbschen near Grimma, about twenty miles south-east of Leipzig, was intended specifically for the daughters of the impecunious nobility, owning sufficient property to be able to accept girls without the usual 'provision'. We know nothing about her parents; her father seems to have died young; three brothers are mentioned, who had to eke out their livings with minor positions at court and took no notice of their sister until she became Frau Doktor Luther. The forty nuns of the convent were kept in strict seclusion: the nuns' choir in the church was latticed, and a latticed window separated a nun from her relatives in the visitors' room, where they were allowed to exchange a few words with her in the presence of the abbess. The *domina* ruled her little republic sternly or leniently as the case might be, but the code itself was strict; the regulations forbade friendships between the nuns, and even dogs were not allowed into the seclusion of the convent. Silence was the rule, as it had been in Luther's monastery at Erfurt, and the nuns were required to walk with lowered heads and slow steps. The daily routine was governed by prayers and hymns. Nevertheless, Katharina learned to read and write and acquired some knowledge of Latin, this last being demanded by the Latin liturgy. One can picture this life as one wishes, as peaceful and happy and dedicated to God, or as an imprisonment unwillingly borne. The more apathetic among the nuns may have been content to be looked after well and be free of cares; at least it was a better life than being married to some impecunious knight, producing a child every year, looking after a husband who was usually drunk, and finally, as was almost inevitable, dying in childbirth and so making way for a successor. It is also possible that, in spite of the rules, the nuns gossiped avidly among themselves; the 'curiosity of nuns' was proverbial. The popular song spoke from the hearts of not a few of the imprisoned nuns: 'God grant him a disastrous year, who forces me to be a nun.'

Perhaps a song on these lines, or one of Luther's writings, had found its way into the convent's latticed seclusion; whatever the reason, nine of the girls, including two pairs of sisters, decided to break out. It was not a very easy thing to do, nor was it without danger, because the punishment for abducting a nun was death, and the surveillance in Duke George's territory was strict. The story of the escape was later somewhat embellished, the nuns allegedly having had to break through a cob wall in order to reach freedom; at all events they had outside assistance. Three citizens of Torgau and the pastor, Gabriel Zwilling, provided a carriage with a large awning to protect the occupants from prying eyes; only on reaching Torgau were they beyond the limits of the 'duchy' of Saxony and the danger of arrest. After a few more days on the road they arrived in Wittenberg, where they were set down outside Luther's monastery. To find homes for the girls among the families in the town presented difficulties; to find employment for them was still harder. As was only natural, most of them wanted to marry as soon as possible, no other occupation being open to an unmarried girl. Luther commended his protégées as 'pretty girls' – almost certainly an exaggeration; most of them were also no longer young by the standards of the day, when fifteen or sixteen was considered the best age to marry. At twenty-four Katharina von Bora was almost beyond marriageable age, but she seems to have been quite determined not to end her life as an old maid. During the first year her attentions were absorbed by the son of a Nuremberg patrician family named Baumgärtner; Luther was overjoyed at the prospects. The father, however, who had obviously heard of the affair and decided to put a stop to it at once, recalled the young man to Nuremberg; he already had a very well-to-do and otherwise suitable bride up his sleeve, whom the son then married. Luther wrote in vain to the young man telling him that if he wanted his Katharina von Bora he must hurry up, otherwise she might turn her attentions to someone else, 'who is at hand. But she has not got over her love for you. It would certainly give me great pleasure to see you united.' The patrician father's decision carried the day.

The other candidate whom Luther had at hand was a pastor in Orlamünde named Glatz, but Katharina refused to have anything to do with him. On the other hand she made it fairly clear that she would like to marry and that if Nikolaus von Amsdorf or Dr Luther would take her she would be happy. Amsdorf, Luther's friend and colleague at the university, had other plans, and Luther himself said later that at first he had had one of the two Schönfeld sisters in mind. He wrote jokingly to Spalatin about his little group of protégées and the talk of marriage: it was strange, he said, that he had not yet made up his mind, 'but if you are looking to me to set an example, you have it here in abundance. For I have three women at the same time and love them all so dearly that I have already lost two of them to other husbands. It is only the third whom I still have on my left arm' – a rather unfortunate allusion to a morganatic marriage. He procrastinated too long for Fräulein Ave von Schönfeld, who settled for a gifted student of medicine; her sister also looked elsewhere. Katharina von Bora remained constant. She became Käthe Luther and the best wife the difficult man could possibly have found.

But she was also made the butt of endless vilification, which continued into the seventeenth and eighteenth centuries with fat, fictitiously elaborated biographies in the most colourful baroque style; in one of these, entitled *Lucifer Wittenbergensis*, the 'morning star' as Luther called his Käthe, was turned into a nymphomaniac virago who jumped into bed with all the students. The fact that the moral indignation continued so long shows how violently this step of Luther's roused people's feelings, more so indeed than other steps of his which were far more significant.

It is unnecessary to expatiate on the subject; we have already seen the level of morals in Luther's day in monasteries, convents, bishops' palaces and Rome itself. One feels more inclined to see this marriage as denoting Luther's entry into a down-to-earth, bourgeois family life; he has, in fact, been held up as a model of the 'healthy philistinism of our German nature'. This again seems an oversimplification. In the ordinary sense his life up to this point had been anything but healthy, and it did not become so in the years that were left to him; in spite of all Käthe's care and attention his physical condition deteriorated steadily, with increasingly frequent illnesses, breakdowns and 'temptations', while the amount of work he got through remained undiminished, if it did not actually increase. He was over forty, and we should not begrudge him the small amount of order and comfort that now entered his life; it was, in any case, modest enough. There is, however, another point that needs to be emphasized: by nature Luther was a sociable person; he was not suited to a solitary life. He had already suffered on this account in the monastery where, when opportunity offered, he formed childlike attachments – with his 'father' Staupitz, for example; he had also welcomed the young Melanchthon with open arms, as he had everyone else in the 'little handful' of people in Wittenberg who got on reasonably well with him, which was not easy. Insisting, perhaps, a little on his role as pastor, but with a deep underlying significance, he enlarged on the subject in his table-talk: 'People sin much more often and more seriously when they are alone than when they are in the company of others. Eve was alone in the Garden of Eden when the devil beguiled her ... Christ promised that when two or three were gathered together in His name He would be in the midst of them. The devil tempted Christ when He was alone. David committed adultery when he was alone and idle. And I also have found that I never lapse into sin more often than when I am alone. God created mankind to be together, not to be alone. A proof of this is that He created them in two sexes, men and women ...'

The solitary genius, who despises his fellow men, exists and can do great things, but rarely without serious harm to himself; he often has to pay for unremitting loneliness with his life. There also exists the gregarious genius, and it was quite logical for Luther, who belonged very definitely to this type, to be led into marriage, a step that signified more than simply defiance and rebellion against the 'papal laws'. Round this marriage he built up his small, intimate circle of friends and pupils; it formed the periphery of his social life, of his work among men. To go beyond this was never granted him.

On the evening of 13 June 1525, according to the custom of the day, he appeared with his bride before a number of his friends as witnesses. The Pomeranian Bugenhagen blessed the couple, who consummated the marriage in front of the witnesses, as Jonas reported the next day: 'Luther has taken Katharina von Bora to wife. I was present yesterday and saw the couple on their marriage bed. As I watched this spectacle I could not hold back my tears.' The bride brought nothing to the marriage; Luther spoke of being able to produce two silver goblets as 'dowry'. A fortnight later, however, he gave a wedding feast which had at least some claims to being a festive occasion; he invited people from far and wide – and his parents had pride of place. The reconciliation with his father was a very significant moment: 'My father took me into his favour, and I became once more his dear son.' The letters which Luther sent out to beg provisions for the celebration read like a last echo of his days as a mendicant friar. To the seneschal Hans von Dolzig he wrote: 'If it is not asking too much, would you be kind enough to let me have some game, and be present yourself and help set the seal on the occasion with joy and whatever else is appropriate?' The town council gave a cask of Einbeck beer, which was considerably stronger than the thin Wittenberg brew, while the university presented a covered silver goblet. The oddest gift of all was twenty guilders sent by none other than Archbishop Albrecht of Mainz; it almost led to the first quarrel between the couple. Luther wanted to send the money straight back, because it came from his first enemy, the 'Nimrod and Giant of Babylon'; the thrifty Katharina, on the other hand, knowing how urgently every guilder was needed for the home, which was bare, saw to it that the present was quietly retained. The explanation of the gift was that this vacillating prince of the Church was once more thinking of following the example of his cousin, the grand master of the Order of Teutonic Knights, taking a wife and turning his archbishopric into a secular duchy. The idea proved altogether too risky, and so Albrecht remained officially celibate while unofficially maintaining his far from unexacting concubines. This episode illustrates yet again the two opposing worlds.

Frau Käthe was not exacting, but she took good care to see that the house was properly run. The Augustinian monastery, which had never been quite finished because the court always hesitated to supply the promised few loads of bricks, was a long, sprawling building containing cramped cells for the monks, some larger rooms for their assemblies, a small tower on the south side, with the little room in which Luther had had his 'tower experience' that led to his doctrine of justification, and a small brewery. One side of the building gave on to the former cemetery and the little chapel where devotions were held; the other side faced the town moat. Luther had been living a meagre existence in one of the cells: 'Before I married, no one had made up my bed for a whole year; the straw was rotting from my sweat. I was tired, and wore myself out with work during the day, so that I just fell into bed oblivious of everything.' Frau Käthe had her hands full. The Elector John made his Doctor a present of the building, in which only Luther and the last prior continued to live, and gradually it was transformed into what finally became the quite imposing Luther home. Frau Käthe had a bathroom fitted out, the sixteenth century being more advanced in this respect than later ages; she also had a cellar built under the house, to eliminate damp from the nearby moat, and the cemetery was turned into a garden, where she grew vegetables. Stables for pig-breeding were added, and land was rented beyond the town gates; later she took over from one of her rather ne'er-do-well brothers a small country estate belonging to the family at Zühlsdorf and put it on its feet. Luther then wrote to her as his 'gracious Miss Katharina Luther of Bora and Zühlsdorf, my darling' – or banteringly

439

as the 'preacher, brewer, gardener and all things else', because she had also taken over and turned to good use the monastery's brewing rights.

The early days of the marriage were not altogether easy for the monk, who was used to being alone; according to his friend Melanchthon Luther was thoroughly depressed. He himself described it more graphically: 'In the first year of marriage a man has strange thoughts. At table he thinks: before you were alone, now there are two of you. In bed, when he wakes up, he sees a pair of pigtails which he never used to see.' At first his wife's mania for talking – she had spent too much time in compulsory silence – got on his nerves: 'During the first year my Käthe used to sit by my side while I was working, and when she was at a loss for something to say would ask me: Doctor, is the Grand Master in Prussia the brother of the Margrave [of Brandeburg]?' As was usual at that time she addressed him by his title, but this did not prevent her calling him to order in front of his pupils and friends, when his language smacked too much of the peasant for the taste of the former aristocrat, and he used those coarse words and illustrations that were all noted down, to the horror of sensitive readers of later ages. She herself had little time for reading, being forced to rise at four o'clock in the morning in order to get through her housework. Six children came at regular intervals, of whom two girls died young.

A new cycle of existence was inaugurated. In the monastery Luther had lived timelessly; now he witnessed the process of passing generations. The monk had devoted himself to abstract, fundamental problems; as head of a family he was concerned with the present and the immediate future. This had its effect on his teaching and work. The *Shorter Catechism*, which grew out of his family experience and was intended for the families of those round him, became the most influential work of his later years. At the conclusion of his exegesis of the Ten Commandments he remarks that the older people, those of his generation, are finished and done with: 'Let us then raise the people who are to follow us and take our places.' The Fourth Commandment – honour thy father and thy mother – which his father Hans had cast in his face when he entered the monastery, had now become one of the most important for him: 'For God has set this estate at the head and to take His place on earth.' Discipline and obedience within the family was the starting-point, 'because everything else flows and develops out of parental authority.' This implied obedience also 'to secular authority, which always occupies the position of father and whose influence extends furthest of all. For to be in this position is to be not one father but as many fathers as there are tenants, citizens or subjects. Therefore such authority is to be respected and honoured.' How far this 'authority' would extend its influence, and how little it would concern itself with 'protection and safety', were matters that did not enter Luther's thoughts. He viewed the relationship entirely patriarchally, and for him the family, with its hearth and home, was still a 'stronghold' in which the head of the family reigned. Undeniably, however, the fatal submissiveness to authority had its origin in this attitude; it became a distinguishing feature of the Protestants and expecially of those who followed Luther. A right to oppose tyrannical authority, such as was recognized and practised by the Calvinists, was rejected categorically by Luther. One had to submit.

In his own little realm, at any rate, he put his precepts into practice. Much time was given to prayer, family prayers were said in the former refectory, the Bible was read and explained; when he was displeased with Käthe, it was because she did not read the Bible enough. 'She busies herself about the place, cultivates the field, grazes and buys cattle, brews beer, etc. Between times she has also started to read the Bible, and I have promised her fifty guilders if she finishes it by Easter. She takes this very seriously! She has already reached Deuteronomy,' he wrote to his friend Jonas, whose wife, also a former aristocrat with numerous children, was a particularly close friend of Käthe's. Jonas married three times; Ambrosius Reuter, another friend and relative, also married three times, but in succession, not simultaneously as was alleged of Wittenberg residents by scandal-mongers outside, and had twenty-three children of whom only twelve survived him. It was one continual round of births and deaths. Luther's sisters, who married and lived in their home town of Mansfeld, also died young, and Käthe took their children to live with her; there were eleven in all. Including her own she had sixteen Luther offspring to look after, and they were not all well behaved by any means.

Where did this remarkable woman get her ability to run the household? She had had only two short years of apprenticeship before her marriage; she seems to have helped, and cast her eyes round, in the large house of Lucas Cranach and his wife Barbara. It sheltered a dozen apprentice painters, a rather boisterous little group who sometimes got into bloody fights with the university students; next door to his studio Cranach had a printing works which reproduced engravings and woodcuts of Luther on a commercial scale for distribution all over the world. But the master's richest source of income was the Wittenberg apothecary's shop, which he also owned and the manager of which married one of the nuns from Nimbschen; attached to it was a wine shop. The painter was one of the three wealthiest men in Wittenberg; another was Lufft, the printer. Dr Luther had only his stipend; it was increased to a hundred guilders when he married, and was later doubled. He received no lecture fees from the students at the university.

A mid-sixteenth-century nursery

He gave without stinting – fugitives and those in need only had to ask him. 'Dear Käthe,' he once wrote, 'if we have no more money the goblets must go. One must give if one wants to have.' Two years after his marriage he still owed a hundred guilders; from time to time he tried to balance his accounts: 'N.B. Curious account between Doctor Martin and Käthe, 1535/6. It covered two half years.' Everything was entered, from parsley to slaughtered oxen; they had eight pigs and two sows for breeding, five cows, nine calves and a goat. But he did not get very far. He reckoned up his yearly consumption of rolls, groaning when the amount came to thirty groschen and four pfennigs – it was too much: 'I never like doing accounts, it depresses me, it always works out to too much. I would not have believed that so much could go on one person! ... Tell me: Where is the money to come from? Won't it mean unpleasantness and debts?' Between the figures he sighed in verse: 'Is there any poor wretch keeps house so ill! For when I need money to pay a bill, and look for it in the place I know, not a penny is there, though I search high and low.' The place he knew was a drawer where the money, always in short supply, was kept and quickly spent again; then the question of the silver goblets had to be raised once more. When his famulus, Rischmann, left he was away and wrote to Käthe telling her to see that he was given a decent parting gift; on this occasion, un-like others, it would be put to good use, 'because he has lost everything. So do what you can! I know there is not much there, but I would willingly give him ten guilders if I had them. But you should not give him less than five because he has no clothes. Don't fail in this, so long as there is still a goblet left. Think where you can get it from. God will give something in its place, that I know.'

To the sixteen children were added the students, whom Käthe took as paying guests: after Luther died this remained one of her chief sources of income. They lived in what had been the monks' cells. There were also other guests; to stay in Dr Luther's house was considered a great honour, and the little town of Wittenberg was badly off for inns. Well-wishers warned a prince who intended to take a room there: 'An odd assortment of young people, students, young girls, widows, old women and children lives in the Doctor's home; this makes for great disquiet in the house, and there are many who pity Luther because of it.'

Even in his study he had no peace, and of order there was still less. Every table, window-sill, chair and stool was covered with letters, books, inquiries from town councils and parishes, petitions, proofs, polemics and tracts; in Nuremberg, so he wrote to his former fellow-Augustinian Link, the city council had a whole office for the purpose. The children came in and played, especially little Hänschen: 'As I sit

443

and write he sings me a song, and if it gets too loud I scold him a little; he goes on singing just the same, but he does it more furtively, becoming rather anxious and shy.' Like Mozart, who was also a 'gregarious genius', worked under similar conditions and even liked to have people round him while he wrote, Luther wrote down only what had long been clear in his head; he repeated himself with complete unconcern, drew broad, practical lessons, let fly furiously when he felt invigorated by a 'lusty anger', or became happy again at the sight of his young son singing away. It is necessary to keep these surroundings in mind when we consider his writings, most of which were improvisations, born of the moment and intended for the moment. He himself never regarded them in any other way and would have liked many of them to be forgotten; this did not apply to his translation of the Bible, his family homilies – in his opinion his best work – or his catechism.

The conversations he held with close friends and at table were also intended for the moment, for the evening hour. They have since become famous as Luther's *Table-Talk*; even during his lifetime everything he let fall, from large mouthfuls to tiny crumbs, was written down and destined for publication. The students often put down their notebooks beside Frau Käthe's bowl of simple fare; they wrote down, in a topsy-turvy mixture of German and Latin, and with abbreviations and many mistakes in hearing, what Luther said or what they understood him to say. When the talk became excessive, Frau Käthe would interrupt with: 'Why don't you eat instead of talking incessantly?' She also cast somewhat unfriendly glances at the notebooks as they grew thicker and thicker, knowing that the students were going to run off to the publishers and make money out of them. Soon after Luther's death, Goldschmied, the last amanuensis, who called himself Aurifaber, published a thick folio volume containing a large number of very dubious additions of his own. Aurifaber became one of the constantly squabbling theologians of the next generation, dealt in Luther relics and Luther sayings, and liked to 'make coarse jokes'; in those days no one thought anything of this, it was the age of coarseness, the age of Rabelais. It was only when the whole literature of the sixteenth century had been forgotten or become an academic study that Luther's works, including his table-talk, were considered shocking and coarse. But there are no salacious stories or obscenities in Luther. He was merely uncouth. He liked illustrations that lend themselves to psycho-analytical interpretations and anal theories. We shall not pursue conclusions about this on the basis of present-day psychology. The disproportionately great importance attached to Luther's statements about his development and experiences is open to suspicion. He naturally interpreted himself in the light of his subsequent teachings and views, and what he said about his life in the monastery, for example, has to be taken with a large grain of salt. And then we cannot be certain what the actual words of his table-talk may have been, scribbled down as they were by students of widely varying intelligence. His phraseology in any case need cause us no embarrassment.

Many of his comments concerned only topics of the day, at a time when news still circulated only by letter and word of mouth, and often in the form of rumours. Thus we see the Doctor presiding over his table. He liked to be surrounded by people, but when he lapsed into his monastic ways and chose to be silent, the others said nothing or spoke in a whisper; Luther would then look round him and say: 'Well, gentlemen, what is the news?' Each contributed what he had heard or read, and the Doctor was expected to extract the lesson and point the moral. This he proceeded to do thoroughly, often at tedious length, though at other times with the pithiness that was his gift. We do not learn very much about the great events of the time, and it is precisely this table-talk that reveals the provincial isolation in which Luther lived, in spite of the fact that he was in touch with so many people in so many places. When the subject of Rome came up, his remarks were generally confined to the familiar invective and abuse; he could barely distinguish between the popes of his own lifetime. Luther's views on the various countries did not transcend the usual prejudices: the French were sensual, the Spaniards brutal, outdoing both the French and Italians in every form of baseness; he saw a certain justice in the fact that they now held the Italians in the most brutal subjection, playing havoc among them 'like a stork among frogs'. He also held forth on the subject of their unnatural vices, their homosexuality and unnatural ways of sleeping together, that were 'contrary to nature'; sodomy he called 'Italian marriage', adding 'God preserve us from this devil! For, thank God, no German mother tongue knows anything of this vice.' But he did not spare his beloved Germans by any means: the 'drunken, gorged' Germans and the 'blind and wanton' Germans were virtually everyday expressions with him.

His answer to the unremitting watch that was kept on him at every meal he ate and every mug he drank was to say placidly: 'If Our Lord is permitted to create nice, large pike and good Rhine wine, presumably I may be allowed to eat and drink.' In spite of this, however, the envious talk of the very strict, who considered that he should live like a 'humble, beaten down' Christian, went on. 'I was a student in Wittenberg for a time,' a Rothenburg schoolmaster wrote, 'but I will not speak of the gold ring on his finger, which vexes many people, or of the pleasant room overlooking the water, where we used to drink and be merry with other doctors and gentlemen, although I and my fellow students often complained of this; nor did I like the way in which we sat drinking beer, to the neglect of so many necessary matters.' Let us leave him there, enjoying a jug of beer or wine with his friends, and forget the 'necessary matters', which only too often were quite unnecessary.

A remarkable feature of this table-talk is Luther's excellent memory; he remembered what he had read, especially, of course, when it concerned his teaching and favourite ideas. When the conversation turned to celibacy and its tyranny, he cited all the Fathers of the Church, starting with Augustine, who still suffered from involuntary ejaculation when almost an old man; and 'Jerome, in his excitement, used to beat his heart with stones but could not beat the maiden from his heart. Francis made snowballs. Benedict lay among thorns. Bernard had so mortified his body that he stank abominably ... These great men were as much slaves to it as we are. Peter had his mother-in-law, I have my wife. James, the brother of Our Lord, was the same; all the apostles were married except John.' He quoted Virgil, which he had taken with him into the monastery, as fluently as the Bible. The great world outside was hardly mentioned, America might as well not have existed; he had no appreciable knowledge of either natural science or history. But he always regretted having learned so little history, and congratulated the younger generation on their better knowledge. In general he was apt to speak of his past as of something that had happened long ago: 'You no longer know what it was like in those days,' or 'how we had to suffer under the papacy, now you can look to the future.'

Superstition was a frequent topic: there were witches who cast spells on Bugenhagen's butter churn; the devil was always present. But he made fun of astrology, of which Melanchthon was an ardent devotee, calling it nothing but blind 'dice-throwing'. He told old tales that he had heard in the monastery at Erfurt, where the silence imposed by the rules was not absolute; he regaled his listeners with wise adages, peasant lore, his views on bringing up children – which were much less harsh than those of his father – and expressed his opinion of women in general and his wife Käthe in particular, who was present and sometimes corrected or contradicted him. The manners of the day required him to sigh on such occasions, which he did: 'If I should ever marry again, I would hew myself an obedient wife out of stone; otherwise in desperation I obey all women.' Or still more harassed: 'I must be patient with the pope, I must be patient with the fanatics, I must be patient with the junkers, I must be patient with the servants, I must be patient with Katharina von Bora, and my patience is so great that my whole life is nothing but patience.' Side by side with this, and such juxtaposition is a commonplace in Luther, we find the highest praise: 'There is no sweeter union than that of a happy marriage and no more cruel parting than that of a happy marriage.' One of Luther's assistants, who had quarrelled with him, wrote in his book: 'Then Frau Käthe, queen of heaven and earth, Juno the wife and sister of Jupiter, who rules her husband as she will, put in a good word for me.' But it is difficult to see how this whole complex of housekeeping, debts, pawned silver goblets, children, guests, students, visitors, as well as a husband with the extremely complex nature of Luther, could have been run without a firm and capable hand. The Wittenbergers' complaints about Frau Käthe's demands were nothing more than the eternal pettiness of German small-town existence and its unwillingness to pay the price of having a great man in its midst.

After her husband's death Frau Käthe, as we have already mentioned, had to earn her livelihood from her paying guests for the rest of her life. Dearly as her Doctor loved her and anxious as he was to provide for her, his incorrigible obstinacy and dislike of lawyers had led him to make a will that was invalid according to the laws of the land; he wanted to make Käthe his sole heir, and to appoint no guardians for the children, being of the opinion that these would only cause quarrels and difficulties. According to the harsh code of Saxon law full power devolved on the children and their successors, while a widow had no claims to anything beyond 'a chair and a distaff'. Frau Käthe was spared this extreme consequence by the intervention of the elector, and she also received a grant. But the pension often failed to materialize, partly owing to the subsequent wars, and she was obliged once more to take paying guests. When Luther's marriage to Käthe is held up as the foundation of the evangelical parsonage and the model of family life, it is as well to remember that the fate of evangelical pastors' widows down the centuries can hardly be counted among the glorious achievements of the German ruling authorities, who owed so much to Luther.

The Augustinian monastery, which was for ever undergoing reconstruction, was no idyll. There were compensating pleasures – delight in the children, pleasant company, 'good friends, loyal neighbours and suchlike' – but illness made constant and severe inroads. Luther's 'pathological' symptoms have often been exaggerated in attempting to explain his character during the first half of his life; for the second half it would be difficult to overstress them. The housewife, occupied though she was with managing the 'business', also had to act as physician and veterinary surgeon. In the remedies Frau Käthe used, not much distinction was made between man and beast. Excrement and urine still held a high place even in the official dispensary, let alone in private practice; modern methods in medicine have revealed once more the secret virtues of mould, of penicillin for example, but it is very doubtful if Frau Käthe's remedies were the right ones. Luther expressed surprise 'that God has placed such high medical properties in dung: pig's dung soothes the blood, horse's dung in wine is good for coughs, human dung for bodily wounds.' On another occasion he wrote peevishly to Käthe: 'Your dung doesn't do me any good either!' The doctors who were called in could not help much; Luther was a difficult and obstinate patient. He prescribed himself strong doses of red wine for gout, and on another occasion claimed to have done himself good by drinking large quantities of water. He scoffed at the doctors who gave him enemas, saying that they 'were only playing with the patient as one plays with a child,' while among themselves they knew better. Here again the devil was the real tormentor; he aimed at one's mind, physical suffering could be endured. The catalogue of Luther's illnesses is a long one: it includes headaches, ringing in the ears, which incapacitated him for weeks on end, severe attacks from gall-stones, and possibly also kidney-stones, which caused him to writhe on the floor and think he was dying. But he expressly denied that overwork was responsible; it was Satan who was tempting him. His Bible was his only hope and comfort. King David, too, could not get warm in his old age, and even Abishag the Shunammite girl was unable to help him, 'because he was so worn out by the temptations in his mind – they rent him so'. Against headaches he used the words from St John's Gospel: 'Ye must be born again ... That is the best I have.'

The Bible gave him a sense of complete protection, even during severe epidemics like the plague, which showed no signs of abating, or the new infectious disease of smallpox. While many people fled from Wittenberg on such occasions, he remained steadfastly at his post, together with Käthe and the children. He was convinced that a great deal of illness was caused only by fear.

Life cannot have been easy for Frau Käthe on these occasions. Her own death occurred during an epidemic of the plague; fleeing with her remaining children to Torgau, the carriage overturned and an attack of pneumonia brought her long and active life to an end. Her strength lay in action. The only words of hers which have survived are those that gave the zealous students an opportunity to note the Doctor's superior wisdom; with very few exceptions her letters were not considered worth keeping. Once when, as often happened, Luther pressed her to read the Bible more assiduously, especially the psalms, she said she had read enough: 'Would to God I lived up to it!' Luther sighed, making the edifying observation that that was how indolence and contempt for the Word began. We are left in doubt whether Frau Käthe had really grasped the doctrine of justification or the principle of the sole authority of the Scriptures; her task was to 'live up to it'. In attempting this the runaway nun justified her life in her own way, and we would go so far as to say that the many small but often difficult steps in her life add up to an admirably straight and narrow path.

# 33

# The Will in Bondage

ACCORDING to Luther it was Käthe who persuaded him to write and publish *De servo arbitrio* ('The Will in Bondage') – his attack on Erasmus. The work appeared at the end of the fateful year of 1525, the year of the Peasants' War, and bears traces of the events of that period. It was Luther's last important treatise both in regard to size and the style it was written in, a Latin carefully revised in order to be worthy of a great opponent. Its thoughtful organization is in sharp contrast to the bluster and fury so characteristic of many of his pamphlets and open letters, especially in this year of intemperate outbursts against the 'blind self-will' of the peasants. He takes up the same theme here, but on an altogether higher plane, developing it thoroughly and logically. He writes of hatred, indeed of God's hatred for mankind, and of the human will, which stands like a beast of burden between God and the devil; either can mount, and 'possess' or 'ride' it; it has to obey. God and the devil quarrel; if the stronger does not triumph, the victim is abandoned to sin and perdition predestined from all eternity. This is the prospect for man's 'free will', which has tried to rebel against the divine order of things.

It was a tragedy that Luther and Erasmus, the two noblest advocates of a new order in secular life and thought and in religious belief and the Church, were forced into mutual opposition. For Erasmus the word 'tragic', which he employed so frequently, signified turmoil and disturbance, something opposed and upsetting to those engaged in quiet scholarship, threatening his ideal of a conciliatory mind or spirit superior to all parties and sects. In many respects it was a matter of clashing temperaments. Luther, by his very way of life, had first appealed to Erasmus as a man who asked nothing for himself, lived modestly, and criticized judiciously the abuses which he himself had denounced with much greater severity. But then Luther had started hitting out, with massive, 'crude' blows, as it seemed to Erasmus, and committed the unforgivable crime of turning to the broad masses of the population. He had dragged sublime and difficult questions, the mysteries that

450

should be the exclusive province of initiates, into the public arena, where they were seized upon and mutilated by the ignorant. Erasmus was convinced that such conduct could lead only to disaster; benign instruction was replaced by wild catchwords, a council of enlightened minds by violent factions that sought to destroy each other, thus causing the downfall of the 'humanities' which he had just brought to an unprecedented pinnacle.

Erasmus had risen to be adviser to kings and popes, an authority on whom the eyes of 'all Europe' were focused; it is understandable that under the circumstances he overestimated his influence and overlooked the extent to which people sought to use him for quite different purposes. He had friends and patrons in high places: the emperor and the men of his entourage; secretaries of state like Alfonso de Valdés, who was the centre of a whole circle of Spanish disciples of Erasmus; the English humanists round Thomas More. He drew a pension from Henry VIII, popes attached the greatest importance to his name, and Hadrian, his countryman, had tried to bring him to Rome; among Luther's most intimate friends there was Melanchthon, his pupil, admirer and secret disciple. But Erasmus had no desire whatever to belong to any faction; this *homo per se* wanted to be true to himself as a human being, and his motive was not only fear, as Hutten and many others alleged. But he was delicate, physically as well as mentally the opposite of Luther. Always shivering with cold, he then suffered agonies from the excessive heat of the large Swiss tiled stoves; he struggled painfully to preserve a mean between cold and heat.

But as the clash intensified beyond hope of appeasement, pressure on his position of splendid isolation became stronger and stronger. Constrained to take sides, he gave way, but only after long resistance. Finally he declared himself against Luther. Luther, and Luther alone, was responsible for the way things had developed; it was against him that this prince among scholars now raised his voice, because the voices of the pope and the emperor had not sufficed. The unique position which Erasmus had won for himself carried with it a degree of recognition that made people constantly appeal to him, as if to a supreme court. He saw himself almost as a one-man Council, not realizing that what people wanted was only the support of his great name.

But Erasmus did not rush to put pen to paper as Luther so often did. He had an unerring instinct for orders of magnitude and subtle distinction. He knew he would achieve nothing by putting Luther in the wrong over some dogmatic question of secondary importance; he also had to bear in mind his own past, since he could not very well retract what he himself had said about the decline of the Church. His sure eye detected the most sensitive spot, the question inherent in religious faith,

451

in decisions about good and evil, and fundamental to all theology and philosophy: the freedom or subjection of the human will. It raised the whole question of God's greatness and the greatness of man. Erasmus defended in its entirety the position of his humanistic philosophy of life, which was based on the assumption that man could train and develop his personality; it was as a pedagogue that he had written his most influential works, 'manuals' for the better instruction of children, for a better marriage structure, for better Christian conduct.

In his treatise on free will, however, Erasmus once more became the prisoner, whose arguments were based not on free will but on acknowledgment of tradition and the authority of the Church. Offering few proofs of his own, he cited in support of his theses passages out of the Bible and the Fathers of the Church; he omitted those which might have damaged his case. In his position as advocate for ecclesiastical tradition Erasmus found himself on dangerous ground, because from the time of the early Councils, the Church had unequivocally condemned the concept of free will, using in evidence the name of Pelagius, which thereafter became synonymous with condemnation. Every declaration of free will was seen as detracting from the greatness and omnipotence of God, and as a dangerous challenge to the Church as the trustee of salvation. Scholasticism had attempted to solve the awkward problem in various ways. Thomas Aquinas wanted to give freedom of the will a small, well-defined scope, but it was difficult to define on Aristotelian principles; nominalism abolished this attempt and once more contrasted God and man as 'unimaginably' far apart. The quarrel has never been resolved. To use the mediaeval terminology still current in his day, Erasmus was semi-Pelagian.

True to his nature he did not affirm anything definitely; he left a great deal open. He confessed frankly that he was really a sceptic, but as an obedient Christian submitted to the Scriptures and their interpretation as authorized by the Church. He declared cautiously that he took 'no pleasure in categorical assertions' and inclined often to doubt; the Scriptures being often enigmatic and by no means as clear and unambiguous as Luther made out, their interpretation had to be left to those appointed by the Church. The greatest danger lay in acquainting the masses with obscure questions – this was really his cardinal point. Finally he turned to the well-worn argument that God could not possibly have allowed the Church to be wrong throughout all the centuries until Luther came and revealed the truth. He concurred with the opinion of those teachers who 'leave something to the freedom of the will, but a great deal to the grace of God.'

Luther had had reservations about Erasmus at a very early stage, almost as soon as he got to know his writings, but had set them aside; it would, in any case, have been stupid to make an enemy of this prince of the humanist world so long as the young movement acclaimed him so enthusiastically. As late as the spring of 1524, a few months before Erasmus's work appeared, Luther proposed a truce; but, in spite of the respectful references to the older man, it was couched in very proud and offensive terms: 'For we observe that the Lord has not granted you sufficient courage or steadfast intention' to proceed against the Church of Rome 'freely and confidently'. 'We do not presume to demand of you what is beyond your powers and talents ...' 'So I ask you only to play the part of observer of our tragedy.' He ended with a sigh: 'There has been enough biting, we must now see that we do not devour each other. That would be a sorry spectacle ...'

The spectacle took place, but it was transformed from a tragedy almost into an ironic comedy. In his reply to Erasmus Luther championed with extreme logic not only his own teachings but those of the Church; Erasmus championed the heretical teachings of Pelagius, views which in another age would have led to violent persecution. Orthodox Catholics have rejected Erasmus's work unreservedly, criticizing it with the utmost severity as not only completely inadequate but actually pernicious; most of his writings were eventually placed on the Index. When it appeared the treatise on free will was received enthusiastically, for no other reason than that this prince of the mind, who reigned over wide areas of literary Europe, had at last come down unequivocally on the side of authority. Erasmus followed his dissertation with a further bulky tract, in which he wrote the words that reflect most clearly his sceptical attitude: 'I have never forsaken the Catholic Church. I know that in this Church, which you [the Lutherans] call the priest-ridden Church, there are many who displease me, but I also see similar people in your Church. The evil to which one is accustomed is the easier to bear. Therefore I shall endure this Church until I find a better, and presumably it in turn is obliged to endure me until I myself have grown better. And the man who steers a middle course between two different evils cannot count himself unfortunate.' The middle course between the two evils relegated the Roman and Lutheran Churches to the roles of Scylla and Charybdis; between them the crafty Odysseus steered his way towards the open sea.

Luther, with an equally sure touch, attacked his opponent on this point, but only after he had paid Erasmus the compliment of telling him that of all his opponents he was the only one who had grasped the 'nerve of the whole matter' and 'seized him by the throat'. Luther answered the sceptic, who refused to take a definite standpoint and yet passed judgment blow by blow; Erasmus, he said, was performing an egg-dance or trying to pick his way between glasses 'without touching one'. 'The Holy Ghost is not a sceptic!' There could be no Christianity without certainty of truth. He banished Erasmus to the Greek scoffers, comparing him to Lucian and the Epicureans, among whom the author of *In Praise of Folly* would undoubtedly have felt more at home than in the world of rigid conclusions and man's total lack of freedom before God.

Luther then set about constructing this world; as with everything he wrote, his strength lay in the fact that he built on his own immediate experience, whereas Erasmus took his stand on authorities in whom he himself believed only to a limited extent, if at all. What disturbed Luther most was that Erasmus so neglected Christ: 'If we believe that Christ has redeemed us by His blood, we are forced to acknowledge that the whole man was lost, otherwise we make Christ superfluous or merely the redeemer of the smallest part of us; this is blasphemy.' With Luther it was always a question of the whole man. He refused to yield an inch either on man's absolute sinfulness or God's absolute grace, which would be diminished were man to presume that his own small efforts could make the slightest contribution. All such presumption stemmed from evil. In the world evil and wickedness reigned; it was a world without grace which therefore needed grace as its only hope. Luther himself was sometimes in despair: 'The fact that God seems so cruel has more than once brought me to the brink of despair, so that I wished I had never been born, until I realized how salutary such despair is and how near in such moments God is with His grace.' This was how man ought to feel: damned and redeemed. The decision was not in his hands but in God's. Man's alleged free will was a 'prisoner, a vassal, a slave, subject to the will of God or the will of Satan.' Absolute faith was demanded – a standpoint it is easy to compare with the totalitarian system of political faith. The limited 'free will' that Erasmus wanted to retain had to be 'subject' to the higher authority of the Church, whose task it was to decide how much scope it might be permitted. 'What, then, is your "impotent" will but no will at all?' Luther mocked – and here again Luther's ideas can be made to support later authorities. Luther then used his irony to still greater effect: 'It would be more accurate to call your "free will" a convertible or inconstant will.' The discussion dealt not only with ecclesiastical questions but with eternal problems, and it is this that makes it so stimulating.

In spite of its animosity the debate was conducted on a high level. One can feel Luther's pleasure in crossing swords for once with an opponent of the highest calibre, instead of the petty, yapping critics for whom he needed only a rough cudgel, and who now bored him so much that as a rule he no longer answered them. He employed the forms of ancient rhetoric and scholastic disputation, showing once again that he had learnt not a little from them; he made use of the terse questions and answers that can be framed so effectively only in Latin. But the lava kept bursting through this outer covering; Paracelsus, a contemporary with a similar temperament, put it epigrammatically: to put one's faith in the papacy is to recline on velvet, to believe in Luther is to sit on a volcano.

Rarely, however, did he curb his eruptive nature as he did here. There is a shadow of deep resignation over *The Will in Bondage*; he had been forced to witness terrible, inexplicable things. The pure, clear Word, in which he had put his trust, had been proved powerless, and all his passionate protestations to Erasmus could not help him, cry out though he might that man had no right to call a single passage in the Scriptures obscure. On the other hand the ways of God, as revealed in what was taking place around him, were obscure, although his faith must not be allowed to waver on that account: 'Rather is this the highest degree of faith, that we recognize God as good even though He leads so few men to salvation and condemns so many.' He himself called this a paradox, finding affirmation for it in the conflict in his own nature and experience, in his constant fight with reason, which had to be reduced to silence before the unfathomable majesty of God; he saw this conflict reflected in world events. Since God's omnipotence and all-pervading activity in the world were not open to doubt, he explained this conflict to himself by the fact that God's will, into which we neither should nor could inquire, was secret and hidden from us. Man was left only with the faith that God had foreseen and foreordained everything throughout all eternity; one could but exclaim with Paul: 'Nay but, O man, who art thou that repliest against God?' There remained the prayer: 'Thy will be done in earth, as it is in heaven.'

If resignation unmistakably pervades *The Will in Bondage*, it is not accompanied by relinquishment of the great struggle. Nothing so aroused Luther's antagonism as Erasmus's desire for 'peace and quiet'; this and similar desires were desires of the flesh – were they to take precedence over faith, conscience, salvation, the Word of God and the glory of Christ? 'I shall acknowledge and defend these to the death, even if it means that the whole world becomes involved in conflict and tumult, yea, even if it has to sink into chaos and oblivion.' Once again he quoted the words of Christ, which he had quoted before the emperor in Worms: 'I came not to bring peace, but a sword.' But his world had grown smaller; then he had addressed 'emperor and empire', the whole nation, now he had a more limited audience. The catastrophe of the Peasants' War had left him with little more than the small half-state of the electorate of Saxony and its elector, Duke John, who was almost sixty and on whose pleasure and goodwill depended his ability to teach and work

455

at all. He was by now very uncertain about the idea of a universal priesthood, and no less uncertain about the free election of pastors by each parish, because so many 'fantasts', as he called them, had seized on the idea with their wild teachings. The need was to establish a Church, to create an institution. The previous organization had collapsed under his blows; a new one must take its place. The bishops, officially still in office everywhere – even in the electorate of Saxony – had proved to be enemies of the new teaching. The question now was – who should assume their functions?

Luther took the fateful step of urging that they be entrusted to the secular authorities; in his eyes the ruling princes and city councils had shown themselves to be the mainstays of order during the Peasants' War. They were now 'invested' with this task, which they accepted the more readily since it accorded with their long-cherished desires and confirmed long-established practice. The Church, it is true, had always protested against this, but with scant success. Now, even in the Catholic countries of the empire, it was no longer in a position to object; for example when the dukes of Bavaria demanded a share in the Church's revenues – a demand that previously would have been answered with the interdict – the Church acquiesced. The great secularization began. The seizure of Church property by Protestant princes and cities has been put forward as one of the main reasons why the Protestant movement spread as it did, and without doubt it was a substantial contributory factor; but the whole distinction between 'ecclesiastical' and 'secular' possessions had become a farce. The 'ecclesiastical' princes ruled territories and came from exactly the same class of higher nobility as their 'secular' neighbours. The grand master of the Order of Teutonic Knights, Albrecht of Brandenburg, the first to take the step of becoming a secular duke, composed impressive confessions of faith and prayers, but we may assume that his decision to take the bold step was dictated by political reasoning. His cousin, Albrecht of Mainz, who thought of doing the same thing, provides a contrasting example: he was not plagued by religious scruples, and abandoned his plan when the dangers of putting it into practice became too great. The many vacillations of other princes present the same picture. They introduced the Reformation when to do so promised advantages; they procured other advantages for themselves when dependence on the Church or the emperor made it more advisable. In national and local history throughout the Christian era princes have always been honoured with the title 'Confessor' and their exceptional piety praised; the older practice of calling a prince the 'Valiant', or an 'Alcibiades', strikes one as more appropriate.

It was Luther's fate to remain dependent on the Elector John;

known as 'the Constant,' he was not one of the vacillating princes. But Luther's Reformation became the history of Saxony. This, of course, does not signify a corresponding limitation of his importance and influence, which extended far beyond the electorate's borders; but the Church he established became a local Saxon Church and the model for Protestant Churches in the other lands of Germany. The ruling prince, the father of his people, took the bishop's place as its head; this was a development Luther had to accept, although with misgivings. Hitherto his position relative to the court had been that of a power with equal rights, almost, indeed, that of a great power confronting a smaller power as his letters to the Elector Frederick show. He had always reserved the right to go elsewhere, 'somewhere under heaven', and this had not been an empty phrase. Now he no longer had any choice; he became a 'servant of the subject will', to use the language of his book. But his letters and statements are sufficient proof that in spite of this he did not become a mere servant to his prince, often though this has been said of him – among others by Thomas Müntzer. He did not kowtow; the German practice of servile kowtowing developed in later centuries. Defiance was a distinctive hall-mark of sixteenth-century men and was not confined to Martin Luther; admirable as a personal quality, it was disastrous in politics and, above all, in theology. Defiant and quarrelsome theologians confronted each other in various camps; men of unmistakable individuality, with hard, angular faces and almost limitless endurance. Some might well be termed the landsknechts of theology; even their clerical dress was 'slit' and torn like that of the soldiers, and their pugnacity was boundless. Others were quiet, dogged and persevering; suffering every jibe in silence, they wandered from place to place in Franciscan poverty, revealing themselves to those with similar convictions by looks and gestures, as the messengers of revolution had done in the Peasants' War.

But in order to establish a Church peace and tranquillity were needed. Luther had a very complex nature, impatient and cautious at the same time. In his basic conceptions he was simple, and it was to their simplicity that his main ideas owed their effectiveness: faith alone, without works; grace alone, without mediators. Now he had to deal with questions of public worship, and they did not lend themselves to absolute, unconditional answers. No mediators? Was everyone to be allowed to preach, as the 'Schwarmgeister' maintained? No works? There were some who found this very convenient. Many people, especially the disillusioned and embittered peasants, wanted to hear no more of the Gospel; not only had it removed none of their burdens, it had added new ones. Directives were needed on the subjects of money, payments, appointments to offices, administration of monastic estates and religious foundations, instruction and the form of divine service. Luther was anxious to avoid unnecessary changes for as long as possible; he wanted to leave things to time so that the new ideas, including those concerned with the form of divine service, would gain acceptance of their own accord. But time, the most essential prerequisite for natural growth of this kind, was not available. Moreover something else was lacking in the tiny land in which he lived. Saxony was a colonial territory, with a very mixed population, few and small towns, and a strong mixture of Wends who, to an even greater extent than other peasants, felt themselves to be helots, and not without reason. Nowhere were there either active and energetic burghers, such as Zwingli had found, or a self-assured peasantry that held meetings and consultations, administered justice and preserved the old forms of community life. An oppressive atmosphere weighed on the Wittenberg district, a blend of servility, hatred and suspicion; when Melanchthon, who was a southern German, first went there it struck him as a place of exile.

Melanchthon was Luther's chief collaborator in the new tasks; a university man and friend of Erasmus, he had much less sympathy for the common people than Luther and clung to authority still more tenaciously than he did – a trait that was to prove fateful. Luther had raged against the peasants; Melanchthon composed a detailed report – but only after the victory of the princes – in which he rejected all the peasants' demands, basing himself on quotations from the Bible. On the question of serfdom, which he regarded as indisputably God-ordained, he did not hesitate to write: 'Indeed a people as savage and ill-bred as the Germans needs to have even less freedom than it has.' Among his proposals for order and discipline there was only one on a subject he had mastered and on which he was to exert a lasting influence: it was essential, he said, for schools to be established; the authorities should provide for this, as well as for correct preaching and Church organization and administration.

Melanchthon undertook to introduce the necessary practical measures. To begin with tours of inspection would have to be made, in order to obtain some idea of conditions in the country. The presence of Luther and Melanchthon in Wittenberg had not turned the electorate of Saxony into a Protestant or Lutheran state. Monasteries were still in existence, some of them partially, and others wholly, deserted. Religious foundations, canons, and preachers conducting services in the old style alternated with the new style of worship; in other places there was no worship at all. Some preachers merely blustered against the monks or against Rome, some kept inns. The whole piteous plight of the ecclesiastical proletariat, the result of decades of neglect, was brought to light during these tours of inspection; the mood of the peasants was also revealed: 'They now despise us as they used to despise the papacy', Luther wrote to Spalatin. Melanchthon drew up instructions, telling the pastors how to preach to the 'common, uncouth man' and how to conduct the services. In the forefront he placed the 'law', the Mosaic law of the Old Testament, and stressed the need for repentance, faith and good works. The Gospels, which for Luther had stood first and 'alone', could be understood only after man had acknowledged and battled with his sinfulness; this necessitated obedience and prayer. About 'other matters, of which the poor, ordinary people had little grasp,' the pastor would do better to say nothing.

There were already intimations of the authoritarian state; but we today, who are subject, though in quite different ways, to the all-powerful state, would be wrong to adopt a superior attitude. The position of the ruling authority in those days is well illustrated in Luther's correspondence with his prince and the court councillors. The Elector John, far from coveting the property of the Church, in fact did not move a finger; like his brother before him he adopted an attitude of wait and see, but he lacked his brother's secret cunning and patriarchal authority. Luther had to coax and goad him into devoting a little more energy to his duties as father of his land and in doing so made himself quite unpopular at court. The university, the apple of the old elector's eye, was neglected and Luther had to petition his successor; nor was anything being done for schools and pastors. The 'bigwigs', the nobility, wanted to annex the abandoned monastic estates. 'There are monasteries, religious foundations, fiefs and endowments and things enough which Your Highness is the only one to look into, settle and arrange'. They ought to be used for the benefit of the university and to support the pastors; where this was inadequate, the government should see that the parishes gave their pastors a decent stipend. The 'secular administration' was also in need of inspection, 'because people every-where are complaining bitterly of bad administration, both in the towns and in the country'; it was up to the duke, 'as head and sovereign of his country', to look into this. Luther first had to explain to the govern-ment that it was indeed a government and had certain obligations to fulfil. Hence, although the first steps had been taken along the road to the authoritarian state, the sovereign was still a very modest potentate; in the case of the Elector John he was also a man of limited intellectual capacity, whose pleasant features differed little if at all from those of the country people. He let things take their course, he brooded, he listened to everyone, to Dr Luther and his opponents alike; he was 'constant' only in his resolute adherence to the new teaching. But he was easily put out by the slightest criticism. People were already saying that Luther was not sufficiently Lutheran and was inclining back again towards the old Church; the Elector, dismayed by this, told Luther it had come to his ears that 'the papists seem to have cause for rejoicing.' Luther shrugged the charge aside: 'We need not pay much attention to opponents who boast that we are creeping back again; it will die down.'

Wittenberg was a very small town and Saxony a very small country, although it was to supply the greatest and most powerful principality in the patchwork of the Holy Roman Empire. The tours of inspection were carried out, the government officials and councillors joining in and leading the way to a future development they understood better than their prince. Originally Luther wanted to enlist him only as 'emergency bishop' for a single occasion; gradually he became permanent bishop. It was impossible to set everything going at once, he wrote resignedly to his elector, and 'lay down how it is to operate. All we have done is to sow the seed; if it comes up there will be so many weeds that we shall be hard put to it pulling them up.'

This, basically, is the formula for the remainder of his life. The church service, a christening service, a marriage service, a German Mass, the smaller catechism for the family, the larger catechism for the pastors, completion of the great collection of homilies and above all of the Bible translation – this was the sowing. The weeding consisted of the never-ending fight against the Schwarmgeister, the 'protestants' within the Protestant movement, the 'left wing' as it has been called in modern terminology, and against the 'right wing' too, which claimed to represent the 'true Luther' as opposed to the watered-down Luther. From the German Mass, and the efforts to replace the Latin liturgy, sprang the most dynamic achievement of Luther's later years: the hymn, sung by the congregation.

Music was the only art that meant anything to him. He had no eye for painting or architecture; when he saw the gothic cathedral at Cologne his reaction was that a church should be a simple place for preaching where nothing distracted attention from the Word. This idea was realized in the Schlosskirche at Torgau, the residence of the electors of Saxony, which was built in the last years of Luther's life and consecrated by him as the first 'Protestant' church: it consists of nothing but a hall for preaching; there is no place set apart for the altar.

The recourse to music, which for the Germans began with Luther, has another special significance. The painters' studios, where the portraits of the saints had been produced, had to shut down, and construction work on building the great cathedrals, which never quite reached completion, began to slacken off. Apart from this, however, there was still great richness of artistic expression; dry tracts were given illustrated borders, the fronts of houses were gaily painted. But it is undeniable that the various reformatory movements, especially the sects, brought an end to artistic expression with varying degrees of suddenness. The 'flight into music', which began with Luther, however, had other causes; that it was precisely the Germans who abandoned themselves to music so completely is not to be explained by the Protestant doctrines alone.

Music is the freest of all the arts; it is by its very nature 'abstract and non-representational'; lending itself to free improvisation, it also submits to strict laws of composition and can, in fact, do both at once. It is 'anonymous' and mocks all attempts at nomenclature. It is international and unsectarian; Bach used the Catholic Mass; atheists find themselves in perfect harmony with his musical concepts. More than all the other arts it makes an appeal on the one hand to basic, primordial feelings, and on the other to the desire for creating forms and structures, to the theoretical world. Schopenhauer claimed to see Platonic ideas reflected in its detachment from all that is earthly; Plato himself said that movement in music was analogous to the movements of the psyche.

Luther sought in it consolation in his states of melancholy and doubt, and this became music's mission for centuries; it revealed an exalted realm beyond the real one, which for most people was wretched and dismal. It corresponded to the world he had outlined in *The Will in Bondage*. It was closer than any other art to the 'mysteries' that were better left untouched, even by words. Music for Luther by no means meant only hymns and the congregational choir; he knew the elaborate compositions of the great masters of his day. Ludwig Senfl, court *Kapellmeister* at Munich, although a Catholic, was his favourite composer; what appealed to him was Senfl's brilliant mastery of his craft. The death of great composers like Josquin, Pierre de la Rue and Heinrich Finck distressed him; he remarked that the world was never worthy of such 'learned people' – meaning by 'learned' mastery of the elaborate style of composition. He admired the contrapuntal music of the great Netherlandish composers, writing on one occasion: 'When natural music is sharpened and polished by art, one sees and observes to some extent (for it cannot be grasped completely), and with great admiration, the great and perfect wisdom of God in his wonderful work of music; what, above all, is unusual and to be admired is the fact that it is possible to sing a simple tune or tenor (as the musicians call it) while at the same time three, four or five other voices are also sung that play and leap around this simple tune or tenor as if in rejoicing, and, embellishing and decorating it wonderfully with various means and sounds, perform as it were a heavenly dance. The result is that those who have some grasp of this music, and are moved by it, are compelled to wonder, averring that there is nothing in the world more unusual than such a song embellished with many voices.' Motets were performed in his house, and it was from the motet that the cantata developed. Three- and four-part round songs were also sung in his day.

Thus the musician in Luther fought against excluding music from the church service, although at first he had come near to it, and the 'radicals' always held the retention of music against him. In 1524 he still had to defend himself apologetically in the preface he wrote to a book of chorales by his friend Walther: 'It is not my view that the Gospel should cause all the arts to be struck down and disappear; on the contrary, I should like to see all the arts, and especially music, used in the service of Him who gave and created them.'

He proceeded carefully in the matter of retaining church music, as he did in other things affecting the church services. The German *Lied* had a long history behind it, so that Luther had abundant riches to draw on; he himself added a great deal. The details of his contributions are disputed, but no one has been able to deny that, in addition to being a great translator and a formidable writer of polemics, he was also a poet. He transcribed Latin hymns, psalms and liturgical chants, as well as composing new texts of his own. It is immaterial which lines are by Luther and which by someone else. Luther's hymns are those that bear his imprint; and their influence has been almost more far-reaching and powerful than that of his Bible.

The first beginnings, typically, were accidental. He enquired from his friends which of them could contribute German hymns for the German Mass. As nothing satisfactory came of this, he sat down himself to have a try; probably no poetry has ever been written with less poetic intent. His hymns were utilitarian poems, written for the use of his congregations. A small volume of hymns in which Luther had no hand was published in Erfurt; a hurriedly compiled speculation on the part of a bookseller, it contained paraphrases of psalms, some of which were by Luther, together with other hymns. In his Bible translation Luther had written '*Aus der Tiefe rufe ich zu dir*' ('I call unto Thee from the deep'); this now became the chorale *Aus tiefer Not schrei ich zu dir* ('In direst need I cry to Thee'). Other writers and other printers joined in, because pirated editions were both permissible and lucrative. Tunes were always added. Luther established a small choir in Wittenberg; he enlisted the services of the excellent singer and subsequent choirmaster Johann Walther, from the elector's residence at Torgau, and of another good musician named Rupff. Georg Rhau, the Leipzig cantor who had composed an elaborate twelve-part Mass for the disputation with Eck and had later gone to Wittenberg as a fugitive, offered his services as publisher. The type was cut in Lucas Cranach's studio, as was the spirited edging for the title with its somersaulting angels. A *Protestant Hymnal* appeared in 1524, the first of a stream of similar publications that continued till well into the eighteenth century. Luther himself wrote about thirty hymns; it is impossible to be certain of the exact number. The first *Liederbuch*, a tiny volume, contained twenty-six items; by Bach's time the great Leipzig hymnal had grown to eight volumes and five thousand items. For almost two centuries German poetry was predominantly religious poetry, and music a source of comfort in very comfortless times.

There is further argument about which of the tunes are by Luther. When preparing his first hymn-book he worked in conjunction with the two professional musicians; they sat at the table with their pens and manuscript paper, while he paced up and down the room. He hummed the old melodies or, as has been supposed, tried them out on the flute; they were tunes he remembered from his choirboy and student days, religious and secular alike, ancient Gregorian chants and modern popular and miners' songs. From the notes themselves one cannot tell whether the music was the work of a minstrel or a monk. The oldest Church melodies often had very worldly or even pagan origins; it was only time that had clothed them with sacral dignity. Luther's greatest and most famous hymn *'Ein feste Burg ist unser Gott'* ('A mighty Fortress is our God') has been subjected to minute analysis which shows that its details derive from 'Gregorian reminiscences'; but Pope Gregory himself, who lived around 600, is an unknown quantity, while still less is known of the sources of the music of his day. At the time when Luther created it, the tune was something new. It, too, has undergone change; in Bach's Luther chorale the original version, which was much more loosely constructed and rhythmically freer, was altered – in order to conform to the changed musical taste of the period – into the much shorter, evenly divided bars we know today. Only then did the hymn receive the march-like, fiercely determined character of a Protestant *Marseillaise* that seems to go so well with the words. If we could hear the hymn performed by Luther and his friends it would, in all probability, sound very strange to our ears, 'indefinite' and much too long drawn out, sad rather than rousing; that, in spite of this, it became the battle hymn and song of defiance of the early Protestants was due to different reasons. In a very short time the hymns composed by Luther and his colleagues ceased to be confined to the Church for which they were intended. Churches were stormed to the accompaniment of singing; a song, hummed clandestinely at first and then more and more brazenly until finally it was shouted, was a characteristic feature of revolutionary movements. Here again, as in the origin of the tunes, the difference between 'secular' and 'sacred' became obliterated and even transposed.

Luther's intentions were strict; he wanted to eliminate the profane songs entirely. How had it happened, he asked, that in the secular field there 'are so many fine poems and so many beautiful songs, while in the religious field we have such rotten, lifeless stuff?' What is undeniable is that he injected his own fire into the genre, wherever the tunes and words may have come from. 'The devil has no need of all the good tunes for himself,' he remarked, and took them away from him. The tone he struck was always manly; he was familiar with the 'cry of deep distress', but whimpering was alien to him. Unlike those who followed him he practised conciseness, nor was he in the least maudlin or sentimental. His verse lacked any self-interest; he wanted to speak to everyone and in the name of everyone. Once he saw that the task of introducing congregational singing had been accomplished he gave up writing verse almost entirely.

In his draft plan for a 'German Mass', compiled in 1526, he stated clearly his didactic intentions and the context he had in mind for this work. It was above all to youth that he turned; he had serious doubts about the old – 'let them go their ways.' For the sake of the younger generation, 'we must read, sing, preach, write, and compose verse, and whenever it was helpful and beneficial I would let all the bells peal, all the organs thunder, and everything sound that could sound.'

The doctrines of the will in bondage and predestination have affected people in very different ways. While they can lead to despondency, they can also fortify and invigorate. Strong and independent natures, in particular, have often been stimulated by them to prove their worth and harness all their powers – much more so than by the more conciliatory teachings of Erasmus. The notion of the will in bondage is capable of releasing remarkable powers of volition, which may be directed to any sphere of human activity. To Luther what mattered was always and exclusively the question of religious faith; by comparison all other problems, whether political or social, receded completely into the background.

# 34

# Sacco di Roma

THE emperor's permanent war with France affected the Germans very little; it was fought on the borders of the empire, and not a few of the German princes sympathized with Francis I. During the battles in Italy and the constitution of the fronts there, whether the pope, as a member of one of the various coalitions, was an ally or an enemy, was of small concern to them; anyhow it was only a smouldering fire. From time to time, however, a flame shot up with unexpected fury, throwing its light into every corner of the world stage. The conquest and sack of the Eternal City, the *Sacco di Roma*, in 1527 by the troops of the Emperor Charles, and the capture of the pope by the Church's most loyal son, had a deeper effect on people at the time than most other events. It was seen as a judgment of God, even by the closest associates of the Curia. Up till this moment almost everyone in Rome had viewed events in Germany calmly, as a passing phase that would soon subside if handled skilfully. Life in Rome had not been touched or changed in any way by it. Only after this blow, which struck within the Castle of St Angelo itself, did a shimmer of awareness begin to dawn. Only as a result of this calamity were those members of the Church who had realized that things could not continue as they were raised to a position of some influence, though they did not prevail for a long time to come.

The extent and horror of the pillaging was compared to the conquest of the city by Alaric and the Goths. Rome had often been conquered and laid waste, but this was forgotten. Few cared to remember that the popes had rarely felt secure in the Holy City, that they had often preferred to reside in better-protected places, that for a long time they had not resided in Rome at all but in Avignon. When, after their long exile there, they returned to the city, a hundred years before the Sacco, they found little more than a heap of ruins. Wolves roamed the streets, the churches were half in ruins, the people lived in poverty-ridden settlements on the banks of the Tiber. During the intervening century, however, Rome had again become a storehouse of treasures and great artistic riches: palaces and fortifications had been erected, a banking quarter had sprung up; architects, painters, sculptors and goldsmiths found employment there. While the Renaissance was a concept for scholars and artists only, the term 'proud Rome' reverberated throughout the world, although with somewhat varied connotations. The hosts of pilgrims still continued to visit the seven pilgrim churches, as Luther had once done. The envoys of the great powers stayed at the famous *Cow Inn*, or at one of the other inns run by Alexander Borgia's clever and able mistress Vanozza. From every country including Germany the large contributions continued to flow into the coffers of the datary; latterly certain difficulties had arisen, especially with the Goths beyond the Alps, but no one took them seriously. Gaiety was the chief characteristic of life in Rome, a robust joy in every manifestation of existence. The painters painted charming delicate scrolls on the ceilings of the palaces; the ecclesiastical calendar held feasts for every day of the year. The city had been unsafe for decades, but the people had grown used to it. Benvenuto Cellini has described the daily murders and the part played in them by the well-aimed thrusts of his own dagger: 'The blade entered between the throat and the nape of the neck, penetrating the bone so deeply that even with all my strength I could not pull it out again.' Between feats of this kind and nocturnal visits to the Colosseum, where a necromancer cast love spells to bring back a faithless mistress, the goldsmith worked at monstrances and chalices for the cardinals, who saved him from arrest when he went on another killing spree; even the pope graciously forgave and absolved him. He had commissioned Cellini to cut the die for a two-sided gold medallion, showing on the obverse Christ with His hands bound and, on the reverse, the pope and the emperor in the act of setting upright a tottering cross; round this was the inscription 'They were of one spirit and one faith' – a much-needed reminder of a great ideal, because at the moment the two powers were at war.

In 1527, during Holy Week, Clement VII pronounced the papal blessing on a concourse of ten thousand of the faithful in the square outside St Peter's. A half-naked man climbed up the statue of St Paul and shouted across to the pope: 'You Sodomite bastard! Because of your sins Rome will be destroyed. Repent and be converted! If you do not believe me, you will see it for yourself in a fortnight!' For the time being the foolhardy man, a preacher from Siena, was shut up.

Pope Clement still thought he held the strings of his puppet theatre in his hands; the performance had been going on successfully for a long time. Immediately after the emperor's overwhelming victory at Pavia he had started to form a new league against the Imperator Mundi; this alliance was christened the Most Holy League, although its purpose was not to fight the Turks or the heretics but to wage war on behalf of His Most Christian Majesty of France against His Most Catholic Majesty of Spain. In making his plans, the Medici pope had been prompted first and foremost by his smaller dynastic aims; in his letters and negotiations, place names occurred that were of interest only to his family, towns like Reggio and Rubiera, unfamiliar to the most ardent traveller in Italy, as well as the more celebrated Parma, Piacenza and Ferrara. Luther's name was not mentioned. The League had had good prospects; Venice was a member, England for the present a sleeping partner. Following his great victory the emperor had fallen victim to a paralysis of will, as he always did after an unexpected success. He did not, like the Italians, think of the wheel of fortune; he trusted in his own very personal God who controlled the fortunes of the House of Burgundy. But the House of Burgundy's succession also had to be assured. The emperor, already betrothed ten times since his childhood, was under heavy pressure from his Spanish subjects to marry at last, and to marry within his own precinct, not into some distant, foreign land. The latest engagement, to the English Mary, was broken off, with serious political consequences, and instead Charles married Isabella of Portugal who brought a dowry of a million ducats. The money was badly needed because this sovereign over a worldwide empire was constantly in monetary straits.

The Imperator's handling of financial matters was the key to his great failures and reverses; his empire was always on the verge of bankruptcy. Who or what swallowed up the hoards of gold from Mexico and Peru has never been satisfactorily settled; whatever the answer, very little found its way into the emperor's treasury. Large sums were obtained by subjecting all those who had taken part in the insurrections of the *comuneros* to ruthless fines and confiscation; these moneys also trickled away. Isabella's dowry was squandered on lavish celebrations. The mines, as has been noted, had been mortgaged to the Fuggers, as had also the revenues of the three great knightly orders, with their vast possessions, the main source of Spain's finances. Only with the greatest difficulty, and as the result of interminable negotiations, were Charles's finance ministers able to wrest approval for taxation from the Spanish estates. The Germans contributed next to nothing to their emperor; the patrimonial lands in Burgundy were squeezed as dry as possible by the regent, but resisted to the utmost. The absolute monarch, exerting absolute control over his country's revenues, did not make his appearance until much later. The Emperor Charles still lived as his grandfather Maximilian had lived, on money borrowed from the great bankers, from hand to mouth, from one draft to the next. When their pay stopped his troops went on strike and the imperial programme was brought to a halt. It was a mutiny of this kind that led to the sack of Rome.

Up until the very last minute Charles's ambassadors in Rome had tried to persuade Pope Clement to opt for peace. High offers had been made. 'Will there be war?' Charles's ambassador had asked; 'You will know when the trumpets sound,' was the reply. A further attempt to persuade the pope to give way elicited only laughter. As the ambassador rode out of the Vatican, his jester was seated behind him on the horse, making grimaces at the people; they were not to be allowed to think that the Spaniards took the pope's sabre-rattling seriously.

The war situation was serious. The emperor wrote urgent letters to his brother Ferdinand, as he had done before Pavia; the Germans were to raise a force of landsknechts. The archduke pawned his jewels and sent the money to Frundsberg, on whom once more all hopes were centred. The condottiere, by now grown stout and apoplectic, approached this new commission with some misgivings; in order to raise sufficient manpower he had to subject his own credit to a severe strain. The recruiting centres were in Bozen and Meran; twelve thousand foot soldiers assembled under experienced officers. His brothers-in-law, the Counts Lodron, guided him over the mountains, because the League held the passes; the artillery had to be left behind. 'The mountains were so high, it made one shudder to look down into the valley. Even Frundsberg had to climb up on foot, although sometimes the soldiers held their long pikes at his side for him to use as handrails. He had grasped the collar of a powerful soldier in front, who pulled him up, while another pushed him from behind, because he was stout and heavy.' This was the description given by Frundsberg's secretary and biographer. The rest of the campaign, in winter and in rain, was arduous. Before Frundsberg's men joined up with the Spaniards, who had come from Milan, they were involved in heavy fighting. Morale was bad; their pay did not materialize.

The only good news came from Rome, where Cardinal Pompeo Colonna, secretly prompted by Moncada, the emperor's ambassador, had launched a powerful attack. What claim to spirituality, apart from his title, this cardinal had is difficult to see; he was renowned as a lover and military leader; thanks to his family's great possessions, he had at his disposal, as his greatest asset, a large following of men capable of carrying arms. He had already stormed the Capitol once under Julius II and proclaimed the republic; now he repeated his attack, but with greater success. His troops forced their way into the virtually unguarded city, Pope Clement had to take refuge in the Castle of St Angelo, and Colonna's men pillaged the city thoroughly, taking large quantities of booty from the palaces, the Vatican and the churches. This was the first, the smaller Sacco, and it did not fail in its effect on Frundsberg's landsknechts. They were furiously jealous. 'To Rome! To Rome!' was the cry in the camp. In itself this was not one of the aims of the war, if indeed there were any definite aims at all. The emperor issued no directives; he left his troops without money and without clear instructions. The League was to be driven back, the pope harassed; how this was to be done was left to the commanders in the field.

Once again the pope was saved; through the agency of Moncada, the emperor's ambassador, he concluded an armistice with the cardinal, swore to turn his back on the Most Holy League, and bestowed a full pardon on Colonna and his men. These last withdrew to their castles and estates in the mountains. Scarcely was Clement reinstalled in the plundered Vatican than he used the moneys which had remained intact in the Castle of St Angelo to raise a papal army and attack Colonna's forces. The plunder of Rome was revenged by plundering the castles; the villages were burnt to the ground and the cardinal solemnly anathematized and excommunicated. Colonna was in no way discouraged because in the meantime Lannoy, the viceroy of Naples, had landed in Gaeta with a strong Spanish force and was approaching. His troops suffered some reverses at the hands of those of the pope, and he negotiated with Clement; the perfidious pope concluded a new armistice, under whose terms the imperial troops were to be withdrawn to Lombardy. At this point another power intervened. Frundsberg's landsknechts and the Spaniards in northern Italy, half starved, soaked to the skin, their rearguard seriously threatened by the League's army, now decided to break out to the front and collect their pay in Rome. They mutinied and this time refused the attempts at appeasement which had been successful after Pavia; Frundsberg had nothing to offer them, and in any case they knew he was heavily in debt. The other army commander, the Bourbon Constable, was a man without land or possessions; moreover, his reputation had been severely damaged by his previous failures against France. No effective supreme command existed at all. Fury over the new pact between the viceroy and the pope exacerbated the atmosphere. Trusting in his mighty voice and his old reputation as a father to his men, Frundsberg drummed them together, paraded them in a circle and, in words charged with emotion, promised to see they were paid. They shouted him down, threatening to run him and the other officers through. The great man sank speechless on to a drum – the victim of a heart attack, or so it was given out. He had himself taken to Ferrara, where he retired to his bed; he did not see his troops again. The Constable returned to his plundered tent and assumed command. He had nothing to command. The master the mercenaries now obeyed was the army itself.

Hitherto the army had manœuvred uncertainly, with conflicting objectives and without any fixed plan. Now its objective was Rome, and it pursued it with an energy rarely seen in these campaigns. It by-passed the towns, plundering only the smaller places, and sent back its artillery to Ferrara; the foot soldiers waded in rain through the rivers and refused to be stopped by anything. By the beginning of May the hordes had reached the hills outside the city; savage and lusting for booty, the majority were old war veterans, still further toughened by the hardships of the past months.

On the morning of 6 May they placed their scaling ladders against the walls surrounding the Vatican quarter, their rough-and-ready storming equipment hastily made from garden fences and bound together with willow thongs. Mist is said to have hampered the de-fenders, especially the excellent cannon of the Castel St Angelo; with the exception of Benvenuto Cellini who, using his infallible musket, claims to have shot the Bourbon leader with his own hand – a deed acclaimed as a great victory by the defenders. The pope fled from the Vatican to his impregnable citadel. Further negotiations took place while some of the soldiers were already beginning to plunder and murder. A number of formations still kept discipline; their officers delivered an ultimatum to the citadel demanding surrender of the city quarters on the near side of the Tiber and payment of three hundred thousand ducats. The pope refused; like many timid people he went wild as soon as he felt himself secure behind the huge castle walls. He gave the order to shoot.

The real battle then began. The bridges over the Tiber had to be stormed; the men still maintained a semblance of order. Towards evening the whole of Rome was in their hands. They paraded in their formations, the Spaniards on the Piazza Navona, the Germans on the Campo dei Fiori. They cannot have felt very safe in the narrow streets of what to them was this huge city, or in front of the great palaces of the cardinals and other notables, many of which were defended by the private troops and retainers of their owners. The cry went up that the camp followers had started looting. This was the signal for disin-tegration; the men had no intention of standing aside and allowing the finest booty to slip out of their hands. The great Sacco began, while it was still night, with the battering down of doors, murder, rape, violence and all that goes with them.

What gave its special character to this Sacco was the duration and thoroughness of the robbing and murdering. It was normal for a con-quered city to be handed over to the troops to plunder; after a few days the commanders usually called a halt. In Rome the gangs of men were left entirely to their own devices, not a vestige of discipline remained. They continued to plunder, not for a few days or a week but for almost six months, breaking off at intervals to retire into the outskirts, because all the provisions had been either eaten or destroyed. The Castel St Angelo, where Clement and some of his cardinals had taken refuge, was surrounded by trenches and subjected to a leisurely siege; the cannon on the walls shot to good effect. Officers who still had men under their command conducted the pillaging somewhat more intelligently; they encircled the fortress-like palaces and opened systematic negotiations for large ransoms. They took care that in the banking quarter the House of Fugger, at least, remained unharmed; they needed it to transfer back to Augsburg the large sums of money gained from their booty. Otherwise no distinction was made between cardinals and aristocrats, Church property and civilian wealth. The preacher from Siena was brought out of prison and led round in triumph. The mercenaries gave him food, but instead of thanking them the brave man shouted at them as he had shouted at the pope: 'Go on with your plundering, take whatever you can find, you will only have to spew it all out again! The spoils of war are as passing as the property of the Church!'

His prophecy came true. The troops retained little or nothing of all they had taken. Large gaming tables were set up in the Campo dei Fiori; round the sides of the square lounged the money changers and buyers who would exchange a gold chalice or a costly piece of brocade for cash. There was a vast amount of drinking, but after a few days all the stocks of food had either been eaten or, to a still larger extent, destroyed, thrown into the streets and burned. No attempt was made to storm Castel St Angelo. Instead the German landsknechts paraded through the streets dressed as cardinals amusing themselves and playing the fool. Frundsberg's sixteenth-century biographer, A. Reissner, records: 'Wilhelm von Sandizell was often to be seen with his men in front of St Angelo, dressed as a pope with the triple crown; the other soldiers, dressed in cardinals' robes, then did obeisance to their pope – holding up their long robes in front with their hands, and letting the trains trail out on the ground behind, they knelt down, their heads and shoulders bowed low, and kissed his hands and feet. Whereupon the mock pope pronounced the blessing with a glassful of wine and drank to Pope Clement. Each of the fake cardinals drank a glassful of wine and toasted the pope in response, shouting that now they intended to appoint truly devout popes and cardinals who would be obedient to the emperor, and not intractable and stubborn like the previous ones, causing wars and shedding blood. Finally they shouted up to the castle at the tops of their voices: we want Luther for pope – all in agreement hold up their hands. They then all raised their hands and shouted "Luther for pope"!'

Scuffles between the Spaniards and Germans, and between the two together and the Italians, were an everyday occurrence. The officers' commands had no effect. St Peter's was ransacked, as it had been by Colonna's men. Schertlin, one of the landsknechts' leaders, took the precious piece of rope with which Judas had hanged himself, and which Luther had seen when he was in Rome, and brought it safely home to Augsburg; one of the other landsknechts tied the head of the holy spear to his own pike. The Spaniards took no part in such sacrilegious acts. Instead, they earned a reputation for employing the most exquisite tortures in order to bring to light hidden treasures; their methods included roasting the soles of victims' feet and hanging them up by the genitals. 'The Spaniards in particular have committed gross and wanton outrages on wives and daughters in full view of their husbands and fathers; there was great distress and misery, and the soldiers were unskilled and wanton,' said a German informant, who maintained that his own countrymen had performed no 'cruel and unnatural' acts. According to the Italians at the time the Neapolitans were the most vicious plunderers; probably they knew more about Rome than the others. In fact none of the participating nations was in a position to cast reproaches at the others.

The dead were left lying in the streets; it was summer and the city began to stink. Water became scarce – Rome was not yet the city of the great baroque fountains. Roman fever, the notorious tertian fever, always a danger to foreigners, combined with the putrefying corpses to produce an epidemic that went by the name of plague. The death rate rose among the victors, giving the preacher from Siena an opportunity to speak once more of the judgment of God, as he had done at the time of the looting. The roll calls held by the officers already showed a marked decrease in numbers. The demands for outstanding pay were heard again; mutinies and ugly threats to the officers remained the order of the day for months to come. The Sacco was followed by a further six months of devastation, interspersed with raids into the surrounding countryside and the plunder of other towns.

Discipline in the Castel St Angelo was not much better than the discipline among the imperial troops. Those cardinals who had succeeded in escaping to the citadel with the pope quarrelled among themselves, or with the pope, as they had always done. Cellini tells how he mounted a culverin on the topmost battlement of the fortress, but hesitated to fire it because the gabions might have fallen on to the terrace below, where two cardinals were engaged in angry altercation. 'Shoot! Shoot!' commanded the pope's major-domo, who was standing at his side; the cannon went off and a gabion fell between the two princes of the Church, who had just stepped slightly apart in a paroxysm of anger. The major-domo whispered in his ear: 'Would to God you had killed the two scoundrels! One is responsible for our great calamity, the other may well have something even worse in store for us.' The 'poor pope, in despair at finding himself betrayed from within and without,' as Cellini put it, ordered the goldsmith to remove the jewels from the triple crown and sew them into the folds of his robe; the gold was melted down. At this time the papacy consisted only of the frightened, helpless Clement and a companion, a former groom whom he had made into a confidant, in whose clothes he hid the remainder of the jewels. He could not count on the cardinals, on his few troops, or on the army of the Most Holy League which, under its commander the duke of Urbino, was encamped at a safe distance on the heights outside Rome, and made not the slightest attempt to intervene and destroy the disbanded formations of the imperial army. Old sins came to roost; the duke had not forgotten how he had been treated by the popes in the past. The worst news to reach Clement came from Florence: the people there had risen and once more proclaimed a republic, driving out his governor and hacking the pope's portrait to pieces in the streets. His own nearest relative, Clarice, the only legitimate Medici, who was married to Filippo Strozzi, had publicly derided him as a bastard worthy neither to be pope nor to be considered a true Medici. The days of the papal supremacy and the glory of the Medicis seemed to be over.

The emperor had played his hand carelessly enough, issuing contradictory orders and differing announcements. Even before Rome was stormed he had put out an extremely threatening publication compiled by his secretary of state, Alfonso de Valdés; it was a sort of 'white paper' containing the notes exchanged between Pope Clement and the emperor. Not since the days of the Hohenstaufen Frederick II had the Curia been spoken to like that; what was new, however, was the tone, the polished, ironic humanist Latin, and the fact that it was addressed to a European public. Whereas Luther's writings had been the voice of a solitary 'presumptuous' monk, this was the voice of the ruler of a world-wide empire, an emperor the steadfastness of whose faith no one had dared to question. 'Here, dear reader, you have the letters of Clement' – the reader could draw his own conclusions; he would have to extract the pope's doctrines from them 'with admiration, with indignation, sometimes with laughter, more often with a sigh.' The whole catalogue of papal intrigues was unrolled, not in the general terms of Luther's accusations but based on an inside knowledge of the international chess play: the machinations of Leo X, the attempt to persuade Pescara to desert the emperor, the wild announcements of anathemas. Such a pope was not a shepherd, but a wolf that had got in among the flock. And what were his aims? All that really mattered to him were possessions like Reggio and Rubiera. 'Are we to believe that Christ's representative here on earth would spill so much as a drop of Christian blood for the sake of such earthly goods? Is that not utterly alien to the teachings of the Gospel?' It was not for this that the holy see had been entrusted to him. Going over the pope's head the emperor addressed the cardinals; they should summon the Council to prevent irreparable harm being done to 'Christ's republic'. The princes should organize a 'universal convention'. Should the pope refuse, the emperor would use his 'imperial office' to apply the necessary remedy. This publication was distributed in various printings as a *Defence of the Divine Charles*. Editions appeared in Antwerp and Mainz, and the booklet even turned up in Rome; it was the most powerful and most important polemic of the day. It reveals the wide variety of levels on which attacks against the papacy were made.

For at this moment, following the capture of Rome, the emperor was at the zenith of his power. He was in a position to order the cardinals to summon a Council, to force the 'wolf' Clement to resign or to have him deposed, as had happened at Constance to his predecessors. Cool, calculating diplomats and statesmen believed the great moment had come, and made detailed proposals. Charles's representative, the nephew of Gattinara, his chancellor, wrote from the plundered city of Rome: 'We await prompt instructions from Your Majesty concerning the government of Rome. Is some form of apostolic see to remain in this city or not?' Leyva, his military commander in Milan, still without pay for his troops, sent a warning: 'God does not work a miracle every day!' His envoy in Genoa was in favour of abolishing the papal states; the papacy should be confined to spiritual duties. After his experiences in negotiating with the Curia, Moncada made the same recommendation: the pope was the worst enemy; he was responsible for all the evils in Christendom. It was the emperor's duty to make it impossible for him to do any further harm, and therefore he must put an end to the temporal sovereignty of the Church. Alfonso de Valdés had still more far-reaching hopes. Now was the time for all warfare among Christians to cease; this would open the way to the great common goal: a crusade against the Turks, the conquest of Constantinople, recapture of the Holy Sepulchre, and thus, 'as many people had prophesied, the whole world would be able to receive our sacred Catholic faith, and the words of Our Saviour would be fulfilled: there will be one Shepherd and one flock.' The philosopher and humanist Vives wrote to his friend Erasmus on the notion of an emperor of peace and world arbitrator: 'Christ has given our age a wonderful opportunity to realize this ideal, thanks to the emperor's great victory and the imprisonment of the pope.'

The emperor was at a loss, unable to decide what to do. When the first news from Rome arrived, he simply went on hunting and enjoying himself. When he saw people looking at him in dismay, he ordered court mourning for the atrocities and murders that had been committed. Quinones, the general of the Franciscan Order, told him to his face that if he did not do his duty in regard to the pope, people would say he was nothing more than Luther's '*capitano*'. Charles had given orders for Clement to be brought to Spain as a prisoner, and then cancelled them. What should have been the emperor's first and most vital concern, the maintenance of an effective fighting force, was neglected to the point of nonchalance. All he thought of was entering into negotiations and making agreements. Through the agency of new intermediaries a compromise was reached: the pope was to be 'free' to carry out the duties of his office, but otherwise was to remain a prisoner in Castel St Angelo. As surety for his good behaviour he was to hand over Ostia and other fortified places in the papal states to the imperial forces, and give the troops their arrears of pay. A detachment of two hundred picked landsknechts mounted guard in the citadel. The rest of the troops continued to plunder and roam the outskirts of the city, mutinying and threatening their officers in a new outburst of indiscipline. Step by step the emperor slipped from the pinnacle he had just attained. Within a few months the great plans of his advisers had evaporated. After paying only a fraction of the indemnity, the pope bribed the guards and escaped from his imprisonment to Orvieto, where, because of the dominating position of the fortress and the proximity of the troops of his League, he felt safer.

In Orvieto Clement, though relatively free, became entangled in a new net – this time not of his own making: he received a visit from envoys of the king of England. Henry VIII was now determined to divorce Catherine and marry Anne Boleyn, who had convinced him she could provide him with a male heir. For this the king, unswerving in his allegiance to canon law, needed the dispensation of the pope, who was to declare his twenty-three-year-old marriage invalid. But Catherine was the emperor's aunt, and he would take this insult to his relative very ill. Clement squirmed under the demands of the two sides – as yet he had no idea that this question was going to lead to England's secession from the Church of Rome. He was ready to agree to every imaginable way out of the impasse, including even bigamy; the king had only to marry his lady-in-waiting, said Clement, and the pope would then legitimate any offspring of the marriage. He could not give an official dispensation because his predecessor, Julius II, had given a dispensation to make the first marriage possible; the unhappy Catherine had been married for six months to Henry's brother, who had died young and allegedly left his widow still a virgin. 'Non-consummation of marriage' had been the grounds for permitting her to marry her deceased husband's brother; canon law, on the authority of a passage in the Old Testament, forbade such a marriage. If Clement were now to rescind a solemn enactment of his predecessor, he would inevitably expose the belief in papal infallibility, which in any case had been severely shaken, to a strain that might prove fatal. On the other hand he urgently needed England as an ally against the emperor. Cardinal Wolsey was also playing for high stakes; he hoped to turn England and the emperor into permanent enemies. He, too, was at the summit of his career and on the threshold of the downfall that followed his inability to effect the desired marriage annulment.

The wheel of fortune turned yet again, this time twice in quick succession. France intervened. A French army advanced through the dazed countryside of Italy, and the scattered positions of the emperor's forces, until it reached the outskirts of Naples. Charles's undisciplined mercenaries were forced to pull out of Rome in order to defend at least this stronghold in the south. The same sort of grandiose plans were now made in the chancelleries of the League as had been made a short time previously by Charles's advisers. Wolsey suggested mobilizing the German princes and deposing the emperor; Venice occupied the ports in Apulia. The emperor was so completely at a loss that he could think of no better solution than solemnly to challenge the perfidious French king to a duel; the farce ended when the heralds-at-arms announced that they were unable to agree on a suitable meeting-place. In view of the fact that in the midst of all this confusion the foundations for the future of Europe were being laid, and the fate of the Reformation decided, it is hard to treat with the requisite historical seriousness all the bargaining over marriages, the challenges to duels, the reciprocal plans to depose kings and popes and subsequent realliances, and the petty haggling over dowries or scraps of Italian soil in which the great powers and princes indulged.

Only his extraordinary luck saved the emperor from the noose that was already almost round his neck; a severe epidemic decimated the French army in its camp outside Naples, leaving only a few survivors. Charles had won another victory without doing anything but stand aside and wait. Pope Clement had at least held sufficiently aloof from the enterprise – on which secretly he had set great hopes – to be able to say he had remained neutral. The total lack of decisive military action everywhere, and of any constructive ideas, resulted in one of the many dishonest peace treaties of the day. In the summer of 1529 terms were drawn up in Barcelona which none of the contracting parties had any intention of keeping. The pope ceded to the emperor sovereignty over upper Italy, Naples and Sicily; in compensation he was promised armed assistance in suppressing the republicans in Florence. France came to an agreement with the emperor; the two women rulers, Margaret, regent of the Netherlands, and Louise, the queen mother of France, were responsible for the 'Paix des Dames' of Cambrai, intended to replace the broken Treaty of Madrid and defer, at any rate for a few years, any further break. As he had done in Madrid, the king of France immediately made reservations and protests; his renunciation of his rights in Italy was only temporary. For the edification of the European public it was announced that all the signatories of the treaty had agreed to take energetic steps against heresy, which had made such great headway during the many years of conflict between the Catholic crowned heads.

In order to seal the pact, and at last to attend to matters in those parts of Italy conquered by his unpaid troops, Charles decided to appear in person. He dared not risk a visit to Rome, and met Clement in Bologna where emperor and pope lived side by side in two adjoining houses separated only by a door, to which Charles and Clement alone had the key. We do not have any details of what passed between them; we know only that Charles, as usual, was never without his notebook, to which he referred constantly. Clement, having only one aim, did not need any memory aids; as there could no longer be any question of liberating Italy, his whole ambition was directed towards the liberation of Florence from republican domination and the establishment in power there of the house of Medici. He had no legitimate candidate at hand; all he had to choose from were two highly suspect bastards: Alessandro and Ippolito Medici. The pope eliminated Ippolito, who was the elder and considered rather the better of the two, by forcing him to become a cardinal, very much against the wishes of the ambitious young man; with him the motley ranks of the cardinals were enriched by the presence of a member who had been appointed to the high title as a punishment. The emperor agreed to everything: he even married Alessandro to his own illegitimate daughter – the offspring of his camp love affair with a middle-class Flemish girl – created his son-in-law a duke and conquered Florence for him with his mercenaries. Those of the landsknechts who were still alive, and who had wanted to hang Clement, were brought from Rome to assist. Michelangelo, a confirmed republican, had vainly tried to bolster the defence of his native city by constructing modern bastions in San Miniato; after resisting bravely for a few months the city was forced to surrender. Alessandro entered Florence, where he inaugurated a reign of terror that only ended when, some years later, another cousin murdered him.

Michelangelo, who had to go into hiding for a time, spent these years working on the huge monument planned for the Medici family

Landsknechts on the march

vault – 'more from fear of Pope Clement than from love of the Medicis,' as Condivi, his pupil and biographer, said. Only two figures of unimportant members of the family were completed; the pope's desire to have the family virtues represented sculpturally in front of the sarcophagi was disregarded. Instead of this Michelangelo created, though never quite finished, his mighty visions in marble known as 'Day and Night, Daybreak and Nightfall', which completely dwarf their confined surroundings in the New Sacristy of San Lorenzo. Even contemporaries were puzzled over their meaning. Perhaps the one that most easily lends itself to interpretation is 'Night', which, if we are prepared to accept the allegorical notions of the time, can be seen as a reference to the darkness that had enveloped Italy and the master's native city.

The solemn alliance between emperor and pope, celebrated in Bologna with a maximum of pomp, parades and costumery, was also an allegory, albeit an empty one. The coronation of the emperor by the pope was performed for the last time in German history. In the eyes of traditionalists it was only half a coronation, because tradition demanded that it be held in Rome; to Germans it was less than half a coronation. Neither the electors nor the knights were represented; only some German landsknechts attended, under the command of the Spaniard Leyva. Apart from these, the emperor's retinue consisted of his Spanish grandees and some Italians, who, taking the place of the electors, bore before him the sceptre, sword and crown; in the rear came heralds of the various Spanish provinces, and this was no longer an empty allegory. The pope placed Charlemagne's crown on Charles's head; the emperor took an oath to defend the Church and all its possessions and privileges. The French envoy reported to Paris that, during the ceremony, he had clearly observed the pope's robes heave with heavy sighs; a good deal more clearly he added that Clement had told him in private audience that he knew perfectly well he would be betrayed but had to act as if he were unaware of it. The emperor wrote to his brother Ferdinand in similar terms.

The pope returned to his ravaged city of Rome; decades were to pass before it recovered from the great Sacco. The emperor, with his Spanish retinue, went to Germany. He had convened a new diet, this time in Augsburg, a city also important to him as his chief source of money. With him he carried a rather pitiful letter of protest from the German electors, complaining that they had not been consulted either over the coronation or over the treaties with the Italian powers. Among his retinue was the papal legate Campeggio, who had with him a report containing more detailed proposals for dealing with the Protestant heretics: attempts should be made to reach an amicable settlement; if these failed fire and sword must follow, or more precisely the fiefs and properties of the rebels were to be confiscated and an inquisition on the Spanish model was to be set up. The emperor's announcement convening the diet sounded a different note; it was couched in the most polite terms. Discord of whatever kind was to be set aside, past mistakes were to be forgotten; the emperor desired 'to listen in love to the views and opinions of everyone.'

# 35

# The Protestants

THE emperor had been away from Germany for almost ten years; during this time the loosely-knit followers of the Wittenberg monk, the 'Lutheran sects', had become the Protestants, not yet a consolidated faction or power group but nevertheless a strong force that had to be reckoned with. For a long time their frontiers remained indeterminate. Religious ties overlapped the plans, aspirations and claims of power politics; large territories still remained neutral, waiting to make up their minds. Almost everywhere people hoped for a reasonably satisfactory solution, an agreement of some sort, a council or a national assembly. There was still an idea that if the emperor appeared in person, he might be able to set things in order; in those days, and not only in Germany, the personal presence of the sovereign had very great significance. In Spain, following the critically dangerous revolts of the *comuneros*, Charles's subjects had quietened down and given in only when he decided to live among them and rule on the spot. The German ruling princes owed their strong position to the fact that they lived in their own lands and were able to exercise a local influence. The strength of France and England lay in the fact that they each had a capital city and a king, and – in the persons of Francis I and Henry VIII – rulers who, in spite of their failings, and partly indeed because of them, represented their people. The Germans had only a 'Roman Emperor', a sovereign who spoke French, and latterly also Spanish, who had an Italian chancellor, Burgundian and Spanish secretaries and councillors, and tucked away in a corner of his privy council an official to report on German affairs. For ten years Germany had been governed on a provisional basis; in reality it had not been governed at all.

The numerous imperial diets, always held in old south German imperial cities like Worms, Speyer, Augsburg and Nuremberg, to the accompaniment of great banquets, hunts and jousts, and scant enactments that were never carried out, had reached conflicting decisions. Of the many and highly important resolutions passed by the Diet of Worms in 1521 – at the end it could not muster a quorum – all that remained was the emperor's edict outlawing Luther and his followers, and over large areas of the empire it, too, had been ignored. The emperor, on the other hand, in his tenacious way, remembered it very well and was constantly reminding people of his edict; the problems of putting it into practice did not concern him in the least. In all his vast correspondence – he wrote incessantly and as we have seen always put his ideas on paper in order to clarify and consolidate them – there is scarcely a word that reveals even a superficial interest in the country whose crown he wore. He had a thorough contempt for the German princes and, like Frederick the Great after him, looked upon them as riff-raff. They were indeed both corrupt and defiant, and seemed to be concerned always and exclusively about money – for their own purposes; there was never any money to be had for the great imperialist plans of the House of Habsburg-Burgundy, or even for the war against the Turks, which was a matter of increasing urgency because the infidels were now threatening the patrimonial lands in Austria. They had already penetrated as far as Vienna and carried out raids in Styria and Carinthia; Hungary was completely exposed. The Turkish question was his main worry; it was to be given priority at the forthcoming diet. The religious problems had to be resolved, for the simple reason that unless all the estates took part, a successful campaign against the sultan was out of the question.

Who were these Protestants who confronted him? People had always protested, reformation had been a constant demand; there had been no lack of great projects at any meetings of the diet. We have seen how a great national assembly was planned to take place in Speyer in 1524, with exhilaratingly far-reaching objectives; the religious questions were to have been solved with the help of expert opinion from the universities. We have also seen how the assembly was prohibited on written orders from Madrid, and how the bold reformers gave in. The same procedure was repeated on many occasions. The various uprisings changed the picture; Sickingen's revolt was the first danger signal, the Peasants' War the gravest warning. Since then the guiding principle had been: no innovations in any sphere. The initial majority of those in favour of a reformation had dwindled from year to year; with each new interpretation of what were frankly compromise formulas they managed to hold their own only with difficulty. At the Diet of Speyer in 1526 the following formula was coined: let each estate 'so conduct itself that it can answer to God and the emperor'; this, basically, was the principle to which the succeeding centuries conformed. At the next meeting of the diet in 1529, also in Speyer, those holding orthodox views were so greatly in the majority that drastically reactionary measures became possible: reintroduction of the old conditions relating to religious belief and property in every country in the empire; repeal of the vague resolutions establishing tolerance. Only a small proportion of the princes and cities objected that a resolution solemnly and unanimously agreed upon could not be rescinded a few years later; they were outvoted. Subsequently they entered a protest, and thereafter became known as the 'Protestants'.

The beginnings of this movement of historic importance were modest in the extreme. Of the seven electors only one, the elector of Saxony, was a signatory, of the princes only Philip, landgrave of Hesse, and of the rest only a few minor figures; the main support came from the cities, and it was in them that the Reformation had made the greatest progress. Even among these some vacillated; Cologne and Frankfurt, for example, originally supported the protest and then withdrew their signatures. Fourteen others, of which Nuremberg and Strasbourg were the most important, remained firm. In parliamentary language these Protestants were no more than a splinter group, a mere handful facing a whole multitude.

But the voting strength at meetings of the diet provides only a surface picture. The movement already had a grip on much larger areas, where it paid as little attention to the meetings of the diet as did the princes. The history of the Reformation is provincial and local history, and it developed so variously and over such long periods of time that only by rigorous manipulation can it be made to conform to the clear 'broad lines' desirable for historic examination. Attention is generally focused on the various coalitions and attempts to form alliances, the Catholics being the first to close their ranks with a meeting in Regensburg; the Protestants followed tentatively with meetings in Gotha and Torgau, after the cities had already set an example on their own. This acting 'on their own' is the keynote of the story, like that of the individual detachments in the Peasants' War. As in that case, there were radical and moderate elements at work, those in favour of quick, decisive action and those who were hesitant. As in the Peasants' War, too, the leaders' personalities were of paramount importance; to this must also be added the difference in generations. The older princes, like the Elector John of Saxony, still continued cautious, slow, and completely enmeshed in their local politics. The young, feverishly restless Philip, landgrave of Hesse, assumed the role of leader of the Protestant party, undaunted by the limited dynastic power at his disposal. He was the driving force in all the thrusts and negotiations over alliances; moving restlessly from one place to the next he negotiated, conspired, and forged grandiose plans that extended far beyond the empire into the great political pattern of Europe. When little more than a boy he had assisted in the overthrow of Sickingen, and later in that of the Thuringian peasants; he knew how to handle his brother nobles in deliberations where heavy drinking, threats, promises and the ability to think quickly were necessary to prevent his clumsy, dull-witted colleagues from growing suspicious and trying to withdraw. He was small and wiry, a totally different type from the shapeless Saxons, whose royal house provided yet another physical colossus in the person of John Frederick, heir to the electorate.

The Catholic party had its own restrictions and difficulties. Bavaria, with a bustling chancellor named Eck – a namesake of Luther's old enemy Dr Eck, still tirelessly active in Ingolstadt – who thought on very up-to-date 'Machiavellian' lines, emerged with particularly ambitious plans of its own. While the new teaching was resolutely suppressed in the Bavarian territories, the other teaching, which aimed at giving the house of Habsburg exclusive sovereignty over the empire, found no support at all. Ferdinand of Austria would have liked to be king of Germany, since his brother, the emperor, was permanently absent; the Bavarian Wittelsbachs, on the other hand, had no doubt whatever that they were of the stuff of which German kings were made. Thus the Catholic camp was split by a network of cross-currents and intrigues that strained this coalition to breaking-point. Side by side with the front against the Protestants there existed a front against the house of Habsburg, extensive negotiations on this subject being conducted with France; the Curia also joined in, because Rome was no more anxious to see a Habsburg as king than it had been to see Charles as emperor. And the fact that the house of Habsburg had once again enjoyed its proverbial good luck made it appear an even greater menace: two thrones had literally fallen into the lap of the Archduke Ferdinand, who until then had reigned very insecurely over his Austrian patrimonial lands, threatened by insurrection and rebellious local diets. In 1526 the Turks had attacked in strength and overrun Hungary. The young Jagellon king Louis, to whose Hungarian throne had been added that of Bohemia, was killed in the Battle of Mohacz; in accordance with one of the contracts of inheritance, which constituted the highly successful family recipe of the house of Habsburg, Ferdinand was able to step into his shoes and so inaugurate the centuries-long Habsburg domination of eastern Europe. On the map this looked impressive even then; in reality, however, it was at first very loose and insecure. The Hungarian magnates elected as king the Transylvanian Zapolya, who enjoyed the Sultan's protection; consequently there were two kings of Hungary, and Ferdinand could assert his authority only on the country's northern borders. After much shilly-shallying the Bohemians, for whose throne the Bavarians were the first among many contenders, finally decided in favour of Ferdinand. The peoples whose existence was at stake had no say in all these surrenders; magnates and aristocratic cliques in both countries were the moving spirits and continued for a long time to hold the reins of power in their hands. This ceaseless play of overlapping interests also explains why the orthodox party, in spite of its overwhelming numerical superiority, never got off the mark; on paper it should have been able to sweep the Protestants off the map, especially as the latter were divided among themselves.

The split in the Catholic ranks was political, the Protestants were at odds over problems of religious belief. In 1521 the papal nuncio Aleander had reported to Rome from Worms that nine-tenths of all Germans had taken up the battle-cry 'Luther'; but the acclaim which had greeted Luther on his first appearance had died away. Other leaders had appeared. The Schwarmgeister had entered the scene and, persecuted, driven out, killed and executed, proved a constant threat, as well as a constant hope to the downtrodden. They were not to be assessed numerically, nor can their numbers be established even approximately, because they lived 'underground', in silent, stubborn opposition. Luther saw in them the 'spirit of Müntzer', but it is questionable how many of Müntzer's ideas lived on in these groups. They rejected all public authority, all force of arms, all oaths, ceremonies and sacraments, and even the appeal to the Scriptures as the ultimate authority; their lodestar was spirit, immediate inspiration, direct intercourse between the elect and God. In this they were radically individualistic, however closely knit they were in their conventicles and however ready they were to share their last crumb of bread. And they are distinguishable only by individual features; the path, and it was a path of suffering, was marked out by individual prophets, whose followers took their names, the followers of Melchior Hofmann being known as Melchiorites, of Jakob Hutter Hutterites, of Menno Simons Mennonites, and of Kaspar Schwenkfeld of Silesia Schwenkfeldians. Luther and his contemporaries made no distinction, nor had they the patience to distinguish between militant and peaceable groups; they called them all anabaptists, or 'sacramentarians' because of their dissenting views on the sacraments of baptism and communion.

Luther now proceeded to label Zwingli and his followers 'Schwarmgeister' and 'sacramentarians', adopting the same brusque attitude towards them – an attitude that was to have particularly disastrous consequences. He was oblivious of the fact that Zwingli was the very opposite of a Schwarmgeist or fanatic, that on the contrary he was a man who, unlike Luther, was both familiar with worldly matters and a considerable politician, and that moreover within his own sphere of influence he also suppressed the anabaptists with every means in his power. The political fate of the movement was also decided by this conflict between the two strongest personalities in the Protestant camp, and the dogmatic differences that culminated in the controversy over the dogma of transubstantiation. Zwingli had found adherents far beyond the confines of Zurich and the Swiss cities. The south German communities were very much more in sympathy with him than with Luther and his ponderous, narrow-minded elector in far-off Saxony. The ties between the empire and the confederation had not yet been severed by any means, and numerous cities in the empire actually entertained the idea of seeking inclusion in the confederation, some even concluding agreements, admittedly only loosely framed ones, expressly for this purpose. A 'greater Switzerland', which would extend to Franconia and Swabia or into the Allgäu, was not just an idle dream; Philip, landgrave of Hesse, promoted this idea enthusiastically, himself taking Swiss nationality and becoming a citizen of Zurich. He did not do this merely on grounds of religious conviction; Switzerland was still regarded as potentially the strongest military power in Europe, and its inclusion in the Protestant camp would, at a single stroke, have made this more powerful than the entire Catholic coalition. Philip strove vainly to bring about a reconciliation between Luther and Zwingli at a three-day religious discussion in Marburg, but like all the disputations of the day it led to nothing.

This thoroughly confused battle-field on which the two opposing camps – and that is the appropriate word – faced each other was the situation that faced the Emperor Charles when he finally approached in person. Those attending the diets and similar assemblies were accompanied not only by delegations; old Germanic custom decreed that they should arrive heavily armed and with considerable troops of horse. The large and costly banquets were also important, the drinking and heavy eating often leading to discussions on the side that were of greater significance than the formal statements made in plenary session. Latterly, since the denominational question had become aggravated, symbolic acts had been added, the Catholics attaching great importance to solemn Masses, which they tried to compel their opponents to attend; the Protestants retaliated by insisting that their preachers preached in the new style.

After all his tribulations the emperor on this occasion appeared as a very powerful sovereign indeed. Spain, which had seemed almost lost when, on his last visit, he attended the Diet of Worms, had been reduced to obedience; Italy had been subdued, France held in check, and the pope humbled by his imprisonment and the plunder of his capital. Charles could command credit again, to an extent that had been impossible for a long time, and the house of Fugger and his other backers were prepared to commit themselves to very large sums. The personal appearance of an emperor involved a shower of cash presents and favours. On his way from Bologna he had made a preliminary stop in Innsbruck to test the mood of the people, the Venetian envoy noting with Italian exactitude that His Majesty had already spent two hundred and seventy thousand thalers. Petitions and repentant sinners were on the spot in a trice. King Christian of Denmark who, driven out of his country, had gone to Wittenberg and joined Luther, threw himself at his brother-in-law Charles's feet and declared he had returned to the old faith. A letter arrived from the emperor's brother Ferdinand telling him that in the meantime he had had talks with the elector of Saxony, admittedly for the sole purpose of holding him off, and that many opportunities existed 'to discipline [the chief rebel] as often as you please – on legal grounds that require no mention of religion.' The emperor, as always, hesitated. His advisers were divided in their opinions. Gattinara, his chancellor, remained close to him, a very sick man already, but still influential; he had not forgotten the pope's martial machinations and was convinced they would be resumed as soon as occasion offered. He opposed the policies of the Curia with all the independence of an Italian and fellow cardinal, and in Bologna had expressed himself very forcefully to Clement; Melanchthon, who heard about this, had great hopes of him. Gattinara died in Innsbruck, before the arrival of the great cavalcade that was making its way to Augsburg. Charles, now in his thirties, prematurely aged and with the features of a man of fifty, never again allowed a chancellor to exert a comparable influence. He had become an absolute monarch, a fact he now made very clear.

According to Burgundian tradition ceremonial was the expression of this, and he took it as seriously as he took the question of religion. First came the entry of the papal legate: the assembled princes, in greater number than ever before, dismounted from their horses on the appearance of the emperor; he and his brother also alighted. The legate, seated on his mule high above the kings and princes, pronounced the blessing; the emperor, King Ferdinand and most of the princes knelt, the Elector John and some of the other Protestant princes remained standing. The great procession then followed, with all the pomp and splendour beloved of that age of pageantry. In the lead came the emperor's bodyguard, consisting of two companies of hastily enlisted landsknechts, among them many with long service who had fought for him in Italy; others, grown rich through booty, marched past in gold-embroidered doublets and silk that was bursting at every seam. After these came the electors' contingents, each wearing its individual colours – that of the elector of Saxony in brown leather jerkins. The emperor rode beneath a tricoloured baldachin, dressed in strictly

Spanish fashion. Connoisseurs of protocol knew that discussions had taken place over something still more provocative: Charles had tried to insist that the papal nuncio ride at his side; the ecclesiastical electors, 'protestants' in matters such as this, objected that this was contrary to all usage. The emperor gave way; Ferdinand and the nuncio rode outside the baldachin. The whole cavalcade proceeded to the cathedral. After a Te Deum had been sung, the princes accompanied the emperor to his quarters in the bishop's palace.

No sooner had they arrived than the first, and quite unrehearsed, altercation took place. After the emperor had summoned the leading Protestant princes into one of the rooms, his brother, who by now had acquired a certain fluency in German, called on them to put an immediate stop to their pastors preaching in the Augsburg churches. The older princes maintained a horrified silence. Philip, landgrave of Hesse, alone of those present, declared that the demand would have to be rejected; the sermons contained nothing but the pure Word of God. The emperor, already very irritable, repeated the order. Now, however, the other princes sided with Philip. The emperor looked up in astonishment. The elderly Hohenzollern, George, margrave of Ansbach, drawing himself stiffly to attention, muttered something and put his hand to his neck. What did he want, demanded the emperor? Ferdinand translated: 'He says he will kneel down here and now and be beheaded by the executioner rather than give up the Gospel.' Charles, not wanting any scenes, regally condescended to utter the only German, or rather half-German half-Flemish, words recorded during his reign: '*Löver Fürst, niet Kop ab, niet Kop ab!*' – 'My dear Prince, not your head off, not your head off!' Once more recourse was had to the old recipe of every diet: time to reflect, fresh consultations. The emperor had yet another new demand to make: all the princes without exception were to take part in the Corpus Christi procession the following day. He had chosen the date of his entry deliberately; it was to be the dress rehearsal for this. The Protestant princes remained obdurate. They had been prepared, they said, to take part in the procession out of loyalty to their sovereign emperor; but now that it had been turned into a doctrinal question, they had no option but to refuse. On the subject of preaching a compromise was reached: the Protestants gave way on the emperor's promise to observe a similar silence; the texts alone would be read out, without any interpretation. The Diet of Augsburg began as the Diet of Compromises.

This was true also of the centre-piece, the so-called Augsburg Confession, which was to acquire historic importance as the confession of Protestant principles for the coming centuries. It was never intended to be a document of such fundamental importance; originally it was called an 'Apology', a defence presented to the emperor for his information. It was still hoped that if he were better informed he might act as arbitrator between the parties and bring about an agreement. Trust in the highest of all secular authorities remained boundless. Even Luther looked expectantly to his emperor, and Melanchthon doubly so because he had been given the role of chief speaker and author of the Apology. The princes' eyes were on the pale, very distinguished-looking sovereign who, in bearing and language, was so different from them and who, uttering scarcely a word, turned to his advisers and experts with brisk, precise movements; he already suffered from gout caused by his hasty and excessive eating and drinking – in this respect so strangely like Luther. He sat silent, gloomy, unapproachable in his black Spanish clothes; in silence, too, he ate his inordinately large helpings of food, against which his doctors and father confessors constantly warned him. One of his few recreations seemed to be music; his excellent band, containing some of the best musicians in Europe, performed the finest and most difficult pieces by the great Netherlandish masters.

The document that was placed before the emperor had been written by Melanchthon. Luther, having been outlawed by the Edict of Worms, could not attend the diet; while it met he stayed in Coburg Castle, his elector's southernmost possession. From there he intervened with an assortment of warnings and advice; but he left his friend to compose the Apology. Melanchthon, a whole-hearted advocate of union, became increasingly the Protestants' spokesman. His paper was intended to demonstrate that Luther's teachings were identical with the old and true teachings of the Latin Church: all that was needed was to put an end to abuses, about which, he admitted, there might be differences of opinion; such abuses, however, were not integral to the decisive questions of belief. The great and delicate problems which had sparked off the conflict had, as far as possible, been omitted: the position of the pope, the position of the priest as mediator, the authority of the bishops – the questions which impinged most directly on living conditions in the various countries. Melanchthon was not left to state his case alone; Luther played his part. He, too, had in mind the restoration of the bishops' authority, enlarging on this in a pamphlet which he addressed to the assembled members of the diet. Between whiles he also thundered, or called on his elector to return home post-haste. Then he put his hopes in the emperor again, declaring in all innocence after the conclusion of the diet that he had 'earned the goodwill and love of everyone', had not intended to condemn the true teaching, and had stood 'firm as a rock'; his advisers were the only ones who had made trouble. This was sheer ingenuousness, and from time to time Luther himself let fall a disarming 'Heavens, what a child I am in such things!' – the things of this world. He could not imagine a world without an emperor. In one of the pamphlets he wrote after the Peasants' War, angered at the thought of revolt of whatever kind, he had declared: 'Just as a rebellious peasant is beheaded, a rebellious nobleman, count or prince should also be beheaded, one the same as the other, and then injustice would be done to no one ...' a dangerous thesis, had it been applied to his elector. Then again he said: 'We teach as we wish, and yet the world continues to do as it wishes,' or, still more gloomily, 'God has cast us into the world under the yoke of the devil, so that we have no paradise here but every hour have to expect every misfortune.' In other words no resistance, only resignation and prayer. Motivated by this fundamental attitude he had also categorically opposed all Protestant alliances. As the Elector Frederick had once said of the younger Luther at Worms, Philip, landgrave of Hesse, was 'much too bold for him'; he mistrusted the landgrave's plans, all of which smelled to him of gunpowder, and his desire to bring in Zwingli increased his aversion. In this he had the support of Melanchthon who, in his first draft of the Augsburg Confession, had been as anxious to make clear his rejection of Zwingli, and his followers among the south German towns, as to draw nearer to the Catholics.

If ever willingness to compromise could have healed a breach that was already past healing, it would have done so at Augsburg. The situation was reflected symbolically in the leading spirits of the day: Luther in Coburg Castle intervening from a distance with contradictory admonitions; Erasmus, who had been pressed by the emperor to give the diet the benefit of his wise counsel, but who remained nervously aloof in his new refuge of Freiburg, contenting himself with guarded warnings by letter of incalculable consequences and the unpredictable fortunes of war; intellectually between them, and in the centre of the stage, Melanchthon, taking his stand before the emperor and the empire. Melanchthon was prepared to give way to such an extent that the Protestants began to suspect he had been bribed by the papists. This, being the normal tactics, may well have been attempted, but on such a point the small, delicate and almost abnormally frail-looking Melanchthon was wholly impregnable; he was no more prepared to accept money or be tempted by high honours than was Luther. In other, less material ways, however, he was vulnerable to influence. Conversing with Alfonso de Valdés, the highly intelligent secretary of state and Spanish follower of Erasmus, who had written the polemics against Pope Clement, he found himself in the presence of a kindred spirit. His newly acquired respect for authority rendered him deeply impressionable to the emperor's majesty. He actually reached agreement on eleven articles of his draft with the indefatigable Dr Eck, the bitterest opponent of all, who had hastened to Augsburg to act as consultant; even Luther in his castle was moved to declare that none of these points was of crucial importance. There was one question, however, on which they did not and could not yield, and this was the Word, the Gospel, the freedom to preach. This freedom was already in operation everywhere; the sermons, it is true, did not always have, indeed they rarely had, a common dogmatic basis, and they were sometimes interspersed with attacks on enemies or brother Protestants – but the freedom existed. It was the new faith, and the authority it claimed was the free Word of the Gospel. This was the Protestants' sole strength and it persisted behind all their internal conflicts. It was much stronger than all the differences over dogma. It was also stronger than the voice of authority, a fact of which it immediately gave proof.

The outward circumstances were as follows: Melanchthon read his Apology – the Protestants claimed this very act as a great success – following which the Catholic theologians composed a refutation; this refutation being accepted by a majority of the diet, the emperor announced that if the Protestants did not now yield he would proceed against them in his capacity of protector of the Church. Melanchthon then produced a 'refutation of the refutation', and finally they dispersed without reaching agreement. The Protestants held to their protest; they consisted of five princes and fourteen cities, including Strasbourg, Frankfurt, Nuremberg and, to the emperor's consternation, Augsburg, the scene of the diet and the seat of his great financial backers. The Protestant princes and delegates left; no one dared restrain them.

The emperor kept the original of the Augsburg Confession; it has since disappeared. Although he had issued an immediate ban on publication, an edition appeared while the diet was still in session, but the Protestants themselves described it as inaccurate. On his return to Wittenberg Melanchthon published an 'authentic' version, with various alterations; over a period of many years he followed this with a whole series of new versions. After his death a bitter controversy arose as to which of the versions was the true Augsburg Confession. In spite of this, however, Melanchthon, with his gift for lucid synopsis, produced a text that served for a considerable time and provided a platform on which conflicting schools of thought could meet.

As with all resolutions passed by the diet, the haughty words of the majority remained on record. The emperor's proclamations themselves had virtually no force behind them; he had no army at his disposal and could not count even on the Catholic powers. Overwhelming might in the hands of the emperor, and this is what victory over the Protestants would have given him, was something they did not want, least of all the

Bavarians; the Curia, always uneasy over the emperor's dominant position, did not want it either. The solution reached was unusually characteristic: the supreme court of the empire was to institute proceedings against the Protestants. In reality this was simply an evasion, an admission of acute embarrassment; the supreme court had been powerless since its foundation, its judges irregularly paid, its files hawked around from place to place. Nevertheless this move had deep significance. From the profound religious questions, over which they had supposedly been wrestling, those concerned had descended to the level of confiscation of estates, possessions, tax revenues and other worldly rights. In so doing they had given tangible proof of what was really at stake, and in the disputes that followed the supreme court itself declared, with all the clarity one could wish, that what was at issue was not religious questions but questions of rights and property.

The emperor's only higher hope for the future lay in the everlastingly postponed Council, which he promised to make the pope convene at last. His conscience had been salved by the expert evidence of the professional theologians. It was at this diet that the professional, in this case the theological expert, appeared for the first time in all his glory, and the most pernicious aspect of this was that, instead of having to give decisions within a specialized field, he was expected to pronounce on the burning questions of the day, these being inextricably linked with the whole hierarchic structure of the Church. The emperor read neither Melanchthon's Apology nor the refutations of his professional theologians. In conversation with a Danish envoy King Henry VIII of England declared, with all the superiority of the amateur theologian he fancied himself to be, that in Augsburg Charles should have given way on the few points that were still in dispute. 'The emperor is uneducated, he does not understand Latin. They should have appointed myself and the king of France as arbitrators. We would have called in the most reputable scholars in Europe, we would have soon brought the matter to a conclusion.' And on the question of electing a king: 'Why do the princes not choose someone else, like the duke of Bavaria who would be quite suitable? They ought not to let themselves be deceived by the emperor as he deceived the pope.' King Henry's remarks were not exactly unbiased, but his criticism of the empire's representatives was devastating; he ended by saying that it would be a disgrace for the emperor if he had to leave Germany without settling the dispute.

He was wrong only on one point: the electors, who chose Ferdinand as king, were not deceived by the emperor; they were paid as they had been at the emperor's election – in cash or in territory. Ferdinand now became king of Germany, in addition to being king of Bohemia and king of Hungary, but he was soon forced sorrowfully to tell his brother the emperor that to the Germans he was no more than any other prince of the empire: 'They do not obey me as king.'

It did not stop at disobedience. The threats made at the diet had taken effect. The Protestants, princes and cities alike, combined to form the Schmalkalden Alliance. Within a few years the little border town of Schmalkalden, in the territory of the landgrave of Hesse and situated in the hollow of a narrow valley on the south-west slopes of the Thuringian Forest, became famous; even foreign powers learned to spell the rather difficult name. The landgrave was the driving force; the elector of Saxony needed some persuasion before he decided to join, but the alliance grew steadily. Although Luther and Melanchthon were suspicious of all 'insurrectionary' alliances, their doubts were allayed by the evidence of the Saxon jurists; the interpretation of Roman law triumphed over the theologians' interpretation of the Bible. It was demonstrated to them that under modern conditions the word 'authority' no longer meant what it did in the days of Paul. The emperor of the Holy Roman Empire was an elected emperor, whereas the princes were hereditary rulers; the empire was not a monarchy but an aristocracy: 'The estates govern side by side with the emperor, and the emperor is not a monarch.' This was precisely what Charles wanted to be, but it was a position the German princes had never conceded to their sovereign. The theologians were forced to retreat, commenting in their embarrassment: 'We did not know that.' To them 'authority' now meant the ruling princes and the city councils. Once again the cities had had a great opportunity; but they remained within their walls, with their excellent artillery, their brilliant craftsmen and artists, their astronomers and their geographers, who traced on their maps the trade routes across the world. When it came to making great decisions, the political paths of their leaders did not extend far beyond their immediate surroundings.

For all this, the Schmalkalden Alliance, embracing both princes and city republics, now became a reality; it even had a sort of constitution. The amounts of the contributions were fixed, and it was decided to create a military organization – both of them problems the empire was never able to solve satisfactorily. A chancellery was set up and something approaching a form of government. France, England and Denmark took a lively interest in the new power group; envoys were sent and returned again. It was an offensive and defensive alliance, the elector of Saxony representing the defensive side and the landgrave of Hesse the offensive. Thus the half-measure, or half-heartedness, the dominating principle of every institution of the age, came into its own again. When agreement could not be reached over the supreme command, it was divided between the Elector John and Philip of Hesse.

The alliance was formed in the first instance for six years, and even this was considered a remarkably long period; the term was then further prolonged, and for fifteen years, from 1530 until 1545, the members of the Schmalkalden Alliance dominated the scene. It was by far the longest span of time that any alliance survived during the sixteenth century. More and more princes and communities joined, including even the arch-Catholic Bavaria. Seriously as they had been taken initially, religious questions had to give way before the need to form a front against the hereditary monarchy of the Habsburgs. The politicians increasingly held the upper hand over the theologians, and this became a distinguishing feature of this second epoch of the Reformation era. The fate of the new movement in Germany no longer depended on Luther. It was decided by princes, by the Landgrave Philip and later by young Maurice of Saxony, who in many respects was very similar to Philip of Hesse: both were 'good Protestants' and neither had too many scruples in joining forces with the emperor and the 'good Catholics' when it suited their own dynastic plans.

The same was true of the other side. The emperor pursued his imperial plans, and these in turn had as their primary objective the glory of the House of Habsburg-Burgundy; as he had done at Worms, on his first visit to the empire, he very soon lost all interest in the ill-defined and inextricably confused conditions in Germany once he left Augsburg. His attempt to bring about agreement had failed, and he had pacified his conscience by demanding a Council. His first abdication came when his brother was elected king: he formally handed over to Ferdinand his imperial authority, retaining only certain rights, the most important of which was the right to decide questions involving the monopolies, on which his finances depended. He had been away almost ten years; he was to stay away another ten years.

The theologians were forced to take second place, but this did not mean that their ideas were no longer influential. On the contrary, it was only now that religious slogans began to exert their pernicious influence in the form of endorsements of, and pretexts for, the exercise of a very different kind of power. Even the papacy had to step down from its position of world domination, although it was a long time before the popes were prepared to admit it.

Luther's remaining span of life coincided exactly with that of the Schmalkalden Alliance. These years, from 1530 to 1546, were his years of resignation. The months he spent in Coburg Castle, where he was kept in semi-captivity as he had been in the Wartburg, were his last months of freedom.

# 36

# The second Reformation

LUTHER spent almost six months, from April until the beginning of October 1530, in Coburg Castle. He has been represented at this period as the trusty guardian, putting things right and guiding his country's destiny from his tower when the others wanted to throw in their hands. It is true that he sent out his fervent letters and warnings, but in spite of all his brave words he was clearly no longer the old Luther. He complained ceaselessly of ringing in his ears, headaches, and gall-stones, and it goes without saying that it was the devil who was tormenting him; in the evenings he would see a fiery snake slide down from the tower and disappear twisting and turning beyond the wood. He was lonely in his fortress and began to feel the loneliness about him.

But the months Luther spent in Coburg Castle were also the last of his creativeness as a master of language. It was as if all the strings of his nature sounded once again. Anger and defiance, when he declared in almost presumptuous words: 'If we go down, Christ will go down with us.' Or his unquenchable confidence when he had witnessed a miracle: 'As I looked out of the window I saw the stars in the heavens and God's whole beautiful vault, and nowhere did I see any pillars on which the master had supported this vault; and yet the heavens did not collapse and the vault still holds fast. Now there are some who look for such pillars, desiring to grasp and feel them. Because they cannot they teeter and tremble, certain the heavens will fall and for no other reason than that they cannot grasp or see the pillars. . . .' His humour, which had almost deserted him, broke through once more. He saw the rooks and other birds that congregated outside his window as a hastily summoned concourse of theologians: 'They chatter away tirelessly and ceaselessly all day long from four o'clock in the morning,' a whole congress of 'sophists' intent on propounding their wisdom – but so far there had been no nightingale among them. He wrote a letter to Hänschen, his small son, with pictures of a paradisical garden; children in golden coats and charming little horses with golden bridles and silver saddles. He composed a sermon for schools addressed to the rising generation, started to put Aesop into German, composed a four-part piece of music, and wrote a fine letter to the great musician Senfl in Munich; he continued to work unflaggingly at his complete translation of the Bible.

But there were now others on the scene, younger men or those with more experience of the world, men like the Swiss Zwingli or the Alsatian Bucer. The latter went to see Luther in an unsuccessful attempt to bring about a reconciliation between him and the south Germans and Swiss; depressed, but respectful, he had to admit that arguing with him only made him more stubborn: 'God has sent him to us, we must make use of him.'

Luther's quarrel with the Swiss was the great turning-point of the Reformation movement, and it cannot be explained simply by the difference in generations. Zwingli was almost his own age; he had a similar peasant background, and the fact that he shared Luther's peasant hard-headedness was responsible in no small measure for their failure to understand one another. But with Calvin, and the movement he created in Geneva, a completely new generation and a world utterly different from that of Luther entered the movement: a precision, which Calvin owed to his Gallic background and legal training, an ability to think and theorize with extreme logic and cogency, a gift for organizing and creating an 'institution', as he called his basic work. We cannot trace this here; it extends far beyond Luther's lifetime. The figure of Zwingli, however, straddles the course of Luther's life, not at his side but confronting him.

Luther appears as the richer character, if only because of his achievements in the realm of language, his translation of the Bible, his songs, his great, early polemic writings. Zwingli also commanded great expressiveness of language, although he usually wrote in Latin, and he composed a moving poem inspired by the plague, but it would be difficult to name any works of his that even approached those of Luther in the range and duration of their influence. Luther was first on the scene, and Zwingli always acknowledged this; it was Luther's great breakthrough that made history. Zwingli reformed Switzerland, or rather half Switzerland, though his influence spread much further than this, to Calvin, the Netherlands and England. The quieter, subterranean influence, that we also find in the case of the anabaptists, is generally underestimated in comparison with that exercised by the 'towering figures', who are easier to comprehend. Zwingli had none of Luther's blazing ardour and none of the lack of moderation that, even when he first appeared on the scene, made the Wittenberg monk an idol to many people and a nightmare to others. In comparison Zwingli strikes one as sober, cautious and very much less controversial; in his case there are no stories of religious battles fought almost to the point of self-annihilation, of constant temptations, breakdowns and passionate resurgence. Continuing on his way methodically and single-mindedly, his development was logical; he was no 'volcano', as Paracelsus had

Ulrich Zwingli

described Luther. He was not, like Luther, thrown into a world infested with devils; the devil never played so decisive a role in his life as it did in Luther's.

Zwingli's point of departure was his home, and he always remained in its close vicinity; he was a Swiss, born and bred in Toggenburg, in the small parish of Wildhaus, high up in the mountains above the line of cultivation of fruit trees. He came of a respected family, his father being mayor and magistrate of the whole valley and by no means badly off; of the many sons three were destined for the Church. Luther grew up without any historical background, whether as a child or in the monastery; to Zwingli Swiss history was one long succession of famous victories, beginning with Tell, the 'God-inspired hero who first raised the cry of freedom in the confederation', the man who with his cross-bow shot the governor from his horse, and going on to victories won by peasant armies against the Austrian and Burgundian knights, and in Zwingli's own lifetime the triumph over the Emperor Maximilian, who recognized the confederation's severance from the empire. He himself had taken part as an army pastor in the Lombardy campaigns, his short sword hanging at his side. Using a somewhat bold simile he liked to describe himself as the 'mercenary of God, His captain', because the fight against the mercenary system of soldiering counted as his first political activity. But what was decisive for him was this starting-point – so entirely different from Luther's: a strong confederation which, though burdened with many inner tensions, had, as the climax of a continuous advance, just reached the zenith of its power and prestige; and within this association the solidly established city republic of Zurich which, unlike Wittenberg, was very far from being a mere colonial village. Before he began his task as reformer Zwingli was already surrounded by a congregation, whereas Luther scarcely ever had anything but listeners, and beyond them readers; this congregation was the basis of Zwingli's work.

Luther was solely and exclusively the religious fighter. Zwingli started as a politician and remained one to the end of his life. Even his reform had a political purpose: he wanted to create a Christian order of society. Authority to him did not mean the emperor, or some other potentate, but the council of the republic of Zurich; what he aimed to to do was to win it, and the population of the little city state, and together with them carry through the new teaching. Luther's 'two kingdoms' did not enter the picture, still less the forced recognition of a secular government, even though it was hostile or bad. Under such circum-stances one resisted fiercely, and over the last three hundred years the Swiss had shown themselves past masters at this. They had made them-selves both feared and sought after, and were in demand everywhere as soldiers; great and powerful cities applied for membership in the confederation, while kings and popes sent their delegations to the national assemblies. In Zwingli's day Switzerland was by no means a 'neutral' country, it was deeply involved in all that went on in Europe. Nor was Zwingli merely a local Zurich politician; his thoughts reached far beyond his native town, much too far as it turned out. The sober, cautious man, with his reputation for 'peasant cunning', became involved in plans for a great Swiss republic, the seat of whose markedly dictatorial government was to be in Zurich; a still larger political structure was to extend far into Germany and Switzerland, in partner-ship with other European powers, was to occupy a dominant position

in it. This was too much for his countrymen, even for the citizens of
Zurich, and they refused him their allegiance. He fell in the civil war.

The unworldly and unpolitical Luther, with his attitude of resignation, was much more in harmony with the course of history, little
though he knew of this and unable though he was to take a constructive
view of it. But Zwingli's intervention in the 'things of this world' was
also closely connected with his religious views and concept of the world.
Brought up on humanist lines, he thought in universal terms. He was
strongly imbued with the ideas of antiquity and ancient Rome; in his
work *On Providence* he speaks of the 'eternal and immutable government and administration of all things', a formula that might have been
used by an ancient Roman. He, too, took the Bible as his starting-point,
but believed that God had not manifested Himself in it alone. Unwilling to forgo Socrates, Seneca and Cicero, Zwingli saw divine wisdom
already revealed in them; the Greek and Roman natural law derived
from God, who was a continuous, active force and of whom nature was
the permanent expression. His notion of the Church, however, he took
from the Bible, the Church for him being unquestionably the congregation, and not the great institution and hierarchy of the Roman *Ecclesia*.
He built his reformation on the congregation, the parish, transforming
this into a Christian state modelled on his ideas. The subsequent great
statesmen of the Protestant world, including dictators like Cromwell,
were disciples of Zwingli, not of Luther.

Compared with Luther's battles, Zwingli's rise was almost effortless.
He had studied in Basle and Vienna, finding nothing to object to
seriously in either scholasticism or the commentaries; in fact, and again
in contrast to Luther, he remained quite content to follow the path of
the old teachings and Aristotle. He became a happy and contented
young humanist and follower of Erasmus; pleasant livings came his
way, and he earned a reputation as a preacher in Glarus and Einsiedeln.
The immensely ambitious and energetic Cardinal Schiner, one of whose
activities was enlisting Swiss soldiery for the pope, interested himself in
his gifted young fellow-countryman; as Schiner's protégé Zwingli continued to rise and was even considered for diplomatic missions in Italy.
For many years he received a regular pension from the pope, and
because of this became involved in the internal conflict over annuities
and bribes that dominated the whole Swiss political scene. Money
poured in from every quarter, the Swiss mercenaries being in demand
as fighters on every front, and like the German landsknechts they sometimes found themselves on opposite sides. This problem, and not a
religious question, was the subject of Zwingli's first literary work.
Switzerland he described as a gorgeously painted bull, led astray by
crafty cats – the French – and warned by faithful dogs not to let itself be

drawn into other countries' affairs. He still remained loyal to Cardinal Schiner, who opposed the French recruitment of Swiss mercenaries while he himself was busy recruiting them for the pope. But Zwingli already had doubts about the whole system of payments and pensions, which had turned Switzerland into a land of 'pensioners'. Cardinal Schiner himself had already encountered bitter opposition on this score in his home canton of Valais and in Sitten, the seat of his bishopric; eventually he was forced to leave Switzerland, and his considerable talents for political intrigue lay fallow until he was appointed councillor to the emperor. He complained bitterly of the roughness and violence of his countrymen, who for centuries had been in the habit of attacking their bishops and masters, strangling them and throwing them out of windows.

It was into this world of bitter disagreement that Zwingli entered when he was appointed to the coveted post of lay-priest at the minster in Zurich, the leading canton of the thirteen cantons that made up the confederation. The Reformation only exacerbated to new bitterness the great tensions that already existed, especially between the city and country cantons; the individuality and stubbornness of the various regions found in it welcome nourishment. Printing had introduced new opportunities for disseminating views, thus ensuring that the fire never died down. The high level of skill and craftsmanship in the country contributed to this; it was a great era of Swiss art, of which there was never again such a wealth on so high a level. Poems, powerful satires, Shrove-tide plays, dramas and mimes made a further contribution; at the time of the Reformation the Swiss drama was by far the most vital of the day, and represented a total mobilization of the spirit of the people in all its nuances, from the coarsest to the finest.

At first Zwingli proceeded cautiously, avoiding roughness and violence. For a long time he held aloof from Luther, maintaining that he had proclaimed his own gospel before ever he set eyes on a line written by the monk of Wittenberg. His sermons dealt with the complete Gospel instead of with the prescribed extracts. He was not a good speaker; his voice did not carry well, and many of those in the church had to sit close to him in order to hear what he said. But people felt the intensity of his nature, and this won him his congregation, the leading members of the city council and the city itself. Most astonishing perhaps was the tolerance with which Zwingli's Reformation was received by the Curia – Switzerland as its most important recruiting ground had to be treated with circumspection. 'We were not spurned or rebuked as renegades,' said Zwingli, 'but rewarded with important titles.'

He had, nonetheless, long been a renegade; in the manner of the day the first contests had taken the form of disputations. The mayor of Zurich decreed that henceforth the unalloyed Gospel, and nothing else, was to be preached; the city shook itself free from the sovereignty of the bishop, and so from the whole hierarchy of the Church. The transformation effected by Zwingli was far more radical and far more rapid than that in Luther's Wittenberg. It had started, as we have seen, with a petty quarrel over the rule of fasting at a Lenten feast given by the publisher Froschauer. Following this the monasteries and religious foundations were done away with, the city council appropriating the estates and revenues for the common good, for poor relief, for payment of schoolteachers, for the establishment for the first time of an evangelical faculty of theology. It was all carried out with Swiss thoroughness; the images were removed with the same thoroughness, not in savage attacks as happened in Thuringia, but on instructions from those in authority. Organ-playing was forbidden; although Zwingli was as good a musician and as keen a music-lover as Luther, he wished to have nothing in church that might interfere with the service. 'And in thirteen days all the churches in the city had been emptied,' wrote the chronicler Bullinger in his description of the action; in other parts of Switzerland there was much greater violence. The most important innovation was the marital law, which until then had come under the jurisdiction of the ecclesiastical authorities and been the cause of much quarrelling over dues and dispensations. These authorities were replaced by a court consisting of four lay members and two pastors; divorce and the right to re-marry were introduced, and a marriage register was kept – it became the model for many other cities, including those within the empire.

Zwingli, however, went further; the marriage court became a court of morals, supervising the entire population of the city; it had its own informers. Householders were made responsible for the conduct of those they housed and of their tenants. Courting couples were spied on in gateways, innkeepers and servants were spied on; even husbands returning home late were reported to the court. Long before Calvin's Geneva, Zwingli's Zurich became the first strictly 'puritanical' city. The head of this community and its leader, although he held no specific post, was Zwingli, preacher, statesman and prophet.

As with all radical movements the 'deviationists' – those who deviated from the radical line and, like the anabaptists in Zwingli's case, wanted to proceed still more radically – were treated with extreme severity and intolerance. In the sixteenth century the idea of tolerance was virtually unknown, except to a very few courageous individuals who were persecuted cruelly for their views. Zwingli struck down the anabaptists mercilessly at the point of the sword. It was his fate to be classed by

Luther with the Schwarmgeister and anabaptists, when in fact his hatred for them was scarcely less intense than Luther's.

Zwingli regarded baptism, which for him was the heart of the matter, as a communal responsibility: the parents and godparents were to be under a binding obligation to bring up the baptized child according to the requirements of a Christian community. The same community idea underlay his celebration of the Communion: those partaking of it sat in orderly rows, the women on the left and the men on the right of the church, while beadles handed round the bread in wooden bowls, each communicant breaking off a morsel, and the wine was passed in wooden beakers; all those attending ate and drank together 'in commemoration' of the first Communion.

But before Zwingli fell out with Luther over this, his reformed city of Zurich encountered violent opposition within Switzerland itself. The city cantons of north Switzerland, such as Basle and Bern, were in sympathy with him and copied him, but the 'old cantons' of the interior opposed him bitterly. The confederation, subjected to a severe test, acquitted itself badly. In an exact parallel to what had happened in the empire, the Catholic cantons, which were in a majority, used a national assembly to place Zurich and Zwingli's work under a ban, citing the Edict of Worms as authority. This meant that the confederation, as a union of free and independent members, was split asunder. The fact that a specifically imperial decree had been invoked, although Switzerland had expressly declared its independence of imperial legislation, inevitably led to the brink of civil war. Both parties sought allies abroad; both were almost equally strong and could not hope to win on their own. The original Catholic cantons turned to Austria and in so doing exposed themselves to the odium of calling in the confederation's old hereditary enemy; Zwingli sounded out the great imperial cities of Strasbourg and Mühlhausen in Alsatia and established contacts with Hesse. At the turn of the century there had been a large influx into the confederation from south Germany; it was then that Basle and Schaffhausen had joined the confederation, and this had already caused great unrest in the country cantons which, in any case, were suspicious of the increasing wealth and power of the cities. Further such additions, they argued, would reduce them to an insignificant minority. Zwingli's plans were, in fact, aimed at placing the leadership in the hands of Zurich and Bern, the two most powerful cities. He began to play for high stakes, involving himself in the whole field of European politics. France was to contain the emperor's western flank, King Zapolya of Hungary to checkmate his rival King Ferdinand in the east. Zwingli had hopes of converting France to the new teaching; Francis I had courageously threatened the pope with defection, a weapon he kept in

# Der Psalter.

I.

Ol dem der nicht wan=delt im rat der Gottlosen/no=ch trit auff den weg der sün=der/Noch sitzt da die Spötter.

(Spötter) Die es fur ei tel narheit halten/was Gott redet vnd thut.

sitzen.

Sondern hat lust zum Gesetz des HERRN/Vnd redet von sei=nem Gesetze tag vnd nacht.

Der ist wie ein bawm gepflantzet an den wasserbechen/ der seine frucht bringet zu seiner zeit/ Vnd seine bletter verwelcken ni=cht/vnd was er machet/das ge=rett wol.

(Gerichte) Das ist/sie werden we=der ampt ha ben / noch sonst jnn der Christen ge=meine bleis ben/ ja sie verweben sich selb/wie die sprew vom korn

Aber so sind die Gottlosen nicht/ Sondern wie sprew / die der wind verstrewet.

Darumb bleiben die Gottlosen nicht im b gerichte/noch die sun

der jnn der Gemeine der gerech=ter.

Denn der HERR kennet den weg der gerechten/Aber der got losen weg vergehet.

II.

Warumb toben die Heiden / Vnd die leute reden so vergeblich?

Die Könige im lande lehnen sich auff / vnd die Herrn ratschla=hen miteinander / Wider den HERRN vnd seinen gesalbe=ten.

Lasset vns zureissen jre bande/vnd von vns werffen jre seile.

Aber der im Himel wonet/lachet jr/Vnd der HERR spottet jr.

Er wird einest mit jnen reden jnn seinem zorn / Vnd mit seinem grim wird er sie schrecken.

Aber ich

Page from Luther's Bible of 1534 (Book of Psalms)

constant readiness and because of which he permitted a certain latitude to the adherents of the new teaching. His sister Margaret of Navarre was allowed to gather round her a whole court of members, or near members, of the reformed Church. Zwingli addressed a comprehensive 'exposition of the faith' to the French king. Strongly tinged with humanism, it pictured heaven as containing a 'round table' at which the 'most devout king' would be able to meet in peaceful union all the saints and sages from the beginning of time; in addition to the apostles and the Virgin Mary he would meet Hercules, Socrates, Scipio, his royal ancestors, Louis the Pious and other monarchs of his line. It is quite conceivable that this, more or less, was the heaven Francis I imagined when he turned his thoughts in that direction but it was something he rarely did, and Zwingli's attempt to win him over remained a chimera.

This grandiose design, which was intended ultimately to extend from the North Sea to Venice and in the east to Transylvania, was weak at its core, no agreement being reached even between the Swiss and south German followers of Zwingli and Luther. The landgrave of Hesse worked unremittingly to bring this about. He summoned the two parties to a religious discussion in Marburg; one of the countless disputations of the time, it was in many respects the most fateful. The two groups were divided over the question of Communion. It is hard today to reconstruct the quarrel, which to us seems like a verbal quibble; but since Luther had raised the Word to the position of supreme authority, no word or phrase was simply a word or phrase any more. When he read in his Bible the words 'This is my body', more than a question of interpretation was involved, and this was doubly true now because, in the years since his return from the Wartburg, he had felt himself to be under constant attack. In his first bold assault he had left the question of Communion virtually aside; but now that it had been raised by the Schwarmgeister, by Karlstadt and Zwingli, he had to accept the challenge and defend himself, and in doing so was constantly led back to his past. To put it crudely, he became more and more Catholic, and the Swiss upbraided him for this. To us it seems that he had always remained much more Catholic than his enforced battle with Rome would lead one to expect; here Zwingli was by far the more determined heretic, although he was never threatened with the stake. But the most pernicious aspect of the dispute was that it stirred up once again all the ancient controversies from the times of the earliest Councils. This was where the root of the problem lay: addicted as early Christendom was to dogmatic definitions – an addiction it owed to the increasing influence of classical thought – it had failed to solve the insoluble problem of defining mysteries in a manner satisfactory to all by the use of terms that were necessarily inadequate. The Trinity as three persons in one, the dual nature of Christ as God and man – the conflict began at once, splitting large groups and sometimes dividing the whole Church. Both Luther and Zwingli still took as their basis the decisions of the Council of Nicaea and the symbols promulgated there; it required further development before even these were doubted, although preliminary intimations were apparent in Luther's lifetime. But Luther's and Zwingli's acceptance of these common symbols did not prevent them from understanding and interpreting them differently. Zwingli, true to his humanist training, kept the two natures of Christ separate: to drag the Deity into this earthly life would have been to profane it; Christ had suffered as a man, because by definition the Deity was incapable of suffering. In Luther's eyes this amounted to blasphemy: did Zwingli then deny God's expiatory death and redemption? Zwingli also regarded the bodily presence of Christ in the bread and wine as a coarsening of the Divine, a link with sensuality; Christ's words 'This is my body' were to be translated, or understood, as 'This signifies my body'. To Luther this was sacrilege; the subject they were discussing was a mystery, a miracle. He explained such miracles in poetic terms: 'When a mirror is broken into a thousand pieces the same picture that before appeared only in the complete mirror is still to be seen in its entirety in each individual piece.' Christ was omnipresent; why should He not be present in the bread and wine? Zwingli argued that because we knew Christ to be in heaven, sitting at the right hand of the Father, He could not at the same time be in the bread and the wine. Luther ridiculed this, saying that Zwingli's heaven was a 'regular conjuring-trick of a heaven, with its golden chair and Christ sitting at the Father's side wearing a cope and a golden crown.'

The ruthless attitude that automatically denied an opponent any true faith is almost incomprehensible to us today. To Luther Zwingli was simply an emissary of the devil, the Swiss celebration of Communion an exhibition of 'gorging and gluttony reminiscent of taverns and fairs'; the Swiss retaliated by calling Luther a 'cannibal'. On the whole, however, they behaved more temperately, whereas Luther raged at them with even less restraint than he had shown towards the pope. For him it was a highly personal battle. He had had to fight the battle out within himself, with the devil who had tried to confuse him with cunningly devised arguments appealing to reason; he had struck him down with his cudgel. Now the devil was raising his head, his many heads, again – Zwingli was only one of them. He sensed in Zwingli the subtle reasoner, the rationalist.

Furthermore, the two men were simply incompatible. Zwingli came to the meeting exuding self-confidence, his short sword hanging at his side; for the moment everything was going splendidly, and his retinue, which included the landgrave of Hesse, was much larger and more powerful than Luther's. Luther was depressed, physically a sick man already, upset by the defection of so many on whom he had counted. He could not even understand what the Swiss said – their 'tangled, matted' dialect, as he called it in obvious allusion to the garment in which the devil habitually appeared. He is unlikely to have made any close study of Zwingli's writings, though he will probably have been aware of the innovations he had introduced in Zurich. He was suspicious of the republic.n nature of the Swiss; he was a patriarchal monarchist and opposed the taking of votes in popular assemblies.

Thus the great three-day discussion in the first days of October 1529 was a fiasco. There is no verbatim record, because Luther expressly rejected the idea; all we have are the later reports of those who took part. One story that has been reliably handed down is the celebrated episode of Luther, with his sense of the dramatically symbolic, writing in chalk on the table in front of him his main proposition: 'This is my body'. He covered it with the velvet tablecloth; lifting this at the climax of the debate he pointed to what stood there: the Word, the Word, there it is, there can be no argument! Apart from this there were few highlights in the proceedings. The two protagonists probed each other thoroughly, and at the end each stuck to the viewpoint with which he had started. They also shouted at one another. When the discussion turned to the question of God's omnipresence, Luther roared angrily: 'God can do much more than any of us have any idea of, we must yield to the Word of God. A servant does not fret over his master's wishes, we must shut our eyes.' Then resorting to paradox, as he so often did, he added still more furiously: 'And if God commanded me to eat dung I should eat it!' Zwingli, who had no intention of shutting his eyes, retorted: 'God does not give that sort of command; He is real and is light, He does not lead man into darkness'; it was wrong, he said, to cling to the human element and the flesh of Christ, we should lift up our spirit to the spiritual Divinity. 'I know of no God but the God who became man, nor do I wish any other,' was Luther's answer. Whatever conciliatory, deeply felt words were uttered from time to time became lost under the table on which the Word was written. Luther's final summing-up was: 'And so our spirit and your spirit are not in harmony.' It had been a confrontation between the humanist and the monk, the 'idealist' and the 'realist'; for Luther reality was the incomprehensible mystery of the 'real presence' of the body of Christ in the bread and the wine.

The landgrave's last-minute attempt to effect some sort of compromise failed. Zwingli and his followers wanted to celebrate Holy

Communion with Luther and his followers as a symbolic act of leave-taking. The suggestion was flatly rejected, and at the four-hundredth anniversary of the meeting at Marburg in 1929 the refusal was repeated.

They parted. The most the landgrave achieved was to get a closing formula accepted which, like the final resolutions of the diets, could be construed as one wished: 'In so far as the conscience of each is able to permit it.' Each side claimed victory. The rupture in the Protestant ranks became a reality before the diet of Augsburg perpetuated the political rupture. As soon as he reached home Luther set down his own *Profession of Faith* as a counter to the Marburg resolutions, which had been intended as *Articles of Union*. Switzerland seceded from the leading Protestant movement. Zwingli's fate was now to be decided within the confines of his own country.

In 1531 civil war broke out. Two years earlier it had been avoided, although the two sides had already taken up arms; at that time Zwingli had given in reluctantly and only under pressure. He was not against war, even a preventive one if it was fought in the 'just cause' of the Gospel. He waged war now with all his might, completely overrating the forces he had at his disposal. An odd change took place in the character of this hitherto exceptionally circumspect man: in 1529, when forces were first mobilized, he had been quick to draft a precise plan of campaign, including detailed instructions for military service, small arms equipment and a signals system; now, in 1531, he ignored all this. He was interested only in grand political schemes, every one of which miscarried. From his prospective allies, from Denmark, Paris and Venice, he received only fair words; even the reformed cities in Switzerland did not give him energetic support. His plan to create a new Switzerland with Zurich and Bern as its 'pillars and foundations', and to subdue, suppress and even 'wipe out' the Catholic cantons, found little favour; an attempt to starve out the five original cantons failed, as such attempts always do. Zwingli also overstrained his position in the city; a 'privy council' had existed for a long time, now Zwingli and his more intimate associates were known as the 'privier privy councillors'. His rule grew stricter. Compulsory church attendance was decreed, the vice-squad used its powers more and more drastically: 'There is fear and suspicion everywhere, among families and officials alike, everyone is afraid to go near the pulpit,' is how a city councillor described the situation. All the posts were held by careerists, even in the army.

The five Catholic cantons attacked in a body, with experienced troops and officers. The Zurich contingent took the field too late and with a pitiful force; in the words of the chronicler: 'Never in its history has the city of Zurich witnessed so wretched and lamentable a sight when its banners were carried forth.' Some two thousand strong, they were met and annihilated by an enemy force of about eight thousand; Zwingli was one of the nine city preachers who fell in the battle. His corpse was solemnly tried by court-martial and sentenced to be quartered, the punishment for high treason, and burned, the punishment for heresy. A still heavier blow than this defeat at Kappel was a second defeat in which the force from Bern, that had hurried to Zurich's aid, was also caught. Lack of discipline was the reason for this disaster; in numbers the armies were evenly matched. It is worth a moment's reflection that the strict discipline introduced by Zwingli, which in the end became dictatorial, stood up so badly to the test of battle. By the second Peace of Kappel Zurich was forced to renounce all its plans for becoming a great power; the foreign alliances were revoked, and the parchment recording the pact with Philip of Hesse torn up. The south German cities reverted to the empire. The Swiss reformation was not brought to an end by this, but henceforth it became a purely Swiss affair. It was forced to adapt itself to parity with the Catholic cantons.

The repercussions of this first Protestant military catastrophe were felt far beyond the borders of Switzerland; it was the first victory of what, in retrospect, came to be known as the Counter-Reformation. Luther saw his views on war and resistance confirmed. Zwingli's death was 'a judgment of God'; clinging stubbornly to his view that Zwingli was a Schwarmgeist and sacramentalist he classed him among the founders of sects, with Thomas Müntzer, Balthasar Hubmair, Hut the anabaptist and others. And with extreme emphasis on his doctrine of the need to suffer and offer no resistance he quoted the Bible: the servant of God would be 'led as a lamb to the slaughter'. 'Zwingli wanted to be a war hero', a 'giant', and Luther doubted whether he would be saved and go to heaven; in his heaven there was no place for those who carried swords.

Zwingli had pictured to the king of France a hereafter that also included the heroes of ancient Greece and Rome, and his death on the battlefield reaffirmed this spiritual affinity. But this typifies only one side of his nature. He could also pray for help from above and practise the submissiveness he expressed in his hymn on the plague, in which he likened himself to an earthen jar, a vessel in the hand of God: 'Make me whole or smash me.' It was his fate to be smashed.

The triumph of his opponents, Luther among them, was brief. But the death of the only leading figure among the Protestants who had any wider conception of the political field was a far more serious blow than the defeat at Kappel, which in itself was of no great importance. Switzerland's secession meant more than the loss of a powerful military ally to the Protestant party; it was the beginning of the end of the cities as the hard core of the Reformation. For a long time those concerned were unaware of this; great centres like Strasbourg, Nuremberg, Augsburg and Ulm regarded themselves as the princes' equals, their power sustaining their claims. With Zurich, Bern and Basle as allies they would have been irresistible. But now they began to feel insecure, and threw in their lot with the elector of Saxony and the princes, who were pursuing their particularist policies. In Wittenberg it was realized with satisfaction that the 'Lutheran cause' would now triumph, and, as far as questions of doctrine and dogmatic formulation were concerned, this was true. But matters of faith were increasingly becoming a pretext for utterly selfish and petty territorial plans. A period of bargaining and haggling began; this very soon led to the most embarrassing volte-face, which local historians had the greatest difficulty in justifying. The heroic age of the Reformation was over. Luther retired further and further into the background. Everywhere voices were raised protesting allegiance to the young, the 'real' Luther, and they were by no means mistaken views; the process has never ceased in the Protestant Church. Luther was overwhelmed with questions, letters and requests for his opinion, and people pestered him with the most trivial and silly problems; he answered as well as he could, but he found it increasingly irksome. His capacity for work remained extraordinary to the end, but he squandered it on things that others could have done as well or better.

The dogmatic controversies, which had come to a head in the fight over Communion, continued, enabling the authorities, whether princes or city councils, increasingly to gain the upper hand. They were forced to intervene and establish some measure of order when preachers constantly abused each other from the pulpit as Satan's messengers and sons of Belial. A whole generation of theologians grew up who knew little more of Luther than his coarse language. He himself, the grand old man, became more and more irritable, his breakdowns, which were partly physical and partly mental, more and more frequent. Himself depressed, he saw the end of the world as an accomplished fact, whereas in his early days it had been a door leading to a new and better age. The organization and progress of his Church went on slowly. 'Secularization' had been simply a catchword; but which secular powers were to take over the privileges and funds? The ruling princes? The nobility? The city councils? This again led to endless haggling, and in many areas absorbed all the available energies for decades to come; the records and registers bear witness to this. This inner conflict, intensified by the unimaginable splintering to which every possession within the empire had been subjected, may have done more harm to the Protestants than the lack of unity among their leaders, although this too was mainly due to quarrels over pieces of land – scraps of a former bishopric, an abbey, or a meadow attached to a monastery. To Luther all these were the things of this world, whose prince was most certainly Satan; he neither understood nor wished to understand them, yet he was for ever being pestered with them. He had placed his Church's cause in the hands of the authorities, and these hands stretched further and further afield. Councillors, syndics and jurists dominated the scene; he had the deepest mistrust of them, which was evidenced even in the way his will was drawn up, but he was at their mercy. The fate of the Reformation was decided by the princes and their advisers.

The Elector John had grown old and died; his place as ruler over the half state of Saxony was taken by his son, John Frederick. The new sovereign excelled his predecessor only in girth and in his capacity for drink; he was suspicious, petty, quick-tempered, stubborn and fell out with everyone with whom he had dealings. He considered Luther and his teaching as a family possession; he was proud of them, and proud too that the Wittenberg teaching was now so generally recognized as the true doctrine. As representative of the new generation he felt so secure that, if it suited his plans for his country, he was able to cultivate ties with King Ferdinand, the emperor and other Catholic princes without endangering his Protestant position; and most people on both sides thought as he did. The great ideas of a comprehensive reform, which would include not only the Church but the whole empire, melted away. Everyone was content to adapt himself to circumstances and try to maintain his position. Luther did the same. His resignation had almost degenerated into faint-heartedness; he cautioned people against all 'experiments' that intruded into territory subject to other 'authority'.

The Catholics were equally tired. There had as yet been no real political test of strength between the two parties; the Peasants' War had been the only decision in the social sphere, and this had had reper-cussions on both sides. No one wanted to jeopardize the tremendous victory that had been won; the latent fear that war might break out again acted as a binding agent, overcoming all confessional barriers. In 1532 the religious Peace of Nuremberg, assuring the Protestants freedom to practise their religion, was signed. Once again a Council, the eternal hope, was demanded to set the seal on this provisional solution. The emperor had to give his consent, because the house of Habsburg was threatened on two sides once more: in the west by France and in the east by the Turks, the allies of the Most Christian King Francis I. The price demanded of the Protestants by Charles for religious tolerance was participation in the Turkish campaign; they agreed.

The Turkish menace was one of the great threats that from time to time overshadowed all other considerations; fear of the Turks dominated people's thinking as much as the coming of the Last Judgment, and it was no mere delusion. Under Sultan Suleiman, the Ottoman Empire had been raised to the pinnacle of its might, both in administrative organization – his chroniclers called him Kamuni, the lawgiver – and in military striking power. He had at his disposal the only standing army in the world, the strongest fleets and an excellent diplomatic corps, and his empire was united by a common faith; he himself copied out the Koran eight times with his own hand. In point of fact, Suleiman was the only true Imperator of his age, and it was as such that he saw himself. He considered it by no means impossible that Europe would succumb to him, especially as he was very accurately informed on the rifts and antagonisms that split its peoples. Hitherto he had made only powerful raids into the alpine regions, penetrating as far as Vienna; now he was approaching with his legendary army. He had had a crown made for his western possessions by Venetian goldsmiths; the Balkans and Hungary were already in his hands. The main secret of his conquest was persistent, steady advance, eroding the frontiers and giving the enemy no real respite; they, on the other hand, could mount only short campaigns of a few weeks' duration, after which they had to return home again because pay for the mercenaries had run out. Suleiman had no worries of this kind; he was independent of both grants from discontented estates and credits from bankers. So far as the emperor was concerned, this campaign, the greatest he had ever undertaken, followed the usual pattern: an impressive gathering of his forces, at which the Protestants were much in evidence, great reviews of the troops – Germans, Spaniards, Italians, landsknechts and contingents from the towns – and skirmishes with the Turks, who had advanced into the alpine regions, after wasting valuable time laying siege to towns in Hungary. At the Austrian border the German forces halted, announced that they had not set out to win Hungary back for Ferdinand, and went home. One might accuse them of shamefully betraying a great cause were it not for the fact that before their very eyes they had evidence that no one was any longer taking the joint operation seriously. Ferdinand was fighting for personal power, the emperor for the greatness of the Burgundian dynasty, and the king of France, in alliance with the Sultan, to force the Habsburgs to their knees or at least to weaken them considerably. International politics reflected faithfully the politics of the petty German states.

In spite of this the cry 'Fight the infidel' still retained some of its ancient allure, a fact of which the emperor was very well aware, hoping to make use of it in the furtherance of his imperialist plans. However, as usual he frittered away his strength. Instead of attacking the Balkans, the only decisive front, he made isolated raids on the north African coast, where a follower of the sultan, the Greek renegade Chaireddin Barbarossa, had established his sovereignty and was making the Mediterranean coasts unsafe with his corsairs. Tunis was captured in 1534, and Charles allowed himself to be rapturously acclaimed as the hero of Christendom. He travelled the length and breadth of Italy where triumphal arches were erected in his honour, one of them bearing the inscription: 'From the Rising to the Setting of the Sun'; this gave rise to the famous saying that Charles ruled over an empire on which the sun never set. The raid was only an episode; a second attack, on Algiers in 1541, was a miserable failure. Campaigns and aid against the Turks remained permanently on the programme, but with no other result than that the Ottoman Empire finally absorbed Hungary for the next hundred and fifty years, and the whole of north Africa remained in the hands of its satellites.

Charles manifested the same inability to carry a favourite idea through to its logical conclusion in the case of his constantly expressed wish for a great Council. Sometimes it was used to exert pressure on the pope, sometimes dangled as a hope before the Protestants, sometimes honestly debated in a desire to bring about a union; but in spite of all his experiences with five popes, Charles could not bring himself to take the only step that held out promise of success, although it had been recommended often enough by his inner circle of advisers. This was to force the Curia. On not a few occasions he had attacked the popes in the strongest terms, and he continued to complain and protest even when finally, though too late, the Council met. Throughout his reign he had to wage unceasing hot or cold war against Rome; but he never dared surrender his respect and reverence for the institution as such, irrespective of its incumbent. Whether this was for the good even of the Roman Church seems to this writer very debatable.

The emperor's attitude to this cardinal question determined events for the rest of his life. The 'Religious Peace', or rather armistice, of Nuremberg, as the provisional settlement was somewhat grandiloquently called, was succeeded by further negotiations, religious discussions, delays and postponements, some of which were as short-termed as the grants for military campaigns or the credit of the bankers. The theologians had the last word; over and over again it seemed almost as if agreement might be possible, but the talks invariably broke down over the Protestants' refusal to submit to the authority of the pope or to a Council presided over by the pope. They demanded a free Council at which they would appear not as the accused but as a partner with equal rights. At times the emperor wavered under the pressure of constant opposition from the Curia, which obstinately supported his enemy France; at other times he threatened to call a National Council, but it remained a threat. When finally the new Pope Paul III actually announced the long-awaited Council, he protested, objecting to Mantua in Italy as the place of convocation; on his insistence it was convened in Trent, in 1544, but with an agenda flatly contradictory to the emperor's wishes, and was then transferred to Bologna where, after ten sittings, it was adjourned for ten years. It met again in 1562 when, as far as the doctrines of the Catholic Church were concerned, it made history for three hundred years. The Emperor Charles did not live to see it; his desire for a thoroughgoing reform of the whole position and function of the Church remained unheeded up to the time when he abdicated. The Protestants no longer took part in the Council. The split in the Church had become permanent.

Luther did not live to see it either; he had condemned the plans for the Council in the most violent terms. In terms of outward expansion the decade from 1535 to 1545 was a glorious age for the Protestant movement, in spite of all the internal dissensions; otherwise there was little that was glorious about it. The distinguishing feature was the subordination of the religious movement to purely political factors and considerations of power. The Schmalkalden Alliance formed the core of the expansion, but it was not a very solid core. Older princes like George of Saxe-Meissen and the margrave of Brandenburg, who had remained loyal to the Church, died, and their territories were reformed. Philip, landgrave of Hesse, conquered Württemberg and gave it back to Duke Ulrich; this territory too was brought into the new faith. Ahead loomed still greater possibilities that would bring almost the whole of Germany into the Reformation: the archbishop of Cologne, Hermann von Wied, wanted to reform his widespread territories, with the approval of the secular estates, and even the archbishopric of Mainz, the greatest of the ecclesiastical electorates, was ready to follow suit; the Palatinate wanted to join. Had there been no outside intervention it is fairly certain that the Reformation, as far as Germany was concerned, would have been virtually complete. This 'outside intervention', however, materialized in the person of the emperor, who was hastening to Germany for his last and longest visit. He changed the picture completely, until after another few years it seemed as if the Reformation had been crushed out of existence in the 'Schmalkalden War' of 1546-7; there was a time when its fate threatened to hang on the resistance of a single city – Magdeburg. Then followed another reversal, the scales being turned by the daring treachery of a single prince, the young Maurice of Saxony, who, having at first supported the emperor, now forced him to relinquish all his conquests again. The balance was restored and, by and large, has remained undisturbed through the centuries. A Protestant north, with strong enclaves in the south, and a Catholic south – this was the picture presented by the map, not only in Germany but far beyond its borders.

We have had to anticipate events. The shadows of what was to come were already falling on Luther in his last years. The Word, in which he had had such boundless faith, still proved effective only in his immediate circle, where it possessed a great and quiet strength. But Luther had become gloomy, suspicious and irritable; his numerous illnesses often merely reflected his state of mind. Everywhere he looked he saw only defection and betrayal of the pure Word. His doctrine of a universal priesthood had long ago narrowed and changed into the doctrine of the invisible Church, whose visible representatives could never be more than small groups of people.

Betrayal was in fact the keynote of the events of these decades. France formed an alliance with the sultan, the pope being a passive partner; the emperor fought against the Curia, supported by Protestant princes although he was firmly determined to exterminate the heresy once and for all. The princes of the Church alternated between changing sides and 'remaining steadfast', steadfast being far too strong a term to describe their attitude. In Luther's immediate vicinity there were already the 'Martinians,' who followed him, and the 'Philippians,' who followed Melanchthon; both united in condemning the 'Zwinglians'. Those who tried to mediate, like the indefatigable Bucer, a revered figure who, however, was physically remote in England, where he eventually died, were suspected and boycotted by both right and left (a 'left wing' being provided by militant groups of anabaptists).

As a postlude to the Peasants' War, and with similarly disastrous consequences, another conflagration issued from these anabaptist circles and threw into relief the confusion of the age. The 'New Jerusalem' and the coming of the millennium had been announced by the anabaptists, and especially by Melchior Hofmann, a furrier whose following extended to the Netherlands; having proclaimed Strasbourg as the seat of the New Kingdom, he was eventually imprisoned there. Prophets, composed of his Dutch followers, moved into neighbouring Westphalia, establishing a foothold in Münster, where religious and social tensions were already very severe, Lutherans quarrelling with the bishop and the lower classes with the patricians on the city council. The anabaptists' preaching transformed the sturdy Westphalian population into a fanatically religious and wildly radical multitude, which blindly accepted the leaders and their predictions of an imminent turning-point in the history of the world. In 1534–5 an anabaptist kingdom was proclaimed and established in Münster; contemporaries regarded it as the quintessence of lunacy and satanic iniquity. The extant accounts all come from enemy sources and are often malicious, but without any doubt there was an outbreak of mass hysteria; hysterical women went into transports of ecstasy, and people entertained absurd hopes of outside help by sympathizers. Communal ownership was proclaimed, as was frequently done in anabaptist communities. Polygamy, compulsory marriage, and the shameless orgies in which the anabaptists were said to indulge stirred people to allege that eleven-year-old girls were forced to take part. Within a very short time the prophets had established a strict dictatorship known, in the terminology of the day, as a 'monarchy', with a royal household and a royal bodyguard. The first leader, John Matthys, was killed in a sortie against the beleaguering troops of the bishop; the landsknechts nailed his genitals to the city gates. Jan Beukelszoon, who came to be known as John of Leiden, an innkeeper and tailor from Leiden, assumed the throne as 'King of Zion'; he initiated a period of ruthless executions, extremely well conceived and implemented defence, and great public festivals at which the ancient spectacle of Dives and Lazarus was performed, in the final scene of which the wretched actor forced to play the part of Dives was actually hanged. It took a whole coalition of princes, a long siege, and numerous mutinies among the landsknechts finally to break down the resistance. Following the pattern of the Peasants' War the prisoners were tortured and King John of Leiden and his followers executed; the iron baskets which contained the mutilated corpses hung for several centuries on the tower of the Lambertikirche.

With this defeat the anabaptists were to all intents and purposes wiped out in Germany. In Holland they found a new organizer in the Frisian Menno Simons, who transformed the communities into quiet and very peaceable groups; finally, after the states general had won their independence, he succeeded in persuading the authorities to tolerate the sect. The Mennonite preacher Cornelis Anslo, whom Rembrandt painted, did not differ in outward appearance from any other citizen of Amsterdam. In its teachings, however, the sect still adhered to the strict rejection of any oath or military service, and carried on the fundamental ideas of the anabaptists, directing them towards practical Christianity and the closest possible cohesion within the community.

But the light from the beacon lit in Münster spread far beyond Germany. Francis i saw in it a warning, and from this moment began persecuting all innovators in deadly and fearful earnest. The slow death by burning, which was the lot of heretics – the victim was hauled up on a specially constructed scaffold and repeatedly lowered into the flames – was carried out with full solemnity in Paris before the king and his people. The age, long brutal in the extreme, became even more brutalized; not only were people executed and burned, whole classes of the population were driven from their homes. The era of the migrations began, and in the ensuing period the exiles made a very substantial contribution to the intellectual and spiritual life of Europe.

The fall of Münster, 1535

Among those hounded and driven out were also the independent spirits who, withdrawing further and further from society, became solitaries like Sebastian Franck – in Luther's opinion one of the most significant of these 'sectarians' – who ended by regarding the world simply as delusion: 'In the eyes of God we are all objects of ridicule, myths and shrovetide plays.'

The shrovetide play also dominated the stage of history, ideological debates being interrupted by colourful figures in jesters' caps and by lovers' quarrels and marriage disputes. Henry VIII made his appearance with the artful and determined Anne Boleyn, and England became a power which, though not exactly Protestant, had nevertheless separated from Rome; Luther was consulted on this affair, too, and sided emphatically with the old Queen Catherine, politically a very imprudent thing to do. Philip, landgrave of Hesse, was enticed into bigamy by an equally forceful young woman and her still more forceful mother, and Luther had to give his blessing; he deluded himself into imagining that the gay and pleasure-loving prince, of whose amorous adventures and wild gambling everyone attending the diets had stories to tell, suffered severe pangs of conscience. Philip pleaded that he could not sleep with his wife because she was ill and incapable of sexual intercourse; he did not want to lead an immoral life, divorce was impossible, and the only way out of his predicament was a second marriage. Moreover, he said, his wife consented. What Philip hid from the reformer was that he had told his wife the exact opposite, promising her by written contract, in addition to financial security, that he would 'be amiable, sleep with her, and exhibit all the friendliness proper between married people, not to a lesser but to a greater extent than before.' Under the seal of secrecy of the confessional Luther gave his consent to a bigamous marriage. The affair did not remain a secret; it became a public scandal and a moral burden that weighed heavily on the Protestants. An even worse consequence was that it drove the landgrave out of the Schmalkalden Alliance which, with considerable effort, he had held together. He demanded of Luther that the step he had taken be given biblical sanction; this Luther refused to do. Luther believed that the unfortunate business could be settled by a 'good strong lie': the landgrave should hide his new wife away for a time, until the excitement had died down. Meanwhile, however, the emperor was approaching. The landgrave became nervous; according to penal legislation introduced by Charles v, and effective in the countries under his control, bigamy was a capital offence. In order, as he said, to save his neck, Philip stuck it into the noose of imperial politics, which then pulled the noose tight. He was offered a pardon on condition that he looked after the emperor's interests in the Schmalkalden Alliance and undertook to ensure that it entered into no foreign agreements.

The affair, which in itself was quite insignificant, having been preceded by so many bigamous marriages, morganatic marriages or benevolently overlooked royal seraglios, with or without dispensations from the popes, and which was to be succeeded by so many others until well into the eighteenth century, was a disaster for the Protestant party. The Alliance's promising connections with Denmark, Sweden and France were broken off; the duke of Cleves, at war with the emperor, was left without help, and starting with this flank the emperor rolled up the whole Protestant front, which for a time had dominated the scene so invincibly. Fräulein Margarethe von der Sale, by whom Philip had eight further children in addition to the nine by his first marriage, became the animating spirit of a bloody political drama.

Above all the case throws a light on the whole company of princes who now awaited the emperor as he finally decided to take a closer look at the German situation. The only reason why Philip of Hesse stands out among his fellows is that he was of somewhat superior intellectual stature, which, however, he tended to overestimate. Hunting was his chief passion, as it was for almost all his peers; it enabled these princelings to enjoy the cheap and deceptive triumph of victory over a whole herd of driven wild boar or deer. Philip once proudly recorded a bag of a thousand boar; stalking his quarry was not his kind of sport. He spent much time reading the German Bible, and enjoyed theological disputations, at which he often showed considerable skill. His hounds, whom he loved extravagantly, would burst in and he would break off to address them in dog language, which one of his clerics in a moment of pique accused him of understanding better than the Greek and Hebrew of the Bible scholars, subjects left by him to the University of Marburg, which he founded. He became involved in risky schemes such as his bigamous marriage. He allowed himself to be outplayed after the Protestants' defeat in the Schmalkalden War, when he trustingly begged the emperor to pardon him; he paid for his foolishness with long years of imprisonment, being dragged from prison to prison until Duke Maurice of Saxony, his successor in the game of reckless political moves, intervened, freed him and turned the landgrave, now old and a veteran of many trials, into a figure of respect for his subjects. He had endearing qualities; his constant attempts to achieve a settlement between the contending theologians, his tolerance even of anabaptists and sectarians and of fugitives to whom no one else would give sanctuary, make him stand out sympathetically among the stubborn absolutists. But he was not a man of the calibre required for these critical years.

The emperor, on the other hand, was such a man. This was apparent at once, even in the outward impression he made on his return to Germany in 1543 after long years of absence: 'Everything was regal, his speech and actions, his look and bearing, even his munificence.' This time he appeared at the head of eight thousand Spanish soldiers, the best and most feared troops in the world. 'There is a great deal he could do if he wished to be a German emperor,' remarked the peripatetic Bucer in concern. Charles, however, had no intention of being any such thing; he was the Imperator, and the empire existed merely to serve his Imperium. He took the measure of the princes, whom hitherto he had known only from hearsay, sizing them up quickly and accurately.

His course of action, which in the past had often been somewhat erratic, became uncannily logical. By ridding himself of the landgrave he broke the back of the Schmalkalden Alliance, from Cleves and Geldern he put an end to the threatened reformation in the archbishoprics of Cologne and Mainz, while the Protestant princes blindly and devotedly helped him to eliminate France's threat to his flank; sacrificing Hungary without a moment's hesitation, he concluded an armistice with the sultan. At the diets he promised religious peace; there were discussions on union, and renewed hopes of a Council. Only in the year of Luther's death, when he had secured himself against attack from every quarter, did he break off to stamp out heresy once and for all. The master-stroke of the emperor's policy was to win over the young Duke Maurice of Saxony who, with even fewer scruples than Philip of Hesse, threw his Protestant land into the scales in order to win the electoral dignity from his cousin in the other half-state of Saxony. After his annihilating victory over the Schmalkalden forces Charles, alone and in grey armour, as Titian painted him, rode over the heath at Mühlberg on which the Reformation seemed to be buried.

But once again, as always in his life, he was unable to exploit and maintain his unprecedented success. The same Maurice, who had betrayed his fellow Protestants, now betrayed the emperor. The war with France, which had never completely died down, revived. Charles's dynastic plans, which he had never relinquished and which were now revealed in his attempt to secure the imperial succession for his Spanish son Philip, enraged all the German princes as well as his own brother Ferdinand. His last campaign against France was brought to a halt outside Metz by the winter weather. The calling of the Council, one of his great political aims, had reached deadlock. He abdicated, and spent the last two years of his life in the beautiful villa opposite the monastery of Yuste near Madrid, where his Italian mechanic Torriano was given the task of synchronizing the innumerable clocks in his collection. He died in 1556, ten years after Luther, regretting even at the end of his life that he had not sent him to the stake; for even in strictly orthodox Spain, and under the eyes of the most rigorous of all inquisitions, cells of heresy had been uncovered. There was no way of eradicating the evil. The moment Charles was dead the Inquisition arrested Torriano as a magician and sorcerer. It also arrested Carranza, archbishop of Toledo, who had administered the last benediction to the emperor. The charge was that he had held the crucifix up to the dying man, saying 'Look on him who has paid the debt for us all'; to the grand inquisitor this was reminiscent of the Lutheran doctrine of justification. The two great enemies, who stamped an entire age, would thus have been remarkably united in a manner transcending all human barriers;

unfortunately highly secular motives also played their part. The archbishop was kept in prison for seventeen years; during all this time, and
in spite of constant protests from the Curia, the royal treasury retained
the revenues, amounting to two million ducats, from the archbishopric
of Toledo. It needed all the money it could lay its hands on, because
Charles had left his empire in a state of total bankruptcy.

As to the bankruptcy of his political life's work, it need not be gone
into here. At the end he was a venerable figure, if only because of his
conduct in misfortune; and there is no doubt that he towered above the
kings and petty princes of his day, and over the popes as well, who
embittered his life and frustrated his efforts to bring about a 'root and
branch' reform. That, within the limitations imposed by his outlook,
his intentions were honourable seems certain. But the clock had moved
on, and the hour of national independence had struck. Neither a world
Imperium nor an empire comprising Spain and Germany was any
longer possible. His death ended an age which may be described, a little
summarily, as the transition from the Middle Ages to modern times.
His inheritance was divided. The inheritance of Luther, his great
antagonist, was also divided, but it remained alive throughout the
emperor's many provinces, as a warning, a challenge and a task.

# 37

# Old age

No GREAT man escapes the tragedy of becoming the 'grand old man'; in Luther's case this lot was especially hard because it had been preceded by unlimited hopes and a triumphal progress of undreamed-of power. The 'almost' that we have seen to be the fate of German history may be applied to him too: 'Only another two years', so he believed in the Wartburg, and the papacy would be finished, along with monasticism and everything that stood in the way of the pure Gospel. He never learnt to calculate either with figures or with men; increasingly he saw those around him becoming slaves to the 'prince of this world', the devil. Not everything he said on the subject should be taken literally. His cheerfulness kept on breaking through. We do not begrudge him his comfortable home, his family life, the large table round which his numerous students sat writing down his every word; there were wise and shrewd words among them, as well as a great deal of blustering and unholy crowing over the deaths of opponents and enemies. But it had not been this he had had in mind when he rushed in and battered down the 'three walls'. He was surrounded by friends, he was world famous, people came to see him from far and wide. While the discussions on union were in progress a papal legate was announced: Luther received him in his best clothes, wearing a fur coat and chain of honour, and with military bearing. The man was not to get the impression that Dr Luther was on his way out, he had every intention of remaining a thorn in the pope's side for a long time yet. But even his closest friends suffered under the endless dogmatic controversies. People frequently deserted him. Melanchthon himself found Luther hard to endure and complained secretly of being coerced. Most distressing of all, perhaps, is a threat Luther once voiced in his indignation over the weak and stubborn souls who would not listen, or else ran after every pied-piper: within three weeks, he declared grimly, he would lead the whole of Wittenberg and the surrounding country back into the old Church if he felt like doing so.

The possibility existed. Again and again talks on union had almost reached agreement. Melanchthon was regarded everywhere as the advocate of reconciliation and was ready to make considerable concessions – not only at Augsburg. For a time his fame eclipsed that of Luther. The king of France wanted him to go to Paris, a project that failed only because the elector refused to let him leave; people in England were interested in him. The tirelessly active Bucer played a similar role in the laborious attempts to prepare the way for some sort of acceptable agreement at least among the Protestants; they too failed, largely because of Luther's stubborn opposition. He had unquestionably grown rigid and intolerant; there was no longer any talk of the cheerful 'clash' of opinions, as he had termed it in the early days when referring to the Schwarmgeister. Even he was now in favour of compulsion, of expelling people. But he never had anyone burned at the stake, as Calvin did when Servet was burned for denying the Trinity, or as was done in ever-increasing numbers in the orthodox countries, where whole populations were secretly wiped out. The king of France exterminated the last remnants of the Waldenses, quiet, hardworking people who had found sanctuary in the wooded valleys of Provence; the few, out of several thousands, who escaped fled higher up into the mountains, where today a few families are all that survive of the first great popular and heretical movement of the Middle Ages.

Luther could still be calm and generous over things he regarded as superficial and unimportant. When Brandenburg was reformed, the Elector Joachim II, a great lover of pomp and ceremony, wanted to retain the greater part of the old ceremonial, especially the processions; a worried provost, who wrote agitatedly to Luther about it, received the humorously mocking answer: the elector could leap and dance like David before the Ark of the Covenant if he wished to, that was not what mattered. But he was completely inflexible over anything that, for him, had become a crucial issue, such as the attempts to interpret the celebration of Holy Communion. It was over this question that the feeble links that Bucer tried to forge with the Swiss had snapped. 'Christ's body is eaten with the bread and crunched with the teeth' was the statement Luther angrily gave Melanchthon for one of the discussions; the latter, quoting it reluctantly, said he was the 'bearer of an alien viewpoint'. New proposals for agreement were sought; the old scholastic interpretations were studied and a formula produced: Christ was present 'in, with and among the bread and wine'. Luther accepted or rejected further versions, and a 'Wittenberg Formula of Concord' was devised which at least enabled the south German cities to join Saxony; but the antagonisms long remained a burning question, and they have never really been resolved. In the last lines he wrote before he died, Melanchthon remarked that at last he would be out of reach of the 'frenzy of the theologians' which, after the death of his friend, descended on him with redoubled fury, accusing him, not entirely without justification, of being a 'secret Calvinist'. As Ignaz von Döllinger, the great Catholic historian, who later joined the 'Old Catholics', put it, Luther had been able to create a new faith but unable to found a new Church. Whether this was necessarily a failing we shall not attempt to decide; at any rate it stemmed from his nature. He achieved his breakthrough by defiance, anger, fearless unhesitating assault, and passionate faith; without these qualities he would have remained a Wittenberg professor, whose well-intentioned suggestions for improvement would have lain buried under proposals for reform accumulated throughout two centuries.

As he looked round him at the end of his life, Luther in fact had reason to feel satisfied; anyone else might well have felt triumphant. The new teaching was advancing everywhere, in the most diverse forms and modifications, and had good prospects of taking hold throughout Germany, the Scandinavian north and England; it had strong footholds in France, and centres had been formed even in Italy, in Venice and Naples, where a highly cultivated circle of people, including Vittoria Colonna and Julia Gonzaga, had collected round Juan, brother of Alfonso de Valdés, the Emperor's secretary of state. Bavaria, Austria and Poland had been captured. The Curia's dominant role in world affairs, like that of the great religious orders, seemed to be finished for ever. Of the forces of the old Church that were gathering to counter-attack Luther could scarcely even have heard; Pope Paul III's attempts finally to convene a great Council must have looked to him simply like a retreat, which to a large extent they were, because there was no intention of undertaking the 'root and branch' reform so often demanded. The Curia stayed as it was; the new pope, a Farnese, still came from the immediate entourage of Alexander Borgia, who had made him a cardinal because he was the brother of his mistress Giulia. Both nepotism on the grand scale and implacable opposition to the emperor remained the order of the day; the duchy of Parma-Piacenza had to be created for the pope's son, Pier Luigi Farnese, and came to an end only when this papal offspring, who was leader of the anti-imperial party in Italy, was murdered on Charles's instructions. Luther hardly gave serious attention to the few cardinals in favour of reform whom Paul added to the consistory, along with his relatives and favourites, nor did their ideas gain acceptance. Among them were some outstanding men, the Englishman Pole, for example, who was of English royal blood, and the Venetian Contarini, a member of the oldest nobility in the republic, whose family had originally come to the Adriatic from Germany and produced eminent leaders as long ago as the first Crusades. As legate to the Regensburg Diet of 1541 he reached agreement with the Protestant theologians on the most important points, above all on Luther's crucial doctrine of justification; but Rome refused its approval, and his treatise on this subject was later put on the Index. The preacher Ochino, at one time Paul III's father confessor, who later exerted wide influence as the roving apostle of strict Franciscan teachings, came so close to Luther's standpoint that he finally had to flee and live as an exile, moving from place to place abroad. The legate Vergerio ended up as a Protestant in Tübingen. The fronts were still fluid.

But Luther had set his boundaries, and his instinct, surer than that of the optimistic mediators, told him that agreement was no longer possible. As to man's receptiveness to the Word, he had reached a state of profound resignation; he complained with increasing bitterness that in spite of now possessing the true word of the Gospel people showed no desire for a change of heart. Nevertheless, he continued tirelessly to work on his translation until he died. And the students? Dissolute and unruly, as they had always been; the authorities, as always, unwilling to intervene. He even thought seriously of leaving Wittenberg, though with no fixed plan; his friends had trouble persuading him to stay. He was on bad terms with the court and the elector's councillors and engaged in bitter feuds with the jurists. His voice now often had the petulant tenor of an old and sick man; people had not really changed for the worse, and his grumblings about the ways of youth sound distinctly sour. But his instincts, as always, were right: the great change which he had hoped for, and regarded as certain, had not materialized. Everything had foundered, the great reform of the empire had sunk ignominiously into oblivion, the Reformation itself, far though it had spread, had not come up to his expectations. The people had not played their part, the individual people whom he had wanted, and finally impatiently commanded, to share his experience of grace, conversion and repentance in the sense of *metanoia*, or fundamental change in one's way of life. They stuck to the old way of life, the old Adam. Nothing had been carried through decisively since he had unleashed the first conflagration, either in the political and social spheres or in the sphere of faith; the fire now was only spluttering, and in many places had already been extinguished. An oppressive atmosphere had settled over the country, to endure for decades to come. He became increasingly preoccupied with thoughts of the end of the world and his calls to prayer as the only hope often had a desperate ring. He even predicted that the Turks must first come to make people listen to the Word of God.

He continued to work and write, now almost exclusively in German,

Luther's handwriting in 1542

and with increasing extravagance; as he felt his own, his Lutheran cause, increasingly threatened, his language grew more raw. Since his pamphlet *The Will in Bondage* he had ceased to address the scholars, regarding them as hopeless. He wanted to appeal to the people, and thought he could reach them only by using the crudest terms. Coarseness being a hallmark of the age, one can find many parallels to Luther's method, and not only in Germany; but he surpassed them all.

He caricatured the orthodox Duke Henry of Brunswick, for example, as 'Hans Worst' (a stage buffoon) and to a similar attack from his princely adversary responded that such blustering 'only pleasantly tickled the bend of his knee.' He became a demagogue, a trait of which he had shown early symptoms but which had been concealed by a pure and deeper passion. His last attack on Rome, *On the Papacy as founded by the Devil*, consisted of monotonous insults that convey a sense of frenzy, as if he were aware of the powerful counter-forces already stirring in the womb of the old Church, little though he understood them.

He saw demons and devilry at work everywhere; he believed the most absurd rumours. He heard from Moravia that the Jews, of whom there were many in the country, were trying to convert the Christians to their faith; of all the calumnies that were circulated this was perhaps the most untrue, because to proselytize among the non-chosen was completely alien to Jewish thought. But he immediately started to rant and rave, as if Christianity were in the gravest danger. The conciliatory attitude he had shown in the Reuchlin quarrel, in his interpretation of the Magnificat and in his earlier writing, pointing out that Jesus Christ had been born a Jew, was forgotten, as was the fact that in those days he had advised leaving the matter entirely to God, who at the appointed time might enlighten and convert the Jews. Now he demanded that they be expelled without mercy. He levelled against them every ancient and modern charge, the pseudo-religious one that the Jews blasphemed against Christ, as well as the material one that they were usurers, or the dark hint that they misused their medical art to do secret harm to Christians. In conversation he even accepted the rumour that the emperor's commander, Freiherr von Katzian, who with his army had suffered ignominious defeat at the hands of the Turks, must have been a Jew; there was no other way to explain his annihilating defeat. This story is only too reminiscent of similar demonism in our own day, when Luther's pamphlet, *On the Jews and their Lies*, and his other work, *Schem Hamphoras*, have been cited with relish.

His followers advised him that the time had come to publish a collected edition of his widely scattered writings. Many were already forgotten and had disappeared, some he himself no longer possessed in the clutter of his study; many more – including those just mentioned – he now considered ephemeral works that were better left to obscurity. But he had become an authority and had to accept the consequences. An initial collection began to appear, in stout folio volumes; significantly, it contained the works written in Latin for the international world of scholarship, with a preface by the Reformer in which he already saw himself in the perspective of history.

It was as a writer that his influence was greatest. In his pamphlet on the need for schools to educate the rising generation, he once defended his work as 'writer' and 'teacher' with great insistence against all those who considered only riding in armour and battling against the enemy and the elements as useful activities, holding the writer's function to be 'easy and unimportant'. Certainly, he said, the pen was an easy implement, one needed only a goose quill and that could be picked up anywhere. 'Nevertheless it is the best part (the head), the noblest member (the tongue) and the highest achievement (speech) of the human body that have to be called into service and do most of the work, whereas other people use only the hand, the foot, the back or some similar part of the body; and they can sing cheerfully and joke freely at the same time, things a writer cannot do. It is said of a writer that three fingers do the work, but his whole body and soul contribute to it.'

The final chapter had been written, he was nearing the last paragraph, the last unease that grips so many people when they are dying. He was ill, and the doctors were unable to help him by bleeding – his body had become abnormally heavy, and the operation left only open wounds – by giving him enemas, or by the dung and urine cures which his wife was not alone in recommending. He was a bad patient and was always breaking loose; he wrote to Käthe from Eisenach saying 'that we are hale and well here, thank goodness, gobble like the Bohemians (though not overmuch), tipple like the Germans (though not a great deal)' – in protest at her concern, which he ascribed to her lack of trust in God. He still travelled round in his clumsy carriage, which must have shaken his sick body excruciatingly on the appalling Thuringian roads. Wittenberg was only a burden to him now; even in his spacious, comfortable home he felt restricted and menaced. The Elector John Frederick embarked on a building programme, but not of schools or lecture rooms for the now world-famous university. Wittenberg was to be turned into a great, impregnable fortress; this was more important than the 'mighty fortress' which Luther had had in mind. The old monastery stood directly on the town moat; the work on the new bastions came closer and closer. Luther already saw his little tower room threatened – 'from which I stormed the papacy'. He could not know that no more than a year after his death this whole costly and up-to-date system of fortifications would fall intact into the emperor's hands, and that the ponderous, hot-tempered, foolish John Frederick would be led away to spend several years in prison, accompanied by Luther's friend Lucas Cranach, now a very old man, who most generously offered to share his elector's misfortune. But Luther heard the sound of the picks and shovels and found it ominous; he heard the rolling of the waggons carrying powder and ammunition. He regarded with the deepest mistrust, and rightly as it turned out, the arming that was going on everywhere and the coalitions, whose brittleness he may have recognized more clearly than the clever councillors.

He longed to go home; Wittenberg had never really been home to him. The sedentary life he led in this small provincial town can easily blind us to the fact that in his heart he remained a pilgrim and a wanderer, even in his faith and teaching. He returned once more to the countryside in which he was born, and shortly before the death to which he looked forward felt himself a 'Mansfelder' again. The families of the ruling counts were quarrelling over their inheritance, as they had been doing for decades, and when he was sent for to arbitrate he was delighted; refusing to listen to all the warnings and advice, or to be deterred by the stormy winter weather, he set out. The river Saale had risen dangerously and crossing it by ferry was a risky business; but he pressed on, and in a letter home made a mocking reference to the 'anabaptists', who had failed to stop him with their tidal waves. The attempts by the representatives of the 'anterior' and 'posterior' lines of the ruling family to find a compromise made very halting progress, and it was only when Luther threatened to leave that a settlement was reached; it lasted no longer than any of the other peace settlements of the day. Luther's sole remaining satisfaction was that the younger generations of the two families held a joint celebration; the last cheerful sound he heard was the ringing of the bells from the great sleigh ride with which the party ended. He had long pinned all his hopes on youth, on the rising generation; the older generation was worn out and a total loss. He was worn out too. If he ever set foot in Wittenberg again, he said, it would be to feed 'a fat doctor to the worms'. He never did. He had to take to his bed in the town where he was born. Doctors, including his elector's personal physician, hurried to his bedside, where they only tormented the helpless, swollen body.

The last lines written by the man who had never spared either his time or his strength were a reminiscence. Thinking back on his schooldays and peasant origin he wrote that no one could understand Virgil's poems on agriculture unless he had spent five years of his life tilling the soil, nor could anyone understand Cicero unless he had spent twenty-five years living in a large community: 'No one can claim to have sufficient experience of the Holy Scriptures unless he has ruled his parish with the Prophets and Apostles for a hundred years.' Not having been granted these hundred years, he closed with the words: 'We are beggars, and that is the truth.'

He died during the night of 17–18 February 1546; his old fellow-student Justus Jonas and a local pastor were at his side. They prayed for him; joining in and speaking with difficulty he committed his

'*Seelichen*' – this was the cautious, modest expression he always used for his soul – to Christ. Towards morning his death struggle ended. Four days later the great funeral procession entered Wittenberg. He was buried beneath the pulpit of the Schlosskirche, the church that had been the starting-point of his career as rebel and reformer. In his funeral oration Melanchthon referred to him as the 'Charioteer of Israel', and the prophet whose doctrine of forgiveness had not been discovered by 'human sagacity' but had been revealed by God; he spoke prophetically gloomy words of severe afflictions to come. A year later the emperor's troops were in Wittenberg. The great bastions, extending as far as Luther's house, fell without a shot being fired. The emperor, against the advice of the absolutists, ordered the tomb to be left untouched. The fight went on.

It is not over yet. The history of Luther's influence on the world is the political, spiritual, intellectual and linguistic history of the succeeding centuries.

# Appendix

# Chronology

| | |
|---|---|
| 1378–1417 | Split in the Western Church, the 'Great Schism', with lines of claimants to the papacy reigning simultaneously in Avignon and Rome. |
| 1414–17 | Council of Constance ends the Schism by deposing the rival popes and electing as Pope Martin V, and condemns John Wyclif [d. 1384] and Jan Hus, who is burned at the stake. |
| 1419–36 | Hussite Wars. |
| 1431–49 | Council of Basle; recognition of separate rights for the Bohemian Church. |
| 1438 | Pragmatic Sanction of Bourges, establishing 'Gallicanism' and prerogatives of the French National Church. |
| 1453 | Constantinople seized by the Turks. |
| 1471 | Sixtus IV as pope. Italian territorial and dynastic policy of the Renaissance popes inaugurated. |
| 1477 | Charles the Bold, duke of Burgundy, killed in battle; marriage of his heiress to Maximilian of Habsburg. Beginning of wars between the House of Habsburg and France. |
| 1483 | Martin Luther born at Eisleben on 11 November. 1484: Luther family move to Mansfeld, where it remains. |
| 1492 | Discovery of New World by Columbus. |
| 1494 | Charles VIII of France invades Italy, starting the European wars in Italy. |
| 1498 | Savonarola burned as a heretic in Florence. |
| 1499 | Swiss Confederation contracts out of the empire, following a war with Maximilian I. |
| 1501–5 | Luther a student at Erfurt University, after attending schools in Mansfeld, Magdeburg and Eisenach. Enters Augustinian monastery in Erfurt, 17 July 1505. Ordained 1507. Journey to Rome, 1510–11, after which begins work as lecturer at Wittenberg |

University. Doctor of Theology 1512. Begins his great lectures. Becomes district vicar of Augustinian congregation.

| | |
|---|---|
| 1506–12 | Pope Julius II's wars in Italy. |
| 1514 | Peasant rising in Württemberg; peasants' war in Hungary. |
| 1515 | Publication of the *Epistolae obscurorum virorum* by humanists in their struggle on behalf of Johannes Reuchlin [d. 1522]. |
| 1516 | New Testament in Greek first published by Erasmus of Rotterdam. Luther publishes *A German Theology*. |
| 1517 | Publication of Luther's *Ninety-five Theses* attacking the sale of indulgences. |
| 1518 | Luther appears before Cardinal Cajetan in Augsburg, November–December. Appointment of Philipp Melanchthon as lecturer at Wittenberg University. |
| 1519 | Charles V elected German Emperor. Disputation at Leipzig in July. Mission of Karl von Miltitz on behalf of the pope. |
| 1520 | Bull of Excommunication. Luther's three primary treatises: *On Improving the Christian Estate, On the Babylonian Captivity of the Church of God, On the Liberty of a Christian Man*. Bull and decretals burned at Wittenberg, 10 December. |
| 1521 | Diet of Worms. Edict issued by the emperor outlawing Luther. Luther secretly removed to the Wartburg. First war between Charles V and Francis I [ends 1526]. The emperor in Spain, where he remains until 1529. |
| 1522 | Unrest in Wittenberg. Luther's return to Wittenberg; his translation of the New Testament published in September. |
| 1523 | Revolt of the knights under Sickingen. Death of Ulrich von Hutten. Diet of Nuremberg. |
| 1524 | National Council planned, but vetoed by the emperor. Catholic princes form league at Regensburg. |
| 1525 | Battle of Pavia. The German Peasants' War. Luther's pamphlets against the peasants; his marriage to Katharina von Bora; publication of his treatise *The Will in Bondage*. |
| 1526 | Pope in league with France against Charles V. Victory of Turks over Hungarians at Mohacz. Death of King Louis II of Hungary; succeeded by Ferdinand of Austria. |
| 1527 | Sack of Rome by the emperor's army. Charles V's second war against France [ends 1529]. Inauguration of church inspections in the electorate of Saxony, and creation of Lutheran Church. |

| | |
|---|---|
| 1528 | Disunity in Germany; clash between theologians in Wittenberg and Switzerland. |
| 1529 | Diet of Speyer. Reversal of policy of tolerance; first solemn protest by certain estates [the 'Protestants']. Disputation between Luther and Zwingli at Marburg. Luther's *Catechism*. |
| 1530 | Diet of Augsburg. *Augsburg Confession* presented. Luther in Coburg Castle. |
| 1531 | Schmalkalden Alliance [ends 1546]. Civil war in Switzerland; Zwingli killed at the Battle of Kappel. |
| 1532 | Diet of Regensburg and religious armistice at Nuremberg. The Turks in Hungary. Charles v abroad again in Spain and Italy, until 1540. |
| 1534 | Württemberg turns Protestant. Anabaptists in Münster [defeated in 1535]. Declaration of independence of Church of England from Rome; Act of Supremacy. Publication of Luther's complete translation of the Bible. |
| 1536 | Denmark turns Protestant. Wittenberg Formula of Concord. Charles v's third war against France [ends 1538]. |
| 1537 | Negotiations over a Council. Luther's *Articles of Schmalkalden*. |
| 1539 | Brandenburg and duchy of Saxony turn Protestant. |
| 1540 | Bigamy of Philip of Hesse. Religious debates at Worms and Regensburg. Society of Jesus [Ignatius Loyola] approved by Pope Paul III. |
| 1541 | Diet of Regensburg. Hungary becomes a Turkish province. Calvin [1509–64] in Geneva. |
| 1542 | Reformation in Cologne. Charles v's fourth war against France [ends 1544]. |
| 1543–4 | Diets of Nuremberg and Speyer. Protestant princes provide armed assistance against France. Francis I defeated: Peace of Crépy. |
| 1545 | Council of Trent convoked by Pope Paul III; final sessions take place in 1563. |
| 1546 | Death of Luther at Eisleben, 2 February. War against Schmalkalden Alliance begins. |
| 1547 | Defeat of the Protestants. Diet of Augsburg provides 'interim' solution. |
| 1552 | Defection of German princes from the emperor, under leadership of Maurice of Saxony and in league with France. |

1555     Diet of Augsburg grants final decision in matters of religion to territorial authorities.

1556     Abdication of Charles v following abortive fifth war against France; succeeded as German emperor by his brother Ferdinand [elected 1558].

# European rulers

### Rome [popes]
Sixtus IV, Rovere, 1471–84
Innocent VIII, 1484–92
Alexander VI, Borgia, 1492–1503
Julius II, della Rovere, 1503–13
Leo X, Medici, 1513–21
Hadrian VI, 1522–3
Clement VII, Medici, 1523–34
Paul III, Farnese, 1534–49

### France
Charles VIII, 1483–98
Louis XII, 1498–1515
Francis I, 1515–47

### England
Henry VII, 1485–1509
Henry VIII, 1509–47

### German princes
Electorate of Saxony:
  Frederick the Wise, 1486–1525
  John, 1525–32
  John Frederick, 1532–47
Duchy of Saxony:
  George, 1500–39
  Henry, 1539–41

Maurice, 1541–53 [from 1548 elector]
Brandenburg:
  Joachim I, 1499–1535
  Joachim II, 1535–71
Hesse:
  Landgrave Philip, 1518–67

### Holy Roman Empire
Frederick III, 1440–93
Maximilian I, 1493–1519
Charles V, 1519–56 [b. 1500, d. 1558; king of Spain from 1516]
Ferdinand I, 1556–64

### Spain
Isabella of Castile, 1474–1504
Ferdinand of Aragon, 1479–1516
Charles I [V], 1516–56

### Scandinavia
Denmark:
  Christian II, 1513–23
  Frederick I, 1523–33
  Christian III, 1534–59
Sweden:
  Gustavus I, Vasa, 1521–60

# Sources

LUTHER

WORKS. The Bonner Studienausgabe, current edition, Berlin, 1963, 8 vols, which gives the original versions of the texts and includes selected letters and table-talk, has formed the basis of my reading; since 1919–22, when I was a student in Berlin and Munich and had the privilege of attending the lectures of Ernst Troeltsch and Max Weber, this edition of Luther's collected works, as well as the faithful reprint of Luther's New Testament of 1522, Berlin, 1918 have been my constant companions. In addition to these I have used the critical Weimar edition of Luther's works, letters, diaries and Bible translations, 1883 ff.; this is now being reprinted and is intended eventually to comprise 110 vols. Its very detailed notes form an essential supplement to existing Luther biographies and monographs. The correspondence has been edited by E.L.Enders, Frankfurt, 1884–1907, 18 vols. Numerous editions exist in modernized German language and spelling and with translations of the Latin works: one edited by H.H.Borcherdt, Munich, 1917–25, 8 vols, and now reprinted; the Calwer edition of 1930, now available in pocket edition, 10 vols, and many others. Full information concerning these, the many modern editions of single works, monographs, and German literature on the Reformation in general is given in *Das evangelische Schrifttum*, Frankfurt, 1966, the catalogue of Protestant publishers (it also contains selected Roman Catholic publications). Detailed reports on current literature are published in the *Luther-Jahrbuch*, Munich, 1919 ff. (vols 1–23 now available in reprint).

English translations: a comprehensive American edition in 55 vols, St Louis-Philadelphia, 1957 ff. is in course of preparation; *Works*, 6 vols, Philadelphia, 1915–23; *Reformation Writings*, ed. R.L.Wolf, London, 1952; *Selections from Luther's Writings*, ed. J.Dillenberger, Chicago and New York, 1961; *Martin Luther: On the Bondage of the Will*, ed. J.L.Packer and O.R. Johnson, London, 1957; *Luther's Reply to Erasmus*, London, 1957. The *Library of Christian Classics*, Philadelphia and London, contains *Luther: Early Theological Works*, ed. James Atkinson, vol. 16, 1962; *Lectures on Romans*, ed. W. Pauck, vol. 15, 1965 and *Letters of Spiritual Counsel*, ed. T.Tappert, vol. 18, 1955. Throughout the present book the English versions of the original texts have been made from the author's own translations.

BIBLIOGRAPHIES. K.Schottenloher, *Bibliographie zur deutschen Geschichte im*

537

*Zeitalter der Glaubensspaltung*, 7 vols, Stuttgart, 1956–61; G.Wolf, *Quellenkunde zur deutschen Reformationsgeschichte*, 3 vols, Gotha, 1915 ff.; K.Aland, *Hilfsbuch zum Lutherstudium*, Gütersloh, 1957. The British Museum's *Short Title Catalogue of Books Printed in the German-speaking Countries 1455–1600*, 1962, is the best available survey of original editions of the whole literature of the period and has served the author as a guide to these texts. In the following notes only some of the works consulted are mentioned. J.Benzing (*Bibliographia Aureliana*, x, Baden, 1963 ff.) is at present the chief authority on original editions of Luther, as well as on those of his contemporaries (Hutten 1956, Reuchlin 1963, and many others).

Among the larger works of reference I would mention *Religion in Geschichte und Gegenwart*, 3rd ed., Tübingen, 1957 ff.; *Realenzyklopädie für protestantische Theologie und Kirche*, 3rd ed., Leipzig, 1896 ff.; *Evangelisches Kirchenlexikon*, Göttingen, 1956; *Lexikon für Theologie und Kirche*, 2nd ed., Freiburg, 1957; *Dictionnaire de théologie catholique*, [Mangenot], 1899 ff.; *The Catholic Encyclopedia*, New York, 1907–18 (new edition in progress).

BIOGRAPHIES. Of Luther's contemporaries, J.Cochläus (Dobneck) published his *Commentaria . . . de actis et scriptis M.Lutheri* in 1549 (in German in 1582); A.Herte in his comprehensive study *Das katholische Lutherbild im Banne der Luther-Kommentare des Cochlaeus*, Münster, 1943 has criticized the influence of this book down the centuries. Luther's faithful pupil J.Matthesius wrote a life of his teacher, Nuremberg, 1566, and reports on his sermons (edited by G.Loesche, Prague, 1906). Dr M.Ratzeberger, the Saxon court physician, told many vivid stories of Luther in his memoirs, ed. C.G. Neudecker, Jena, 1850.

German biographies: J.Koestlin's *Martin Luther. Sein Leben und seine Schriften*, Eberfeld, 1875 (*Martin Luther. His life and writings*, London, 1883) and 5th edition ed. G.Kawerau, 1903, is still quoted; that by T.Kolde, 2 vols, Gotha, 1884–93, is dry but reliable; A.Hausrath, *Luthers Leben*, 2 vols, Berlin, 1913, though written by an expert, was intended for a wider public; A.E.Berger, *Luther in kulturhistorischer Darstellung*, 4 vols, Berlin, 1895–1921. In the series *Sammlung Deutscher Literatur in Entwicklungsreihen*, 1930–42, Berger also edited seven valuable volumes of extracts from works, pamphlets, autobiographies and literary documents of the period. A new critical biography was begun by O.Scheel, but only 2 vols, covering Luther's development up to his monastery days, have appeared – *Martin Luther: Vom Katholizismus zur Reformation*, Tübingen, 1917; the work is supplemented by the very important anthology *Dokumente zu Luthers Entwicklung bis 1519*, 2nd ed., Tübingen, 1929. Finally there are H.Boehmer's *Luther im Lichte der neueren Forschung*, 5th ed., Leipzig, 1918 (*Luther and the Reformation in the Light of Modern Research*, London, 1930); and *Der junge Luther*, 5th edition ed. H. Bornkamm, Stuttgart, 1962.

English and American biographies: Roland H.Bainton, *Here I Stand*, New York, 1950 and London, 1951; E.G.Schwiebert, *Luther and his Times*, St Louis, 1950; R.H.Fife, *The Revolt of Martin Luther*, New York, 1957; E. Gordon Rupp, *Luther's Progress to the Diet of Worms*, London and Chicago,

1951; J.MacKinnon, *Luther and the Reformation*, 4 vols, London and New York, 1925 ff.

Among French biographies Lucien Febvre's *Un Destin, Martin Luther*, Paris, 1928 (*A Destiny. Martin Luther*, London and New York, 1930) stands out as a study by a writer of encyclopaedic knowledge who commands a beautiful style. By the same author is *Un cœur religieux du XVIe siècle*, Paris, 1957. Of books that have contributed to our knowledge of Luther's early development: H.Strohl, *L'Evolution religieuse de Luther*, Paris, 1922; *L'Épanouissement de la pensée religieuse de Luther*, Paris, 1924; *Luther, sa vie et sa pensée*, Paris, 1953. The Abbé L.Christiani's *Luther tel qu'il fût*, Paris, 1963 also contains an introduction by Henri Daniel-Rops, whose extensive history of the Church I have consulted in the volumes *L'Eglise de la Renaissance et de la Réforme*, Paris, 1955 (*History of the Church of Christ*, London and New York, 1957) in addition to the Church histories by the theologians. Of Italian works, I found E.Buonaiuti's *Lutero e la Riforma in Germania*, Bologna, 1926, and Giovanni Miegge's *Lutero*, Torre Pellice, 1946, most useful.

H.Denifle, O.P., *Luther und Luthertum*, continued by A.M.Weiss, 2nd ed., Mainz, 1904–6 (*Luther and Lutherdom*, 2nd revised ed., Ohio, 1917) was epoch-making, as I have mentioned in the text. Hartmann Grisar, S.J., *Luther*, Freiburg, 1921 ff. (London, 1911, New York, 1913) in three large volumes and supplemented by six further issues of *Luther-Studien*, is the chief work of Roman Catholic research, although it is more an exhaustive collection of notes and material than a biography proper. These books were followed by long controversial debates; of this material I shall mention only *Luthers theologische Quellen* by the former Dominican A.V.Müller, Giessen, 1912. An entirely new chapter in the discussion on Luther from the Roman Catholic side was inaugurated by Joseph Lortz in *Die Reformation in Deutschland*, 2 vols, 5th ed., Freiburg, 1962 (*The Reformation in Germany*, New York, 1964); John M.Todd, in his *Martin Luther, A Biographical Study*, London, 1964, has also attempted a more oecumenical interpretation of the subject. See, in addition: H.Lilje, *Luther, Anbruch und Krise der Neuzeit*, Berlin, 1946; H. Bornkamm, *Luthers geistige Welt*, Leipzig, 1947; F.Lau, *Luther*, Berlin, 1959 (London and Philadelphia, 1963) and the pictorial biographies by O. Thulin, Berlin, 1958 (*Life of Luther*, Philadelphia, 1966) and H.Lilje, *Martin Luther. Eine Bildmonographie*, Hamburg, 1964.

Jacques Maritain in *Trois réformateurs*, Paris, 1925 (*Three Reformers*, London, 1928) saw Luther as the 'father of individualism' and at the head of a great decline that led via Descartes to J.J.Rousseau. Gerhard Ritter's study appeared in various editions, finally as *Luther, Gestalt und Tat*, 6th ed., Munich, 1959 (*Luther: His Life and Work*, London and New York, 1963). Of the psychological and psychiatric studies I would mention Erik H. Erikson's *Young Man Luther: A Study in Psychoanalysis and History*, New York, 1958 and London, 1959, partly based on Paul J.Reiter's *Martin Luthers Umwelt, Character und Psychose*, 2 vols, Copenhagen, 1937–41. On the medical history of Luther's life see W.Ebstein, *Dr Martin Luthers Krankheiten*, Stuttgart, 1908, and Frh. von Nothafft, 1929. In the eighteenth century F.S. Keil had already produced, in Leipzig, 1764, a quarto volume on 'the saintly man, . . . the medical state of his body, his sore tribulations, and the state of his mind.' On individual topics, in addition to works listed below, J. Luther, *Legenden um Luther*, Berlin, 1933. A Luther Dictionary, though urgently needed, is still lacking; a first attempt in 1870, by P.Dietz, was never completed. There is a short dictionary on early modern German by A. Götze, 1912, and for Luther's language: O.Francke, *Grundzüge der Schrift-sprache Luthers*, Halle, 1913–22; P.Meinhold, *Luthers Sprachphilosophie*, Berlin, 1958; H.Bornkamm, *Luther als Schriftsteller*, Heidelberg, 1965.

LUTHER AND POSTERITY. H.Bornkamm, *Luther im Spiegel der deutschen Geistesgeschichte*, Heidelberg, 1955. E.W.Zeeden, *Martin Luther und die Reformation im Urteil des deutschen Luthertums*, 2 vols, Freiburg, 1950–2 (*The Legacy of Luther*, London, 1954) and W. von Löwenich, *Luther und der Neu-protestantismus*, Witten, 1963, are both works intimately connected with the interpretation of Luther's theology. The Berlin professor Karl Holl has made a particularly useful contribution with his lectures and essays (*Gesammelte Aufsätze*, 3 vols, 5th ed., Tübingen, 1927), and has also contributed to the much discussed subject of Thomas Müntzer and the spiritualist radicals. Brian A.Garrish, *Grace and Reason*, Oxford, 1962, E.G.Rupp, *The Righteous-ness of God*, London and New York, 1953, and P.S.Watson, *Let God be God!* London, 1947, are among the most discussed contributions to the subject of Luther's theology and its development.

HISTORY OF THE REFORMATION PERIOD. The first true 'history of the Refor-mation' was written by Baron Veit Ludwig von Seckendorf in his enormous *Commentarius historicus et apologeticus de Lutheranismo* in 1692; despite its some-what odd presentation – it was written to refute the work on the same sub-ject by the French Jesuit Maimbourg – it was a work of great erudition. L. von Ranke, *Deutsche Geschichte im Zeitalter der Reformation*, 1839, reprinted by the Berlin Academy in six vols, 1925 (*History of the Reformation in Germany*, London and New York, 1905) is a classic. This was followed by F. von Bezold, *Geschichte der deutschen Reformation*, Berlin, 1890; dealing for the first time with social problems, it showed an independence rare in those days. J. Janssen, *Geschichte des deutschen Volkes seit dem Ausgang des Mittelalters*, Freiburg, 1877 ff., later edited by his pupil Pastor in ten vols, 1898 ff. (*History of the German People at the close of the Middle Ages*, London, 1896–1910), written with a strong Roman Catholic bias, caused heated discussions, but presents a great deal of information, especially in the field of cultural history. Pastor continued the work in ten supplementary volumes by other authors, in-cluding F.Lauchert on Luther's Italian opponents, 1912, and Nikolaus Paulus, a tireless apologist of the Roman Catholic Church, on the German Dominicans in their fight against Luther, 1903. Karl Brandi, *Deutsche Reformation und Gegenreformation*, 2 vols, Leipzig, 1927, and Paul Joachimsen, *Das Zeitalter der religiösen Umwälzungen*, Berlin, 1930, represent the older historical school of the beginning of this century. P.Imbart de la Tour, *Les Origines de la Réforme*, 4 vols, Paris, 1907–14, goes into much detail. E.G. Leonard, in vol. I of his *Histoire générale du Protestantisme*, Paris, 1950, gives a good survey (*A History of Protestantism*, London, 1966 with an excellent and detailed bibliography). The *New Cambridge History*, vols 1 and 2 (1493–1559), with individual contributions by specialists. Owen Chadwick, *The Reformation*, London and Grand Rapids, 1965; Harold J.Grimm, *The Reformation Era*, New York, 1954; and Hajo Holborn, same title, New York, 1959 are the more recent textbooks.

I should like to mention also Ricarda Huch, *Das Zeitalter der Glaubensspaltung*, Berlin and Zurich, 1937; W.E.Peuckert, *Die Grosse Wende*, Hamburg, 1948; and an anthology by H.J.Hillerbrand, *The Reformation in its Own Words*, London 1964.

HISTORY OF THE POPES. Leopold von Ranke, *Die römischen Päpste*, 10th ed., Leipzig, 1900 (*The Popes of Rome*, London, 1941). The leading work is L. von Pastor, *Geschichte der Päpste*, Freiburg, 1866 ff. and many subsequent editions and translations. M.Creighton, *History of the Papacy from the Great Schism to the Sack of Rome*, 6 vols, 2nd ed., London and New York, 1897. Recent Roman Catholic interpretation: F.X.Seppelt and G.Schwaiger, *Geschichte der Päpste*, vol. 4, Munich, 1957. In Luther's day the most widely read history of the popes was that by Platina (Bartholomaeus Sacchi); I consulted the edition of 1529 and C.Hedio's German translation of 1546. Contemporaries were indispensable to me; they wrote and reported, especially in the period before the great conflagration, with refreshing realism. There are the diaries of papal dignitaries like Paris de Grassis and Johannes Burchardus (ed. L.Celani, Citta di Castello, 1910 ff. English translation by G.Parker, London, 1963), and the extremely instructive reports of the Venetian diplomats, the best observers of the contemporary scene; M. Sanuto incorporated many of these reports in his vast diary (58 vols, Venice, 1879–1903). F.Guicciardini, in his *Historia d'Italia*, Florence, 1561 wrote with great independence about the popes he served as a high official, and was still more outspoken in his posthumous *Scritti Politici* (*Collected Works*, ed. C. Panigada and R.Palmarocchi, Bari, 1929–36). Paolo Giovio, a prototype of the modern reporter, also amassed pictorial material; he was venal, like the great men who paid him; collected edition, Basle, 1578. The cardinals, together with documentary evidence of their nepotism and pluralism, are faithfully recorded in C.Eubel, *Hierarchia Catholica*, vols 2 and 3, Munich, 1901–23. No scholarly history of the cardinalate exists, a fact mentioned by J.Haller in his *Das Papsttum, Idee und Wirklichkeit*, 5 vols, Basle, 1965. The financial history of the Curia, which has been treated thoroughly in modern works on the Avignon period, has been explored to some extent in publications about the Fuggers (see below).

PRE-REFORMATION ERA. H.B.Workman, *Wyclif. A Study of the English Medieval Church*, 2 vols, Oxford, 1926; Johann Loserth, *Hus und Wiclif*, 2nd ed., Munich and Berlin, 1925. M.Spinka, *John Hus and the Czech Reform*, Chicago, 1941, and *Johannes Hus at the Council of Constance*, New York, 1965. U. von Richental, *Chronik des Konzils* (of Constance), Stuttgart, 1882. F.G.

Heyman, *John Ziska and the Hussite Revolution*, London and Princeton, 1955, and *George of Bohemia, King of Heretics*, Princeton, 1964.

Brian Tierney, *Foundations of the Conciliar Theory*, Cambridge, 1955. Willy Andreas, *Deutschland vor der Reformation*, 6th ed., Stuttgart, 1959. J.Huizinga, *Herbst des Mittelalters*, Munich, 1928 (*The Waning of the Middle Ages*, London, 1924) and *Men and Ideas*, London and Cleveland, Ohio, 1960. J.Hashagen, *Staat und Kirche vor der Reformation*, Essen, 1931. A.Dempf, *Sacrum Imperium*, Munich and Berlin, 1929.

SOCIAL AND ECONOMIC HISTORY. E.Troeltsch, *Die Soziallehren der Christlichen Kirchen*, Tübingen, 1912 (*The Social Teaching of the Christian Churches*, London and New York, 1931); collected works, 4 vols, Tübingen, 1912–25. H.Hauser, *Les Débuts du capitalisme*, Paris, 1927; H.Barge, *Luther und der Frühkapitalismus*, Gütersloh, 1951. R.Pascal, *The Social Basis of the German Reformation*, London, 1933; F.Rörig, *Mittelalterliche Weltwirtschaft*, Jena, 1933. On the Fuggers: A.Schulte, *Die Fugger in Rom*, 2 vols, Leipzig, 1904; Götz. Freiherr von Pöllnitz, *Jakob Fugger*, 2 vols, Tübingen, 1951, and *Anton Fugger* 2 vols, Tübingen, 1963; Léon Schick, *Un grand homme d'affaires au début du 16e siècle: Jakob Fugger*, Paris, 1957, written with a businessman's experience.

## SOURCES

GERMAN DOCUMENTS RELATING TO THE IMPERIAL DIETS. *Die Reichstagsakten, jüngere Reihe*, Gotha, 1893 ff.

Pamphlets, etc. O.Schade, *Satiren und Pasquille der Reformationszeit*, 3 vols. Hanover, 1855–8; O.Clemen, *Flugschriften der ersten Jahre der Reformationszeit*, 4 vols, Leipzig and New York, 1906–13; M.Gravier, *Luther et l'opinion publique*, Sorbonne thesis, Paris, 1924; K.Schottenloher, *Flugblatt und Zeitung*, Berlin, 1922, a survey by a great expert which also contains a valuable bibliography. Single sheets and posters, an important weapon in the propaganda war, edited in facsimile by M.Geisberg in *Der deutsche Einblattholzschnitt*, 40 vols, Munich, 1923; concise illustrated catalogue, Munich, 1930. Letters are listed under individual writers. A sort of press service, employing handwritten or printed information sheets, already existed; see, for example, *Briefbuch* by the Nuremberg syndic Christoph Scheurl, ed. F. von Soden, 2 vols, Potsdam, 1867 ff. A similar role was played in the world of international politics by the Italian aristocratic Petrus Martyr of Anghiera in his *Opus epistolarum*, Alcalá, 1530, and Amsterdam, 1670.

CHRONICLES OF GERMAN TOWNS. Some written officially by the town clerk or syndic and some by individual citizens, these have been published very fully; some, like the *Chronik der schwäbischen Städte*, vol. 6, by the Augsburg painter Georg Preu (1512–37), are highly critical, to the point of being revolutionary; among the best are those by Swiss chroniclers; Pellicanus, ed. B.Riggenback, Basle, 1877, and T.Vulpius, Strasbourg, 1892; J.Kessler of St Gallen, *Sabbata*, ed. E.Egli, St Gallen, 1902. J.Oldecop, ed. Euling, 1891, was a student at Wittenberg and later an anti-Lutheran. The chronicle of the Zimmern family (1538–94), available in a new six-volume edition,

*Zimmerische Chronik*, 1963, is a mine of information about people and customs of the time. Götz von Berlichingen, edited by Pistorius, 1731. S.Schertlin, a leading mercenary (ed. O.F.H.Schönhut, Münster, 1858), described the life of the landsknechts, a picture of which is also to be found in A.Reissner, *Georg von Frundsberg*, Frankfurt, 1568, and often reprinted. The wretched life led by the poor schoolboys, and the beginnings of the Reformation in Switzerland, are described in *Thomas und Felix Platter, zur Sittengeschichte des sechzehenten Jahrhunderts*, ed. H.Boos, Leipzig, 1878, and the life of the great merchants by the Augsburg patrician Lucas Rem, ed. B.Greiff, 1861. Among the many printed chronicles, mostly in praise of their native town or country-side, Sebastian Franck's *Germaniae Chronicon*, Frankfurt, 1538, is justly famous for its powerful language and independence of judgement. The commentaries of *J.Sleidanus* (Philippson), 1555 (German translation 1557 and English translation 1560) on the reign of Charles v were the first attempt to write history on a larger scale.

LITERATURE. Devoted almost entirely to topical problems, the literature of the day forms an essential part of its history. Historical folk-songs and ballads, which were often news-sheets in rhyme, were collected by R. von Liliencron, 1865 ff., in an edition entitled *Die historischen Volkslieder der Deutschen vom 13 bis 16 Jahrhundert*. Dramatic productions were often lively and highly controversial satires; of these Derek van Abbé gives a good survey in his *Drama in Renaissance Germany and Switzerland*, Melbourne, 1961. *Die Geschichte der deutschen Literatur 1480–1600*, East Berlin, 1961, written by various contributors, is a Marxist interpretation with very full notes. Carl Goedeke's *Grundriss zur Geschichte der deutschen Dichtung*, 2nd ed., Dresden, 1885, vol. 2, is still the only comprehensive survey of the subject.

*Sources for individual chapters*

*Part One*

1. THE MINER'S SON OF PEASANT STOCK. C.Spangenberg, *Mansfeldische Chronica*, Eisleben, 1572; K.Krumhaar, *Die Grafschaft Mansfeld im Reformationszeitalter*, Eisleben, 1855; *Die Grafen von Mansfeld*, Eisleben, 1872; G.Agricola, *Vom Bergwerk*, Basle, 1557. F.Paulsen, *Geschichte des gelehrten Unterrichts*, 3rd ed., Leipzig, 1919 ff.

2. AT ERFURT UNIVERSITY. W.Kampschulte, *Die Universität Erfurt*, 2 vols. Trier, 1858–60; G.Oergel, *Vom jungen Luther*, Erfurt, 1917, F.Benary, *Geschichte der Stadt und Universität am Ausgang des Mittelalters*, Gotha, 1919, P.K.Kalkoff, *Humanismus und Reformation in Erfurt*, Halle, 1926, Euricius Cordus, *Epigrammata* (1520), ed. K.Krause, Berlin, 1892; *Helius Eobanus Hessus*, ed. K.Krause, 2 vols, Gotha, 1879, G.Kaufmann, *Geschichte der deutschen Universitäten*, 2 vols, Stuttgart, 1888 ff. H.Rashdall, *The University of Europe in the Middle Ages*, ed. F.M.Powicke and A.B.Emden, 3 vols, 2nd ed., Oxford, 1936.

3. THE MONK. T.Kolde, *Die deutsche Augustiner – Kongregation*, Gotha, 1879. K.Benrath, *Luther im Kloster*, Halle, 1905; H.Lietzmann, *Geschichte der alten Kirche*, vol. 4, Berlin and Leipzig, 1944; K.Heussi, *Der Ursprung des Mönchtums*, Tübingen, 1936. The *Vitae Patrum*, many editions starting in the fifteenth century; *The Desert Fathers*, translations from the Latin by Helen Waddell, London, 1936. J.Bühler, *Klosterleben im deutschen Mittelalter* (selected texts), Leipzig, 1921. B.Lohse, *Mönchtum und Reformation*, Göttingen, 1962.

4. LIFE IN THE MONASTERY. I have quoted from G.Steinhausen's *Deutsche Privatbriefe des Mittelalters*, vol. 2, Berlin, 1907, and the *Legenda aurea*, ed. T. Graesse, Dresden, 1846 (*The Golden Legend of Jacobus de Voragine*, London, 1941 and New York, 1948).

5. BATTLE WITH THE COMMENTARIES. On scholasticism: the survey by my Academy teacher Clemens Baeumker in *Die Philosophie der Gegenwart*, Leipzig, 1928, still seems to me an excellent introduction. M.Grabmann, *Geschichte der scholastischen Methode*, Freiburg, 1909–11, supplemented by his collected articles, 3 vols, 1956; E.Gilson, *L'Esprit de la philosophie médiévale*, 2 vols, Paris, 1932; Gordon Leff, *Medieval Thought*, London, 1958 and Chicago, 1960; G.Ritter, *Via antiqua und via moderna*, 2nd ed., Heidelberg, 1963; L.Baudry, *Guillaume d'Occam*, Paris, 1949; Heiko A.Obermann, *The Harvest of Medieval Theology*, Cambridge, Mass., 1963, a new estimate of late scholasticism, in particular of G.Biel. – On Luther's teachers: N.Paulus, *Der Augustiner Bartholomäus Arnoldi von Usingen*, Freiburg, 1893; G.Plitt, *J. Trutfetter*, Erlangen, 1875.

6. ARRIVAL IN WITTENBERG. On Staupitz: A.Jeremias, *J. von Staupitz*, with selected writings by Staupitz, Berlin, 1926; E.Wolf, *Staupitz und Luther*, Leipzig, 1927. On Wittenberg: O.Oppermann, *Das sächsische Amt Wittenberg im Anfang des 16. Jahrhunderts*, Leipzig, 1897; W.Friedensburg, *Geschichte der Universität Wittenberg*, Halle, 1917; O.Thulin, *Lutherstadt Wittenberg*, 5th ed., Berlin, 1964. – On the Saxon dukes: G.Spalatin on Frederick the Wise, ed. C.G.Neudecker, Jena, 1851; T.Kolde, *Friedrich der Weise und die Anfänge der Reformation*, Erlangen, 1881; P.Kirn, *Friedrich der Weise und die Kirche*, Leipzig, 1926; C.Gurlitt, *Die Kunst unter Friedrich dem Weisen*, Dresden, 1897, and R.Bruck on the same subject, Strasbourg, 1903. – On Lucas Cranach: C. Schuchardt, 3 vols, Leipzig, 1851–71; C.Glaser, Leipzig, 1923. *Heiltumsbuch der Stiftskirche*, illustrated by Cranach, in facsimile, Munich, 1884; the *Hallesche Heiltum* (of Archbishop Albrecht of Mainz), ed. P.M.Halm, Berlin, 1931.

7. JOURNEY TO ROME. A.Hausrath, *Martin Luthers Romfahrt*, Berlin, 1894; H.Boehmer, *Luthers Romfahrt*, Leipzig, 1914; L. von Pastor, *Die Stadt Rom zu Ende der Renaissance*, Freiburg, 2nd ed. 1925; *Die römischen Skissenbücher von Martin von Heemskerck*, ed. C.Hülsen, 2 vols, Berlin, 1913–16; Aegidius Sadeler, *Vestigi delle Antichità di Roma*, Prague, 1596. – On Julius II: M. Brosch, *Papst Julius II*, Gotha, 1878, in addition to the histories of the popes listed above.

9. THE FIRST CONTROVERSIAL LECTURES. J.Ficker, *Luthers Vorlesung über den Römerbrief*, Leipzig, 1908; P.Althaus, *Der Brief an die Römer*, 9th ed. Göttingen, 1959, with extensive commentary; E.Vogelsang, *Die Anfänge von Luthers Christologies*, Berlin, 1929. K.A.Meissinger, *Luthers Exegese in der Frühzeit*, Leipzig, 1910; E.Hirsch, *Luthers Vorlesung über den Hebräerbrief*, Berlin and Leipzig, 1929.

10. REBEL AND REFORMER. On Reuchlin: L.Geiger, biography, Leipzig, 1871 and correspondence 1876; *Festschriften der Stadt Pforzheim*, 1922 and 1955. – On the Cabbala: G.Scholem, *Die jüdische Mystik*, Jersualem, 1941 [*Major Trends in Jewish Mysticism*, New York, 1946 and London, 1955]; *Epistolae obscurorum virorum*, ed. A.Bömer, 2 vols, Berlin 1924. – On the Cologne Dominicans: N.Paulus, in *Die deutschen Dominikaner im Kampfe gegen Luther*, Freiburg, 1903 (supplement to Janssen). – On the humanists: G.Ellinger, *Geschichte der neulateinischen Literatur*, 3 vols, Berlin and Leipzig, 1929–33. – On the mystics (only works immediately connected with the text are mentioned): *Der Franckforter* ('A German Theology'), ed. W.Uhl, Bonn, 1912; *Die Predigten Taulers*, ed. F.Vetter, Berlin, 1911; Tauler, *Sermones*, Augsburg, 1508 (British Museum); A.Spamer, *Texte aus der deutschen Mystik des 14. und 15. Jahrhunderts*, Jena, 1912; A.Hyma, *History of the Devotio Moderna*, Grand Rapids, 1925.

## Part Two

11. THE NINETY-FIVE THESES. W.Köhler, *Dokumente zum Ablassstreit*, Leipzig, 1902; E.Iserloh, *Luther zwischen Reform und Reformation*, Münster, 1967 (*Luther between Reform and Reformation*, London and Dublin, 1968); J. Luther, *Vorbereitung und Verbreitung von Martin Luthers 95 Thesen*, Berlin-Leipzig, 1933; N.Paulus, *Johann Tetzel*, Mainz, 1899. – On indulgences: N. Paulus, *Geschichte des Ablasses im Mittelalter*, 3 vols, Paderborn, 1922–3 (*Indulgences as a Social Factor in the Middle Ages*, New York, 1922); T.Brieger, *Das Wesen des Ablasses am Ausgang des Mittelalters*, Halle, 1897; H.C.Lea, *A History of Auricular Confession and Indulgences in the Latin Church*, 3 vols, London and Philadelphia, 1896; P.Brezzi, *Storia degli anni santi*, Milan, 1949.

12. THE HOLY ROMAN EMPIRE. K.Zeumer, *Heiliges römisches Reich Deutscher Nation*, Weimar, 1910; A.Dempf, *Sacrum Imperium*, Munich and Berlin, 1929; James Bryce, *The Holy Roman Empire*, 1864 and often reprinted. – On Albrecht of Mainz: Jakob May, *Der Kurfürst Cardinal und Erzbischof Albrecht II*, 2 vols, Munich, 1867–75. On the humanists and history: P.Joachimsen, *Geschichtsauffassung und Geschichtsschreibung in Deutschland unter dem Einfluss der Humanismus*, Leipzig, 1910. – On Maximilian I: H.Ulmann, *Kaiser Maximilian I*, 2 vols, Stuttgart, 1884–91; Documents published by the Stuttgart Literary Society, vol. 10, 1843. – Bernard Moeller, *Reichsstädte und Reformation*, Gütersloh, 1962; *Die Sogenannte Reformation Kaiser Siegmunds*, Monumenta Germaniae historica, new ed., Stuttgart, 1966; F.L.Carsten, *Princes and Parliaments in Germany* (fifteenth to eighteenth centuries), Oxford, 1959.

13. AUGUSTINIANS AND DOMINICANS. Many special papers have been written on the trial for heresy; Paul Kalkoff made a very detailed study in nine contributions to the *Zeitschrift für Kirchengeschichte*, 1904–27. – On Johann Eck: T.Wiedemann, Regensburg, 1865; J.Greving, Münster, 1905 and 1908. Six of Eck's main works have been published in the *Corpus Catholicorum*, a series of Roman Catholic authors of the sixteenth century with informative introductions, Münster, 1919 ff. The satirical *Eckius Dedolatus*, ed. S.Szamatolski, Berlin, 1892. – On Mazzolini (Prierias): F.Lauchert in *Die Italienischen literarischen Gegner Luthers*, Freiburg, 1912; a Latin dissertation on him by F.Michalski, Münster, 1892.

14. EXAMINATION BEFORE CARDINAL CAJETAN IN AUGSBURG. J.F.Groner. *Cardinal Cajetan*, Louvain, 1951; articles by various authors in the *Revue Thomiste*, new series XXVII Saint Maximin, 1935; Cajetan's work on the authority of the pope, *Corpus Catholicorum*, vol. 10, Münster, 1925; F.Roth, *Augsburgs Reformationsgeschichte*, Munich, 1881.

15. THE MILTITZ INTERLUDE. J.K.Seidemann, *Karl von Miltitz*, Dresden, 1844; H.A.Creutzberg, *Karl von Miltitz*, Freiburg, 1907; P.Kalkoff, *Die Miltitziade*, Leipzig, 1911. – On Charles V: K.Brandi, *Kaiser Karl V*, Munich, 1937 (*The Emperor Charles V*, London and New York, 1939). H.Baumgarten (Brandi's teacher), *Geschichte Karls V* (to 1539 only), 3 vols, Stuttgart, 1885–9; Royall Tyler, *The Emperor Charles V*, London and Fair Lawn, NJ, 1956; *Historiographie de Charles-Quint*, ed. A.P.V.Morel-Fatio, Paris, 1913. On financial history: E.J.Hamilton, *American Treasure and the Price Revolution in Spain*, Cambridge, Mass., 1934; R.Carande, *Los Banqueros de Carlos Quinto*, Madrid 1944. – H.Angles, *La música en la Corte de Carlos V*, 2 vols, Barcelona, 1965. B.Weicker, *Historische Studien XXII*, Berlin, 1901, on Charles's election.

16. SEVENTEEN DAYS' DISPUTATION. Recently a whole literature has appeared on Joachim de Fiore and the Antichrist: see F.Russo, *Bibliografia Gioachimita*, Florence, 1954. Here I shall mention only H.Grundmann, *Studien über Joachim von Floris*, Leipzig and Berlin, 1927; E.Benz, *Ecclesia spiritualis*, Stuttgart, 1934; R.Bainton, *Studies of the Reformation*, London and Boston, Mass., 1965. – On Karlstadt: H.Barge, *Andreas Bodenstein von Karlstadt*, 2 vols, Leipzig, 1905; Karl Müller, *Luther und Karlstadt*, Tübingen, 1907; E.Hertsch, *Karlstadt und seine Bedeutung für das Luthertum*, Halle, 1932. J.K.Seidemann, *Die Leipziger Disputation*, Dresden, 1843; *Der authentische Text*, ed. O.Seitz, Berlin, 1903. – On Duke Georg: O.Vossler in *Geist und Geschichte*, collected essays, Munich, 1964. On Pelagius the theologians have been very reticent; the subject has been treated by the classical philologist John Ferguson in his *Pelagius*, Cambridge, 1956.

17. THE THREE PRIMARY TREATISES. W.Köhler, *Die Quellen zu Luthers Schrift an den christlichen Adel*, Halle, 1895; E.Kohlmeyer, *Die Entstehung der Schrift Luthers an den christlichen Adel deutscher Nation*, Gütersloh, 1922. On the gift of Constantine: J.Haller in vol. I of his history of the papacy, *Das Papsttum. Idee und Wirklichkeit*, Basle, 1951–3. – On Melanchthon: K. Hartfelder, *Philipp Melanchthon als Praeceptor Germaniae*, Berlin, 1889; G.

Ellinger, *Philipp Melanchthon*, Berlin, 1902; Clyde Manschreck, *Melanchthon the Quiet Reformer*, New York, 1958; R.Stupperich, *Der unbekannte Melanchthon*, Stuttgart, 1961; W.Maurer, *Der junge Melanchthon*, 2 vols, Göttingen, 1967.

18. ULRICH VON HUTTEN. *Werke*, ed. E.Böcking, Leipzig, 1858 ff.; *Ulrich von Huttens deutsche Schriften*, Strasbourg, 1891. D.F.Strauss, *Ulrich von Hutten*, 2nd ed., Leipzig, 1871 (*Ulrich von Hutten: His Life and Times*, London, 1874); P.Kalkoff (very critical of Hutten), *Ulrich von Hutten und die Reformation*, Leipzig, 1920 and *Huttens Vagantenzeit und Untergang*, Weimar, 1925; F. Walser, *Die politische Entwicklung Huttens*, Munich and Berlin, 1928; H. Grimm on the young Hutten, *Ulrich von Hutten. Lehrjahre an der Universität*, Berlin, 1938; Hajo Holborn, *Ulrich von Hutten and the German Reformation*, New Haven, Conn., 1937.

19. THE BULL OF EXCOMMUNICATION. On heresy and the Inquisition: H.C.Lea, *History of the Inquisition of the Middle Ages*, 3 vols, London and New York, 1888 and often reprinted, and continued in four further volumes dealing with the Spanish Inquisition, New York, 1906–7; J.Guiraud, *Histoire de l'Inquisition au Moyen-Age*, Paris, 1935 (*The Medieval Inquisition*, London and New York, 1939); *Bibliography of works on the Inquisition* by E. van der Vekené, Hildesheim, 1964; Gordon Leff, *Heresy in the Later Middle Ages*, 2 vols, Manchester and New York, 1967; H.Flatten, *Der Häresieverdacht im codex iuris canonici*, Amsterdam, 1963. – On the burning of the Bull: J.Luther and M. Perlbach, *Ein neuer Bericht über Luthers Verbrennung der Bannbulle*, Berlin, 1907; H.Grisar in the *Historisches Jahrbuch der Görres-Gesellschaft* 42, Fulda, 1922.

20. SUMMONS BEFORE THE EMPEROR. H. von Schubert, proceedings of the Heidelberg Academy, 1912. – On Aleander: J.Paquier, *L'Humanisme et la Réforme*, Paris, 1900; T.Brieger, *Aleander und Luther*, Gotha, 1884; P.Kalkoff, *Die Depeschen des Nuntius Aleander*, 2nd ed., Halle, 1897, *Aleander gegen Luther*, Leipzig and New York, 1908, and *Erasmus, Luther und Friedrich der Weise*, Leipzig, 1919; *Journal autobiographique*, ed. H.Omont, Paris, 1896. – On Erasmus: J.Huizinga, Haarlem, 1924 (London and New York, 1924); P.S.Allen, *The Age of Erasmus*, Oxford, 1914, and *Opus epistolarum*, Oxford, 1906–47; *Julius exclusus in Erasmi Opuscula*, ed. W.K.Ferguson, The Hague, 1933; R.H.Murray, *Erasmus and Luther*, London, 1920; J.B.Pineau, *Erasme, sa pensée religieuse*, Paris, 1924, and *Erasme et la papauté*, Paris, 1924; J.C. Margolin, *Erasme par lui-même*, Paris, 1965.

21. THE DIET OF WORMS and following chapters. *Reichstagsakten* under Charles v, vol. 2, ed. A.Wrede, Gotha, 1896; P.Kalkoff, *Der Wormser Reichstag*, Munich and Berlin, 1922, and letters, dispatches, etc., about Luther in German translation, Halle, 1898; E.Walder, *Kaiser, Reich und Reformation 1517–1525*, Bern, 1944; P.Kalkoff, *Die Entstehung des Wormser Edikts*, Leipzig, 1913.

24. THE GERMAN BIBLE. W.Walther, *Die deutschen Bibelübersetzungen des Mittelalters*, Brunswick, 1889, and *Luthers deutsche Bibel*, Berlin, 1917. Detailed

commentaries in the Weimar Edition, Section III, 12 vols; H.Volz, *Bibel und Bibeldruck in Deutschland im 15. und 16. Jahrhundert*, Mainz, 1960, and *Hundert Jahre Wittenberger Bibeldruck*, 1522–1626, Göttingen, 1954; W.Mejer, *Der Buchdrucker H.Lufft*, Leipzig, 1923; *The Cambridge History of the Bible. The West from the Reformation to the Present Day*, ed. S.L.Greenslade with contributions by R.Bainton, H.Volz and others, New York and Cambridge, 1963.

25. UNREST IN WITTENBERG AND BEYOND. Nikolaus Müller, *Die Wittenberger Bewegung*, Leipzig, 1911; K.Holl, *Gesammelte Aufsatze zur Kirchengeschichte*, vol. 1, Tübingen, 1927. – On the spiritualists, radicals and anabaptists: G.H.Williams, *The Radical Reformation*, London, 1962, and a selection of texts in the *Library of Christian Classics*, vol. 25, Philadelphia, 1957, containing bibliographical notes; H.Fast, *Der linke Flügel der Reformation*, Bremen, 1962; R.H.Bainton in *Studies on the Reformation*, London and Boston, 1964. There are now numerous editions of collected works by formerly neglected men like H.Denck and B.Hubmeier as well as specialist studies on them. G.Zschäbitz, *Zur mitteldeutschen Wiedertäuferbewegung*, Berlin, 1958, is a Marxist interpretation.

26. FALSE SPRING. On Bugenhagen: *Johann Bugenhagen: Beiträge zu seinem 400. Todestag*, ed. W.Rautenberg, Berlin, 1958. – On Jonas: H.G.Hasse, *Justas Jonas Leben*, Leipzig, 1862; correspondence, ed. D.G.Kawerau, Leipzig, 1884–5. – On Thomas Murner: Collected works ed. F.Schultz, 1818–31; T. von Liebenau, *Der Franziskaner Dr Thomas Murner*, Freiburg, 1913. – On the iconoclasts: E.J.Martin, *A History of the Iconoclastic Controversy* (in Byzantium), London, 1930. I have quoted J.Kessler's *Sabbata*, ed. E. Egli, St Gallen, 1902. – On Sebastian Franck: a new collected edition is planned; his *Paradoxa*, modernized version by Ziegler, Jena, 1909; W.E. Peuckert, *Sebastian Franck*, Munich, 1943.

27. A DUTCHMAN AS POPE. G.Pasolini, *Adriano* VI, Rome, 1913; E. Hocks, *Der letzte deutsche Papst*, Freiburg, 1939. Pope Hadrian's correspondence with Charles V, ed. L.P.Gachard, Brussels, 1865.

28. SICKINGEN AND THE END OF THE KNIGHTS. H.Ulmann, *Franz von Sickingen*, Leipzig, 1872; *Die Flersheimer Chronik*, ed. O.Waltz, Leipzig, 1874; J.Becker, *Sickingen und Luther*, Leipzig, 1890; Caspar Sturm (the Imperial Herald who escorted Luther to Worms), *Wie die drey kriegsfürsten Frantzen von Sickingen überzogen*, 1523 (British Museum). – On Luther's political views: J.W.Allen, *A History of Political Thought in the 16th Century*, London and New York, 1960; P.Meinhold, *Römer 13*, Stuttgart, 1960; G.Törnwall, *Geistliches und weltliches Regiment bei Luther*, 2nd ed., Munich, 1947; H.R.Gerstenkorn, *Weltlich und Regiment zwischen Gottesreich und Teufelsmacht: Die staatstheoretischen Auffassungen Luthers*, Bonn, 1956. Heinz Zahrnt, *Die Sache mit Gott*, Munich, 1966, deals with present-day discussion of the subject. As I have pointed out in the text, no clearly defined theories about the state are to be found in the writings of either Luther or any of his German contemporaries; they did not appear until the seventeenth century.

29. TWILIGHT. On Henry VIII: E.Doernberg, *Henry VIII and Luther*, London and Stanford, Calif., 1961, and literature mentioned there. – On economic problems: A.M.Knoll, *Der Zins in der Scholastik*, Innsbruck, 1933; P.Cleary, *Church and Usury*, Dublin, 1914; J.Höffner, *Wirtschaftsethik und Monopole im 15./16. Jahrhundert*, Jena, 1941. – On the Reformation in other countries: E.H.Dunkley, *The Reformation in Denmark*, London and New York, 1949; H.Holmquist, *Die schwedische Reformation* (translation), Leipzig, 1925; G. Schwaiger, *Die Reformation in den nordischen Ländern*, Munich, 1962; W. Hubatsch, *Albrecht von Brandenburg, Deutschordensmeister und Herzog in Preussen*, Heidelberg, 1960. – A.Richter, *Der Reichstag zu Nürnberg 1524*, Leipzig, 1888. E.V.Cardinal, *Cardinal Lorenzo Campeggio*, Boston, 1935.

30. THE BATTLE OF PAVIA. On the mercenaries: A.Reissner, *Georg und Kaspar von Frundsberg*, Frankfurt, 1568–72; Leonard Fronsperger, *Kriegsbuch*, 3 parts, Frankfurt, 1573; H.Delbrück, *Geschichte der Kriegskunst*, vol. 3, 2nd ed., Berlin, 1920; E. von Frauenholz, *Das Heerwesen in der Zeit des freien Söldnertums*, 2 vols, Munich, 1936–7; Max Jähns, *Die Schlacht von Pavia*, in collected essays, Berlin, 1903; Jean Giono, *Le Désastre de Pavie*, Paris, 1963, with introduction by G.Walter on the situation in France. – On Francis I: C.Terrasse, *François I*, 2 vols, Paris, 1943–8; F.A.M.Mignet, *La Rivalité de François I et Charles V*, Paris, 1875; M.Göhring, *Weg und Sieg der modernen Staatsidee in Frankreich*, 2nd ed., Tübingen, 1947; G.Duchamel, *La Captivité de François I*, Paris, 1958. Frundsberg's report, *Newe zeytung wie es fuer Pavia in der Schlacht ergangen ist*, Strasbourg, 1525 (British Museum). – On Pescara: De Leyva, *Storia documentata di Carlo V in Correlazione all'Italia*, 5 vols, Bologna, 1863–94; J.Igel, *Die Versuchung des Pescara*, Tübingen, 1911.

31. THE PEASANTS' WAR. A.Rosenkranz, *Der Bundschuh*, 2 vols, 1927. – On the Hungarian Peasants' war: St Taurimus, *Cruciatorum servile bellum*, Vienna, 1519, reprinted in *Monumenta Ungarica*, 1809. – Wilhelm Zimmermann, *Allgemeine Geschichte des grossen Bauernkriegs*, 3 vols, Stuttgart, 1841–3, still the fullest account; it was from Zimmermann that Friedrich Engels took the material for his little book *Der deutsche Bauernkrieg* published in 1850, shortly after the abortive German revolution of 1848, and frequently reprinted (*The Peasant War*, New York, 1926 and London, 1927). After this many documents and results of local investigations were published by Schreiber, Baumann, Böhmer, Barge, and more recently by Merx, Franz and Fuchs, 1923–42; in 1925 O.H.Brandt published a useful selection. – A new account was written by G.Franz, *Der deutsche Bauernkrieg*, Munich, and Berlin, 1934, and dedicated to the National Socialist 'Peasants' Day'; new edition 1963, with a separate volume of documents. – P.Althaus, *Luther-Jahrbuch*, VII, 1925, an interpretation of Luther's attitude in the war. – On Thomas Müntzer: O.H.Brandt, *Thomas Müntzer: Sein Leben und seine Schriften*, Jena, 1932; J.K.Seidemann, *Thomas Müntzer*, Dresden and Leipzig, 1842; K. Holl in *Gesammelte Aufsätze*, vol. I, Tübingen, 1927; A.Lohmann, *Zur geistlichen Entwicklung Thomas Müntzers*, Leipzig and Berlin, 1931; P. Wappeler, *Thomas Müntzer in Zwickau*, 1965; C.Hinrich, *Luther und Müntzer*, Berlin, 1952; W.Elliger, *Thomas Müntzer*, Berlin, 1960. Ernst Bloch, *Thomas*

*Müntzer als Theologe der Revolution*, Munich, 1921, opened the new debate on Müntzer; M.M.Smirin, *Die Volksreformation des Thomas Müntzer* (translated from the Russian), Berlin, 1952. Müntzer's correspondence, edited by Boehmer and Kirn, Leipzig, 1931. – There is no comprehensive study of the actual fighting and the widely scattered campaigns.

## Part Three

32. FRAU DOKTOR LUTHER. Biographies of Katharina von Bora by A. Thoma, Berlin, 1910, and E.Kroker, 5th ed., Leipzig, 1959. – On Lemnius: G.E.Lessing, *Schriften*, vol. 2, Berlin, 1753; the satire was reprinted in Munich 1919 by G.Vorberg. – Eusebius Engelhard (properly Kuenen), *Lucifer Wittenbergensis*, 2 vols, Landsperg, 1747; refuted by J.G.Walch, *Wahrhaftige Geschichte der seligen Frau Catharina von Bora*, Halle, 1757.

33. THE WILL IN BONDAGE. Erasmus, *De libero arbitrio*, ed. J. von Walter, Leipzig, 1910; R.Will, *La Liberté chrétienne*, Strasbourg, 1922; H.J.Iwand in *Gesammelte Aufsätze*, Munich, 1959; Otto Veit, *Soziologie der Freiheit*, Frankfurt, 1957, discusses the wider aspects of the problem. – On Luther and music: H.J.Moser in vol. 35 of the Weimar edition and *Die evangelische Kirchenmusik*, Stuttgart, 1954; F.Blume, *Geschichte der evangelischen Kirchenmusik*, Kassel, 1965 (*A History of Evangelical Church Music*, London and New York, 1965); A.Schweitzer, *J.S.Bach*, Wiesbaden, 1952 (London, 1911); P.Wackernagel, *Das deutsche Kirchenlied*, Leipzig, 1863 ff. Facsimile editions of the early hymn-books have been published by the Baerenreiter Verlag, Kassel (the Erfurt hymn-book of 1524, the German Mass of 1526, and many others).

34. SACCO DI ROMA. C.Milanesi, *Il sacco di Roma*, Florence, 1867 (contemporary reports); H.Schulz, *Der Sacco*, Halle, 1894; A.Rodriguez Villa, *Memorias para la historia del Saqueo di Roma*, Madrid, 1875; J.E.Longhurst, *Alfonso de Valdes and the Sack of Rome*, Albuquerque, 1952; (by Valdes) *Pro divo Carolo quinto*, Mainz, 1527, and 1587 (British Museum).

35. THE PROTESTANTS. C.E.Förstemann, *Urkundenbuch zum Reichstag von Augsburg*, Halle, 1833–5; *Die Bekenntnisschriften der evangelisch-Lutherischen Kirche*, 5th ed., 1964. O.Winckelmann, *Der Schmalkaldische Bund*, Strasbourg, 1892; K.Köhler, *Luther und die Juristen*, Gotha, 1873.

36. THE SECOND REFORMATION. On Zwingli: W.Köhler, *Huldrych Zwingli*, 2nd ed., Leipzig, 1954, and *Zwingli und Luther*, 2 vols, Leipzig, 1924, 1953; O. Farner, *H.Zwingli*, 1943 ff. (*Ulrich Zwingli*, London, 1952). – On Philip of Hesse: C. von Rommel, *Philipp der Grossmütige*, 3 vols, Giessen, 1830; *Festschrift*, Marburg, 1904, ed. J.R.Dietrich; Rockwell, *Die Doppelehe Philipps von Hessen*, Marburg, 1904. – On the Turks: S.A.Fischer-Gelati, *The Turkish Impact on the German Reformation*, Cambridge, Mass., 1949. – A. von Druffel, *Karl V und die Kurie*, Munich, 1877. – On the anabaptists in Münster: C.A. Cornelius, *Geschichte des münsterschen Aufruhrs*, 2 vols, Leipzig, 1853. A good selection of contemporary reports and documents edited by K.Löffler, Jena, 1923.

37. OLD AGE. R.Stupperich, *Der Humanismus und die Wiedervereinigung der Konfessionen*, Leipzig, 1936; F.W.Kantzenbach, *Das Ringen um die Einheit der Kirche*, Stuttgart, 1957; Hubert Jedin, *Das Konzil von Trient*, Freiburg, 1950 ff., containing in vol. 1 a comprehensive history of the events leading up to it (*A History of the Council of Trent*, 2 vols, London, 1961 and New York, 1962). – On Luther and superstition: E.Klingner, *Luther und der deutsche Volksaberglaube*, Berlin, 1912. – On Luther and the Jews: R.Lewin, *Luthers Stellung zu den Juden*, Leipzig, 1911; Otto Veit in *Christlich-jüdische Koexistenz*, Frankfurt, 1965. – On the impact of the Reformation: G.Ritter, *Welterwirkung der Reformation*, Munich, 1959; H.Schöffler, *Wirkungen der Reformation*, Frankfurt, 1960. – On Italy: B.Nicolini, *Ideali e passioni nell'Italia religiosa del Cinquecento*, Bologna, 1962; D.Cantimori, *Eretici italiani del sec. XVI*, Rome, 1937. – On Luther's death: C.Schubart, *Die Berichte über Luthers Tod und Begräbnis*, Weimar, 1917.

# Index

'ML' refers throughout to Martin Luther.
Figures in italics refer to illustrations in the text;
figures in bold type refer to plate numbers.

Henry VIII—*cont.*
451; divorce crisis, 475–6, 515–16; on Augsburg Diet, 491
Henry, duke of Brunswick, 525
hermits, 31–2, 35–6
Hesse, 501
Hessus, Eobanus, 19–20
Hieronymus of Prague, 341
Hildebrand, *see* Gregory VII, pope
Hilten, Johannes, 13
Hipler, Wendelin, 410, 415
historians, 344
Höchstetter, House of, 152, 416
Hochstraten, Jakob van, 114–15
Hocker, Jodokus, *The Devil in Person*, 332
Hofmann, Melchior, 484, 513
Hohenzollern family, 145–6
Holbein, Hans, 28, 212, *256*, 337
Holland, anabaptists in, 514
Holy Junta, 266
Holy League, 89–90
Holy Roman Empire, 6, 144, 148–56, 355–6
Homer, 65, 108
Honorius, pope, 247
Hubmair, Balthasar, 507
humanists, 107–10, 115, 148, 157, 257, 332, 377
Hungary, 408–9, 483, 510, 511
Hus, Jan, 58, 136–7, 246, 306–7; influence on ML, 206, 207, 211; essay, *On the Church*, 211
Hüssgen, Johannes (Oekolampadius), 360
Hussite Wars, 4, 68, 164, 206, 207, 404
Hutten, Hans, 233
Hutten, Ulrich von, 109, 110, 147, 230–9, *235*, 298; intervenes in Reuchlin case, 115; on ML controversy, 157; on Cajetan, 174; publishes Valla's exposé, 219; calls for popular rising, 273, 363; use of German language by, 293; book, *On the Roman Trinity*, 235–6
Hutten, Ursula, 233
Hutter, Jakob, 484
hymns, 460–4

iconoclasm, 70, 316, 336–40, 419–20
indulgences, 59, 83, 106, 127–8, 130–42, 193; sale of, woodcuts of, *139*,

221; not established dogma, 180–1; official doctrine drafted, 185, published, 199
Ingolstadt University, 388
Innocent I, pope, 203
Innocent VIII, pope, 88, 110
Innsbruck, emperor in, 486
Inquisition, 113, 246, 248, 341, 518
Institoris, Heinrich, 110
Isabella (the Catholic), queen of Castile, 113
Isabella, queen of Denmark, 382, 387
Isabella of Portugal, 467
Ivan III, Grand duke, Tsar, 4

Jena, students meet ML in, 323–4, 327
Jerome, St, 309
Jews, 116, 525; taxation of, 356; *see also* Cabbala
Joachim, I, elector of Brandenburg, 145, 272, 282, 289, 386, 512
Joachim II, elector of Brandenburg, 521
Joachim de Fiore, 37, 178, 197–8, 294, 419
Joan, legendary female pope, 86
Joanna (the Mad), queen of Castile, 194, 263, 265, 266
John XII, pope, 250
John XXII, antipope, 136
John (Zapolya), king of Hungary, 409, 483
John (the Constant), elector of Saxony, 68, *177*; and Müntzer, 420, 421, 422–3; succeeds as elector, 428; gives monastery building to ML, 439; role in Saxon Church, 456–7, 459–60; 'protests' at Speyer, 482; at Diet of Augsburg, 486; joins Schmalkalden Alliance, 492; death, 509
John of Leiden (Jan Beukelszoon), 514
John Frederick, elector of Saxony, 483, 509, 526, **13**
Jonas, Justus, 329, 527; quoted, 27, 438
jousting, 363
Jubilee Year, 135
Julius II, pope, 79–81, 82, 88, *89*, 89–92, 200, 475
'Junker Jörg', 286, *323*
jurists, 343–4
Jutta (legendary female pope), 86

Kafka, Franz, 29